PHIL SHERIDAN
and His Army

Paul Andrew Hutton

PHIL SHERIDAN
and His Army

Foreword by Robert M. Utley

University of Oklahoma Press
NORMAN

To Martin Ridge

Frontispiece: General Philip H. Sheridan, by L. Hart Darragh.
Courtesy of West Point Museum Collections, United States Military Academy.

All of the maps except the Division of the Missouri, 1869–83 are reprinted by
permission from Robert M. Utley's *Frontier Regulars: The United States Army and the
Indian, 1866–1891* (New York: Macmillan, 1973), copyright © 1973 by Robert
M. Utley

Portions of Chapter 8 originally appeared in "Phil Sheridan's Pyrrhic Victory:
The Piegan Massacre, Army Politics, and the Transfer Debate," *Montana: The
Magazine of Western History* 32 (Winter 1982): 32–43.

Library of Congress Cataloging-in-Publication Data

Hutton, Paul Andrew, 1949–
     Phil Sheridan and his army / Paul Andrew Hutton ; foreword by
Robert M. Utley. — Oklahoma paperbacks ed.
        p.   cm.
     Includes bibliographical references and index.
     ISBN 978-0-8061-3188-7 (paper)
        1. Sheridan, Philip Henry, 1831–1888.   2. Indians of North America—
Wars—1866–1895.   3. West (U.S.)—History.   4. Generals—United States—
Biography.   5. United States.   Army—Biography.   I Title.
E83.866.S49H87   1999
973.8'092—dc21
     [B]   99-28700
                                                                          CIP

The paper in this book meets the guidelines for permanence and durbility of
the Committee on Production Guidelines for Book Longevity of the Council on
Library Resources, Inc. ∞

Oklahoma Paperbacks edition published by the University of Oklahoma Press,
Norman, Publishing Division of the University. Manufactured in the U.S.A. First
edition, 1985. First printing of the University of Oklahoma Press edition, with
foreword and nine new illustrations, 1999.

CONTENTS

MAPS

ILLUSTRATIONS

FOREWORD

In the last two decades American Indians have asserted their cultural heritage and ethnic identity within the American nation, and scholars have flooded the historiography of the westward movement with Indian studies. Public awareness and understanding of peoples marginalized by earlier generations has been enriched. No longer are Indians mere foils in the saga of sturdy white pioneers carving civilization out of the wilderness. Robust civilizations already existed in the wilderness, and we may now vicariously identify with them and watch the overpowering advance of the newcomers.

Neither in the burgeoning literature nor in public perceptions have the Indian-fighting soldiers fared well. Motion pictures and television, popular works, and even scholarly studies have portrayed them as the villains of the story and often as bloodthirsty butchers. The image is no more accurate than the earlier public image of Indians as savages barring the path to civilization. The U.S. Army played a significant role in the Indian wars, one entitled to the same canons of scholarship that should govern all examinations of the past.

In *Phil Sheridan and His Army*, Paul Andrew Hutton applied those canons rigorously, at a time when Indian studies were gaining momentum. His book revealed the true significance of the frontier soldiers without romanticizing them or being condescending to their Indian adversaries. In contrast to most works in this field, his book is no mere chronicle of campaigns and battles—it is also a study in command.

Philip Henry Sheridan was a scrappy combat cavalryman who won deserved fame as a battlefield leader in the Civil War. He had distinct limitations of intellect and personality, however, and he did not function very well as a desk-bound commander in the postwar years. Nevertheless, from 1869 until 1883 he held the most important command in the final years of Indian warfare, the Military Division of the

Missouri. Its jurisdiction stretched from the Missouri River to the Rocky Mountains and from Mexico to Canada, and all the operations on the Great Plains occurred under his generalship. His Chicago desk afforded an ideal perspective from which to view the challenges of high command in Indian warfare. This is Paul Hutton's unique contribution to scholarship. The campaigns and battles are there, but they are placed within the context of high command.

That *Phil Sheridan and His Army* offered superior history and reading when first published in 1985 was attested to not only by highly favorable media reviews but also by the awarding of three prestigious prizes: the Billington Prize of the Organization of American Historians, the Spur Award of the Western Writers of America, and the Evans Biography Award. That it has stood the test of time is demonstrated by the decision of the University of Oklahoma Press to bring out this new edition fourteen years later.

Hutton's impeccable scholarship, sharp insights, and engaging writing style ensure that *Phil Sheridan and His Army* will endure as an honest and balanced treatment of a central cast of characters in the drama of the American West.

ROBERT M. UTLEY

January 1999

PREFACE

Philip Henry Sheridan is most often remembered as one of the great captains who saved the Union during the Civil War. Yet the majority of his years in the army, both before and after the Civil War, were spent in connection with the expanding frontier. As the nation's chief Indian fighter from 1867 until he assumed overall command of the army in November 1883, he planned and directed the greatest Indian campaigns of the century. He was the nation's preeminent western soldier, commanding a large frontier region for a longer period of time than any other officer in the history of the Republic.

Considering Sheridan's important role in national expansion, it is surprising that so little has been written. Only two monographs have given any consideration to his western career. Richard O'Connor's *Sheridan the Inevitable* (1955) is the only modern biography of the general. Although journalistic and sparingly documented, it serves well the mass audience for which it was intended. Less than a third of the book, however, concerns Sheridan's post–Civil War service. Carl Coke Rister's brief *Border Command: General Phil Sheridan in the West* (1944) is limited in scope, concentrating on the southern plains campaigns, offers no documentation, has a shallow analysis of frontier warfare, and is repeatedly marred by an antiquated viewpoint toward Native Americans. The present study provides a look at Sheridan's post–Civil War career in a broader context: one that places emphasis on the army as an institution as well as on the man.

Sheridan left few private papers, and so this biography concentrates on his professional life. An attempt has been made to expand the boundaries of biography to profile not only the general's life but also his army. Emphasis has been placed on those personal and professional connections that dominated his career and the institution in which he served. These connections went beyond the military to include the northern capitalists who had emerged triumphant in the Civil War. In the Gilded Age atmosphere of laissez-faire capitalism, Sheridan's army often acted as agents of expansion for this business community.

Sheridan and his frontier army did not exist in a void, untouched by national and international affairs. One of the goals of this book is to place the military frontier in a balanced perspective. To national policy-makers, frontier expansion was an inevitable process that could be subordinated to more pressing political or economic needs in the East. Indian resistance was a minor irritant already anachronistic to Gilded Age Americans, and soldiers were unhesitatingly called from conflicts in the West to meet greater threats to national order in the East. As a result, the role of Sheridan and his army in Reconstruction, the contested election of 1876, and the labor strife of 1877 forms an important part of this story.

Phil Sheridan's pragmatism and elastic ethics made him the perfect soldier for the Gilded Age. He carried out the dictates of his government, ruthlessly quashing opponents, be they southern redeemers, northern workingmen, or western Indians. He never faltered in the belief that what he did was right and in the best interest of his nation. The author has, for the most part, left to the reader the final moral judgment on those actions.

Like all books, this study could not have been completed without the assistance of others. My greatest debt is to Martin Ridge, who suggested the topic, patiently guided the research, and carefully supervised the writing. His high standards of excellence set a lofty mark to work toward. It is an honor to work with him, and to dedicate this book to him.

Robert M. Utley provided essential research materials and shared his vast knowledge of the frontier military with me. He read an earlier draft of this manuscript and suggested several critical revisions. This monograph, in common with all books on the frontier military, owes an enormous debt to Utley's pathbreaking books and articles in the field. He professionalized this field of study and laid firm foundations for others to build on. I am also grateful to Utley for generously allowing the use of maps from his *Frontier Regulars: The United States Army and the Indian, 1866–1891*.

At Indiana University, Robert Gunderson, Walter Nugent, and

James Madison all read an earlier version of this book. They made many useful suggestions to improve the manuscript.

My colleagues at Utah State University were constant sources of encouragement. In particular, thanks are due S. George Ellsworth, Norman L. Jones, Clyde A. Milner, Charles S. Peterson, and F. Ross Peterson. Barbara Stewart supervised the typing of several versions of this manuscript and generally acted as able midwife to this book. Evelyn Lawrence and D. Teddy Diggs provided ready assistance in the gathering of research materials and the preparation of the final manuscript.

Research materials and other types of assistance were provided by Annette Atkins, Dennis Berge, John M. Carroll, Raymond DeMallie, Bruce Dinges, Brian W. Dippie, Lawrence Frost, Paul Hedren, Vincent Heier, Jon James, Marvin Kroeker, William Lang, Roger Miller, Michael Moss, Fred Nicklason, Brian Pohanka, Joseph Porter, Joseph Rosa, Tom Swinford, and Douglas Youngkin.

Some of my research for this study was conducted as a Fellow at the DeGolyer Library, Southern Methodist University, where Clifton H. Jones and his fine staff were most helpful. Thanks are also due Art DeBacker of the Kansas State Historical Society and Archie Motley of the Chicago Historical Society.

A very personal debt of gratitude is due my parents, Paul and Louise Hutton, who, although denied their own chance for schooling by the Great Depression, always impressed upon me the power of education. My wife, Vicki, despite her own busy career as an educator, took time to assist me with this book in innumerable ways. Her contribution is evident on every page. It is our mutual dream that our daughter, Laura, grow up in a world that no longer has need of the terrible skills of a Phil Sheridan.

Finally, I should note that brevet rank often leads to some confusion in studies of the post–Civil War army. Brevets were honorary promotions given for distinguished military service. They were, however, not hollow awards, for officers were assigned to special commands and staff assignments by brevet rank. When mixed units (for example, when cavalry and infantry were combined) and when volunteer and regular units served together, brevet rank prevailed. Officers wore the insignia of their brevet rank and were addressed, both officially and socially, by their brevet rank. In 1869 and 1870 congressional reformers passed regulations forbidding officers to wear brevet insignia or be addressed in official correspondence by brevet rank and ruled that brevet rank could no longer take precedence over regular rank. Brevets, however, still retained predominance in social intercourse as officers continued to be referred to by brevet rank in military circles, by the press, and occasionally in official correspondence. In this book, when an officer is first mentioned, his brevet rank is given in parentheses after his regular rank. Otherwise, officers are referred to by their regular rank.

CHAPTER 1

The Making of a General:
"Worth His Weight in Gold"

On September 5, 1867, Major General Philip Henry Sheridan left New Orleans for Fort Leavenworth, Kansas, to assume command of the Department of the Missouri. His new command embraced the states of Missouri and Kansas, the Indian Territory, and the territories of Colorado and New Mexico. Only three years before, he had led forty-five thousand men to victory in the Shenandoah Valley; now he commanded but six thousand troopers scattered about a vast territory. Nevertheless, he was happy to be rid of the thankless duty of reconstructing Louisiana and Texas.

A massive torchlight parade staged by Carl Schurz, local commander of the Grand Army of the Republic, greeted him when he reached St. Louis. Veterans from twenty organizations enthusiastically cheered Sheridan and loudly condemned President Andrew Johnson for dismissing their hero from command of the Fifth Military District.

After a hurried trip to Fort Leavenworth to assume command of the department, Sheridan began his first extended leave—six months —since entering the army nineteen years earlier. He visited his home in Somerset, Ohio, but remained only a few days, for he would never again be satisfied with a sleepy Ohio village. He had acquired grander tastes and now claimed among his friends famous generals, powerful politicians, business tycoons, and the leaders of fashionable society.

Many of New York's socially prominent citizens, none of whom normally would have associated with an Irishman from the Ohio back country, fawned over Sheridan. The stubby little general, even in his medal-bedecked dress uniform, could not have been very impressive to the admirers who crowded around him. Abraham Lincoln once described him as "a brown, chunky little chap, with a long body, short legs, not enough neck to hang him, and such long arms that if his ankles itch he can skratch [sic] them without stooping." With the hard days of campaigning behind him, he gained weight, his barrel-shaped torso reaching such proportions that it was a marvel his stumpy legs and tiny feet supported the mass. Moreover, his oversized, bullet-shaped head, from which protruded in back two large bumps, made it almost impossible for him to wear a hat. His head was crowned by a growth of coarse, short hair that, as one wag remarked, resembled "a coat of black paint." Below heavy, arched eyebrows, however, Sheridan's dark eyes, long and narrow, sparkled with a fire that betrayed him as the victor at Missionary Ridge, the warrior who had turned an army around at Cedar Creek, and the commander who had broken Lee's forces at Five Forks. John Schuyler Crosby, one of Sheridan's closest friends, insisted that "one could tell from his eyes in a moment whether he was serious, sad, or humorous, without noticing another feature of his face." Another admirer admitted that the "stumpy, quadrangular little man" had a "forehead of no promise," but added that "his eye and his mouth shew force" and marked him as a fierce warrior. His facial features disclosed his Irish descent, but his voice carried no trace of a brogue. Some thought Sheridan a drunkard because his face was always flushed, but this was in reality the result of an abnormally rapid heartbeat which, combined with a fondness for rich food and fine liquor, would send him to an early grave.[1]

The exact place of Sheridan's birth is unknown. He confused the issue himself, giving Boston and Somerset on various official documents before finally settling on Albany, New York. A strong case can also be made for County Cavan, Ireland, where his parents worked as tenant farmers before migrating to America. Some authorities have suggested that he was born on the way over. To assert their claim, the city fathers of Albany in 1916 lavished twenty-five thousand dollars on an equestrian statue, even though there is no record of his birth there.[2]

Philip, born March 6, 1831, was the third of six children of John and Mary Sheridan. He was only an infant when the family settled in Somerset, a hamlet of slightly more than one thousand residents, where John Sheridan found work on the Cumberland Road. Because the internal improvements boom kept John Sheridan employed but away from home most of the time, Philip was reared by his mother, a quiet, strong woman with firm convictions on honesty, piety, industry, and patriotism. She led her family faithfully to Somerset's Church of Saint Joseph, the oldest Catholic church in Ohio.

Things military were all the rage among Somerset's boys, and, next to Christmas, the Fourth of July was the most important day of the year. Every year on that day, after the amateur orators were exhausted, Somerset's own genuine veteran of the revolutionary war would hobble out to greet the crowd. While the town's tiny brass cannon sputtered salutes and the crowd cheered wildly, young Sheridan would gawk at the ancient warrior. "I never saw Phil's brown eyes open so wide or gaze with such interest," noted his playmate Henry Greiner, "as they did on this old Revolutionary relic." Little wonder that Ohio was a miniature Prussia in the first half of the nineteenth century! It produced sixty-four Civil War generals, including Ulysses S. Grant, William T. Sherman, William B. Hazen, George A. Custer, James Forsyth, David S. Stanley, and George Crook. These officers proved important to Sheridan's career. But military fervor had its limits. When Richard M. Johnson, the reputed slayer of Tecumseh and Democratic vice-presidential candidate, campaigned in Somerset, Philip refused to shake his hand, even though he admired the Indian fighter, declaring it improper for a Whig to shake with a Democrat. Loyalty, be it to a political party, the Union, or a comrade, was early Sheridan's first consideration.[3]

Sheridan attended Somerset's one-room schoolhouse. He had two teachers. The first was an itinerant Irishman named Patrick McNaly, who believed that education could be beaten into students; the second, a more progressive educator named Thorn, introduced the slate-board to Somerset, much to the dismay of many citizens who feared the children would spend their time drawing pictures. Although one of Sheridan's classmates remembered McNaly as a drunken brute, Phil recalled with admiration that the Irishman consistently punished every "guilty mischief-maker" by whipping the whole class when unable to detect the actual culprit. At age fourteen, with "a smattering of geography and history, and . . . the mysteries of Pike's Arithmetic and Bullions' English Grammer" somewhat mastered,

Sheridan secured a clerk's position in a local general store. He soon became a bookkeeper in the town's largest dry goods shop. Although neither widely read nor given to philosophizing, he had a profound respect for education. It was "the little white schoolhouse of the North [that] made us superior to the South," he once remarked: "Education is invincible."[4]

Sheridan's love of the military, doubtless reinforced by glorious tales originating in the Mexican War, led him to apply for nomination to West Point in 1848. Congressman Thomas Ritchie, who knew both Philip and his father, was pleased to make the appointment. His family had misgivings, and a local Dominican priest suggested that it would be better to cut the boy's throat than send him to a den of heretics. David S. Stanley, Sheridan's classmate at West Point, traveled with him from Ohio to the academy. The trip was the first meeting for the two future generals, and Stanley remembered Sheridan as "small and red faced, [with] long black wavy hair, bright eyes, very animated and neatly dressed in a brown broadcloth sack suit." The wavy locks were soon shorn, the suit exchanged for the uniform brown linen jacket, or "plebe skin," of the freshman cadet. Sheridan's diminutive figure was not flattered; Stanley described him as "the most insignificant looking little fellow I ever saw."[5]

The seventeen-year-old plebe found little to admire at the academy. Unimpressed, he found taking the oath of allegiance and receiving the cadet warrant on February 17, 1849, all quite pompous. The ceremony reminded him of the Dominican priest's plea to cut his throat, for as he stared at the imposing row of officers in full dress uniform and sword, he could think only that "it looked just like they were going to cut somebody to pieces."[6]

A momentary respite from depression was provided when some twenty colors captured during the Mexican War arrived at the academy. Sheridan received a flag taken at Chapultepec. As he carried the tattered banner up the hill from the dock, amidst the roar of forty eighteen-pounders, he could not help dreaming of military glory. Within a month, however, his colorful daydreams faded, while the gray buildings, dark wintry skies, and rocky landscape reinforced the monotonous regimen of cadet life. "It is colder than Greenland here," he complained to his sister in February 1849. Even the climate conspired against him.[7]

Sheridan's days at the academy tested him. His grades ranged from modest to dismal, and it was only through the tutoring of his roommate that he managed to pass his examinations.[8] Although he found solace in the company of a trio of Ohio cadets—George Crook, Joshua Sill, and John Nugen—Sheridan never fit into the aristocratic, southern clique that dominated social affairs at West Point. Rural, Irish Catholic, and Whig, he felt ill at ease with the southerners, who prized refined manners and stately posturing. Traditional hazing frayed his short temper, and in a significant break with his conservative nature he came to regard it as "a senseless custom which an improved civilization" would, he hoped, eradicate.[9]

His pent-up resentment and frustration finally broke forth in September 1851. On the drill field late one afternoon cadet Sergeant William R. Terrill of Virginia ordered Sheridan to align himself properly in the ranks. There may have been more to it than that, perhaps some previous altercation. Terrill's imperious manner enraged Sheridan, and he lunged forward with his bayonet to strike at his tormentor. For an instant, all the demons that hounded him for being Irish, Catholic, short, and ugly were loose, but he regained control before disaster and pulled back. A horrified Terrill reported the incident to his superiors, as duty required. Further enraged, Sheridan immediately sought out Terrill and attacked him, but this time with his fists. At a wiry five-foot-six, Sheridan was no match for the larger Virginian and was saved from a sound thrashing by the intervention of an officer.

His first outburst compounded by the second, Sheridan gloomily awaited the deliberations of his superiors. He knew that expulsion would not be unwarranted, and although unrepentant and convinced that his actions were justified, he thought long and hard on the wages of an uncontrolled temper. Only the intervention of the superintendent of the academy, Captain Henry Brewerton, saved Sheridan from dismissal. Since Sheridan's conduct record had been good up until the time of his outburst, he received only a year's suspension.[10]

Although fortunate to have avoided expulsion, Sheridan harbored deep resentment against all the parties involved in the incident. He spent nine humiliating months as a bookkeeper in Somerset before reentering the academy in August 1852. His attitude was, if anything, worse than before his suspension, and at the time of his graduation he lacked but eleven demerits for expulsion. Graduating thirty-four in a

Brevet Second Lieutenant George Crook, Cadet Philip H. Sheridan, and Brevet Second Lieutenant John Nugen posed together in 1853. Crook and Nugen had just graduated and were awaiting assignment, as signified by their brevet rank, while Sheridan's transgressions had forced him to miss graduating with his Ohio pals. (*United States Military Academy Archives*)

class of fifty-two, he ranked too low to win an immediate position and was assigned as a brevet second lieutenant until a vacancy occurred.[11]

The fresh shavetail was assigned to the First Infantry and ordered to Fort Duncan, Texas. Although the most desolate and primitive post in all the army, to Sheridan it was an improvement over West Point. He occupied his time with hunting, amateur ornithology, and excursions over the Rio Grande to the Mexican hamlet of Piedras Negras for dances with the local senoritas. He was impressed by the Mexicans, by "their graceful manners and their humility before the cross." But he still considered them "a half-breed population." To Sheridan, the mixing of "wild Indian blood" with that of the Spaniards had produced a bastardized people, too weak to protect themselves from the Indian raids that devastated their land. If the Mexicans were a degraded lot, the "blood-thirsty savages" that terrorized them were even more contemptible. His few glimpses of raiding Lipans and Comanches, or their handiwork, disabused him of any latent image of "noble savages."[12]

Sheridan's next assignment, as second lieutenant of the Fourth Infantry stationed at Fort Reading, California, gave him a much closer look at Indians. Fort Reading stood at the northern end of the Sacramento Valley, an area filled with all varieties of the world's humanity in search of a quick fortune in the gold fields. Prices were so exorbitant that in 1851 Congress voted to increase the pay of soldiers serving in California and Oregon. The extra pay, however, was insufficient, and some Fourth Infantry officers—Sheridan's friend George Crook, for example—leased land and raised wheat to earn extra money. Since common laborers received higher wages than army officers, morale was low, and the desertion rate high. Many of the officers succumbed to alcohol, an occupational hazard of frontier service; still others "were petty tyrants . . . in command of small posts so long that their habits and minds had narrowed down to their surroundings."[13]

Following the Cayuse War of 1847, Indian relations in the Pacific Northwest had steadily deteriorated. For years, the Indians had been abused by miners and squatters who "would about as soon shoot an Indian as eat supper." The Indians—Pit Rivers, Rogue Rivers, Walla Wallas, Cayuses, Nez Perces, Spokanes, and Yakimas—responded in kind. The settlers were incited by the governor of Washington Territory, Isaac Stevens, who hoped to clear all Indian land titles, open up the Northwest to white settlement, and encourage Congress to adopt the northern route for the proposed transcontinental railway. Stevens negotiated a series of specious treaties with the tribes which, coinciding with discovery of gold at Colville, Washington, drove the Yakimas and Rogue Rivers to war. Pugnacious General John Wool, commanding the department, viewed the conflict as "one of plunder of the Indians and the treasury of the United States." Stevens and Oregon's Governor George Curry, to "promote their own ambitious schemes and that of pecuniary speculators," wanted General Wool to deal more harshly with the Indians.[14]

Crook, agreeing with General Wool, viewed Indian-white relations in the region as "the fable of the wolf and the lamb. It was no unfrequent occurrence," he noted, "for an Indian to be shot down in cold blood, or a squaw to be raped by some brute," and the white culprit to escape punishment. Crook was frustrated because the army was powerless to aid the oppressed, but when the Indians "were pushed beyond endurance and would go on the war path we had to fight when our sympathies were with the Indians." Sheridan, however, was unmoved by the Indians' plight. It was, after all, but the natural pressure of civilization that threatened to dispossess them of their lands and homes. He was disgusted by the "miserable wretches" native to the region, and the fact that their "naked, hungry and cadaverous" condition resulted from white thievery did not elicit sympathy. Sheridan's consistent demonstration of cruelty toward those he designated as enemies is nowhere more apparent than in his inability to perceive the tragedy of the northwestern tribes.[15]

Sheridan's first campaign against the Indians was a pathetic affair. A detachment of 350 regular troops and a regiment of Oregon mounted volunteers was dispatched under the command of Major Gabriel Rains in October 1855 against the Yakimas. Although the campaign gave Sheridan his first look at warriors massed for battle—"a scene of picturesque barbarism, fascinating but repulsive"—it yielded no results. The Indians fled before the advancing troops, who had to satisfy themselves with burning a Catholic mission on the Yakima River that had tended the Indians. Their inability to force the Yakimas to fight was fortunate, for the soldiers were an inept lot. On one occasion Sheridan, in command of an advance column, galloped in pursuit of a party of supposed Indians for two miles before discovering them to be a company of Oregon mounted volunteers. Winter snows ended the campaign, and the officer's conversations quickly degenerated into recriminations about who was to blame for the failure. Captain Edward O. C. Ord brought charges of incompetency against Major Rains, who replied in kind by accusing Ord of stealing a pair of shoes from the Catholic mission before it was burned. General Wool properly ignored them both.[16]

Sheridan, wintering at Fort Vancouver, spent a few relatively quiet months while the army reorganized and prepared for a spring campaign. Colonel George Wright, an experienced veteran who brought ten companies of the Ninth Infantry from the East, replaced the ineffectual Rains. Colonel Wright moved his troops to Fort Dallas and prepared for a spring invasion of the Walla Walla Valley. The

Indians however, struck the first blow. On March 26, 1856, a large party of Yakimas, assisted by Klikitat and Chinook renegades, attacked the white settlement at the Cascades, a six-mile stretch of rapids whose portage afforded the only connection between eastern and western Oregon. The band captured the Lower Cascade, killing seventeen whites and besieged the surviving settlers in cabins at the Upper Cascade and a military blockhouse on the Middle Cascade. News of the attack reached Fort Vancouver that night, and Sheridan led forty dragoons to retake the Cascades. Moving his men upriver aboard the steamboat *Belle*, he stormed the Lower Cascade with the aid of a small cannon and fought his way to the blockhouse. The Indians, although outnumbering the soldiers, retreated before the cannon and only engaged in skirmishing. During the fight a bullet grazed the bridge of Sheridan's nose and killed the soldier beside him. On the morning of March 28, soon after Sheridan reached the blockhouse, Colonel Wright arrived with reinforcements from Fort Dalles, and the Yakimas withdrew.[17]

Sheridan next unleashed his fury on the Cascade tribe, whose village was near the rapids. He easily rounded up the demoralized Indians. Although the warriors protested their innocence, Sheridan found freshly burned powder in several of their muskets. He arrested thirteen warriors and turned them over to Wright, who immediately held a drumhead court-martial and sentenced nine to death. The soldiers unceremoniously fastened a rope to a handy cottonwood limb, stacked two barrels underneath it, and hanged the warriors. Among those executed was Tumult, a Cascade Indian who on the morning of the attack had warned many settlers and guided one old white man to safety. Sheridan believed that the "summary punishment inflicted on the nine Indians . . . had a most salutary effect on the [Indian] confederation, and was the entering wedge to its disintegration."[18]

A few days after the executions, Joseph Meek, the famed mountain man, arrived at Sheridan's camp at the Cascades, inquiring after the family of a friendly Chinook chief named Spencer who had been acting as an interpreter for the army. Spencer's family had been sent from Fort Dalles to Fort Vancouver several days before and were overdue. A search party soon found the family, all dead. Spencer's wife, two young sons, three daughters, and an infant lay in a semicircle near the Middle Cascade, the rope used to strangle them still around

9

their necks. The murderers, who went unpunished, were settlers living near the military blockhouse, and for once Sheridan sympathized with the Indians. "Greater and more atrocious massacres have been committed often by Indians," Sheridan later wrote. "Their savage nature modifies one's ideas, however, as to the inhumanity of their acts, but when such wholesale murder as this is done by whites, and the victims not only innocent, but helpless, no defense can be made for those who perpetrated the crime, if they claim to be civilized beings."[19]

Sheridan spent his remaining years in the Northwest within the relative quiet of the Grande Ronde Indian Reservation in western Oregon. Various tribes—Rogue Rivers, Coquilles, Klamaths, Modocs, and Chinooks—lived on the reservation, and Sheridan's troops guarded them. Ill fitted by temperament for this type of work, Sheridan attempted, as he did in every endeavor, to do his best.

He learned the Chinook language, greatly aided no doubt by Frances, a Rogue River Indian girl who lived with him during his remaining years in the territory. There was no chance, however, of Sheridan going native; he seemed to gain no appreciation or understanding of the Indian way of life from this liaison.[20]

Sheridan was horrified by the "absurdly superstitious practices" followed by the natives in mourning their dead. They often destroyed household utensils, tepees, and clothing and killed their horses on the graves of the recently deceased. Even more disturbing to the young officer was the execution of Indian doctors upon the death of a patient. This custom led to the slaying of a Rogue River woman by sixteen members of her tribe on the parade ground at Fort Yamhill. Sheridan angrily reacted to this "flagrant and defiant outrage committed in the teeth of the military authority" by arresting all sixteen killers, fastening them in ball and chain, and forcing them to labor at the fort "until their rebellious spirit was broken." Such tactics eventually succeeded, so the officer could proudly report that the cowed Indians were "compelled to cultivate their land, to attend church, and to send their children to school." This early success convinced Sheridan that "the most effectual measures for lifting [the Indian] from a state of barbarism would be a practical supervision at the outset, coupled with a firm control and mild discipline." This simplistic plan for Indian control would, in the future, be unwaveringly applied by Sheridan to every situation. He did not seem to realize, or was unwilling to admit, that the Rogue River Indians had been completely subjugated by the military before his arrival. They could offer no serious resistence. Moreover, their sedentary life enabled them to adjust fairly easily to agriculture on the rich Oregon lands. For the powerful nomadic tribes of the Great Plains such adjustments would be more traumatic and difficult.[21]

Sheridan's experiments in "uplifting savages from barbarism" ended in September 1861, soon after the advent of the Civil War, when he was promoted to captain and ordered to join the Thirteenth Infantry. Sheridan hurried east, fearing the war would end before he could join his regiment. Patriotism was the guiding principle of his life, and he took great pride in it being "untainted by politics." He was probably truthful when he later remarked that his mind had never "been disturbed by any discussion of the questions out of which the war grew" and his only desire was to aid in preserving the Union.[22]

The thirty-year-old captain from the West entered the war with high hopes. If it lasted long enough, he told a friend, he might "have a chance to earn a major's commission."[23] This was not false modesty; Sheridan had no powerful friends in the army, War Department, or Congress to help him win promotion. He was a latecomer to the fighting. Ulyssess S. Grant had already won victories at Forts Henry and Donelson, and William T. Sherman commanded a division by the time Sheridan assumed a desk job at General Henry W. Halleck's Missouri headquarters. Sheridan straightened out the confused accounts of Halleck's predecessor, General John C. Frémont, so well that he was appointed chief quartermaster for General Samuel R. Curtis's Army of the Southwest.

Sheridan's fellow officers saw him as a "modest, quiet little man," and his bashfulness became a legend in the Army of the Southwest, especially as it related to the ladies. Attracted to a young lady in Springfield, the nervous captain proved too shy to press his attentions and sent off his clerk to take the lady riding, while he provided horse and carriage. This proxy courtship proved agreeable to Sheridan, although his fellow officers expressed both amazement and delight at such an enterprise. The novel experiment never reached fruition, however, for the bashful captain soon faced more pressing problems.[24]

Sheridan's promising career as a quartermaster came to an abrupt end in March 1862 when he refused to obey General Curtis's order to purchase stolen horses. "I will not jayhawk or steal on any order," Sheridan impertinently wrote Curtis, "nor will I acknowledge the right of any person under my supervision in this District to do so." Charges were drawn up against him for "disobedience of orders and neglect of duty," but never pressed, and he rejoined General Halleck's staff.[25]

Still eager for a field command, Sheridan requested appointment as colonel of the Second Michigan Cavalry. General Halleck, sorry to lose an excellent staff officer, reluctantly agreed to Sheridan's transfer. Within thirty-five days the new colonel of volunteers led his regiment into a half-dozen skirmishes, a daring 180-mile raid, and a masterful battle at Booneville, Mississippi, where his 750 troopers routed 4,000 Confederates.

His superiors were impressed. General William S. Rosecrans and four of his brigadiers telegraphed Halleck, now general in chief in Washington: "Brigadiers scarce; good ones scarcer. . . . The undersigned respectfully beg that you will obtain the promotion of Sheridan. He is worth his weight in gold." Sheridan, meanwhile, marched on to Louisville, Kentucky, to reinforce General Don Carlos Buell's Army of the Ohio. Upon his arrival, he received a promotion to brigadier general of volunteers.[26]

He did a superb job arranging the defense of Louisville and was rewarded with command of the newly organized Eleventh Division. On October 8, 1862, his troops repelled five rebel assaults at Perryville, Kentucky, to hold the line and save the Union army. The northern press, starved for authentic heroes, hailed Sheridan as the "paladin of Perryville."

Rosecrans replaced General Buell soon after Perryville as commander of the redesignated Army of the Cumberland, but victories came no more easily. In January 1863 at Stones River—near Murfreesboro, Tennessee—Sheridan tenaciously held on amidst great slaughter to form the anchor that allowed George Thomas's line to stand. Rosecrans seemed ready to retreat after a day of terrible carnage at Stones River, but was dissuaded by Thomas and Sheridan at a midnight council of war. Sheridan consented to lead the counterstroke that eventually brought a grisly but important victory to the Union.[27]

Stones River confirmed Sheridan's growing reputation for tenacity and courage. "I knew it was infernal in there before I got in," declared Major General Lovell Rousseau in describing the battle, "but I was convinced of it when I saw Phil Sheridan, with hat in one hand and sword in the other, fighting as if he were the devil incarnate, and swearing as if he had a fresh indulgence from Father Tracy every five minutes."[28]

The stand at Stones River earned Sheridan another star in the volunteers, but his actions at Chattanooga won him Grant's esteem and secured his future. Sheridan had shared in the humiliation of the Army of the Cumberland, first defeated at Chickamauga and then besieged in Chattanooga. Now he shared in the determination of his men to redeem themselves in front of reinforcing troops from the Army of the Potomac under Joe Hooker and the Army of the Tennessee under Sherman. Grant, placed in overall command west of the Alleghenies to meet the Chattanooga crisis, seemed determined to deny the Cumberlanders an opportunity for redemption. Sheridan's soldiers seethed when they learned that they would be held in reserve. The assaults against the Confederate positions high above the city on Lookout Mountain and Missionary Ridge were entrusted to Sherman and Hooker.

The Cumberlanders' chance finally came on November 25, 1863. Sherman's men had been repulsed four times from the north slope of Missionary when Grant ordered the Cumberlanders forward to assault the rifle pits at the base of the central ridge. The maneuver was intended to take pressure off Sherman's men. Sheridan's Second Division, one of four in the assault, overran the rifle pits with ease, but faced a murderous fire from the crest of the ridge, some four hundred feet above them. To advance up the ridge appeared suicidal, but to stay in the rifle pits was equally deadly. Sheridan sent an aide off to his commander, Gordon Granger, begging permission to take the ridge. When the officer returned with Granger's assent, Sheridan beamed.

Taking a pewter flask from his aide, Sheridan toasted the Confederate headquarters directly above him. As he gulped down the brandy, the Confederate batteries answered with a mighty volley that sent dirt and rock flying all around him. Cursing rebel rudeness, Sheridan tossed the flask up the ridge, mounted his black charger, Rienzi, and led his division roaring up Missionary Ridge.

Afterward the newspapers called it the miracle of Missionary Ridge. The Cumberlanders swept up the face of the ridge as one, each regiment pushing to plant its colors on the crest first. Sheridan, unlike

13

the other Union commanders, did not halt on the summit, but pushed on after the retreating rebels to Chickamauga Station.[29]

"Sheridan showed his genius in that battle," declared a delighted Grant, "and to him I owe the capture of most of the prisoners that were taken. Although commanding a division only, he saw in the crisis of that engagement that it was necessary to advance beyond the point indicated by his orders . . . and with the instinct of military genius pushed ahead."[30] Sheridan never quit, and Grant prized him for it. When Grant went east in March 1864 as general in chief, he offered Sheridan command of the cavalry of the Army of the Potomac.

General George Gordon Meade, commanding the Army of the Potomac, believed the role of cavalry was to provide heavy escorts for provision trains and infantry columns and do picket duty. Sheridan and Meade argued incessantly, for the new cavalry commander believed that cavalry ought to fight cavalry and infantry fight infantry. Sheridan wanted to concentrate his ten thousand troopers and engage J. E. B. Stuart's supposedly invincible horsemen. Grant eventually interceded, overruled Meade, and ordered Sheridan's three divisions of cavalry to attack Stuart. Sheridan's troopers proceeded to avenge three years of humiliation by brushing aside the Confederate cavalry at Yellow Tavern, mortally wounding Stuart in the process, and then galloping to the gates of Richmond before rejoining the Union army.

Sheridan's role in the fighting now increased. When Lee sent General Jubal Early up the Shenandoah Valley to threaten Washington and relieve the pressure on Richmond, Grant countered by placing Sheridan in command of the Army of the Shenandoah. Lincoln objected because of Sheridan's youth, but youthful audacity was essential if the North was to seal off the Shenandoah breadbasket from Lee. The reputations of Frémont, Banks, Shields, Sigel, and Hunter were shattered campaigning in the valley, but Sheridan fared better. In September 1864 he soundly defeated Early at Winchester and Fisher's Hill. These victories won him a brigadier's star in the regular army.

At Cedar Creek, however, the rebels caught the federals napping while Sheridan was absent and routed a portion of the army. Sheridan, returning from a conference in Washington, heard the sounds of battle and raced to the field, where his presence so electrified his stricken army that it rallied and crushed the Confederates. The

Just before departing for the Shenandoah Valley campaign, Sheridan posed with several of his cavalry commanders. Left to right: General Henry E. Davies, who later wrote a biography of Sheridan and a book on their buffalo hunting adventures in the West; General David McMurtrie Gregg, able commander of the Second Division who remained with the Army of the Potomac when the others departed for the Valley; Sheridan, fully bearded for one of the few times in his life; General Wesley Merritt, a great favorite with Sheridan who eventually commanded the Fifth Cavalry in the Indian Wars; General Alfred T. A. Torbert, who became chief of cavalry in the Valley campaign but failed to live up to Sheridan's expectations; and General James H. Wilson, able commander of the Third Division who became Sherman's chief of cavalry in October 1864. (*U.S. Signal Corps photo, National Archives*)

victory came on the eve of the presidential election and proved a tonic for Lincoln and the Republicans. The president commissioned Sheridan a major general in the regular army, and Congress tendered its thanks. He now stood firmly with Grant and Sherman in the front rank of Union generals.

At Cedar Creek Sheridan had eliminated the Confederate army in the Shenandoah, but he had been ordered to destroy not only the enemy but also his resources. Sheridan's Robbers, as his army was

The nation was captivated by Sheridan's dramatic ride to rally his army at Cedar Creek, October 19, 1864. It became one of the best-known episodes of the war, repeatedly told in song, poem, and painting. This version by Louis Prang depicts the general riding between the lines to encourage his stricken troops. They cheered him and then crushed their Confederate foes. The victory won Sheridan promotion to major general in the regular army and secured his place among the top echelon of Union generals. (*Chicago Historical Society*)

thereafter known, so effectively ravaged Virginia's most bountiful valley that Sheridan could boast, with little exaggeration, that "a crow would be compelled to carry his own rations" when crossing the Shenandoah.[31]

Sheridan knew that the war would soon end, and eager to have his cavalry "be in at the death," he hurriedly rejoined Grant.[32] At Five Forks his forces destroyed the right flank of Lee's army, at Sailor's Creek his men captured Ewell and the right wing of the Army of Northern Virginia, and at Appomattox he blocked the line of retreat of Lee's forces. With Lee's surrender the thirty-four-year-old Sheridan reached the zenith of his military career.

War had been a tonic to Sheridan. "He was a wonderful man on the battle field," one of his officers recalled, "and never in as good humor as when under fire." Like a Spartan warrior the comradeship of camp and field gave him his fondest memories, and he retained a fierce loyalty to those who had served him well. His view of war was not romantic, for Sheridan was a modern warrior.[33]

Sheridan shared Sherman's view that "war is simply power unrestrained by constitution or compact." Power was to be used to cripple an enemy people as well as an enemy army. "I do not hold war to mean simply that lines of men shall engage each other in battle," Sheridan wrote. "This is but a duel, in which one combatant seeks the other's life; war means much more, and is far worse than this." The key to success in war is in ravaging the enemy homeland and destroying his will, "for the loss of property weighs heavy with the most of mankind; heavier often, than the sacrifices made on the field of battle." The torch, to Sheridan was as effective a weapon as the sword, because "reduction to poverty brings prayers for peace more surely and more quickly than does the destruction of human life."[34]

Sheridan quickly learned the effect of terror on a hostile civilian population. When Confederate partisans killed one of his messengers, he responded by ordering every house within a five-mile radius of the incident burned. Unable to injure the source of his irritation, the redoubtable Confederate ranger John Mosby, Sheridan wreaked vengeance upon the innocent, convinced they would identify Mosby as the source of their misfortune and turn against him. "I have made a scapegoat of [Mosby] for the destruction of private rights," Sheridan wrote Halleck. "Now there is going to be an intense hatred of him in that portion of this Valley which is nearly a desert. I will soon commence on Loudoun County, and let them know there is a God in Israel." Exasperated when such measures failed to stop Mosby, Sheridan received permission from Grant to hang captured partisans without trial, arrest as suspected guerrillas all the male citizens of Loudoun County under fifty, and incarcerate as hostages the wives and children of known partisans. Sheridan was always ruthless in battle, pursuing a routed foe until either annihilation or surrender resulted, but the frustration of guerrilla warfare completely brutalized him. When Mosby's rangers eluded him, Sheridan vented his anger on the innocent and guilty alike.[35]

Sheridans heartlessness toward an enemy contrasted sharply with his compassion for the men of his command. He not only selected campsites but also went to great pains to ensure that his men were well fed and clothed. In his view there was a social contract between officers and enlisted men with obligations on each side, and if an officer fulfilled his obligations, "recompense would surely come through the hearty response that soldiers always make to conscientious exertion on the part of their superiors." An officer who failed in his obligations was worthless, for "a General lacking the confidence of his men is not less helpless than a general without an Army."[36]

Although often described as the embodiment of the reckless cavalryman, Sheridan rarely exposed his men to needless danger. Unlike many other officers, he respected the intelligence of the common soldier and understood that "none realized more quickly than they the blundering that often takes place on the field of battle." If soldiers were to be called on to die, they must have "some tangible indemnity for the loss of life." He never sought glory at the expense of his men. At Richmond in May 1864 he turned aside, although the city was practically undefended and a raid into it would have made him "the hero of the hour," because his men "would have known as well as I that the sacrifice was for no permanent advantage."[37] Sheridan's soldiers responded to his concern with unqualified devotion. Few generals could claim such influence over their men as Sheridan demonstrated at Cedar Creek, when by his mere presence on the field he rallied a routed army. Yet, recalled John Schuyler Crosby, "Sheridan rarely expressed any strong approval other than a quiet smile . . . [for] it was inconceivable to him that a man should expect any reward for performing the service required of him."[38]

If, however, an officer or soldier failed to perform his duty, or even failed to share Sheridan's zeal, the general's wrath was unrelenting and unmerciful. At Stones River he observed three officers—"three things wearing shoulder straps" was how he described them—skulking from the battlefield. He had them arrested and a few days later marched out on dress parade. Forming the division in a hollow square, with himself and the skulking officers in the center, Sheridan harangued the troops on the obligations of officers. Unwilling to ask any of his troopers to degrade themselves by touching the cowards, he then called forward his black servant to tear off the shoulder straps and buttons from the officers. Sheridan was proud of the fact that thereafter his division's casualties in officers exceeded those of other units.[39]

In February 1865, at the close of the Shenandoah campaign, Sheridan replaced General Alfred T. A. Torbert, long his chief of cavalry, with Wesley Merritt. Torbert was not replaced because of failure—on the contrary, his corps had succeeded spectacularly—but because on two occasions, at Luray Valley and Gordonsville, he was not aggressive enough. When the army was reorganized after the war, with most of Sheridan's division commanders receiving regiments, Torbert was given only the rank of captain. For the same reason Sheridan removed General Gouverneur K. Warren, a hero at Gettysburg, from command of the Fifth Corps at Five Forks. Warren simply moved his troops into position too slowly and displayed a quiet calm in the face of the enemy, which the excitable Sheridan attributed to apathy.[40]

Sheridan was a good hater, especially if someone was beyond his power to punish. His contempt for Meade was notorious, but his persecution of General William B. Hazen displayed even more glaringly a cruel pettiness. After Missionary Ridge, Sheridan and Hazen argued over whose troops reached the crest first and captured eleven rebel cannons. Although Grant sided with Sheridan, the controversy continued, and Sheridan never forgave Hazen.[41]

Sheridan emerged from the Civil War as the premier Union combat leader. Rarely innovative, he nevertheless developed the cavalry into a more powerful force by dismounting them in battle and supplying them with artillery support. He utilized techniques of scouting and spying at a level far above his colleagues and always had a reputation as the best-informed general on any field. Although cautious and painstaking in planning battles, on the field he could be quick-thinking and bold to the point of rashness. "A persevering terrier dog" is how Sherman viewed him—"honest, modest, plucky and smart enough."[42]

Adam Badeau, Grant's military secretary, described the relationship between Sheridan and Grant as "the love of strong men who had stood side by side in war, and watched each other's deeds. . . . The affection was founded on admiration; the intimacy grew out of achievement. It was the strange, rich fruit of battle, watered by blood and ripened by patriotism into a close and tender regard." Grant's affections often caused him to exercise poor judgment, and his opinion of Sheridan was sometimes given over to hyperbole. Yet this estimate which Grant expressed to Senator George F. Hoar is probably true: "I

Matthew Brady photographed Sheridan and four of his best generals in 1865, just before they all embarked on new careers as Indian fighters. Left to right are Wesley Merritt, Sheridan, George Crook, James W. Forsyth, and George A. Custer. (*United States Military Academy Archives*)

believe General Sheridan has no superior as a general, either living or dead, and perhaps not an equal. . . . He has judgment, prudence, foresight and power to deal with dispositions needed in a great war. I entertained this opinion of him before he became generally known in the late war."[43]

With the close of the Civil War, Grant immediately ordered Sheridan to Texas. He was told to establish a large force on the Rio Grande, supposedly to force the surrender of Kirby Smith's rebel forces but actually to be ready to move against Maximilian, Louis

Napoleon's puppet in Mexico. Both Grant and Sheridan viewed the French intervention in Mexico as an extension of the American rebellion, "because of the encouragement that invasion had received from the Confederacy." Indeed, several prominent former Confederates had enlisted under Maximilian's banner in return for promises of land grants and peon labor. Grant wanted the Johnson administration to issue a peremptory demand for the withdrawal of the French and, in case of noncompliance, to let Sheridan unite with Benito Juárez and attack the imperialists. Grant gave Sheridan command of fifty-two thousand men and suggested that "he was not to be over-cautious about provoking the Imperial forces." Sheridan considered Maximilian no better than "the buccaneer, Morgan, on a more extended scale" and relished the possibility of confronting the French in battle. He felt the Union army at the close of the war to be the finest in the world, and he hoped for any opportunity to prove it. Without taking time to appear in the grand victory parade in Washington, an event he hated to miss, Sheridan hurried to the Rio Grande.[44]

Secretary of State William H. Seward, however, was not going to allow Grant and Sheridan to stampede the nation into a war with France. Under intense pressure from the French ministry, Seward ordered Sheridan to "preserve a strict neutrality" along the border. Exasperated, Sheridan declared that "it required the patience of Job to abide the slow and poky methods" of the State Department.

Since patience was not one of Sheridan's virtues, he construed "strict neutrality" in the loosest possible way. He constantly moved his troops along the border and sent a pontoon train to Brownsville, Texas. Sheridan also held a review of the Fourth Corps and Wesley Merritt's cavalry division at San Antonio, loudly proclaiming them ready for combat. Proceeding to his old post, Fort Duncan, with a regiment of cavalry, he opened communications with Juárez, inquiring about roads into Mexico and the availability of forage. At the same time, huge quantities of arms and ammunition were declared surplus or condemned and deposited on the Rio Grande for Juárez's troops. During the winter of 1866 more than thirty thousand muskets from the Baton Rouge arsenal alone were turned over to Juárez. Sheridan's maneuvers had the double effect of strengthening Juárez while bluffing Maximilian's army out of northern Mexico.[45]

In January 1867 Sheridan's spies brought word that the French were abandoning Maximilian, expecting to withdraw all their troops by March 15. The imperialist enterprise moved swiftly to its melancholy finale, and although Sheridan sent one of his scouts to Juárez with a plea from Seward to spare Maximilian, the pretender was executed. Sheridan took pride in the significant part played by his command in restoring republican government to Mexico, doubting "whether such results could have been achieved without the presence of an American army on the Rio Grande."[46]

Although preoccupied with Mexico, Sheridan kept a wary eye on civil affairs in Louisiana and Texas. He cooperated with A. J. Hamilton, the Unionist provisional governor of Texas, and distributed troops at critical points throughout the state to suppress night-riding former rebels and to assist civil agents in enforcing the law. The inauguration of James W. Throckmorton as governor of Texas on August 9, 1866, brought an end to such cooperation. Throckmorton immediately requested President Johnson to order the military to quit interfering in civil matters. Johnson promptly complied, much to Sheridan's chagrin. The state quickly enacted various apprentice and vagrancy laws—Black Codes—which Sheridan declared resulted in "a policy of gross injustice toward the colored people on the part of the courts, and a reign of lawlessness and disorder ensued."[47]

Sheridan further enraged the citizens of Texas with a flippant remark to a newspaper reporter. Arriving in Galveston after a long day's ride at the conclusion of an inspection tour along the Rio Grande, Sheridan was checking into a local hotel when approached by a stranger wishing to know how he liked Texas. While slapping a cloud of trail dust off his uniform the general replied, "If I owned hell and Texas, I would rent Texas out and live in hell!" That quip quickly became one of the West's most famous quotations. The reporter had gotten a better story than he could ever have hoped for, and Sheridan's "hell and Texas" remark made good copy throughout the Lone Star State. The general took little interest in the uproar. But he did derive some pleasure from an editorial in a small border-county paper praising him for sticking up for his place of origin.[48]

In Louisiana, where Unionists were engaged in a heated political struggle with resurgent former Confederates, there was a crisis. Unionists, with the dubious support of Governor James M. Wells, called a convention to assemble in New Orleans and remodel the state's

1864 constitution. They were opposed by the state's lieutenant governor, attorney general, and the mayor of New Orleans, John T. Monroe. The anticonventionists unsuccessfully requested General Absalom Baird, the senior military officer present while Sheridan was in Texas, to arrest the convention leaders. Upon receiving assurances from President Johnson that the military would not interfere, the anticonvention forces decided to arrest the Unionists themselves. On July 30, 1866, thirty convention delegates and several hundred black supporters were attacked by Mayor Monroe's police force and a mob of white citizens. Thirty-seven blacks were killed, many of them pursued and clubbed to death blocks from the convention site, while over a hundred were wounded. General Baird, arriving with his troops too late to save the Unionists, declared martial law. When he arrived in New Orleans the day after the riot, Sheridan disgustedly declared the affair to be "an absolute massacre by the police . . . perpetrated without the shadow of a necessity."[49]

Sheridan sent Grant a report on the riot, labeling the convention leaders "political agitators and revolutionary men," but firmly placing blame for the violence on Mayor Monroe and his police force. The report was forwarded to Johnson, who released it to the press with the key passage blaming Monroe deleted. Outraged when he realized his report had been distorted, Sheridan officially protested "this breach of military honor." He felt that Johnson was "governed less by patriotic motives than by personal ambitions" and cared nothing for the safety of the freedmen and southern Unionists.[50]

Sheridan was hardly a crusader, clearly subscribing to the racial prejudices of his era, but he was determined to protect the emancipated blacks. He had not forgotten that during the terrible "mud-march" of March 1865, when his army was bogged down in Virginia, some two thousand blacks who had attached themselves to his column literally lifted the wagons out of the mud, allowing the army to proceed to Petersburg. They had earned their freedom, and "it was the plain duty of those in authority to make it secure" and "see that they had a fair chance in the battle of life."[51]

No matter how much he might sympathize with the blacks, Sheridan's basic conservatism led him to oppose government interference in the racial situation beyond providing protection. "I believe the best thing that Congress or State can do is to legislate as little as possible in reference to the colored man beyond giving him security in his person and property," Sheridan declared. "His social status will be worked out by the logic of the necessity for his labor."[52]

Grant urged Sheridan to "persevere exactly in the course your own good judgment dictates," assuring him that "the purity of your motives will never be impeached by the public." The general in chief, while strongly disagreeing with Johnson's position on Reconstruction, felt compelled by respect for the presidency to remain publicly silent. Grant had no reluctance, however, in urging Sheridan to pursue a policy in direct contradiction of the president's wishes. Sheridan followed Grant instead of Johnson; his loyalty was to the general. Secretary of the Navy Gideon Welles, no lover of either Grant or Sheridan, correctly saw that Sheridan was "really but a secondary personage after all in the business. He would never have pursued the course he has if not prompted and encouraged by others to whom he looked—from whom he received advice if not orders."[53]

Sheridan's position was bolstered in March 1867, when Congress overrode Johnson's vetoes and the first two Reconstruction acts became law. As commander of the Fifth Military District (Texas and Louisiana) Sheridan was determined to see a "zealous execution" of the new laws, although he knew that Johnson would endeavor to embarrass him "by every means in his power, not only on account of his pronounced personal hostility, but also because of his determination not to execute but to obstruct the measures enacted by Congress." Eight days after the laws went into effect, Sheridan removed from office Mayor Monroe of New Orleans, the attorney general of Louisiana, and a district judge who had worked against the Unionist convention. In June he removed Louisiana Governor Wells, who, he felt, was attempting to defraud the state by packing the Board of Levee Commissioners with his cronies. In all these acts Sheridan was supported by Grant, who assured his friend that, if Johnson removed him from command, it would not damage his military career.[54]

The second Reconstruction Act authorized the registration of voters to elect delegates for state constitutional conventions, but who was allowed to register remained unclear. Sheridan asked the administration for clarification and received an opinion from Attorney General Henry Stanbery that interpreted the law liberally, limiting the power of registration boards and allowing anyone to vote who was willing to take an oath of allegiance. Sheridan disapproved of Stanbery's ruling and asked Grant whether he had to abide by it. Grant urged him to enforce his "own construction of the military bill until ordered to do otherwise." He assured Sheridan that Stanbery's opinion lacked "the force of an order." In this Grant directly contradicted the president's wishes. Congress settled the question with the third Reconstruction Act in July 1867, which gave registration boards the right to deny registration to anyone they believed was disfranchised.[55]

Congress also stripped Johnson of most of his power over Reconstruction, but, as commander in chief, he could still assign military personnel wherever he pleased. He used that power, against the advice of all his cabinet members except Welles, to remove Sheridan on July 31, 1867, from command of the Fifth Military District. Johnson had long considered such action, feeling that Sheridan's rule had been "one of absolute tyranny, without reference to the principles of our government." Sheridan's dispute with Governor Throckmorton of Texas prompted the decision.[56]

Sheridan and Throckmorton had argued over transferring troops from the interior of the state to protect frontier settlers from raiding Comanches. When Sheridan refused to move any men, Throckmorton appealed to the administration for redress, and the general was overruled. Sheridan angrily noted, "If a white man is killed by the Indians on an extensive Indian frontier, the greatest excitement will take place, but over the killing of many freedmen in the settlements, nothing is done." He retaliated by removing Throckmorton from office and was himself removed from command the next day.[57]

Grant had tried to dissuade Johnson from relieving Sheridan by reminding the president that it was "unmistakably the wish of the country that Gen. Sheridan not be removed." When his efforts failed, Grant acidly pointed out to the president that his well-publicized opposition to Sheridan had "emboldened the opponents to the laws of Congress . . . to oppose [Sheridan] in every way in their power, and has rendered necessary measures which otherwise might never have been necessary."[58] Johnson was not persuaded and declared that "patriotic considerations demand that he [Sheridan] should be superseded by an officer, who, while he will faithfully execute the law, will at the same time give more general satisfaction to the whole people, white and black, North and South." In other words, Johnson desired a more

Artist Theodore Davis made this informal sketch of Sheridan in New Orleans during the summer of 1866. Davis used the sketch to illustrate his brief article on the general that appeared in the June 1892 issue of *Cosmopolitan*. Davis described the inspiration for the drawing, entitled "On His Rostrum," thus: "In work Sheridan, while methodical, was liable at any moment to break off writing, and literally turn his back on this, his hardest labor. Then, when he spoke, looking from my drawing I saw a coatless rotund form seated squarely on the desk, his chair a footstool."

pliable officer who would conform to the presidential concept of Reconstruction, and in Major General Winfield Scott Hancock he found such an officer. Grant reassured Sheridan that his "personal welfare" would not suffer as a result of Johnson's action and promised to continue defending his administration of the district, "not from personal feeling or partiality, but because you were right."[59]

Sheridan had executed the laws of Congress in the Fifth Military District with the same rigor with which he had charged up Missionary Ridge, treating civil officials as if they were subordinates in his army. Many aspects of his administration were admirable, especially his zealous regard for the safety of the freedmen, and there is no reason to regard his tenure as a failure. His stubbornness, candor, quick temper, prejudices, dislike of the president and sympathy with the Radicals in Congress made it impossible for Sheridan to win the support of the defeated people he governed, but that was not the intent of the Reconstruction acts. He was sustained in his course by Secretary of War Edwin Stanton, a majority of the Congress, and, most importantly, General Grant.

Sheridan looked back on his command of the district with grim satisfaction, for he had done his best, and he looked forward to new opportunities in the Department of the Missouri, where he could again take the field. He would once again go west, this time as a general.

CHAPTER 2

Sheridan's Campaign: "The Enemies of Our Race"

The arrival of the new year, 1868, found Sheridan relaxing in Washington, D.C., enjoying the good life while serving on a board with Lieutenant General Sherman and Brigadier General (Brevet Major General) Christopher C. Augur to compile a code of articles of war and army regulations. "I am pushing Sheridan as hard as I can to work, but he don't want to hurry through," complained Sherman to his wife. "He rather enjoys the parties." Sheridan was in no particular hurry to return to the West, because Indian affairs had been taken out of military hands and turned over to a peace commission charged with negotiating an end to warfare and settling the tribes on suitable reservations. It was February 29, 1868, before he arrived at Fort Leavenworth to take charge of his department, officially relieving the temporary commander, Colonel (Brevet Major General) Andrew J. Smith, on March 2.[1]

The 100th meridian, neatly dividing the Department of the Missouri in half, also marked the beginning of semiarid lands. To the east grew tall grasses over rolling plains, often cut by shallow streambeds bordered with timber. To the west rose high, flat plains covered with a matting of short grass and stretching to the Rocky Mountains. These grasslands provided forage for great herds of buffalo. During the summers hot southwesterly winds, wrung dry of moisture by the Rockies, turned the region into a blast furnace, while in the fall and winter violent north winds sent the temperature plunging and, when accompanied by sleet and snow, spelled doom for the unprotected traveler.

The department was divided into four military districts, each designed to expedite the control of particular Indian tribes. These districts were manned by a total of approximately six thousand soldiers, scattered about in twenty-seven forts and camps.[2] The District of New Mexico, commanded by Colonel (Brevet Major General) George W. Getty, had been relatively quiet since the Navajo War of 1863–64, save for sporadic Apache raids. Within Getty's district lived the Navajos, Utes, some Apaches, and a scattering of smaller tribes. New Mexico was an old military district, well supplied with forts, with headquarters at Santa Fe. Elements of the Thirty-seventh Infantry, Thirty-eighth Infantry, and Third Cavalry garrisoned Forts Union, Craig, Sumner, Selden, Stanton, Bascom, Bayard, Wingate, Lowell, Cummings, and McRae.

The District of the Indian Territory, commanded by Colonel (Brevet Major General) Benjamin H. Grierson as of May 1868, was the home of numerous tribes—Cherokees, Chickasaws, Choctaws, Creeks, Seminoles, and Osages. The 1867 Treaty of Medicine Lodge marked out new reservations for the Kiowas, Comanches, Arapahos, and Cheyennes within this district, but the tribes had not taken up residence when Sheridan took command of the department. Elements of the Tenth Cavalry and Sixth Infantry were stationed at the two posts within the district, Forts Gibson and Arbuckle.[3]

The District of Kansas was commanded by Colonel (Brevet Major General) William Hoffman of the Third Infantry, with headquarters at Fort Leavenworth. The only other post in the district was Fort Riley, but a few companies of the Tenth Cavalry were placed in strategic camps to guard against raiding Indians.[4]

Most of Colorado, and all of Kansas west of Fort Harker, formed the District of the Upper Arkansas, commanded by Major (Brevet Lieutenant Colonel) Thomas C. English. It was through this district that the major stage and wagon roads, the Smokey Hill and Santa Fe trails, directed commerce toward Colorado and New Mexico. More important, along the Smokey Hill Road the Kansas Pacific Railroad was methodically moving toward Denver. These routes were guarded by components of the Seventh and Tenth Cavalry, and the Third, Fifth, and Thirty-eighth Infantry stationed at Forts Harker,

Hays, and Wallace along the line of the Kansas Pacific, and at Forts Zarah, Dodge, Larned, Lyon, and Reynolds, along the Santa Fe Trail. The district included lands claimed by the Cheyennes, Arapahos, Kiowas, and Comanches and over which bands of Sioux, Northern Cheyennes, and Northern Arapahos also hunted. Within the district Sheridan had a force of about twelve hundred cavalry and fourteen hundred infantry, composed mainly of new recruits. This was hardly sufficient to deal with the estimated six thousand warriors roaming the area should hostilities commence.[5]

Indian-white relations from the Platte River on the north to the Red River on the south had been in disarray since 1864, when Governor John Evans of Colorado Territory and Colonel John M. Chivington of the Colorado volunteers began a war of extermination against the Cheyennes. Chivington's massacre of a peaceful Cheyenne village along Sand Creek near Fort Lyon in November 1864 enraged the plains tribes. Public indignation over the Sand Creek affair and a year of costly, futile campaigning, led the government to send a peace commission to negotiate a settlement with the Indians. By the treaties of the Little Arkansas, signed with various chiefs of the Cheyennes, Arapahos, Comanches, Kiowas, and Kiowa-Apaches in October 1865, the Indians agreed to give up their lands in Colorado, cease warfare, and accept reservations in the Indian Territory, southern Kansas, and the Texas Panhandle. The states of Texas and Kansas, however, refused to allow any reservations within their boundaries, and Congress, more concerned with Reconstruction, dallied for two years with the treaties. In the meantime, the tribes roamed across the plains, following the buffalo herds and grumbling over the ever-increasing white population.

Major General Winfield Scott Hancock, appointed commander of the Department of the Missouri in 1866, marched into the Indian country in April 1867 with seven companies of infantry, eleven companies of cavalry, and an artillery battery to investigate rumors of Indian depredations. At first the Cheyenne Dog Soldiers and their Oglala Sioux allies promised to parley with Hancock, but when he approached their village on the Pawnee Fork of the Arkansas River, they fled. One Sand Creek massacre was enough. Enraged, Hancock ordered Lieutenant Colonel (Brevet Major General) George A. Custer to pursue the Indians with eight companies of the Seventh Cavalry.[6]

Lieutenant Colonel George Armstrong Custer, photographed in
1869, dressed and bearded as he appeared during the Washita
campaign. "If there was any poetry or romance in war he could
develop it," said Sheridan of his flamboyant protégé. (*Little Bighorn
Battlefield National Monument, National Park Service*)

Custer, who would lead the major strike forces for both Hancock and Sheridan on the southern plains, was the embodiment of the romantic cavalryman, a stereotype he sought and nurtured. Graduated from West Point as the goat of the class of 1861, Custer had, through good fortune and hard work, won a brigadier's star at the age of twenty-three in 1863. The press labeled him "the Boy General with his flowing yellow curls," and they reported his wild charges from Gettysburg to Appomattox, where as major general of volunteers under Sheridan he helped cut off Lee's retreat. Sheridan purchased the table on which the surrender terms were written and presented it to Elizabeth Custer, declaring that "there is scarcely an individual in our service who has contributed more to bring about this desirable result than your very gallant husband." In the army reorganization following the war Custer was awarded the lieutenant-colonelcy of the new Seventh Cavalry. Custer was Sheridan's protégé, and the older general fondly remembered that "if there was any poetry or romance in war he [Custer] could develop it." But Sheridan also recognized the volatile side of Custer's character, for he "was as boyish as he was brave" and "always needed someone to restrain him." Sheridan admired nothing more than audacity and aggressiveness, but Custer "was too impetuous, without deliberation; he thought himself invincible and having a charmed life."[7]

Most observers failed to understand Custer, their eyes blinded by either the gallant cavalier or the eccentric egomaniac. Those who served with him in battle tended to remember him with "a pistol in his boot, jangling spurs on his heels, and a ponderous claymore swinging at his side—a wild daredevil of a general, and a prince of advance guards, quick to see and act." But to many who rode with him on the frustrating Indian hunts of 1867 he was "an incarnate fiend" and a "complete example of a petty tyrant," who spared neither man nor beast in his search for added laurels.[8]

Custer found no glory chasing Indians in the summer of 1867. By the time he reached Smokey Hill Road, the band had broken into small parties and scattered. He reported his failure to Hancock along with the news that warriors had struck all along the road, burning stage stations, killing the inhabitants, and driving off stock. Custer pointed out that the depredations were committed before the Indians from

Pawnee Fork could have reached the road, thus exonerating them from participation in the crimes.[9]

Hancock responded by burning the deserted Indian camp and property at Pawnee Fork, an act that undercut the position of the peace advocates among the tribes and allowed the war factions to gain control. Guerrilla war soon swept the plains from the Platte to the Red River.[10]

Hancock could see that his campaign was a failure, and in frustration searched for a scapegoat. He soon found one. Custer had engaged in a fruitless search for Indians to the north, finally marching and countermarching himself into arrest. Weary of chasing Indian will-o'-the-wisps, he made a forced march from Fort Wallace to Fort Harker in mid-July, supposedly to speed along needed supplies, but actually, as a court-martial later ruled, to visit his wife. The boy general was suspended from rank and pay for one year. Custer was convinced, and Sheridan agreed, that the trial was "an attempt by Hancock to cover up the failure of the Indian expedition."[11]

With Custer's court-martial, Hancock's campaign came to a sorry close. The expedition had accomplished much, but none of it good from the government's viewpoint. Indian raids were on the increase; even army posts were struck. Workers on the Union Pacific were continually harrassed, while a combination of high water and Indians brought construction of the Kansas Pacific to a grinding halt. The United States Treasury was several million dollars poorer, and the bright reputations of Hancock and Custer were tarnished.[12]

An exasperated Congress passed an act on July 20, 1867, creating an Indian Peace Commission to negotiate a peaceful settlement with the hostile tribes. The commission consisted of General Sherman; General William S. Harney; General Alfred H. Terry; Senator John B. Henderson, chairman of the Senate Committee on Indian Affairs; Nathaniel G. Taylor, commissioner of Indian Affairs; John B. Sanborn, Minnesota lawyer and former general of volunteers; and Samuel F. Tappan, who had presided over the investigation of the Sand Creek massacre. While the work of the commission was in progress, Sherman ordered a halt to all offensive operations against the tribes. The commission, with General Christopher C. Augur taking the temporarily absent Sherman's place, met with the southern tribes on Medicine

Lodge Creek, about seventy miles south of Fort Larned. Treaties were signed with the Kiowas, Kiowa-Apaches, and Comanches on October 21, and then with the Cheyennes and Arapahos on October 28. By the treaties the tribes agreed to accept reservations in the Indian Territory, although they retained the right to hunt buffalo south of the Arkansas River. The Cheyennes were given permission to hunt north of the Arkansas until the buffalo were all killed off, but this provision was later changed without their knowledge. They were to give up their claims to all other territory, cease opposition to the railroads, and stay away from the major roads and settlements. In return the government was to provide them with specified amounts of food, clothing, and other provisions, as well as doctors, schools, teachers, and tradesmen. After the signing the commissioners distributed presents, which is what most of the Indians had really come for, and returned east much pleased with their accomplishment.[13]

Of course, the celebrated treaty was misunderstood. In the last speech given before the Cheyennes signed the treaty, Buffalo Chief clearly stated the Cheyenne position: "We sprung from the prairie, we live by it, we prefer to do so, and, as yet, we do not want the blessings of civilization. We do not claim this country south of the Arkansas, but that country between the Arkansas and the Platte is ours. . . . You give us presents and then take our land; that produces war." Captain Albert Barnitz, of the Seventh Cavalry, noted in his diary that the Cheyennes "had *no idea that* they are giving up, or that they have ever given up the country which they claim as their own—the country north of the Arkansas. The treaty all amounts to nothing, and we will certainly have another war sooner or later with the Cheyennes."[14]

Congress, preoccupied with the impeachment of President Johnson, took no action on the treaties, so the promised annuities were delayed and the proposed Indian Territory reservations unopened. It was late July 1868 before five hundred thousand dollars was appropriated to fulfill the obligations of Medicine Lodge.[15]

Congressional insensitivity brought General Sherman to take up the Indian's cause. "The poor Indians are starving," he wrote his wife from Kansas. "We kill them if they attempt to hunt and if they keep within the Reservations they starve. Of course we [the peace commission] recommended they should receive certain food for a time

... but Congress makes no provision and of course nothing is done. I wish Congress could be impeached."[16]

Sheridan, however, was less concerned with congressional hot air than with Indian hotheads. Rumors of war abounded, and soon after his arrival in Kansas he embarked on an inspection tour of Forts Zarah, Larned, and Dodge. Large bands of Cheyennes, Kiowas, and Arapahos camped along Pawnee Creek near Fort Larned, and Sheridan visited their villages to measure their temper. He found them "reckless and defiant" of the military and outspoken in their contempt for the Treaty of Medicine Lodge. At a council at Fort Larned the Cheyenne chief Stone Calf told Sheridan: "Let your soldiers grow long hair, so that we can have some honor in killing them." Sheridan smiled, replying that he could not comply since his soldiers would then get lice.[17]

Sheridan discovered that Brulé and Oglala Sioux had come south with tales of how Red Cloud's warriors had swept aside the soldiers at Fort Phil Kearny and closed the Bozeman Trail. The delays in delivery of promised annuities, especially of arms and ammunition, increased the influence of the war factions. Sheridan found these warriors disdainful of his troopers. When, on one occasion, he refused the Indians arms and ammunition with the declaration that they might use them against the soldiers, the warriors promised to use guns only against buffalo, adding that they could "chase soldier and drive way with sticks."[18]

Never one to shun a fight, Sheridan nevertheless realized that his troops could not hope to protect the extended frontier line. To buy time he issued army rations to the Indians in order to keep at least one of the government's many unfilled promises. This, however, was a case of too little too late.

As was his custom, Sheridan quickly developed an intelligence-gathering system to keep him informed of Indian mood, plans, and movements. It was no easy task to find the right men for the job, for although so-called Indian scouts were plentiful, Sheridan found "the real scout—that is, a guide and trailer knowing the habits of the Indians—was very scarce."[19]

The best scouts were often men with Indian wives, such as Ben Clark, John Simpson Smith, and Amos Chapman, who lived among the

Sheridan's Scouts

Ben Clark. (*Kansas State Historical Society, Topeka*)

William "Medicine Bill" Comstock. (*Joseph J. Pennell Collection, Kansas Collections, University of Kansas Libraries, Lawrence*)

tribes and knew them well. The sympathies of such men, however, were often more with the Indians than with their military employers. More trustworthy were several men who had won reputations in the bloody internecine struggle that had consumed the Kansas border long before Fort Sumter. Numbered among these were William "Buffalo Bill" Cody and James "Wild Bill" Hickok. Sheridan enjoyed the company of these exponents of rugged individualism and kept up lifetime friendships with Cody and Clark.

To watch over the Indians the general employed three men: William "Medicine Bill" Comstock, who was considered by Custer, whom he had served the previous summer, as "the superior of all men who were scouts by profession"; Abner "Sharp" Grover; and Richard Parr. Sheridan's spies, or "mediators" as he liked to call them, were put

Moses "California Joe" Milner. *(Kansas State Historical Society, Topeka)*

William "Buffalo Bill" Cody. *(Author's Collection)*

under the command of Lieutenant Frederick H. Beecher, Third Infantry, a nephew of Henry Ward Beecher, and one of the most promising subalterns in the service. Beecher, lamed by a shell fragment at Gettysburg, had a reputation for heavy drinking, but he was an especially intelligent, well-educated officer. Sheridan placed much faith in him.[20]

Beecher sent his spies out among the tribes, Comstock and Grover mingling with the Cheyennes while Parr visited the Kiowas and Comanches. The lieutenant reported to Sheridan at least once a week. The Indians, while unhappy, did not commit any serious depredations, and as the summer faded into autumn, Sheridan began to think that hostilities might yet be avoided.

In June, however, a party of Cheyennes had raided a Kaw Indian village near Council Grove, Kansas, running off some stock. Learning of this, Indian Superintendent Thomas Murphy ordered Edward W. Wynkoop, agent for the Cheyennes and Arapahos, to withhold from the Indian annuities the arms and ammunition prom-

37

ised at Medicine Lodge. The Cheyennes were furious at this; they had carefully avoided clashes with white men and refused to accept any of their annuities until the guns were supplied. An outbreak seemed imminent when Wynkoop consulted with Lieutenant Colonel (Brevet Brigadier General) Alfred Sully, an old Indian fighter who had taken command of the District of the Upper Arkansas in May. Sully and Wynkoop agreed that issuing the arms would placate the Cheyennes, and they persuaded the Indian Bureau to give in. On August 9 the Cheyennes at Fort Larned were issued 160 pistols and eighty Lancaster rifles, as well as supplies of powder and lead.

Sheridan, alarmed that "Indian diplomacy had overreached Sully's experience," believed issuing the arms was "a fatal mistake." The fatal mistake, however, may have been in withholding the arms in the first place. A few days before the Indian Bureau relented, a sullen party of two hundred Cheyenne warriors moved north to raid the Pawnees. Joined by some Sioux and Arapahos, the war party decided against going after Pawnees and turned instead toward the white settlements on the Saline and Solomon rivers. Between August 10 and 12 they ravaged the countryside, killing fifteen men and raping five women.[21]

Beecher, camped at Walnut Creek with his scouts, heard rumors of the clashes on the Solomon and Saline and sent Grover and Comstock to the village of Turkey Legs on the Solomon River. Sheridan's spies were greeted warmly, but it soon became clear to them that they were in danger. They quickly left the village, accompanied by seven warriors, supposedly to guard them. Not far from the village the warriors opened fire, killing Comstock instantly. Grover, gravely wounded, managed to make his escape in the dark, traveling on foot to the Kansas Pacific tracks, where a train picked him up.[22]

News of the raids against the Solomon and Saline settlements and the attack on the scouts reached Sheridan at about the same time. He immediately began to prepare for a campaign, convinced that "there was not the slightest provocation offered by the soldiers or citizens for the commencement of this war by the Indians." To Sheridan's mind, the only way to ensure peace was that the Indians "be soundly whipped, and the ringleaders in the present trouble hung, their ponies killed, and such destruction of their property as will make them very poor."[23]

To oversee military operations, Sheridan transferred his head-quarters from Fort Leavenworth to Fort Hays, a small post that was then the railhead of the Kansas Pacific Railroad. The protection of the railroad was Sheridan's primary concern. As soon as he could discern which bands were hostile, he planned to send his cavalry out to attack their stock and families in order to "break them up completely and effectively." No concerted effort would be made to pursue the small raiding parties that did all of the damage against the settlements; instead, some troops would be massed in order to attack Indian villages and others dispersed in forts along the line of the railroad.

Sheridan was not alone in his concern for the safety and progress of the railroad. The military establishment was tied by bonds of self-interest, blood, and past fellowship to the railroaders. Officers took pride in the belief that "the civil war trained the men who built that great National Highway" and that the workers could " 'deploy as skirmishers,' and fight the marauding Indians just as they had learned to fight the rebels down at Atlanta."[24] The construction bosses, surveyors, and engineers were almost all former military men with close ties to the postwar military hierarchy. Grenville M. Dodge, chief engineer for the Union Pacific, had commanded the Sixteenth Corps during the Atlanta campaign and had been commander of the Department of the Missouri during 1865. He was a close personal friend to Grant, Sherman, and Sheridan. William J. Palmer, president of the Kansas Pacific, had commanded one of Sherman's cavalry brigades, while W. W. Wright, superintendent of the Kansas Pacific, also a former general, had managed Sherman's railroad operations during the Georgia campaigns. These personal relationships resulted in close cooperation between the military and the railroads, with railroadmen often calling on post commanders for supplies and protection. In turn, railroad passes were liberally dispensed to military officers and their families.

Nothing displayed the close bond between the former generals on the railroad and the military establishment better than the conflict between Dodge and Union Pacific vice-president Thomas C. Durant over the Union Pacific's route. Durant, who hoped to secure more government grants, changed Dodge's route, and the chief engineer threatened to resign, which was exactly what Durant wanted. The argument brought presidential nominee U. S. Grant, Generals Sher-

The close relationship between the soldiers and the railroaders is vividly documented in this photograph taken at Fort Sanders, Wyoming (near present Laramie) in July 1868. U. S. Grant, left of center, backed by an impressive array of military brass, has just forced Union Pacific vice-president Thomas C. Durant (perched atop the fence at far right) to back off his efforts to change chief engineer Grenville Dodge's route. The triumphant Dodge hovers in the doorway behind his two Civil War comrades, Grant and Sherman. From left to right: Sidney Dillon, Union Pacific Board of Directors, later president of the railroad; Major General Philip H. Sheridan; unknown (behind Sheridan); Mrs. J. H. Potter; Brigadier General Frederick Dent; Mrs. John Gibbon; Colonel John Gibbon; unknown boy; General U. S. Grant; Katherine Gibbon; unknown nursemaid; Grenville M. Dodge; Francis Gibbon; Lieutenant General William T. Sherman; unknown (behind Sherman); Major General William S. Harney; Thomas C. Durant, vice-president, Union Pacific; Lieutenant Colonel Joseph H. Potter. (*Courtesy of Golden Spike National Historic Site, National Park Service*)

man and Sheridan, and a number of other high-ranking officers, to Laramie, Wyoming, in late July 1868 for a meeting with Dodge and Durant. Grant insisted that changes in Dodge's lines would not be tolerated and that Dodge must remain as chief engineer. Durant quickly backed down, and Dodge escorted his wartime comrades, Grant, Sherman, and Sheridan, to his home at Council Bluffs, Iowa, for a working holiday.[25]

This alliance was only natural, considering the heavy federal investment in the roads. It was in the best interest of the government, the military, the capitalists, and the American people to have the roads completed as rapidly as possible. From the military standpoint the railroad would enable rapid transport of troops and supplies as well as allow the abandonment of numerous forts. Even more important, the roads would bring in more settlers, spell doom for the buffalo, and split the northern Indians from the southern Indians. Sherman, in 1867, correctly foresaw that the completion of the transcontinental railroad was "the solution of the Indian question."[26]

Sheridan's immediate concern was separating hostile from peaceful Indians. Indian campaigns, by both state and federal troops, had often been tarnished by accusations that peaceful Indians had been slaughtered while the more elusive guilty ones went unpunished. Arriving at Fort Harker on August 20, Sheridan met with Cheyenne-Arapaho agent Wynkoop, who was surprised and perplexed by the recent outrages. Wynkoop, a courageous, unselfish public servant and true friend of the Indian, had a blind spot toward those in his charge. He could blame the outbreak only on outsiders, in this case "a medicine man of the Sioux." Wynkoop was especially concerned for the safety of Little Rock's band of Cheyennes who, he was sure, had had no hand in the Solomon raids. Sheridan pledged to protect them if they would turn over the guilty Indians as required by the Treaty of Medicine Lodge and congregate at Fort Larned. Neither Little Rock nor any other chief could accomplish the former, and they would not perform the latter. They had well learned the lessons of Sand Creek and Pawnee Fork. Wynkoop, his hopes for lasting peace disintegrating, applied for a leave of absence and went east.[27]

Sheridan next met with Little Raven and other Arapaho chiefs at Fort Dodge on September 3, 1868. Again he demanded the surrender of any warriors involved in the recent raids and promised the Arapahos sanctuary if they would move south of the Kansas line to their reservation as stipulated in the Treaty of Medicine Lodge. Four Arapaho warriors were involved in the Solomon raids, and one of them was Little Raven's son. Although the chiefs told Sheridan they would comply, the Arapaho bands soon scattered, and some engaged in depredations along the Kansas frontier.[28]

The peace had been tenuous at best, and all the chiefs realized this. After the raids in northern Kansas they fully expected war with the whites. In the old days, when the young men raided another tribe, retaliation came swiftly; and it did not fall only on the guilty warriors. The Indians expected the whites to react in the same manner. They would not willingly place themselves in the hands of the military or peacefully surrender their young men to the white man's laws. Furthermore, the plains tribes had no reason to assume that white retaliation could reach them. Hancock's campaign and Sioux victories in the Powder River country had vividly demonstrated the impotence of the white warriors. Loss of life at Sand Creek and loss of property at Pawnee Fork were the result of trusting white promises of protection. Now Sheridan was asking the supposedly peaceful Cheyennes and Arapahos to gather under his protection. This they quite logically, and perhaps wisely, refused to do.

The noncompliance of these bands made the chore of distinguishing hostiles from friendlies rather simple for the military authorities. All of the Cheyenne and Arapaho bands were designated hostile; the Kiowas, Comanches, and Kiowa-Apaches, who were not involved in the Kansas raids, were considered friendly. "We have selected and provided reservations for all, off the road," declared Sherman. "All who cling to their old hunting grounds are hostile and will remain so till killed off."[29]

In September 1868 Sherman instructed Colonel (Brevet Major General) William B. Hazen to order the friendly bands of Indians to the Indian Territory, using Fort Cobb as their agency. Hazen, who was Sherman's personal agent in the area, would have charge of all the Indians. Congress had appropriated five hundred thousand dollars for the Indian annuity goods promised by the Medicine Lodge and Laramie treaties negotiated by the 1867 peace commission. The money, however, was turned over to General Sherman for disbursement, instead of the distrusted Indian Bureau. In reality, if not by law, this signaled the transfer of Indian affairs from the Interior Department to the army. Sherman created two new military districts covering the area of the new northern and southern Indian reservations. General William S. Harney was given command of the northern district and Hazen the southern. Hazen was directly responsible only to Sherman, except in matters relating to military personnel in the district. Then he had to answer to Sheridan. In this manner, with the military in control of all aspects of Indian affairs, Sherman believed that a "double process of peace *within* their reservations and war *without* must soon bring this matter to a conclusion."[30]

Hazen had served Sherman well during the Civil War, commanding the Second Division of the Fifteenth Corps during the

Atlanta campaign and March to the Sea, and the two men had formed a lasting friendship. To Sherman, Hazen was "an officer of the highest professional attainments, [and] of the best possible habits" whose "military record from the day of his first commission is perfect."[31] Sherman recognized in Hazen a keen, probing mind, not unlike his own, and used him often after the war as an inspector. Hazen also shared Sherman's views on Indians. In 1859 Hazen had been wounded in a fray with Comanches, and he carried their bullet in his side for the rest of his life, which caused him pain and disability. Little wonder that he regarded the Indian as "a dirty beggar and thief . . . [who] knows no sentiment but revenge and fear, and cares only to live in his vagrancy." He had written in 1866 that the solution to the Indian problem was to "allot to each tribe, arbitrarily, its territory or reservation, and make vigorous, unceasing war on all that do not obey and remain upon their grounds."[32]

Hazen's actions were directed by a strong code of personal ethics and professional duty. He would not shirk his obligation to protect his Indian charges. This sense of ethics, which was on occasion self-serving, kept him embroiled in controversy through much of his military career. When he died in 1887, the *Army and Navy Journal* unkindly reported, "No one in the Service had a more unfortunate faculty for involving himself in controversies, and it has not been easy in all cases to determine to what traits his difficulties were chargeable."[33]

He made many enemies, and among the most bitter was Phil Sheridan. Still nurturing a grudge over who captured the rebel cannon on Missionary Ridge, Sheridan tormented Hazen throughout his military career, using every opportunity to retard his advancement. For his part, Hazen returned Sheridan's animosity in full measure. "Sheridan and I have a sort of mutual dislike," Hazen wrote his close friend, congressman and future president James A. Garfield, in 1871: "I think him a selfish, weak, unscrupulous man, admitting his dashing qualities as a leader in battle, but without a particle of administrative capacity."[34] Unfortunately for those Indians seeking a federal sanctuary, their safety depended on the cooperation of these two soldiers who were still fighting the Battle of Missionary Ridge.

While Hazen hurried south to distribute supplies to those Indians who sought his protection, Sheridan busied himself with military preparations to drive the recalcitrants south of the Kansas line. After

43

Colonel William B. Hazen. This photograph was taken during the Civil War, when the feud between Hazen and Sheridan began. "Sheridan and I have a sort of mutual dislike," wrote Hazen in 1871. (U.S. Signal Corps photo, no. 111-13-4968, Brady Collection, National Archives)

making garrison assignments to the forts along the two major roads, Sheridan had but eleven companies of cavalry left for offensive operations, about eight hundred men. Eager to mount some type of offensive, he called on his assistant inspector general, Major (Brevet Colonel) George A. Forsyth to "employ fifty (50) first-class hardy frontiersmen to be used as scouts against the hostile Indians."[35] Sheridan had long been fascinated with the concept of using partisan ranger detachments to fight an enemy on his own ground. The tactic proved successful in the Civil War, especially in Tennessee and the Shenandoah (although Mosby's men had wiped out one such detachment in northern Virginia). Using mobile rangers in Indian fighting was, of course, hardly novel. Ranger detachments dated back at least to Robert Rogers in the French and Indian War, but Sheridan would not have much success with his experiment.

The rangers' lack of success was not for lack of energy and daring on the part of their commander, George Forsyth. Known to his comrades as Sandy, to help distinguish him from Sheridan's inspector general Major (Brevet Brigadier General) James W. Forsyth, he was one of those bright, ingratiating fellows whose optimistic outlook brightened everyone's disposition. He had enlisted as a private in 1861, eventually gaining a commission in the Eighth Illinois Cavalry. Joining Sheridan's staff during the Wilderness campaign, he served thereafter as a member of the general's official family. In the Shenandoah he made the famed ride from Winchester at Sheridan's side. Forsyth emerged from the war with four wounds, a colonel's brevet, and the warm support of his chief. Sheridan's patronage helped Forsyth win an appointment as major of the Ninth Cavalry in the postwar regular army, as well as a position on the general's staff. Years of staff duty had left him chafing for a field command. The assignment as commander of the scouts, while hardly commensurate with his rank and reputation, was the best Sheridan could offer without appearing unfair to the other officers equally eager to get into the field. Forsyth, happy with any chance to see action, readily accepted the command.[36]

Forsyth had no problem enlisting his men, signing up thirty at Fort Harker and the rest at Fort Hays on August 20. Many of the new scouts, but by no means all, were experienced frontiersmen or former soldiers. Sharp Grover signed on as guide. William McCall, a former brevet brigadier general in the Union Army, was appointed first sergeant. Forsyth was also fortunate in having Lieutenant Beecher as second in command.

On August 29, Sheridan ordered Forsyth to take the field, scout Beaver Creek to Fort Wallace, and then await instructions. Determined to make good use of his opportunity for fame, Forsyth dismissed the warnings of fellow officers with a display of confidence "of being able to whip all the Indians he would meet on the plains with his select company of scouts." The major led his men from Fort Hays in a drizzling rain, warmed by the "fascination that the danger of campaigning in an enemy's country ever holds for a soldier"[37]

No Indians were sighted between Hays and Wallace, but no sooner had the detachment reached Fort Wallace on September 5 than word came from the town of Sheridan, thirteen miles to the east, that Indians had attacked a freighter's train, killing two teamsters. Forsyth immediately pursued this war party, which was estimated to number twenty-five warriors. Moving northwesterly in search of the Indians, the scouts found a fresh trail on September 14. They followed it along the Arickaree Fork of the Republican River into Colorado. All the while the trail grew larger "until finally it was a broad beaten road along which had been driven horses, cattle, and trains carrying heavy loads of Indian tent-poles that had worn great ruts into the earth." The men became increasingly anxious, and a delegation approached Forsyth concerning the wisdom of continuing. Like a hound onto a fresh scent, the major could not be deterred, interrupting his nervous men by contemptuously asking, "Did [they] not hire with him to fight Indians?"[38]

On September 16 they camped in a well-grassed valley on the north bank of the Arickaree. The river was little more than a trickle. In the middle lay a small timbered island about two hundred feet long by forty feet wide. Only a dozen miles away were three large villages of Brulé Sioux, Northern Arapahos, and Cheyennes under Pawnee Killer, Bull Bear, and Tall Bull. Although the scouts were ignorant of this, the Indians were well aware of the fifty-one white soldiers.

At dawn a small raiding party made a dash for the horses, but was driven off. Just as Forsyth's men mounted to move out of the valley, hundreds of Indians appeared, swarming over the nearby hills. The scouts hurried onto the island and carved out entrenchments in the soft sand.

As Forsyth's men frantically dug, the Indians poured in a deadly fire, killing all the horses. Then the warriors charged, only to be met by steady fire from seven-shot Spencer carbines. Forsyth, cool as if directing target practice, walked from man to man urging them to stay calm and aim low. When at last the situation seemed under control, the Indians breaking off their charge and contenting themselves with long-range sniping, he took cover in the sand. No sooner had he gotten down than a bullet crashed into his thigh and another shot shattered the bone in his lower left leg. He was moved into a sand pit at the lower end of the island, where assistant surgeon John H. Mooers could work on him. But Forsyth refused to stay down, and his determination to command resulted in another Indian shot glancing off his skull, fracturing it and momentarily blinding him. As Dr. Mooers attempted to aid Forsyth, he was shot through the forehead.

Three times that day the warriors charged the island, but each time the scouts' Spencers broke the charges. The Indians suffered heavily in their charges on the island, and young Lieutenant Beecher, who seemed as joyful as if on a holiday, declared it to be "like shooting sparrows."[39] Beecher's holiday suddenly ended when a bullet cracked his spine. He repeatedly begged his comrades to end his agony, before death mercifully silenced him at sunset.

With night came a slight rain, which cooled the exhausted men. Beecher and three of the scouts were dead, and surgeon Mooers and two others mortally wounded. Nineteen others, including the major, were wounded. Forsyth, so wracked with pain and fatigue that he could barely focus his thoughts, called for volunteers to try and sneak through the Indian lines to Fort Wallace, eighty-five miles away. After dining on horsemeat, two volunteers crept away, accompanied by the throb of drums and death wail of mourners from the Indian camp.[40]

Sheridan was at Fort Hays on September 22, 1868, when a telegram from Captain (Brevet Colonel) Henry C. Bankhead, commander at Fort Wallace, informed him that Forsyth's messengers had reported. Sheridan ordered Bankhead to spare neither men nor horses in rescuing the scouts. On September 28, another telegram from Bankhead brought the welcome news that a detachment of the Tenth Cavalry had reached Beecher's Island on September 25. Forsyth was alive, although blood poisoning had set in.[41]

Forsyth and his wounded men were hospitalized at Fort Wallace, while the remaining scouts were reorganized under the command of Lieutenant Silas (Lewis) Pepoon of the Tenth Cavalry. It would be two years before Forsyth recovered, and he would remain partially crippled by his wounds. Sheridan hurried to Fort Wallace to comfort his aide, praising the scouts and their leader in general field orders and later securing a brigadier's brevet for Forsyth. The battle, of course, had accomplished nothing except to prove to the Indians that the white soldier could indeed fight. Sheridan's experiment had worked in one respect: the scouts had been able to find the hostiles, but the results were disappointing. Thereafter, the reorganized scout detachment under Pepoon was not used for independent offensive operations.[42]

At the same time that Forsyth's scouts maneuvered along the Kansas Pacific line, Sheridan concentrated eight companies of the Seventh Cavalry and one company of the Third Infantry, with a small howitzer, under District of the Upper Arkansas commander Alfred Sully at Fort Dodge. These troops intended to move south across the Arkansas River and attack the families of the Cheyennes and Arapahos reportedly camped along the Cimarron River. Such pressure, Sheridan hoped, would pull Indian raiding parties down out of Kansas to protect their exposed villages.[43]

Sully had earned Sheridan's displeasure by allowing the distribution of arms to the Indians in early August, and had another officer been available, it is unlikely that he would have been given command of the expedition. Sully's excellent reputation as an Indian fighter was earned against the Seminoles soon after graduating from West Point in 1841 and against the rebellious Minnesota Sioux in 1863–65. But Sheridan gave slight consideration to past glories. Sully was not Sheridan's type of soldier. As one officer recalled, Sully was "a very pleasant, genial sociable man in manner and appearance," whose only common characteristic with Sheridan was that he always took "a little whiskey very regularly."[44]

On September 7, Sheridan reviewed Sully's column of over five hundred men and thirty wagons as it crossed the Arkansas River. He was eager to go along, but the duties of department commander kept him out of the field. He could only salute the troops as they passed. Sully's column, reaching the Cimarron on September 10, found evidence of Indians, and the column's scouts, Amos Chapman, John

Smith, and Ben Clark, were surprised by a small Cheyenne war party but were rescued by the troops.[45]

Sully disgusted his cavalry officers by leading the column from a military ambulance, and he lost their confidence altogether when he arrested two officers for pursuing a war party that had captured two stragglers.[46] The command plodded along the Cimarron, turning south into Indian Territory, where the wagons became mired in the sand hills along the North Canadian River. Now the Cheyennes sallied forth in force, melting before cavalry charges only to attack again. His wagons useless, his horses and troops fatigued, and all the while the Indians gaining in strength, Sully ordered a retreat on September 14.[47]

For the frustrated Sheridan, the return of Sully's column to Fort Dodge on September 18 climaxed a dismal initiation to plains Indian warfare. Within the boundaries of Sheridan's command, since the Kansas raids of early August, 110 civilians had been killed, thirteen women had been raped, over a thousand head of stock stolen, farms, stage buildings and rolling stock destroyed, and unescorted travel stopped on all the major roads. His troops were engaged in numerous fights with the Indians, almost always being bested, and not once inflicting serious injury to the natives. Eighteen of his troopers were dead and forty-five wounded. His aide-de-camp was critically wounded, and his company of scouts, of whom so much had been expected, had been badly shot up in their first engagement with the enemy. And now Sully, grumbling about short rations, endless sand hills, and elusive Cheyennes, came creeping back to Fort Dodge like a dog with his tail tucked between his legs. It was obvious to Sheridan that if he was going to catch the Indians, he had to have more troops, and field commanders aggressive enough to lead them into battle.[48]

Sherman, determined to crush Cheyenne resistance once and for all, promptly complied with Sheridan's request for more men. Six companies of the Twenty-seventh Infantry and two companies of the Second Cavalry had already been ordered south from the Department of the Platte to operate along the Republican River. These troops, under Lieutenant Colonel (Brevet Brigadier General) Luther P. Bradley, reached their destination in time to assist in rescuing Forsyth's men on the Arickaree. But Bradley's infantry would be of little use in offensive operations. For that reason Sheridan secured authority to have Governor Samuel J. Crawford of Kansas call out a regiment of volunteer cavalry (twelve hundred men). Kansas militia, with arms, ammunition, and rations supplied by the federal government, had already taken the place of regular troops on garrison duty in eastern Kansas. But the new regiment, the Nineteenth Kansas Cavalry, would actively participate in offensive operations. Governor Crawford, who had long advocated such action, resigned his office and sewed colonel's eagles on his shoulders. Dead Indians meant live voters on America's frontiers.[49]

Sheridan's main new offensive force would be the Fifth Cavalry, seven companies of which were ordered to Kansas from Reconstruction duties in the South. These troops, gathered at Fort Harker by September 29, moved north to scout along Beaver Creek, a tributary of the Republican, in hopes of catching the Indians who had fought Forsyth. They were commanded by Major (Brevet Colonel) William B. Royall until Major (Brevet Major General) Eugene A. Carr could escape from Washington staff duties and take charge of the regiment.

Sheridan hoped that the Fifth Cavalry under Carr would be able to search out and destroy the hostiles along the Republican River. Sheridan had known Carr during the 1862 campaigns leading to the Battle of Pea Ridge, where Carr, leading the Fourth Division of the Army of the Southwest, held the line at a critical moment and won the Congressional Medal of Honor. With full Cossack beard and erect bearing, Carr inspired confidence in those around him and, as Sheridan noted, was "always active, competent and brave."[50] After graduation from West Point in 1850, Carr had been assigned to the Mounted Rifles and served on the frontier from 1852 to 1860 in campaigns against the Sioux, Kiowas, Comanches, and Apaches. During the Civil War he saw action in the western theater, eventually becoming a brevet major general in both volunteer and regular grades. His proven abilities as a leader, especially his long service against the plains Indians, made him an important part of Sheridan's plans.[51]

Carr arrived at Fort Wallace on October 12, with orders from Sheridan to secure an escort and proceed to his command in the field, supposedly on Beaver Creek. On October 14 Carr and about a hundred Tenth Cavalry troopers left the fort with Sharp Grover as guide. They reached Beaver Creek without incident and traveled fifty miles along the stream without finding Royall. They did, however, find the

Indians. At dawn on October 17 a large war party of the same Cheyennes that had fought Forsyth surprised Carr's detachment. After eight hours of off-and-on-again battle, the Buffalo Soldiers managed to beat off the Indians and retreated to Fort Wallace.[52]

Carr learned that the Fifth was at the Buffalo Tank station of the Kansas Pacific Railroad. Royall, who had also been surprised by Tall Bull's Cheyenne Dog Soldiers, had lost two troopers and twenty-six horses on October 14. Carr joined his regiment on October 22, and with seven companies of the Fifth and Pepoon's scouts he took the field in search of Tall Bull's Cheyennes. He found them on October 25 along Beaver Creek. For the next five days there was a running fight, but Carr could never close in for the kill, and by October 31 the Indians had vanished. The weary troops moved south to Fort Wallace to refit. Unlike Sully, Carr at least had not failed for want of effort.[53]

Although confident of good results with Carr in command of the Fifth, Sheridan still sought another energetic field officer to lead the Seventh. Sully was out of the question, and the Seventh's senior officer in the field, Major Joel Elliot, had not proven particularly effective either. Sheridan wanted Custer, whose dash and bravado were just the ingredients needed to snap the Seventh back into shape and make it an effective weapon in the forthcoming campaign. Neither short rations and sand hills nor casualties and massed warriors would stop Custer. Short on prudence but long on pluck and grit, Custer's fierce determination to find and fight the enemy had endeared him to Sheridan since their first Civil War campaign together in 1864.

Audacity was what was needed now, so Sheridan wired Sherman that he wanted Custer's court-martial sentence suspended. He also telegraphed Custer on September 24, notifying the Boy General of his efforts to get the remaining two months of the sentence remanded. An exuberant Custer, without waiting for orders from Washington but fully aware that any request from Sheridan would be honored, boarded a train the next morning and ate breakfast with Sheridan at Fort Hays on October 4. The general promised his eager warrior that a major winter campaign was in preparation, with the Seventh to play a central role and its commander to have a free hand. On October 10 the Seventh's camp thirty miles southeast of Fort Dodge awoke to the hubbub of Custer's triumphant return, "with his hair cut short and a perfect menagerie of Scotch fox hounds!"[54]

51

After a month of relative inaction the regiment was swept into the maelstrom of activity that, for good or bad, always swirled around Custer. The first evening he had patrols out scouring the countryside for Cheyenne horse thieves, and three days later he moved the whole command away from the relative comforts of their permanent camp to search for Indians along Medicine Lodge Creek. Except for a brief skirmish between the rear guard and a small war party, a mistaken charge upon the cavalry by drunken chief scout California Joe Milner, and Custer's hounds tearing a prairie wolf apart, the march was uneventful. Custer intended to toughen his troops and to restore their enthusiasm for an offensive, and in this he felt successful. After a few days scouting, he led the regiment to the Arkansas River and camped some ten miles below Fort Dodge. "I can move on the proposed campaign in *good* condition in half an hour's notice," Custer assured Sheridan on October 28, and added that he felt "great confidence in being able to do something decisive."[55]

Decisive action was essential. The War Department was beseiged by demands from western political and business interests to settle the Indian problem. The military establishment, which had emerged from the Civil War with a proud self-image as one of the great modern armies of the world, suffered humiliation at the hands of a few thousand poorly armed nomadic natives.

Sheridan and his officers, haunted by their inability to protect the settlers, felt especially concerned about the fate of white women who fell into the Indians' clutches. As he planned his winter campaign, Sheridan received a plaintive letter from W. T. Harrington, whose daughter, Clara Blinn, along with her child, had been captured by the Arapahos. Harrington begged Sheridan to rescue his daughter and grandchild, enclosing in his letter a message written by Clara pleading with her family and race: "Save us if you can. We are with them." It was a story as old as white America, and always effective—the innocent white mother held captive by savages. Sheridan, who heartily subscribed to notions of man's role as woman's protector, could not help being moved.[56]

The salvation of Clara Blinn, and others like her across the exposed frontier, depended on the success of a winter campaign to crush the hostiles. On October 9, 1868, Sheridan received Sherman's permission to proceed. Sherman promised to do everything in his power to ensure that "these Indians, the enemies of our race and of our civilization, shall not again be able to begin and carry on their barbarous warfare." He endorsed a harsh winter campaign, even if "it ends in the utter annihilation of these Indians." Sherman extended complete freedom of action to Sheridan, promising to "back you with my whole authority, and stand between you and any efforts that may be attempted in your rear to restrain your purpose or check your troops." All Indians who did not join Hazen at Fort Cobb were to be outlawed and killed. Sheridan was to launch a race war of vengeance—with no quarter asked or given.[57]

Sheridan assumed that most of the hostiles would be in the vicinity of the North Fork of the Red River, just south of the Antelope Hills. The movements of Carr and Bradley along the Republican and its tributaries, as well as the need to seek a more sheltered area to winter in, had forced the Indians south. Three converging columns would be used, with one coming southeast from Fort Lyon, Colorado, one moving due east from Fort Bascom, New Mexico, along the South Canadian, and another striking south from Fort Dodge.[58]

At Fort Bascom Colonel George Getty organized a column consisting of six companies of the Third Cavalry, two companies of the Thirty-seventh Infantry, and four mountain howitzers. This command, numbering 563 men, moved eastward on November 18, 1868, under Major (Brevet Lieutenant Colonel) Andrew W. Evans. He was to scour the Canadian for Indians until January or as long as supplies lasted. Major Carr marched southeast from Fort Lyon with seven companies of the Fifth Cavalry. On the North Canadian he joined four companies of the Tenth Cavalry and one company of the Seventh Cavalry already in the field under Captain (Brevet Brigadier General) William H. Penrose. This combined force of 650 men planned to proceed toward the Antelope Hills as long as supplies could be forwarded from Colorado.

Sheridan did not expect these two columns to do much damage to the Indians, but hoped they might drive them toward the Antelope Hills. When the main column from Fort Dodge struck the killing blow, Evans and Carr would block any escape. This central strike force, technically commanded by Sully but with Sheridan present, consisted of one company of the Fifth Infantry, one company of the Thirty-eighth Infantry, and three companies of the Third Infantry, all commanded by Captain (Brevet Major) J. H. Page, eleven companies of the Seventh Cavalry under Custer, and Crawford's Nineteenth Kansas Cavalry. Crawford's command, except for two companies en route to Fort Hays by rail for escort duty, was to march overland from Topeka to the point where Wolf and Beaver creeks joined to form the North Canadian River. At that place Page's infantry would establish a supply depot and await Crawford. As soon as all columns were in motion, Sheridan planned to join this combined force of over two thousand men at the supply depot and commence offensive operations.[59]

A winter campaign on the plains was universally viewed as a bold, innovative plan, if not a bit reckless. Sheridan had no experience with Great Plains winters, and no amount of description could do justice to the sudden temperature changes and heavy snows that could accompany a norther. When old frontiersman Jim Bridger heard of Sheridan's plans, he came out from Saint Louis to talk the general out of his folly. Even the ebullient Custer warned his commander that "a hard campaign . . . in that country must necessarily reduce the condition of our horses," and even if especially good care was taken of the animals, he should not be surprised "if at the end of our campaign you find our stock pretty well run down."[60]

Campaigning in winter against Indians was not new. General Arthur St. Clair had led a blundering campaign into the Ohio wilderness in November 1791, only to have his army decimated by the Miami Confederacy. William Henry Harrison, however, effectively campaigned against the followers of the Prophet in November 1811, destroying an Indian village along Indiana's Tippecanoe River. As a young officer Sheridan had participated in a late autumn campaign against the Yakimas in 1855, which met with little success. General Patrick Connor, however, marched three hundred men from Fort Douglas near Salt Lake City amid snow and bitter cold to a Shoshone-Bannock village along Bear River (near the Utah-Idaho border) in January 1863 and routed the Indians. Just one year later Brigadier General James Carleton and Colonel Kit Carson pursued a scorched-earth campaign that broke the power of the Navajos in January 1864. Sheridan was probably unaware of all these winter campaigns, for he always referred to his 1868 winter war as a novel concept. It certainly was the first major military operation to test the endurance of troops against a Great Plains winter, with its extremes of temperature.

The perils of a winter campaign were somewhat offset by its advantages. Winter, with its numbing cold and heavy snows, limited the Indians' mobility, which was their greatest advantage. No longer would their grass-fed ponies be able to outrun the larger, grain-fed warhorses of the troopers. The ponies would be weakened by scarce fodder, while their owners would seek the shelter of their tepees, lulled into a false sense of security by the weather. For years they had followed the same successful pattern of raiding throughout the warm months and then relaxing the winter away in some secluded camp protected from all enemies by distance and climate. But the railroad had wiped out the advantage of distance, for supplies could now be quickly shipped to depots and give troops greater mobility. Sheridan had devoted much of his time and energy to accumulating large quantities of supplies and forage at Forts Dodge, Lyon, Gibson, and Arbuckle to feed his troops in the field. And now Sheridan was ready to challenge the climate, reasoning that his well-fed-and-clothed soldiers could withstand severe weather long enough to strike a hard blow. Time was his enemy, for prolonged exposure would weaken men and stock. That was one of the reasons he had wanted Carr and Custer: he knew he could depend on their energy. He was not so sure about Sully, and so he decided to accompany the main column.[61]

At eight o'clock on the morning of November 15, two mule-drawn military ambulances and a light baggage wagon pulled out of Fort Hays carrying the department commander, his staff, and newspaper correspondent D. B. R. Keim. Twenty miles from the fort they picked up a twenty-man escort and moved south, hoping to make Fort Dodge within two days. A more disagreeable day could hardly have been found, for it had rained heavily the previous night, and a soaking mist permeated the air. The wind blew strong and cold from the north, reminding Sheridan of Bridger's warning.[62] But the fears of an old mountain man were hardly enough to daunt the spirit of the conqueror of the Shenandoah. He once more felt the exhilaration of the chase after the most desperate of quarries—man. Sheridan was in the field.

CHAPTER 3

Battle of the Washita:
"Kill or Hang All Warriors"

From the north and the west Sheridan's troopers began to move
across the southern plains, accompanied by a strong, cold wind that
seemed to foretell a harsh winter to come. The Cheyennes, Arapahos,
Kiowas, and Comanches pulled in before the troops, retreating toward
the Antelope Hills. As usual, they were seriously divided over what
action to take. Trusted white friends, like government interpreter
John Smith, warned Kiowa and Comanche chiefs to be on the lookout
for treachery and avoid Forts Larned and Cobb. The Cheyennes had
lost their good friend, Wynkoop. The Indian agent was visiting in the
East when he received orders to return to his agency and gather in his
charges at Fort Cobb. It had been Wynkoop, then a major in the
Colorado volunteers, who had persuaded the Cheyennes to place
themselves under military protection at Fort Lyon in November 1864.
The Sand Creek massacre resulted. Wynkoop, the horror of Sand
Creek in mind, declined to obey the order, refusing "to again be the
instrument of the murder of innocent women and children," and
resigned his post.[1]

Colonel Hazen arrived at Fort Cobb on November 7 to find
some seventeen hundred Comanches, Caddos, Wichitas, Wacos and
affiliated bands encamped nearby. Rations were low, for the government had not anticipated so large a gathering, and some hungry
warriors threatened to return to the plains to hunt. The main bands of
Kiowas and Comanches, whose chiefs had met with Hazen and Sher-

56

idan at Fort Larned, had still not come in. Although their arrival would increase his logistical headaches, Hazen was eager for their safety. He knew that Sheridan's troops would attack any Indians they found on the plains, regardless of tribe.

By the middle of November most of the Kiowa and Comanche bands reached the vicinity of Fort Cobb, and the principal chiefs, Satanta, Satank, and Lone Wolf, met with Hazen. He issued rations and urged them to move in near the fort, lest they run afoul of one of Sheridan's columns. Hazen believed that the Kiowas and Comanches were peaceful and that they held no threat to the whites "excepting their old habit of thieving and murdering in Texas."[2]

Hazen offered the Kiowa and Comanche bands sanctuary, despite their Texas forays, because they had not been implicated in the Kansas raids, but he denied it to the Cheyennes and Arapahos. They visited Fort Cobb on November 20 to seek protection. Big Mouth spoke for the Southern Arapahos and Black Kettle for his Cheyenne band, and each declared his dedication to peace and his regret over the present state of hostilities. Black Kettle repeated the familiar complaint of Indian leaders: "I have always done my best to keep my young men quiet, but some will not listen, and since the fighting began I have not been able to keep them at home. But we all want peace." Although he had not been able to control his people all summer, Black Kettle promised Hazen that if sanctuary was given his band, he "could then keep them all quietly near camp."[3]

Hazen was in a difficult position. The leaders of the Indian bands that had been declared renegade now offered to make peace, but he was not empowered to negotiate with them. Sherman had warned Hazen that Sheridan might invade the reservation in pursuit of hostiles. Hazen feared that granting sanctuary to these Indians would invite another Sand Creek massacre. He was in a position to bring the war quickly to a close, but if the peace were broken again, he would have to shoulder the blame. He was unwilling to take that risk.[4]

Turning Black Kettle and Big Mouth away, Hazen told them to make their peace with Sheridan: "I am sent here as a peace chief; all here is to be peace; but north of the Arkansas is General Sheridan, the great war chief, and I do not control him; and he has all the soldiers who are fighting the Arapahos and Cheyennes. Therefore you must go back to your country, and if the soldiers come to fight, you must

57

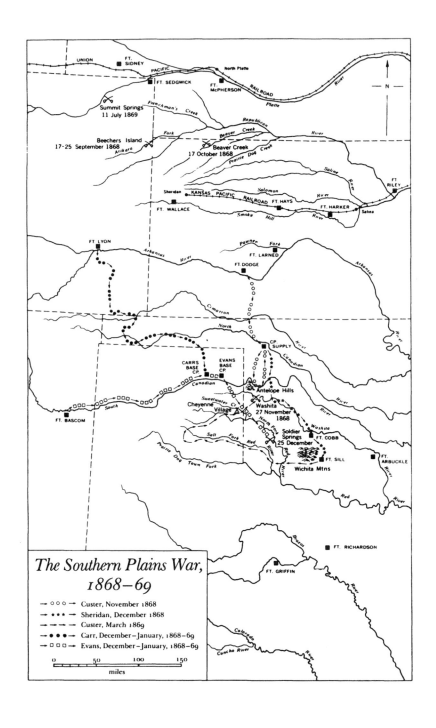

The Southern Plains War,
1868–69

→ o o o → Custer, November 1868
→ • • • → Sheridan, December 1868
→ – – – → Custer, March 1869
→ ● ● ● → Carr, December–January, 1868–69
→ □ □ □ → Evans, December–January, 1868–69

0   50   100   150
miles

remember they are not from me, but from the great war chief, and with him you must make peace."[5]

The council broke up, and the Cheyennes and Arapahos departed for their camps nearly a hundred miles to the northwest in a broad valley along the Washita River. The chiefs were disappointed, but the young warriors who had accompanied them to Fort Cobb were overjoyed with the failure of the negotiations. As they passed through Kiowa and Comanche camps on their way north, some of the warriors called on all the Indians to join them on the warpath, for "that next spring the Sioux and other northern bands were coming down and would clean out this entire country."[6]

Soon after the departure of Black Kettle, a melancholy letter reached Hazen that further called into question the dedication of the Cheyennes and Arapahos to peace. The letter was from Clara Blinn, the young woman who, along with her two-year-old son, had been captured in October near Fort Lyon and whose sad fate had been brought to Sheridan's attention. In the letter addressed to "Kind Friend," she begged for someone to buy her from the Indians, for her child was weak and she feared that she would soon be sold into slavery in Mexico. Hazen authorized a local Indian trader, William "Dutch Bill" Griffenstein, "to spare no expense in his efforts to reclaim these parties."[7]

The hostile attitude of Black Kettle's warriors worried Hazen, for Fort Cobb offered little protection in case of attack. Furthermore, the Comanches and Kiowas were becoming increasingly restless because, as Hazen put it, "they could not have everything there is at the post." The Indians had become accustomed to liberal annuity disbursements, secured by inflating the declared population of the various bands. The Indians had also forced their civilian agents into giving them allotments of sugar and coffee, valuable trade commodities, instead of regular rations. Hazen tried to correct these abuses, but was confronted with an immediate and angry response from the Indians. He quickly realized that the old system "had to be endured at the risk of revolt." The civilian Indian agents who were responsible for abuses in the annuity system were conspicuously absent from Fort Cobb, although they had been ordered there by the Indian Bureau. Hazen, with the able assistance of Captain Henry Alvord of the Tenth Cavalry, had to improvise. To satisfy the Indians he requested more funds, for the fifty thousand dollars given him by Sherman had been quickly exhausted. He also requested two companies of the Tenth Cavalry and two howitzers with a hundred shells for each.[8]

While Hazen struggled to gather in the supposedly peaceful Indians to Fort Cobb, Sheridan moved south to join his strike force in the field. His small column reached Fort Dodge on November 16, where they spent a pleasant evening in the company of the fort's commandant, Captain Mike Sheridan of the Seventh Cavalry, the general's younger brother.

When the column moved out the following morning, it kept closer together, alert for any Indian activity. Just before the general's arrival at Fort Dodge a party of Indians had galloped through the post, shooting a trooper before making their escape. War parties prowled the countryside, and the column was on the watch for trouble. A small band of Kaw Indian guides led the way, followed by the reorganized Forsyth scouts under Lieutenant Pepoon. The column's twenty mule-drawn wagons lumbered behind Pepoon's men, closely followed by Lieutenant Thomas Lebo's troop of the Tenth Cavalry. Caution was well advised, for after a difficult crossing of the Arkansas River a party of warriors was spied in the distance. The Indians made no threatening action, but everyone was nevertheless relieved to reach Bluff Creek. They were joined there by two companies of the Nineteenth Kansas Volunteers that Sully had detailed to escort the department commander to the main camp.[9]

Concern over an Indian ambush now eased, for Sheridan's party numbered over three hundred. Indian warriors, however, were not easily intimidated by numbers, and the next evening they struck the camp. The column had camped on an island in Beaver Creek late in the afternoon on November 19. Several small herds of buffalo grazed in the valley surrounding the campsite, and a number of hunting parties went out. In order to observe the hunters, Sheridan and newspaper correspondent Keim hiked to a knoll about a mile from camp. Sheridan not only watched the hunters through his binoculars but also studied the low hills bordering the valley, trying to get a feel for the terrain he would be campaigning in. His attention was captured by a number of figures moving about on the distant hills, silhouetted against the darkening sky. It was too far to make out clearly whether they were buffalo or Indians, but Sheridan feared the latter. Since it was almost dark, the two men hurried back to the camp, discovering along the way fresh pony tracks in a dry channel of Beaver Creek. The Indians, concealed by the timbered banks of the stream, had passed between Sheridan and his camp—and had missed a grand opportunity to capture or kill the department commander.[10]

Sheridan detailed an extra officer of the guard for night watch and left a reserve force under arms all night. Twice during the night small parties of warriors crept up on the camp, only to be fired upon by the alert pickets. A dawn attack was fully expected, so Sheridan had the camp roused and the troopers under arms by three in the morning. But the attack never materialized, and at sunrise they continued their march to the southeast. Not long after leaving Beaver Creek, Sheridan's scouts reported a good-sized trail leading to the northeast, and, they concluded, it had been made by a large war party coming up from the headwaters of the Washita River. Sheridan's already optimistic mood was further bolstered by this discovery. He was positive that his plan of winter campaign would succeed if only the Indians could be located. Now here was their trail, clear and fresh before him.[11]

Sully's trail was also clear, and they followed it at as rapid a gait as possible. At two in the afternoon the smoke of Sully's campfires was spied. Within an hour Sheridan reached the confluence of Beaver and Wolf creeks, where the new military post, Camp Supply, was under construction.

Captain (Brevet Lieutenant Colonel) Thomas Moore, Sheridan's aide-de-camp, rode ahead to inform the camp of the general's approach. This news sent Custer galloping out on the plains to meet his mentor. He was full of news for Sheridan, none of it reflecting well on Sully. Custer's Osage scouts had also located the Indian trail near Beaver Creek, which they estimated to mark a war party of over a hundred warriors. But when Custer had requested permission to follow the trail and attack the warriors, Sully refused. This was only the beginning of their troubles. No sooner had they reached their destination and started building Camp Supply than a quarrel over rank began when Sully started issuing orders under his rank of brevet brigadier general and district commander. The expected arrival of Crawford's Kansas Volunteers would cause a problem of rank, since Colonel Crawford outranked Lieutenant Colonels Sully and Custer. Military regulations, however, stipulated that when volunteer and regular army units served together, the officer with the highest brevet rank would command. But Sully was outranked by Custer's brevet of major general, and, since they were no longer in the District of the Upper Arkansas, Custer argued that he was in command. The arrival of Sheridan made the squabble over rank meaningless, but Sully's continued lack of aggressiveness was another matter. Soon after he reached the camp, Sheridan resolved the matter by ordering Sully back to his district headquarters at Fort Harker.[12]

The evening of Sheridan's arrival, Custer and the officers of the Seventh, accompanied by the band, proceeded to serenade the general. He received them in front of his tent "in his genial way, shaking hands with all," and they gathered around a large campfire to listen to the band and discuss the campaign. For many of the officers it was the first meeting with the hero of the great war, and they hung on his every word, hoping for some hint of when they would take the field. "Like Grant, Sheridan is a man of few words," wrote captain Albert Barnitz to his wife later that evening, "but he always looks very animated, and although he really does not say much, you come away with the impression that you have had a prolonged and interesting conversation with him!" Barnitz noted that Sheridan's displeasure with Sully was made obvious that evening: "He would have preferred that General Sully would have allowed us to at once to go in search of Indians." As the party broke up and Custer's men walked the six hundred yards back to their camp, it began to snow steadily. The officers were pleased, for the snow would make it easy to track their enemies, and Sheridan had promised that they would take the field on November 23.[13]

The snow continued all night, followed by a day of alternating sleet and snow. The weather increased Sheridan's concern over the absent volunteers, but he was eager to have Custer in the field and did not want to delay any longer on account of Crawford. Camp Supply bustled with activity throughout the day as the Seventh prepared to march. Thirty days' supplies were loaded onto wagons. Troopers carefully packed their belongings, putting aside extra clothing and furnishings. They were to carry only what was essential—even tents were not allowed. Magazine-load Spencer carbines and Colt revolvers were checked and rechecked and the horses inspected and given extra grain. Custer, decked out in a pair of buffalo overshoes and a fur cap given him by Sheridan, picked a sturdy brown horse from the remuda of new horses brought in with Sheridan and named him Dandy. Most of his troopers also had new horses, for Custer had recently ordered all company commanders to exchange horses so each company would have a uniform color. This caused considerable unease among some officers, who felt it unwise to make such a change just before the campaign. It had dissatisfied many of the men as well, for they had become attached to the animals they rode. But show and appearance meant everything to Custer, so complaints were ignored, and the reissue was made.[14]

Reveille sounded at four in the morning and the soldiers emerged from their scant canvas shelters to find over a foot of snow on the ground and the storm continuing unabated. Breakfast was quickly dispensed with, for the freezing troopers had little appetite. By six the horses were groomed and packed, and as "Boots and Saddles" signaled each trooper to saddle his mount, Custer galloped over to Sheridan's tent. The general looked out of his tent at the blinding clouds of snow, which, in the predawn light, cut visibility to almost zero, and asked Custer whether he thought he should move in the storm. Custer looked on the snow as a godsend, for it would isolate the Indians and prevent their movement while the troops closed in. If only the snow would remain on the ground another week, he promised, he would catch the Indians. Custer always had the right answer for Sheridan.[15]

Sheridan's orders were simple and direct: "To proceed south in the direction of the Antelope Hills, thence towards the Washita River, the supposed winter seat of the hostile tribes; to destroy their villages and ponies; to kill or hang all warriors, and bring back all women and children."[16]

With an admonition to keep him informed and his best wishes for success, Sheridan bade Custer farewell. The young officer galloped back to the head of his command and quickly had the Seventh in motion. The Osage guides took the lead, followed by the band playing the old military tune "The Girl I Left behind Me." As the infantry cheered, the eleven companies of the Seventh vanished into the blizzard swelling up from the south.[17]

The storm kept up all day on the twenty-third, but by the next morning it had passed and began to melt almost as quickly as it had fallen. There was still no word from Crawford's column, and Sheridan's concern increased. The volunteers had left Topeka on November 5, with only enough rations to carry them to Camp Supply. By now their supplies would be exhausted and men and animals starving.[18]

Sheridan was perplexed. He had personally provided Crawford with two scouts who knew the country: William "Apache Bill" Seamans, who worked out of Fort Dodge, and young Jack Stilwell, who had fought with Forsyth on the Arickaree. He assumed that the Kansans had holed up during the storm, but this could not explain their continued absence. Numbering more than a thousand men Crawford's force was too formidable to have been ambushed by Indians, but Sheridan realized that prolonged exposure and starvation could cause as much damage as bullets.

Late the afternoon of November 25, Sheridan's concern was somewhat eased by the appearance of Captain Allison J. Pliley, who also had been one of Forsyth's scouts, and fifty of the Kansas Volunteers. Pliley reported to Sheridan that he had left Crawford on the evening of November 22, holed up on the Cimarron and facing the prospect of subsisting on mule meat. Half of the supplies that were supposed to be waiting for the volunteers at Camp Beecher on the Arkansas River had been consumed by the troops attached to that post, and only a small amount of damaged forage was made available for the horses. Colonel Crawford had decided to press on anyway and live off the land. At first all had gone well, for the buffalo were plentiful and the march fairly easy. On November 18, affairs had taken a turn for the worse when a freak accident sent six hundred of the regiment's horses stampeding through the camp, nearly one hundred of them being lost. Then on November 21 had come the blizzard, further debilitating the starving men and horses and covering all the landmarks with a snowy blanket. Everything now collapsed: Apache Bill announced that he was lost; the buffalo vanished; and despite the constant efforts of the men to secure grass from under the snow, the horses died on the picket lines from hunger and cold. Pliley had been given the best fifty men and horses with instructions to push through to Camp Supply and bring back help.[19]

Pliley and his exhausted men were made comfortable for the night and in the morning set out with a detachment of Pepoon's scouts and a train of supply wagons to bring in the starving volunteers. In his march to the east, however, the captain missed Crawford and the main body of volunteers. They had pushed on ahead, leaving the wagons and 360 weak, disabled, and dismounted men behind at what came to be known as Camp Starvation. Crawford and his men reached Camp Supply on November 28, to find that Sheridan already had tents, bedding, and rations prepared for them. On December 1, Pliley brought in the rest of the battered volunteers. Fortunately no lives had been lost.[20]

The terrible march of the Nineteenth Kansas Volunteers dealt a severe blow to Sheridan's campaign. The regiment was supposed to have been at Camp Supply when Sheridan arrived, and if they had been on time, they would have gone with Custer after the Indians. This would have doubled Custer's force and allowed him more flexibility. Events conspired to place Custer in a position where he sorely needed those extra troops, and if he had had them, the campaign would probably have drawn to a successful conclusion that November. Even if Crawford's regiment had arrived late, but in good condition, Sheridan could have put them to immediate use. The men, however, were worn out and many of their horses dead or completely broken down, so that at least a week of rest and refitting was required.[21]

Sheridan blamed the situation on Crawford, who he felt had "undertaken to strike through the canons of the Cimarron" instead of relying on the guides and had wound up "floundering about for days without being able to extricate his command." Crawford retorted that Sheridan had been misinformed about the competence of the scouts, "whose reputations and wages depended largely on their skills as liars." The general feeling in the regiment seemed to be that the scouts were incompetent, and Apache Bill narrowly escaped being lynched by angry volunteers at Camp Starvation. One volunteer spread blame for the disaster to everyone, observing that "the universal ignorance of the country, including that of Sheridan himself, was at the bottom of it all."[22]

While men and mounts of the Nineteenth Kansas Volunteers recuperated, Sheridan dispatched his quartermaster, Major Henry Inman, with a train of 250 wagons to draw supplies at Fort Dodge. Adequate quantities of rations, ammunition, and forage were to be stockpiled at Camp Supply for a prolonged campaign. Construction of the fort also moved along smoothly, with log buildings replacing the large tents that had sheltered perishable supplies. Upon completion, however, the post could not house many members of Sheridan's large command, and most of the troopers remained in tents.[23]

To conserve supplies hunting parties were sent out daily, although they were not allowed to stray too far from Camp Supply. Sheridan, for whom hunting was an absolute passion, often accompanied these parties. Although still quite cold, the climate had moderated considerably since Custer had marched away. The sun shone brightly most days and caused the snow to retreat. There was still enough snow, however, to make tracking game easy. As a result, the post was well supplied with buffalo, elk, deer, antelope, and especially wild turkey and rabbit. This abundance of wild game increased Sheridan's distrust of the Indian Bureau, which had often claimed that the Indians in this area were starving because there was no game to hunt.

Sheridan and his staff celebrated the new national holiday of Thanksgiving with a banquet prepared by the general's German cook. The grand feast consisted entirely of game killed in the vicinity of the post, with the exception of vegetables, desserts, and imported liquid refreshment. The Thanksgiving turkey alone weighed in at thirty pounds dressed. For Sheridan, campaigning in the western wilderness was certainly not all privation and strife.[24]

An added reason for thanksgiving arrived at Camp Supply mid-morning on November 29, in the persons of Custer's scouts, Moses "California Joe" Milner and Jack Corbin. California Joe, over six feet tall with full red beard and long, matted hair, wore a huge sombrero with rim tied down about his ears. His hair was "well powdered with a series of layers of dust, intermingled with stray blades of dry grass, leaves, and chips," and his clothing exhibited the same general appearance. Joe and Sheridan were old friends, having met in Oregon where Joe had tried his hand at raising a family and a few head of cattle in the mid-fifties. The ranch and family had not worked out, and while Sheridan was winning glory on eastern battlefields, Joe had adventured across the West, prospecting for gold in Idaho and Montana and scouting for the army on the southern plains. Now chance had thrown them together again. Sheridan enjoyed swapping tall tales in Chinook with Joe and reminiscing about their youthful days "on the slope."[25]

Custer had selected the flamboyant California Joe as his chief of scouts, despite the advice of several officers who preferred the more reliable Ben Clark, who had served as chief scout during Custer's absence. Joe promptly got roaring drunk to celebrate his appointment and was demoted; Clark was reappointed chief scout.

When he was sober, which was not that often, Joe was a good scout, and both Custer and Sheridan thought highly of him. For his part, Joe returned their friendship, saying of Sheridan:

> Why bless my soul, I knowed Shuridun way up in Oregon more'n fifteen years ago, an' he wuz only a second lootenant uv infantry. He wuz quartermaster of the foot or something uv that sort, an' I hed the contract uv furnishin' wood to that post, and, would ye b'lieve it? I hed a kind of sneaking notion then that he'd hurt somebody ef they'd ever turn him loose. Lord, but ain't he old lightin?[26]

From Joe's manner as he rode up to Sheridan's tent, it was obvious he carried good news. He handed the general a packet of letters from Custer. Sheridan's staff officers and correspondent Keim anxiously watched the general's face as he glanced over Custer's report. With California Joe regularly interjecting colorful descriptions, Sheridan read the report to those standing around him.

On the morning of November 26, Custer's column had discovered the fresh trail of an Indian war party estimated to number one hundred warriors. The heavy snow made following the Indians relatively easy, so the troops had corralled the supply wagons and left behind all heavy accouterments in an effort to catch the war party. From dawn until half past one the next morning the pursuit kept up, with only an hour's rest for men and animals during the entire march. The discovery of an Indian village by the Osage scouts halted the Seventh just above the Washita River. Custer divided his command into four attack columns. They quietly took up positions surrounding the village. Custer, ever the romantic, reported that "the moment the charge was ordered the band struck up 'Garry Owen,' and with cheers that strongly reminded one of scenes during the war, every trooper, led by his officer, rushed towards the village. The Indians were caught napping for once."[27] Within ten minutes the village was in possession of the troops, although it took several hours to wipe out Indian resistance from nearby ravines and underbrush. Custer reported a mighty victory. The village, consisting of fifty lodges, had been populated by Cheyennes under Black Kettle. The dead bodies of 103 warriors, including Black Kettle, had been counted on the field, and fifty-three women and children had been taken prisoner. Although he gave no

James E. Taylor's "The Attack at Dawn" captures the fury of Custer's assault on Black Kettle's camp. (*Little Bighorn Battlefield National Monument, National Park Service*)

numbers, Custer admitted that "in the excitement of the fight, as well as in self-defence, it so happened that some of the squaws and a few children were killed or wounded."[28] Enormous quantities of food-stuffs, clothing, shelter material, and weaponry had been captured and burned as contraband. Cheyenne mobility and wealth had been struck a devastating blow by the slaughter of over eight hundred of their ponies and mules.[29]

Black Kettle's village had been only one part of a great Indian encampment spread along the Washita. According to Custer, these other villages belonged to Kiowas and Arapahos under Satanta and Little Raven. These chiefs had led their warriors against his troops in a vain effort to rescue the Cheyennes. Custer would have liked to chastise all these Indians, but with his men exhausted and supplies and forage depleted, he had to fall back on his supply caravan. The victory had been a costly one for the Seventh, with Major Joel Elliott, Captain Louis Hamilton, and nineteen enlisted men dead and three officers and eleven enlisted men wounded.[30]

68

Sheridan was elated. His campaign could not have had a more promising beginning. He hurriedly penned a letter of congratulations for Custer and his men and ordered Corbin and Milner to backtrack and deliver it to the troops in the field.

When Custer received Sheridan's congratulatory note, he went wild with joy, for the opinion of his "beloved commander," as he referred to Sheridan, was critical to him. Custer promptly forwarded the note to his wife and gushed: "Oh, is it not gratifying to be so thought of by one whose opinion is above all price?" Sheridan also sent off a communication to Sherman summarizing Custer's report. He assured his division commander that it was "Black Kettle's band who committed the first depredation on the Saline and Soloman rivers" and that "if we can get one or two more good blows there will be no more Indian troubles in my Department."[31]

Sherman, who received Sheridan's brief report at division headquarters in Saint Louis, was well satisfied. He passed on Sheridan's report to the adjutant general's office in Washington, adding that the "bands of *Black Kettle*, Little Raven and Satanta are well known to us, and are the same that have been along the Smokey Hill the past five years, and as General *Sheridan* reports embrace the very men who first began this war on the Saline and Solomon." Sherman felt certain that the Indians would not escape this time, nor, he assured the War Department, would innocent Indians suffer at Sheridan's hands, for "his very presence there will give assurance that the troops will act with energy and that nothing will be done but what is right."[32]

Sherman telegraphed his congratulations to Sheridan and Custer on the "decisive and conclusive" battle on the Washita. It looked to him as if the war would be over by Christmas and "all these Indians begging for their lives." He reminded Sheridan to turn over all surrendering hostiles to Hazen after, of course, "having executed every Indian who began this war." Sherman was soon leaving for Chicago for meetings with the Indian Peace Commission, and he promised Sheridan to look after the interests of the troops in the field and prevent the humanitarian friends of the Indians from misrepresenting the battle as a massacre.[33]

While the lieutenant general prepared to give battle to the eastern humanitarians, the conquering heroes arrived at Camp Supply on December 2. Custer had sent a messenger ahead to inform Sheridan just when his troops would reach the post so they might pass in review before the general and his staff. The glory days of the Civil War might be gone, but Custer still hungered after the old military pomp and ceremony, even in the wilderness. Just after noon the Seventh appeared on the hills about a mile from Camp Supply, announcing its arrival with hurrahs and rifle fire. The fort's animal herd was startled by this and stampeded toward the post, but no damage was done. The segment of the Nineteenth Kansas that had arrived at Camp Supply was marched over from their camp to the main parade ground about eleven o'clock so that they could witness the return. At the approach of Custer's column, Sheridan and his staff mounted their horses and took position to view the parade. The day was bright and sunny, the snow now completely gone, and the temperature almost as warm as the soldier's spirits.

Like a conquering Roman chieftain, his enemies marching in chains behind him, Custer led his army in review before his leader and his men-at-arms. It was a scene of startling barbaric splendor. First came a dozen Osage trailers, wildly painted and chanting their shrill war songs. Their ponies and lances were decorated with the scalps of the Washita victims. Little Beaver, their chief, rode quietly but haughtily in the front, followed by the young warrior Trotter, who carried on his spear the prize trophy of the battle—the scalp of Black Kettle. Over and over the Osages fired their rifles into the air, and louder and louder came their chants of war. Suddenly Little Beaver broke his proud silence and shouted, "they call us Americans; we are Osages!"— and his warriors whooped in approval. Fighting the Cheyennes had been the duty of Osage warriors long before the white man arrived.

Next came the white scouts, riding abreast, decked out in buck-skins and displaying a small arsenal of knives, pistols, and rifles. Everyone recognized California Joe astride his faithful mule with his pipe clenched between his teeth. With Joe rode his partner, Jack Corbin, trailed by a heavy-set Mexican lad called Raphael Romero who had long lived among the Indians and served as an interpreter, two part-Arapaho scouts, Jack Fitzpatrick and John Poysell, and chief of scouts Ben Clark. Clark, more reflective than the others and a friend of the Cheyennes, was probably, of all those in the gaudy parade, the least pleased with the slaughter on the Washita.

Then rode Custer, looking far different from the young Beau

Sabreur of the Civil War. The long golden locks were now accompanied by a full beard hiding the sharp features of his face. Dressed like his scouts in full buckskins with a fur cap perched atop his head, he looked every inch a Cossack chieftain. Many of the soldiers of the Nineteenth Kansas, eager to get a look at the war hero, did not even recognize Custer, mistaking him for one of the scouts.

Behind Custer and his staff rode the Cheyenne captives, many wrapped in bright red trade blankets that stood out in sharp contrast to the dark costumes of Custer and his scouts. Mounted on their small ponies, sometimes as many as three to a horse, they stared straight ahead at their conqueror's back. The mothers pulled their blankets and robes high around their faces as if to shield themselves and their children from the stares of the enemy. Around them rode a military guard, as if this pitiful remnant could offer resistance.

Not far behind marched the regiment, preceded by the band playing the jaunty "Garry Owen." As each officer passed before General Sheridan, he flashed his saber in salute, to which the general lifted his cap in recognition and smiled. The regiment marched on through camp and about half a mile up Beaver Creek, taking the cacophony of Osage war songs, military commands, hurrahs, rifle shots, and Irish marching tunes with them. There the Seventh settled into camp.[34]

As soon as the Seventh's camp was well established, the officers of that regiment met with Sheridan and his staff to discuss the battle. Custer showed the general hard evidence of the hostile nature of Black Kettle's camp. There were household photographs captured in the raids along the Saline and Solomon, letters taken from a captured army courier, a large blank book displaying drawings of the recent history of Cheyenne fights with the whites, and army mules found in the Indian camp.[35]

Sheridan was especially concerned about Major Elliott and his troops, for it now became apparent that there was no evidence that they had been killed as first reported by Custer. Lieutenant Owen Hale reported that he had seen Elliott and a small group of troopers in pursuit of Indians who were trying to escape to the east of the village. As he rode by Hale, Elliott had turned and shouted, "Here goes for a brevet or a coffin!" Lieutenant Edward Godfrey had heard heavy firing in that direction some time later, but when he reported it to Custer, it was discounted, since no one else had reported it. As evening approached on the day of the battle, a small party had gone out in search of Elliott and the seventeen missing troopers, but could find no trace of them. Meanwhile, hundreds of warriors had swarmed up from the villages downstream, threatening to overrun Custer's tired detachment. Considering the great numbers of warriors coming toward him from the east, Custer assumed that Elliott had been surprised by them and killed. The best they could hope for, he theorized to Sheridan, was that Elliott's group had become lost and would eventually make it in to Camp Supply or Fort Dodge. This, Sheridan felt, was "a very unsatisfactory view of the matter," but it was now too late to do anything about it.[36]

Custer's desertion of Major Elliott lost him the confidence of a sizable faction of the Seventh's officers. Sheridan was also disturbed by the rather cavalier fashion by which Custer had written off a detachment of eighteen soldiers that included the regiment's major and sergeant-major. Sheridan felt that the "disappearance of Major Elliott and his party was the only damper upon our pleasure, and the only drawback to the very successful expedition."[37]

It was not too late, however, to follow up Custer's strike by marching back to the Washita and hitting the other tribes. A few more hard blows would force all the tribes onto their reservations and end the campaign. This was the same tactic employed in the Shenandoah in 1864, a "whirling movement," reinforced by winter cold and snow, to press the hostiles incessantly, keeping them always off balance until cold, starvation, and bullets broke them forever.

With all of Crawford's men now at Camp Supply, Sheridan finally had the troops to crush the hostiles. But time remained his enemy. While the Indians who had battled Custer scattered from the Washita, Sheridan would be forced to delay his follow-up stroke to allow Crawford's exhausted men and horses to recover. Custer's men and animals were still in fairly good shape, but they also needed to be rested before more campaigning. But Sheridan could not afford too much time; Sherman wanted him in Washington for Grant's inauguration as president March 4. He decided that December 7 would be the date of the departure. That would give the troops time to refit and also allow Major Inman time to arrive from Fort Dodge with additional supplies. Rations for at least thirty days were needed in order to retrace

Custer's route to Washita and then move south toward the Wichita Mountains, using Fort Cobb as a base.[38]

After the officers adjourned their meeting, some of them proceeded over to the banks of Beaver Creek at sunset, for the Osages were to celebrate a scalp dance. With Sheridan and his officers standing silently as spectators, the Indians "distorted their bodies in every conceivable shape" as they danced around a large log fire chanting war songs, displaying their grisly trophies, and recounting their heroic deeds against the Cheyennes. Correspondent Keim was particularly fascinated, if not a little horrified, by the dance, later writing that during "almost the entire night, long after the officers and men, assembled to witness the occasion, had departed, the Indian drum and the shout of the warriors could be heard, borne upon the still air."[39]

The captive women and children were kept at the Seventh Cavalry camp, constantly watched by a chain of sentinels. They expected to be slaughtered at any moment. So great was this conviction among them that the wounded refused to be separated from the group to have their wounds tended, fearing that they would be taken away for torture and a lonely death.

Finally Mah-wis-sa, a middle-aged Cheyenne woman who claimed to be Black Kettle's sister, asked to be taken before the white chief. Upon arriving at Sheridan's headquarters, she promptly asked through interpreter Dick Curtis when the prisoners could expect to be killed. When Sheridan informed her that that was not the custom of white men, her countenance quickly changed. She became quite talkative, informing Sheridan that the trail Custer had followed to her village had been made by a Cheyenne-Arapaho war party returning from a Kansas raid with fresh white scalps. She also revealed that three white women had been held captive in the Indian camps further downstream. Those camps consisted of seventy additional Cheyenne lodges, plus Kiowas, Arapahos, Comanches, and Apaches.[40]

Mah-wis-sa was prepared to tell her captors anything that would secure their favor and save the lives of her people. She was successful in this gambit, for both Sheridan and Custer developed a high opinion of her talents, gave her special treatment, and made use of her as an emissary. The interpreter Raphael Romero, however, did not share their opinion of Mah-wis-sa. He warned Custer: "She knows they are in

73

your power, and her object is to make friends with you as far as possible. But you don't believe anything she tells you, do you? Why, that squaw—give her the chance, and she'd lift your or my scalp for us and never wink."[41]

When Mah-wis-sa told the prisoners that they were not to be killed, their mood improved. They now allowed the military doctors to clean and dress their wounds, and also happily accepted the rations offered by the soldiers. The frolicking Indian children were soon a common fixture about the cavalry camp and won many a trooper's heart. Several of the Seventh's officers were especially attracted to some of the young Cheyenne women. The Mexican interpreter, Romero, who was in charge of the captives, acted as a procurer for the officers and sent young women around to their tents at night. Among the officers of the regiment, Romero was fondly nicknamed Romeo.[42]

On December 5, Major Inman returned with 250 heavily loaded supply wagons. They provided Sheridan with enough forage and rations for at least thirty days of campaigning and enough wagons for easy transport. Inman also reported that on his return he had discovered what was left of the bodies of scouts Bill Davis and Nate Marshall, surrounded by the signs of a desperate struggle. Davis and Marshall had been carrying dispatches for Sheridan to Fort Dodge, and it was items from their mail pouches that Custer had recovered from Black Kettle's village.[43]

Soon after Inman arrived, another violent snowstorm set in. The men awoke on December 6 to find eight inches on the ground and several of their horses dead from exposure. At first it seemed as if the storm would delay the expedition's departure, but when no more snow fell, Sheridan decided to move ahead as planned.

Captain John Page of the Third Infantry was given command of Camp Supply and was assigned three companies of his regiment, one of the Fifth Infantry and another of the Thirty-eighth Infantry, to garrison the new fort. Lieutenant Thomas Lebo's company of Buffalo Soldiers was attached to the post for scouting and escort duty, and two companies of the Kansas Volunteers were left to act as escort for Major Inman's supply trains. Even with the main body of troops leaving the post, it remained the vital link connecting Sheridan with supplies and communication from Fort Dodge.[44]

"The Indian War—Sheridan on the Move" was the title that war correspondent and artist Theodore Davis gave to his on-the-scene sketch published in *Harper's Weekly* on December 5, 1868.

The men left at Camp Supply hardly diminished the strength of Sheridan's army, for on the morning of December 7 he fielded a force of about seventeen hundred men. They would be more than a match for anything the combined tribes could muster. Custer retained nominal overall command of the strike force composed of eleven companies of the Seventh, ten companies of the Nineteenth Kansas Volunteers under Crawford, Lieutenant Pepoon's scouts, and a motley crew of between twenty and thirty white, Osage, and Kaw guides and trailers led by chief of scouts Ben Clark. Three hundred wagons accompanied the expedition, carrying equipment, tents, baggage, and thirty days of supplies and forage. In one of the wagons rode Mah-wissa, accompanied by a fifty-year-old Sioux woman and an attractive Cheyenne girl called Mo-nah-se-tah, whom Custer had befriended.

The rest of the Washita captives were sent to Fort Hays for safekeeping, but these three were to act as intermediaries with any Indians the expedition confronted. Although Sheridan was pleased to allow his ambitious young protégé official command of the troops, he still rode to the front of the column, accompanied by his staff, and personally gave the order, "Forward."[45]

CHAPTER 4

Winter War:
"The Most Sacred Promise
of Protection"

While Sheridan prepared to move southward, the Indian chiefs and leading warriors gathered in a grand council at the mouth of Sweetwater Creek on the north fork of the Red River. The Washita bands had fled to the Sweetwater after Custer's attack, being joined en route by Satanta and Satank with almost half the Kiowas who had been encamped near Fort Cobb. They now joined with the Kiowa bands of Woman's Heart and Big Bow, who had been camped on the Washita and had given battle to Custer. Mow-way and his Kotchateka Comanches, with members of several smaller Comanche bands, also had stampeded from Cobb at the news of the battle and joined the hostiles. It was a great encampment, numbering about five hundred lodges, the majority of which were Cheyenne and Arapaho.

All during the day on December 2, the Cheyenne and Arapaho chiefs tried to sway the other tribal leaders to the warpath. But their calls for vengeance and unity went unheeded. The peace faction prevailed among the Kiowas, with even bold Satanta deciding to rejoin the Kiowas under Lone Wolf and Black Eagle, who had remained near Fort Cobb. Only the small Kiowa bands of Big Bow and Woman's Heart declared for war. Mow-way of the Comanches spoke what was in the hearts of many when he declared that he wanted no part in this war of the Cheyennes and Arapahos, but he wanted no dealings with the

77

white men at Fort Cobb either. He would take his people out onto the safety of the Staked Plain.

So the Cheyennes and Arapahos would have to stand alone. They declared themselves well prepared and strong enough to do so. The Indians who sought sanctuary at Fort Cobb were to be regarded as friends, even though they would not join in the war. Through Kicking Bird and Little Heart, Kiowa chiefs representing the Fort Cobb faction at the council, a message was sent back to both Indians and whites. The Kiowas, Apaches, Comanches, Wichitas, Chickasaws, and other tribes on the reservation, as well as all white people, both soldier and civilian, south of the Sweetwater were to be regarded as friends by the Cheyennes and Arapahos. They would not be attacked unless they struck first. In return, they expected these tribes to be generous in sharing their surplus government annuities with those tribes out on the plains who would be cut off from the government larder. But against the Navajos, Utes, Osages, and all the white soldiers and settlers north and west of the Sweetwater, there was to be only war.[1]

War was just what Sheridan's troopers wanted as they prowled southward from Camp Supply in search of new prey. Ben Clark, California Joe, and the other scouts led the way with a pioneer corps to ensure suitable stream crossings for the wagons. Clark was also charged with finding camp sites with enough timber to enable warm fires to be built at night. Since only shelter tents were provided, good fires were essential. Hard Rope, the Osage leader, had other ideas on how to keep warm, announcing to all that he "would capture a Cheyenne squaw to keep his back warm."[2]

Although desolate at times, the snow-covered country was abundantly blessed with wildlife. On the second day of the march, vast herds of buffalo and antelope were encountered. The buffalo became so thick that they stampeded some of the army mules, threatening the safety of the column. Sheridan finally ordered the column's flankers to shoot the leading bulls and turn the buffalo herds away from the line of march. The wolf packs that had begun following the column to feed on the spent mules were now provided even richer fare.

Nothing could stand before this great armada; nothing seemed capable of stopping it. Great animal herds, deep showdrifts, jagged ice floes, and the harsh badlands of the Canadian were all swept under as the column plodded on. A norther struck on the second night out, continuing all the next day with sleet, snow, and biting wind. Temperatures hovered between ten degrees and zero, so that even thick buffalo gloves and boots could not protect the troopers from frostbite. It became too cold to ride, so the men dismounted and led their suffering horses. Often making less than a mile an hour, Sheridan's army crept on, the blue-painted military wagons moving in four columns in the center with the Seventh abreast of the train on the right flank and the Kansans on the left flank, each regiment in column of fours. With each mile they made, the old West of the Indian and buffalo drew that much closer to extinction.[3]

On the evening of December 10 the weary troops made camp in the Washita valley about six miles below the site of Custer's battle. Here the command was rested for a day to enable search parties to look for Elliott's lost command. An escort squadron of the Seventh and several Indian scouts accompanied Sheridan, Custer, Keim, and a number of staff, Seventh Cavalry, and volunteer officers to the battlefield early on December 11. A sharp, cold wind blew in the men's faces as they moved quickly up the north side of the Washita, reaching the site of the battle in an hour and a half. As they entered the battlefield, thousands of ravens and crows, disturbed in their feasting, rose as one in a black cloud of movement and flew overhead screeching in protest. Wolves skulked off on every side, retreating to nearby summits to sit and watch the invaders until it was safe to return. The trooper's horses gingerly picked their way through the village, avoiding the charred remains of Indian lodges and property. Most of the Indian bodies had been removed, although some, mostly women and children, remained on the battle site, wrapped in blankets in preparation for burial. Several more bodies, including thirty together in one place, were later found wrapped for burial in the nearby hills.

Sheridan and several of his officers rode onto a nearby ridge to view the entire field. Here Custer explained the battle, pointing out the location of the lodges, the movement of his troops, and the area to the right of the village, covering several acres, where lay the eight hundred slaughtered ponies.

Now the troops were divided into search parties to locate Elliott and his men. Sheridan and Custer, accompanied by Keim and a small detachment of men, worked their way down the south bank of the Washita in the direction Elliott had last been seen moving. They had not gone a hundred yards when the nearly beheaded body of Sergeant Major Walter Kennedy, last seen with Elliott, was discovered. Two hundred yards beyond that, in the center of a broad plain, the naked, frozen corpses of all but one of the missing men were found.

Sheridan dismounted to examine the scene and try to reconstruct the struggle. The bodies were all within a circle of twenty paces, piles of spent cartridge shells beside each—mute testimony that their struggle had been hard and protracted. It was not difficult to imagine them, ammunition almost gone, holding off the warriors from downstream while straining their ears for the bugle notes of the rescue column from Custer that never came.

Finding the men dead was no surprise, but the terrible mutilations inflicted on the bodies still wrenched at the stomach. Some of the men had been beheaded, some scalped, most hacked repeatedly with knives and hatchets, and all had numerous bullet and arrow wounds. Major Elliott lay with his men, three bullet wounds in his head, his throat cut, a hand cut off and a foot almost so, and his body otherwise slashed and cut in a most gruesome manner. Carnage had been a part of Sheridan's life for many years, and he neither feared nor shied from it. He had witnessed the deaths of hundreds of men in a single hour and had seen bodies torn asunder by saber and cannon. Yet the mauled bodies of this young officer and his troopers were of a different nature. Sheridan was both incapable of and unwilling to accept a rational, cultural explanation for such mutilations. He viewed it as the animalistic behavior of devilish savages. Such a people could only understand force, and Sheridan was now more ready than ever to give them a full measure of it.[4]

Sheridan and his party returned to the main camp by riding down the river through the area lately occupied by the other Indian villages. Only now did the size of the encampment become evident, for the abandoned campsites spread through the timber along the Washita for eight miles. Buffalo robes, jerked meat, domestic utensils, and other Indian goods were littered about in evidence of the haste with which the camps had been abandoned. The officers estimated the number of abandoned lodge sites at between six hundred and one thousand. Custer had been fortunate indeed to escape on November 27. Sheridan ordered the Indian property gathered and burned, and then hurried back to camp.[5]

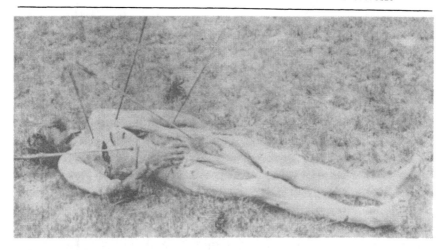

When Sheridan discovered the bodies of Major Joel Elliott and his men on the Washita battlefield they had been mutilated in a fashion similar to this soldier, Sergeant Frederick Wyllyams of the Seventh Cavalry, who was killed on June 26, 1867, by Cheyenne Dog Soldiers. The cultural reasons for such mutilations were lost on Sheridan. He saw them as evidence of the innate savagery of the Indian and used them to justify his own brutal military policy. (*Kansas State Historical Society, Topeka*)

Captain Milton Stewart of the volunteers soon reported to Sheridan that he had discovered a dead white woman and her infant beside the river near one of the abandoned villages. The general ordered the bodies brought into camp. He had the woman and child laid out on a blanket so that the Kansans could get a look and perhaps identify them. She was a young woman, perhaps twenty years old, "of more than ordinary beauty," though her face had been disfigured by gunpowder when she had been shot in the forehead from point-blank range. She had also been scalped. Sheridan sadly concluded that cruel as her death was, it "no doubt brought her welcome release." Her baby had a bruise on the side of his head, which caused Sheridan to decide that it had been picked up by the feet and bashed against a tree. Finally, one of the Kansas troopers recognized the pair as Clara Blinn and her two-year-old son. This was the woman whose father had written Sheridan early in November begging the general to save his child and grandchild. Yet the frustrating truth was that Sheridan, with all his armed might, could not rescue them. Now he could only have them gently wrapped in blankets and, along with Major Elliott, carried to Fort Arbuckle for burial. Here was one more score to settle with the Indians.[6]

Mah-wis-sa was brought before Sheridan. The general wanted to know what tribes had occupied the other camps along the Washita. The Arapahos under Little Raven, the Kiowas led by Satanta and Lone Wolf, and then other mixed Cheyenne, Arapaho, Comanche, and Lipan Apache bands was her answer. Sheridan wanted to know whose village Clara Blinn had belonged to. It was the village of Satanta, replied the sister of Black Kettle. Sheridan burned with righteous anger as he envisioned the lovely white woman "being reserved to gratify the brutal lust of the chief, Satanta" and then cruelly murdered when her rescue was almost at hand. He could not know, and never realized, that Mah-wis-sa was lying. Clara Blinn had been the captive of the Arapahos, the faithful allies of Mah-wis-sa's people. Satanta had had no part in this sad affair, but Mah-wis-sa was quick to blame the pompous Kiowa in order to protect her friends from Sheridan's wrath.[7]

At dawn on December 12 the expedition departed from its Washita encampment. The Indian trail was plain and broad, leading down the Washita in the direction of Fort Cobb. Another trail, which had recently been made by the fleeing Cheyennes, Arapahos, and Kiowas who had been camped with Black Kettle, struck off to the west toward the Red River. Sheridan, however, could not discern the origin of the trails, and since it was essential to reach Fort Cobb for supplies and intelligence reports, the Washita Indian trail was followed.[8]

It was difficult going, with upwards of three hundred men regularly employed as pioneer corps to clear obstructions and bridge ravines and creeks so that the wagons could advance. Nor did the weather moderate. Mornings would find tents, saddles, and harnesses frozen solid to the ground, and many a cut and frozen finger resulted from efforts to prepare to move out. The snow often made it impossible to reach dry grass for the horses, the troopers cutting young cottonwood branches for the starving animals.

The morning of December 17 found the column halted near Rainy Mountain Creek, some twenty miles from Fort Cobb, while the pioneer corps bridged a deep ravine. At about ten o'clock Osage scouts reported a party of Indians approaching under a white flag. The Indians sent forward a lone rider, who turned out to be a messenger from Fort Cobb with a dispatch from Hazen addressed to "the Officer, commanding troops in the field." Sheridan quickly read the note, dated 9:00 P.M., December 16:

> Indians have just brought in word that our troops today reached the Washita some twenty miles above here. I send this to say that all the camps this side of the point reported to have been reached are friendly, and have not been on the war path this season. If this reaches you, it would be well to communicate at once with Satanta or Black Eagle, chiefs of the Kiowas, near where you now are, who will readily inform you of the position of the Cheyennes and Arapahoes, also of my camp.

The messenger also informed Sheridan that Satanta, Lone Wolf, and a large party of Kiowas were holding another courier hostage not a mile away and that they desired a parley.[9]

This was unbelievable. For seven grueling days Sheridan had led his men across rough terrain in vicious weather to bag these very Indians, and now that they were within his grasp, Hazen dared to throw a protective cloak around them. Sheridan could only marvel at Hazen's stupidity, describing the letter as "a pretty good joke." He was already furious at Hazen for issuing flour, sugar, and coffee to the hostiles. Custer had discovered these government rations in Black Kettle's camp, and Sheridan had immediately fired off a letter to Sherman condemning Hazen for feeding the savage enemies of the Republic. The fact that Hazen had previously been drawn into serious controversies with both Sheridan and Custer certainly colored the manner in which both men viewed the supplies in Black Kettle's camp and the message now before them. They were quick to put the worst possible interpretation on anything concerning their professional enemy.[10]

Custer wanted to attack. A mile away was bloody Satanta, probably displaying the scalps of Clara Blinn and Major Elliott on his lance. There could be no doubt of the guilt of the Kiowas. Mah-wis-sa had told of their perfidy, and their trail had been followed directly from the Washita battlefield. Hazen had been "readily and completely deceived as to their real character," or he had been won over by the bleeding hearts of the Indian Bureau. But Sheridan would not unleash Custer. Hazen was Sherman's personal appointee, and Sheridan had been ordered to cooperate closely with him. Sheridan would not cross Sherman by disregarding Hazen's message, no matter how much he wanted Satanta's hide or how sure he was that Hazen had been deceived.[11]

It was not Hazen, however, who had been misinformed. Because of their reliance on Mah-wis-sa, their predisposition to punish the Kiowas, and their prejudice toward Hazen, both Sheridan and Custer misread the entire situation and were wrong on every point. The supplies in Black Kettle's camp had been purchased from Indian trader Bill Griffenstein behind Hazen's back when Black Kettle visited Fort Cobb. Hazen knew exactly who the declared hostiles were and was not about to issue them rations. Furthermore, Hazen had been kept well informed of Indian movements by Captain Alvord and a small corps of Comanche scouts. He was absolutely positive that the Kiowas, as a tribe, had not taken part in the Battle of the Washita. Small Kiowa bands under Woman's Heart and Big Bow had been there and had fought Custer's men, but they had fled southwest with the Cheyennes and Arapahos. Satanta, Satank, and Lone Wolf had spent the night of November 26 at Fort Cobb, and while Custer was fighting on the Washita, they were having breakfast at Hazen's tent. The trail that Sheridan and Custer had followed from the battlefield was an old one, made over a week before the Washita fight by the Kiowas moving from the big Indian encampment to the sanctuary promised by the government at Fort Cobb. Hazen also knew that Clara Blinn had not been Satanta's prisoner, but had been held by the Arapahos. He had been negotiating for her release through Griffenstein when Custer's attack doomed her. Hazen had no love for Satanta and company; he knew of many recent raids into Texas, but he was bound to protect them. The war had been specifically declared against the Indians who had raided in Kansas and endangered the railroad, no one much caring at the time about the ex-Confederates in Texas. The Kiowas had taken no part in those Kansas raids, and they had reported to Fort Cobb as ordered by the government. Hazen rightly felt that it would be "a most gross neglect of duty" to allow Sheridan to attack the Kiowas while "they were resting under the most sacred promise of protection."[12]

No amount of evidence would ever change Sheridan's obsessive conviction that Satanta's Kiowas had fought Custer on the Washita. But since he could not disregard the wishes of the commander of the Southern Indian Military District, he decided to send Custer forward to parley with the Kiowas. Accompanied by two interpreters, correspondent Keim, Sheridan's aide-de-camp Lieutenant (Brevet Lieutenant Colonel) J. Schuyler Crosby, several other officers, and Pepoon's fifty scouts, Custer galloped off toward the waiting Kiowas. As they moved down the valley, the soldiers could see several hundred warriors in nearby ravines and lined along the surrounding hilltops. Many of them pranced back and forth on their ponies, brandishing their weapons and shrieking war cries. Hazen's letter was looking more absurd by the minute. Two Indians waited in the valley floor for the approach of the troops. They were Satanta and Lone Wolf, and the interpreters went forward to meet them. Momentarily a sign was made that the Indians wanted to speak with the white chief, and Custer, Crosby, and Keim, rifles at the ready, joined the interpreters.[13]

Satanta was impressive: "quite large and very strongly built," recalled one of Custer's men, "much more noble looking than the others who are darker and just ordinary looking Indians." Assuming Crosby to be the commander because of his uniform, Satanta extended his hand and "with an air of arrogance exclaimed 'How.'" Arrogance not belonging only to Kiowas chiefs, Crosby scowled and refused Satanta's hand. Satanta flew into a rage, beating his chest and loudly exclaiming, "Me Kiowa!" He seemed about to signal his warriors when Sheridan, with the rest of the troops, appeared over a hill about a mile away. Satanta quickly calmed down and approached Custer, whom he had first mistaken for a scout because of his buckskins, extending his hand again. "I never shake hands with any one unless I know him to be a friend," declared the long-haired cavalryman. This seemed to satisfy Satanta, who promptly began a tirade on how much he loved the white man. Custer demanded that Satanta release Hazen's courier to prove his friendship, and this was complied with. Custer then informed the chiefs that Hazen's letter would be honored, but only if the Kiowas came into Fort Cobb as a sign of good faith. This was also agreeable to Satanta and Lone Wolf. As further evidence of their dedication to peace they agreed to accompany the military column to Fort Cobb. Several important warriors would also join the column, but the main village would have to move slower on account of the poor condition of their ponies. This was fine with Custer, and the two Kiowas, joined by a Comanche chief, accompanied the soldiers back to the main column.[14]

The consensus among Sheridan's officers was that the Kiowas

"Custer's Demand" by Charles Schreyvogel depicts the dramatic confrontation between Custer and the Kiowa chiefs, December 17, 1868. The soldiers were in peril and would undoubtedly have been attacked except for the timely arrival of Sheridan with the rest of the troops. From left to right are Little Heart, Lone Wolf, Kicking Bird, Satanta, Abner "Sharp" Grover (who was not in reality present), Lieutenant Colonel George Custer, Lieutenant Tom Custer (the colonel's brother), Lieutenant Colonel John Schuyler Crosby, and General Sheridan (in front of the distant troops). (*The Thomas Gilcrease Institute of American History and Art, Tulsa, Oklahoma*)

would have attacked Custer's small force unless the main column had come up. Since the whites were too numerous to fight, reasoned the officers, the Indians had decided to pretend friendship in order to stall for time while their villages escaped. For once the soldiers were exactly right, for while Lone Wolf and Satanta were soon joined in Sheridan's camp by twenty more Kiowa, Comanche, and Kiowa-Apache warriors and chiefs, the main village was moving in the opposite direction as rapidly as possible.[15]

By dawn on December 18, when the troops broke camp for their last day's march to Fort Cobb, most of the Indians who had agreed to join the column were gone. As the day progressed, the rest of the warriors, one at a time, took their leave in order, they claimed, to hurry along the village. Finally only Lone Wolf and Satanta were left. About mid-afternoon Satanta allowed his pony to drift beyond the column's flank, then jerking his pony about, made a dash for safety. Several of Sheridan's officers saw him and gave chase, overtaking him within half a mile. Satanta's attempted escape confirmed Sheridan's suspicions. He promptly placed a guard around the two chiefs, announcing that they would be held as hostages until their people surrendered. Not long after this the eldest son of Satanta, Tsa'lante, a strikingly handsome warrior about twenty years of age, approached the column to see what was delaying his father and Lone Wolf. He was informed of Sheridan's demand and was sent back to convey the message to his people, a role he would perform many times over the next few days.[16]

After dark on December 18, the column reached Fort Cobb, having completed a march of almost 190 miles during some of the winter's worst weather. When the troops were about a mile from Fort Cobb, Colonel Hazen rode out to greet them. He promptly became aware that Sheridan and Custer held him "accountable for seriously marring the success of their operations," and that "their opinions, that the Kiowas had fought them at the battle of Washita, were so firmly fixed, that . . . it [was] futile and unwise to endeavor them to correct their impressions." Hazen, however, could clear the air somewhat by presenting specific instructions he had received from Sherman that "every appearance about Ft. Cobb should be suggestive of an earnest desire to afford a place of refuge where the peaceable Indians may receive food and be safe against our troops, as well as against the hostile Indians who may try to involve them in the common war." The gruesome specter of Sand Creek was still fresh in Sherman's mind as he reminded Hazen that if he had "not notified General Sheridan of the fact that some of your Kiowas are peaceful, get word to him some way or other, lest he pursue them and stampede your whole family."[17]

A stampede had occurred when Sheridan's columns were first spotted. Hazen described the Indians "as uncontrollable as a herd of scared buffalo." No matter what Lone Wolf and Satanta's intentions had been when they first conferred with Custer, Hazen doubted whether they could bring in their panicky people. Nor were the Kiowas alone in their mistrust of the whites, for the rest of Hazen's Indians were huddled in camps behind Fort Cobb with ponies saddled and goods packed, ready to run for their lives if necessary.[18]

With three hundred Indian lodges as well as the tents of the troops, Fort Cobb resembled a mining camp tent city more than a fortified outpost of the United States government. Sheridan posted his headquarters in a wall tent in the Seventh Cavalry camp, around which a low fence of rough poles was constructed. Most of the regular officers shared wall tents, while the volunteer officers and the regular troops had smaller A-tents. The volunteer soldiers had to make do with tiny dog tents, which caused considerable grumbling about inequality. To remedy their cramped living conditions, the volunteers began digging square pits about the size of their tents, but deep enough to stand up in, to which a sod fireplace was added. These dugouts proved quite comfortable, but the ridiculous nature of their dwellings led the men to amuse themselves by "poking their heads out and barking at the occupants of adjacent huts in imitation of the prairie-dog." Soon after the men reached Fort Cobb, however, persistent rains flooded most of the dugouts.[19]

The torrents of rain and resulting mud, which made transporting supplies nearly impossible, challenged even Sheridan's famous reputation as a blasphemer. Everything seemed to conspire to displease him: essential forage was scarce around Fort Cobb, and the place was indefensible; supplies and mail from Arbuckle were delayed; the rain caked everything and everybody in mud, while the accompanying high winds played havoc with his wall tent; and the Kiowas still were not in sight. Sheridan might not be able to do anything about the weather, but the Indians were another matter. These Kiowas, he wrote Sherman, "have attempted to brow-beat General Hazen since he came here." But their day was over, for Sheridan assured Sherman that he would "take some of the starch out of them before I get through with them." Sheridan proposed to accomplish this by hanging Satanta and Lone Wolf unless their people came in as promised. The general refused to have anything to do with the two chiefs himself, so he summoned Custer to give them his ultimatum.[20]

"This matter has gone on long enough, and must be stopped," Sheridan told Custer, "as we have to look after the other tribes before spring overtakes us." Sheridan branded the two captive chiefs "guilty of untold murders and outrages," for which they richly deserved punishment. He ordered Custer to inform Satanta and Lone Wolf that if their people were not in by sundown the next day, they would be hanged, and the soldiers sent after their villages.[21]

Custer delivered his message to the surprised chiefs. Tsa'lante was sent galloping across the plains by his father, with the earnest admonition to hurry along the village. Satanta was not sanguine concerning his chances. A volunteer officer saw him "sit down by the side of the tent, then swaying back and forth, chant the most doleful and monotonous death-song. Then stooping over he would scoop up sand and dirt and put it into his mouth." This ritual was followed by a walk to the southwest side of the tent to study the horizon in hopes of seeing his people approach.[22]

Satanta's gaze was rewarded when, at about two o'clock on December 20, a large party of warriors led by Black Eagle rode into Fort Cobb. There was a warm reunion between Black Eagle and his two friends, and then the chief informed Custer that he and his warriors had come in as hostages until the rest of the Kiowas, who had been camped some forty miles west on Elk Creek, could arrive. True to Black Eagle's word, most of the other Fort Cobb Kiowas soon arrived, establishing their villages on the Washita about a mile from Sheridan's camp. The general's ploy had worked perfectly, but he was not entirely pleased with the outcome. "I will always regret, however," he wrote in his report of the affair, "that I did not hang these Indians; they had deserved it many times; and I shall also regret that I did not punish the whole tribe when I first met them."[23]

Compelling the Fort Cobb Kiowas to settle on their reservation under military supervision had proven relatively easy, but now Sheridan turned his attention to the hard-core nonreservation bands. The Cheyennes of Medicine Arrows (Rock Forehead) and Little Robe were still encamped on Sweetwater Creek, while the Arapahos under Little Raven and Yellow Bear had moved eastward from the Sweetwater camp to another tributary of the Red River, Mulberry Creek. Horse Back's Nakoni Comanches, sixty lodges strong, had moved beside Soldier Spring on the north fork of the Red River, with the nonreservation Kiowas under Woman's Heart and Big Bow camped nearby. Horse Back's people had fled from Fort Cobb after news of the Washita fight reached them, while Woman's Heart and Big Bow had never reported to Hazen at the fort. Mow-way's Kotchateka Comanches, as well as the Kwahadis (Quohadas), remained safe from the military out on the vast Staked Plain of the Texas Panhandle.[24]

Sheridan decided to work through local Indians in order to persuade the reluctant bands to surrender. Since he knew the general location of the Cheyennes and Arapahos, he selected a local Kiowa-Apache chief, Iron Shirt, to carry a message to the hostiles. Mah-wis-sa was to accompany Iron Shirt back to her people. They were to inform the hostile chiefs that if they immediately brought their people onto the reservation, all past grievances would be forgotten and no punishment inflicted on anyone. If, however, this offer was not agreed to, the soldiers would be sent out to destroy them.[25]

This represented quite a mellowing of the general's hard-line position of hanging all guilty warriors. As tough as Sheridan talked, he always accommodated himself to the reality of a situation. He realized that if the war were to be concluded soon, the Indians would have to be given honorable terms for coming onto the reservation. Foremost in Sheridan's mind was how to bring about peace in the shortest time with the minimum expenditure of blood and treasure.

Taking a cue from Captain Alvord, the general employed the services of several Penateka Comanches as scouts. Varying in size, depending on Sheridan's need for information, this band of scouts kept him well informed on the attitude of the local tribes as well as on the location of hostile bands. The Penatekas were paid well in goods for their work and were happy to be kept busy, since Sheridan's soldiers made their usual raids against the Texas settlements inconvenient for a while.[26]

While Sheridan's peace message went out to the Cheyennes and Arapahos and his Indian spies kept track of other nonreservation bands, the garrison at Fort Cobb settled down to await developments and celebrate a soggy Christmas. The rains continued, turning the fort grounds into a quagmire. Sheridan made up his mind that this would be the last Christmas any troops spent at Cobb. Not only was the climate bad, but forage was poor, defenses inadequate, and the location too far north properly to supervise the Kiowa-Comanche reservation. A new fort was needed to watch over the reservation and protect the exposed Texas frontier. With Fort Arbuckle to the east and Camp Supply to the north, a new post further south would allow supervision of Indian activity and provide a good base from which to launch future expeditions.

Sheridan selected Colonel (Brevet Major General) Benjamin Grierson, who had explored the region the previous May, to pick a site for this important new post. Grierson would be accompanied by Major James Forsyth of Sheridan's staff, Colonel Hazen, correspondent Keim, several officers, and forty Tenth Cavalry troopers. They would join in Christmas festivities at Fort Cobb and then strike out for the Wichita Mountains on December 28.

A violent wind storm marked Christmas Day. Although the tents were often in danger of tearing loose, Sheridan's officers attempted to ignore the winds and spent the day in celebration. First there was a cocktail party in Hazen's tent, the sole beverage being a milk punch made with condensed milk, sugar, and some home-brew brought up from Texas. When the punch had been exhausted, the officers removed themselves to Sheridan's quarters for a banquet. There was much Christmas cheer, even though, as Keim noted, the dinner "was not so bountifully supplied with the game of the country as the feast of Thanksgiving-day at Camp Supply."[27]

Out on the north fork of the Red River, just west of Soldier Spring Creek, the three hundred freezing troopers of Major Andrew Evans's column were spending Christmas in quite a different manner. Since leaving Fost Bascom, New Mexico, on November 18, they had struggled across the barren plains, giving battle to cold and hunger but finding no Indians. The foul weather and lack of success had done nothing to lessen Major Evans's well-deserved reputation as one of the worst-tempered officers in the service. One observer characterized him as "having, to all appearance, registered a vow never to smile, in any sense." His mood brightened a bit on December 24, when scouts reported warriors spying on the column and numerous Indian trail markings visible on the frozen ground. Evans decided to rest his men on Christmas day and then attempt to follow the main Indian trail in the evening. He dispatched Captain (Brevet Major) Elisha Tarlton with a company of the Third Cavalry to scout the nearby countryside.[28]

Tarlton's men skirmished with a large party of warriors and, reinforced by two more companies of cavalry, pursued the Indians to their encampment, sixty lodges strong. Warriors swarmed out of the village, and for a moment it seemed as if Tarlton's command might be

Satanta, or White Bear, although not a principal chief
among the Kiowas, was an important leader of the war
faction. He wears an army captain's shoulder straps as
decoration in this 1870 photograph. "It will always be a
matter of regret to me that I did not hang Satanta when
I had him a prisoner in the winter of 1868," Sheridan
wrote in 1873. "He has repeatedly merited such a
punishment." (*Bureau of American Ethnology, Smithsonian
Institution*)

encircled. Major Evans arrived just in time with the rest of the troops, and the Indians were thrown back.[29]

The warriors now withdrew, although some desultory skirmishing continued throughout the day and into the night. Since Evans's horses were too broken down to pursue the Indians, he contented himself with making camp in their village and burning everything in sight. Evans's men reported twenty warriors killed, although no bodies were found, with only one trooper mortally wounded. The major could content himself with a good Christmas Day's work.[30]

The village had belonged to Horse Back's Nakoni Comanches, and these people were now completely impoverished. They had been supported in the fight by Woman's Heart's Kiowas, who had played the same role at Washita a month before. The Indians now scattered east and west, some eventually straggling into Forts Cobb and Bascom to surrender, while others joined the Kwahadis on the Staked Plain. Evans had dealt them a hard blow, not in lives lost, but in property destroyed.

The Indian camps around Fort Cobb buzzed with rumors of the battle at Soldier Spring. At first Sheridan discounted the stories, but the arrival of a messenger from Evans on December 30 confirmed them. The general was delighted, even going so far as to inform Sherman prematurely that the battle "gave the final blow to the backbone of the Indian rebellion." Sheridan sent congratulations back to Evans along with rations and instructions to return to his supply depot on the Canadian River in Texas and await further orders.[31]

Near midnight on New Year's Eve a delegation of twenty-one Cheyenne and Arapaho warriors led by Chiefs Little Robe and Yellow Bear limped into Fort Cobb. They had received the message carried by Iron Shirt and Mah-wis-sa and, no doubt given impetus by Evans's battle, had hurried in to confer with Sheridan, their weakened ponies giving out on the way. They first met with Custer and then were taken before Sheridan the next day. These were the men the general had vowed to hang, but in their present condition he could only pity them.

The chiefs reported their people in mourning, their food gone, even the "dogs all eaten up," and no buffalo or small game to be found in the rough country where they were hiding. Peace was all they now desired, on whatever terms Sheridan would allow. They asked only for

93

a letter to protect them from the soldiers while they packed the villages and moved to Fort Cobb.[32]

This was agreeable to Sheridan, but he made it clear that the bands could not "come in here and make peace with me now, and then commence killing white people again in the spring." For all he cared, they could remain on the plains, and he would gladly "make war on them winter and summer as long as I live, or until they are wiped out." This was not to be a peace like those made before, but rather a "peace which will last." Sheridan warned the chiefs that "if they commit robberies and murders afterwards they must be punished." Their choice was clear, he declared, either a lasting peace or a war of annihilation.

The chiefs listened quietly, offering no argument, and when Sheridan was finished, Little Robe sadly replied, "It is for you to say what we have to do."[33]

Sheridan ordered the chiefs to send messages to their people ordering them to report to the reservation. As a sign of their good faith, which neither Sheridan nor Custer doubted, Little Robe and Yellow Bear remained at Fort Cobb. They asked Sheridan not to be impatient, since the weakened condition of the stock would delay the arrival of their people. Sheridan assured the chiefs that he would hold back his soldiers and wait for the Indians to come in. Couriers were sent out informing Evans and Carr of the surrender and instructing them to cease hostile operations for the time being. Sheridan believed that the "Arapahos and Cheyennes [had] hollered Enough" and that the campaign was at an end.[34]

CHAPTER 5

Campaign's End:
"This Shameless Disregard
for Justice"

The violent struggle with the Indians was a conflict Sheridan could understand. But in the East a political war raged, which left him baffled and embittered. The friends of the Indians had risen in unison to decry the "massacre" at Washita and the foul murder of peace-loving Black Kettle. Their letters and editorials splashed across newspaper pages across the country.

"I cannot but feel that the innocent parties have been made to suffer for the crimes of others," lamented Superintendent of Indian Affairs Thomas Murphy. Black Kettle, Murphy asserted, was "one of the truest friends the whites have ever had among the Indians" and was no doubt on his way to Fort Cobb when he was slain. Former agent Wynkoop quickly chimed in: "Black Kettle had proceeded to the point at which he was killed with the understanding that it was the locality where all those Indians who were friendly disposed should assemble." Samuel F. Tappan, a member of the Peace Commission, demanded an "immediate and unconditional abandonment of the present war policy," for it could only result in the spilling of more innocent blood. "This shameless disregard for justice has been the most foolhardy course we could have pursued," preached Reverend Henry B. Whipple, the Episcopal bishop for Minnesota. Over and over the chorus of protest reechoed the charge that Washita had been another Sand Creek massacre.[1]

Nor were such sentiments found only in the East. When William Griffenstein, the Fort Cobb Indian trader, made the mistake of publicly stating that Custer had attacked friendly Indians on the Washita, Sheridan ordered him out of the Indian Territory and threatened to hang him if he returned. Griffenstein, however, was not the only westerner to label the fight a massacre. James S. Morrison, who had served Wynkoop as a scout, wrote his former employer a brief report of the fight. Morrison declared that twice as many women and children as warriors had been killed. As his source for this information he cited John Poysell and Jack Fitzpatrick, two of Custer's scouts who were involved in the fight. This letter soon found its way into print.[2]

Nor was criticism leveled only by civilians. The *St. Louis Democrat* and the *New York Times* published a description of the battle by an anonymous Seventh Cavalry officer which depicted Custer as taking sadistic pleasure in slaughtering the Indian ponies and dogs, while callously abandoning Major Elliott to his fate. The article, while not favorable to Black Kettle, also alluded to the killing of innocent women and children. Custer was so enraged when he saw the newspaper that he called his officers together and, pacing to and fro striking a rawhide riding crop against his leg, threatened to whip the author if he had the courage to step forward. Captain (Brevet Lieutenant Colonel) Frederick Benteen, a vitriolic Virginian who commanded H Company, promptly stepped up to Custer and admitted writing the article as a letter to a friend. Benteen then snarled at Custer to begin whipping, at the same time unsnapping his holster. Custer dismissed the officers, and the affair ended, although some have felt that its reverberations continued until Little Big Horn, when Custer would be stranded and Benteen would leave him to his fate.[3]

Randolph Keim learned of the episode and reported it to Sheridan. Upset by Custer's behavior, Sheridan, as Benteen soon learned, gave his young friend "a piece of his mind about the matter." Benteen was convinced that the general "was rapidly beginning to learn more about the characteristics of [Custer], and . . . cared but little for him thereafter." Benteen, who could hate better than most men, and hated Custer more than any other man, misread the situation. Sheridan may well have dressed down Custer for high-handed behavior, but it had no lasting effect on their relationship. Sheridan had worked with Custer long enough to understand his strengths and weaknesses. Although strained on occasion by Custer's penchant for controversy, their friendship, both professional and personal, remained warm and close until Custer's death.[4]

Colonel Grierson, commander of the Tenth Cavalry and the District of Indian Territory, was not a Custer partisan either. He was, however, more discreet than Benteen, wisely keeping his thoughts on the battle out of the press. But to his father-in-law he wrote that "Custer's fight was a big thing on paper—the 102 warriors he reported killed has dwindled down according to Indian *count* to just *eighteen* and he reported more material captured and destroyed than all the hostile Indians had put together." Grierson's opinion reflected more than just a dispassioned review of the evidence, for he also tellingly grumbled that "so far as any gain or glory is concerned I am merely left here to hold the empty bag."[5]

Sheridan acted quickly to counteract such sentiments. "I see it alleged by Indian agents that Black Kettle's band was on their reservation at the time attacked," he complained to division headquarters, "[and] it is also alleged the band was friendly. No one could make such an assertion who had any regard for truth." These were the very Indians who had commenced hostilities in the first place, Sheridan asserted, and as evidence he listed the government mail, settler domestic items and photographs, army mules, and other booty found in the camp by Custer's men. He reminded headquarters that Black Kettle— "a worn out and worthless old cypher"—and his people had been offered a chance to surrender at Fort Larned in September 1868, but had refused to come in.[6]

A solid front being essential to discredit the claims of the Indian Bureau, Colonel Hazen was pressed into service to send a similar letter to Sherman. Hazen declared that Black Kettle's people "were those engaged in the trouble on the Soloman [sic], and their reservation was not in this vicinity at all." To make the military position appear even sounder, Hazen twisted Black Kettle's statements made at their November 20 meeting. The chief had frankly and contritely confessed to being unable to control some of his young warriors, but Hazen now made it appear that Black Kettle had boasted that "many of his men were then on the warpath, and that their people did not want peace with the people above the Arkansas."[7]

Further to buttress his case, Sheridan had his aide-de-camp, Crosby, prepare an affidavit from Edmund Guerrier, a sometime government interpreter who had resided with Little Rock's Cheyennes at the time of the Saline-Solomon raids. Guerrier testified that "nearly all the different bands of Cheyennes had some of their young men in this war party," and several of the warriors, including one of the two leaders, were from Black Kettle's village.[8]

As the debate heated up, so did Sheridan's rhetoric. He could see sinister forces manipulating the humanitarian outcry, declaring that "the hue and cry was raised through the influence of the Indian ring." Now the Indian Ring was a nebulous combination of crooked politicians, conniving federal bureaucrats, profiteering businessmen, and thieving Indian agents who, while never specifically identified, operated in the collective military mind as a grand conspiracy to defraud the Indians and the government. Since the army was the only obstacle to the complete success of the ring's villainous schemes, it had to be discredited and emasculated. While the level of fraud in the Indian service seems to have been great, although certainly not unprecedented by Gilded Age standards, there is no evidence of an organized conspiracy. But it proved a handy whipping boy for the military, and Sheridan could handle a whip with the best of them. "Good and pious ecclesiastics" had aided the ring in disparaging the army and thus became, to Sheridan's way of thinking, "the aiders and abettors of savages who murdered, without mercy, men, women and children; in all cases ravishing the women sometimes as often as forty and fifty times in succession, and while insensible from brutality and exhaustion forced sticks up their persons, and, in one instance, the fortieth or fiftieth savage drew his saber and used it on the person of the woman in the same manner." Far from being murderers of helpless Indians, Sheridan saw Custer and his men as the defenders of female virtue who had allowed no obstacle to prevent them from destroying "old Black Kettle and his murderers and rapers of helpless women." Sheridan could not understand how anyone could dare criticize brave, self-sacrificing soldiers who were combatting so hellish a foe. "I do not know exactly how far these humanitarians should be excused on account of their ignorance," he wrote in his annual report to the War Department, "but surely it is the only excuse that gives a shadow of justification for aiding and abetting such horrid crimes."[9]

The Victorian era's social standard of propriety certainly did not condone such a vivid description of rape as Sheridan presented in his annual report. The passage gives some insight into Sheridan's breeding, but also into his unconventional nature, his inability to cope rationally with criticism, and his quick reliance on any tactic to discredit those he perceived as enemies.

General Sherman attempted to calm Sheridan, assuring his department commander that he was "well satisfied with *Custer's* attack, and would not have wept if he could have served Satanta's and Bull Bear's bands in the same style." Sherman promised Sheridan that strong efforts would be made both within the government and through the press to "meet the cry raised by Tappan, Taylor & Co." There was, however, only so much that could be done, and Sherman urged Sheridan to have faith in the wisdom of the American people. "This you know is a free country," Sherman reminded his agitated friend, "and people have the lawful right to misrepresent as much as they please, and to print them, but the great mass of our people cannot be humbugged into the belief that Black Kettle's camp was friendly."[10]

Sheridan's faith in the people had been sorely tried. He had been royally treated as a conquering hero for over five years, his every action greeted with national praise. Even when President Johnson had opposed his Louisiana policy, the people had supported him and rejected the president. Suddenly, while fighting a difficult war against a brutal adversary, the cheering had stopped. The criticism stung Sheridan deeply, forever embittering him toward the hero status he had so recently enjoyed. "I have the greatest horror of popular demonstrations," he later confided to an associate, "[for] those very men who deafen you with their cheers today are capable tomorrow of throwing stones and mud at you."[11]

Although the fight on the Washita was most assuredly one-sided, it was not a massacre. Black Kettle's Cheyennes were not un-armed innocents living under the impression that they were not at war. Several of Black Kettle's warriors had recently fought the soldiers, and the chief had been informed by Hazen that there could be no peace until he surrendered to Sheridan. The soldiers were not under orders to kill everyone, for Custer personally stopped the slaying of noncombatants, and fifty-three prisoners were taken by the troops. The reports of Sheridan and Custer on the Battle of the Washita did not accurately reflect the tragic nature of that sad affair, but neither did the harsh epithet of massacre that was leveled by their critics.

The Civil War had forever changed the nature of American combat—Grant, Sherman, and Sheridan had seen to that. They thought nothing of destroying the property, and sometimes the lives, of enemy populations. Confederate cities, with large noncombatant populations, were bombarded mercilessly to force surrender. These soldiers could hardly see any difference between a cannonade against the population of Vicksburg and a surprise attack on an Indian village. There is little doubt, however, that feelings of racial and cultural superiority made the killing of Indian noncombatants less disturbing to the soldiers. But to the new military thinkers, war was a ghastly business which was to be waged against enemy populations, not just hostile soldiers. In that way it could be brought to a speedy close with the least expenditure of blood and treasure.

Sheridan soon found himself too busy to dwell for long on his critics, for Grierson returned with news of an excellent location for a new post near Medicine Bluff, a beautiful cliff formation not far from the base of the Wichita Mountains. Grierson and his party reached Fort Cobb on December 29, and Sheridan would have started his whole command on the thirty-two miles south to the new post site the next day but for the continuing rains, which made travel all but impossible.[12]

The sky finally cleared on January 6, 1869, and Sheridan put his army on the march. More rains came the next day, which made traveling toilsome, but most of the troops were encamped near Medicine Bluff by January 10. Sheridan had his headquarters tent pitched beside a nook of swollen Medicine Bluff Creek. He was pleased with Grierson's site selection, for the area was perfect for the establishment of a large, permanent military post.[13]

Sheridan personally supervised the staking out of the post. Grierson's Tenth Cavalry was charged with constructing the fort, a type of duty the black soldiers were finding to be more and more their lot, while their white cohorts assumed the choicer combat assignments. At first the encampment was known only as Camp Wichita, with the officers of the Seventh arguing in favor of a permanent name of Fort

Elliott. But Sheridan named it for his West Point classmate and close friend Brigadier General Joshua Sill, killed leading one of Sheridan's brigades at Stones River.[14]

As soon as the soldiers were well established in their new camp, Colonel Hazen and Captain Alvord moved the agency Indians down to the Medicine Bluff area. For safekeeping, the agency supplies were located within the military camp, in a large tent near Sheridan's headquarters.[15]

Hazen had a large and sometimes sullen Indian population to contend with. There were two hundred lodges of Comanches—Penatekas, Yapparikas, and Horse Back's recently surrendered Nakonis—amounting to around eight hundred men, women, and children. The Kiowa bands of Satanta, Lone Wolf, Kicking Bird, Black Eagle, and Timbered Mountain also totaled about eight hundred souls. These bands were a special problem, since the Kiowas remained "restive, with troublesome young men," because Satanta and Lone Wolf were still in custody. Camped with the Kiowas, but "quiet and well disposed," were the sixty lodges of Wolf-Sleeves's Kiowa-Apaches, some 290 people. Of no worry whatsoever were the 900 Wichitas, Caddos, Wacos, Kichais, Tawakonis, and Delawares camped in the Washita Valley. All these Indians, around 2,800, looked to Hazen for rations, annuities, and protection.[16]

Of more concern to Sheridan, however, were the Indians who still remained off the reservations. Captain Alvord's Comanche scouts were employed to ascertain the strength, location, and disposition of these nonreservation bands. Alvord estimated that two thousand Comanches still resided on the desolate Staked Plain. These were mostly Kwahadis, a band that had never signed treaties or taken government annuities, and who confined most of their raids to Old Mexico. Mow-way's sixty lodges of Kotchateka Comanches were also on the Staked Plain. But Alvord's scouts reported Mow-way leaning toward surrender, and they were soon proven correct when that chief appeared at Fort Bascom to seek terms. Between three hundred and five hundred Kiowas remained out on the plains, but while they professed a desire for independence, they were not necessarily hostile to the whites. Most of these belonged to the bands of Satank and Little Heart who had been at Fort Cobb before the battle at Washita and would eventually return to their reservation. But the Kiowas of Big Bow and Woman's

The Peace Chiefs

Little Robe, Cheyenne. (*Bureau of American Ethnology, Smithsonian Institution*)

Little Raven, Arapaho. (*Bureau of American Ethnology, Smithsonian Institution*)

Heart had fought both Custer and Evans and would remain aloof and hostile for some time to come. All these bands were reported to be in Texas and thus officially out of Sheridan's military jurisdiction.[17]

The Cheyennes and Arapahos, however, were assumed to still be in the Indian Territory and were estimated to number around twenty-two hundred. Even if they should cross out of his department, Sheridan was prepared to follow them anywhere, since they constituted the campaign's primary target. He hoped this would not be necessary, for Little Robe and Yellow Bear steadfastly held to their promise that their bands would come in and surrender. But as the weeks passed without sign of the Indians, Sheridan's suspicion grew that this was just another ploy to delay his campaign until spring grass enabled the Indians to strengthen their pony herds and renew the fight.[18]

This increasing suspicion of Indian duplicity combined with continued inactivity was especially hard on Custer—"as impatient as a crazed animal to have them come in." Unable to wait any longer, Custer suggested to Sheridan that he accompany Yellow Bear and Little Robe to their villages to hurry the Indians along. Since a large force would indicate hostile intentions, Custer desired only forty troopers to ride with him. At first Sheridan was hesitant, fearing that so small a party would invite the Cheyennes to avenge Black Kettle, but he soon relented. He declined, however, to issue Custer orders for the expedition, feeling that its risky nature called for volunteers only.[19]

Custer selected most of his forty troopers from the Seventh's elite sharpshooter company. As guides Custer had Yellow Bear and Little Robe, as well as an old Blackfeet warrior called Neva, who claimed to have guided one of Frémont's expeditions. Romero agreed to go along as interpreter, and a young Kansas settler, Daniel Brewster, who was seeking a sister held captive by the Cheyennes, was also allowed to share the expedition's dangers.

Sheridan and his officers grimly watched as Custer and his little band rode out of Camp Wichita on the evening of January 22. So certain was one officer of the recklessness of the venture that he slipped a small pocket derringer into Custer's hand as they shook farewell—the weapon's single bullet to be reserved for its owner in case the party was overwhelmed.[20]

Around noon on the fifth day out, after some eighty miles of hard riding, Little Raven's Arapaho village was reached, along Mulberry Creek near the middle fork of the Red River. The Arapahos, some sixty lodges strong, remained divided on the question of moving onto their reservation, but Custer and Yellow Bear managed to convince Little Raven that it would be safe to place his people under the power of the soldiers. The day following the conference the Arapahos packed their belongings and began moving toward Camp Wichita.

There was still no sign of the Cheyennes, the Arapahos reporting that their allies had moved farther to the northwest into Texas. Although reluctant to part with the chief, Custer allowed Little Robe to go ahead in quest of the Cheyennes. He hoped to persuade them to move eastward and meet the troops halfway. Custer delayed for three days on Mulberry Creek until Lieutenant William W. Cooke arrived with additional supplies as well as California Joe and a dozen more troopers. Cooke also carried a note from a worried Sheridan, admonishing Custer: "Keep close watch to prevent Cheyennes and Arapahoes from getting the advantage of you." Custer tucked the note into his buckskins and was off the next morning following the trail marked by Little Robe.[21]

Before moving out, Custer dispatched a message to Sheridan, which described the Arapahos as "half starved, the people naked, and the whole outfit poverty stricken in every particular." If these were a fair specimen of the hostiles out on the plains, Custer brashly declared himself ready "to take a turn at the whole crowd" with his fifty men. Sheridan, Custer announced, might soon hear of "the biggest fight yet" if the Cheyennes and Arapahos did not show the proper respect, for he was ready to "clean out the whole institution." This bravado notwithstanding, the news of Little Raven's surrender pleased Sheridan and justified the risk of the expedition. Sharing Custer's confidence in a quick end to the hostilities, he began preparations to depart by February 10 in order to reach Washington in time for Grant's inauguration. Some of the other officers, however, were not so confident. Captain Alvord wrote Grierson: "So much for Custer—a good deal of *talk* as usual."[22]

Alvord's estimation was correct, for Custer's expedition soon fizzled out. He marched westward, daily expecting to reach the Cheyenne encampment, but found no trace of the Indians and soon even lost Little Robe's trail. A few miles from the mouth of Sweetwater Creek, on the north fork of the Red River, Custer gave up the search and turned east. The men were fortunate to survive, for their provisions were exhausted, and they had to subsist on parched corn and horseflesh. Riding a mule, Custer reached Camp Wichita on February 7 after a journey of four hundred miles. Sheridan was astonished. After Custer's letter he expected next to hear of the surrender of the Cheyennes. Still, he was pleased to see the men back safely, and after hearing Custer's story, he endorsed the wisdom of giving up the search. Sheridan now had to reassess all his plans, since, as Captain Alvord wryly noted, Custer's sudden return "places matters in a very different shape."[23]

Custer was surprised to learn that Little Raven's Arapahos had still not reached Camp Wichita. Alvord's Comanche scouts reported them twenty miles away and having second thoughts. Little Raven's people were showing a decided lack of enthusiasm for placing themselves at the mercy of the soldiers. Sheridan responded by dispatching

Captain Thomas Weir on February 8, with a detachment of the Seventh to escort the Arapahos in.[24]

Weir surrounded the Arapaho camp, conversed with Little Raven, and had the Indians at Camp Wichita within two days. Little Raven hurried to parley with Sheridan and Custer to explain the delay. The weakened condition of the ponies and the rain-swollen streams were first offered as excuses, but eventually Little Raven admitted that George Bent and John Smith had warned his people to avoid the soldiers. This had caused dissension and delay. Both of these men had at one time been employed by the Indian Bureau as interpreters, and Little Raven's statement increased Sheridan's conviction that the Indians "had only been kept out by the influence of the Indian Ring."[25]

The surrender of this main Arapaho band left only the Cheyennes and a few Arapahos at large, and Sheridan began preparing another expedition. Some of the officers feared that the Cheyennes would cross into Texas, escaping from Sheridan's military jurisdiction. But the general made it clear that he would cross the Texas line without hesitation. Camp Wichita was alive with speculation, but no one was informed of the general's plans. "Sheridan is evidently arranging," Alvord wrote Grierson, "but keeps his own counsels."[26]

Ever since arriving at Camp Wichita, Sheridan had been plagued by failures in supply and mail. The road between his camp and the supply depot at Fort Arbuckle had become a swamp. To this natural impediment was added the quartermaster's gross inefficiency at both Arbuckle and department headquarters. Supplies, supposedly stockpiled at Arbuckle, were still far to the east at Fort Gibson.

Feeling that his presence might clean up the mess, Sheridan traveled to Fort Arbuckle with his quartermaster officer, Captain (Brevet Colonel) Andrew Jackson McGonnigle, California Joe, and a small detachment of troops. Sheridan could do nothing about the roads, one of which he dubbed "boggy bottom," but he promptly put every available mule at Arbuckle to hauling supplies. This speeded up delivery. He also purchased several fields of corn near the post from the Chickasaws and Choctaws. He ordered horses from Camp Wichita driven to Fort Arbuckle in shifts and fattened on the corn to prepare them for more campaigning. The mail problem was easily handled by taking the courier service out of the hands of local officers and turning it over to Crosby.[27]

Eager to return to Camp Wichita, Sheridan rushed to complete his business, but at the appointed departure time California Joe could not be found. Believing that Joe's services as guide were essential for the return trip, Sheridan sent out search parties. He was located, hopelessly drunk. Disgusted, Sheridan delayed his departure a day while his scout sobered up. Although a guard was assigned to watch over Joe, the next morning he was still "gloriously tipsy." Infuriated at having wasted a day, but a bit in awe of Joe's talent for procuring home-brew, Sheridan had his guide thrown into a Dougherty wagon, and they all headed back to Camp Wichita.[28]

With supplies arriving in quantity, Sheridan could concentrate on organizing his strike force. The main problem was horses. Both the Seventh and the volunteers had numerous weak or broken-down animals. To remedy the situation Sheridan dismounted the volunteers, except officers, and designated them as infantry. The volunteers had only 550 horses of the 1,200 they had brought, and these were combined with the Seventh's 600 serviceable horses (of 750). The regulars picked the best animals from the combined herd; the rest were sent to Arbuckle for reconditioning. Sheridan ordered the horses turned over to Grierson's Tenth Cavalry when again serviceable.[29]

The necessity of tracking the Cheyennes made it impossible for Sheridan to attend Grant's inauguration on March 4. He dispatched his aide, Major James Forsyth, to represent him at the ceremonies. Camp gossips quickly deduced that there was more to Forsyth's mission than met the eye. Grant's presidency would elevate Sherman to command of the army, and, as Captain Alvord noted, Forsyth had gone "to represent Sheridan's interests in the new deal which is due to take place at Army Hd. Qts. when Sherman gets there."[30]

With the supply and courier situation corrected, the Seventh mounted on sound horses, and his own political interests looked after, Sheridan turned to assure peaceful relations with the reservation Indians after the departure of his army. His main tactic was the release of Satanta and Lone Wolf from the guardhouse on February 15. To mark their release Sheridan held a grand council with the reservation tribal leaders on February 16. Fifty chiefs and leading warriors sat in a semicircle in front of Sheridan's headquarters tent while the general lectured them:

Your people must now consider me their chief, just as much as I am the chief of the white people in this country. When the white people do wrong—commit murders and robberies—we always punish them, and hereafter if you commit any crimes I am going to punish you just the same as the white people are punished.

Sheridan proposed an anmesty for past crimes if the Indians would agree to live by the white man's rules. Satanta and Lone Wolf had already assented to live in peace and to stop their warriors from committing crimes. Now Sheridan demanded a similar pledge from the assembled Indians.[31]

One by one the chiefs rose to give their pledge and thank Sheridan for releasing the two Kiowa chiefs. When the warriors completed their speeches, with each giving a solemn pledge of eternal peace, they approached Sheridan and "shook the General vigorously by the hand, exclaiming emphatically, 'How! How!' "[32]

Sheridan planned to leave a strong force at Camp Wichita to watch over them. Both Sherman and Hazen wanted Grierson to command the new post, and Sheridan complied with their wishes. As a further favor to Sherman, who was Grierson's friend and patron, Sheridan assigned all the Tenth Cavalry to the Indian Territory. Half of Grierson's regiment would garrison the new post, while the rest would operate out of Camp Supply.[33]

Sheridan expected Grierson to watch the reservation tribes carefully and "allow no intercourse or assistance to be given to the hostile Indians by Indians on the reservation or by white people." Grierson was to block any effort by the Indian Bureau or Colonel Hazen to deal with the hostiles, but he could accept the unconditional surrender of the Indians. Sheridan worried about Grierson, whom he correctly perceived to be sympathetic toward the Indians. "No people, especially those in a savage state," he lectured, "can be expected to behave themselves where there are no laws providing punishment for crime." Sheridan demanded that Grierson deal promptly and firmly with Indian "criminals," even to the point of taking hostages from the bands to which they belonged if he could not capture the offenders. The Indians were to be "coddled" no longer, because in Sheridan's view "the trouble heretofore with Indians has been caused by the absence of all punishment of crimes committed against the settlements."[34]

Sheridan now prepared to take to the field. He planned for Custer to march west from Camp Wichita with a fifteen-hundred-man force consisting of the Seventh Cavalry and the dismounted Kansas volunteers. Sheridan would, meanwhile, travel to Camp Supply and arrange the establishment of a supply depot at the mouth of Salt Creek on the north fork of the Red River. Custer was to proceed to this supply depot, where Sheridan would rejoin the column and continue the pursuit.[35]

Custer would operate on his own, for Carr's column had returned to Fort Lyon. Carr had left Fort Lyon on November 29, with seven companies of the Fifth Cavalry, but had not been able to join Captain Penrose's column until a week before Christmas. Both commands suffered terribly from the cold, and Penrose's five companies had almost starved before joining Carr, losing two hundred horses and mules. After sending back for more supplies, the combined columns scouted south along both branches of the Canadian. On December 28, Carr encamped on the South Canadian just a few miles west of Evans's supply depot.[36]

Carr's command had not found one Indian. The only action the troopers saw was a successful raid by scouts Buffalo Bill Cody and Wild Bill Hickok on a party of sutlers from Fort Union who were taking, among other items, kegs of beer to Evans's command. The diverted beer was one of the few bright spots in over two months of unrelenting hardship. Unable to keep his men supplied, Carr yielded in the unequal contest and returned to Fort Lyon, arriving on February 19. Although he had not struck the Indians, as had the other two columns, he still fulfilled his role in the campaign. The presence of the troopers on the South Canadian had kept the Indians moving, and thus weakened, and had been a major factor in the surrender of the Comanches and Arapahos.[37]

Carr's troops were already recuperating at Fort Lyon when Sheridan left Camp Wichita on February 23. The general was accompanied by McGonnigle, Crosby, and Surgeon Morris Asch of his staff, correspondent Keim, guide Ben Clark, and thirty-eight of Pepoon's scouts as escort. The Seventh Cavalry and Kansas volunteers were assembled to view Sheridan's departure, and "cheers to the General rose, as he rode through the lines of men." The troopers hated to see him go, since a "jovial" commander who "does not put on much style" was a cherished commodity in any army. As David Spotts of the volunteers confided to his diary: "General Sheridan has been with us ever since we left Camp Supply and had his headquarters with us, camping in a tent when the weather was fair or foul, marching at our head in snow and rain, enduring all the hardships of wind and weather." The twenty-one-year-old trooper marveled that Sheridan could withstand the ordeal: "He is not a young man either, between 35 and 40 years old."[38]

The weather stayed fair, and Sheridan's party made good time, arriving at Camp Supply on March 1. Here the general found a telegram from President-elect Grant requesting that he report to Washington immediately. Grant's telegram overruled his plans to join Custer on Salt Creek. Sheridan ordered the supplies sent on to Custer—some twenty-four thousand rations and two hundred thousand pounds of forage—to see the troops through to Camp Supply. He instructed Custer to "draw in the 7th, and terminate this campaign," mustering out the Kansas volunteers since their maintenance could no longer be afforded. "Should you be able to strike the rascals on your way up," Custer was told, "so much the better." But Sheridan had decided that all the Indians would soon surrender anyway, and he did not "anticipate further trouble" in his department.[39]

Custer marched out of Camp Wichita on March 2, traveling along the southern rim of the Wichita Mountains. On March 5, he divided his command, sending the weak and disabled to the Washita battlefield, while he continued on with eight hundred men in search of the Cheyennes. With rations exhausted and horses worn out, Custer finally discovered 260 Cheyenne lodges along Sweetwater Creek on March 15.

Although his men, and especially the volunteers, were anxious to attack, Custer decided to parley instead. Meeting with the Cheyenne leader Medicine Arrows, he discovered that the Indians were in an even more weakened condition than his own men and that they held two white women captive in their camp. As a result, Custer held his tense soldiers in check, but when the Cheyennes came into his camp for another parley, he seized three warriors as hostages. By threatening to hang the warriors he secured the release of the white women, one of whom turned out to be the lost sister of young Brewster.

Custer informed the Cheyennes that their three warriors and the prisoners taken at Washita would be freed when all the Indians surrendered at Camp Supply or Camp Wichita. Medicine Arrows, Little Robe, and the other chiefs agreed to bring their people in. With his weary troopers in danger of starving, Custer had no choice but to take the Cheyennes at their word. His command staggered into Camp Supply on March 28, 1869.[40]

True to their word, many of the remaining Cheyenne and Arapaho bands drifted back to their reservation. Most of the Arapahos, about one hundred lodges led by Little Big Mouth, unconditionally surrendered to Grierson at Camp Wichita on April 3, 1869. Four days later they were joined by sixty-seven Cheyenne lodges, estimated at four hundred people, under chiefs Little Robe, Minimac, Red Moon, and Grey Eyes.[41]

The rest of the Cheyennes, under Medicine Arrows and Buffalo Head, remained camped along the Canadian River near the Texas boundary. They were rejoined in late April by the bands of Little Robe, Minimac, and Red Moon, who had bolted from Camp Wichita when Hazen attempted to move them to their designated reservation near Camp Supply. More councils and debates followed as the sorely divided Cheyennes attempted to formulate a unified plan of action. But all unity was gone. Little Robe and Minimac left the encampment and took their bands into Camp Supply. The belligerent Dog Soldier warrior society, representing some 165 lodges under Tall Bull, White Horse, and Bull Bear, moved north to join the Sioux and Northern Cheyennes and continue the old way of life. Medicine Arrows and Buffalo Head, with two hundred lodges, decided to avoid both the reservation and open hostilities by remaining in the Canadian River country. They would wait and watch to see what happened to the Dog Soldiers and to Little Robe's peace faction.[42]

They were not kept waiting long. Tall Bull's Dog Soldiers moved into their favored Republican River haunts, once more threatening the railroad and the settlements. To counter the Dog Soldier threat, Sheridan transferred Carr and the Fifth from Fort Lyon to Fort McPherson, on Nebraska's Platte River. In May a detachment of the Fifth clashed with a large party of Cheyennes and Sioux near Beaver Creek, and this was followed by devastating Indian raids on the Kansas Pacific line and against the settlers along the Republican River.[43]

Carr, with eight companies of the Fifth and three companies of Pawnee Indian scouts, pursued the raiders. After a determined month-long hunt he surprised Tall Bull's Cheyennes on July 11, at Summit Springs, on the South Platte in northeastern Colorado. In a fierce battle the Dog Soldiers were routed, their eighty-four lodges and all their property were captured and destroyed, and fifty-two Indians were killed and seventeen women and children taken prisoner. Among the dead was Tall Bull, supposedly slain by scout Bill Cody. There could be no debate over this battle. Tall Bull's people were notoriously hostile, and the village contained two white women captives as well as booty from the recent Kansas raids. Sheridan's goal of clearing the Republican River country of Indians was finally achieved. The railroad lines and settlements were now secure from Indian harrassment. The power of the Cheyenne war faction was broken by Carr's victory at Summit Springs.[44]

The defeat of the Dog Soldiers had an immediate effect on the remaining nonreservation Cheyennes. White Horse led his Dog Soldier band across the Platte, where they joined the Northern Cheyennes in Wyoming, but most of the Dog Soldiers and their families eventually followed Bull Bear into Camp Supply to surrender. Convinced of the futility of further resistance nearly all of the other Cheyenne bands went onto the reservation, although some, like Medicine Arrows, found it exceedingly difficult to remain for long.[45]

Thus Sheridan's campaign, with Carr's Republican River expedition included as its final episode, proved a success. The campaign's three major goals had been achieved: the Indians had been removed from the land between the Platte and the Arkansas and the security of the railroads and settlers assured; the Indians involved in the Kansas raids had been punished, if sometimes in an indirect manner; and the major southern plains tribes had been settled on their reservations as stipulated in the Medicine Lodge treaty. Furthermore, the campaign had disabused the Indians of the idea that winter would afford them security and had taught them a new respect for the white soldiers as a relentless and ruthless enemy.

Sheridan had proven the feasibility of winter campaigning, and

Charles Schreyvogel's 1908 painting, "The Summit Springs Rescue 1869," presents Buffalo Bill Cody and Eugene Carr in heroic action. Cody is depicted shooting the warrior who has just slain a white captive, Mrs. Susanna Alderdice. The other captive, Mrs. Maria Weichel, was rescued. Actually, Cody took no part in the rescue of the surviving captive, but he was responsible for the death of Tall Bull, leader of the Dog Soldiers. The power of the Cheyenne war faction was broken by Carr's victory at Summit Springs. (*Courtesy of the Buffalo Bill Historical Center, Cody, Wyoming*)

it became his favorite Indian-fighting strategy. His faith that well-clothed and well-fed troops could endure severe weather conditions and find the enemy had been justified. Even though most of the men had only shelter tents and were at times compelled to subsist without standard rations, the incidence of frostbite proved minimal, and the percentage of men left unfit for duty remained under 3 percent. In fact, the incidence of men on sick report in the Seventh remained below the level during the preceding summer months. Animals did not fare as well, suffering terribly from starvation and exposure: over 50 percent of them died or became unfit for further service. It had proven impossible to move enough forage from Forts Bascom, Lyon, and Arbuckle properly to feed all the animals used in the field.[46]

The supply problem, for men as well as animals, had proven to be Sheridan's biggest headache. Improper movement of supplies had prematurely ended operations by Evans and Carr, had delayed Crawford's volunteers at a critical time, and had often compromised Custer's movements. Such quartermaster problems were nothing new to Sheridan, and he did not view them as unique to winter campaigning, only more intensified. The campaign's results, however, justified the costs.

Although a success, Sheridan's campaign was not decisive. It was the beginning of a war of attrition that by 1876 broke the power of the southern plains tribes. At the conclusion of Sherdan's campaign the tribes retained considerable power, and the military authorities and Indian Bureau were hard pressed to keep them on the reservation. The Kiowas and Comanches soon resumed their destructive raids against the Texas settlers, ignoring their pledges to Sheridan at Camp Wichita. The Cheyennes, having felt Sheridan's power more fully, initially resisted the blandishments of Satanta and Lone Wolf to join in the Texas raids, but they were eventually engulfed by a rising tide of conflict. The Red River War of 1874–75 completed the harsh work initiated by Sheridan in 1868 and resulted in the complete subjugation of the southern tribes.

On March 6, 1869, as Sheridan and his party moved rapidly toward Fort Hays and the railroad that would speed them to Washington in compliance with Grant's order, the general was feeling proud of his winter campaign and confident that he had broken the tribes. As the little party approached the Smokey Hill River, just a few miles from their destination, a courier was spied galloping southward. Suspecting that the courier's pouch might contain mail for him, Sheridan sent a trooper to bring the rider back.

The courier rode up to Sheridan's ambulance, saluted smartly, and to the surprise and delight of all remarked, "I have the honor to deliver a dispatch to the Lieutenant General."

The staff and correspondent Keim were surprised to see the unusually unflappable Sheridan for once deeply moved. With face flushed and voice choking with emotion, Sheridan read aloud the telegram announcing his promotion to the army's second highest position. The general then reached into his pack and produced a small bottle of whiskey which he announced he had "been keeping for an emergency."

There on the wind-swept banks of the Smokey Hill Sheridan's staff offered a ringing toast: "To the health of the Lieutenant General and the close of the campaign."[47]

CHAPTER 6

Division of the Missouri:
Personalities, Politics,
and Policies

Sheridan's promotion to lieutenant general came as a surprise to many. The president-elect was silent on the question until the day of his inauguration, but sentiment in Washington held that General George Meade would receive the position. Those who knew Grant, however, and recognized his penchant for cronyism, felt that Sheridan had the inside track even though both Henry Halleck and Meade outranked him. Just before Grant's inauguration, General Sherman confided to his brother, Senator John Sherman: "The only trouble is in my successor. Halleck is out of the question. Meade comes next on the list, but is not a favorite. Sheridan comes next in order and is Grant's preference, I *think*." General Sherman hoped that his old friend George Thomas would get the position.[1]

Thomas had indeed hoped for the lieutenant generalcy, but was not at all surprised when Sheridan was appointed. Thomas told an army colleague that he had "always supposed the President would exercise the right to appoint his friend to an office in preference to another, whom he did not particularly like. I much prefer to deserve the place and not have it than to get it without having deserved it." Thomas, given his choice of the remaining commands, reluctantly decided on the Division of the Pacific, which consisted of the present states of California, Nevada, Arizona, Oregon, Washington, and Idaho.[2]

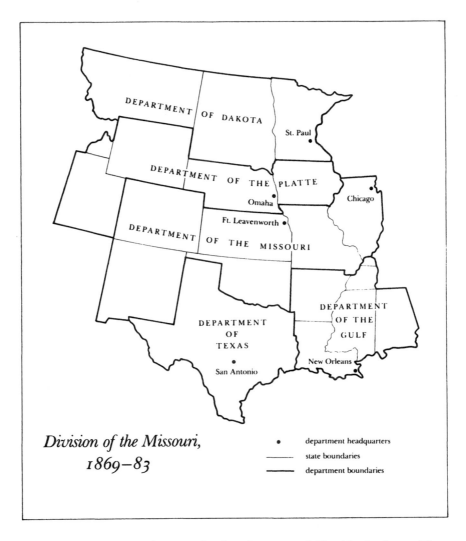

Division of the Missouri,
1869–83

- • department headquarters
- —— state boundaries
- —— department boundaries

General Meade, a professional enemy of Sheridan's since 1864, had felt certain that the lieutenant generalcy would be his, and could only, as he wrote his wife, "find consolation in the consciousness we have that it is the cruelest and meanest act of injustice." Some of the northeastern newspapers, unhappy with Sheridan ever since he relieved Warren at Five Forks, echoed Meade's sentiments. The *Philadelphia Age* branded the affair "a gross and unjustifiable act of personal favoritism."[3]

Grant offered Sheridan his choice of assignments, including a return to the Fifth Military District. Declining to become entangled again with the Reconstruction tar baby, Sheridan instead chose the Division of the Missouri, which held the promise of work more congenial to his temperament.[4] His vast new command extended from Chicago on the east to the western borders of New Mexico, Utah, and Montana, and from the Canadian boundary on the north to the Texas line on the south. The boundaries of the division, however, were far from static. As Reconstruction tensions eased and concern over Indian depredations increased, Texas was added to the Division of the Missouri on November 1, 1871, extending Sheridan's command south to the Rio Grande. Reconstruction difficulties led to the addition of the Department of the Gulf, embracing the states of Louisiana, Arkansas, and Mississippi, on January 4, 1875. Alabama and the parts of Kentucky and Tennessee west of the Tennessee River were added to the department on June 26, 1876. This emergency expansion was temporary, and the Department of the Gulf was transferred to the Division of the Atlantic on May 1, 1877. In June 1875 the division boundary was extended westward to include Fort Hall, Idaho, and the Bannock Indian reservation.[5]

Scattered throughout the million square miles of Sheridan's command lived most of the Indian population of the United States: the Sioux, Northern and Southern Cheyennes, Kiowas, Comanches, Arapahos, Utes, and Apaches would all engage Sheridan's troops in conflict. Indian bands from Old Mexico also raided into Sheridan's jurisdiction, while Indians from the Division of the Pacific, most notably the Nez Perces, Bannocks, and Arizona Apaches, fought battles with Sheridan's men. No accurate census of Indian strength in the division was ever made, but in 1882 Sheridan's headquarters staff estimated the Indians to number about 175,000.[6]

The division was divided into four geographic military departments, which were, at the discretion of their commander, subdivided into military districts. These departments were titled Missouri, Dakota, Platte, and Texas (this does not include the brief tenure of the Department of the Gulf in the division). By 1874 each department had its headquarters well situated on the line of a railroad and was within telegraphic communication with all but the most isolated posts.

In 1869 the Department of the Missouri was commanded by Sheridan's scholarly and dependable West Point classmate, Major

Sheridan's Department Commanders

Edward O. C. Ord. (*U.S. Army Corps photo no. 111-B-4550, Brady Collection, National Archives*)

Christopher C. Augur. (*Everhard Collection. Courtesy of the Amon Carter Museum, Fort Worth, Texas*)

General John M. Schofield. He had served with distinction as a corps commander under Sherman and Thomas in the Civil War and had temporarily been secretary of war in 1868. Although his relationship with Sheridan was cordial, it was not close; and his professional ties were with Sherman.[7]

Schofield's successor in the Department of the Missouri was Brigadier General (Brevet Major General) John Pope. In a profession studded with egomaniacs, few could match the temperament of Pope. A member of no military clique, unless it be his own, Pope was never deferential to his superiors. During the Civil War he had displayed flashes of brilliance in the 1862 Mississippi River operations, which led to his appointment as brigadier general and commander of the Army of Virginia. The Radical Republicans had viewed him as a champion who could discredit the Democratic general, George McClellan, but

John Pope. (*U.S. Army Corps photo no. BA-230, Brady Collection, National Archives*). (at left, above)

Alfred H. Terry. (*Custer Battlefield National Monument, National Park Service*). (at right, above)

John M. Schofield. (*U.S. Army Corps photo no. BA-212, Brady Collection, National Archives*). (at left) their hopes were crushed, along with Pope's army, at the Second Battle of Bull Run in August 1862. Pope was soon relieved of command and transferred to Minnesota, where he performed impressively against the Sioux. Well suited by experience, both in administration and Indian warfare, to command the department, Pope handled those responsibilities ably until 1883, when he was promoted to division command.[8]

Sheridan's relationship with Pope was stormy. Pope, who could be active and energetic when it suited his purpose, often acted so slowly that Sheridan found himself repeatedly complaining, "Pope does everything so reluctantly that to move him on matters affecting his own Department requires preemptory [sic] orders." Sheridan liked to give his department commanders considerable latitude and freedom of action, but with Pope that was impossible. "I am sorry to say I do not like the spirit manifested by Brig. Gen. Pope to reasonable and legitimate orders," declared Sheridan in 1876. "He seems to be getting into such a condition that it is disagreeable to him to perform his proper duties if they conflict with his opinion."[9] Pope, driven by a bloated self-image and tormented by his failure in the Civil War, could never be satisfied with any post that placed him in a subordinate position.[10]

The Department of the Missouri, embracing Illinois, Missouri, Kansas, part of Arkansas, Colorado Territory, New Mexico Territory, and the Indian Territory, was virtually at peace by the end of 1869 as a result of Sheridan's campaign. It was clear that the Indians' day was almost done. The great southern buffalo herd, essential both economically and culturally to the survival of the plains Indians, was quickly vanishing. When Sheridan observed that massive herd in 1868, he estimated its number at three million head. The herd traversed the country between the Platte Valley and the Concho River in Texas, and when it moved south in the fall, Sheridan described it as "one large mass, with a front of from 50 to 60 miles in extent, and a depth of from five to ten miles." The herd scattered after crossing the Red River "and seemed to cover the whole of Northern Texas." But professional hunters soon discovered the profit in buffalo robes, and by 1870 the bleached bones of the once seemingly innumerable beasts were being plowed under by an ever-increasing phalanx of farmers.[11]

The department was well supplied with railroads, so essential to the rapid and economical movement of troops and supplies. The

Kansas Pacific reached Denver in the fall of 1870, absorbed the Denver Pacific, and constructed a connecting link from Denver to the Union Pacific line at Cheyenne, Wyoming. The Atchison, Topeka and Santa Fe had, by 1873, reached Granada, Colorado, and was in stiff competition with the narrow-gauge Denver and Rio Grande for the southern Colorado traffic. This rapid railroad development within the department placed added escort and guard-detail burdens on the military, but also diminished the advantage of space and distance that the Indians had so long enjoyed.[12]

Much of the Department of the Platte, consisting of Iowa, Nebraska, and the territories of Utah and Wyoming (and extended westward in 1875 to include Fort Hall, Idaho), was also fairly settled by the end of 1869. The completion of the transcontinental railroad in May 1869 connected the population centers in Iowa and Nebraska with the Mormon communities of northern Utah, but the interior regions of the department, most notably in Wyoming, remained sparsely settled and vulnerable to Indian depredations. The Sioux, Northern Cheyennes, and Northern Arapahos, while not openly professing war, remained sullen and haughty. The Sioux, at the peak of their power, were, in fact, expanding their domain across the northern plains at the expense of the Pawnees, Crows, Arikaras, and other tribes. It was already clear to the military authorities headquartered at Omaha that conflict was inevitable as mining and other commercial interests expanded into the Sioux country. But in the first few years of Sheridan's tenure as division commander almost all of the department's resources were concentrated in posts along the line of the Union Pacific. In the first full year of operation nearly 150,000 passengers rode the line between Omaha and Sacramento, and within a dozen years that number increased to almost 1,000,000. Sheridan believed the primary duty of the troopers of the Department of the Platte was to secure that fragile national link from harm.[13]

The department also shared a somewhat distasteful duty usually reserved for troops on Reconstruction duty in the South. On the benchland just above the Mormon metropolis of Salt Lake City, the cannons of Fort Douglas pointed toward the town. Sheridan described the fort as being in "somewhat the position of an American consulate in a foreign city—a place where persecuted Gentiles can take refuge and have protection under the American flag." Sheridan, however, did not share the extreme views then current of the dangers of Mormonism. He felt that if the Mormons were left alone, trouble could be avoided and urged his officers to use discretion and avoid conflict "except when called upon by the proper civil officers."[14]

Brigadier General (Brevet Major General) Christopher Augur commanded the Department of the Platte from January 1867 to November 1871. The ever-dependable Augur commanded, at various times, the departments of Texas, Missouri, and the Gulf. A West Pointer, class of 1843, he had seen service in the Mexican War and on the Oregon frontier. Augur had been a captain during that dismal 1855 campaign against the Yakimas that had initiated Second Lieutenant Sheridan to Indian warfare. During the Civil War he had ably commanded the Twenty-second Corps and after the war had been entrusted with the investigation of the Lincoln assassination conspiracy. Modest and bewhiskered, he proved an able administrator but left campaigning to more vigorous officers. Like Schofield, he did not share Sheridan's brutal views on how to handle the Indians, but subscribed to the old frontier adage that it was cheaper to feed the Indians than to fight them. With a perceptive knowledge born of service on the 1867 Peace Commission, Augur argued, "Bread and meat are the only things these indians now want—they say they have had enough talk."[15]

When Augur was transferred to command of the Department of Texas in November 1871, he was replaced in the Department of the Platte by Brigadier General (Brevet Major General) Edward O. C. Ord. Graduating from West Point in 1839, Ord had seen service in Florida against the Seminoles and in California during the Mexican War. As a captain of the Third Infantry, he had known Sheridan during the Yakima Indian war, and they had served together throughout some of the Civil War as well. Ord commanded corps with distinction throughout the Vicksburg campaign in the West and the Shenandoah and Appomattox campaigns in the East. With deep-set eyes under heavy brows and a mass of white hair, old Ord appeared reflective and calm, but his expression belied the vigorous, even rash, nature of the man. Sherman characterized Ord as "a rough diamond, always at work on the most distant frontier." Friends at the academy, they had served together in Florida and California. To Sherman, there was no "more unselfish and manly person" than this friend of his youth.[16]

This close friendship with Sherman eventually set Ord at odds with Sheridan. Ord developed a habit of ignoring the chain of command and corresponding directly with Sherman on military matters. Moreover, Ord, who was thirteen years Sheridan's senior and had outranked him throughout the Civil War, was not inclined to accept this subordinate position with good grace. Sheridan came to doubt Ord's "motives in some of his recommendations for the expenditure of public money and even in his calls for and disposition of troops." He lost all confidence in Ord's soldierly honor, viewing him as an opportunist. Sheridan blocked Ord's attempts to transfer departmental headquarters to Council Bluffs and to Denver, on both occasions feeling that Ord was working in collusion with business and civic leaders against the best interest of the service. He even intervened in some of Ord's purely departmental personnel matters.[17]

Their relationship completely collapsed after Ord assumed command of the Department of Texas in 1875. The zealous manner in which he allowed his troops to cross into Mexico, his failure to report fully to division headquarters, his unjustified reluctance to allow troop transfers out of his department, and his stated reasons (Sheridan suspected lies) for these actions led Sheridan to cease all personal correspondence with him. By 1877 military affairs in the Department of Texas suffered as a result of their relationship, and Sheridan requested that Sherman agree to relieve Ord of his command. Sherman, however, protected his old friend, pointing out to Sheridan that Ord was held in high esteem by the Texas congressional delegation, whose support Sherman needed to block congressional attempts to reduce the size of the army. Sheridan temporarily relented, but renewed his request in 1879, complaining: "General Ord's eccentricity of character, and the devious methods he employs to accomplish his ends some time since forced me to doubt his motives in some of his official actions— . . . [and] occasioned in my mind a distrust of General Ord's management of affairs in Texas—I feel that we want there an officer free from schemes." The dispute between the two men clearly displayed the limits of Sheridan's military power. He could not effectively control or discipline a subordinate who had powerful friends in the military or in government. Nor was this situation unique to Ord, for Sheridan faced similar problems with other officers.[18]

Sheridan probably expected a closer working relationship with the last of his three Department of the Platte commanders, Brigadier

General (Brevet Major General) George Crook. Boyhood pals who had become the best of friends at West Point—sharing membership in a small clique of Ohio cadets—Crook and Sheridan had both seen combat against the Indians of the Pacific Northwest. At the outbreak of the Civil War, Crook's Ohio political connections got him the colonelcy of the Thirty-sixth Ohio Volunteer Infantry. It was another nine months before Sheridan earned by merit what well-placed friends had secured for Crook, but after that he quickly passed his friend in volunteer rank, reaching brigadier a month before Crook (by date of commission) and major general almost two years before. In regular rank the difference was, of course, much greater; at the end of the war Sheridan was a major general, while Crook was but a captain (and brevet major general).[19]

Although Sheridan had surpassed him in rank, Crook had served with distinction in the early years of the Civil War. When Grant sent Sheridan to stop General Jubal Early in the Shenandoah, Crook took command of one of the three corps of Sheridan's Army of the Shenandoah and was promoted to major general of volunteers. Pleased to have his old friend serving with him, Sheridan "placed implicit faith in his experience and qualifications as a general."[20]

Sheridan's faith was fully justified by the performance of Crook's Eighth Corps in the Shenandoah, but their friendship suffered as a result of the campaign. Crook, generally regarded as the most unassuming, even-tempered, and humble of Sheridan's western commanders, was scarcely less a slave to ambition than Nelson Miles or George Custer; he was merely more subtle. Convinced that he had received too little recognition for his exploits in the Shenandoah, Crook fumed the rest of his life. Sheridan became the focus of Crook's hidden anger and frustration, no doubt tinged by some jealousy that the fortunes of war had elevated his friend so far above him.

Crook's enmity was, in particular, the result of the battles at Fisher's Hill, September 22, 1864, and Cedar Creek, October 19, 1864. Sheridan's great victory at Fisher's Hill was the result of a brilliant flanking attack on Early's left and rear that had been Crook's idea, and he was incensed when Sheridan's battle report failed to acknowledge him as the author of the plan of attack. Future President Rutherford B. Hayes, then a brigadier under Crook, shared his chief's consternation and noted in a letter to his uncle that "the turning of the Rebel left was planned and executed by Crook against the opinions of the other Corps generals." Hayes had a high regard for Crook, which the passing years did not diminish, and Sheridan paled in comparison to his idol. During the Shenandoah campaign he wrote: "General Sheridan is a whole-souled, brave man, and believes in Crook, his old class and roommate at West Point. Intellectually he is not Crook's equal, so . . . General Crook is the brains of this army."[21]

Cedar Creek, on the other hand, proved to be a great embarrassment to Crook when his corps was surprised and routed by Early's Confederates in a dawn attack. Sheridan's return from Winchester turned defeat into victory, catapulted him into the forefront of Union generals—along with Grant and Sherman—and won him a major general's commission in the regular army. Crook burned with envy. He later claimed that after the battle Sheridan had confessed: "Crook, I am going to get much more credit for this than I deserve, for, had I been here in the morning the same thing would have taken place."[22] Despite Sheridan's kind comments, the responsibility for the surprise was Crook's. Sheridan's remarks were probably intended to calm and reassure his distraught friend. But Crook was not to be consoled; the wound to his pride never healed.[23]

On December 26, 1889, twenty-five years after the battles and only five months after Sheridan's death, Crook toured the battlefields at Fisher's Hill and Cedar Creek. That evening he wrote lines in his diary that show only too well the depth of his bitterness and the degree to which his thoughts, like those of many of his military contemporaries, were consumed by the past:

> After examining the grounds and the position of the troops after twenty five years which have elapsed and in the light of subsequent events, it renders General Sheridan's claims and his subsequent actions in allowing the general public to remain under the impressions regarding his part in these battles, when he knew they were fiction, all the more contemptible. The adulations heaped on him by a grateful nation for his supposed genius turned his head, which, added to his natural disposition, caused him to bloat his little carcass with debauchery and dissipation, which carried him off prematurely.[24]

After Cedar Creek the war went dismally for Crook. Later taken prisoner and then exchanged, he was assigned by Grant to command a division of cavalry in the Army of the Potomac. Once more Crook felt cheated by Sheridan, for he was under the impression that Grant intended to give him command of all the Army of the Potomac's cavalry, but the sudden appearance of Sheridan with his army from the Shenandoah ended that possibility. Crook had to content himself with command of that portion of the cavalry that remained back with Meade and thus found scant opportunity to distinguish himself in the Appomattox campaign. He looked back on that period with regret, noting that he had "learned too late that it was not what a person did, but it was what he got credit of doing that give him a reputation and at the close of the war gave him position."[25]

Crook emerged from the war a major general of volunteers, but still only a captain in regular rank. Appointed lieutenant colonel of the Twenty-third Infantry on July 28, 1866, he was ordered to Fort Boise, Idaho, and within a week of his arrival, was off after raiding Paiutes. He kept up a stubborn two-year campaign that broke the power of that tribe and brought peace to the southwestern Idaho gold fields for the first time in four years. Here, at last, was a Civil War general who could fight Indians, and Crook's superiors appointed him commander of the Department of the Columbia.[26]

In 1871, through the personal intervention of President Grant and against the advice of Sherman and Secretary of War William Belknap, Crook was given command of the Department of Arizona. He was assigned under his brevet rank since in regular rank he was junior to at least forty other officers. The region had been torn by bitter conflict with the Apaches for years, but Crook felt confident that he could quickly end the war. "All that I require," he wrote Division of the Pacific commander Schofield, "are a few more horses & to be let alone." It proved to be no idle boast, for in the brilliant Tonto Basin campaign of 1872–73 Crook's forces tenaciously pursued the Apaches, keeping them insecure, poor, and hungry, and forcing them onto their reservation. Crook was rewarded in 1873 by promotion to brigadier general, earning the enmity of many officers within a military establishment wedded to the seniority system.[27]

Crook, always a bit eccentric, now grew a full beard, with elongated points on each side, took to riding a mule on campaign and to sporting a canvas hunting suit and pith helmet. "Crook was the last man in the world to seek notoriety," claimed the general's aide, Captain John G. Bourke. Yet Crook was no less interested in a favorable press

Brigadier General George Crook, dressed in a private's overcoat
for this 1877 photograph, had once been Sheridan's best friend.
They shared the warm camaraderie of tent and field as West
Point cadets, as shavetails in the Pacific Northwest, and as ambitious young officers in the Civil War. Professional jealousy and divergent opinions on Indian policy eventually turned them into
bitter enemies. (*Fort Laramie National Historic Site, National Park
Service*)

than his peers, and his unique clothing became as distinctive and self-conscious a trademark as Custer's fancy buckskins. But Crook's unconventionality paid rich dividends in Indian warfare. His close study of Indian life and culture, his determination to know fully the terrain he operated in, his wise use of mule pack trains instead of wagons for supply transport, and his intelligent exploitation of Indians as military scouts and auxiliaries marked him, as President Grant bluntly declared, "the best, wiliest Indian fighter in this country."[28]

Crook's well-deserved reputation resulted in his transfer, in the spring of 1875, to command of the Department of the Platte. There, during the 1876–77 Sioux campaign, his performance in one of the few conventional Indian wars was, at best, mediocre. Both Sherman and Sheridan were sorely disappointed.[29] Sheridan was also dismayed by his friend's well-publicized sympathy with the Indians. Crook insisted that the "Indians have never had any redress for the wrongs committed against them," and he was willing to defend the natives against unscrupulous government functionaries, be they civilian or military. Committed to the belief that the "American Indian was a human being, gifted with the same god-like apprehension as the white man, and like him inspired by noble impulses, [and] ambition for progress and advancement," Crook cooperated with humanitarian groups, most notably Herbert Welsh's Indian Rights Association, in their efforts to turn the natives into stockmen and farmers. In Arizona Crook put the defeated Apaches to work, under the direction of his officers, tilling gardens and then purchased their crops for his troops.[30]

While his fellow officers gave faint lip service to the Indians' plight, Crook acted. When the Poncas fled their Indian Territory reservation and returned to their traditional lands in Nebraska, Crook defended them. In 1879 he spoke out for the embattled Bannocks and Dull Knife's Cheyenne fugitives, members of both groups having served him as scouts against the Sioux. He worked with General Howard, Herbert Welsh, and Senator Henry Dawes to transfer Chiricahua prisoners sent to Florida by Nelson Miles to the Indian Territory, endorsed both the Coke and Dawes Indian reform bills, and advocated voting rights for the Indians. His sympathy with the Indians led him to disobey Sheridan's instructions to disarm Indians at the Red Cloud Agency in 1876 and to soften government terms for the surrender of Geronimo in 1886. Such actions endeared him to the white humanitarians and to the Indians, if not to his military superiors. Red Cloud, the great Oglala leader, left as good an epitaph for Crook as any: "Then General Crook came; he, at least, had never lied to us. His words gave the people hope, He died. Their hope died again. Despair came again."[31]

Sheridan, who tended to see sinister motivation behind every action he disagreed with, viewed Crook's gestures of moderation at the Red Cloud Agency in 1876 and with Geronimo in 1886 as self-serving actions to win glory by having the Indians surrender to him. By 1879 Sheridan was disgusted with Crook's handling of the Department of the Platte. "I am sorry to say that but very few things have been well done in that Department since Crook came in command of it," Sheridan confessed to Sherman in a letter marked "strickly confidential." Crook's troops, Sheridan felt, had no confidence in their commander, who seemed to return their disdain in kind, which meant that the army "must expect indifference and bad results" in that department. "I am a warm personal friend of Crooks and have stuck by him," Sheridan concluded, "but he has given me a good deal of disappointment."[32]

Thus, Sheridan and Crook, the Ohio boyhood pals who weathered West Point and distant Indian wars in the Pacific Northwest together, gradually outgrew their youthful friendship. Professional jealousy and differences on policy eventually destroyed their relationship, but the wonder is, not that it ended, but that it ever existed. Two men could hardly have been more different. Crook avoided both alcohol and tobacco and was never heard to employ a profane word, while Sheridan was the army's most notorious blasphemer and was as famous a drinker and cigar smoker as Grant. Henry A. DuPont, scion of the Delaware industrialist family and Crook's artillery chief in the Shenandoah, noted that "there was a radical difference in temperments" between Sheridan and Crook. Sheridan was "naturally eager and impulsive" while Crook remained "genial, patient, slow-speaking, and inclined to reticence," a man who never flustered. Sheridan saw everything in blacks and whites—in the West it was the clear-cut struggle of civilization against barbarism—but it was not so simple for Crook. He was a man of keener vision—for he could see the grays.[33]

The Department of Dakota, headquartered at Saint Paul, Minnesota, had only two commanders during Sheridan's tenure as division commander. The first, Major General Winfield Scott Hancock, assumed command in May 1869 and served until December 3, 1872, when he moved to command of the Division of the Atlantic. Hancock's unhappy experiences against the Cheyennes in 1867 had given him more respect for the complexities of Indian affairs, and he proved an able administrator and forceful advocate for the needs of his command. The Indians remained comparatively quiet during his time in command of the department.

Sheridan and Hancock were not friends. The reserved, aristocratic hero of Gettysburg had little in common with the plebeian, Irish cavalryman, but it was not temperament alone that separated them. Sheridan never forgave the strongly Democratic Hancock for accepting President Johnson's order to replace him in the Fifth Military District in 1867. George Thomas had refused the command, and Sheridan felt that Hancock should have done the same. Sheridan had been further angered by the almost simultaneous court-martial of his protégé, Custer, by Hancock in 1867. Sheridan viewed this as an effort by Hancock to use a court-martial smoke screen to cover up the failure of his Indian campaign.[34]

Brigadier General (Brevet Major General) Alfred H. Terry followed Hancock in command of the department and continued in that position until 1886. Terry was the only one of Sheridan's department commanders who had not graduated from West Point. A member of a wealthy and distinguished New England family, he was a lawyer by profession. He had entered the military service at the outbreak of the Civil War as colonel of a ninety-day militia regiment. Most of Terry's campaigning was against Confederate coastal defenses in Georgia and the Carolinas, and it was his capture of Fort Fisher in January 1865, thus closing off the Confederacy's last port, that won him the thanks of Congress and a brigadier's commission in the regulars. In the closing months of the war Terry served with Schofield and Sherman, forming warm friendships with each.[35]

Scholarly and quiet, Terry was so modest that he hesitated to accept his brigadier's appointment because it would displace older, professional officers. This self-effacing attitude and mild demeanor led some younger officers, most notably Miles and Custer, to exploit Terry's kindness and disregard his authority. Although an able administrator, Terry had difficulty disciplining such vigorous men, but in that he was hardly alone.[36]

Terry had no experience as an Indian fighter and preferred to leave campaigning to younger officers. He was not, however, inexperienced with Indians. He had come fresh from the Civil War to command the newly formed Department of Dakota in 1866. The department was formed by dividing the Department of the Platte, which had proven too unwieldy to deal effectively with increased traffic to the Montana mines. Terry's new command was immediately put on the defensive against Red Cloud's Sioux, and the general was forced to expand the chain of forts that protected overland and steamboat travelers on their way to Montana. Terry also served with the 1867 Peace Commission, following Sherman's lead and helping to lay the groundwork for the concentration concept that became the mainstay of Grant's celebrated Indian Peace Policy of 1869. From May 18, 1867, until December 3, 1872, he was on Reconstruction duty in the South, but then returned to his former command in the West.[37]

Embracing the state of Minnesota and the territories of Montana and Dakota, the Department of Dakota was the most unsettled, and its Indians regarded as the strongest and most dangerous, of any of Sheridan's departments. Minnesota, devastated by the Sioux uprising of 1862, was now free from Indian threat, as was Dakota east of the Missouri River. But the river formed the border of Sioux country, and west of that line no settler or traveler dared let down his guard. Under the stipulations of the 1868 Treaty of Fort Laramie, which established a Great Sioux Reservation covering present South Dakota west of the Missouri River, the various Sioux bands were to attach themselves to agencies built on the Missouri—the Cheyenne River Agency for the Miniconjous, Sans Arcs, Blackfeet, and Two Kettles; the Grand River Agency (moved a short distance and renamed Standing Rock Agency in 1875) for the Hunkpapas, Yanktonais, and some Blackfeet; and three smaller agencies. Retired General William S. Harney, superintendent for the northern tribes was repeatedly frustrated in his efforts to cajole the Sioux under Red Cloud and Spotted Tail to associate with the agencies. These uncowed chiefs eventually forced the government to establish their agencies in the northwestern tip of Nebraska, along the White River just below the Black Hills, in 1873. Northern Cheyennes and Northern Arapahos joined the Oglalas at Red Cloud Agency, swelling the number of Indians drawing rations to an estimated 12,500. Perhaps 8,000 Brulés attached themselves to the Spotted Tail

Agency, while the Grand River and Cheyenne River agencies were each claiming 7,000 Indians by 1875. These Indians, however, were not permanently settled at the agencies, and roamed throughout the reservation and often beyond, while several thousand Sioux never attached themselves to any agency and were regarded as hostiles.[38]

In this wild and often desolate country, through which flowed the Missouri and its great tributaries the Yellowstone, Milk, Little Missouri, and Cheyenne rivers, vast herds of buffalo still roamed. No accurate count was ever made, but the herds were so large that in 1867 the steamer *Stockade*, Captain Grant Marsh at the helm, was stopped for hours in the waters of the upper Missouri while a mighty herd crossed the river. No white hunters dared challenge the Sioux until the late 1870s, and estimates of a half million buffalo near Miles City, Montana, were not uncommon as late as 1881. Thus the Indian commissary in the Department of Dakota was well stocked.[39]

Both settlement and military activity in the department were retarded by the lack of railroads. The transcontinental Northern Pacific Railroad, chartered in 1864, did not reach the Missouri River until 1873 and was then promptly halted by the collapse of Jay Cooke's financial empire and the resulting panic of 1873. The railroad was not completed until 1883. Nevertheless, military authorities were amazed at the rapidity with which farmers and stockmen moved onto the supposedly barren northern plains.[40]

To protect these people, friendly Indians, and the mining and railroad interests in the department, a line of forts was maintained along the Missouri River, and blockhouses were constructed at the agencies. These isolated posts, a "picket line of civilization" as Sherman described them, were by no means exempt from Indian harassment. In 1869, Sheridan declared that "the post at Fort Buford [near the confluence of the Yellowstone and Missouri Rivers] has been in a state of seige for two or three years." Fort Abraham Lincoln, founded in August 1872 on the west bank of the Missouri at the point where the Northern Pacific reached the river, became a favorite target of Sioux raiding parties from the time of its construction. As early as 1871 Sheridan became convinced that a major campaign would be necessary to subdue the Sioux, and Sherman fully agreed.[41]

The Department of Texas was added to Sheridan's division on November 1, 1871, with Colonel (Brevet Major General) Joseph J.

Reynolds, Third Cavalry, serving temporarily as commander. Reynolds, graduated from West Point in 1843, numbered among his friends his academy classmate U. S. Grant. Although he resigned his commission in 1857 to pursue business interests, Reynolds returned to the military as a commander of Indiana volunteer troops during the Civil War. He had done well enough as a division and corps commander in the war to secure a colonelcy in the postwar army reorganization. Reynolds had served on Reconstruction duty in Texas since 1867, and, when the state was readmitted to the Union on March 30, 1870, thus changing from the Fifth Military District to a department in the Division of the South, he was the logical choice as commander. The genial, gray-haired officer would serve for almost two years before being ordered to rejoin his regiment.[42]

Brigadier General Augur replaced Reynolds as commander on January 29, 1872, and at the same time the boundaries of the department were extended to include that part of the Indian Territory north of Texas and south of Kansas. (A month later, for supply reasons, the post of Camp Supply, Indian Territory, was put under the control of the Department of the Missouri.) This was done to assist in countering Kiowa and Comanche raiding parties originating in the Indian Territory. After the tribes were finally crushed in the Red River War, the Indian Territory was returned to the Department of the Missouri. At the same time, March 11, 1875, Brigadier General Ord replaced Augur as commander. Augur, however, would resume command of the department after Ord's retirement in December 1880.[43]

The guardians of the exposed northern Texas frontier were three posts established in 1867—Fort Richardson, half a mile from Jacksboro; Fort Griffin, on the Clear Fork of the Brazos; and Fort Concho, at the confluence of the North Concho and main Concho Rivers. Although the troops at these forts were able to act against the Kwahadi Comanches who raided south from the headwaters of the Brazos in the Staked Plain, they were powerless to pursue raiding Kiowas and Comanches across the Red River into Indian Territory. The November 1871 department boundary change was meant to rectify that situation, but the troops were still barred from entering the Fort Sill Indian reservation, to which many of the raiding parties fled. It would take another major campaign in 1874–75 to curtail the raids.

Texas also faced hostile incursions from across its southern border. Lipan, Mescalero Apache, and Kickapoo Indian raiding parties as well as bands of Mexican bandits made life and property insecure in southwest Texas during all the years of Sheridan's divisional command. Forts Bliss, Quitman, Davis, Stockton, McKavett, Clark, Duncan, McIntosh, Ringgold, and Brown stood sentinel on the border from El Paso to Brownsville. This situation played havoc with United States–Mexican relations and required the assignment of a large percentage of Sheridan's forces to the region.[45]

Sheridan's department commanders were all veteran officers with distinguished military careers, each having reached the rank of brevet major general in the Civil War (with Hancock and Schofield holding that rank in the regulars). They were also fairly young for general officers. In 1874, for example, the average age of all the officers who would serve Sheridan as department commanders was only fifty. Sheridan, however, was younger than all of the department commanders except Schofield, who was the same age. This meant that there would be slight turnover in department command positions. Although Sheridan could shuffle the officers around, he could scarcely hope for new blood.[46]

The age situation among field grade officers was quite similar. In 1874 the average age of the sixteen line colonels serving in Sheridan's division was only forty-eight. Most of them had been brevet generals in the Civil War, and half of them had served in the Mexican War. Nine of Sheridan's sixteen colonels were graduates of West Point, with the rest coming out of Civil War volunteer units. The sixteen lieutenant colonels stationed in the Division of the Missouri in 1874 were remarkably similar in age and experience to the full colonels. Since mandatory retirement (at age sixty-four) was not introduced into the army until 1882, few of these field grade officers could hope for promotion. In fact, between 1867 and 1880 there were only two promotions to brigadier general of the line—Augur in 1869 and Crook in 1873. This bottleneck in promotions continued on downward, so that the prospects for officers commissioned after 1865 were particularly dismal. The Civil War veterans provided Sheridan with a cadre of able and experienced field officers, but in most cases they would grow old in the ranks they achieved in the 1866 army reorganization.[47]

Sheridan recognized this situation and was hard pressed to reward officers who performed conspicuously well in the Indian campaigns. The lieutenant general urged his superiors to give line promotions only to "officers who have rendered the best services on the frontier since the close of the Civil War." The promotions and appointments that came with the army reorganization had, in Sheridan's mind at least, rendered "all accounts closed and the books balanced" for Civil War service. "We cannot expect officers to strive hard, take risks and perform distinguished services on our frontiers," Sheridan lectured the secretary of war in 1881, "if we permit other officers to come in and take the opening on what they did during the rebellion."[48]

Several of the younger colonels in the division, notably Mackenzie, Miles, Custer, Merritt, and Carr, proved to be vigorous, effective Indian fighters. These officers—and especially the boy generals of the Civil War, Mackenzie, Miles, and Custer—hounded both Sheridan and Sherman on the question of promotion. As his own retirement approached, Sherman came to view these upstarts as vultures anxiously awaiting a faltering step from the old war-horses. He confided in his wife that in particular Mackenzie and Miles were "ambitious and troublesome" and that they "count the days till age will compel the Retirement of all above them that they may be in chief command." Sherman took comfort in the fact that their rise to command "is a long way off and no man is wise enough to guess what may happen meantime, yet they fret and chafe over it like young horses in harness."[49] The ambition so openly displayed by Mackenzie, Miles, and Custer seemed, at times, to border on the compulsive, but it was accompanied by some impressive campaigning that speeded the Indian wars to a conclusion. In the end Nelson Miles finally achieved his goal of commanding the army, but that harsh race for preferment and position may well have cost Mackenzie his sanity and Custer his life.

It was an article of faith among nonacademy officers that in the tight competition for preferment a West Point graduate had the edge as a result of the old-boys'-school philosophy. There was considerable antiacademy sentiment in the country, and it was fueled regularly by the statements of Senator John Logan, the champion of a volunteer army, southerners anxious to strike at the Union military in any way, and reformers who found West Point a bastion of undemocratic, aristocratic philosophy. The occasional pontifications of the army's brightest non–West Point officer, Nelson Miles, also contributed to antiacademy feelings. As Miles clawed his way to the top, he insisted

Sheridan's Field Commanders

Wesley Merritt. (*Custer Battlefield National Monument, National Park Service*)

Eugene A. Carr. (*United States Military Academy Archives*)

that West Point cliques blocked him at every turn. Nonacademy officers like Miles tended to agree with Captain Albert Barnitz of the Seventh Cavalry that a West Point education was "a positive detriment to the individual" rather than an advantage.[50]

Sheridan prided himself on having no prejudice against the mustang, the nongraduate of West Point officer. His own less-than-happy experiences at West Point gave him a rather dim view of that institution. In a speech to the graduating class of 1878 Sheridan was quick to warn the cadets that the "academic restraints of this National School" were not enough to make good officers of them. Now that the "education of the cadet has ceased," Sheridan declared, "the education of the faithful and accomplished officer is about to begin." Only by hard work and experience could they reach that goal.[51]

Despite Sheridan's professed feelings, West Pointers made up a disproportionate share of the general and field grade officers in the

Nelson A. Miles. (*Courtesy Paul Hedren Collection*)

Ranald S. Mackenzie. (*U.S. Signal Corps photo no. sc-87407, National Archives*)

Division of the Missouri. In the 1866 army reorganization Congress had ruled that in selecting officers for the new Twentieth through Forty-fifth infantry regiments and Seventh through Tenth cavalry regiments all grades above first lieutenant had to be filled equally by Civil War regular and volunteer officers, and that all lieutenancies were to be filled from volunteer regiments. (Regular officers who had held volunteer ranks were still considered regulars.) But the army appropriation acts of 1869, 1870, and 1874 cut the size of the army establishment from fifty-four thousand to just over twenty-seven thousand, with a resulting loss of nine hundred officers. The retiring boards and Benzine Boards, who were to ferret out substandard officers, were especially hard on volunteer and civil-appointee officers. Although West Pointers represented but 34 percent of the total number of army officers, they made up almost 60 percent of the colonels in Sheridan's division in 1864, and 65 percent of the lieutenant colonels.

137

West Pointers represented 39 percent of Sheridan's majors, which is somewhat nearer their proprotionate share, but it is interesting to note that all but one of the five academy graduates who were majors in 1874 reached full colonel before leaving the army, while only four of the thirteen nonacademy majors ever reached that rank.[52]

Obviously, the West Point connection was important in reaching high rank, at least on the frontier. The superior training of academy graduates may have played a part in their success over other officers, as did the fact that many of them had been in the service longer and were thus promoted by seniority. The complaints of Miles and Barnitz about the West Point clique at least had some basis. The poor showing of nonacademy majors in the race for promotion tends to support such charges. It should also be noted, however, that the high percentage of West Pointers on the frontier may have reflected the ability of well-connected civil-appointee officers (who made up 57 percent of all officers in 1875) to secure better assignments with the staff or at eastern stations. Nevertheless, in Sheridan's frontier division the West Pointers held sway with 54 percent of all field grade officers, and completely dominated the high ranks. Of course, there were only two nonacademy graduates serving as general officers under Sheridan during his tenure as division commander—Terry, promoted in 1866, and Miles, promoted in 1880.

There were other professional and political connections at least as important as (perhaps more than) the West Point connection. Some officers could look to powerful political patrons, usually men they had served with in the Civil War. Hazen had such a relationship with James A. Garfield; it secured him a general's star when Garfield became president. Crook had a similar relationship with Rutherford B. Hayes, while Sheridan's friendship with Grant was obviously instrumental in furthering his career. Officers also looked to their former Civil War commanders for protection and patronage throughout the postwar era. More often than not, cliques were formed on the basis of this Civil War connection, and junior officers were anxious to serve in regiments commanded by officers they had served under during the war, or at the very least an officer who had served in the same theater of conflict. The chief division was between Sheridan and Sherman men, but every general officer had a clique of supporters. Officers such as Custer and Merritt looked to Sheridan for desirable assignments, extended leaves, recommendations, staff assignments for friends or colleagues, support in disputes with other officers, and a host of other personal and professional opportunities. In the same way, Sherman's Civil War comrades, like Hazen, Grierson, Howard, and Ord, looked to him for support. This often led to professional disputes and bypassing of the normal channels of military communication.

Nevertheless, Sheridan and Sherman had a warm professional friendship. Sherman gave Sheridan a free hand and tried to avoid interfering in divisional affairs. His time was taken up with increasingly strained relations with the staff bureaus, various secretaries of war, and with Congress. While he worked to "sustain the authority of the Generals in command of Divisions and Departments—without the aid of the President and Secretary of War," Sherman left frontier matters to Sheridan. At the same time, the commanding general repeatedly urged Sheridan to keep him "advised of [his] views on all material points." He reminded him, "In time you will feel the same trouble that I have experienced." Concerned to make the eventual transition of army commanders as smooth as possible, Sherman kept Sheridan well informed of all important matters at headquarters. Some officers were not pleased with this command arrangement. Miles complained in 1876, "Sheridan represents the honor of the army without studying or confidence in anything but cavalry; and Sherman unfortunately does not take that interest or positive action in the organization and details of the army that it sadly needs." But Sherman was taking the long view and eventually sought early retirement so that Sheridan could take overall command while fairly young, feeling that is was "but fair he should have his chance."[53]

Another vital connection was of family, for the post–Civil War military was an incestuous profession. High-ranking officers often secured civil appointments in the army for relatives, or at least found them some employment connected with the military. Custer's penchant for nepotism almost wiped out the male line of his family. He had secured commissions in the Seventh Cavalry for his brother and brother-in-law, Thomas W. Custer and James Calhoun, as well as for a close personal friend, George Yates. In 1876 Custer also arranged military employment for another brother and a nephew, Boston Custer and Armstrong Reed. They all died on the same hill above the Little Big Horn on June 25, 1876.[54]

Custer was an extreme example of a fairly common, and generally accepted, practice. When Schofield commanded the Department of the Missouri, he promptly appointed his brother, Major George W. Schofield, as acting assistant inspector general. General Howard did not hesitate to use his influence with Sherman and Grant to secure a civil appointment for his son, Guy Howard, and then appointed the new officer to serve on his staff. Wesley Merritt obtained a commission in the Ninth Cavalry for his younger brother, despite the fact that he failed the qualifying examination. Sheridan had appointed his younger brother, Michael V. Sheridan, to his staff during the Civil War. Mike continued in various positions on the staff until his brother's death.[55]

The most famous family relationship in the army is also one of the most perplexing. Nelson Miles's marriage to General Sherman's niece would seem to have put him in a highly favorable position, especially when it is considered that another uncle-in-law was Senator John Sherman, long-time chairman of the Military Affairs Committee. Nor were Miles and his wife the least bit shy about pressing his claims for preferment on their illustrious relatives. Although Miles received important field commands and rapid promotion, it remains unclear how much influence his uncles-in-law had on this. Miles came to feel that his family ties to General Sherman actually hurt him more than helped, and he probably was right. Sherman was often exasperated with Miles's aggressive self-glorification. In 1879 an angry, frustrated Sherman complained to Sheridan, "Miles was running off with the bit in his teeth, determined to ignore Terry, you and me for the purpose of making a little personal fame and capital."[56]

Many officers, however, did not understand Sherman's feelings about Miles. Custer, who was Miles's friendly rival until his death, complained to Wesley Merritt in 1875 that Miles had received a transfer out of command of a "Colored Regiment" and into command of a white one through the influence of General Sherman. Custer feared that Miles's next goal was transfer to the cavalry, and he was convinced that "Sherman would gladly advance Miles' interests and would give little thought to the outrage such a transfer would be to us." He urged Merritt to join with him in beseeching Sheridan to block Miles's plans. Their fears were unfounded, but Miles's ambition, and use of powerful relatives, would sting many officers in the years to come.[57]

His nephew-in-law was not the only one who pressed Sherman for preferment. In 1872 Sherman became involved in a drawn-out dispute with Mrs. Julia Grant, the president's wife, because he refused to appoint her son to his staff. Sherman rigidly adhered to the army regulation that required officers to serve three years in a line regiment before becoming eligible for staff duty. President Grant understood Sherman's position and did not try to sway him, but Mrs. Grant was furious. Sheridan, hardly the stickler for the finer points of regulations that Sherman was, intervened and appointed young Frederick Grant to his own staff in order to end the feud and keep peace in the president's family. Young Grant wound up spending most of his military career on Sheridan's staff, serving as an aide from 1873 to 1881, when he resigned from the service.[58]

Although nepotism was not necessarily considered unethical in army circles, it could have negative consequences for the service. This was true when Quartermaster General M. C. Meigs was forced to retire in February 1882. Meigs, a superb quartermaster general who had been instrumental in marshaling the resources that fueled the Union war machine during the Civil War, was, at sixty-five, quite healthy and far from senile. President Chester Arthur still used his option to force Meigs out, just as Ord had been forcibly retired by Hayes in 1880. (The president could forcibly retire any officer of forty-two years' service or sixty-two years of age if he judged that officer incapable of performing his duty or in need of rest.) It was Meigs's misfortune to have an officer waiting to succeed him who was desperate to secure the quartermaster general title before he died. That officer was Colonel D. H. Rucker, aged seventy, and Sheridan's father-in-law. The dutiful son-in-law applied all his influence to force the retirement of Meigs to make way for Rucker, and he was successful. Rucker served in the position for only ten days before he also retired, but voluntarily. This established a tradition of sorts, in which elderly officers were given a brief moment at the top and then quickly retired. As a result the quartermaster general office retained no effective, prolonged leadership; there were seven quartermasters general between 1882 and 1898. This bad example was followed by the other staff bureaus, as the army rushed to honor aging Civil War veterans at the sacrifice of building a professional military service to meet future emergencies.[59]

Rucker's promotion, and the part Sheridan played in securing it, was so blatant an instance of nepotism that even a generation whose sensibilities had been blunted by the excesses of Gilded Age politics was outraged. Even Sherman felt compelled to chide Sheridan over the affair, pointing out that when compared to Rucker, "Meigs has equal mental & physical vigor and possesses more the confidence of the congress & country." The *Philadelphia Evening Telegram* was blunter: "A Good many features of the Grant era have been revived of late, but the feature of nepotism has hitherto lingered in the background. Now, it seems, we are to have this too, with the other elements of 'Stalwartism.' "[60]

Some, including the editors of the prestigious *Army and Navy Journal*, felt that some of the unethical qualities of the Gilded Age originated in the military. Commenting upon the 1876 scandal implicating Secretary of War William Belknap in the sale of post traderships, the editors lamented that the former general had "brought from the camp one of its legacies." Such behavior was common in the army where "few post commanders did not accept an occasional delicacy for the mess-table at headquarters from the post sutler, who desired to keep on the right side of those in authority." Many military men thought it only natural then for the secretary of war to extract payment for favors from one of those "who always grow rich, and who without harm [should] be made to lay down a fraction of their extortionate gains." It was clear to the editors that "this camp-argument had its evil effect [on Belknap], as many other camp arguments and camp customs have had here at Washington since the surrender at Appomattox."[61]

Despite the nepotism, favoritism, and fierce rivalries, Sheridan and his officers viewed themselves as a cast of extraordinarily honorable men. This high moral sense, which was carefully guarded through peer pressure and self-policing, was viewed by the officers as setting them above the rest of society during the Gilded Age. This officer corps's self-image was of chivalrous knights in Union blue who sacrificed themselves so that civilization might possess the wilderness. A chronicler from their own ranks, Captain Charles King of the Fifth Cavalry, devoted his life to immortalizing that sacrifice in a series of novels about knightly officers who went forward into the wilderness with "absolutely nothing to hold [them] soldier stern and steadfast to the bitter end, but the solemn sense of Soldier Duty."[62]

Such ideas were also prevalent in the pages of the *Army and Navy Journal*, where the editors reminded their readers that the "sentiment of military honor, the best part of the legacy left by medieval chivalry, cannot be cherished too dearly." This sense of honor impelled the officer "to patience, fortitude, courage, temperance, chastity, probity, and that large charity and self-forgetfulness which would sacrifice life for the protection of the weak and helpless." The *Army and Navy Journal* could see that these virtues "have descended to us from the chivalry of the Middle Ages, and are embodied to-day in our ideal of military honor."[63]

Implicit within this strict code of honor was the protection and chaste adoration of women. Sometimes, however, their special position came into conflict with the demands of military honor, which called for some twisting of logic. Sheridan, for example, interceded in the case of a young second lieutenant of the Tenth Cavalry, the relative of a close friend, who had been caught in an adulterous relationship with the wife of a fellow officer. Sheridan personally visited Fort Sill, questioned all the parties, and discovered that the woman had been driven to the liaison by her husband, "a drunken, worthless man who used up his salary for drink and left his wife open to even the temptation of supplying herself with articles of ordinary comfort by offering her person." Despite these circumstances, Sheridan demanded the young lieutenant's resignation since "officers have on account of the contingencies of the service to be often absent from their wives & we cannot well let down the high standard of honor which should be observed." Sheridan, although no Victorian prude, demanded that his officers live by the same high moral code that he followed, but he failed to understand the weaknesses of others. He elevated the rule or law above the circumstances, be it in relation to the Reconstruction of the South, the straying of starving Indians off the reservation, or the affair of a desperate woman and a lieutenant fresh from West Point. In the last case, however, he could throw all the blame on the woman. "There is a strong rule and a very worthy one existing generally in the Army," he wrote in summing up the Fort Sill episode, "that no matter how vicious & depraved the woman or wife may be there should be a profound honor which should protect her, if only for the honor of the absent husband and the service."[64]

Sheridan was as willing as any late-nineteenth century man to place women upon a pedestal, but only as long as she quietly and unobtrusively remained there. He would remain a bachelor most of his life, not marrying until age forty-four and then taking a wife young enough to be his daughter. Yet he was fond of the ladies, seemingly as much at home on the dance floor as on the battlefield. But Sheridan worried about the extra burdens a wife brought upon a soldier, and frequently told Elizabeth Custer that her husband was the only one of his officers "who had not been spoiled by marriage."[65]

If an officer could be spoiled by marriage, then a wife could be forever tainted by any deviation from her position on the pedestal. It made no matter whether she deviated by free choice, as had the officer's wife at Fort Sill, or by accident; she was still ruined. In 1872 Sheridan refused to authorize the payment of five ponies to ransom a white woman held captive by the Indians. She was now forever tainted by her captivity. "I cannot give my approval to any reward for the delivery of this white woman," declared Sheridan. "After having her husband and friends murdered, and her own person subjected to the fearful bestiality of perhaps the whole tribe, it is mock humanity to secure what is left of her for the consideration of five ponies."[66] That highly valued chivalric military code of honor could indeed become bizarrely convoluted.

If Sheridan's Indian-fighting army looked to the medieval past for its code of honor, it did not have to look back so far for what it considered the American army's most glorious days. For most of Sheridan's officers the Civil War had been the most important event in their lives, and they looked back to "the great conflict and its marvellous experiences." There were few who could not agree with the cavalry officer's wife who jotted in her diary that the Indian conflicts were "so different from our late war—when we gave up our loved ones to go into battle we felt that it was our duty and we had the strength to make the sacrifice—now it is a real *business* and we endure all the misery for *money!*"[67]

The army, as an institution, looked backward throughout the whole period of Sheridan's post–Civil War service. Undoubtedly, this obsession with the glorious days of the Civil War retarded progress in military thought and reform in the years between 1865 and 1890. Sheridan was rarely an advocate of change in any form. His response to proposals for army reform is best summarized in his rejoinder to a request to support changes in the antiquated staff bureaus: "It answered well during the war, and we ought to be contented with it in time of peace."[68]

His statement regarding the "time of peace" is significant, since it was made in 1873, just before Sheridan's division embarked on four years of difficult, protracted conflict with the mounted tribes of the southern and northern plains. The conflict on the plains simply was not real war in the minds of men who had won their stars in the great struggle of 1861–65. Civil War major generals who had commanded corps and divisions tended to be more interested in refighting Gettysburg or Five Forks in their memoirs than in formulating new strategies of unconventional warfare to deal with their Indian foe.

The fact that the officers had little respect for their Indian enemy played a part in their nostalgia for the real war. Their sympathy for the terrible plight of the Indian, however, made their employment more a necessary evil than a glorious enterprise. A few officers, and Sheridan was one, suffered no pangs of conscience over dispossessing the Indians of the West, but most recognized the great wrong that was being perpetrated on the tribes. Even Custer, who unlike most of his peers received as much contemporary fame in his new role as an Indian fighter as he had as a leader of cavalry in the Civil War, could only sympathize with the Indians. "If I were an Indian," wrote Custer in 1874, "I often think I would greatly prefer to cast my lot among those of my people adhered to the free open plains rather than submit to the confined limits of a reservation, there to be the recipient of the blessed benefits of civilization, with its vices thrown in without stint or measure."[69]

Such feelings do not mean that Custer and the numerous other officers who wrote kindly of the Indian did not consider their foe to be savages—for that would be a misrepresentation. The officers simply recognized that even a savage could be fighting in the right. Charles King probably expressed the feelings of most of Sheridan's officers when he lamented that the frontier army was "fighting ofttimes against a foe for whom we felt naught but sympathy, yet knew the response could only be a deathless hate." To King, "no army in Christendom" was ever called on to undertake so thankless a task: "Who of our number would willingly at the outset have dealt a blow to the Christian Nez Perces? Who of our number would not gladly have spared the heroic band that broke from the prison pen at Robinson and died disdaining to surrender? Who of our number did not feel a thrill of soldier pity when the gallant fellow, Crazy Horse, was done to death resisting unlooked for arrest at old Camp Robinson?" Perhaps Phil Sheridan would have answered in the affirmative to the rhetorical questions that Charles King put to a group of veterans, but the vast majority of Sheridan's officers would have agreed with King that duty against the Indians held little glory.[70]

As the melancholy Indian wars consumed their efforts, Sheridan's soldiers could look warmly back to a time when, as the general put it, "no treacherous Indian, no effeminate Mexican . . . was their foeman, but their own countrymen met them face to face on the field, struggling for the mastery. When volunteer meets volunteer 'then comes the tug of war.'" Not only was the Civil War a real war as opposed to the guerrilla fighting in the West, but Sheridan and his officers believed that the soldier "reared in the camps of the great contending armies of the Civil War . . . stands as the soldier of the future . . . [and] the peers of the soldiers of the world." Sheridan was absolutely dedicated to the idea that there never was "so effective a body of officers and men as the armies of the Union at the close of our rebellion." His observation of European troops, both in times of war and peace, left him "fully satisfied that there is no nation in Europe which has so perfect an army system as ourselves." Such smug conceit concerning the might of the American army, even though it may well have been correct in 1865, made the police work on the western plains even more galling. It also evoked feelings of complacency that stymied reform.[71]

Sheridan's uninterest in military reform emerged from his firm belief that the nation faced no threat of conflict from abroad. "I do not believe such a war will ever occur," Sheridan told an 1880 army reunion. "We have the ocean as a fortification," he continued. "It would take more than all the shipping in Europe to bring men sufficient to this country to make one campaign. I mean all the shipping of Europe, unmolested, if it were permitted to sail, couldn't carry men and material sufficient for one campaign, to meet the force we could command. It would take more than all Europe could do."[72]

Sheridan could also see the day coming when he and other soldiers would be obsolete, for new technologies would soon make war

Sheridan always looked forward to military reunions, but not just to relive glorious bygone days if this illustration from *Frank Leslie's Illustrated Newspaper,* November 8, 1873, is to be believed. At a reception for President Grant on October 16, 1873, during the reunion of the Army of the Tennessee in Toledo, Ohio, the Union's three greatest heroes and the frontier's best-known combat officer launched a campaign to kiss all the ladies in attendance. Holding firm on this picket line of civilization are Lieutenant Colonel Custer, President Grant, Lieutenant General Sheridan, and General Sherman. (*Courtesy of Lawrence A. Frost*)

impossible. At Philadelphia, in 1887, in a speech given on occasion of the centennial of the signing of the Constitution, Sheridan saw banishment of warfare on the horizon:

> There is one thing that you should appreciate, and that is that the improvement in guns and in the material of war, in dynamite and other explosives, and in breech-loading guns, is rapidly bringing us to a period when war will eliminate itself; when we can no longer stand up and fight each other in battle, and when we will have to resort to something else. Now what will that "something else" be? It will be arbitration. I mean what I say when I express the belief that if any one now present here could live until the next centennial he would find that arbitration will rule the world.[73]

So while they waited for the lofty goal of world peace to be reached, the Civil War veterans joined together in numerous groups to do honor to their dead and to themselves. Sheridan loved these veterans' conclaves and attended as many as he could. He was a member of the Grand Army of the Republic, commander of the Loyal Legion, and a member of the veteran societies of the Armies of the Mississippi, Ohio, Cumberland, Potomac, and Shenandoah. He served as an officer in several of these, and he attempted to direct the organizations away from political uses, for which the Grand Army of the Republic was no notorious, and toward being vehicles for comradeship and nostalgia. At the Army of the Potomac meeting in 1878 he criticized several speakers for turning the occasion into a political forum:

> I never yet have heard a single address by any one in this army society that I thought embodied what the society most wanted to hear. They all want to talk about the cause which led to the war, and about emancipation, and all such things. We do not care about hearing that. It is all over. The problem is worked out. What we now want to hear is something about our old comrades and about the battles we fought, and the good times we had, and the bad times we had—and things of that kind.[74]

This preoccupation with the Civil War manifested itself most dramatically in the professional and personality disputes that plagued the army in the postwar years. Colonel (Brevet Major General) David S. Stanley and Colonel Hazen engaged in an acrimonious and unrelenting feud throughout their military careers, beginning at the Battle of Shiloh in 1862. Stanley hounded Hazen with accusations of cowardice and of deserting his men during that battle. He later tacked on charges that Hazen had falsely claimed the capture of certain cannons on Missionary Ridge in 1863. This charge may well have been a bid for Sheridan's support, since he and Hazen continued to argue over the captured guns. If this was Stanley's intent, it failed, for Sheridan firmly opposed Stanley's efforts to have Hazen court-martialed on the charges. "I think it would be a great misfortune to let the Stanley and Hazen trouble go as far as the ordering of a courtmartial," Sheridan told Sherman in 1879. "I do not see much in their quarrel, and I know there must be a large portion of the Army who thinks about it as I do. The investigation of it . . . will result in the exposition of the personal habits of both, and I beg that the Army may be saved from the burden of what will, or what might be developed."[75]

148

The Stanley-Hazen feud reopened the public debate between Hazen and Sheridan over whose troops captured Confederate guns on Missionary Ridge. This debate might seem inconsequential, even ridiculous after the passage of many years, but it interfered with the operation of military affairs in the Division of the Missouri. The feud had made it virtually impossible for Sheridan, and his protégé Custer, to cooperate with Hazen in the administration of Indian affairs in the Indian Territory in 1868–69. Their hostility became even more pointed over Hazen's alleged protection of guilty Indians. This inability of two army officers, one charged with supervision of peaceful Indians and the other with power over the hostile ones, to work together undercut military efforts to take control of Indian affairs from the Department of the Interior. It was obvious that even when the military was in complete control, the same old arguments over jurisdiction and over which Indians were hostile continued to prevail.

In 1872 Hazen and his regiment, the Sixth Infantry, were transferred from Kansas to Fort Buford, far up the Missouri River in the northernmost part of Dakota Territory. Sheridan personally made the final decision on the transfer. There was some speculation that his feud with Hazen as well as the colonel's recent statements regarding the sale of army sutlerships at Fort Sill played a part in the assignment. Hazen was dismayed at what he viewed as "banishment" to the most remote and desolate post in the country. His obvious reluctance to go to Fort Buford was noted by Sheridan, and, when Hazen asked for thirty days' leave for the fall of 1872 because of pain resulting from an old wound, Sheridan hesitated to comply. He finally approved the leave but added a damning conclusion to his half-hearted endorsement:

> The disability which Col. Hazen now has seems to have come on him about the time his Regiment was ordered to the Dept. of Dakota. I would regret very much to do injustice to Col. Hazen, but must confess that he has done much injury to the discipline of the Army by his reluctance to do duty with his regiment (which should be his pride) and I find it impossible to remove from my mind the impression that this reluctance is the foundation of his present disability.[76]

Such insinuations continued for years. In 1874 Hazen charged that Sheridan had ordered the Seventh Cavalry to Fort Abraham Lincoln in order to benefit the sutler at the post. The charge was so obviously ridiculous that nothing came of it, but Sheridan was quick to note that he doubted whether "any officer's honor is safe under such a system." Hazen's involvement in the 1876 impeachment of Secretary of War Belknap further angered Sheridan. When time came to confront the Sioux on the northern plains, Colonel Hazen was conspicuously absent from the action despite the fact that he was stationed near the scenes of combat. The final triumph, however, went to Hazen in 1880 when his friend Garfield was elected President. Hazen was promptly promoted to brigadier general and made chief signal officer, finally escaping the reach of Sheridan's persecution.[77]

Two officers, William W. Averell and Gouverner K. Warren, who were not as fortunate as Hazen, saw their military careers destroyed by Sheridan. Along with their friends in and out of the army, they were among Sheridan's worst enemies. Averell, commander of a cavalry division under Sheridan in the Shenandoah Valley, had been relieved from command for failing to press the retreating enemy after Fisher's Hill. He finished the war as brevet major general, but resigned his regular army commission in 1865 and went into business. He became a successful and wealthy inventor, but he never forgot his humiliation at Sheridan's hands in the Shenandoah. While on his way to meet with Grant in 1869, Sheridan happened on Averell in a hotel lobby and offered his hand in greeting. It was accepted, but Sheridan soon received a coldly worded note from Averell: "Your proffered courtesy at an unexpected meeting today surprised me but it being a public place . . . I was determined to await some more fitting occasion to make a proper statement of my sentiments. . . . I was the victim of a grievous wrong and cannot permit you to entertain the impression I am willing to resume friendly intercourse with you."[78]

Averell left the military service, but Gouverner Warren remained in the army and diligently worked from within to clear his name. The hero of the second day at Gettysburg had been removed from command of the Fifth Corps at Five Forks by Sheridan just a few days before Lee's surrender. Sheridan's reasons for removing Warren were essentially the same as those for Averell; the officer was simply not aggressive enough. Soon after the dismissal Warren resigned his commission as a major general of volunteers and reverted to his regular army rank of major in the engineers.

During the postwar years Warren performed routine engineering and surveying work in the upper Mississippi Valley, all the while petitioning higher authorities to grant him a court of inquiry. President Hayes finally relented, and in 1879 a military court met to decide whether Warren had been deserving of removal at Five Forks.[79]

It was 1882 before the court published its finding, a full seventeen years after the battle in question, and Warren was exonerated on three of the four reasons on which Sheridan had based his removal. The verdict was a blow to Sheridan's pride, and he loudly complained that the findings were "more in the nature of apologies than annunciation of the facts as shown in the evidence." Senator John Logan of Illinois, national commander of the Grand Army of the Republic from 1868 to 1874 and the chairman of the Senate Committee on Military Affairs, was in full agreement and promised to stop the organization of these "pretend 'Courts' for the purpose of plastering up the reputation of some who could not gain an enviable reputation by their own course of conduct during the war." Sherman did not let his friend down either, making it clear to all that he felt "General Sheridan was perfectly justified in his action in this case, and he must be fully and entirely sustained if the United States expects great victories by her armies in the future." It was all to no avail anyway, as far as Warren was concerned, for that brave but tainted officer died months before the court vindicated him. Warren's death, according to his supporters, had resulted directly from worry and anguish over the prolonged fight for vindication.[80]

The period between 1865 and 1880 has been labeled as the "army's dark ages," and one of the main causes of that condition was the long shadow cast by the Civil War.[81] Instead of looking to the future, too many men, both within and outside the military, seemed captivated by their memory of the past, be that memory tragic or glorious. Sheridan, while certainly not as guilty of this as others, was still in many ways a captive of the past. Compounding this problem was the miserly attitude of Congress, whose meager appropriations made it rare for the tiny, scattered army even to bring whole regiments together at one place for training or maneuvers. As the army lost vitality, its enemies grew stronger.

Senator John Logan, a sharp critic of the regular army ever since Sherman passed him over during the Civil War and gave command of the Army of the Tennessee to West Pointer Oliver O.

Howard, championed the cause of a nonprofessional, volunteer army. He was joined by former Confederates with little sympathy for their former enemies, by humanitarians outraged over the treatment of the Indians, and by those who sought to trim the federal budget at all times. Sheridan, who during the Civil War had proven to be quite original in his approach to problems, now failed as a result of these internal and external problems, as well as of his own personality, to provide the Division of the Missouri with innovative and imaginative leadership.

Traditionalism set the tone of Sheridan's post–Civil War career. Deeply conservative and distrustful of change, he was hardly suited to lead a military renaissance. Even the innovative, cerebral Sherman could not overcome the solid conservatism of the army and the nation and institute lasting change. Sheridan would not even try. He did not have much time to concern himself with changing the system anyway, since his division command kept him busy, not only with Indian affairs but also with a myriad of other duties as well.

CHAPTER 7

Varied Duties
of Division Command

One of Sheridan's first acts as commander of the Division of the Missouri was to transfer division headquarters from Saint Louis to Chicago. Bustling, vibrant, loud, and bombastic, this was a city with a character to match the general's. Chicago became Sheridan's first extended place of residence since Somerset. He considered the city his home, took an active part in civic and social affairs, and numbered among his personal friends many of Chicago's elite, including Marshall Field, Potter Palmer, E. B. Washburn, Levi Leiter, and William Strong. Most of the prominent social clubs listed him as an honorary member, and as a great horse racing fan, he was elected president of the Washington Park Club. Division headquarters was located at the corner of Washington and LaSalle, across from the central square with its impressive limestone courthouse. Sheridan selected for his personal residence an attractive, two-story home at 708 South Michigan Avenue, which he shared with his brother Michael.

Establishing his new headquarters posed few problems for Sheridan, since he already had a close-knit and highly skilled military staff to oversee office operations. He liked to surround himself with friends and had a clannish outlook toward his staff officers, several of whom had served with him since the Civil War. James W. "Tony" Forsyth, appointed division aide-de-camp with the rank of lieutenant colonel, had been with Sheridan since April 1864 and was his constant companion and close friend. They had known each other at West

Point, although in different graduating classes, and had served together in the Pacific Northwest. Tall and thin with a ramrod straight, even imperious, military bearing that belied his warm, gregarious nature, Forsyth was a "champion story-teller." He served Sheridan as aide-de-camp until 1873 and as military secretary until 1878, when he was promoted to lieutenant colonel, First Cavalry, and joined his regiment. In 1886 he became colonel of the Seventh Cavalry and commanded the troops that brought the curtain down on the Indian wars with the terrible slaughter at Wounded Knee.[1]

Further staff continuity was provided by the appointment of John Schuyler Crosby, another of Sheridan's personal friends, as aide-de-camp. But Crosby, a New York aristocrat, resigned his commission in December 1870 to pursue a career in business and politics, serving in various diplomatic positions and as territorial governor of Montana from 1882 to 1884. George "Sandy" Forsyth also continued to serve Sheridan, first as military secretary until 1873, and then as aide-de-camp until 1881, when he was promoted to lieutenant colonel, Fourth Cavalry, and joined his regiment in the Southwest. Captain Michael V. Sheridan, who had served on his brother's staff since the Civil War, received an appointment as acting adjutant general and, in 1870, replaced Crosby as aide-de-camp with the rank of lieutenant colonel. He would serve on the staff longer than the others, eventually becoming his brother's military secretary from 1878 to 1888. Other members of Sheridan's inner circle included Morris Asch, staff surgeon, and A. J. McGonnigle, who became Chicago depot quartermaster. These and other appointments provided Sheridan with a loyal and competent staff to administer the Division of the Missouri. The ability of his staff enabled Sheridan to escape much of the minutiae of daily administration.[2]

Sheridan was authorized to employ eleven men from the General Services Detachment at this Chicago headquarters. The chief clerk on Sheridan's staff was Corporal Daniel O. Drennan, an Irish immigrant who did not even become a citizen until 1874 but who faithfully served the general from 1865 to 1888. Drennan's work was endless, since each mail delivery brought a stream of requests for recommendations and endorsements, applications for work, petitions from citizens, pleas for clemency or reinstatement to rank, complaints from deserted army wives, requisitions, bills, and invitations to every sort of social, historic, and political affair.[3]

Much time was consumed in writing letters of introduction and applications for pensions for veterans of Sheridan's Civil War commands or their widows. The general's loyalty to those who had served with him was unshakable, and he always tried to do his best for them.[4] But letters of introduction were refused to friends and acquaintances traveling on business matters. Sheridan also refused to endorse army officers for special positions "on ground that his endorsement of any one of them would be an injustice to others equally deserving, who desired the same appointment." When exceptions were made to this policy, they were kept secret.[5]

Sheridan, perhaps in deference to his days as a quartermaster, paid close attention to the details of his command, especially to financial accounts such as requests for funds for buildings, repairs, and supplies, or the cost of escort duty. He carefully diagramed a complete record-keeping system for Drennan, which allowed easy access to any papers concerning present and past commands.[6]

The voluminous paperwork of army record-keeping strained Sheridan's patience, and he denounced the absurdities of the system to Sherman:

> Before returning this paper to the Commanding General Dept. of Dakota, I desire to call the attention of the General of the Army, as a matter of curiosity, to the number of endorsements thereon. Coming from the office of the Post Quartermaster at Helena, Montana, and addressed to the Post Adjutant there, it is forwarded by the Commanding Officer of the Post to the Headquarters of the District of Montana, at Fort Shaw whence it is returned to Helena in order that it may be sent direct to Department Headquarters at St. Paul. Leaving Helena once more, it reached St. Paul two months after the date of its inception. The adjutant General of the Department refers it without endorsement to the Chief Quartermaster, who returns it approved. It is then forwarded to the Adjutant General of the Division, who passed it along to the Chief Quartermaster, who refers it to the Quartermaster in charge of Jeffersonville Depot, by whom it is referred to the military storekeeper there to fill the requisiton for one field desk. None, however, are on hand there, and the storekeeper returns the paper to the Depot Quartermaster, and he to the Chief Quartermaster of the Division. It is next forwarded to the Quartermaster General in Washington,

who refers the unfortunate requisition to Col. Rucker in Philadelphia with directions that if he cannot fill it, it is to be transmitted to Col. Easton in New York City. Accordingly, after being referred by Col. Rucker to Maj. Dana in Philadelphia, and by him to the military storekeeper there, it is returned by the same channel to Col. Rucker who forwards it to New York, but still without success, and Col. Easton therefore returns it to Washington unfilled. It now commences the homeward trip with the decision that no one has the desk asked for and that there are no funds available to purchase one.

Reaching these headquarters, it received an endorsement from the Chief Quartermaster of the Division, suggesting that the desk be manufactured at the post of Helena with the means available there.[7]

Decisions on the establishment, construction, maintenance, and abandonment of the forts within the Division of the Missouri took up a large portion of Sheridan's time and energy. A parsimonious Congress never appropriated the funds to build new posts and keep established forts in even a modest state of repair. "There is one fact which we must recognize," Sheridan lectured Hancock in 1872, "that for every new post we establish an old one must be given up."[8] This meant that older, sometimes better constructed and larger quarters had to be sacrificed to keep troops on the rapidly moving frontier line. More often than not the troops suffered in the quality of their housing as a result. Important decisions on where to construct posts became increasingly difficult, since conditions on the frontier were "so rapidly changed by the progress of Railroads that what may appear right and proper one year becomes, to some extent if not entirely, useless the next year."[9]

Western communities competed for forts, depots, or headquarters offices, because any government construction meant added economic growth. Sheridan guarded his construction funds carefully and repeatedly confronted irate citizens, congressmen, and even his own officers, who favored some project that he considered against the "public service." His office often received petitions from citizens demanding construction of a new post in their region or protesting the abandonment of an existing fort. A hard-bitten Sheridan told one group of petitioners: "If the wishes of the settlers on the frontier were to be gratified, we would have a military post in every county, and the Army two or three hundred thousand strong." When the citizens near Fort Gibson, Indian Territory, protested its abandonment, Sheridan caustically remarked that the fort "for years had been a source of profit

No one save his brother Mike was closer to Sheridan than James W. Forsyth. He served on Sheridan's staff from 1864 until 1878, became colonel of the Seventh Cavalry in 1886, and commanded that regiment at Wounded Knee. They are pictured together with an unidentified civilian in 1865. (*Author's Collection*)

to them" and their self-interest was now overruled by "more pressing interests."[10]

Territorial delegates and western congressmen clamored to have their state or territory designated an independent military department. Sheridan attempted to meet their basic complaint—centralization in the disbursement of public funds—by locating district headquarters in the major western cities. Since he worked diligently to open the West to settlement, Sheridan resented any accusation that he was retarding development in the territories. When Montana's territorial delegate chided Sheridan for not constructing forts in his region, the general angrily reminded him, "Nearly everything done for the opening of a way to Montana for the last two years has been ordered by me, or on my recommendation." Sheridan was not exaggerating, for his power was substantial.[11] When he discovered an effort by citizens of North Platte, Nebraska, to transfer Fort McPherson to their city, Sheridan told his superiors that he saw no reason to move the fort, "unless it is done in the interest of town lot speculators [at North Platte] who keep agitating the subject whenever they get a chance."[12]

Sometimes Sheridan was too late to stop the waste of public funds, as in the case of the construction of Fort Abraham Lincoln near Bismarck, North Dakota. Upon a personal inspection of the site selected by a board of officers, Sheridan was "utterly astonished" to find that "every possible public interest in the way of economy, comfort and convenience for the troops seems to have been neglected." The site chosen was on a wind-swept bluff that rose 270 feet above the Missouri River. There was no excuse for such an "error" of judgment since a "beautiful plain at least five miles long spreading from the base of the bluff southward" provided a superb location for the post. Sheridan ruefully concluded that since the anticipated route of the Northern Pacific Railroad crossed in a westwardly direction over the plain, the board of officers had forgotten "the public interest in order to let the Railroad Company have the land for speculating purposes in the way of town lots." The situation was partially rectified by the construction of a portion of the fort on the plain, but since construction of the barracks on the bluff was already well advanced when Sheridan visited the post in September 1872, it was allowed to proceed.[13]

Western municipalities, eager to secure military depots, often were aided by influential officers. The citizens of Council Bluffs, Iowa, enlisted the support of General Ord in 1873 to transfer the Department of the Platte headquarters across the Missouri River from Omaha to their city. The city fathers even offered the government a gift of land for the military depot. Sheridan vetoed the plan, warning the secretary of war that "the Government should enter into no terms with towns or cities that would bind it to remain at any given point," since military necessity might require the moving of depots and department headquarters at any time. The affair further shook Sheridan's dwindling faith in Ord, whom he perceived to be in dishonorable collusion with the city boosters of Council Bluffs.[14]

Sheridan's opposition was not always enough to halt pork-barrel military construction. A proposed military depot at San Antonio, Texas, in 1876 provides a good example. Sheridan and Department of Texas commander Augur both opposed the depot as a waste of money, since the advance of a railroad across northern Texas changed supply routes and made it "only a good place for cobwebs" before its construction. Sheridan angrily denounced the scheme as "conceived and carried on, and sneaked through Congress, not in the interest of the public service, but for the benefit of San Antonio." He could only console himself in blocking anticipated construction cost overruns by requesting that the War Department "issue an order forbidding the construction of a building exceeding the sum appropriated, and requiring a plan with specifications to hold down cost." Sheridan feared that the specified cost of one hundred thousand dollars would be greatly exceeded in order "to gratify the artistic taste of the Quartermaster General, or the interests of the City of San Antonio."[15]

Such extravagance was especially annoying to Sheridan when Congress failed to appropriate enough money for critical post construction elsewhere. The danger was made especially obvious by Sheridan's repeatedly ignored requests for funds to build posts on the Tongue and Big Horn Rivers in the Yellowstone Valley in order to control the Sioux. Two years after Sheridan's initial funding request, the Seventh Cavalry was slaughtered on the Little Big Horn. The construction of the forts would have, in all likelihood, averted the disaster, and Congress belatedly appropriated funds. The two forts, finally constructed in 1877, were named for Custer and one of his troop commanders, Myles Keogh. Little wonder that Sheridan so despised those who would needlessly squander military construction funds.[16]

Despite the press of daily affairs, Sheridan took an interest in all aspects of the military service. As an avid marksman he took particular interest in the movement to impose a well-regulated system of target practice on the army. In 1871, as a result of the efforts of William C. Church, editor of the *Army and Navy Journal*, and Captain George W. Wingate of the New York National Guard, the National Rifle Association was formed. Through the sponsorship of rifle matches, like those held at the Creedmoor Rifle Range on Long Island, and editorials in the *Army and Navy Journal,* Church and the National Rifle Association won the regular army over to their philosophy. In 1879 the army adopted a regulated system of target practice, with each soldier allowed twenty rounds of ammunition per month for that purpose and prizes given for the best shooting scores. Various army teams participated in the Creedmoor matches, the Division of the Missouri team winning in 1880, and Sheridan served as an early president of the National Rifle Association. In 1885 Sheridan introduced company skirmish firing practice at dummy targets of men. This enabled company commanders to perfect the fire discipline of their men in a combat simulation.[17]

The logic of target practice was clear to Sheridan, but he was not so easily won over to the merits of that long-standard weapon of war, the bayonet. He considered "all bayonets humbugs" and felt the army could do away with the weapon altogether, since "one side or the other runs before the bayonet can be used." He expressed special concern that the bayonet was too useful as a digging tool, and that the "men are liable to commence covering themselves too soon, if the tools are convenient." His quixotic advice was ignored.[18]

Sheridan also took a keen interest in military scholarship and, along with Sherman, sponsored the work of Colonel (Brevet Major General) Emory Upton. Sheridan early recognized that Upton combined a scholar's brilliant mind with all the aggressiveness, courage, and dash that any soldier could hope for. A West Point graduate in 1861, Upton quickly established an enviable reputation as a commander in all three combat arms. He served under Sheridan in the Shenandoah, commanding first a brigade of cavalry and then a division of infantry. Seriously wounded at Winchester, he was transferred upon his recovery to command a division of Sherman's cavalry, participating in the great raid through Alabama and Georgia at the close of the war. In the 1866 reorganization Upton was promoted to lieutenant colonel of infantry, and from 1870 to 1875 he served as commandant of cadets at West Point.

Upton was the natural choice of the army high command to go on a world tour and observe the armies of Europe and Asia. Sherman hoped that Upton's observations of the British army in India could lead to new techniques of Indian fighting for the western army, but this goal was frustrated by Secretary of War Belknap's instructions that Upton concentrate on studying the German war machine. Upton found Belknap's orders more agreeable to his own desires and so followed them instead of Sherman's. Joining Upton in this grand tour of Japan, China, India, Russia, and the major European powers was George Forsyth, Sheridan's trusted aide of fourteen years. Forsyth kept Sheridan well informed of the details of the journey and on the composition of the various armies observed. It was as a result of the trip that Upton wrote his important book, *The Armies of Asia and Europe*, which not only encompassed a report of the tour, but also proposed organizational reforms for the United States Army based on the German system.[19]

Upton, who suffered from a brain tumor, committed suicide in 1881, but the spirit of military scholarship that he represented was given institutional life through the creation of the School of Application for Infantry and Cavalry at Fort Leavenworth, Kansas, founded that same year. Here one lieutenant from each infantry and cavalry regiment was to serve a two-year period of advanced training in tactics and military science. Sheridan followed Sherman's lead and gave his full support to the school, continually working to upgrade faculty and curriculum. The Fort Leavenworth school, the Fort Monroe Artillery School, and the Engineering School of Application were carefully nurtured by Sherman and Sheridan so that they could offer solid, postgraduate courses to officers who might otherwise be isolated from current military thought.[20]

Professionalizing the officer's corps was not the only reason behind Sherman's sponsorship of the Fort Leavenworth school, or so he told Sheridan as they planned to open the school: "I confess I made the order as a concession to the everlasting demand of friends & families to have their boys detailed to signal duty, or to the school at Fort Monroe to escape company duty in the Indian Country. This school at Leavenworth may do some good, and be a safely valve for those who are resolved to escape from the drudgery of Garrison life at small posts."[21]

The Leavenworth schools pointed toward a future that was far removed from the Indian campaigns of Sheridan's day. The era of Indian campaigning was almost over. Upton realized this, and he warned that the years of frontier fighting had kept the army from developing modern command and staff systems comparable to the European armies. As early as the 1840s Henry Halleck had also seen that the transitory nature of Indian warfare meant that the army must seek out new functions if it was to survive. There were many advocates of this view. General Hancock wrote in 1876 that Indian warfare need not be given consideration, since it "is of secondary importance, and is comparatively temporary in its nature." Hancock felt that since Indian warfare "furnishes only incidental duty for part of the army," it was "entitled to no weight" in formulating long-term military policy.[22]

Despite the opinions of Upton, Halleck, and Hancock, keeping the peace on the Indian frontier remained Sheridan's primary duty throughout his tenure as division commander. Even during periods of Indian unrest, however, labor agitation or political disturbances could pull military attention away from the frontier. At the same time, the tasks of the division went far beyond engaging in Indian campaigns, for Sheridan's men belonged to a truly multipurpose army.

One of the more unusual duties performed by Sheridan's command was the distribution of food and clothing to indigent frontier settlers in 1874–75. Twin plagues of drought and grasshopper infestation destroyed crops throughout the Great Plains from Fort Worth, Texas, to Saint Paul, Minnesota, during the summer of 1874. The grasshoppers, declared a Kansas editor, "came upon us in great numbers, in untold millions, in clouds upon clouds, until their fluttering wings looked like a sweeping snowstorm in the heavens, until their dark bodies covered everything green upon the earth." Sherman, who was visiting with Pope at Fort Leavenworth in May 1875, wrote Sheridan that the fort was "being literally devoured by the Grasshoppers."[23]

General Ord, at Omaha, was especially moved by the plight of the destitute settlers, many of whom were newly arrived and had not been able to harvest a crop. In response to a barrage of letters from Ord during the fall of 1874, President Grant authorized the distribution of surplus army clothing to the settlers. Throughout the winter of 1874–75 the army gave out more than sixteen thousand coats, over twenty thousand pairs of boots and shoes, over eight thousand blankets, and thousands of other items of clothing to the needy in western Kansas, Nebraska, Dakota, and Minnesota.[24]

What the settlers really needed, however, was food. Even after the distribution of clothing was agreed to by the president, General Ord continued to press for permission to distribute army rations to the starving settlers. Sheridan, who had distributed army rations to both needy displaced white settlers and to Indians during the 1868–69 Indian war, now decided that such direct federal relief measures would "compromise the Government." He claimed that if further aid in the form of army rations were offered to the settlers, they were likely to exaggerate their plight in order to bilk the federal government of free food.[25]

Fortunately for the hard-pressed settlers on the plains, Sheridan's views did not prevail. A rising chorus of pleas for assistance from western soldiers, farmers, and politicians led Congress to appropriate $150,000 to enable army officers to distribute food and clothing to the needy on the frontier. On February 12, 1875, the War Department instructed the commanders of the Departments of the Missouri, Platte, and Dakota to designate officers to draw up a roll of citizens who qualified for federal relief and to distribute army rations to them. Betweeen February and August 1875, army officers gave away 1,957,108 rations to 107,535 citizens in Kansas, Colorado, Nebraska, Iowa, Dakota, and Minnesota.[26]

A more traditional and less controversial duty was exploration. While the heroic age of the army explorers, such as Long, Pike, and Frémont, was over, the exploration and surveying of uncharted regions remained an important military duty throughout most of Sheridan's years in Chicago. The last blank spaces on the Division of the Missouri maps were filled in by military officers during this period, providing interested easterners with details of marvels of nature as well as descriptions of the economic potential of the new lands.

Northwestern Wyoming, for example, was the focus of much of Sheridan's interest. While on a May 1870 inspection tour of military posts in Utah and Montana, Sheridan heard marvelous tales from an old mountain man of the natural wonders of the region where the Yellowstone River originated. Wild stories of a hellish land of mud volcanoes, steam geysers, and petrified forests had been circulating for years on the frontier, but had generally been dismissed as flights of fancy. The tale, however, fascinated Sheridan, and when he reached Helena, Montana, he sought out confirmation of the story. Three respected citizens of Diamond City, forty miles south of Helena, had explored a portion of the Yellowstone country in the fall of 1869, and their descriptions of natural wonders matched the stories of Sheridan's chance acquaintance.

At Helena, Sheridan found several leading citizens eager to explore this unknown country. The general extended his support to this enterprise and authorized an escort of one officer and five men from Fort Ellis to accompany the civilians. If this party, led by Henry D. Washburn, the surveyor general of Montana, and Nathaniel P. Langford of Helena, supported the tales of Yellowstone's marvels, Sheridan planned to send a larger military expedition the next year to examine the region.[27]

The Washburn-Langford expedition confirmed the incredible tales of a wilderness land so diverse as to encompass all the lush beauties of Eden alongside bizarre thermal marvels straight out of hell. Lieutenant Gustavus C. Doane, who led the military escort, wrote a detailed report that was published by the government and had quite an impact on Congress. Langford and Washburn, who appreciated the tourist bonanza to be derived from careful exploitation of Yellowstone, wrote articles, gave lectures, and urged Congress to designate the region a national park. Congress responded by authorizing a major expedition under Ferdinand Hayden, the famed geologist, who headed up the Department of Interior's geological survey of the territories.[28]

Sheridan, undeterred by the congressional backing of the Hayden expedition, proceeded with his own plans for the military exploration of Yellowstone. Meeting with Captain John W. Barlow, chief engineer officer for the Division of the Missouri, and Captain David P. Heap, engineer officer for the Department of Dakota, at division headquarters, he mapped out a six-week reconnaissance of the region. The officers would travel through Yellowstone in conjunction with the Hayden expedition in order to take advantage of the troop of the Second Cavalry provided as escort for the civilians, but the military expedition would operate independently. In contrast to the numerous members of Hayden's party, Captains Barlow and Heap would have but six soldiers and six civilian employees.[29]

Barlow and Heap followed essentially the same route as Hayden's party, but the soldiers made a much more extensive survey of the country to the south of Yellowstone Lake. While in that region

Barlow thoughtfully christened a 10,308 foot peak just west of Heart Lake as Mount Sheridan. Barlow returned to division headquarters with a mass of field notes, meteorological and topographical data, astronomic observations, and some two hundred photographs, just in time to have it all lost in the great Chicago fire of October 1871. Luckily, Heap had taken enough of their notes to his Saint Paul office so that the army was able to construct the first accurate map of the once-mysterious region. The map was far superior to those prepared by Hayden, but the military expedition remained in the shadow of the better-publicized and more elaborate civilian enterprise. Still, Sheridan's expedition made a substantial contribution to knowledge, and its report undoubtedly aided in persuading Congress to establish the Yellowstone region as a national park in 1872.[30]

Three other military expeditions explored northwestern Wyoming. In the summer of 1873 Captain William Jones trekked north from Fort Bridger, Wyoming, to survey a route from the line of the Union Pacific Railroad to the national park. Jones mapped two passes through the Absoraka Range: Two Oceans Pass, between the park and Jackson Hole; and Togwotee Pass, into the Wind River Valley.

A military road was planned to follow Jones's trail from the Union Pacific railroad to Fort Ellis, Montana, via Yellowstone Lake. The citizens of Montana, isolated as they were from rail transportation, strongly advocated a military road, but Sheridan crushed their hopes. Although pleased with Jones's expedition, he opposed the road. "If the Government desires to make appropriations for the benefit of the mining population at Atlantic City," declared Sheridan, "I have no objections; but I am not prepared to give even a shadow of support to anything so absurd as the military necessity for such a road."[31]

In August 1875 Captain William Ludlow led a small party that included the famous scout Charley Reynolds and the soon-to-be-famous scientist and author George Bird Grinnell into the park on a routine reconnaissance. As a consequence of their visit both Ludlow and Grinnell championed the cause of military control of the park to prevent vandalism and the slaughter of wildlife. A year after Ludlow's expedition Sheridan ordered Lieutenant Doane to explore the Snake River from Yellowstone Lake to the Columbia River. Unfortunately, Doane was recalled for service with his regiment before his small company could cover much more territory than had already been explored.[32]

Despite his fascination with the region that was to become Yellowstone National Park, much of Sheridan's attention was drawn to the northeast, in the Yellowstone River Valley. The Sioux treaty of 1868 designated most of this area as "unceded Indian Territory," which Sheridan interpreted to mean that the Sioux had the right to hunt there but did not own the land. He believed the region to be of great strategic importance in the struggle with the Sioux and thought that once the Indians were cleared from the valley, it would be of significant economic importance to the West. As a result he sent out three small reconnaissance parties.

In March 1873 Sheridan ordered George Forsyth to explore the Yellowstone River from Fort Buford to the mouth of the Powder River and to identify a suitable site on the river for a military supply depot in anticipation of Colonel David Stanley's summer expedition escorting railroad survey parties. Forsyth was told to make a thorough sounding of the Yellowstone River channel, carefully pinpoint all dangerous rapids, and fully report on the Yellowstone Valley, "especially in reference to timber and soil, etc." Forsyth proceeded to Fort Abraham Lincoln in May and enlisted Captain Grant Marsh, acknowledged the best pilot on the western rivers, to take him up the Missouri to Fort Buford and then up the Yellowstone on the steamboat *Key West*. Forsyth also recruited Luther Kelly to serve as scout. Kelly, later to win the sobriquet of Yellowstone Kelly, was familiar with some of the country through which they traveled and provided Forsyth with information known by few men. Marsh piloted the *Key West* as far as Wolf Rapids, about three miles below the mouth of Powder River, with a good spot for the supply depot located along the way at Glendive Creek. Forsyth reported to Sheridan that the Yellowstone River was "a better stream to navigate than the Upper Missouri above Buford," with the Wolf Rapids easily navigable during the spring flood period, and the country rich.[33]

Sheridan ordered further exploration of the Yellowstone River in May 1875 for the purpose of locating sites for two forts and ascertaining the navigability of the river. James Forsyth and Fred Grant were dispatched from Chicago with orders to examine not only the Yellowstone River but also its tributaries, the Tongue, Rosebud, and

Big Horn. This time Grant Marsh piloted the steamer *Josephine*, with Charley Reynolds along as guide. Marsh managed to ease the *Josephine* through some particularly treacherous rapids until, about two miles east of present Billings, Montana, the steamer turned back. Forsyth and Grant recommended sites at the mouths of the Tongue and Big Horn Rivers for forts, submitted a detailed report on river navigation, and reported glowingly on the prospects of the Yellowstone Valley for white settlement.[34]

The 1874 Black Hills expedition was certainly the most impressive military exploring party ordered out by Sheridan. Lieutenant Colonel Custer, who Sheridan felt "especially fitted for such an undertaking," assembled ten companies of the Seventh Cavalry, two infantry companies, three Gatling guns, and a three-inch Rodman cannon in order to make a peaceful reconnaissance of the relatively unknown South Dakota hills. As his personal representatives on the expedition, Sheridan dispatched two of his aides, Major George Forsyth, who commanded one of Custer's two cavalry battalions under his brevet rank of brigadier general, and Lieutenant (Brevet Lieutenant Colonel) Fred Grant.[35]

Attached to the Black Hills Expedition was a small corps of scientists consisting of Professor Newton H. Winchell, the state geologist of Minnesota, his assistants A. B. Donaldson, a botanist, and George Bird Grinnell, a Yale paleontologist, and Grinnell's assistant, Luther North, coleader of a Pawnee battalion of Indian scouts. Winchell and Donaldson went at the insistence of Custer and engineer officer William Ludlow: both officers wanted competent men along to search for gold. Grinnell and North, however, went because of Sheridan's interest in science. In May 1874 Sheridan invited an old acquaintance, Professor O. C. Marsh of Yale, to accompany Custer, but he declined and sent young Grinnell in his place.[36]

Sheridan attempted to aid scientific study within the limits of his command whenever it was feasible. In 1870 he had provided Marsh and a group of his students with a military escort, which included scouts Frank North and Bill Cody, to enable them to search for fossils along Nebraska's North Platte River. Marsh returned to the West in 1871, 1872, and 1873, and each time the army aided his scientific quests. When Marsh wanted to explore Nebraska's Niobrara River between Antelope Creek and Rapid Creek in the summer of 1873,

Sheridan ordered out a military scouting expedition for the sole purpose of helping the scientists. Sheridan requested the commander of Fort McPherson to provide horses and supplies for the visitors and "to show all the kindness possible to Professor Marsh & boys with him, & especially to give them every protection."[37]

Colonel Stanley's 1873 Yellowstone expedition, escorting surveyors for the Northern Pacific Railroad, was accompanied by a large contingent of scientists, who were provided by the army with rations, saddle horses, two spring wagons, and a special escort. On this occasion Sheridan worried about the safety of the scientists, since he feared there would be fighting. Although happy to "let them gather as many bugs as they may desire," he noted that "in the present expedition it is best to have as few deadheads as possible." Despite his reservations, he declared that "all officers and persons on the expedition are charged with the duty of contributing as much as may be in their power to aid in the collection and preservation of . . . knowledge."[38]

Sheridan consistently supported scientific causes. Through his support of Marsh's expeditions, the work of Stanley's scientists, the various expeditions into Yellowstone National Park, the sponsorship of Grinnell with the 1874 Black Hills expedition, and the four-hundred-man escort to geologist Walter Jenney's 1875 Black Hills expedition, Sheridan contributed more than his share to what one historian has labeled "the newer, more sophisticated academic approaches to scientific exploration in the West."[39]

Gold, not scientific exploration, however, haunted the public's mind in the summer of 1874 when they thought of Custer's Black Hills expedition. Custer quickly gave them just what they wanted when he sent scout Charley Reynolds on a daring ride southwest to Fort Laramie. Reynolds carried newspaper dispatches and Custer's report of the expedition, which contained a rather restrained account of the discovery of gold by miners with his command. From Laramie the telegraph carried the news of gold eastward. By the time Custer reached Fort Abraham Lincoln on August 30, the press was trumpeting a major gold strike in the Black Hills.[40]

The expedition's leading officers supported the exaggerated claims of gold that appeared in newspapers. Custer told a *Bismarck Tribune* reporter that the strike in the Black Hills would rival "the richest regions in Colorado." He added that "no country in the world is superior for stock growing" and that he personally would "recommend the extinguishment of the Indian title at the earliest moment practicable for military reasons."[41]

Sandy Forsyth, in a diary of the expedition that he forwarded to Sheridan for release to the press, extolled the Black Hills. "Taken all in all," Forsyth declared, "I do not know of a country west of the Missouri that begins to offer the inducement to stock and sheep growers that this will as soon as civilization shall push this way." When the *New York Times* asserted that the claims of gold were a promotional scheme cooked up by the Northern Pacific Railroad and western boomers, Forsyth quickly countered "that gold has been found in Custer's Gulch and that . . . it will be found in such quantities as to pay good average wages to industrious miners." Sheridan backed up his officers, declaring that he had "the utmost confidence in the statements of General Custer and General Forsyth."[42]

This active promotion of western lands by Sheridan and his loyal subordinates gave succor to the capitalists who were attempting to push through the Northern Pacific Railroad in the face of an economic depression, and to the business interests of various western communities who stood to profit by increased trade and settlement. These groups viewed themselves as natural allies in the exploitation of the West.[43]

There was, however, at least one notable military dissenter: Sheridan's old adversary, Colonel Hazen. Incensed by the glowing reports of rich agricultural land west of the 100th meridian put out by the owners of the Northern Pacific Railroad and their allies, Hazen published three stinging rejoinders. First in a long letter to the *New York Tribune* in 1874, then in an 1875 article in the *North American Review*, and finally in a booklet entitled *Our Barren Lands*, Hazen characterized the railroad builders as manipulative and deceitful men whose "scheme has been wicked beyond the power of words to express." Hazen declared the land proposed for the railroad route "not worth a penny an acre," and totally unfit for agriculture, its climate harsh, its water scarce, and its multitudinous insects ravenous.[44]

Nor did Hazen spare his military colleagues. To Custer's glowing reports of the agricultural potential of the Black Hills, Hazen retorted: "Where General Custer saw plenty of water, the [newspaper] correspondents noticed it was stagnant, and for 155 miles they saw not

169

a drop of it running. Where the General saw grass in abundance for his stock, the citizens noticed the country was all dried up, and the good grass only in occasional patches; and where the commander saw wood for fuel, the others noticed that it grew scraggily and sparsely, and only near water."[45]

Thomas Rosser, an engineer for the Northern Pacific Railroad, sent a copy of Hazen's first essay to Custer and requested that the lieutenant colonel of the Seventh Cavalry "render us a great service" by rebutting Hazen's contentions. Rosser had been Custer's classmate at West Point before joining the Confederate Army, and they remained warm friends. Custer promptly complied with Rosser's request, and his reply to Hazen was published in the *Minneapolis Tribune*. The officials of the Northern Pacific Railroad were delighted. A. B. Nettleton, trustees' agent for the line, thanked Custer profusely and promised to have the railroad publish Custer's reply so it could have wider circulation. Rosser and W. Milnor Roberts, chief engineer for the Northern Pacific line, also joined Custer in attacking Hazen in the press. (The close relationship of railroad and military men is further highlighted by the fact that Roberts's daughter was married to one of Custer's troop captains.) The trio of writers accused Hazen of ignorance and of blocking progress. The development of these lands by the Northern Pacific Railroad, Custer and friends commented, would bring prosperity to the new settlers and the entire region.[46]

General Sherman, who was under no illusions concerning the agricultural potential of the northern plains, having once half seriously suggested that Fort Abraham Lincoln be named "Fort Desolation or Damnation," also saw the railroad as a military necessity. "That Northern Pacific road is going to give you a great deal of trouble, and I expect to stand back and do the hollowing while you and younger men go in," Sherman warned Sheridan in 1872. "My notion is that all the way from the Missouri River about Stevenson till you enter Montana about Fort Ellis the land is miserable and the Indians will be hostile in an extreme degree. Yet I think our interest is to favor the undertaking of the Road, as it will help to bring the Indian problem to a final solution."[47] All his predictions proved resoundingly true, but the financial problems faced by the railroad forced Sherman to modify his statements on the value of the land. By 1877 he willingly suggested that there was "a great deal of valuable country along the line of the Northern Pacific railroad."

Like Sheridan, Sherman was most concerned with the hotly contested Yellowstone country, and he pressured the administration to help the railroad complete the line from Bismarck to the mouth of Powder River, which would cut 450 miles of river transport for the army. "I do not know a single enterprise in which the United States has more interest," Sherman told the secretary of war, "than in the extension of the Northern Pacific railroad from its present terminus at Bismarck to the mouth of Powder river on the Yellowstone."[48]

The military provided the railroaders with more than just verbal support. Military operations within the Division of the Missouri almost revolved around the needs of the Northern Pacific Railroad for several years. Sheridan, before submitting his financial requests for the 1873 fiscal year, requested a full report from the management of the Northern Pacific so that he might "be able to meet the wants of the company, by the concentration of the necessary number of troops to give adequate protection and in order to be able to get authority from Congress for the construction of one or more military posts between the crossing of the Missouri and the mouth of Powder River, on the line of the Railroad."[49]

Whole regiments were transferred to the Department of Dakota to protect railroad survey and construction parties. Requests for funds for new posts were made to accommodate the needs of the railroad. A slight change in the railroad's route could instantly alter expansion plans at already existent posts, as at Fort Buford in 1872.[50] The demands of the railroaders were so heavy and Sheridan's troops so few that other obligations had to be slighted in order to oblige the railroad. In 1872, for instance, Sheridan was unable to provide a substantial escort for the Department of the Interior's Hayden expedition to Yellowstone because of the demands of the Northern Pacific for survey party escorts.[51]

These railroad survey parties were no minor operation. Initial Northern Pacific Railroad survey parties, in 1870 and 1871, had only small escorts, but the signs of potentially hostile Indians encountered by these parties persuaded the army to provide larger escorts. The military escorts that accompanied survey parties from Fort Rice and Fort Ellis in 1872 clashed with hostile Sioux on several occasions, and even more troops were ordered to protect the railroadmen and overawe the Sioux. Accordingly, Sheridan moved the Seventh Cavalry from Reconstruction duty to the Department of Dakota to protect the 1873 survey party.[52]

The survey escort for 1873 consisted of 1,451 men and 80 officers under the command of Colonel David S. Stanley. Eight troops of the Seventh Cavalry, commanded by Custer, were detailed on the expedition, along with twenty companies of infantry. There were also 373 civilian employees to handle the 275 wagons, 2,321 mules and horses, and 600 cattle. Of the wagons used, 150 were newly constructed in Philadelphia for the expedition. With 254 six-mule wagon teams needed, it was necessary to purchase 900 mules in Saint Louis, as well as buy new harnesses for them. The task of coordinating these purchases and concentrating the material fell on Sheridan's headquarters staff. All funds for these purchases, as well as all expenses connected with the expedition, came from the Division of the Missouri and constituted a government subsidy for the railroad.[53]

This massive expedition, which successfully completed its summer's work, but not without clashing with the angry Sioux, demonstrated the most obvious example of the close cooperation between the army and the railroadmen in mapping the West. The Northern Pacific engineers received the results of the careful exploration of the Yellowstone River made by Sheridan's staff officers in 1873 and 1875 as well as the report of Sheridan's personal exploration of the Yellowstone region in 1877. Sharing information was clearly in the best interest of the nation, but the railroadmen viewed such action as special favors which they promised to repay. Rosser of the Northern Pacific was not shy about reminding George Forsyth that the railroad was "much gratified at the interest which the officers of the Army take in our enterprise, and should we prosper, we will not forget those who have been our friends."[54]

A tangible sign of the railroaders' gratitude was the liberal manner in which they dispensed valuable railroad passes to important army officers. Throughout 1873, for example, Sheridan held passes for a dozen western and midwestern railroads. These were often renewed. Railroads, and most notably the Northern Pacific, proffered Sheridan the use of a private car when he traveled on their line.[55] Sheridan unhesitatingly requested extra passes for staff members or friends, even if the anticipated travel was for pleasure. When Sheridan visited Wyoming in June 1877 for a personal reconnaissance of the Big

Horn Mountains and Yellowstone Basin, he wrote Sidney Dillon of the Union Pacific to request passes for his entire party, reminding the railroad president that the knowledge gained by the exploration "will be a valuable interest to the Union Pacific Railroad and any branches you may hereafter build to the north."[56] Likewise, when Sheridan and four friends wanted to go to southern Colorado in 1879 to inspect "this interesting country and for a little good fishing in the mountains of Northern New Mexico," he secured passes on the Kansas Pacific Railroad from Jay Gould.[57]

Sheridan never dreamed that by accepting favors he compromised his integrity. Honor meant everything to him, and although a pragmatist, he would not have sold himself for a fortune in gold, much less a railroad pass. The railroaders could not buy Sheridan's favor. They did not have to try, for the general dedicated himself both personally and professionally to their success. He was proud to "have been connected with the great development of the country west of the Mississippi river by protecting every interest so far as in my power, and in a fair and honorable way, without acquiring a single personal interest to mar or blur myself or my profession." Scandal never tainted Sheridan's name, nor did he become wealthy, though the opportunities to a man in his position were legion. "All I can leave my family is my name," he told a friend toward the end of his life, "and I will try and see that it is never tarnished."[58]

Sheridan helped the railroaders when it was in the public interest, but he quickly spurned their requests when he felt they were trying to exploit the army for financial gain without public purpose. Railroaders repeatedly requested troops to guard their lines. Sheridan, often obliged to turn them down, sometimes displayed an alarming lack of tactfulness, as when he rejected a plea from the Missouri, Kansas, Texas Railroad. He reminded railroad officials that five companies were already protecting the line, which he felt was "as much as we can do and as much as the road should ask," bluntly adding that "if the chief engineer will only prevent his hair from standing on end with fear or thrilling excitement everytime he hears a frontier story, he will be a happier and wiser man."[59]

Even Sheridan's old friend Grenville Dodge suffered the general's wrath when he attempted to exploit his army connections in behalf of his employer, the Texas and Pacific Railroad. Dodge attempted to use his influence to have the forts that guarded the northern frontier of Texas moved south onto the line of his railroad, supposedly to protect the line. When Sheridan discovered the scheme, he refused to move the forts, insisting that "to remove them to the Railroad would be equivalent to ordering the inhabitants of the whole line of frontier from Jacksboro to Fort Concho to pick up their traps and come down to the Railroad."[60] Sheridan refused to abandon the settlers of northern Texas in order to improve the financial position of the railroaders. "We are willing to give to Gen. Dodge full protection to his road and hope he will hurry it along," Sheridan declared, "but we refuse to be a party to create a doubt in the minds of the settlers that the posts will be removed so as to intimidate them from settling on lands which in that case may ultimately come into the hands of the railroad, or to other speculative monopolies."[61] The forts were not moved.

No friend was so dear, nor ally so valuable, that Sheridan would stay his disapproval if his actions contravened the public's interest or threatened honor. But Sheridan's attacks on the railroaders were infrequent, for he recognized them as "amongst our strongest allies in the march of civilization upon the frontier." Their contribution was enormous, and Sheridan was quick to praise the railroads for their potential to "add to the security of our advancing settlements and assist greatly in developing our country." Most important, he viewed them as "new factors that cannot be ignored in the settlement of the Indian question."[62]

Near the end of his memoir of plains Indian warfare, Captain Eugene F. Ware stated: "Soon the Union Pacific Railroad was built, and the Indian problem was solved."[63] This was no exaggeration, for the wave of whites brought by the railroads quickly pushed the Indian from his range, destroyed the game, and fenced the land. The greatly increased mobility afforded the army by the railroads spelled doom for the nomadic tribes. Not only did the railroad mean quicker movement of men and supplies, it also meant cheaper movement. Troops could be transported by rail for about five cents a mile as compared to twelve and a half cents by stagecoach. Savings on supply transport were equally dramatic. Nineteen cents a hundred pounds per hundred miles was the average rate by rail, as compared to $1.45 to $1.99 for an equal distance by freight wagon. During emergencies the railroaders were quick to provide special trains to move men and supplies for their army friends.[64]

Expansion of the roads also increased the morale at previously isolated army posts by expediting the import of luxuries and opening communication with the East. The railroads overthrew the tyranny of distance that had for so long plagued the soldier. This allowed the army to abandon forts for additional financial savings and eventually to end the long-standing policy of establishing many small outposts throughout the frontier. "The extension of the railroads," Sheridan wrote in 1882, "affords an opportunity for a much-needed concentration of the small companies of troops into larger garrisons where they can be more economically supplied and their discipline and efficiency increased—conditions hitherto almost impossible, when weak companies were scattered at numerous small military posts."[65]

This natural alliance between the railroad capitalists and the military was vividly displayed during the great railroad strikes of 1877. That year, in reaction to a deepening economic depression, some railroads cut wages and increased employee workloads. When, in July 1877, the Baltimore and Ohio Railroad decreased wages by 10 percent for the third time, forty furious laborers at Martinsburg, West Virginia, walked off the job and attempted to halt further movement on the rails. Workers in Maryland followed their example, and the strike spread westward to the major rail centers in Ohio, Indiana, Illinois, and Missouri. Railroad property was destroyed, and bands of strikers clashed with strikebreakers as well as with state and local police and militia forces. Governors, under intense pressure from railroad managers, called on President Hayes for federal troops to quell the riots. Hayes responded by placing federal troops under the direction of state officials to stamp out the "insurrection." Army officers were ordered to "protect public property, assist in executing United States civil process, or to display such strength as to serve the moral purpose of keeping the peace."[66]

Nearly a week after the inauguration of the strikes, work stopped in Chicago. On July 24 Colonel (Brevet Brigadier General) Richard C. Drum, assistant adjutant general for the Division of the Missouri, wired Washington that all the trunk lines into Chicago would be closed by strikers by nightfall. Sheridan was in the West on a reconnaissance of the Big Horn Mountains and Yellowstone Basin, so Colonel Drum took charge, working closely with local officials. Chicago Mayor Monroe Heath hesitated before calling for federal troops, fearing that their presence would aggravate the situation. Nevertheless, Secretary of War George McCrary directed that six companies of the Twenty-second Infantry, then en route from service in the Department of Dakota to new stations in the East, stop off in Chicago. McCrary felt that more troops were needed, and so ordered in several companies from Indian campaigning to meet what he perceived to be the greater threat. Eight infantry companies and three dismounted companies of the Fifth Cavalry arrived in Chicago from Omaha, and two companies of infantry from Fort Randall, Dakota Territory, soon joined them. Sheridan, upon reaching Bismarck on July 27, found a telegram from the War Department ordering him to return promptly to Chicago to take charge of troops facing the strikers. The Northern Pacific Railroad put a special train at the general's disposal, and two days later he reached Chicago.[67]

Sheridan found a quiet but tense city. On July 26 Chicago police had fought a fierce battle with five thousand rioters. Routed, the laborers dispersed, but throughout the day and night groups of workers clashed with detachments of police, mounted militia, and so-called special police, or goons, financed by the wealthier citizens under the leadership of Sheridan's friend, Marshall Field. The governor of Illinois had requested federal troops to "protect the law-abiding citizens in their rights," and Drum complied with instructions to place his soldiers under the governor's orders. By the evening of July 26 twelve companies of infantry were at the disposal of the forces arrayed against the strikers of Chicago and their working-class allies.[68]

But the blue-clad foot soldiers, many of them Germans and Irishmen fresh from campaigning in Wyoming and Montana against the Sioux, never clashed with their immigrant cousins in the streets of Chicago. Late on July 26 a mob on Kinzie Street stoned a detachment of the Twenty-second Infantry, but a single shot in the air dispersed the crowd. That proved to be the only confrontation of strikers and regulars; thereafter, the troops spent their time guarding the municipal gas and water works and government warehouses. A *Chicago Tribune* headline, declaring "The Fight with the Communists is at an

End," greeted Sheridan when he arrived to take charge of the troops. The general concluded that the peaceful status of the city was the direct result of the troops in Chicago. He kept them in the city until August 20, but they were never actively used, for the power of the strikers had been broken.[69]

Elsewhere in Sheridan's division Saint Louis also was the scene of serious labor disturbances, and General Pope distributed five hundred stands of small arms from the Rock Island arsenal to local officials. Colonel (Brevet Major General) Jefferson C. Davis, commanding fourteen companies and a battery of gatling guns in Saint Louis, aided local authorities on July 27 and 28 in seizing railyards and bridges from the strikers. By August 2 business in Saint Louis was back to normal, and Pope reported that his troops had done neither "too little nor too much" but that "the effect of their presence in giving confidence and moral support . . . was very manifest."[70]

Troops within Sheridan's division were not so blatantly employed as strikebreakers as were troops in the Division of the Atlantic, but their very presence was nevertheless an act of government strikebreaking. Under the guise of keeping order, the troopers aided management and prevented the workers from achieving their goals. Certainly Sheridan's officer corps, with its numerous contacts with railroad managers and business leaders, identified with the business community and could thus hardly act in the labor dispute as a neutral party. Some officers even went so far as to view the army's position as "a national police force for the maintenence of order" since "Communistic principles have struck their roots into the social soil of the nation."[71]

This class identification was vividly expressed in Captain George F. Price's 1885 essay on army-civilian relations, which won the best-essay prize from the Military Service Institution. Price warned the nation to sustain a strong standing army, since "ignorant suffrage and unrestricted emigration are now sowing the seeds of future peril." The captain of the Fifth Cavalry could see "the pernicious doctrines of communism" everywhere: "The criminal and ignorant classes are as powerful, man for man, at the polls as are the law-abiding and intelligent classes. The misguided voting of the former may threaten the public safety—perhaps jeopardize the existence of the nation. Would it not be better, therefore, if the country had an army of sufficient numbers ready to obey the summons of rightfull authority in case such an emergency should arize?" If only the "intelligent classes" would heed his call and keep the army strong, declared Price, they need have no fear, for "the vicious classes in every community cower before the strong arm of military power when it is uplifted in defence of life and property."[72]

The labor disturbances of 1877 led Sheridan to recommend that full regiments be permanently stationed at Saint Paul, Omaha, and Fort Leavenworth in order to meet any further labor agitation. While conceding that conditions on the frontier required the use of all the troops in the division, Sheridan warned his superiors that "there is no telling when greater troubles than the Indian difficulties on the plains may exist nearer home." Troops would be needed near urban centers to deal with the special problems created by "labor dissatisfaction" and "speedily suppress the agitation."[73]

As the years passed, Sheridan's concern over civil unrest increased. By the mid-1880s, with the Indians defeated and no foreign threat on the horizon, the general worried more about this internal threat. "It should be remembered that destructive explosives are easily made," he warned in 1884, "and that banks, United States subtreasuries, public buildings, and large mercantile houses can be readily demolished and the commerce of entire cities destroyed by infuriated people." If the army were properly prepared for domestic trouble, if the National Guard were continually upgraded, and "if both capital and labor will only be conservative," Sheridan hoped, upheaval in the cities could be avoided.[74]

Such sentiments won the son of an Irish laborer the affection and plaudits of the midwestern capitalists. They could see in Sheridan a man who would defend their interests. In 1883, when he was transferred to Washington to assume command of the army, the leading citizens of Chicago gave a dinner in his honor at the Commercial Club. J. W. Doane, the speaker of the evening and one of the society's prominent members, warmly recalled how "when the Communist riots (so destructive to other places) threatened Chicago, the general, by making a rapid journey of 1,000 miles, by appearing quickly upon the scene, and by his wise and decisive action, rescued us . . . from what might have been a public misfortune of no ordinary kind." "Believe me, general," he concluded, "a grateful people will embalm your memory in their innermost hearts."[75]

Sheridan had come a long way from his humble origins, and any early working class identification had vanished in the smoke of a hundred battles, the blinding glory of heady honors, and the self-serving friendship of the great in business and politics.

CHAPTER 8

Forming Military Indian Policy: "The Only Good Indian Is a Dead Indian"

Nothing is so closely identified with Phil Sheridan's western career as the infamous remark that "the only good Indian is a dead Indian." It has the ring of typical Sheridan rhetoric. His enemies used it against him during his lifetime, and historians have repeated it as an example of military myopia and viciousness. According to Mike Sheridan, the statement was attributed to the general by a Montana acquaintance during the Piegan controversy of 1870. But Captain Charles Nordstrom, Tenth Cavalry, claimed that Sheridan uttered the famous remark in his presence at Fort Cobb in January 1869. According to Nordstrom, the Comanche leader Toch-a-way had approached Sheridan, striking his chest and declaring, "Me, Toch-a-way; me good Injun." To which Sheridan gave a "quizzical smile" and replied, "The only good Indians I ever saw were dead." That Sheridan repeatedly denied ever making such a statement has had little impact on his image as a bigot and Indian hater. "The only good Indian is a dead Indian" became synonymous with Sheridan's Indian policy.[1]

Sheridan agreed with the so-called friends of the Indian that the ultimate goal of the government's Indian policy should be the conversion of the nomadic tribes from their old culture to an agricultural way of life built around mainstream American white culture. He disagreed with them, however, on the means to achieve this end. Sheridan regarded all Indians as savages, with "only one profession, that of arms, and every one of them belongs to it, and they never can resist the natural desire to join in a fight if it happens to be in their vicinity."[2] To curb this "natural inclination" to war, the Indians had to be severely punished after every crime. Sheridan liked to make the point that "an attempt has been made to control the Indians, a wild and savage people, by moral suasion, while we all know that the most stringent laws have to be enacted for the government of civilized white people."[3] His oft-repeated maxim on Indian affairs, according to Daniel Drennan, was "protection for the good, punishment for the bad."[4]

Sheridan agreed with the reservation policy. He was convinced that contact between the two races should be avoided for the benefit of each, but he disagreed with what he viewed as overly mild treatment accorded the reservation tribes. "I have the interest of the Indian at heart as much as anyone, and sympathize with his fading out race," Sheridan told his superiors, "but many years of experiences have taught me that to civilize and Christianize the wild Indian it is not only necessary to put him on Reservations but it is also necessary to exercise some strong authority over him."[5] Sheridan believed that such firm control could be exercised only by the army and repeatedly recommended, along with almost all his military colleagues, that control of Indian affairs be transferred from the Department of the Interior to the War Department, where it had resided until 1849. He held the employees of the Department of the Interior's Indian Bureau in contempt, feeling that "the admirable system of civilizing and providing for the wild tribes is constantly being thrown into chaos by the impracticable, unbusinesslike actions of some of the men engaged in carrying it out."[6] The obvious failings of the Indian Bureau, some caused by corruption and others by an overdose of humanitarian zeal, could be rectified by the use of army officers as Indian agents and by the stationing of military contingents on the reservations.

Sheridan argued that transfer would result in a savings in both lives and money. Repeatedly in testimony on this issue he emphasized that the army could better control the Indians because of the great moral force that officers had over the warriors. He contended that the western army officers' long experience with the tribes made them far better candidates for such service than the political hacks and church missionaries who worked for the Indian Bureau. With the military on the ground at the reservations, further Indian outbreaks could be halted before they began. The general failed to mention in his many arguments for transfer that it would provide employment for the hundreds of army officers facing displacement through reductions in the military establishment. Although this was certainly not the only reason he supported transfer, Sheridan's concern over army reductions influenced his position.

On firmer ground when he declared that transfer could save the government money, Sheridan wrote the chairman of the House Committee on Military Affairs, "It is my belief that the present expenses of the government in lasting care of the Indians would be reduced at least one third by the transfer." Sheridan held that "the army is very perfect in its administration and organization with carefully systematized machinery to promptly or economically carry out its promises to the various tribes of Indians."[7] The transfer would lower the cost of the Indian service by several million dollars, Sheridan contended, and save the army $3,500,000 a year in the matter of transportation and forts because it would enable military consolidation. Further savings would result, the general declared, because the Indians would be more honorably dealt with by army officers as a result of more regular habits of doing business and greater penalties for malfeasance than existed in the Indian Bureau. Sheridan foresaw a golden age of Indian administration, where the tribes would no longer be cheated and the government no longer robbed, if only Congress would authorize transfer of Indian affairs to the army. Several congressional attempts to pass a transfer bill succumbed to a coalition of politicians worried over the loss of patronage and humanitarians concerned over ruthless army officers. The best chance the army ever had of taking complete control over Indian affairs came in 1870 with the transfer rider attached to the army appropriation bill, but the actions of Sheridan and his officers in the field destroyed the opportunity for passage.[8]

Sheridan's primary concern, however, was not with the treatment of Indians on the reservations, but rather with the causes of the Indian wars. He identified two distinct causal factors leading to conflict. The first was inevitable and would have occurred no matter what policy the government might have adopted. "We took away their country and their means of support," the general commented, "broke up their mode of living, their habits of life, introduced disease and decay among them, and it was for this and against this they made war. Could any one expect less?" Ever the pragmatist, he made no moral judgment on this dispossession, but was content to admit that "we could not deprive these primitive people of their homes, where they had lived in barbarous contentment for centuries, without war."[9] The responsibility for the second cause of conflict, the failure of the reservation system adequately to feed and clothe the Indians, Sheridan laid squarely on the government. With rare insight, he came to view the reservation Indian as truly tragic: "After he has lost his country, and finds himself compelled to remain on reservations, his limits circumscribed, his opportunities of hunting abridged, his game disappearing, sickness in his lodge from change of life and food, and insufficiency of the latter, and this irregularly supplied, and the reflection coming to him of what he was, and what he now is, and pinched by hunger, creates a feeling of dissatisfaction which . . . starts him on the war-path again."[10]

Sheridan chided Congress over miserly appropriations for Indian subsistence and reminded the officials that all the county between the Missouri River and the Rocky Mountains had been recently wrested from the Indians and taken over by miners, ranchers, and farmers who reaped millions from the land. It seemed that "such beneficial results as these should induce Congress to furnish the poor people from whom this country had been taken with sufficient food to enable them to live without suffering the pangs of hunger." Little wonder that the Indians fought; Sheridan could easily imagine "how exasperating it must be to a warrior to find himself limited to a meager ration of Texas beef and to see his women and children suffering for food before his eyes."[11] Only "'kind treatment," he believed, "administered with steadiness and justice, would relieve our Western frontier of all its appalling horrors arising from Indian outbreaks," while at the same time with such treatment "the Indian can be redeemed and made self-supporting."[12] Such a call for justice was not unusual in late-nineteenth-century America, but it may well have surprised many who unfairly regarded Sheridan as an advocate of Indian extermination.

Sheridan viewed his troops as playing a dual role in regard to the reservation Indians. The troops would first compel the Indians to move to the reservation and then keep them from leaving. But Sheridan also felt that the reservation Indian could "only be protected in his rights while there by the troops keeping off the emigrants who encrouch on his land."[13] Sheridan often deployed his forces to protect the Indian reserves from white invasion. Sometimes, as with the Black Hills gold rush of 1874–75, his heart was not in the protection of the Indians' rights, but on other occasions, such as the white invasion of the Ute reservation in 1872–73, or the squatter invasion of the Indian Territory in 1879, he aggressively defended the tribes.[14]

The plight of tribes that had remained friendly to the whites was of special concern. Sheridan felt that "the government shamefully neglects in many cases the broken down & tractable Indians while spending large sums of money on those hostile & worthless." He realized that the logic, or illogic, of the government's policy was not lost on the Indians, for it was "known to every hostile Indian & is one of the principle objections they have to adopting civilization & Christianity."[15] A conference in 1869 between Sheridan's old adversary Satanta and Colonel Benjamin Grierson validated this statement. To Grierson's demand that the Kiowas give up their profitable Texas raids and follow the path of the white man, Satanta replied that the Caddos and Wichitas, who were the friend of the white man, got nothing, while his tribe was fawned upon and courted, invited to councils, and given presents and annuities. "It is plain that Grierson is mad," declared Satanta in conclusion. "Let's keep what we have, and see how much more we can get."[16]

It would be a mistake, however, to view Sheridan as a consistent defender of Indian rights. Like most men, the sight of obvious injustice moved him. But the fact that he used his position to aid the oppressed Indian on occasion does not by any means make him a friend of the Indian. Sheridan, a man of his era, viewed the Indians as members of an inferior race that embraced a primitive culture. In war he felt them to be inordinately barbarous, and he attributed this to a natural, ingrained savageness. In his official capacity as division commander he saw the tribes as a Stone Age barrier to an inevitable progress resulting from the expansion of white, Christian civilization. Not only did he favor such progress, he proudly saw himself as its instrument.

What bothered Sheridan most about Indian warfare was not the morality or immorality of subjugating the tribes and taking their lands, but rather the lack of a firm national consensus on the righteousness of the conquest. During the Civil War his every action had been applauded by a grateful nation, even when he had waged war on civilian populations. But now he found himself sharply criticized for pursuing the same tactics against the Indians. The 1868–69 campaign on the southern plains had given Sheridan his first taste of public condemnation, and it wounded him deeply. In the years to come, the attacks, coming from many of the same people who had once praised him lavishly, would not subside.

Never able to fathom why so many opposed his methods of Indian campaigning, Sheridan believed that he had learned from the errors of previous campaigns, which had employed conventional military methods and failed. The army could not, he insisted, "successfully fight Indians on the principle of high-toned warfare; that is where the mistake had been." "In taking the offensive," he explained to Sherman in defense of his methods, "I have to select that season when I can catch the fiends; and if a village is attacked and women and children killed, the responsibility is not with the soldiers but with the people whose crimes necessitated the attack. During the war did any one hesitate to attack a village or town occupied by the enemy because women or children were within its limits? Did we cease to throw shells into Vicksburg or Atlanta because women and children were there?"[17]

Sheridan always contended that his soldiers had no desire to kill Indians. The soldiers, he asserted, were "the only good, practical friends the Indians have."[18] His straightforward, blunt approach to the Indians—that punishment should follow crime and that they must promptly conform to the government's wishes or be destroyed—was in many ways no worse than the slow cultural strangulation that the Indians' humanitarian friends had in mind for the tribes. Sheridan's position was at least made clear to the Indians.

It was a no-win situation for Sheridan. "We cannot avoid being abused by one side or the other," he mused in 1870. "If we allow the defenseless people on the frontier to be scalped and ravished, we are burnt in effigy and execrated as soulless monsters, insensible to the sufferings of humanity. If the Indian is punished to give security to these people, we are the same soulless monsters from the other side." Sheridan consciously, even combatively, threw in his lot with the settlers who resided on the extended frontier line encompassed by his military division. Soon after assuming division command, he made his position clear to his eastern critics:

My duties are to protect these people [settlers]. I have nothing to do with Indians but in this connection. There is scarcely a day in which I do not receive the most heart rendering appeals to save settlers . . . and I am forced to the alternative of choosing whether I shall regard their appeals or allow them to be butchered in order to save myself from the hue and cry of the people who know not the Indians and whose families have not the fear, morning, noon, and night, of being ravished and scalped by them. The wife of the man at the center of wealth and civilization and refinement is not more dear to him than is the wife of the pioneer of the frontier. I have no hesitation in making my choice. I am going to stand by the people over whom I am placed and give them what protection I can.[19]

Such sentiments endeared Sheridan to the westerners, who soon came to regard him as their special advocate. Only a simple choice existed: "Shall we Williampennize or Sheridanize the Indians?" asked the *Platte Journal* of Columbus, Nebraska, in 1870. An angry Texan provided an answer in an 1870 letter to the *Chicago Tribune*: "Give us Phil Sheridan and send Philanthropy to the devil!"[20] But Indiana's Democratic Congressman Daniel Voorhees, the Tall Sycamore of the Wabash, spoke for many in the East when he rose in the House to denounce the "curious spectacle" of President Grant "upon the one hand welcoming his Indian agents in their peaceful garments and broadbrims coming to tell him what they have done as missionaries of a gospel of peace and of a beneficent Government, and upon the other hand welcoming this man, General Sheridan, stained with the blood of innocent women and children!"[21]

Sheridan, as division commander, was first plagued by this lack of national consensus when prosecuting a campaign against the Piegans, a faction of the Blackfeet tribe, early in 1870. Hostility between the Piegans and the expanding white settlements of northern Montana had been in progress before Sheridan assumed his position as division commander, and seems to have been caused by lawless elements prevalent among both races. The willingness of employees of the Hudson's Bay Company, across the nearby Canadian border, to purchase goods and horses stolen by the Indians and the presence of a flourishing liquor and arms trade with the Indians encouraged conflict between the races. Indian dissatisfaction was further intensified by a smallpox epidemic in late 1869, which they attributed to the whites. Mountain Chief was the leader of the Piegan band most hostile to the

Lieutenant Colonel Alfred Sully, shown in this 1862 photograph as a brigadier general of Civil War volunteers, earned an excellent reputation as an Indian fighter battling the Florida Seminoles in the 1840s and the Minnesota Sioux from 1863 to 1865. But the genial Sully did not possess the aggressive spirit that Sheridan demanded of his officers and was distrusted by his commander. (*Minnesota Historical Society*)

whites, but the reported depredations were sporadic and related more to the lawless actions of a few malcontents than to the organized resistance of any band of Piegans.[22]

As Sheridan attempted to clarify the confused situation in Montana, his efforts were hampered by conflict between the two ranking officers in the field: Lieutenant Colonel Alfred Sully, serving as superintendent of Indian affairs in Montana, and Colonel (Brevet Brigadier General) Philippe Régis de Trobriand, commander of the Military District of Montana. Sully, of course, had served under Sheridan on the southern plains and had incurred the lieutenant general's wrath. Sully's temporary assignment to the Indian Bureau further alienated him from Sheridan, for since his squabbles with Hazen and the bureau in 1868, the general distrusted all those connected with it. Sherman shared Sheridan's doubts about Sully's loyalties and warned his friend to place his faith in de Trobriand because Sully was "apt to identify himself with the people rather than with the troops."[23] Colonel de Trobriand, a naturalized citizen born in France who had volunteered at the outbreak of the Civil War and risen to division command in the Army of the Potomac, had served since 1867 on the northern plains. Although not as experienced with Indians as Sully, his impressive Civil War record gave him a greater reputation as a soldier. He was highly regarded in military circles as an intelligent officer of great integrity.[24]

The dispute between Sully and de Trobriand centered on the condition of Indian affairs. Not long after his arrival in Montana to assume his new duties as superintendent for the Indians, Sully requested more troops, claiming that the settlements might well be overrun. When no troops were forthcoming, he proposed to raise a force of three hundred civilian volunteers and lead them against the Piegans himself. He even sought permission to cross the line into Canada in pursuit of the suspected hostiles. Colonel de Trobriand, who felt the accounts of Indian depredations to be exaggerated, opposed the plan. De Trobriand willingly conceded that some Montana Indians, especially the Piegan band under Mountain Chief, had raided the white settlements, but his chief concern was that it would prove impossible to distinguish the guilty from the innocent. The number of raids, he felt, did not justify mounting a major campaign against all the Piegans. De Trobriand suspected that Sully was conspiring with business and mining interests in Montana, who were suffering from two years of economic depression, to bring in additional military forces in order to secure lucrative contracts and increase local civilian employment. De Trobriand believed Sully was especially close with certain Montana trading interests and went so far as to suggest to Sheridan that Sully was involved in smuggling whiskey into the territory and selling it to the Indians. Sheridan, deeply prejudiced against Sully as a result of the 1868 campaign, accepted de Trobriand's charges.[25]

Despite Sheridan's negative opinion of Sully, the Indian superintendant's reports forced him to proceed with military operations. The secretary of the interior, in response to Sully, demanded that Sherman and Sheridan chastise the hostile Piegans. Sherman, no more impressed with Sully's reports than Sheridan, had heard the clamor from Montana for troops before: "The same Indians, the same men, and the same stories," Sherman wearily characterized the situation.[26] Nevertheless, on November 4, 1869, Sherman authorized Sheridan to proceed with military operations. Sheridan called Major (Brevet Colonel) Eugene M. Baker of the Second Cavalry, then in Chicago en route to Fort Ellis, Montana, to division headquarters for a war council. Baker had served under Sheridan in the Shenandoah—he was breveted for gallantry at the Battle of Winchester—and had distinguished himself campaigning against Indians on the northern plains from 1866 to 1868. After the conference, Sheridan wired General Hancock, commanding the Department of Dakota, authorizing a strike against the Piegans and suggesting that Baker was "a most excellent man to be intrusted with any party you may see fit to send out."[27]

Even after his conference with Baker and his authorization to Hancock to proceed against the Indians, Sheridan retained nagging doubts about the veracity of Sully's reports of Piegan depredations. Two reports from de Trobriand, contradicting Sully's account of Indian hostilities, increased Sheridan's concern. The firestorm of public condemnation that had followed Custer's battle on the Washita had made the general more cautious. He was determined to avoid a slaughter of innocent Indians that might give credence to the arguments of the army's enemies. Therefore, he instructed his division inspector general, Colonel (Brevet Major General) James A. Hardie, to proceed to Montana and investigate the situation. Hardie left Chicago on December 27, 1869, with broad powers to suspend all military operations in Montana "if there is any danger of Indians being molested who are friendly."[28]

Hardie reached Fort Shaw on January 7 and spent the next few days interviewing de Trobriand, Sully, Lieutenant William B. Pease, agent for the Blackfeet, and several others, both military and civilian, who had knowledge of the situation. To his amazement, Hardie found a complete reversal of opinion between Sully and de Trobriand. Since de Trobriand's last communication with division headquarters, bands of Piegans and Bloods had moved south of the Canadian line into camp on the Marias River. The colonel had not expected their return before the end of January or February and had thus opposed military operations until he could be sure of bagging the guilty warriors. The movement onto the Marias had provided just such an opportunity, for Mountain Chief's band was among those encamped near the river. De Trobriand felt confident that by employing competent scouts he could isolate Mountain Chief's camp from the friendly Piegans and destroy it. Sully, whose reports of Indian hostilities had precipitated the crisis, now urged restraint until he could negotiate further with the Piegans. Hardie found Sully especially concerned that military operations might jeopardize the operations of the Northwest Fur Company. The inspector general puzzled over the fact that Sully had been anxious for war when he thought the military command might be his, but now opposed it when it became clear to him that others would take the field. Hardie wired the facts, as he saw them, to Sheridan on January 13, throwing his full support behind de Trobriand's plan.[29]

Sheridan's reply was prompt and terse: "If the lives and property of the citizens of Montana can best be protected by striking Mountain Chief's band, I want them struck. Tell Baker to strike them hard."[30]

Major Baker departed Fort Ellis on January 6, 1870, with two companies of the Second Cavalry and marched north to Fort Shaw, where two companies of infantry, one of them mounted, joined his command. Two scouts, Joe Kipp and Joseph Cobell, also joined Baker's detachment at Fort Shaw. These two men, both intimately acquainted with the Piegans, were to lead Baker to Mountain Chief's village, directing the soldiers away from the camps of innocent Piegans and Bloods.

Near mid-morning on January 19, Baker led his detachment

out of the fort and north toward the Marias River. Late on January 22 a five-lodge Piegan camp was discovered and the occupants easily captured. They nervously declared bigger game to be six or seven miles downstream where the villages of Big Horn and Red Horn, hostile Piegan chiefs, were to be found.

After a forced march over broken terrain the soldiers discovered thirty-two Piegan lodges in the bottom land along the Marias River. Baker's men were concealed from the village by steep bluffs, and it was along this natural firing range that the major deployed his soldiers. The strict silence that Baker had ordered during this deployment was suddenly broken by scout Kipp, who came running toward the major shouting that he had recognized the village as belonging to Heavy Runner, a Piegan chief that Colonel de Trobriand had specifically ordered to be left alone. Baker, fearing his surprise attack would be thwarted, ordered Kipp arrested. The scout later claimed that Baker was drunk at the time.

Kipp had been heard in the village, and Chief Heavy Runner suddenly emerged from one of the lodges. Shouting and waving a sheet of paper—a safe conduct from the Indian Bureau—the chief ran directly toward the soldiers on the bluffs. There was a single shot, and he crumpled to the ground. Scout Joe Cobell later claimed to have fired the shot that killed Heavy Runner. He did so in order to divert the soldiers from attacking the camp of Mountain Chief, which he knew to be ten miles further downstream—he was married to Mountain Chief's sister. Cobell's desperate ploy worked; the whole line of soldiers opened fire as soon as Heavy Runner fell. It was a terrible and effective cross fire that poured into the helpless village, and after an hour of it Baker sent a mounted detachment into the camp to finish the job. By eleven o'clock the soldiers had possession of the camp and had rounded up 140 prisoners, mostly women and children. A hasty count revealed 173 dead Indians, 53 of whom (according to Baker) were women and children. Baker's casualties were one man killed and another suffering a broken leg from falling off his horse. Lieutenant Gustavus Doane, one of Sheridan's chief explorers, took a prominent part in the fight and characterized it as a complete slaughter.[31]

From his prisoners Baker learned of the location of Mountain Chief's village. Leaving Lieutenant Doane and his company to guard the prisoners and captured pony herd, Baker hurried downstream after the true goal of the expedition: the village of Mountain Chief. The Piegans, however, had been warned and had escaped north across the nearby Canadian line. Baker had to console himself with destroying the seven abandoned lodges of his elusive quarry. When he returned to the battle site, the major was informed that many of his prisoners were infected with smallpox. Baker set them at liberty, and by January 29 the victorious soldiers were back at Fort Shaw.[32]

A jubilant Colonel de Trobriand reported to his superiors that the expedition had been "a complete success, with most of the murderers, and marauders of last summer . . . killed." Sheridan received de Trobriand's initial report on January 29 and forwarded it to Sherman with a characteristically brash endorsement that "this will end Indian troubles in Montana." Upon receiving Sheridan's message, a more subdued Sherman warned his friend to "look out for the cries of those who think the Indians are so harmless, and obtain all possible evidence concerning the murders charged on them."[33]

Sherman's warning proved prophetic, for the outcry against the Marias slaughter was both quick and vociferous. The first to take up the pen in defense of the Piegans was Vincent Colyer, secretary to the Board of Indian Commmissioners. Colyer charged in a letter read in the House of Representatives that Baker's troops had killed but 15 warriors, the remainder of the 173 slain being noncombatants. Fifty of these noncombatants, claimed the outraged secretary, had been children under the age of twelve, many of whom "were in their parents' arms." Furthermore, Colyer claimed that the village had been defenseless because of a raging smallpox epidemic. Colyer's sources for this information were both army officers: Lieutenant William Pease, the Blackfeet agent headquartered at Fort Benton, and Lieutenant Colonel Sully.[34]

Outraged by Colyer's charges, Sheridan went at the secretary with the same fury that had blackened the Shenandoah Valley. "I see that Mr. Vincent Collyer [sic] is out again in a sensational letter," Sheridan wrote Sherman in a letter promptly made public. Sheridan slandered Colyer's reputation by accusing the secretary of "deceiving the kind-hearted public . . . to further the end of the old Indian ring, doubtless in whose interest he is writing." A grand conspiracy was forming in Sheridan's fertile imagination whereby "the old Indian ring

Colonel Philippe Régis de Trobriand served Sheridan in Montana during the Piegan troubles and later in the Louisiana crisis. Born near Tours, France, in 1816, he married a New York heiress and became a naturalized citizen just before the war began. His distinguished career with the Army of the Potomac won him high regard in military circles, which was further enhanced by his military writings after the war. (*Fort Laramie National Historic Site, National Park Service*)

193

has set itself to work to get possession of Indian affairs so that the treasury can be more successfully plundered."[35]

Self-restraint was hardly a Sheridan virtue, but in his attack on Colyer he outdid himself in unreasonable vituperation. As he had done in his defense of Custer's Washita battle, Sheridan trotted out Indian atrocity stories, rather salaciously dwelling upon their sexual nature. He claimed that "since 1862 at least 800 men, women and children have been murderd within the limits of my present command, in the most fiendish manner; the men usually scalped and mutilated, their ——— cut off and placed in their mouths; women ravished sometimes fifty and sixty times in succession, then killed and scalped, sticks stuck up their persons, before and after death." From his own experiences on the plains the general related woeful tales of white women taken captive by the Indians, presenting a poignant picture of innocents in the hands of brute savages. "I have myself conversed with one woman," Sheridan claimed, "who while some months gone in pregnancy was ravished over thirty times successively by different Indians, becoming insensible two or three times during this fearful ordeal; and each time on recovering consciousness mutely appealing for mercy, if not for herself, for her unborn child." Sheridan did not claim that these atrocities were the handiwork of the Montana Piegans, rather, he implied that the actions of one tribe of Indians (in this case the southern Cheyennes) would be repeated by all Indians. In his rhetoric the general lumped all Indians together as savages in order to sway the gullible minds of a nation raised on stories of dark and bloody deeds. In a remarkable example of logical gymnastics the general concluded that since Colyer had defended the Piegans, and since the Piegans were Indians, and since Indians committed such atrocities, then clearly "It would appear that Mr. Vincent Collyer [sic] wants this work to go on."[36]

Poor Colyer deserved better than an irrational personal attack from the army's second-ranking officer. He was a sincere humanitarian, a leader of the YMCA, former secretary to the United States Christian Commission during the Civil War, and member of the civilian United States Indian Commission, who felt that soldiers made fine policemen for the reservations, but poor civilizers. Sheridan's rantings must have reinforced that view, and undoubtedly further convinced Colyer's wide range of influential eastern friends that men like Sheridan should be the last ones to be entrusted with the future of the natives. Far from being a tool of the ever-unidentified Indian Ring, Colyer worked diligently to remove control of the reservations from the politicians and turn it over to the churches.[37]

Colyer issued a subdued public response to Sheridan, although he did note that the general "strikes out at me almost wildly as he did at the poor Piegans, and with about as much justice." Sheridan's logic on Colyer's support of Indian atrocities had naturally proven a puzzle to the secretary. Colyer gently lectured the general, advising him that "Because I pull aside the curtain and let the American people see what you call a 'great victory over the Indians,' it don't follow that we do not want the *men* who perpetrate the horrid crimes you portray with so much zest justly punished. Strike, if you must strike, the guilty—not the innocent."[38]

Sherman stood firmly behind his subordinates despite Colyer's charges. He soothed Sheridan, urging his excitable friend not to be "unhappy about Indian affairs." Sherman reminded Sheridan that there were "two classes of people, one demanding the utter extinction of the Indians, and the other full of love for their conversion to civilization and Christianity. Unfortunately the army stands between and gets the cuff from both sides." The best the army could do was to put forward a solid front to meet the attack of Colyer and his friends, for there was little hope of converting the humanitarians from their position. More concrete steps, however, could be taken to shore up the military position by purging backsliders from within the ranks, and that, Sherman assured Sheridan, would be the fate of Sully. Sherman reminded Sheridan that it had been Sully who had persuaded the Department of the Interior to request that the army punish the Piegans in the first place and that "these should now be shocked at the result of their own requisition and endeavor to cast blame on you and Colonel Baker is unfair. General Sully, by communicating by telegraph for the use of Mr. Collyer [*sic*] did an unofficerlike and wrong act, and this will in the end stand to his discredit."[39]

Sherman was enough of a realist to comprehend that the army did not have adequate information to mount an able refutation of Colyer's massacre charge. He complained to Sheridan that Baker's report of the Marias fight was insufficient, for "Colonel Baker should have reported more exactly the number, sex, and kind of Indians killed; and in view of the severe stricture in Congress on this act as one of horrible cruelty to women and children, I wish you would require Baker to report specifically on this point."[40]

On March 23, 1870, exactly two months after the Marias River fight, Baker submitted an estimate of Indian casualties to Sheridan. Baker briefly asserted that but 53 of the 173 Indian dead were women and children and that "every effort was made by officers and men to save the non-combatants." Most of Baker's report, however, consisted of a calculated attempt to discredit Sully. "The reports published in the Eastern papers, purporting to come from General Alfred Sully," declared Baker, "are wholly and maliciously false." The major demanded a full military inquiry into the campaign in order to clear himself and his men.[41]

Many in the nation were far from satisfied, and the army eventually paid a high price for Baker's victory. The *New York Times*, a supporter of Sheridan during the Washita controversy, changed its position completely. The newspaper supported Colyer's description of the Marias attack as a "sickening slaughter" and declared that Baker's own report only confirmed that characterization. The editors of the *New York Times* went on to demand that the control of Indian affairs be retained by the Department of the Interior rather than be turned over to the brutal militarists as recommended in a bill before Congress.[42]

Wendell Phillips, the famed Boston abolitionist now working for Indian rights, declared Sheridan's hands to be "foul with Indian blood." "I only know the names of three savages upon the Plains," Phillips trumpeted at a Reform League meeting, "Colonel Baker, General Custer, and at the head of all, General Sheridan."[43]

Lydia Maria Child scolded the general for subscribing to the theory that "the approved method of teaching red men not to commit murder is to slaughter their wives and children! . . . Shame on General Sheridan for perpetrating such outrages on a people because they were poor, and weak, and despised!" William Lloyd Garrison added his condemnation to the rising chorus by protesting the "terrible vindictiveness" of Sheridan's spirit.[44]

The most important of the humanitarian protests, a resolution in the spring of 1870 by a national convention of reformers meeting in New York and sponsored by the United States Indian Commission, condemned the Piegan massacre in the strongest terms and called on President Grant to recognize that the "present military policy is unwise, unjust, oppressive, extravagant, and incompatible with Christian civilization."[45]

The repercussions of the slaughter on Montana's far-away Marias River were felt not just among the nation's dedicated reformers, for the halls of Congress echoed with cries of outrage over the fate of the Piegans. Daniel Voorhees declared himself filled with horror that the army evidently "proposed to change our mode of warfare and smite not merely the warrior, but the woman and the babe in her arms." Illinois Congressman John Logan suddenly reversed his position on the transfer bill, declaring: "I have always believed the War Department to be the proper place for the Indian Bureau; but I went the other day and heard the history of the Piegan massacre, as reported by an Army Officer, and I say now to you Mr. Speaker, and to the country, that it made my blood run cold in my veins. It satisfied me; and I shall therefore move to strike out this section at the proper time and let the Indian Bureau remain where it is."[46]

The measure to transfer the control of Indian affairs from the Department of the Interior to the War Department had seemed near passage as a rider to the army appropriation bill until the controversy over the Piegans. Major Baker massacred the chances of the transfer measure on the same bloody day that he massacred the Piegans. The *Army and Navy Journal* bemoaned the fate of the transfer rider, noting that where once it had known wide support, it now "seems to have been stricken out by general consent, and it has no friends to say a word for it."[47]

Another army casualty of Baker's massacre was the policy of assigning military officers as Indian agents. When President Grant had formulated his Indian Peace Policy in 1869, he had asked the Quakers, chosen because of the antiwar stance they symbolized, to submit recommendations for Indian agents and superintendants from among their own ranks. The Quakers, however, were intent on beginning their new task on a fairly manageable scale and so only filled positions in the Central and Southern Superintendencies, comprising agencies in Nebraska, Kansas, and the Indian Territory. Army officers detailed for duty with the Indian Bureau filled the other Indian agency and superintendent positions. Congress, by the army appropriation bill of July 15, 1870, ended this practice by forbidding army officers to hold civilian appointments. The Piegan massacre provided the excuse, and the necessary votes, to remove the military Indian agents, but the hard core of opposition to the practice remained more concerned with lost patronage in the Indian Bureau than with dead Indians. Grant, however, frustrated their intent by extending the agency appointments to other denominations besides the Quaker. This, of course, gave his Indian policy an even greater antimilitary appearance and placed many of the reservations in the hands of men mistrustful of the army. The Indians were temporarily saved from the political spoilsmen, but the military officer corps was nevertheless denied essential employment during a period of repeated reduction.[48]

Phil Sheridan was loyal to a fault, and that was never more apparent than in his unwise defense of Major Baker. By his determination to support Baker, Sheridan sacrificed both justice for the Piegans and the best interest of the army. Instead of properly investigating the charges leveled against Baker, Sheridan lashed out at his critics in an irrational, and certainly nonpolitic, manner. As a result he discredited himself and the army with an influential segment of the population and assisted the army's enemies in defeating transfer and removing military Indian agents. All this was sacrificed in defense of morally reprehensible actions that were in disobedience of military orders.

De Trobriand had clearly specified in written orders that Baker was not to molest Heavy Runner's band, and yet the major, despite the warning from scout Kipp, destroyed that very group of Piegans. It can either be assumed that Baker was so anxious for glory that he was determined to destroy the largest village he could find, or that, as Kipp later charged, the major was so drunk that he ignored the warning. Baker, either willfully disobedient or incompetent, did not deserve to have his actions sustained. Despite the official support that he received from his superiors, the Marias massacre destroyed Baker's career. Thereafter known in army circles as Piegan Baker, he never rose above his 1869 rank of major and seems to have taken more and more to the bottle for solace. In August 1872, while escorting surveyors for the Northern Pacific Railroad, Baker's command was surprised in camp by a Sioux war party, but he was so drunk that he refused to acknowledge that a battle was in progress. The command was saved by the prompt action of other officers.[49] It was for such an officer that Sheridan sacrificed so much.

The massacre on the Marias clearly illustrated the complex

problems that dogged Sheridan throughout the Indian wars period, making it exceedingly difficult to punish hostile Indians while protecting friendly Indians. Despite the fact that Sheridan's officers were in complete control of both Indian and military affairs in Montana, there was still no centralized management or planning. Military authorities proved as incapable of working together as would military and civilian officials when authority over the Indians was taken away from the army. The failure of military control of the Indians in Montana glaringly contradicted Sheridan's arguments in favor of transfer.

The personal prejudices and petty cliques that so dominated Sheridan's officer corps were combined in Montana with divergent civilian interest groups. There was a sharp division between the wishes of the settler-miner white population and that segment of the white and mixed-blood population that derived a livelihood from the Indian trade. The settlers wished the Indians destroyed, while the traders wanted their business protected. This divergence of opinion led to personal and professional enmity between Colonel de Trobriand, representing the interests of the military and the settlers, and Lieutenant Colonel Sully, supporting the interests of the Indian Bureau and the traders. This clash resulted in conflicting reports, both before and after Baker's massacre, from the two ranking army officers in the field.

Such divisions, however, were not limited to the whites. The Piegans were also divided, with Heavy Runner representing the accommodationist, or peace, faction, and Mountain Chief advocating the traditionalist, or war, faction. That well-known hostiles like Big Horn and Red Horn were killed in Heavy Runner's village does not mean that the chief was insincere regarding peaceful accomodation with the whites. It simply indicates the decentralized nature of Piegan leadership and an understandable tendency toward racial solidarity in the face of the white onslaught. Essentially it reflects the same situation that Sheridan had confronted in 1868 when Custer destroyed Black Kettle's village. That Cheyenne village was a similar mixture of Indians representing both war and peace factions, although Black Kettle was well known as an advocate of accommodation.

The divisions between the military, Montana whites, and the Indians were also reflected in the actions of Baker's scouts, Kipp and Cobell, both of whom were engaged in the Indian trade. Kipp, a friend of Heavy Runner, would eventually marry the chief's daughter. Cobell was a friend of the hostile Mountain Chief and was married to his sister. The conflicting desires of Montana whites and Indians, combined with the personal ambition, or incompetence, of Major Baker, put Cobell in a position to save Mountain Chief's village by murdering Heavy Runner.

While Sheridan, representing the army, and Colyer, representing the reformers and the Board of Indian Commissioners, argued over the best way to bring the Indian into the mainstream of Anglo-Saxon culture, white and red men in the West settled personal, professional, and economic conflicts with guns. The situation on the Marias was not unique, but reflected the fact that the Indian wars were far more complicated than the clear-cut struggle between barbarism and civilization so hotly debated by Phil Sheridan and Vincent Colyer.

CHAPTER 9

Diplomacy at Home and Abroad

Although the limits of Sheridan's geographical command were clearly prescribed by the borders of the Division of the Missouri, his position as the nation's second-ranking army officer opened up a much larger field of operation. Despite his quick temper and blunt demeanor, the lieutenant general was called on to perform several missions of a diplomatic or political nature. Sheridan's close friendship with Grant made him an especially reliable agent for the president.

Throughout the spring of 1870, Prussia and France prepared for war. The ambitions of Napoleon III, who labored under the megalomania of his namesake though devoid of his talents, and of Count Otto von Bismarck, singlemindedly driven to unite the German states under the Prussian king, seemed certain to result in war. Sheridan, eager to study the conflict, was in Helena, Montana, when dispatches reached him declaring hostilities imminent. He hurried east to secure Grant's permission to observe the war. The president quickly approved, but requested that Sheridan stop to see him at Long Branch, New Jersey, before setting sail.

Grant wanted to know which army Sheridan planned to accompany, since the presence of the second-ranking military officer of the United States with one army or the other was an important diplomatic statement. Sheridan was adamant in choosing the German army, for he was confident it would prove to be victorious. Grant welcomed this choice for, like Sheridan, he held Napoleon III in contempt because of the Mexican intervention. The president wished Sheridan well, providing him with a letter of introduction describing the bearer as "one of the most skillful, brave and deserving soldiers developed by the great struggle through which the United States Government has just passed."[1]

Accompanied by James Forsyth, Sheridan joined the German army at Pont-à-Mousson on August 17, 1870, after first stopping in London, Brussels, and Berlin. His first experience with German efficiency was hardly glamorous; he and Forsyth were forced to travel in a hay wagon from a railroad station to German field headquarters. This minor blow to his dignity was forgotten when he met Bismarck and King William I. Sheridan was not accustomed to hobnobbing with royalty. He fretted over what uniform to wear—an undress uniform, minus sword, suggested the helpful Bismarck—and whether he should remove his cap when addressing the king or not—not if out-of-doors, Bismarck told him. Sheridan soon adjusted to this new environment, finding William I to be a cordial old gentleman of seventy-three and quite interested in how the Americans viewed the war. The king honored Sheridan by inviting him to accompany his personal head-quarters, and the general gratefully agreed. The American officer's modesty and simplicity charmed his hosts. Dr. Moritz Busch, longtime confidant to Bismarck, fondly remembered Sheridan as "a small, corpulent gentleman of about forty-five, with dark moustache and chin tuft, [who] spoke the purest Yankee dialect."[2]

Sheridan thus secured the best possible vantage point from which to observe the combat. He was also able to watch closely the Prussian high command, for numbered among his companions were William I, Bismarck, War Minister Albrecht von Roon, and Chief of Staff General Helmuth von Moltke. In this select company Sheridan witnessed the French defeats at Gravelotte, Beaumont, and Sedan, as well as Napoleon III's humiliating surrender on September 1, 1870.

At Gravelotte, on August 18, 1870, Sheridan's quick eye saved his German hosts from disaster. The day had gone well for the Germans, although their cavalry had been mismanaged by General von Steinmetz, suffering terribly as a result. Sheridan, already at ease with Bismarck, commented: "Your infantry is the best in the world; but it was wrong of your generals to advance their cavalry as they did." The chancellor agreed, grumbling that Steinmetz "was a spendthrift of blood."[3]

Despite the slaughter of the German cavalry it was soon considered safe for the Prussian king to move his headquarters from the village of Gravelotte to a high point to the northeast where he might observe the battle's progress. The hill selected for headquarters was open and exposed, but the French artillery had been quiet for some time, and the Germans were confident that their Krupps had destroyed the French guns. Sheridan did not share their confidence.

The impressive group that gathered on that wind-swept knoll included William I, wearing helmet, light-blue overcoat, and high boots and surrounded by a glittering array of staff officers and advisers—among them Bismarck, Moltke, and the king's nephew, General Frederick Charles, the famous Red Prince. The Germans were nearly all tall men, and their height and brilliant uniforms contrasted sharply with the stocky figure in faded blue who stood near them. With feet planted wide apart to steady himself, Sheridan slowly surveyed the battlefield with a long field glass. Spying French troops moving to the right of the advancing German columns, he realized that the French artillery would undoubtedly open up on the Germans to support this flanking movement. The king's position would soon be exposed to this fire.

Calling Bismarck aside, Sheridan advised him of the danger. Agreeing, Bismarck pleaded with the king to retire, but William steadfastly refused to budge. Within minutes two hundred French guns opened fire on the Germans, several shells exploding near the king's position. The royal entourage promptly withdrew, amidst many favorable comments on Sheridan's foresight. Bismarck was deeply impressed. "Sheridan had seen it from the beginning," he remarked. "I wish I had so quick an eye."[4]

During the campaign Sheridan came under fire on a number of other occasions. Twice German soldiers mistook him for a Frenchman, the design of the American uniform of that period having been greatly influenced by the French, and only the intervention of German officers saved him from rough handling, or worse. Even more dangerous was his rather foolhardy attempt to get a close-up view of some French rifle pits at Brie. He exposed himself to volleys from the entrenched Frenchmen, who seemed to take little notice of the design of his uniform. After extricating himself from this predicament—without seeing the rifle pits—he was quick to admit, "My hair was all on end, and I was about as badly scared as ever I had been in my life."[5]

Bismarck, who was the only member of the royal party who spoke fluent English, took a liking to his American guest, so that much of Sheridan's time with the Germans was spent in the company of the Iron Chancellor. They bunked together on occasion, messed together quite often (which, one morning, produced a minor foraging competition between the two—Sheridan producing some large sausages but Bismarck coming up with eggs and brandy, so that the contest ended as a tie), and shared the hazards of the battlefield, comparing notes on the fighting and generally enjoying the warm comradeship of the military camp. Sheridan's tales of life on the western frontier fascinated Bismarck, especially those related to hunting. Bismarck was also a great hunter, and a lively swapping of hunting yarns went on for hours over dinner and drinks. As the years passed, and Bismarck's fame reached even greater heights, the chancellor continued to inquire of visiting American dignitaries for news of his old friend. He was always quick to share his firm opinion that "that man has a great military head on his shoulders."[6]

By mid-October the war had settled into a siege as the French National Guard dug in around Paris, and the Germans, unwilling to waste lives in an assault on the city, waited for the French to run out of food. Although Napoleon III had surrendered, the French refused to concede defeat. French guerrillas made it dangerous for the Germans to let down their guard in the countryside. A debate began at the highest levels of the German command over how to deal with the guerrillas. Bismarck turned to Sheridan for advice.

Sheridan responded that the Germans had been too mild and humane and advised Bismarck to adopt the tactics he had so effectively employed in the Shenandoah and on the southern plains. "The proper strategy," he told the Prussian, "consists in the first place in inflicting as telling blows as possible upon the enemy's army, and then causing the inhabitants so much suffering that they must long for peace, and force their government to demand it. The people must be left nothing but their eyes to weep with over the war."[7]

Dr. Busch, who was present at the discussion between Sheridan and Bismarck, remarked that the American's ideas were "somewhat heartless . . . but perhaps worthy of consideration."[8] Bismarck embraced Sheridan's words wholeheartedly. He soon issued orders to burn any village to the ground, hanging all male inhabitants, where guerrilla acts were committed. To show mercy was "culpable laziness in killing," declared the chancellor. German reprisals against the French guerrillas soon reached levels of brutality worthy of a Sheridan campaign.[9]

Sheridan, bored by the relative inactivity of the siege of Paris, hurried off with Forsyth to explore the continent. They traveled from Brussels to Vienna to Budapest, dining with royalty and prime ministers all along the way.

At Constantinople Sheridan was disappointed that religious ceremonies made it impossible for him to meet the sultan, although his feelings were somewhat mollified when he was allowed to view the sultan's harem on parade. As if reviewing a foreign army the general noted the strengths—"now and then a pretty face"—and the weaknesses—"many were plump, even to corpulence . . . since with the Turk obesity is the chief element of comeliness"—of this female host. Sheridan and Forsyth must have looked particularly dashing that day, for the general clearly noticed that as the carriages carrying the women passed, "every now and then an occupant, unable or unwilling to repress her natural promptings, would indulge in a mild flirtation, making overtures by casting demure side-glances, throwing us coquettish kisses, or waving strings of amber beads with significant gestures, seeming to say: 'Why don't you follow?' " Sheridan's *Arabian Nights* fantasy soon ended, even though "the temptations to linger in Constantinople were many indeed."[10]

After quick tours of Greece, where King George and Queen Olga took special pains to entertain the Americans, and Italy, with King Victor Emmanuel II proving equally hospitable, it was back to Paris. Sheridan arrived just in time to witness the triumphant Germans march into the French capital on March 1, 1871. Sheridan found his friend Bismarck at Versailles, where the peace treaty had recently been signed and William I declared German emperor. Bismarck was in a grand mood, and Sheridan noted that "along with his towering strength of mind and body . . . he plainly showed his light-heartedness and gratification at success." Sheridan knew well the triumphal emotions that warmed the Iron Chancellor, for Bismarck's war aim had been the same that had directed Sheridan half a decade before—the unification of his nation. The war with France had welded the German states together in a compact which Sheridan felt "no power in Europe could disrupt."[11]

Sheridan did not have long to share in his friend's triumph, for a letter from Sherman reminded him that there were pressing duties at home. "The great game of war has dwindled down to the little game of politics," Sherman noted, "so that I doubt if it will afford you instruction or amusement."[12] Sheridan agreed, for he had seen enough of European war. He had not been impressed. As he confessed in a letter to Grant, "I . . . have had my imagination clipped, in seeing these battles, of many of the errors it had run into in its conceptions of what might be expected of the trained troops of Europe." Sheridan was particularly disgusted with the French, declaring that "all my boyhood fancies of the soldiers of the great Napoleon have been dissipated, or else the soldiers of the Little Corporal have lost their elan in the pampered parade soldiers of the Man of Destiny." The Prussians were more impressive, being "very good brave fellows, all young, scarcely a man over twenty-seven in the first levies," and possessors of that military spirit so admired by Sheridan whereby "they had gone into each battle with the determination to win." Still, Sheridan was satisfied to conclude, "There is nothing to be learned here professionally . . . [and] there is much, however, which Europeans could learn from us."[13] Even as good as the Germans were, Sheridan prophetically mused, "they would never know what real fighting was until they should meet in a popular war, American or British troops."[14]

Sheridan's chauvinism colored his opinion of European military might. When his ship, the *Russia*, docked in New York he was met by Custer, who was in the city on personal business. He gave his young friend a detailed account of the war. "Custer, I wish you had been with me," Sheridan declared. "Custer, you with that 3rd Division could have captured King William six times over."[15]

In his memoirs Sheridan devoted nearly a hundred pages to his observations during the Franco-Prussian War. This discourse is not uninteresting, but it is nevertheless revealing that he expends so much space on this episode while spending much less, or ignoring, events on the frontier in which he played a more important role. The excitement and uniqueness of this excusion abroad gave it greater importance in his mind than it merited.[16]

Upon his return home Sheridan had to hurry west, for a grand buffalo hunt on the plains had been organized in his absence by Mike Sheridan and Morris Asch. With the general acting as host, a distinguished party of business and civic leaders was to be treated to a taste, albeit a romanticized one, of frontier life. What better way to impress influential citizens with the role of the frontier army than to take them on a junket to the West? A few exciting days on the plains might well dispose important capitalists and newspapermen toward the army.

On the morning of September 20,1871, Sheridan gathered his notable company into a spacious palace car provided by the Northwestern Railroad. The hunters included two newspaper editors, James Gordon Bennett of the *New York Herald* and Charles L. Wilson of the *Chicago Evening Journal*; Anson Stager of Western Union; Leonard W. Jerome, New York financier and grandfather of Winston Churchill; Henry E. Davies, commander of one of Sheridan's cavalry divisions in the Shenandoah; Colonel (Brevet Major General) Daniel H. Rucker, assistant quartermaster general and Sheridan's future father-in-law; John Schuyler Crosby, late of the general's staff; and several prominent New York and Chicago businessmen.[17]

Upon reaching Fort McPherson, Nebraska, on September 22, the tourists were treated to five companies of the Fifth Cavalry, led by Major Carr, passing in review before Sheridan. These veterans of Summit Springs handsomely took the salute of their commander.[18]

Sheridan requested the services of a young scout who had won his admiration three years before during the southern plains campaign. He could hardly have made a more fortunate choice, for Bill Cody, already the star of a Ned Buntline newspaper serial, was developing the glossy image he eventually perfected on eastern stages. Henry Davies glowingly recalled how Buffalo Bill, mounted on a white charger, galloped into camp dressed in "light buckskin, trimmed along the seams with fringes of the same leather, his costume lighted by the crimson shirt worn under his open coat, a broad sombrero on his head." Davies and his friends agreed that Cody "realized to perfection the bold hunter and gallant sportsman of the plains."[19]

Cody was determined to put on a good show for Sheridan's guests. The general had secured Cody's appointment as chief of scouts for the Fifth Cavalry in 1868 and had made sure that the scout remained on the army payroll. Cody was eager to repay his debt. "I rose fresh and eager for the trip," Bill noted, "and as it was a nobby and high-toned outfit which I was to accompany, I determined to put on a little style myself."[20] So Buffalo Bill and Phil Sheridan busied themselves inventing the Wild West Show that autumn on the western plains.

Captain (Brevet Major) William H. Brown led a one-hundred-man Fifth Cavalry escort for the hunters, accompanied by sixteen wagons, including one loaded with ice, and three army ambulances for passengers and baggage. Wall tents were provided to house the tourists, their servants, and cooks.

Covering almost two hundred miles in ten days, the hunters left a trail of empty champagne bottles and animal carcasses from Fort McPherson to Fort Hays, Kansas. Over six hundred buffalo were slaughtered, along with hundreds of elk, antelope, and wild turkeys. Sheridan had brought an English greyhound back with him from Europe, and he delighted in the chase until an accident prematurely ended the dog's career.

Cody was such a success that Sheridan enlisted his services for an even larger hunt to come when the Russian Grand Duke Alexis, then en route to America, visited the plains. As the hunt ended, the *Salt Lake Tribune* wondered whether enough game would be left "for the Grand Duke Alexis when he takes a scurry over the hunting grounds."[21]

Reaching Fort Hays on October 1, the hunters bade a fond farewell to Cody and Captain Brown, and then sped off on the train to Chicago. They gathered together a final time on October 5 for an elegant dinner at the Chicago Club hosted by Anson Stager and then went their separate ways, brimful of good will for Phil Sheridan and his army.[22]

The general had no time to reflect on this public relations triumph, for planning of the hunt for the Russian grand duke was already in advanced stages when he returned to Chicago. The September junket had been an excellent practice run for the royal hunt. The Grand Duke Alexis, third son of the czar, was eager to visit the frontier and get a taste of western hunting and soldiering during his 1871–72 tour of the United States. The grand duke's party would be busy visiting major American cities until January 1872, so Sheridan still had plenty of time to make the necessary arrangements for a lavish hunt.[23]

But all thoughts of visiting royalty were suddenly swept away in the great conflagration that devastated Chicago and Sheridan's headquarters. Like most Chicago citizens, Sheridan paid little attention to the fire when it was first reported around nine o'clock Sunday evening, October 8. There had been thirty blazes in the preceding week, and only the previous evening four blocks on the west side had been consumed before the city's two hundred exhausted fire fighters could put out the flames. But there was no stopping the new fire, and from the O'Leary barn near Halsted and Twelfth streets it swept north and east, whipped into a frenzy by dry, thirty-mile-an-hour winds. Neither the wooden shanties of the wretched Irish slum, Conley's Patch, nor the elegant Palmer House and Grand Pacific hotels were spared; the fire was scrupulously egalitarian. From the first alarm, the great bell in the central courthouse clanged its warning until, at 2:00 A.M., it came toppling down as fire gutted the building. Across the street the building that harbored the headquarters of the military Division of the Missouri was also consumed by the flames.

Sheridan learned of the fire's devastation shortly before midnight. From his residence on the city's south side he hurried toward the corner of LaSalle and Washington streets, where division headquarters were located, but was stopped by intense flames several blocks southeast. He could see how rapidly the fire was spreading, high winds carrying fiery brands great distances through the air; so he set about attempting to pull together remnants of the harried fire department. Messages were also sent to his staff officers, several of whom had been burned out, ordering them to report to him on the south side fire line. By early Monday morning he was prepared to make a stand and, securing gunpowder, ordered the destruction of buildings at key points to form a fire break. The blowing up of buildings adjacent to the Wabash Avenue Methodist Church at Harrison and Wabash finally deflected the flames to the north so that, in the south side at least, the fire was checked. By late Monday afternoon the fire began to wane, and that evening, some twenty-seven hours after the first alarm, a welcome rain fell and extinguished the last flames.[24]

Chicago was devastated. A three-and-a-half-square-mile area was destroyed, with a property loss later estimated at $200,000,000. At least 250 were known dead; another 100,000 were homeless. Sheridan's headquarters were destroyed, along with most of his personal and professional papers. All military property had been lost, except for one express wagon and a few horses and mules. Among the horses that did not survive was a gray pacer that Sheridan had captured from a Confederate officer on Missionary Ridge and had ridden often on campaigns during the war.[25]

Widespread looting convinced many demoralized Chicagoans that anarchy was imminent, and on October 9 a delegation of citizens pleaded with Sheridan to take charge of the city. When word reached Sheridan that Mayor R. B. Mason was in full agreement with this sentiment, he agreed.[26] Sheridan immediately ordered two companies of infantry from Omaha and four more from Kansas to Chicago. This force, however, proved too small to allay the fears of Chicago's property owners, and so Sheridan, in consultation with city officials, organized a thousand-man regiment of volunteers to patrol the city. A prominent Chicagoan, Francis T. Sherman, a former general of volunteers who had commanded one of Sheridan's brigades in the charge up Missionary Ridge, was selected to command the regiment. The volunteers, called the Sheridan Guards, were on the streets by October 12, but Sheridan soon found "it difficult to make good guards of citizens," and requested four companies of infantry from Kentucky and two more from Nebraska.[27]

Relief operations were promptly undertaken. Sheridan soon had three hundred thousand rations and several thousand army tents and blankets ready for distribution to the needy. By the evening of October 10, thousands of men, women, and children were being fed and sheltered by the army. This would be no short-term relief project. Sheridan wrote President Grant explaining that "nearly all those made very poor will have to be cared for during the winter."[28] Government and army officials sustained Sheridan's actions. Sherman assured Sheridan of the government's support, and advised, "Use your power of relief to the maximum, giving away field blankets, overcoats, shoes & socks without stint. The U.S. Govt. can better afford this means of relief than any other body."[29]

The leading citizens of Chicago were deeply impressed by Sheridan's quick actions, but they also remained fearful of mob violence. So on October 11 another delegation approached Sheridan, this time to request that he "assume entire control of the city." This he properly refused to do, pointing out that Chicago's elected officials were entrusted with the operation of the city, but he did agree to assume all responsibility for the "peace and good order of the city," if the mayor would issue a proclamation to that effect. Mayor Mason consented and published a proclamation turning over all city police powers to the lieutenant general. Sheridan dictated the final paragraph of the proclamation, which declared his intent "to preserve the peace of the city without interfering with the functions of the city government."[30]

Sheridan's troops patrolled the streets as a visible sign of law and order. William Bross, publisher of the *Chicago Tribune*, was especially warmed: "I saw Sheridan's boys, with knapsack and musket, march proudly by. *Never did deeper emotions of joy over come me.* . . . Had it not been for General Sheridan's prompt, bold, and patriotic action, I verily believe what was left of the city would have been nearly, if not entirely, destroyed by the cutthroats and vagabonds who flocked here like vultures from every point of the compass."[31]

Not only "cutthroats and vagabonds" had reason to fear Sheridan; determined that no one should profit from the catastrophe, he took a dim view of profiteers of any stripe. When he was told that the proprietor of one of the few remaining hotels had raised his rates from $2.50 to $6.00 a day, Sheridan stormed into the establishment. He ejected the manager and put one of his officers in his place with orders to return the hotel rates to their prefire level.[32]

Just as affairs seemed to be under control, with Sheridan hailed everywhere as the savior of Chicago, an attempt to discredit the general was launched from a most unlikely source. Governor of Illinois John M. Palmer wrote a scathing letter to Mayor Mason on October 21, accusing him of illegally abdicating his authority to Sheridan when state militia were ready and able to restore order to Chicago. He further accused Sheridan of unconstitutional acts in raising Frank Sherman's volunteer regiment. Sheridan was shocked by Palmer's letter, for the governor was an old army comrade of the Tennessee campaigns. But times had changed. Palmer held a grudge against the West Point clique that ruled the army, feeling that it had discriminated against him during the war. Elected governor as a Republican in 1868, he promptly came out as a strong advocate of states' rights. Soon after his criticism of Sheridan's Chicago activities, Palmer allied himself with the anti-Grant faction of the Republican Party, and after the 1872 election he declared as a Democrat.[33]

Palmer spared no effort to discredit Sheridan. A prominent citizen, Thomas Grosvenor, got into an argument with one of Frank Sherman's volunteers and was killed on the evening of October 20. Palmer attempted to have Sheridan, Mayor Mason, Frank Sherman, and the volunteer indicted for murder by the Cook County grand jury. When Roscoe Conkling, the New York politician, heard of this, he promptly wired Sheridan that "should legal proceedings be set on foot against you I will come & defend you & all the just people of the state will be indignant at such an attempt to annoy you."[34] The Cook County grand jury must have been made up of "just people," for they were rightly indignant at Palmer's charge and threw it out of court. The governor, however, was not to be stilled and took the question of the constitutionality of Sheridan's use of federal troops in Chicago without first consulting the governor of the state to the Illinois Supreme Court. The court upheld the governor's position.[35]

Stung by Palmer's actions, Sheridan consoled himself that the governor's conduct was based "on the ground that my action here popularized the Army here and throughout the West, and he and other politicians thought it would be best to destroy this good opinion as much as possible by a very unjust attack on me."[36] The troops that so offended the governor departed for their western and southern posts on October 24, and on the same day Frank Sherman's volunteers disbanded. Sheridan could take solace, however, in the almost universal condemnation of Palmer by Americans everywhere, but most decidedly by the citizens of Chicago. They agreed with General Sherman, who lavishly praised Sheridan for "by means of a very few soldiers you kept substantive good order amidst the chaos of ruin, and probably saved the city."[37]

With Chicago in order and Governor Palmer finally quiet, Sheridan once again turned his attention to the grand duke's buffalo hunt. There was a more urgent diplomatic reason to get Alexis onto the western plains than simple entertainment. President Grant wanted Alexis away from the East, since the diplomatic atmosphere in Washington had been poisoned by a bitter feud between Secretary of State Hamilton Fish and the Russian minister, Constantine Catacazy. Despite the fact that Catacazy was now persona non grata in Washington, Grant eagerly sought to retain the especially warm relations that existed between the United States and Russia ever since Czar Alexander II had firmly supported the Union during the Civil War. Thus a buffalo hunt was decided upon as a fine diversion for the twenty-one-year-old Romanoff, and Grant picked Sheridan to host it.[38]

The buffalo hunt was to be on a truly spectacular scale. Dr. Asch and Sandy Forsyth were sent out from division headquarters to coordinate preparations in the field. Pope sent out scouting parties to locate and track the southern buffalo herd, and Ord established a supply depot for the hunting party at Omaha. Colonel (Brevet Major General) Innis N. Palmer, Second Cavalry, was put in command of the escort, which was to consist of two companies of infantry, two cavalry companies, and the Second Cavalry's regimental band. Special arrangements were made so that Cody, who was supposed to accompany the Fifth Cavalry to Arizona, could instead remain in Nebraska to take part in the hunt. To be sure the grand duke could see a famous Indian fighter, a special invitation was extended to Lieutenant Colonel Custer, then stationed in Kentucky.[39]

To make this Wild West Show on the plains complete, some Indians were needed. Sheridan sent Cody off to find Chief Spotted Tail and request that he bring one hundred of his Brulé Sioux to join in the hunt and put on some dances to entertain the grand duke. This was agreeable to the chief, and he soon had his party on the move toward the designated hunting camp on Red Willow Creek, situated between the Platte and Republican rivers some sixty miles from Fort McPherson.[40]

On January 12 Sheridan, accompanied by James and Sandy Forsyth, surgeon Asch, and Mike Sheridan, all of his staff, as well as Lieutenant Colonel Custer, Colonel Palmer, General Ord, and Major (Brevet Brigadier General) Nelson B. Sweitzer of Ord's staff, met the grand duke and his seven-member retinue in Omaha. They boarded a special train provided by the Union Pacific Railroad and were whisked off to North Platte, Nebraska. A company of the Second Cavalry and Cody awaited them with wagons, and the party scurried off toward Red Willow Creek, which was reached before sunset on January 13.[41]

The hunt proved a grand success; the plains were soon littered with over two dozen dead buffalos. The Brulé women of Spotted Tail's camp made good use of the fallen beasts, so that the victims of the royal sportsman were not left to rot. The Indians provided a war dance to climax the entertainment, and Buffalo Bill regaled the visitors with tall

The grand duke's hunting party posed for this group portrait in the Topeka, Kansas, photograph gallery of J. Lee Knight. Left to right, top row: Frank Thompson, Dr. Vladimir Kadrin, Lieutenant Colonel George A. Forsyth, Count Olsonfieff, Dr. Morris J. Asch, Major Nelson B. Sweitzer, Russian Naval Lieutenant Tudeer; middle: Russian Consul General at New York Waldemar Bodisco, Russian Councillor of State W. F. Machin, Lieutenant General Philip H. Sheridan, Grand Duke Alexis, Russian Admiral Possiet, Lieutenant Colonel George A. Custer; bottom: Lieutenant Colonel James W. Forsyth, Russian Naval Lieutenant Sterlegoff, and Lieutenant Colonel Michael V. Sheridan. (*Courtesy of Lawrence A. Frost*)

tales until it was time to turn in. After two days of hunting the party decamped for the railroad, by which they would travel on to Denver.[42]

Cody left the royal party at North Platte, but not before Alexis, who was quite taken with the picturesque plainsman, gave him several valuable gifts. Sheridan gave the young scout some advice that proved to be of considerable more value than the grand duke's presents. At the conclusion of their September hunt, James Gordon Bennet, editor of the *New York Herald*, had invited Cody to be his guest in New York. Sheridan told Cody that he would "never have a better opportunity to accept that invitation than now" and secured the scout a leave of absence with pay from Fort McPherson and a railroad pass to New York City. Cody, who had never visited the East, soon decided to take the general's advice. He first journeyed to Chicago, staying with the Sheridan brothers at their Michigan Avenue home. Sheridan took his frontier friend in hand and introduced him to Chicago society, a chore poor Bill found quite trying, since he "had not yet become accustomed to being stared at."[43]After a few days in Chicago Cody moved on to greater triumphs in New York, his fame having preceded him, falling in with a promoter named Ned Buntline, who could see a great future ahead for the shy frontiersman on eastern stages. About three weeks after Cody's arrival in New York, Sheridan passed through and checked to see how his friend was faring. Cody replied that he "had struck the best camp I had ever seen," and requested an extension of his leave.[44] Within a year Cody was a hit before the footlights, but he never forgot his debt to Sheridan. When, in 1879, he published an autobiography, he dedicated it to the general whose sage advice had started him on the greasepaint road to fame and fortune.

While Cody was contemplating Sheridan's advice, the general was entertaining the royal tourist. After a tour of Denver and nearby mining camps on January 19, the party was off to Kit Carson, Colorado, where another large buffalo herd had been located. This hunt was highly successful, for the animals proved more spirited than their Nebraska cousins.

The hunters also nearly bagged the army's lieutenant general as a trophy. After his horse had taken a couple of bad falls, Sheridan decided to sit out the rest of the day's hunt. Spying a couple of wounded buffalos, however, he and a few others started up a small hill on foot to put the animals out of their misery. Suddenly a gang of mounted hunters came over the top of the hill from the opposite direction firing wildly at the wounded animals. With bullets thick about them, Sheridan's companions took off down the hill while the general, his short legs not much for running, threw himself flat on the ground. The hunters, Custer and Alexis among them, quickly realized their error and ceased fire, but it was too late to appease the lieutenant general.

Sheridan got to his feet, his face flushed and temper boiling— "the maddest man I ever saw," noted an eyewitness. "I don't know what kind of language Pa Romanoff used to Alexis when he got mad," declared an impressed hunter in describing the scene, "but that slip of royalty got a cussing from Phil Sheridan that day that I bet he will never

The hunt was a great success, with dozens of buffalos soon littering the frozen ground. The Brulé women of Spotted Tail's camp put the slain beasts to good use. This modern painting of the royal hunt by noted Texas artist Joe Grandee depicts George Custer, Bill Cody, the Grand Duke Alexis, and Sheridan engaging in the frosty chase. (*Courtesy of Joe Grandee*)

forget." The hunter detected the spirit of democracy in the cussing, for Sheridan "didn't spare anybody in the bunch, not even Custer and the grand duke, and he included all their kinsfolk, direct and collateral. It was a liberal education in profanity to hear him."[45]

The whole party soon headed east by special train to Saint Louis. Here the general departed for Chicago, putting Alexis under Custer's care for a tour of several southern cities. Upon reaching Chicago, Sheridan wired his superiors the news of the hunt's success, declaring himself confident "that it gave more pleasure to the Grand Duke than any other event." And indeed it had, for Sheridan soon found himself the recipient of a decoration from the czar in recognition of his services to the imperial family.[46]

Sheridan found his next foray into the realm of diplomacy to be far more difficult than his days hunting buffalo with the grand duke.

The Rio Grande border was a source of constant irritation to Sheridan, at times consuming nearly one-third of his total division forces for garrison duty. Kiowas, Comanches, Apaches, and Cheyennes raided south into Mexico with impunity, while Kickapoos, Lipans, and Apaches returned the favor by sweeping north across the river, striking the settlements in Texas. Meanwhile, assorted bandits, both American and Mexican, and groups of Mexican pseudorevolutionaries added to the unhealthy climate along the great river from El Paso to Brownsville.

From the close of the Civil War until 1873 the thorniest problem was caused by Kickapoo raiders who resided just across the international boundary in Coahuila. The Kickapoos, originally from the United States, had been induced by the Mexican government to settle in Coahuila and act as a buffer against raiding Comanches, Apaches, and Kiowas from the north. In return for their actions as mercenaries the Kickapoos received a substantial land grant from the Mexicans. So attractive was the Mexican offer, and so unattractive was life in Kansas, that by 1865 all the southern Kickapoos had settled in Nacimiento Canyon along the Sabinas River, about 120 miles northwest of Piedras Negras. Numbering about thirteen hundred, they were the merciless enemies of Texas as a result of Texan attacks on peaceful Kickapoo emigrant parties in 1862 and 1865. A bold, stealthy enemy, the Kickapoos made life and property insecure throughout the Nueces River ranch country north of Laredo and southwest of San Antonio.[47]

Not only did the Kickapoos find sanctuary across the Rio Grande, they also found a ready market for their Texas booty among the Mexican merchants. Mexican customs officers at Piedras Negras and Nuevo Laredo supplied these merchants with transfer papers that made their purchases legal before Mexican courts. Efforts by the United States Department of State to secure permission to cross the border and chastise the raiders had failed, as had an 1871 attempt by the Indian Bureau to induce the Kickapoos to return to the United States. The Mexican central government made faint promises concerning control of the Kickapoos, but in reality it had no power in the border states of Coahuila or Tamaulipas.

Sheridan's intelligence sources reported no Mexican federal forces on the Rio Grande except for a small battalion of infantry stationed at Matamoros, across from the southern tip of Texas.

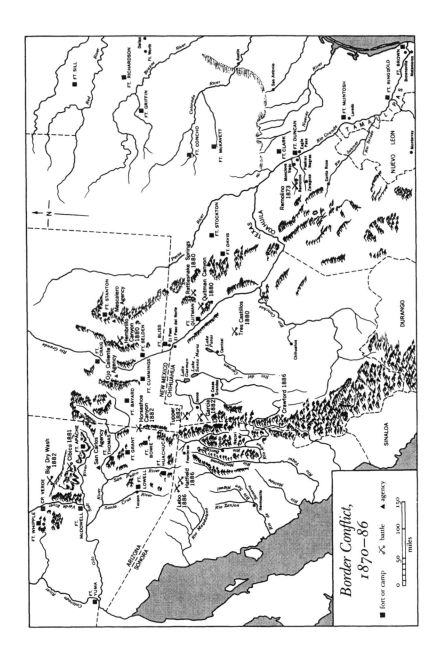

Border Conflict, 1870–86

■ fort or camp   ✗ battle   ▲ agency

miles
0   50   100   150

Coahuila could boast but fifty or sixty state troops stationed at Piedras Negras, opposite the United States post at Fort Duncan. The real power on the border was the Mexican war lord of Tamaulipas, General Cortinas, who held more power in that region than either the state or federal governments. "The real Mexican government so far as affairs on the Rio Grande are concerned," department commander Brigadier General Christopher C. Augur reported to Sheridan in 1873, "is whoever controls the great crowd of idle and vicious Mexicans who have been attached for years past to that line by prospect of plunder and robbery of the Texas frontier, and who are still retained there by their continued success in this business." In short, there was no Mexican government to negotiate with concerning Rio Grande depredations. The Kickapoos and Cortinas held the power, and Augur felt that the only way to deal with them was by the sword.[48]

Sheridan agreed with Augur. Fort Duncan had been the first assignment for shavetail Sheridan in 1854, and the prejudices he then formed against the Indians and Mexicans living along the Rio Grande were never erased. He viewed the inhabitants of the region as "a mixed race of Indian and Spanish blood, in which the Indian blood largely predominates," who felt no "restraint from law and order or from any public sentiment in regard to national or international rights." Sheridan had no more regard for the American citizens of Mexican descent who resided in Texas. He believed they were "in full sympathy with their Mexican friends and relatives," and accused them of protecting Mexican criminals and Indian raiders from United States troops. So contemptuous was he of the Mexican central government that Sheridan once seriously recommended to Sherman that the United States seize that part of Mexico from the Rio Grande River to the Sierra Madre and establish law and order.[49] Sheridan was not a man to be bothered with the fetters of international law.

If the Rio Grande raids were to be stopped, it was essential for Sheridan to place an energetic, trustworthy officer on the border. That was accomplished in February 1873, when President Grant personally ordered the transfer of Colonel (Brevet Major General) Ranald S. Mackenzie and his Fourth Cavalry to the border.[50] Mackenzie, only thirty-two years old when ordered to the Rio Grande, had graduated first in his 1862 West Point class. Serving as an engineer officer in the Army of the Potomac from June 1862 until June 1864, Mackenzie found little opportunity to distinguish himself. He nevertheless received both a serious wound and a brevet at Second Bull Run and won promotions up to captain by hard, effective work. On June 10, 1864, General Meade appointed him colonel of the Second Connecticut Heavy Artillery, a volunteer regiment serving as infantry. A few days later the young colonel was leading his regiment against Petersburg, where he was to win another brevet and suffer another wound, this time losing two fingers on his right hand. This disfigurement later won him the sobriquet Bad Hand from the western Indians.

After a short disability leave Mackenzie rejoined his regiment in defending the capital from Jubal Early's troops and soon found himself transferred to Sheridan's Shenandoah command. It was a fortunate transfer, for under Sheridan he experienced a phenomenal rise in rank, first commanding a brigade and then a division of cavalry. When Sheridan made his dramatic ride from Winchester to his stricken army at Cedar Creek, one of the first officers to welcome him was a wounded Mackenzie. The beardless boy colonel refused to obey his commander's order to retire from the field and see a doctor, and won by this disobedience Sheridan's lasting respect.[51] War's end found Mackenzie, at twenty-four, a brigadier general of volunteers with brevets up to major general in the volunteers and brigadier in the regulars, as well as scars from six severe wounds. More important than the brevets, however, was the impression he had made on Generals Grant and Sheridan. Grant felt Mackenzie "the most promising young officer in the army," and the passing years would justify that estimation.[52]

In the army reorganization of 1866 Mackenzie's impressive war record won him an appointment as colonel of the Forty-first Infantry. Although stationed on the lower Rio Grande, the black regiment was given no opportunity to distinguish itself, and Mackenzie was undoubtedly pleased when transferred to the command of the Fourth Cavalry in January 1871. A hard, no-nonsense commander, he drove his new regiment relentlessly and with good results, for the Fourth's dogged campaigns of 1871–72 against the Comanches and Kiowas on the Staked Plain won it a reputation as the best cavalry regiment in the service.[53]

Mackenzie's cold, almost emotionless hawk face matched an irascible, eccentric temperament. His Civil War wounds, and another leg wound in 1871 from a Comanche barbed arrow, left him in torment and undoubtedly exaggerated a surly, impatient temper. Irritability may well be a virtue in a soldier, for Mackenzie's superiors could rarely find fault in him. General John Pope once pleaded with Sheridan to transfer half a regiment out of his department rather than take away the fretful colonel.[54] Within a few years of assuming division command, Sheridan came to regard Mackenzie as his finest field officer and the best Indian fighter in the army.[55]

Sheridan felt confident that Mackenzie was the man to put an end to the forays of the Mexican Kickapoos, and to ensure that desired result he departed Chicago on April 1, 1873, for San Antonio. He made his Texas visit in conjunction with Secretary of War William Belknap, who was anxious to inspect some of the posts in that region, but the general's true purpose was to meet with General Augur and Colonel Mackenzie and instruct them to end the Kickapoo raids, even if it meant violating the international boundary. This was risky business. Sheridan kept his own counsel, not even informing Sherman of his plan. Failure might result in severe international and domestic repercussions, but a successful raid into the Kickapoo's Mexican sanctuary would bring security to southwestern Texas.[56]

Colonel Mackenzie, after putting his regiment in motion toward Fort Clark, left Fort Concho on March 24 and hurried to San Antonio to confer with Sheridan, Belknap, and Augur. He found the visiting dignitaries eager to be off on the 130-mile journey to Fort Clark to inspect the Fourth Cavalry and get a closer look at the troubled border area.

Fort Clark, which Sheridan and his party reached on April 11, had been established in 1852 as a substantial post with stone buildings set amidst an oak grove, but by 1873 it was fairly run down. Lieutenant Colonel (Brevet Major General) Wesley Merritt, another of Sheridan's Civil War protégés, commanded the departing Ninth Cavalry at Fort Clark, and he honored the visiting dignitaries with a dance on the evening of their arrival.

The newly arrived Fourth Cavalry ladies were naturally delighted at the prospect of dancing with Phil Sheridan and the illustrious secretary of war, but as many of them prepared their hair for the evening's festivities, they discovered one of the hazards of life on the southwestern frontier. Their hair had been invaded by an army of lice, and all strategies to eradicate this horrid enemy proved fruitless, in some cases doing more damage to the battlefield than to the foe. Undaunted, the ladies made a pact not to reveal their dark secret to the officers and proceeded bravely to the dance. Sheridan displayed his usual warm interest in dancing with the ladies, unaware of how he was exposing himself to invasion by a foreign host. He probably had little reason for alarm even had he known of the ladies' predicament, for his closely cropped hair, which he kept as short as possible because he disliked its natural curl, was hardly an inviting nest for even the most desperate nit.[57]

On the following day Sheridan and Belknap secluded themselves with Mackenzie for a long conference held in Merritt's quarters. Sheridan explained to Mackenzie that he had been ordered to the border to take action against the Kickapoos. "I want you to *control* and *hold down* the situation, and *do it in your own way*," Sheridan told Mackenzie. "I want you to be bold, enterprising, and at all times *full of energy*, when you begin, let it be a campaign of *annihilation, obliteration* and *complete destruction*. . . . I think you understand what I want done, and the way you should employ your force."

Mackenzie was momentarily silent, obsessed with Sheridan's manner. Even Mackenzie hesitated to take so much responsibility on his own initiative. "Gen. Sheridan, under whose orders and upon what authority am I to act?" he asked. "Have you any plans to suggest, or will you issue me the necessary orders for my action?"

"Damn the *orders*! Damn the *authority*," Sheridan exclaimed, slamming his fist onto the table and gesturing vehemently for emphasis. "You are to go ahead on your own plan of action, and your authority and backing shall be Gen. Grant and myslf. With us behind you in whatever you do to clean up this situation, you can rest assured of the fullest support. You must assume the risk. We will assume the final responsibility should any result."[58]

Their business completed, Sheridan and Belknap left for San Antonio on April 12, from where they continued their inspection of Texas forts before departing by boat from Brazos on April 28 for New Orleans. The general was back in Chicago by May 5.

While Sheridan was en route home, Mackenzie busied himself preparing his regiment for a secret raid. He trusted Sheridan's pledge of support and was prepared to risk castigation by the humanitarians, the press, and even the international community, in order to strike the

Mexican Indians. Scouts were sent across the border to spy on the Indian villages, and late in the evening of May 16 they brought Mackenzie the message he wanted to hear. All the warriors had departed that morning from the important Kickapoo village situated near the small Mexican town of Remolino, some forty miles west of the Rio Grande.

At dusk the next day Mackenzie splashed across the Rio Grande, followed by six companies of the Fourth Cavalry, about four hundred men, and two dozen Seminole-Negro scouts under Lieutenant John Bullis from Fort Duncan. An all-night march put the soldiers at the Kickapoo village at six o'clock on the morning of May 18. Mackenzie wasted no time. His troopers charged into the village by platoon, carbines blazing. The surprised Kickapoo women, children, and old men tried vainly to escape, and even managed to kill one of the white soldiers and wound two others before they were rounded up by the troopers. At least nineteen were killed with another forty taken prisoner. Mackenzie sent his men on to two nearby villages, one Lipan and the other Mescalero, but the occupants had fled. All three villages were destroyed, and the cavalrymen hurried back toward the Rio Grande with their captives and sixty-five Indian ponies. Mackenzie dared not rest inside Mexico, and it was only after an exhausting march that he let his men bivouac on the American side of the river, some sixty sleepless hours after the expedition began.[59]

Sheridan was elated when word of Mackenzie's raid reached his Chicago headquarters. The first military reports carried no word of a border crossing, but Sheridan sent them on to Belknap with the warning: "It is more than probable that Mackenzie crossed into Mexico and had his fight on that side of the Rio Grande. We must back him."[60] When word from Augur on May 27 confirmed the crossing, Sheridan promptly sent back a warm endorsement, instructing his department commander to "send word to Mackenzie that he is all right and will be sustained, that he has done a good thing."[61]

Sheridan's personal approval was not enough to protect Mackenzie if his violation of an international border were condemned by the powerful in the press, government, and society at large, and the lieutenant general sent off a barrage of telegrams in defense of his field officer. He begged the secretary of war to make every effort to uphold Mackenzie, warning that "if our government disavows the act of his crossing into Mexico than [*sic*] all hope of stopping Indian raids & cattle thieving on the Rio Grande is at an end." Sheridan reiterated his conviction that the weak Mexican government was unable, or even unwilling, to put a stop to the Indian raids and his soldiers could "only stop the bad work by the fact that we may cross the river and exterminate the murderers and thieves. But if we make the acknowledgement of an error on part of Mackenzie there never will be any fear of our crossing again, and murdering our people & stealing our property will continue with increasing abandon."[62]

Sheridan also wired Sherman, who had not been previously informed of any plans to cross the border, and assured him that Mackenzie was only following his wishes. "I have for a long time been satisfied that it is the only course to pursue to bring safety to life and property on our side of the Rio Grande," declared Sheridan. He asked Sherman to use his influence to sustain Mackenzie, adding that "there should be no boundaryline when we are driven to the necessity of defending our lives and property against murderers and robbers."[63]

Sherman was not pleased, but he nevertheless stood behind his subordinates. "McKenzie [*sic*] will of course be sustained," he told Sheridan, "but for the sake of history, I would like to have him report clearly the facts that induced him to know that the Indians he attacked & captured were of the identical Indians then engaged in raiding Texas. Had he followed a fresh trail there would be law to back him." Sherman reminded Sheridan that Indians from the north side of the border were constantly raiding into Mexico as well, "and taking lesson by McKenzie [*sic*] I would not be surprised to hear that the Greasers had invaded Arizona to pitch into the Indians." There were larger political and diplomatic questions involved, Sherman lectured his friend, than the problems on the Rio Grande. President Sebastián Lerdo de Tejada of Mexico, who was reasonably friendly toward the United States, could not "preserve his popularity if he submits to positive insults from us, the 'Gringos.'" President Grant, Secretary of State Hamilton Fish, and Sherman were anxious for Lerdo de Tejada to hold his office, and Mackenzie's raid had compromised their friend in Mexico City.[64]

Sherman was naturally angry over Sheridan's failure to consult with him on Mackenzie's raid. Belknap's involvement in the conspiracy further exacerbated the situation, for Sherman despised the secretary of war. In fact, one of the reasons for Sherman's being left in the dark was that he and Belknap had ceased to talk to each other. The cross-border raid, however, caused no rift in the warm friendship between Sherman and Sheridan. Still, despite Sherman's public position, he never approved of Sheridan's actions. When, in 1879, Colonel Nelson Miles used Mackenzie's raid as a precedent when requesting Sherman's blessing for a raid into Canada against the Sioux, the flinty commanding general angrily refused. "Because as you explained Generals Sheridan and Mackenzie once consented to act unlawfully in defiance of my authority in a certain political contingency," Sherman told Miles, "is no reason why I should imitate so bad an example."[65]

The administration, like General Sherman, publicly supported Sheridan and Mackenzie despite the diplomatic problems caused by the raid. Belknap assured Sheridan that the president, secretary of state, and attorney general all agreed: "You and Mackenzie will be sustained as thoroughly as possible, there is no difference of opinion among us on the subject."[66]

The decision to support Sheridan and Mackenzie was doubtless made easier by the positive public reaction to the raid. Most newspapers reported favorably on Mackenzie's actions, and those in the West were laudatory in their comments. The Texas state legislature passed a joint resolution in praise of the colonel and his regiment. There was a brief storm of outrage in Mexico, but President Lerdo de Tejada weathered it well enough, and his government did no more than lodge a mild protest with Secretary of State Fish.[67]

Meanwhile, two American commissioners representing the Indian Bureau were in Mexico negotiating for the return of all the Kickapoos to their reservation in the United States. As a prerequisite to negotiations the Kickapoos demanded the return of Mackenzie's captives. The commissioners agreed to this, and they visited General Augur in San Antonio to press the Kickapoo demand. Their arguments persuaded Augur, but when he sent his recommendation to Sheridan, it was flatly rejected. Sheridan instructed Augur to send the Kickapoo prisoners on to their reservation in the Indian Territory and to send word to the Indians in Mexico that they would have to join them there if they ever wished to see them again. "You can also tell them that if their people elect to remain in Mexico," warned Sheridan, "and still continue to murder and rob, the Rio Grande will not be regarded as a boundary line by our troops . . . no odds what may be the consequences."[68]

The commissioners returned to the Kickapoos in Mexico and informed them that the only way they could hope for a reunion with their relatives was to return to the United States. The use of the captives as bait to lure the Indians to the United States, combined with a generous distribution of cash payments to influential Kickapoos, resulted in the migration of over one-half of the Mexican Kickapoos to the Indian Territory in the fall of 1873.[69]

Mackenzie's raid thus proved to be a resounding success, and it resulted in several years of relative peace on the Rio Grande border. His attack on the Kickapoo village after he knew the warriors had left appears reprehensible at first glance, but when the expedition is viewed as the kidnapping raid that it really was, Mackenzie's action seems more reasonable, although still a gross violation of international law. The raid brought an immediate settlement of the Kickapoo problem, thus saving many lives, both red and white, that would have been lost if the raids and counterraids had continued for several more years. The return of the Kickapoos to the United States proved the wisdom of Sheridan's strategy and of Mackenzie's tactics.

The new quiet on the Rio Grande allowed Sheridan to call on Mackenzie for another campaign. To the north the Comanches, Cheyennes, and Kiowas, eager to avenge a long list of white abuses, flailed out at their oppressors in a desperate uprising in June 1874. Similar to the events in Montana in 1869, the background to the Red River War of 1874–75 was marked with military factionalism, which in turn caused confusion and suspicion among the officers charged with watching over the Indians.

CHAPTER 10

Military Factionalism and Indian Policy: "The Nest at Fort Sill Should Be Broken Up"

Colonel Benjamin H. Grierson, Tenth Cavalry, commanding Fort Sill from 1869 until 1872, disliked both Phil Sheridan and his methods of dealing with the Indians. A decidedly unconventional cavalryman in background and personal philosophy, Grierson was not Sheridan's type of officer. One critic described the former Illinois music teacher as "a common bone-rattler in a minstrel troupe."[1]

At the outbreak of war in 1861, Grierson enlisted in the volunteers. Although afraid of horses as a result of a boyhood accident that had permanently scarred his face, Grierson found himself assigned to the cavalry. Yet by 1862 he was colonel of the Sixth Illinois Cavalry, and in April 1863 he led his regiment and two others on a daring raid from La Grange, Tennessee, to Baton Rouge, Louisiana, that contributed significantly to Grant's victory at Vicksburg. Grierson's six-hundred-mile raid made him a national hero. General Grant proclaimed it the most brilliant expedition of the war. Grierson then served as a division and corps commander under Sherman, rising to major general of volunteers. Sherman shared Grant's assessment of Grierson, characterizing him as "one of the most willing, ardent, and dashing cavalry officers I ever had—always ready, day or night—against equal and superior foes he handled his men with great skill, doing some of the prettiest work of the war."[2]

In the reorganization of the army after the war the amateur cavalryman was offered command of the Tenth Cavalry and, after some soul-searching, accepted. Although Grierson rejected the practice of war and the camaraderie of tent and field, he craved the security offered by a military career. "Army life has many drawbacks," he admitted, "but there is a permanency about it after all—which is pleasant to contemplate."[3]

Grierson's appointment as colonel, coupled with a brevet as major general in the regulars, reflected his favored position as a friend of Grant and Sherman, but it was also a wise choice from the standpoint of the black soldiers of the Tenth Cavalry. Grierson had been a firm Lincoln Republican before the war, and there were few officers in the army as enlightened on the race issue. He waged an unrelenting campaign against the "distinctions between white and Negro troops," demanding equal treatment for his men. He realized that many army officers were convinced that the experiment with black regiments would fail, while some even worked to ensure that it did. Grierson held to his conviction that "colored troops will hold their place in the Army of the United States as long as the government lasts."[4] To Grierson one of Sheridan's few redemptive qualties was that he seemed "to be entirely without prejudice in regard to Colored troopers."[5]

Grierson, however, came to view Sheridan as a nemesis, stepping in to block his every favorable assignment or chance for promotion. He entered Sheridan's command first in the summer of 1865, when preparations were underway to send troops into Texas as a warning to Maximilian. Stationed in New Orleans at the time, Grierson expected command of a brigade or division of Sheridan's cavalry, but found himself instead "quickly and preemptoraly [sic] relieved and ordered to my home by Sheridan—with the view and hope that he would thus not only get rid of me but have me mustered out of the service." Grierson felt favoritism guided Sheridan's every action in making troop assignments, and he regarded his removal in 1865 to be "for no just cause but for the purpose of making a place for two of his toadies—Custer and Merritt."[6]

When Grierson again came under Sheridan's direct command during the 1868 Washita campaign, he suffered the same treatment. Although the colonel had spent long months preparing his regiment for the field, Sheridan ordered him to Fort Gibson with only his

Colonel Benjamin H. Grierson was a decidedly unconventional cavalryman. His warm support of Grant's Peace Policy and his quick defense of Indian rights often led him into conflict with Sheridan. He viewed his commander, whom he labeled "Sherry-dan," as a nemesis dedicated to breaking him. "But thank God my back is not broken," he declared in 1875, "and mark what I tell you, sooner or later I will get even with this man." (*Fort Davis National Historic Site, National Park Service*)

headquarters, while half his regiment campaigned under one of his majors. "This," Grierson complained, "was so I would not come in contact with Custer—whom I outranked—he being a Lieut. Col." Despite this injustice, Grierson diligently compiled a good record as commander of the District of Indian Territory, only to have it "cut to pieces by *Sherry-dan* and from a district comdr. I was placed in command of merely the Kiowa and Comanche Reservations—thus he took three-fourths of my command from me—and other orders since have been of the same stripe." In Grierson's mind Sheridan meant to break him and force him out of the army. "But thank God my back is not broken," Grierson proclaimed to his wife, "and mark what I tell you, sooner or later I will get even with this man."[7]

Despite these vindictive feelings, Colonel Grierson was a kind, generous man, brimful of warmth and compassion, attributes that made him suspect as a soldier to hard, serious Sheridan. The general undoubtedly agreed with Anson Mills's characterization of the colonel as a big-hearted man "too prone to forgive offenses and trust for reform, which rendered the discipline and reputation of the regiment poor."[8]

The central issue clouding the relationship between Sheridan and Grierson was not the colonel's laxity of discipline, but rather his position on Indian affairs. While Sheridan grudgingly supported Grant's Peace Policy out of respect for his old friend, Grierson warmly embraced it as an enlightened experiment to save a wronged people. Grierson's enthusiasm for the Peace Policy condemned him in Sheridan's eyes.

Grierson believed that the single cause of all Indian disturbances was the failure of the government to fulfill its obligations to the tribes. He advocated the expansion of the reservations, since their inadequate size, combined with outrageous irregularity in the supplying of the confined Indians, made it impossible for the warriors adequately to provide for their families. Grierson decried the vicious pattern that he saw in the Indian Territory, whereby the government did not provide promised rations and the starving Indians then left the reservation to hunt in the Staked Plain or Kansas. When the Indians jumped the reservation, he would be ordered "to use force to keep them upon the reservation." "To do so," he felt," is gross injustice." Grierson often fed the Indians from Tenth Cavalry supplies to rectify this situation, a practice that Sheridan also followed on occasion, and at the same time sent a stream of complaints to his superiors describing the Indians' plight.[9]

Grierson and Sheridan differed radically on the role of the military in controlling the Indians. "I will pursue such a course as to control the Indians & prevent depredations without loosing sight of the object contemplated by the phylanthropic [sic] and good people of the land," Grierson promised Indian agent Lawrie Tatum, *without bringing on a war for the purpose of gaining an opportunity of killing off Indians*. Let those who may wish it done (either on account of material interests or *personal advancement*) grumble as they may. I will do only what I believe to be just & right—even at a sacrifice of my position and commission in the Army."[10]

Such sentiments endeared Grierson to the humanitarians who temporarily controlled Indian affairs under Grant's Peace Policy. Indian agent Tatum, a Quaker farmer from Iowa appointed to oversee the Kiowas and Comanches in 1869, was impressed with this army officer who "evidently would prefer to lead, than to attempt to drive the aborigines into civilization." In Tatum's estimation, if the reputation of an army officer was to be judged by how little blood and treasure were expended in conquering the foe, then "the commanding officer here will rank high."[11]

Grierson's sentiments were sincere, but he shamelessly exploited them in his efforts to secure promotion. Realizing that his lenient attitude toward the Indians on the Fort Sill reservation had angered Sheridan, Grierson made it clear to Tatum, "If you wish me to remain here with you, it will be necessary for you to take the matter in hand at once . . . with the combined influence of the Friends and [Board of Indian] Commissioners, I believe you can, by bringing the matter before the President defeat those who conspire against me to have me removed from the military affairs of this Reservation."[12]

Grierson found an even stronger ally in Felix R. Brunot, the Pittsburgh industrialist who chaired the Board of Indian Commissioners from 1869 to 1874. The colonel kept Brunot informed on the situation around the Fort Sill reservation and even sent him copies of his yearly official report before it was transmitted through military channels. Brunot released some of Grierson's letters to the press to bolster the humanitarian position. Grierson repeatedly urged Brunot to work for his promotion to brigadier general so that he might "be placed in military charge of the Indian Territory, with sufficient rank and powers to put this thing [the Peace Policy] through."[13] Brunot tried to aid Grierson, lobbying both military officers and government officials, but he met with little success; and when approaching Sheridan on the subject, he encountered outright hostility. Brunot found the general convinced that the Board of Indian Commissioners was his enemy because of the controversy over Baker's Piegan massacre. Brunot learned that Sheridan was unwilling to promote Grierson and discovered a "disposition in military quarters to censure" the colonel for his activities on behalf of the humanitarians.[14]

Nevertheless, army politics limited Sheridan's options in dealing with the colonel. Grierson's strong personal relationship with Grant and Sherman gave him a leverage over Sheridan not held by many officers. After all, Grant had initially secured a colonel's berth in the regulars for Grierson, and Sherman's recommendation had induced Sheridan to assign Grierson to command so vital a post as Fort Sill.

The Fort Sill Indian reservation was home to most of the Kiowa and Comanche bands, although the Kwahadis disdained to draw government rations and continued to roam at will across the Staked Plain. The Kwahadis taunted their relatives to the east and urged them to join the hunt on the plains. The reservation bands, however, were prospering under the Peace Policy. They drew government rations and continued their profitable raids into old Mexico and Texas. Since the Peace Policy forbade troops to enter an Indian reservation the warriors enjoyed a sanctuary. They also found their benevolent Quaker agent to be a dependable ransomer for white children kidnapped from the Texas settlements. Thus raiding parties under Satanta, Satank, Big Bow, Lone Wolf, and other warriors preyed upon the Texans and then scurried across the Red River to the safety of their reservation.[15]

At first Tatum thought that the stories of Indian raids coming from Texas were exaggerated. He could not believe that his charges might be the culprits, and he blamed the raids on Apaches from Arizona and New Mexico as well as the Kwahadi Comanches. When, in June 1870, a band of Kiowas raided the agency horse herd, killing one agency employee and wounding another, Tatum reluctantly faced the truth. He then put his trust in the Lord to "restrain the evil intentions and passions of the Indians," and turned to Colonel Grierson for

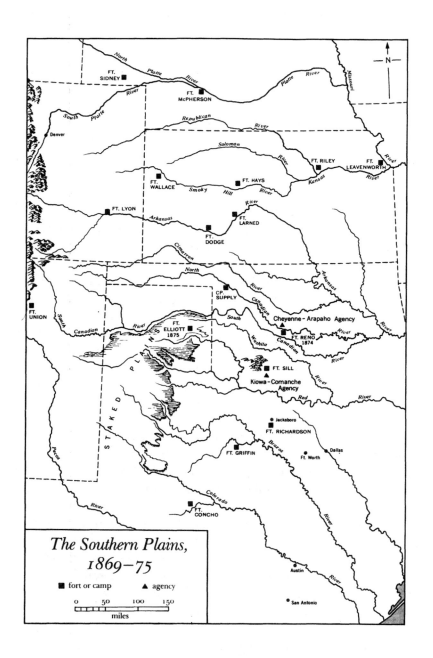

The Southern Plains,
1869–75

■ fort or camp   ▲ agency

0   50   100   150
miles

advice and some guards.[16] Despite this, Grierson, whose faith in the Peace Policy was unshaken, went so far as to instruct his officers to remain silent about the Indian raids so that the president's policy might have a chance to succeed.[17]

Texas newspaper editorials reviled the government for protecting the Kiowa and Comanche raiders at Fort Sill. The Texas state legislature passed a resolution declaring that between 1866 and 1871 the Indians had "not only retarded the settlement of the frontier counties of the State, but have almost depopulated several counties thereof."[18] Some frustrated Texans even claimed that Tatum and Grierson provided arms and ammunition to the hostile Indians. Colonel (Brevet Brigadier General) James Oakes, commandant at Fort Richardson, supported the charge that Tatum was arming the Indians and accused Grierson of making no effort to stop raids.[19]

With Sheridan in Europe observing the Franco-Prussian War, the responsibility of answering the charges leveled by the Texans fell to General Sherman. He did not have a high regard for the wild charges emanating from Texas, especially the one regarding the authorities at Fort Sill arming Indians. "That Genl. Grierson and the Indian Agent Mr. Tatum (a Quaker) should wink at or connive in this is simply absurd," he noted. Sherman tended to agree with Grierson that many of the Texas raids were the work of whites disguised as Indians.[20]

To resolve the issue Sherman decided on a personal inspection of the Texas frontier. He traveled to San Antonio for a conference with department commander Joseph J. Reynolds, and then set out on May 2, 1871, to inspect Forts McKavett, Concho, Griffin, and Richardson.[21] By the time Sherman reached Fort Richardson on May 17, he was even more firmly convinced that the tales of Indian raids were grossly exaggerated. A delegation of angry citizens from the nearby hamlet of Jacksboro could not dissuade the general from his conviction.[22]

Late the next night a wounded teamster staggered into Fort Richardson with a tale of horror that immediately changed Sherman's opinion and set in motion a chain of events that would lead to the departure of Tatum and Grierson from Fort Sill, the arrest of three prominent Kiowas, and the outbreak of a final war for control of the southern plains. The man declared that Indians had attacked Henry Warren's ten wagons carrying corn to Fort Griffin, killing seven of the twelve teamsters, destroying the wagons, and making off with forty-one mules. The slaughter had occurred to the west of Fort Richardson on Salt Creek Prairie, on the very road that Sherman had traveled the previous day.[23]

Ranald Mackenzie was in command at Fort Richardson, the Fourth Cavalry having recently replaced the lethargic Sixth Cavalry there, and Sherman ordered him to take a strong force and investigate the teamster's story. If the story proved true, Mackenzie was to pursue the Indians and destroy them. He was then to join Sherman at Fort Sill.

Mackenzie departed the fort on May 19 with four cavalry companies and headed toward Salt Creek Prairie, where he found the gruesome handiwork of the Indian raiders. Sherman headed northeast the next day in his Daughtery ambulance for Fort Sill, his new respect for Texan accounts of Indian depredations evidenced by the Winchester rifle across his lap. Reaching Fort Sill on May 23, he conferred with Grierson and Tatum to see whether any bands were off the reservation.[24]

Satanta, Lone Wolf, Big Tree, Satank, and other leading Kiowas came to the agency on May 27 to draw rations, and Tatum confronted them with Sherman's story of the Salt Creek Prairie massacre. Sheridan's old foe Satanta lived up to his reputation as the Orator of the Plains by boldly proclaiming that he had led the attack himself, and naming the other leading warriors who had gone with him. He castigated Tatum for refusing to supply the Kiowas with arms and ammunition and declared that as a result a new order was dawning. Warming to his subject, Satanta denounced Sheridan for forcing him onto the reservation in the first place: "Some years ago they took us by the hair and pulled us here close to Texas where we have to fight them. More recently I was arrested by the soldiers and kept in confinement several days. But that is played out now. There is never to be any more Kiowa Indians arrested."[25]

Satanta, seemingly determined to brag himself into a hangman's noose, next went to the fort and demanded to meet the big soldier chief from Washington. When Sherman stepped forward to question Satanta about the wagon train massacre, the proud chief readily admitted his leading role in the raid. In response, Sherman promptly had Satanta, Satank, and Big Tree arrested.[26]

When Mackenzie reached Fort Sill on June 4, he was ordered to deliver the three Kiowas to civilian authorities in Jacksboro for trial.

Kiowa War Chiefs

Lone Wolf. (*Bureau of American Ethnol-ogy, Smithsonain Institution*)

Satank. (*Bureau of American Ethnology, Smithsonian Institution*)

Four days later the three chained prisoners were placed in wagons for the journey to Texas. Not far from Fort Sill old Satank pulled a knife and stabbed one of his guards. The troopers shot him and left him mortally wounded by the side of the road to Texas. Upon receiving word from Mackenzie of Satank's death, Sherman grumbled, "Hanging would have been better, but we can be content that he is now extinct."[27]

Satanta and Big Tree soon faced a Jacksboro jury and were condemned to death. Edmund J. Davis, the Republican Reconstruction governor of Texas, now found himself the unwitting recipient of intense pressure from Washington to commute the sentence to life imprisonment. President Grant, Enoch Hoag, head of the Central Indian Superintendency, Lawrie Tatum, and others finally convinced the governor to commute the sentence to life imprisonment. The two hapless Kiowas were removed to the state prison at Huntsville.[28]

A letter from Sherman on the deterioration of Indian affairs on the southern plains persuaded Sheridan to leave Europe and return to his headquarters late in the summer of 1871. Clearly some changes in division boundary lines were essential if the Indians on the Staked Plain and in the Indian Territory were to be cowed effectively. As of November 1, 1871, the Indian Territory, except for Camp Supply, was transferred to the Department of Texas, and the entire department was moved from the Division of the South into Sheridan's division. At the same time the ever-reliable General Augur was ordered to replace Colonel Reynolds as department commander. It would be late January, however, before Augur could assume his new duties.[29]

Colonel Reynolds had the misfortune to become embroiled in a heated dispute with Mackenzie. The choleric, uncompromising commander of the Fourth Cavalry charged his department commander with fraudulent practices in the disbursement of army contracts, to which Reynolds responded by sending formal court-martial proceedings against Mackenzie to Sheridan. The lieutenant general's response was not at all what Reynolds hoped for. Mackenzie was tenderly tapped on the knuckles for not according proper respect to a superior officer, the court-martial charges were ignored, and Reynolds was removed as department commander and ordered to rejoin his regiment, the Third Cavalry, in the Department of the Platte.[30]

Back at Fort Sill, Colonel Grierson fretted over these changes. In May Sherman had agreed to transfer the Tenth Cavalry companies at Camp Supply to Fort Sill so that Grierson would have a larger command, but Sheridan vetoed the idea. Grierson was also worried about Augur. Reports reached him that Augur had been prejudiced against him "by a number of persons on one side of this matter" and that the new department commander was notorious for treating "the Colonels who were not West Pointers, with indifference and injustice."[31]

Grierson's support of Tatum and the Peace Policy had irretrievably damaged his reputation. So suspicious were other officers of his actions that they tended to place the worst possible interpretation on everything that he did. In August 1871, Mackenzie crossed into the Indian Territory with ten companies of his regiment in search of Kicking Bird's Kiowas, who had fled the reservation after the arrest of the three Kiowas in May. Grierson met him with six companies of the

Tenth, on Otter Creek, and they devised a plan to scout along divergent trails in search of the Kiowas. The day after the two regiments parted, Mackenzie received a message from Grierson that angered and frustrated the young colonel and essentially ended the campaign before it began. Mackenzie did not share the dispatch with his officers, but rumor had it that the nefarious Indian Ring had somehow managed to circumvent or overrule the wishes of General Sherman and had placed Grierson in command of both columns so that he could prevent Mackenzie from attacking the Indians. The camp gossip went that Grierson, the ever-willing tool of the Indian Ring, had then ordered Mackenzie away from the Kiowas so that he might reach them first. Despite this evil scheme to save the Kiowas from their deserved chastisement, Mackenzie was almost upon them when a messenger from Grierson reached the Indians and warned them to hurry back onto their reservation before the soldiers could attack. Thus the Kiowas escaped, according to Captain Robert Carter of the Fourth Cavalry, because "of the most wily and diplomatic 'side step,' and 'double cross,' our partner in this game of 'hide and go seek' (Grierson), had played upon his friend (?) Mackenzie." Carter noted, "For this act Mackenzie never quite forgave Grierson."[32]

In reality Grierson had received new orders, not from the Indian Ring, but from Sherman. The commanding general had reiterated his conviction that Grierson could handle affairs in the Indian Territory and that Mackenzie was not to cross into that country unless called upon by Grierson or in hot pursuit of hostiles. Grierson had then learned that the frightened Kiowas had restored all the property taken by Satanta and friends in the May raid into Texas, and desired peace. Accordingly, in compliance with his firm belief that it was better to reach accommodation with the Indians than seek military glory by slaughtering them, Grierson warned the Kiowas to move back onto their reservation. They did, and the brief campaign ended without bloodshed.[33] Far from reflecting Grierson's connivance with the Indian Ring, the episode reflected Sherman's confidence in his wartime comrade. Nevertheless, Grierson's position was fast becoming untenable, with his every move held suspect by his brother officers.

Sheridan moved promptly to solve this problem by transferring Grierson away from Fort Sill. Even though Grierson might well reflect the position of a large portion of the public, Sheridan was not obliged to suffer officers who failed to uphold his views on Indians if he could help it. He was determined to purge those who failed to support his official position in the face of civilian criticism. In June 1872 Grierson was ordered to move his headquarters to Fort Gibson, in the Cherokee Nation near the eastern border of the Indian Territory. The stated reason for this change was to deal with white intruders on the reservation, but that was simply an excuse, since Sheridan felt that there were "but few persons in that portion of the territory assigned to Grierson." Although rid of Grierson at Fort Sill, Sheridan worried nonetheless that the colonel would attempt to recoup his eclipsed fortunes by making "much out of little" over the question of white intruders. Sheridan warned General Augur "not to let Grierson make too much out of Gibson. He is fond of the place & will get his whole regiment there if a half a chance is given to him. I know him & you can take my judgement about him quite safely."[34]

Grierson never had time to "make too much out of Gibson," for in January 1873 he was ordered to Saint Louis as superintendent of the Mounted Recruiting Station, and Lieutenant Colonel (Brevet Major General) John W. Davidson assumed command of the Tenth Cavalry. This was a hard blow to Grierson and those Tenth Cavalry officers who were loyal to him, for the regiment, like the Third and Seventh cavalry regiments, was fiercely divided into cliques supporting the colonel and lieutenant colonel. Grierson soon learned that Davidson had secured command of the regiment by having "assisted himself into favor, if not made himself *entirely* so, by his concurrance in the expressed antagonism to you and your administration."[35]

Grierson never returned to Fort Sill. When his recruiting assignment ended in 1875, he assumed command of Fort Concho, in west Texas. Grierson viewed this as another blow from "Sherry-dan," and bitterly complained to his wife: "When he found that I was about to return to the Ind-Terr. at Ft. Sill he hurridly issued an order directing me to proceed to Fort Concho—transferred my Hd. Qrtrs on paper but actually separated me from my Rgt. and men. This last order—after rushing at great expense to the Government my Regt out of the Ind-Terr.—was the order issued to break *the camels back*."[36]

Despite Grierson's not unjustified paranoia, Sheridan did not transfer the regiment simply to banish him to the Texas desert. The transfer was also aimed at rotating the Tenth Cavalry with the Eighth

Cavalry and at punishing Lieutenant Colonel Davidson and his clique of officers for what Sheridan considered severe breaches of military honor. Black Jack Davidson was something of a brass-buttoned martinet. After graduating from West Point in 1845, he had served against the southwestern Indians before the Civil War, and while doing so had suffered severe sunstroke, which led to strange behavior on occasion. As Indian affairs became increasingly delicate around Fort Sill, Sheridan found Davidson's conduct to be "mixed and unexplained for." By the fall of 1874 he was so distrustful of Davidson's ability to cope with conditions around Fort Sill that he requested that Augur temporarily remain at the post.[37]

It was Davidson's social conduct, however, and not his military activities that brought Sheridan's wrath down fully on him. In the summer of 1874 a young lieutenant in the Tenth Cavalry was hauled before a "social court of officers," chaired by Davidson, and forced to resign his commission because of a liaison with a fellow officer's wife. The lieutenant was related to one of Sheridan's friends, and the lieutenant general was outraged with Davidson's treatment of the case. Sheridan visited Fort Sill and investigated the case of the young lieutenant as well as the Tenth Cavalry officer corps in general. Displeased, he decided that "the nest as Ft. Sill should be broken up—the companies scattered. Davidson has never been the proper man for that place." If the scattering of the companies did not suffice to break up the cliques and cabals, Sheridan proposed to "aid in putting the standard of social honor a little higher than it seems to have been at Ft. Sill by helping some of those concerned out of the service."[38] The most damaging result of all this was that the experiment of using black soldiers in the regular army was compromised and undermined by the personal disputes of the white officers in command of the Tenth Cavalry. Because of his distrust of Grierson and distaste for Davidson, Sheridan was delighted to have a good excuse to break up the regiment and scatter it about on a less critical frontier line. He spurned criticism of this action, declaring that the Tenth "may be considered as having had fair treatment."[39]

Following the imprisonment of Satanta and Big Tree, and the abortive Grierson-Mackenzie campaign of August 1871, a quiet settled around the Fort Sill reservation. This was largely due to the tireless efforts of Kicking Bird (Striking Eagle), leader of the Kiowa peace faction, and Indian agent Tatum. Colonel Mackenzie, barred from the reservation, turned his attention to the notorious Kwahadis, still roaming unpunished across the Staked Plain. In a month-long campaign Mackenzie covered over five hundred miles, but never managed to catch his elusive foe.[40]

The restraint displayed by the Fort Sill Kiowas lasted only until the spring of 1872, when White Horse and Big Bow led a large raiding party into Texas. On April 20 they struck a government contractor's wagon train at Howard's Wells, on the road from San Antonio to El Paso, killed all seventeen teamsters, and made off with a rich cargo of small arms and ammunition. On June 9 White Horse led a small party back into Texas and struck the home of Abel Lee, whose cabin was a few miles from Fort Griffin, killed him, his wife, and fourteen-year-old daughter, and carried three younger children back to the reservation. Kiowa raids continued throughout the summer, with even the military horse herd at Fort Sill depleted by prowling Indians.[41]

The summer raids, and especially the massacre at Howard's Wells, led to renewed criticism of the military for their inability to protect the frontier. Sheridan's old rival, Colonel Hazen, then en route to his banishment at Fort Buford in northern Dakota Territory, seized on the Howard's Wells tragedy as a vehicle to take some parting shots at his professional enemies. In a letter to the *New York Tribune* that was reprinted in the *Army and Navy Journal* and other papers, Hazen lashed out at both Sheridan and Grierson, accusing them of grievously mismanaging affairs around Fort Sill. Hazen accused Grierson of encouraging the Kiowa raids and insisted that, had Sheridan only left him in command, the Indians would have been crushed long before. Hazen's charges struck Henry Alvord, a former Tenth Cavalry captain prominent in the Indian reform movement, as being rather bizarre considering Hazen's protective attitude toward the Indians when he commanded in the area. "Is General Hazen still sore because he could not have your fine command—and post," Alvord asked Grierson, "or, being lately moved against his will does he take Howard's Wells as a club to hit at both Gen. Sheridan and you at once—on old scores generally—while saying, as usual a good word for his backer—Gen. Sherman?"[42]

Sheridan, for once in the same camp with Grierson, registered a defense of his actions with the War Department. "[Hazen] seems to have forgotten in his recent newspaper communication where he censures the Government for not chastising these Indians," declared Sheridan, "that when I had my sabers drawn to do it, that he pronounced them in the name of the Peace Commission friendly." Had it not been for Hazen's actions in 1868, Sheridan angrily reiterated, "the Texas frontier would be in a better condition than now." Sheridan confessed that he was powerless to punish the Kiowas because his troops could not operate on the reservation. "If I only had some authority to manage and punish the Kiowas," Sheridan lamented. "I would not stop until I had caused them *to respect* human life and the rights of property." Sheridan felt that it was high time to reconsider the wisdom of the Peace Policy, for "the Government will not be able for a much longer time to avoid the demands of progress and settlement, and must resort to measures which will render every portion of our extensive frontier safe for a citizen to travel over or occupy."[43]

Lawrie Tatum, more disillusioned than ever, halted disbursement of rations to his charges until the Lee children were turned over. The agent's effort to force the return of the children was soon overruled by the chief clerk to the Central Indian Superintendency, Cyrus Beede, a man characterized by Sheridan as "a little too simple for this earth."[44] Beede called a council with the Kiowas and Comanches, as well as representatives of the Cheyennes, Arapahos, Caddos, Wichitas, and affiliated tribes, for late July. Far from proving submissive, the Kiowas and Comanches were in a belligerent mood. White Horse declared that the Kiowas did not want peace with the whites and would raid when and where they pleased. As for the Lee children, Lone Wolf asserted that they would not be freed until Satanta and Big Tree were released from prison, all the forts were removed from Indian Territory, and the Kiowa's reservation was extended from the Rio Grande to the Missouri River.[45]

Despite Lone Wolf's declaration on the captive children, their release was soon secured by Tatum working through Kicking Bird. The return of the captives did not make Tatum sanguine about a lasting peace. He realized that it represented only the momentary triumph of Kicking Bird's counsel. "He whom I endeavor to serve has, I believe, enlightened my understanding in times of need," declared Tatum in attempting to explain his new-found pragmatism to his Quaker superiors. After the summer raids of 1872 he was convinced that only the army could stop the Fort Sill Indians from raiding Texas, and he recommended such a course of action. This recommendation was promptly disapproved by Superintendent Hoag and the commissioner of Indian affairs.[46]

Sheridan, of course, heartily approved Tatum's suggestion to call in the troops. He endorsed the recommendation and sent it on to the secretary of war with the pledge that "if the Government is willing to entrust me the settlement of this Texas frontier question and give me full support, I will promise peace to the frontier of Texas for ever, and I think in side of one year."[47] The general was exasperated with the blind optimism of those who administered the bankrupt Peace Policy. The Indians could not be relied on to punish their own people, and if the military did not take action, the murdering and stealing in Texas would continue unabated. "If a white man in this country commits a murder we hang him, if he steals a horse we put him in the penitentiary," Sheridan lectured the politicians in the War Department. "If an Indian commits these crimes we give him better food & more blankets. I think I may with reason say under this policy the civilization of the Wild Red Man will progress slowly."[48]

Permission to invade the reservation was not forthcoming, but the Kiowas and Comanches quieted down anyway in the fall of 1872. Far to the west of Fort Sill, on the north fork of the Red River near McClellan Creek, Colonel Mackenzie surprised Mow-way's Kotchateka Comanche village on September 29, 1872, killed between 23 and 52 Indians, and captured another 130, mostly women and children. Mackenzie destroyed the village and all the Indian property and incarcerated the captives at Fort Concho to ensure the good behavior of their people. Mackenzie's victory led several Comanche bands to report to Tatum's agency, including the Kwahadis. The Comanche defeat had a sobering effect on the Fort Sill Indians, since the release of Mackenzie's prisoners was made contingent on the good behavior of all the tribes. Another reason to suspend the Texas raids was provided in October by the commissioner of Indian affairs, who promised to secure the release of Satanta and Big Tree within six months if the Fort Sill Indians halted their depredations.[49]

Governor Davis of Texas could well testify to the lack of a national consensus on Indian affairs; he received intense pressure from both sides of the issue while considering whether to comply with the federal government's request to free Satanta and Big Tree. Reports even circulated that Sheridan had recommended a full pardon for the two Kiowas. Sheridan wrote the governor to make his position clear, and minced no words. He branded Satanta a murderer and the Kiowas "a small tribe—the most cowardly, & most untrustworthy on the plains. It will always be a matter of regret to me that I did not hang Satanta when I had him a prisoner in the winter of 1868. He has repeatedly merited such a punishment."[50] Sheridan's words were wasted, for the governor was won over by the argument of the commissioner of Indian affairs that the Texas courts had no jurisdiction over the Kiowas since they were not citizens, but wards of the government. The release was temporarily delayed when public sentiment swung against the Indians after the murder of Brigadier General Edward R. S. Canby during an April 1873 peace conference with insurgent Modocs in California, but in October 1873 Satanta and Big Tree were finally returned to their people.[51]

Tatum vigorously opposed the release of Satanta, but was ignored by his superiors. Feeling that Satanta's return would undercut his relationship with the Kiowas, and stung by the lack of confidence in him evidenced by his superiors, Tatum resigned his post, effective March 31, 1873. He sadly left the scene of his long labors, burdened with the conviction that Satanta's release "was like a dark and rolling cloud in the Western horizon, and when he should be restored to his people in freedom, it might burst like a tornado upon innocent and unsuspecting parties."[52]

CHAPTER 11

The Red River War:
"Instruct Them to Act
with Vindictive Earnestness"

As Indian ponies fattened on the spring grass, the Kiowa and Comanche raids into Texas picked up. Moreover, Cheyennes from their agency on the Canadian River increasingly joined in these incursions, launching some solo raids into Kansas as well. The depredations of white thieves on the Indian herds, the influence of a scourge of whiskey traders, poor government rations, racial hatred, the wanton slaughter of the buffalo herds by white hunters, and the desire of a new generation of young men to obtain social standing by winning war honors all combined to make a major outbreak inevitable by the summer of 1874.[1]

On June 27, 1874, several hundred Comanches and Cheyennes attacked a buffalo hunter stronghold at Adobe Walls, on the north fork of the Canadian River in the Texas Panhandle. The hunters beat off their assailants, but far from subduing the martial spirit among the Indians, the victory of the buffalo hunters added vengeance to the Indian tally of reasons for war.[2]

When word of the fight at Adobe Walls reached the governor of Kansas, he called upon Department of the Missouri commander John Pope to send troops to the relief of the buffalo hunters. Adobe Walls was not in Pope's department to begin with, and the general was not about to help the hunters. If he sent any troops into that region, Pope declared, it would be to "break up the grogshops and trading establishments rather than protect them." Pope considered the Adobe Walls trading post to have been established illegally in the Texas Panhandle "to trade with the Cheyennes and Arapahoes, and such other Indians as might come there, but mainly to supply the buffalo hunters, whose continuous pursuit and wholesale slaughter of the buffalo, both summer and winter, had driven the great herds down into the Indian Reservations." Pope felt that the traders were selling whiskey and guns to the Indians as well as to the white hunters and thus "did not consider it proper or right to defend such traffic."[3]

The buffalo hunters did not need Pope's help; they were more than capable of taking care of themselves, but his refusal to aid them enraged Sheridan. The division commander heartily approved of the activities of the buffalo hunters, feeling that they were doing the public a great service by depleting the Indians' shaggy commissary.

Sheridan felt it imperative to deprive the Indians of excuses to continue to hunt buffalo, because it led them off the reservation and into collision with the whites. Since several treaties, like the 1868 Sioux treaty, gave the Indians the legal right to hunt in certain areas off the reservation so long as the buffalo ranged in such numbers as "to justify the chase," Sheridan wanted quickly to reduce the buffalo population so as to terminate the hunting right. When, in 1881, the government considered protecting what was left of the herds, Sheridan vigorously opposed such action. "If I could learn that every buffalo in the northern herd were killed I would be glad," the general wrote his superiors. "The destruction of this herd would do more to keep Indians quiet than anything else that could happen. Since the destruction of the southern herd, which formerly roamed from Texas to the Platte, the Indians in that section have given us no trouble. If the Secretary of the Interior will authorize me to protect all other kinds of game in the far west I will engage to do so to the best of my ability."[4]

Pope's attitude toward the buffalo hunters particularly galled Sheridan. Never warm, the relationship between the two men had recently been strained by Sheridan's unhappiness over Pope's deployment of cavalry along the southern border of Kansas. As Sheridan saw it, Pope was using the Sixth Cavalry to throw up a defensive cordon. He complained to Sherman that Pope "shows great reluctance to giving up his defensive line, which, if held, is equivalent to doing nothing."[5]

Pope's refusal to assist the white men at Adobe Walls stoked

Sheridan's smoldering temper. He fired off a stinging letter to Sherman on July 16, criticizing Pope in the strongest terms. To Sheridan's dismay someone in Sherman's office leaked the letter to the press. "I am sorry it was done as Pope is very sensitive and may feel badly about it," Sheridan complained to Sherman. "Its publication gives me some embarrassment also." Sheridan suggested that Sherman plug up the leaks among his office staff, which led the general of the army to instigate an in-house investigation to discover how the confidential letter got into the hands of the reporters.[6]

Pope, notoriously thin-skinned, angrily complained to Sheridan about the letter. Sheridan, however, refused to back down. He wrote Pope, confessing regret over the publication of the dispatch, but reminding him that as division commander he had "the right to criticize the military actions of the officers under me, in accordance with my best judgment. Sheridan then delivered Pope a brief lecture on his duties as department commander,

> "You are in the charge of a large command, with powers to act in emergencies, or ordinarily, without order from me. You should have sent to the relief of the hunters or traders closed in at Adobe Wells [sic]. No odds what may have been the character of these men, they were in distress, and they came near being all massacred, and they had the legal right to hunt or trade at that point, for it is in Texas. . . . You should have used the troops for the protection of life and property wherever it might have been."[7]

Conciliatory words came hard to Sheridan, but he tried his best to soothe Pope's wounded pride. "There are few of us so far-sighted and perfect as not to make errors," wrote Sheridan, attempting without much success to be generous. "Your judgment was probably made up to the protection of the line of settlement in your Department—mine imbraced that and the Department of Texas also. I shall deeply regret that a friendship on my part existing during the last twelve or thirteen years, and which was often agreeably taxed in your defense, should be jeopardized by the blunder of some clerk about the Department in Washington, in letting my dispatch be published."[8]

Pope, declaring himself "very greatly chagrined" over the episode, informed Sheridan that he was not satisfied with the statement of regret. Exasperated, Sheridan turned the whole matter over to Sherman, who finally stepped between his two squabbling subordinates. He wrote both Sheridan and Pope, urging an end to their quarrel before it got out of hand. He agreed with Sheridan's right to criticize Pope, and reiterated his previously expressed conviction that it had been "absurd to use cavalry on the defensive" as Pope had tried. "No two men can perfectly agree," Sherman reminded Sheridan, "and therefore the necessity of the Junior yielding promptly & graciously to the Senior. We have a fine good set of General officers now, and I hope & pray we may all be friends—If I can do nothing else I can try to be Peace Maker, and if Genl Pope makes allusions to it I know you will meet him more than half way."[9]

The argument with Pope was disagreeable, but it did not distract Sheridan from formulating a campaign strategy for the southern plains. He received permission from the secretary of war on July 20, 1874 to proceed against the hostile Kiowas, Comanches, and Cheyennes. The secretary of the interior and commissioner of Indian affairs agreed to the campaign, but only on the condition that measures be taken to separate hostile from friendly Indians. All friendly Indians were to be enrolled at their agencies and carefully accounted for while the campaign was underway to prevent fraternization with the hostiles to the west. The concentration of the peaceful Indians near the agencies allowed Sheridan to invade the reservations. He had reiterated the need for permission to move onto the reservations when requesting authority to undertake the campaign; without such freedom of movement there was no hope of success. The opening of the reservations to Sheridan's troopers ended the Peace Policy's main tenet of peace within the reservation and war without and deprived the warriors of their last sanctuary.[10]

"If you order the Cavalry Regiment to penetrate the Reserve, I would advise that you instruct them to act with vindictive earnestness, and to make every Kiowa & Comanche knuckle down," suggested Sherman. He had no worry along those lines, for Sheridan was as earnest as ever, and was determined to crush his old foes of 1868 once and for all. "I propose now, if let alone," Sheridan assured his chief, "to settle this Indian matter in the Southwest forever."[11]

Sheridan's strategy was a copy of his 1868 campaign, except on a larger scale and without winter as an immediate ally. From Fort Dodge, Colonel (Brevet Major General) Nelson Miles was to move south and invade the Indian Territory with four companies of his own regiment, the Fifth Infantry, and eight companies of the Sixth Cavalry. Fiercely ambitious, Miles planned to make good on his first opportunity to prove himself as an Indian fighter. Major (Brevet Brigadier General) William R. Price, with four companies of his Eighth Cavalry, was ordered to move eastward, down the Canadian River, from Fort Bascom, New Mexico. These columns, both operating out of the Department of the Missouri, were under the overall command of General Pope.[12]

In the Department of Texas, General Augur ordered three more columns to move against the hostiles in the Texas Panhandle. Sheridan had Augur recall Mackenzie from the Rio Grande and move eight companies of the Fourth Cavalry to Fort Concho. Mackenzie was to push north from Concho toward the headwaters of the Red River, with eight companies of cavalry, as well as five infantry companies to escort his supply train and guard a supply base on the freshwater fork of the Brazos River. Lieutenant Colonel (Brevet Brigadier General) George P. Buell was to advance northwestward from Fort Griffin with six companies of Ninth and Tenth Cavalry Buffalo Soldiers, as well as two companies of his own Eleventh Infantry. From Fort Sill, Lieutenant Colonel Davidson would scour westward with six companies of the Tenth Cavalry and two companies of the Eleventh Infantry. Davidson was also charged with overseeing the enrollment of friendly Indians at the nearby Kiowa-Comanche agency. At the Cheyenne-Arapaho agency, on the Canadian River between Fort Sill and Camp Supply, a similar duty fell to Lieutenant Colonel (Brevet Major General) Thomas H. Neill, Sixth Cavalry. Known in army circles as Beau Neill because of his elegant dress and suave manners, he had been a staff officer for Sheridan during the Shenandoah campaign.[13]

Sheridan made it clear that troop commanders were not to concern themselves with military department lines or the Indian reservation boundaries, but were to pursue and punish guilty Indians wherever found. It was estimated that the troops would face between eight hundred and twelve hundred hostile Kiowas, Comanches, and Cheyennes. The Cheyennes were Sheridan's main concern, for he considered them "the most formidable" of the southern plains tribes. Once they were chastised, he felt confident that Indian resistance would collapse. As in his winter campaign of 1868–69, Sheridan hoped to harry the Indians incessantly, keeping them ever on the move,

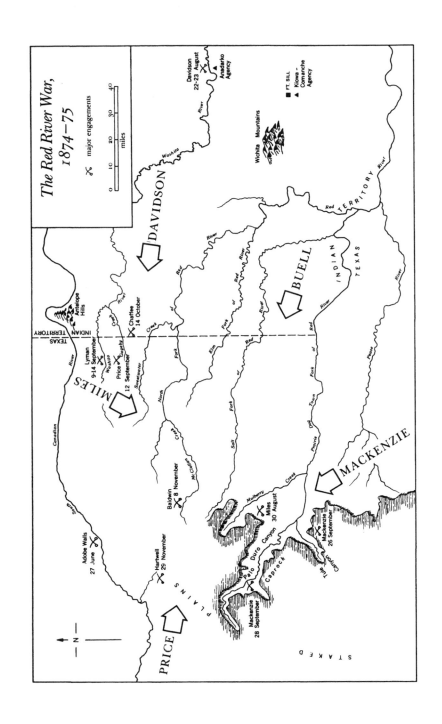

The Red River War, 1874–75

✗ major engagements

miles
0 10 20 30 40

DAVIDSON

Davidson
22–23 August ✗

Anadarko
Agency

■ FT. SILL
▲ Kiowa–
Comanche
Agency

Wichita Mountains

Washita River

Red

River

Red River

Fork

of

Red

River

BUELL

North Fork

of

Red

River

INDIAN

TEXAS

River

Red

River

TERRITORY

Antelope
Hills

INDIAN TERRITORY
TEXAS

Chaffee
14 October ✗

Sweetwater Creek

Lyman
9–14 September ✗
Price ✗
12 September

Gageby Creek

Washita River

MILES

McClellan Creek

North Fork

Salt Fork

Elm

Fork

or

Red

Fork

Double

Mountain

Fork of

Brazos

Prairie Dog Town Fork

of

Red

River

Pease

River

TEXAS

MACKENZIE

Baldwin
8 November ✗

Canadian River

South

Canadian

River

Adobe Walls
27 June

Hartwell
25 November ✗

PRICE

Mulberry Creek

Miles
30 August ✗

Palo Duro Canyon

CAPROCK

Mackenzie
28 September ✗

Tule Canyon

Mackenzie
26 September ✗

STAKED
PLAINS

N

preventing them from hunting or grazing their stock, and thus starving them into submission or slowing them down enough so that one of the columns could strike them. As in the Washita campaign, he hoped that one of the converging columns would eventually drive the weary Indians into another of the columns.[14]

The Indians branded as hostile were not to be allowed to surrender at the agencies, nor were their women and children to be allowed to come in. Sheridan realized that the families would slow down the warriors, tax their food supply, and make them more anxious. The fact that the noncombatants would undoubtedly be caught in the cross fire of any engagement with troops, and that this could be prevented by allowing them to move onto their agencies, was of no concern to Sheridan. "All captured Indians must be treated as prisoners of war, and all captured stock regarded as government property," Sheridan instructed his field commanders. "All surrenders must be total and absolute, and arms of every description delivered up."[15]

Sheridan regretted that events forced him to lose the use of winter as an ally against the tribes, but he wanted to move promptly against the raiders. "I am not at all sanguine that much can be done at this season of the year," he complained to Pope, "but if we let the Indians run unrestrained, nearly all those who are for peace may have to join them. We will keep at them so long as we have the present authority, and will be sure to get them in the end."[16]

The weather, however, turned out to be the soldiers' ally. A devastating drought, accompanied by temperatures over one hundred degrees, scorched the Staked Plain, dried up water holes, and forced the Indians eastward. This calamity, accompanied by a locust plague, consumed whatever sparse vegetation survived the heat. These were hard blows to both soldier and warrior, but the natives suffered more, since they depended on the land for survival. Still, the drought delayed Mackenzie and afflicted Miles's men so terribly that on one occasion they opened the veins in their arms and moistened their parched and swollen lips with blood.[17]

First action of the campaign was seen by Davidson at the Wichita Indian agency at Anadarko, some thirty miles north of Fort Sill. The agent at Anadarko requested Davidson's help when a band of Nakoni Comanches, known to have been raiding in Texas, attempted to enroll as friendlies at the agency. Permission had been granted to the troops to move among the friendly Indians at the agencies in search of hostiles, and so Davidson, with four troops of his regiment, marched on Anadarko to demand the surrender of the Nakonis. A fight broke out betweeen the soldiers and the Comanches, who were joined in the engagement by Kiowas under Lone Wolf and Satanta. Little blood was spilled, but the Nakonis and their Kiowa allies were sent scurrying westward, up the Washita River, clearly branded as hostile.[18]

A week after the fight at Anadarko Agency, Colonel Miles's troops clashed with two hundred Cheyenne warriors along the bluffs that marked the border of the Staked Plain. The Indians retreated after a five-hour running battle, but Miles could not follow them on to the Staked Plain for want of supplies. He contented himself with destroying the Cheyennes' abandoned property and then turned back toward the Antelope Hills to resupply. Miles's line of supply, however, was in danger of being severed by the fugitives from the Anadarko fight. On September 9 a large party of Comanches and Kiowas, including Lone Wolf, Satanta, and Big Tree, swooped down upon one of Miles's supply trains near the Washita River and besieged it for three days until troops under Major Price approached. Another running fight followed as the warriors covered the retreat of their families and then withdrew. Price, also low on supplies, did not pursue.

Miles, increasingly frustrated by logistical problems and worried that Mackenzie would strike hostiles on the Staked Plain first and reap all the glory, took his wrath out on Major Price. Angered that Price had not pursued the hostiles after his September 12 fight, Miles merged the major's column with his own and assumed full command. "I would like to know if Sheridan is going to take any interest in this Indian affair," fretted Miles in a letter to his wife while awaiting supplies. "I am satisfied that there must be gross mismanagement somewhere in our rear. . . . I must remain here, much as it is disagreeable for me, until I can obtain supplies and then go for them again, unless Mackenzie and Davidson finish it up in the meantime."[19]

The fulminations of Colonel Miles notwithstanding, Sheridan was taking an intense interest in the troops' progress. Miles's activity particularly pleased him. "I desire to say that Colonel Miles' conduct throughout the campaign so far, mee s my decided approval," Sheridan wrote the department adjutant general upon receiving Miles's report. Sheridan pronounced himself so satisfied with Miles's ability that he did "not wish even to embarrass him with any suggestions," at the same time reassuring the anxious colonel that "his action in returning for supplies is perfectly satisfactory."[20]

The supply problems that so bedeviled Colonel Miles and the other column commanders were nothing new to Sheridan. He had confronted the same shortfalls in 1868–69. Sheridan viewed such shortages as the unavoidable price of campaigning in so vast a region on so large a scale with so little time to prepare. "All these columns were pushed out much sooner than desirable, especially that of Colonel Miles and Major Price," Sheridan conceded on October 1, "but I deemed it necessary that we should take the field at once to prevent the hostile Indians from forcing out those of their tribes who had made up their minds to remain at peace, and also to prevent the accumulation of winter supplies from the buffalo herds."[21]

In order more closely to supervise operations, Sheridan departed Chicago on October 8 for Fort Sill. His arrival at the fort nine days later coincided with the return of Black Jack Davidson's column from a fruitless 335-mile march that had netted but three stray Indians killed for over a month of campaigning. A tragic conclusion to the march occurred on October 16 when Lieutenant Silas Pepoon, whom Sheridan had selected to command the reorganized Forsyth scouts in 1868, committed suicide. If the troopers had any hopes of resting before renewing their campaign, they were sorely disappointed. Sheridan ordered Davidson to continue his search for hostiles on October 21, with but four days to resupply and refit.

Sheridan had already decided to remove the unsatisfactory Davidson from command of Fort Sill and transfer the Tenth Cavalry out of the Indian Territory. His meeting with the lieutenant colonel only reinforced that conviction. Sheridan realized that troop transfers would have to await the defeat of the hostiles, but after meeting with Davidson he informed Belknap that he intended, "as soon as it can properly be brought about," to "scatter the companies at Fort Sill & bring Mackenzie there with the best part of his regiment."[22]

While at Fort Sill Sheridan renewed his acquaintance with First Lieutenant (Brevet Captain) Richard Henry Pratt of the Tenth Cavalry. They had first met in Tennessee while serving in the Army of the Cumberland during the Civil War. The young officer had again come to the general's attention during the 1868–69 Indian war. Pratt now commanded a detachment of Indian scouts, and after conferring with Sheridan he was authorized to increase their number from twenty-five to eighty-five. During Sheridan's second evening at Fort Sill, Pratt's scouts staged a war dance on the post parade ground for the benefit of the general and his staff. When the Indian scouts departed Fort Sill on October 21, Sheridan came out to review them. The mounted warriors marched by in column by twos, loudly singing their war song to the beat of two gourd rattles. Clapping his hands in appreciation, Sheridan congratulated Pratt on his handling of the Indians.[23]

White men who could open up channels of communication with the Indians and deal effectively with them always impressed Sheridan. Over the years he found men like Ben Clark, Hugh Scott, John Bourke, Frank and Luther North, and William P. Clark quite useful to him. He now tagged Lieutenant Pratt as such a man. Sheridan would later have an important job for him.

After the departure of the Tenth Cavalry, Sheridan remained at Fort Sill for three more days, conferring with Augur and interviewing chiefs from the friendly bands on the nearby reservation. On October 25 Sheridan departed for the Cheyenne-Arapaho agency, learning upon his arrival that Major George W. Schofield, with three companies of the Tenth Cavalry, had surprised a large Comanche camp on Elk Creek the day before, taking 69 warriors and 250 women and children prisoner. These Indians had been forced eastward by the operations of Buell and Mackenzie.

Mackenzie had been particularly successful, routing a large Indian village in Palo Duro Canyon, on the eastern edge of the Staked Plain, on September 28. The Indians, a combination of Comanches, Kiowas, and Cheyennes, had escaped with a loss of but three warriors killed, but the battle nevertheless proved to be a devastating defeat. Several hundred lodges were burned, along with vast quantities of foodstuffs and other Indian property, and over one thousand Indian ponies were shot by Mackenzie's troopers. From the Cheyenne-Arapaho agency Sheridan wired Sherman news of the Indian defeats, along with his assurance that with luck the war would be over before winter set in.[24]

"I wish the troops had managed to kill more bucks," Sherman replied, "but when they are disarmed & unhorsed and collected on their Reservation under military surveillance they will likely behave themselves for a time, at least until the Quakers manipulate them a while longer." Despite such pessimism, Sherman was pleased with the campaign's progress, and especially with the movement of the troops. "I am charmed at the handsome conduct of our troops in the Field," reflected the commanding general, in a nostalgic mood. "They go in with the relish that used to make our hearts *glad* in 1864–5."[25]

Sheridan, like Sherman, worried over what would happen to the hostiles once the Indian Bureau had control of them again. While at the Cheyenne-Arapaho agency, he met with several of the peace chiefs, many of whom he knew from his last campaign, to seek their opinion on how to handle the surrendering hostiles. The Cheyennes were pleased to talk again with Hotohci o Niis (Three Stars), as they now called Sheridan. They urged him to punish the war faction. If the hostiles were not severely punished, the position of the peace faction would be undercut and the lives of the Cheyenne and Arapaho peace chiefs endangered. Sheridan had found the Kiowa and Comanche peace faction at Fort Sill in agreement with this sentiment.[26]

The meetings with the Indian peace chiefs reinforced Sheridan's conviction that some special mode of punishment should be meted out to the leaders of the hostile faction of the tribes. Before departing for Fort Sill, he had secured permission from the president and the secretary of war to institute a three fold plan for punishing the Indians. Those warriors who had committed murder or stolen horses and cattle, Sheridan wanted tried by a military commission. This had been the method used in July 1873 to deal with the remnants of the California Modocs who had assassinated Brigadier General Canby, and it seemed the surest method to ensure the execution of the hostile leaders. Those Indians who might escape the military commission for lack of evidence, yet who were known ringleaders in the war, Sheridan wished imprisoned far to the east at some suitable fort. In order to punish the entire hostile faction, Sheridan desired that they be completely disarmed, with all their horses sold at auction and the proceeds invested in cattle for the friendly faction of the tribes. This plan was approved on October 6 by Grant and Belknap.[27]

Sheridan hoped to move swiftly with his military commission. He instructed Pope and Augur to see that there was a good "example made in the way of punishment," for "if a few of the murderers can be hanged, the effect will be salutary." Sheridan's department commanders urged him to delay the trials, fearing that some of the worst hostiles, like Lone Wolf and Big Bear, would not surrender if they knew what was in store for them. Sheridan reluctantly agreed.[28]

There was one notorious warrior, however, that Sheridan did not have to delay punishing. That was Satanta. The Kiowa chief had surrendered to Beau Neill at the Cheyenne-Arapaho agency on October 4. Although Satanta claimed to have taken no part in the war and to have fled the reservation only because of fright over the Anadarko affair, he found himself back in chains. Sheridan ordered that his foe be immediately transported back to Huntsville State Prison. Four years later the despondent Satanta committed suicide.[29]

Sheridan disagreed with General Pope and others that the Indians had been driven to hostilities by the incursion of white thieves and whiskey peddlers. Writing on October 1, he had declared: "This outbreak does not look to me, as being originated by the actions of bad white men, or the sale of whiskey to Indians by traders. It is the result of the restless nature of the Indian, who has no profession but arms and naturally seeks war and plunder when the grazing gets high enough to feed his ponies."[30] But while at the Cheyenne-Arapaho agency the lieutenant general got a firsthand glimpse at the audacity of the white horse thieves from Kansas. Late on October 27 the outlaws made off with seventy-five of the friendly Indians' horses. Enraged, Sheridan ordered out a detachment of cavalry with instructions to "pursue and punish at all hazards" the outlaws. The cavalry caught the thieves on the north fork of the Pawnee River, killing two and recovering most of the horses.[31]

Sheridan left the agency on October 28, moving up the North Canadian to Camp Supply. After inspecting the post he traveled to Fort Dodge, which he reached on November 3, and from there took the railroad back to Chicago. He was confident that the war was almost over, feeling that all the Comanches, save perhaps the Kwahadis, would surrender in November. "If we can get a few more turns at them, the end will be at hand," Sheridan assured Miles while en route to Fort Dodge. "The cold weather will be bad medicine for them in their present destitute state."[32]

George Forsyth was left in the Indian Territory to keep Sheridan informed on the progress of the campaign and to search out a site for a new post to be built to the west of the Kiowa-Comanche reservation. Sheridan hoped to complete the encirclement of the Indian reservation and cut off the Staked Plain from malcontents. Forsyth soon located a suitable location about a mile south of the head of Sweetwater Creek, some 146 miles northwest of Fort Sill. Colonel Miles, whose column Forsyth joined to observe the campaign, established a permanent supply cantonment at the Sweetwater site. In 1875 the supply post was officially established as Fort Elliott, named in honor of the Seventh Cavalry major slain at the Washita.[33]

The Red River War moved swiftly to its conclusion. While the summer days of the campaign had been marked by fierce heat and severe drought, after September 5 heavy rains came, making travel over the muddy plains difficult and earning from the Indians the title Wrinkled-Hand Chase for the last months of conflict. On November 8 a detachment from Miles's column struck a large Cheyenne encampment near the headwaters of McClellan Creek, rescuing two young white girl captives. The fleeing Cheyennes were relentlessly pursued. The rain soon turned to snow, but still Miles kept portions of his command in the field scouring the frozen country longer than any of the other columns, until he finally disbanded his expedition in late January. The Cheyennes, in ever-increasing numbers came into their agency throughout the winter to surrender, 820 giving up on March 6 alone. A few, under leaders such as Bull Elk and old Medicine Arrows, fled to the north, where they joined the Sioux and Northern Cheyennes.[34]

The Kiowas and Comanches, with the exception of the lucky Kwahadis, were harried from their haunts on the Staked Plain by the movements of Buell and Mackenzie. Lieutenant Colonel Buell, after destroying four Indian villages along the salt fork of the Red River and pursuing the fugitives upriver, was finally forced to pull back because of bad weather and supply shortages and terminate his campaign in early December. Mackenzie, after his victory at Palo Duro Canyon, combed the southern reaches of the Staked Plain until late December and then disbursed his command to Forts Concho, McKavett, and Richardson. The colonel proceeded to Fort Sill to assume command of the post and the Kiowa-Comanche reservation. As with the Cheyennes, small parties of Kiowas and Comanches had surrendered at Fort Sill as early as October, but it was not until January that larger bands came in. On February 26, 1875, Lone Wolf, the principal Kiowa war chief,

257

surrendered with over 250 of his followers. It was not until spring, however, that the Comanches came in, with the Kotchatekas under Mow-way surrendering on April 18, and the independent Kwahadis, over 400 strong, finally submitting to Mackenzie on June 2.[35]

With most of the Indians back on their reservations, Sheridan's plan for punishing the war faction was put into operation. There would, however, be no military commission. The attorney general had ruled that the law required the existence of a state of war to warrant trial by such a court and that it was impossible for war to exist between a nation and its wards. This ruling saved President Grant from damaging his relationship with the humanitarians, by allowing him gracefully to retreat from his initial approval of Sheridan's plan. Obviously there would be no hangings such as Sheridan desired, but he was allowed to continue with his program of selecting leading hostiles for imprisonment on the East Coast.

The selection of seventy-two warriors to be imprisoned at Fort Marion, Florida, was accomplished in a rather arbitrary manner. It was necessary for the army officers charged with selecting the internees, Lieutenant Colonel Neill at the Cheyenne-Arapaho agency and Lieutenant Pratt at Fort Sill, to rely heavily on Indian informants. Many old intratribal feuds and jealousies played an important role in who was fingered as guilty of crimes. Neill marked thirty-three Cheyennes and two Arapahos for internment. The attempted escape of one of Neill's prisoners at the Cheyenne agency resulted in some stray shots striking the main Cheyenne village, panicking the Indians into fleeing the reservation. Eleven Cheyennes were killed by Neill's troops on April 6 before they could escape to the west. Most of these Indians soon returned to the reservation, but a detachment of the Sixth Cavalry clashed with a band of Cheyenne fugitives in northwestern Kansas, killing twenty-seven. This last clash of the Red River War had the highest Indian casualty figure of the conflict.[36]

Pratt selected nine Comanches, twenty-seven Kiowas, and one Caddo for internment. Among the Kiowa prisoners were Lone Wolf, the tribal war chief, and Woman's Heart, an implacable foe of the whites who battled Custer and Evans in 1868 and took a leading role in the 1874 outbreak. Most of the prisoners, however, were men of no rank or influence. They were selected by the Kiowa peace chief, Kicking Bird. This melancholy task was his last on behalf of the whites, for

Kicking Bird, or Striking Eagle, the leader of the Kiowa peace faction who tirelessly worked to avoid war. It was his melancholy task
to select warriors to be imprisoned for their part in the Red River
War. In retaliation he was murdered. "I have taken the white
man's road, and am not sorry," he declared as he lay dying from
strychnine poisoning. "Tell my people to keep the good path."
(*Bureau of American Ethnology, Smithsonian Institution*)

Kicking Bird died of strychnine poisoning a few days later. The Comanches, who had contributed more warriors to the fighting than the Kiowas, had fewer banished as a result of earlier agreements reached with Davidson and Mackenzie granting immunity from punishment in exchange for their surrender. Lieutenant Pratt was quick to confess to Sheridan the inequity of the prisoner selection, pointing out that "most of the young men being sent away have simply been following their leaders, much as a soldier obeys his officers, and are not really so culpable."[37]

During his October visit to Fort Sill, Sheridan had told Pratt to call on him if he ever needed assistance, and the young officer took the general at his word, writing in late April 1875 to request the detail of supervising the imprisonment of the Indians. This was agreeable to Sheridan, and he recommended Pratt's appointment to the secretary of war. On April 26, 1875, Pratt led his sad entourage eastward from Fort Sill, accompanied by the interpreter Romero, who had served in the same capacity for Sheridan and Custer in 1868. For Pratt it was the beginning of a momentous journey that would lead him to found the Carlisle Indian School and win him recognition as one of the leading reformers and humanitarians of the century. It was indeed ironic that Phil Sheridan's patronage should give birth to the lifetime crusade of the Red Man's Moses.[38]

When Sherman inspected Fort Sill in November 1875, he was well satisfied with the subdued Kiowas and Comanches. "I am sure if Mckenzie [sic] can have the entire control," Sherman assured Sheridan, "we will have no more trouble with these Indians."[39] They had been disarmed and dismounted, their pony herds sold at a great loss and the proceeds used under Sheridan's order to purchase New Mexico sheep for the once-mighty buffalo hunters. Their chiefs scattered to white prisons and their young men held hostage far to the east, the Kiowas and Comanches were never again to be a threat to white expansion.

The Red River War of 1874–75, or Indian Territory Campaign as the army officially called it, completed the subjugation of the southern plains tribes that Sheridan had undertaken in 1868. It had not been a particularly graceful campaign, with monumental logistical problems repeatedly interfering with troop movements, and the lack of a central commander for the various columns leading to arguments over command. Massive stock losses were incurred by the military as a result of the weather—first the drought, and then severe winter storms—and the soldiers likewise suffered from exposure to the extreme climate. Little blood had been shed, with but eight soldiers killed and another thirty-six wounded in over six months of campaigning. The army claimed to have killed eighty-three Indians, amost half of whom died as a result of the April 1875 panic at the Cheyenne agency. It has not been loss of life in battle that had defeated the Indians, but, rather, the terrible toll wrought by starvation, exposure, stock and property losses, and constant insecurity. The campaign had reaffirmed the effectiveness of Sheridan's philosophy of total war. "This campaign was not only very comprehensive," Sheridan boasted, "but was the most successful of any Indian campaign in this country since its settlement by the whites."[40]

CHAPTER 12

Reconstructing Louisiana:
"To Charge upon the Liberties
of His Fellow-Citizens"

Never was the low priority given the frontier by government officials more apparent than in 1875–76, when Sheridan was twice ordered to Louisiana. The nation's chief Indian fighter was called from the frontier at that critical moment when the Red River War was winding down and the Great Sioux War beginning. At that time, as always, national policy-makers were far more concerned with eastern political needs than with the prosecution of Indian conflicts far to the west.

By the winter of 1874 political affairs in ever-turbulent Louisiana were in chaos, and the president decided to send Sheridan as his personal representative to investigate matters and take charge of the state if necessary. Sheridan was, of course, firmly prejudiced against the unreconstructed rebels of Louisiana as a result of his previous duty in that state and was ill suited by temperament for such a delicate and potentially explosive chore. Grant, however, wanted someone in Louisiana that he could depend on for unquestioning loyalty and prompt action.

The bitter animosities that had marked Louisiana politics since the end of the war climaxed in the 1872 gubernatorial election. It was impossible to tell the real winner because of open fraud and the violent intimidation of voters. Two rival governments claimed to rule the state. In March 1873 the impasse seemingly had been resolved when police forces loyal to the Republican government dispersed the Democratic government after the latter attempted to raise a militia force in New Orleans. The Republicans, under Governor William P. Kellogg, retained de facto control of the state until September 1874, when an army of White Leaguers and Democratic militia captured the statehouse and forced Kellogg to seek sanctuary in the customs house. Federal troops restored Kellogg to his office, and passions ran high as the voters went to the polls the next month. Once more violence and fraud were the rule. The election returns gave the Democrats a majority in the state legislature, but a Republican-controlled election return board contravened the rule of the ballot and decided that fifty-three Republicans and fifty-three Democrats had been elected, with five seats left to be decided by the legislature. It was clear that in January there would be trouble when the legislature convened.[1]

President Grant had carefully monitored these developments. The congressional elections of 1874 had gone against the Republicans, with the Democrats capturing the House of Representatives for the first time since the war. The North seemed weary of bloody shirt politics, accompanied as it was by Republican corruption both North and South, while at the same time the Ku Klux Klan, White League, and other white terrorist organizations sapped Republican strength in the South by intimidating black voters. This did not bode well for the Republican standard-bearer in 1876. It was essential, then, that the power of the southern terrorists be broken and as much of the South as possible be held in the Republican fold. Grant saw Sheridan as just the man to restore order in Louisiana, save the unpopular regime from being overthrown, and set an example for the rest of the South.[2]

On Christmas Eve, Sheridan received secret instructions from Secretary of War Belknap to inspect Mississippi and Louisiana, with special regard to New Orleans, and "ascertain the true condition of affairs" for the president. This order was not to be recorded in the division record books unless "action is taken under it," but Sheridan was extended extraordinary latitude in what action he might take. This included authority to assume command of the Division of the South, if he deemed it necessary. Neither General Sherman nor Major General Irvin McDowell, commander of the Division of the South, was informed of Sheridan's mission. Belknap's orders instructed Sheridan to report only to the secretary of war, and to use cipher when doing so.[3]

Sherman, when finally informed of Sheridan's mission, instantly saw through the cloak-and-dagger melodrama to the fact that the army's second in command was being used as the iron fist of a crude political power play. The flinty army commander took it stoically, but grumbled to his brother, Senator John Sherman, "I have all along tried to save our officers and soldiers from the dirty work imposed on them . . . and may, thereby, have incurred the suspicion of the President that I did not cordially sustain his force." It was Sheridan, not the secretary of war, who first informed Sherman of the mission. Sherman assured Sheridan of his support, but made it clear that he hoped he would not assume command in New Orleans.[4]

The Louisiana state legislature was to convene on January 4, 1875, and Sheridan and several members of his staff as well as a number of ladies, including Miss Irene Rucker, the winsome young daughter of his quartermaster general, arrived in New Orleans a few days before. Rumors that he would assume command abounded, but Sheridan denied them, declaring that he was on his way to Havana with Miss Rucker and the other ladies. The *New Orleans Picayune* was not fooled, and proceeded to condemn him soundly as soon as he arrived: "We know him for the man who desolated the valley of the Shenandoah, and brought fire and the sword and famine among its people; and to whom Louisiana was a desolation to which that of fire and sword and famine might well be regarded as preferable. Yes, we know General Phil Sheridan well enough; and because we know him for what he is, he has been sent here by the President in order to add this crowning outrage to the outrages which have already been heaped upon us."[5]

As soon as he reached New Orleans, Sheridan met with Colonel (Brevet Major General) William H. Emory, commander of the Department of the Gulf (the states of Louisiana, Mississippi, and Arkansas), to look over the disposition of troops in the area. Emory had an infantry regiment in the city, cavalry farther inland, and considerable reserve power at Jackson Barracks and on nearby warships. Governor Kellogg had requested that troops be stationed near the statehouse on January 4, and Emory had agreed to comply.

Sheridan approved of these arrangements, but found himself disenchanted with Emory, worrying about the colonel's "ability to keep things steady and inspire confidence."[6] Emory was an old comrade in arms, having commanded a corps in the Shenandoah campaign, but

Sheridan now characterized him to Belknap as a "very weak old man, entirely unfitted for this place." Sheridan's prejudice against older officers, so evident in his dealings with Colonel Sully and General Ord, colored his opinion of the sixty-three-year-old Emory. However, the fact that the colonel was a Marylander also played a part; Sheridan was convinced that Emory "was not at any time on the side of the Government."[7] Sheridan recommended that Emory be forced to retire from the army, or at the very least be relieved of his command. In his place Sheridan wanted young Colonel Mackenzie. Because of his distrust of Emory and since an immediate change in department commanders was impossible, Sheridan decided, on January 2, to annex the Department of the Gulf to his division on the day that the Louisiana legislature convened.[8]

When the legislature met at noon on January 4, there were fifty-two Republicans and fifty Democrats present. Before the roll could be tabulated, a Democratic representative suddenly nominated one of his colleagues, Louis Wiltz, for temporary speaker. Wiltz rushed to the rostrum, seized the gavel, began accepting nominations for clerk and sergeant-at-arms, and in the confusion declared them elected. The bewildered Republicans, taken off guard by the well-planned Democratic coup, now attempted to leave the building so as to prevent a quorum. From the rear of the chamber appeared armed men displaying badges marked assistant sergeant-at-arms, and they forcibly detained enough Republicans to keep the house in session. The Democrats then busied themselves seating five of their number in the contested seats left unfilled by the returning board. Meanwhile, those Republicans who had escaped gathered in the halls outside the chamber and harangued their supporters among the crowd. Violence appeared imminent. Amazingly, Colonel Philippe Régis de Trobriand, commanding the troops stationed at the statehouse, responded to the request of the illegally elected speaker, Wiltz, and cleared the hallways. The Democrats had been protected by the army, but not for long.[9]

The Republican legislators who had escaped appeared before the governor to request assistance in regaining their seats and restoring the legislature to order. Kellogg called on the federal troops to reseat the Republicans and eject the five illegally seated Democrats. Within two hours of the Democratic coup Colonel de Trobriand was back in the house chamber with his soldiers. With bayonets fixed they forcibly ejected the five newly seated Democrats, whereupon Wiltz and the rest of the Democrats stamped out in protest to sit in a rump session elsewhere. The Republicans, guarded by de Trobriand and his men, then organized the house with their own speaker. It was a gloomy day for constitutional procedure, but Grant had the Republican government in Louisiana that he wanted.[10]

Sheridan now moved to annex the Department of the Gulf to his command, an act which became official at nine that evening. He reported the day's activities to Belknap, characterizing the role played by his troops as that of a neutral party. To support his claim he pointed to de Trobriand's rescue of the Democrats following the noon coup.[11] Clearly, Sheridan was grasping at straws to excuse what he must have realized was too heavy-handed an action, for it was clear to everyone that the army firmly supported the Republicans, who now controlled both the governor's chair and the legislature from behind a wall of bayonets.

Sheridan, however, was far from satisfied with the day's work. On January 5, he sent a telegram to Belknap, its contents soon famous throughout the nation, branding his opposition as "banditti," and suggesting that "the terrorism now existing in Louisiana, Mississippi, and Arkansas could be entirely removed and confidence and fair dealing established by the arrest and trial of the ring-leaders of the armed white leagues." The paramilitary White League, which used economic and physical intimidation, social ostracism, lynching, and assassination to achieve its goal of subjugating the blacks and over-throwing the Republicans, numbered among its members many of the region's most prominent citizens. Members of the White League were considered patriotic heroes by most white citizens of the region, so Sheridan's statement was regarded as a virtual declaration of war. But the feisty general was not interested in name-calling. He promised Belknap, if Congress or the president "would issue a proclamation declaring them banditti that no further action need be taken except that which would desolve [sic] upon me." The action that Sheridan had in mind was arrest and trial by military commission.[12]

There was precedent to back Sheridan's request. In October 1871 President Grant had issued a proclamation suspending habeas corpus in nine South Carolina counties better to enable army troops and federal marshals to combat the Ku Klux Klan. In July 1873 a military commission had sat in judgment over six Modoc Indians charged with assassinating Brigadier General Edward R. S. Canby and sentenced the defendants to death. Just the previous October, Grant and Belknap had approved Sheridan's request of trial by military commission for the Indian leaders in the Red River War. Sheridan had good reason to expect that his present request would also be approved.[13]

Sheridan, ready to fight, wanted to dispose of bothersome laws that tied his hands, preventing him from quickly crushing the White League. Congressman George F. Hoar of Massachusetts, chairman of a House Committee investigating the rival state governments, was in New Orleans, and Sheridan called on him to press his views. More people have been killed within the last four years in Louisiana for their political opinions, Sheridan lectured the congressman, than were slain during the Mexican War. "What you want to do, Mr. Hoar, when you get back to Washington, is to suspend the what-do-you-call-it," sputtered the general! He meant, of course, the habeas corpus. Congressman Hoar, a firm admirer of the general, found Sheridan's simplicity amusing.[14] Many in the country, however, were not blessed with the congressman's sense of humor.

The Democratic press had a field day at the expense of the president and his general, while embarrassed Republican newspapers generally remained silent. The *New York Tribune* warned that next the president was likely to "decide who shall belong to the next Congress and enforce his decisions by five or six regiments of United States troops, commanded by the truthful and just man, General Sheridan." The *Cincinnati Inquirer* denounced Sheridan's action as the "crowning iniquity of a Federal administration not wanting in iniquities," while an Atlanta paper suggested, "If any hanging or shooting is to be done, it is just possible that a braggart and dirty tool of an upstart like Sheridan may ornament a lamp-post quite as rapidly as any White League 'ringleader' may grace a gallows." The *Shreveport Times* paid homage to the general's ethnicity and also took a slap at his Indian policy by tagging him "Piegan H. Sheridan" and noting that his recent actions displayed all the "brush instincts of the lowest class of Irish." The *New Orleans Picayune* despaired that "any attempt to influence General Sheridan by any rational argument would be as futile as the effort to make a Maori chieftan understand the binomial theorem."[15]

William Cullen Bryant, at a mass meeting held in New York's Cooper Institute, declared that Sheridan should "tear off his epaulets and break his sword and fling the fragments into the Potomac, rather than go upon so impious an errand."[16] Stern protests of Sheridan's actions were also forthcoming from Charles Francis Adams, Jr., and William Evarts. Senator Thomas Bayard rose in Congress to condemn Sheridan, accusing him of riding "rough-shod" over the Bill of Rights. "If the cavalry officer," thundered Bayard, "with whatever of renown he may have gained with his bloody sword, shall be stronger than these guarantees of personal liberty which we supposed were secured to us, let us know it now." Sheridan, concluded Bayard, was not "even fit to breathe the air of a Republican government."[17]

Although the wrath of Bayard and other Democrats in Congress was heavily tinged with political partisanship, it was clear that their indignation was shared by many Republicans. Senator Carl Schurz, speaking for the Republican moderate wing, branded Sheridan's banditti proposal "so appalling that every American citizen who loves his liberty stands aghast," and bemoaned the fact that the nation should witness "the hero of the ride of Winchester and of the charge at the Five Forks stain that name by an attempt to ride over the law and the Constitution of the country and to charge upon the liberties of his fellow-citizens."[18]

The state legislatures of Ohio, Illinois, Pennsylvania, Virginia, Missouri, Georgia, Tennessee, and New York passed resolutions condemning Sheridan's actions. In Congress, a Republican caucus was sharply divided over the issue, and the army's firm friend, Congressman James A. Garfield, declared himself "shocked and distressed beyond measure" at Sheridan's use of troops.[19] Even the cabinet was divided, with Secretary of State Hamilton Fish, Postmaster General Marshall Jewell, and Secretary of the Treasury Benjamin Bristow urging the president not to sustain Sheridan. In a stormy cabinet meeting on January 9, Fish denounced Sheridan's telegram as "unwise and very objectionable," and declared that such intemperate rhetoric "did not allow me to have confidence in him in his present position, or to approve his course, and I am unwilling to appear before the public as having such confidence or as approving Sheridan's course."[20]

Sheridan was surprised by the firestorm of condemnation that followed his telegram of January 5, but it did not deter him from his course. When news of the banditti telegram hit New Orleans, a mass meeting was called. Hundreds of angry citizens met in the rotunda of the St. Charles Hotel, where Sheridan was staying, to protest the general's actions. Threats of assassination were loudly proclaimed, but if the mob hoped to cow the general, they were sorely mistaken. "Some of the Banditti made idle threats last night that they would assasinate [sic] me because I dared to tell the truth," Sheridan informed Belknap. "I am not afraid and will not be stopped from informing the government that there are localities in this Department where the very air has been impregnated with assasination [sic] for some years." Belknap's reply was just what Sheridan wanted to hear: "The President and all of us have full confidence and thoroughly approve your course."[21]

Fortified by the confidence of Grant and Belknap, Sheridan appeared unruffled by the abuse that dogged him as he went about his daily activities. He made a point of taking his meals in the dining room of the St. Charles Hotel, although whenever he appeared, the other guests greeted him with loud groans and hisses. The local newspapers, of course, overflowed with abusive diatribes against the general, and the other diners took these papers, underlined a particularly imaginative insult, and sent it to Sheridan via the waiter. Sheridan invariably glanced quickly at the paper, then smiled and bowed toward the sender.[22] When moving about New Orleans, he was usually followed by a hostile crowd to which he paid no attention, although James Forsyth, who accompanied his chief everywhere, discreetly carried a pistol in his coat pocket. Unflattering caricatures of the general were displayed in shopwindows throughout the city. One of the more imaginative portrayed him in plaster as a fierce bulldog with a collar around his neck, from which hung a card with the words, "I am not afraid." In the bulldog's mouth was a rather limp banditti. Some Sheridan partisan— and there were a few in New Orleans—finally could bear this particular insult no longer and shattered the window, and presumably the plaster bulldog.[23] This, however, was one of the few acts of violence in the city. New Orleans had felt Sheridan's iron hand before. The White Leaguers knew that the military reaction to any acts of violence on their part would be swift and harsh. As early as January 9 Sheridan felt confident enough to wire Belknap: "The dog is dead. White leaguers here are trying to make arrangements to surrender to the civil authorities fearing to come under my jurisdiction."[24]

The dog, however, was far from dead, although he might be pretending to be so, for the tension in New Orleans continued to mount. That it finally had an effect on Sheridan became evident one night at New Orleans's New Varieties Theater. Famed actor Lawrence Barrett, in town with his touring company for a production of *Richelieu*, was acquainted with Sheridan through Custer, who was the actor's close friend, and so sent the general and his staff complimentary tickets to the performance. In act 2 of the play, Barrett, as Richelieu, forcefully delivered the line, "Take away the sword; States can be saved without it!" The audience jumped to their feet, cheering and applauding this topical declaration. Poor Barrett, when the curtain fell on the act, found Sheridan waiting in his dressing room. Amidst a flourish of curses Sheridan demanded to know why the actor had inserted the line into the play. Barrett could only assure the outraged general that no offense had been meant, for the lines had been put in the play many years before by the playwright.[25] Clearly, the general was as untutored in literature as he was in constitutional law.

Grant, despite the crushing blow that Sheridan's actions had dealt his dream of a third term, remained firm in support of his friend. Against all political expediency Grant delivered a message to the Senate on January 13 defending Sheridan. The president contended that the military had intervened at the request of the legal state government and had prevented bloodshed on January 4. He reminded the Senate that "nobody was disturbed by the military who had a legal right at that time to occupy a seat in the legislature." Yet, he declared, the Democrats had plotted fraud, violence, and intimidation to seize control of the legislature illegally with the ultimate aim of deposing Kellogg. The army had thwarted "their lawless and desperate schemes."[26]

As for General Sheridan, the president proclaimed that "no party motives nor prejudices" could be imputed to him. Grant assured the Senate that Sheridan had "never proposed to do an illegal act nor expressed determination to proceed beyond what the law in the future might authorize for the punishment of the atrocities." Barely giving an inch to his critics, Grant defended Sheridan's characterization of the White League as banditti while at the same time assuring the senators that the general's proposed method of dealing with this group would not be adopted. Yet the president refused to disavow the proposal and regretted that Sheridan could not be turned loose, since his tactics "would, if legal, soon put an end to the troubles and disorders in that State."[27]

While Grant insisted that he had "no desire to have United States troops interfere in the domestic concerns of Louisiana or any other State," he was nevertheless determined that no "Kuklux Klans, White Leagues, nor any other association using arms and violence . . . be permitted in that way to govern any part of this country." If errors were committed by his soldiers, the president concluded, they were committed "on the side of the preservation of good order, the maintenance of law, and the protection of life."[28]

Grant's message, a tonic for the beleaguered Sheridan, was received warmly by all but the most violently partisan of legislators. It was especially gratifying to loyal Republicans worried about a party split over the Louisiana issue. The New York Times found the message to be "a moderate, strong, and sensible document."[29]

The House of Representatives sent a committee to New Orleans to investigate the situation and make a full report to Congress. Headed by George Hoar, the committee spent three weeks in Louisiana collecting information. Sheridan worked closely with the committee, providing the congressmen with an imposing list of White League atrocities, including a list of 2,141 political murders committed in Louisiana between 1866 and 1875. Unfortunately, in his zeal to condemn the White Leaguers, Sheridan compiled his figures from some highly dubious scources that were later easily contradicted. To make matters worse he presented different murder statistics on various occasions, claiming on January 10 that nearly 3,500 had been killed and on February 8 that 4,256 was the proper figure. Such inconsistency damaged his credibility and tended to undercut the fact that white terrorists had indeed murdered black and white Republicans for years in Louisiana and gone unpunished.[30]

Hoar's committee, however, accepted Sheridan's claims as fact and submitted an impressive list of atrocities to Congress. The committee also defended Sheridan's use of troops on January 4, claiming that only the presence of de Trobriand and his men prevented bloodshed. At the same time, the committee castigated the Kellogg regime for corruption. More important, however, one member of the committee, future vice-president William A. Wheeler of New York, won the confidence of the Louisiana Democrats while in New Orleans and managed to work out a compromise that temporarily settled the political war. By the terms of the Wheeler Compromise the Democrats were awarded control of the Louisiana House, the Senate went to the Republicans, and the Democrats promised to make no effort to unseat Governor Kellogg until the expiration of his term. The compromise brought relative peace to Louisiana, at least until the 1876 election.[31]

Sheridan, under no illusions about the durability of the Wheeler Compromise, saw southern conspirators everywhere. He was convinced "that the next rebellion was to be fought under the stars and stripes and in the north as well as the south; that the mistake made in 1861 was to have had their own flag." He warned Grant's secretary, Orville Babcock, that the threat of a new, more sinister, underground rebellion was real "and had better be looked after." Sheridan was pleased that his presence had deflated the schemes of the "traitors" in Louisiana, and bragged to Babcock, "When I first reached here the common topic of conversation was about killing people who did not agree politically with these malcontents: It is not so now." But Sheridan was hardly optimistic, believing that the rebel element "have only gone back into their holes and will come out again as soon as the sun shines."[32]

In anticipation of the renewal of strife in Louisiana, Sheridan was determined to have a dependable officer in command of the Department of the Gulf. It quickly became obvious that his effort to replace Colonel Emory with Colonel Mackenzie was untenable because of the latter's youth and lack of seniority. He decided, in late February, to withdraw his request for Mackenzie and ask instead for Brigadier General Augur, then commanding the Department of Texas. "I wish to give as much personal attention to this Dept. as possible," Sheridan told Belknap, "and Augur and myself could and have always worked together like one man." In an interesting comment on military courtesy, Sheridan declared that the only reason he had not requested Augur in the first place was on account of his large family. By late February, however, Sheridan had decided that Augur's services were needed too urgently to let his family stand in the way: "Besides," Sheridan reminded Belknap, "the Govt. has provided for three of his oldest children by commissions, and one of his daughters is married to an officer."[33] Sheridan's request was complied with, and on March 27, 1875, Augur assumed command of the Department of the Gulf, a position he retained until May 1, 1877, when the department was transferred to the Division of the Atlantic.[34]

With Augur in residence in New Orleans and the White League quiet, Sheridan returned to his Chicago headquarters. In order to remain well informed on the Louisiana situation, however, he left George Forsyth behind in Shreveport to keep an eye on the surrounding parishes. Forsyth was also instructed to gather information on oppression of the black citizens of the region. Sheridan's every action in Louisiana had been influenced by his conviction that the military had an obligation to ensure the blacks their right to vote, so that eventually they could use the franchise as a weapon to protect themselves. It did not take Forsyth long to uncover numerous instances where the blacks had "been trodden down and intimidated during the last eight years," by the "White Mans Party." Forsyth was convinced that the information he was gathering, when made public, would result in "such a howl of indignation as is rarely witnessed."[35] He was, of course, mistaken.

The North had wearied of military reconstruction. Fiery tales of the plight of the blacks could not rekindle enthusiasm for a policy that was regarded as bankrupt. Insatiable greed for the momentary advantage, both political and pecuniary, on the part of Republicans at the state level, like Louisiana Governor Kellogg, and the national level, like Secretary of War Belknap, had undercut the idealistic, righteous goal of securing political justice for southern blacks. One staunch Republican, in January 1875, lamented the repudiation of his party and its Reconstruction policy: "Genl Sheridan told the simple truth—but the truth is our people are tired out with this worn out cry of 'southern outrages'!!! Hard times & heavy taxes make them wish the 'nigger,' 'everlasting nigger,' were in ―――― or Africa. . . . It looks to me as though the game was up for 1876."[36]

Sheridan wished to put politics out of his mind during the spring of 1875, for he was a man in love. The preceding spring he had met Irene Rucker, the youngest daughter of Colonel Daniel H. Rucker, at a military wedding where she had been one of the bridesmaids. The petite brunette of twenty-two won his heart, and he courted her with the same vigor that had marked his military campaigns.

Irene was an army brat. Her grandfather had served as captain in the Second Infantry, and both her brothers were cavalry officers. Born at Fort Union in 1853, where her father was depot quartermaster, Irene's first three years were spent at the isolated frontier post. But in 1856 her father had been transferred to Washington, D.C., and it was there that she grew up. A devout Catholic, she had been educated at the Academy of the Visitation in Georgetown, and at Saint Frances Mary Xavier's Catholic convent in Philadelphia.[37]

Within a month of Sheridan's return from New Orleans it was announced that the wedding would be held on June 3, 1875. Sherman, who knew the Ruckers well—he had once courted Irene's mother—was delighted. He congratulated Sheridan on "selecting a bright young lady whose whole heart and interests will be yours . . . and who can go with you to the camp or a palace with equal grace and happiness."[38]

The recent death of Sheridan's father kept the wedding private and simple. Only family members and a small number of Sheridan's military associates—Sherman, Pope, Terry, Ord, Augur, and a few others—were in attendance. The ceremony was performed at the house of the bride's father, Bishop Foley of Detroit presiding. An informal reception that evening at Sheridan's Michigan Avenue home quietly concluded the ceremonies. "Of the many weddings with which the elite of Chicago have been regaled," noted the *Army and Navy Journal*, "this event will bear off the prize for simplicity."[39]

The newspapers avidly reported every bit of information on the wedding that they could gather, the *Chicago Inter-Ocean* headlining: "Great Cavalry Leader Vanquished By A Blonde." The *Shreveport Times* snidely wished the newlyweds "many little banditti."[40] Most of the press attention angered Sheridan, who was becoming more and more a private man distrustful of publicity, but he was highly pleased with the full page drawing that appeared on the cover of *Harper's Weekly* for June 5. The sketch by Thomas Nast, as firm a partisan as Sheridan and the army could hope for, portrayed a humbled Sheridan, chained by garlands, being led to the "Union Altar" by little cupids. The cupids were all labeled as "banditti," and under the drawing of Sheridan were the words "I am not afraid."[41]

The age difference between the bride and groom did not go unnoticed. Colonel Benjamin Grierson noted sarcastically that he had received an announcement card for the wedding which listed the couple as "General and Mrs. Sheridan." In a letter to his wife the

When the famed cartoonist Thomas Nast heard rumors of Sheridan's im-
pending marriage, he wrote his old friend to see if the reports were true.
"I am to be married on the 3d of June, coming, unless there is a slip between the cup and the lip, which is scarcely possible," the prospective
groom replied. "I am very happy but wish it was all over." To commemo-
rate the wedding, Nast prepared a cover illustration for the June 5, 1875,
Harper's Weekly. With Louisiana still fresh in everyone's mind, Nast depicted a humbled Sheridan led to the Union alter by "Banditti" cupids. "I
am not afraid," brave Phil exclaims. The general loved the drawing.
(*Chicago Historical Society*)

colonel could not resist a vindictive swipe: "Miss Irene Rucker is the lady's maiden name. It is evident to my mind that the card states the matter all right, the *Lady* married the *Lieut. General*, more than she did *Sherry-dan*. Any one who would marry the latter for love I think would be rather hard up for a lover."[42] Other observers were more charitable. Lieutenant John G. Bourke, of General Crook's staff, was "delighted with Mrs. Sheridan, a beautiful and refined lady, dignified but cordial in her manners." Another officer concluded that marriage had mellowed the general's fierce temper: "After his marriage a marked change was visible. His voice, once noticeable for its piercing shrillness, was soon equally marked for its softness, and his whole manner showed the refining influence of the beautiful and cultivated woman he was so fortunate as to marry."[43]

The newlyweds did not go on a honeymoon, but in mid-August took a three-month trip to Oregon and California accompanied by Mike Sheridan and his wife. The trip was a pleasant one, allowing Sheridan to reacquaint himself with old friends from his days in the Pacific Northwest, but it had to be cut short when rising tension over the presidential election and Indian hostilities on the northern plains made it imperative that he return to Chicago.[44]

Few elections in American history rival the 1876 election for fraud and violence, and once more Grant found it necessary to call on Sheridan for duty in the South. Republican Rutherford B. Hayes, who had served as a colonel under Sheridan in the Shenandoah, appeared soundly defeated by Democrat Samuel J. Tilden in the November 7 presidential election. It became evident, however, that despite the popular vote count, all the electoral votes of South Carolina, Florida, and Louisiana, as well as a single vote from Oregon, were in dispute. Tilden, who had 184 undisputed electoral votes, needed but one more vote to be the next president, while Hayes would need all the disputed electoral votes to be elected. As Grant reviewed the situation, he became convinced that Florida and South Carolina had honestly gone to Hayes, but that Louisiana, and the presidency, had clearly been won by Tilden. This did not bother him much, since he personally preferred Tilden to Hayes anyway, although he was too stalwart a party man to make such views known.[45] Fearing violence in Louisiana, Grant ordered more troops to that state to protect the election canvassing board. Grant, determined to secure an honest count, believed that "no man worthy of the office of President should be willing to hold it if counted in or placed there by fraud."[46] Toward this end he ordered Sheridan to proceed to New Orleans on November 10.

Sheridan, preoccupied with the Great Sioux War, was displeased with this third assignment to Louisiana. Nevertheless, he was, as always, dedicated to the service to his old friend and commander. Sheridan's return to the Crescent City on November 15 caused a stir. The general attempted to allay the fears of the Democrats by assuring them that his only duty was to protect the constituted authorities in the discharge of their duty. He would have nothing to do with the canvassing of the returns except to assure that only authorized representatives of the two political parties were present at the canvass.[47]

The chairman of the returning board was former Louisiana governor James Madison Wells, who had been removed from office for malfeasance by Sheridan in 1867. Sheridan considered Wells to be "a political trickster and a dishonest man," whose conduct was "as sinuous as the mark left in the dust by the movement of a snake."[48] Louisiana law required that the returning board include representatives of both parties, but the only Democratic member had resigned, leaving four Republicans. It was a surprise to no one when the returning board threw out enough Democratic votes to change a Tilden majority of almost 9,000 to a Hayes majority of over 3,000.[49]

Thoroughly disgusted with his assignment, Sheridan pleaded with his superiors to end his mission. "There is no military necessity for my presence here," he told Sherman. "It is not fair to Augur and I doubt if it is fair to me." Sherman persuaded Grant to let Sheridan go, and on November 26 the general departed New Orleans for the last time.[50]

When on December 6, 1876, electors met in each of the thirty-eight states to cast their ballots for president and forward them on to Washington, duplicate sets of electoral votes were sent from Louisiana, South Carolina, and Florida, as well as one duplicate vote from Oregon. The Democrats who controlled the House of Representatives announced that they would contest any attempt to inaugurate Hayes until the legality of his election was established.

Sober men were deeply troubled, for it had been a disputed election that had resulted in civil war just fifteen years before. Ominous rumblings came from the Democrats. Tilden "minute men" were enrolled by the Democratic Veteran Soldiers Association in fifteen states to oppose by force the inauguration of Hayes. The Democratic *New York Express* blustered about "the use of the sword" to overthrow Hayes and the phrase "Tilden or blood" was becoming common. The *Albany Argus* warned that the Republicans planned to strike first and that terrible Phil Sheridan would soon take command of the East from Hancock and, with troops and warships, "bulldoze" New York City. The Republicans, however, remained restrained, sneering a bit at the Democratic hotheads and reminding them that General Grant, not old Buchanan, now held power in Washington. Still, it has been justifiably asserted that more citizens feared civil war over the election of 1876 than had anticipated such a conflict in 1860.[51]

The army was in a delicate and dangerous position, but Sheridan and Sherman were as one in the crisis. They were both stalwart Republicans and viewed with dread the election of a Democrat as president. Sherman was convinced that the election of Tilden would mean "a four year struggle for existence" for the army and result in insecurity for the highest-ranking officers as well.[52] Sherman looked with disdain upon the newfound political power of the Democratic party. He felt it was controlled by the southerners, who "though defeated by us in war are *conquering* us in Politics." He was convinced that a southern plot was in operation "to cut down the Army so as to afterward increase it by New Regiments commanded by the Southern officers who *deserted* in 1861."[53] All the death and sacrifice of the Civil War would be for naught, if the old enemy won by the ballot what he could not win with the bayonet.

Sheridan was even more likely to see lurking southern conspirators than Sherman, and his political partisanship was far more visible than his commander's. He had drifted to the Republican party at its formation from the Whig and antislavery associations of his youth. Although the circumstances of his life as a soldier at distant outposts prevented him from voting until 1864, the first ballot he ever cast was for Lincoln. His stand in Louisiana and Texas in 1867 against Johnson had clearly branded him as a Radical Republican, and he never avoided such an identification. He vigorously defended the interests of the Republican capitalist class that had emerged triumphant from the war, both against Indians' blocking business expansion westward and workers' striking in the cities. Although he had no personal political ambitions, Sheridan scrupulously supported the Republicans and their economic and political interests at all times.[54]

The worst possible series of events, as far as the two ranking army officers were concerned, would be for the Republican Senate to declare Hayes president, while the Democratic House might assert that since there was no result from the election, the choice of president devolved upon them, and they would naturally select Tilden. This would result in two presidents, each claiming to be rightful commander in chief of the army. The one president would control the cabinet and executive departments while the other would have control of the Treasury. Since neither could effectively govern, civil war would likely result. This time, however, the war would not be sectional, but would be along party lines.[55]

"Personally and officially," Sherman advised Sheridan in a confidential letter on December 11, "we are not charged with the determination of the question as to who is President, but we must sustain the President who is declared to have been elected." If no acceptable president emerged, Sherman intended to "obey the legitimate authority so long as such authority exists." But he warned his colleague to be ready to act, for "if Revolution is inevitable then we must act when the time comes as occasion demands."[56] Until midnight on March 4, 1877, however, there was a "legitimate authority" in the person of President Grant, and both generals looked to their old commander for direction.

Grant wanted Sheridan to pull in his troops on the frontier, where most of them were engaged in a fierce struggle with the Sioux, and collect them into fairly large garrisons so they could move east quickly. He felt that he might need four thousand men in Washington to preserve order, and Sheridan would have to provide most of them. Soon after the election Grant had quietly started to build up land and naval forces around the capital, relying on eastern troops, but he feared these might prove inadequate. By December 21, in response to Grant's request for western troops, Sheridan had stripped Forts Sill and Reno of all their artillery companies and had them on trains heading east.[57] Colonel Mackenzie was ordered to Washington from Wyoming, where he was in the midst of a campaign against the Sioux and Cheyennes, to take charge of the troops guarding the nation's capital.

While Sheridan and Sherman quietly prepared for a new rebellion, the politicians were hard at work devising a compromise to settle the election crisis. On January 31, an electoral commission was organized consisting of seven Democrats and eight Republicans, and it soon ruled along partisan lines in favor of Hayes, but in what was a surprise to many, the Democrats acquiesced in this decision. A bargain had been struck by the Democrats, who had no stomach for war and had grown disenchanted with Tilden because he displayed a marked lack of leadership during the crisis. The most important part of this compromise, from the military's standpoint, was an agreement to withdraw most of the federal troops from the South. The blacks and the southern Republican governments were to be abandoned to the mercies of the former rebels in order to secure the White House for Hayes and avoid conflict.[58]

By the end of January the crisis was over. "This by universal consent terminates the deadlock which has so long existed and which made military precautions necessary," Sherman wrote Sheridan. "You will not be called on for any troops, and you had better arrange for the further prosecution of active operations against the hostile Sioux as early as your judgment may approve."[59] The compromise, so welcome to all who remembered the horrors of civil strife, was bad news indeed for the Indians far to the west, who never had any idea of how close they came to receiving a reprieve from conquest.

Sherman hated to see the white southerners gain home rule at the expense of white and black Republicans, but he was realistic enough to see it coming. Unlike Sheridan, Sherman had no faith in the use of military power to coerce a people into social or political change, and for this reason he had opposed Sheridan's missions to New Orleans. "I was always embarrassed by the plain, palpable fact, that the Union whites are cowardly," he wrote his senator brother in response to Sheridan's 1875 mission, "and allow the rebel element that loves to fight, to cow them." Sherman was convinced that "until the Union whites, and negroes too, *fight* for their own rights they will be trodden down." Federal bayonets were a crutch that had eventually to be discarded because of the small size of the army, and Sherman could forsee that the white southerners "have the votes, the will, and will in the end prevail." The political compromise to seat Hayes proved the keenness of Sherman's vision. He was happy to have his army out of Reconstruction, for he felt, "Our soldiers hate that kind of duty terribly, and not one of our officers but would prefer to go to the plains against the Indians, rather than encounter a street mob, or serve a civil process."[60]

Sheridan, while clearly preferring duty against the Indians on the plains to the thankless chore of Reconstruction, did not share his friend's view on the use of military power for political ends. The roots for this disagreement can be found in the men's backgrounds, for Sheridan had known nothing but the soldier's life, while Sherman had spent several years in banking, law, and education before resuming his military career at the outbreak of the Civil War. Sheridan tended to view every situation in light of how military power could be brought into play to achieve a desired result. Whether dealing with rebellious southerners or recalcitrant Indians, each group in its own way seeking home rule, Sheridan felt that he could force them into conforming to his government's wishes by the application of enough force.

Sheridan was the perfect man to protect the blacks and uphold the Republican regime with the sword, but by 1875–76 the time for such tactics had passed. The country would support them no longer. That Sheridan's motives were laudable, in that he was genuinely dedicated to the preservation of the political rights of the black and white southern Republicans, cannot be denied. That his missions to Louisiana were but a momentary reprieve from the inevitability of a Democratic political triumph is also clear. As such, Sheridan's missions achieved little that was positive, resulting instead in increasing tensions and bitterness on both sides and directing undeserved national sympathy to Louisiana Democrats. Undoubtedly, however, Sheridan's presence in Louisiana prevented bloodshed, for the white terrorists feared his wrath.

With the southern question settled, Sheridan could again focus his attention on the Indian country. The Louisiana missions and the election crisis diverted him from military affairs on the plains at a critical time, but now he could give the West his full care. It was important that he be able to, for on the northern plains segments of several tribes, some culturally conservative and wishing to adhere to the old ways at any cost and others simply unable to bear any longer the daily humiliation of subjugation on the reservation, were making their last stand against the white invasion.

CHAPTER 13

Crisis on the Northern Plains: "Sooner or Later These Sioux Have to Be Wiped Out"

In Red Cloud's war of 1866–68 the army had been beaten, and the knowledge of that humiliation focused Sheridan's resentment against the Sioux. The 1868 treaty that temporarily ended conflict on the northern plains established a reservation for the Sioux that included most of present South Dakota west of the Missouri River. Several agencies were established on the Missouri River, allowing close military supervision as well as an economical movement of Indian supplies by steamboat.

Despite Sheridan's objection, Red Cloud and Spotted Tail induced the Indian Bureau to move their agencies to the White River in Nebraska, southeast of the Black Hills and completely off the Sioux reservation. Sheridan repeatedly urged that the different bands of Sioux "be forced back with their agencies on the Missouri River." He admitted that "the original plan of this North Indian Territory was well conceived," in deference to General Sherman who had helped create it. "But I think it was unfortunate to let any agency go back from the Missouri River and the sooner we can get them again upon the River the better it will be."[1]

Such concessions only added to the confidence of the undefeated, unbowed Sioux and led Sheridan and Sherman to expect war at any time.

As Sherman surveyed the promises made to Red Cloud during a visit to Washington in June 1870—such as honest agents, bountiful presents, hunting rights west of the reservation, and the right to live off the reservation—he saw no hope for peace. "I told Genl. Cox [secretary of the interior] yesterday in the presence of the President," Sherman informed Sheridan, "that with these promises war was as certain as anything could be and that right soon."[2]

Of particular concern to Sheridan was the concession of hunting rights to the Sioux between the Black Hills and the Big Horn Mountains and north of the Platte River. The movement of Indian hunting parties through this vast region was a constant source of worry, since collision with whites moving through the same area was inevitable. Furthermore, neither the Indians nor the whites respected established boundary lines.

The 1868 treaty gave the Sioux hunting rights in these regions so long as the buffalo ranged in sufficient numbers to "justify the chase," and Sheridan was forbidden to interfere with this right. The intent of the peace commissioners in 1868 was that the right to hunt would be temporary. They assumed that the buffalo would soon be exterminated and that by extending hunting rights to the Sioux, the Indians would assist in their destruction. This would end their right to hunt. In this the peace commissioners had been overly optimistic, for the buffalo continued to range across the northern plains in large numbers throughout the 1870s, long after increased white immigration into the region made abrogation of the Sioux hunting right essential.[3]

General Augur, commanding the Department of the Platte from 1867 to 1871, lamented the impact that this Sioux hunting right had on the citizens of Wyoming, "who see themselves cut off from nearly a third of their entire Territory, and that the best part, and all for the benefit of hostile tribes, who by their depredations render another third of their Territory unsafe for general settlement." Augur claimed that "there has hardly been a month, except during winters, since the day the [1868] treaty was made," that Sioux raiding parties had not struck the Wyoming settlements.[4]

That Sioux raiding parties made a standard practice of striking the whites in Wyoming and Montana there can be no doubt, but tales of such raids were often exaggerated and sometimes fabricated. In 1874,

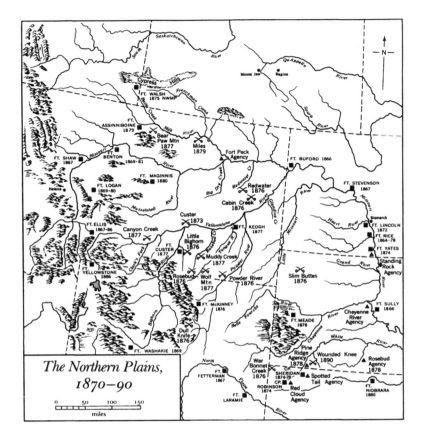

The Northern Plains,
1870–90

0   50   100   150
miles

for example, Sheridan uncovered a scheme by town promoters in Carroll, Montana, to instigate an Indian scare by giving out false reports of Sioux raids. The purpose of these wild tales was to discourage the efforts of rival promoters to establish a town on the head of navigation of the Yellowstone River and thus capture a water connection with the Northern Pacific Railroad. General Alfred H. Terry had already ordered troops at Fort Ellis to move against the nonexistent Sioux before Sheridan uncovered the true facts and called back the soldiers. The lieutenant general proposed "to let these parties fight their own battle," and turned his attention to the real threat posed by Sioux parties elsewhere on the northern plains.[5]

The Sioux were clearly a barrier to the advancing white frontier, for the tribe's military power blocked the rapid advance into the

Dakotas, Wyoming, and Montana that many promoters hoped for, but the brunt of Sioux aggression was borne by other Indians, such as the Mandans, Crows, Arikaras, Shoshones, and Pawnees. These tribes had been fighting the aggressive, expansive Sioux long before the white man came onto the Great Plains, and they allied themselves with the white newcomers in a continuation of the conflict. But the whites made poor allies, exploiting the friendly tribes in time of war and forgetting them as soon as peace returned. Their agents interfered with their efforts to battle the Sioux during so-called periods of peace, and yet the white army provided little protection for them from Sioux raiders.

Although Sheridan recognized the problem, manpower shortages and Indian Bureau interference frustrated his efforts to resolve it. He was forced to reassess his long-standing, blanket opposition to the giving of arms and ammunition to Indians, for the plight of the friendly tribes led him occasionally to recommend that they be supplied with arms with which to repel the Sioux.

On occasion Sheridan had his troops act in conjunction with friendly Indians in action against the Sioux. When inspecting Camp Brown, Wyoming, and the Shoshone Indian Reservation in July 1874, Sheridan learned of just such an opportunity when scouts reported a large party of Sioux with their Northern Cheyenne and Arapaho allies camped but ninety miles away. Sheridan ordered out a company of the Second Cavalry to cooperate with Chief Washakie and 150 of his warriors in a surprise attack on the hostiles. In a July 4 battle on the Bad Water branch of Wind River the combined force of troopers and Shoshones killed or wounded fifty hostiles and captured over a hundred of their ponies. Such cooperative cavalry-Indian war parties, however, were the exception rather than the rule.[6]

Sheridan summed up the quandary of the friendly tribes in an 1872 request that a small delegation of Mandans be allowed to visit the president. As usual, these friendly chiefs had been ignored, while the leaders of the Sioux and Cheyenne were treated royally in the nation's capital. Sheridan vigorously protested such shabby treatment:

> If it is considered to be a virtue on part of an Indian to be peaceful, just, manly and brave then the Mandans are by their conduct fully entitled to this virtue and greater consideration than the granting of their simple request to go to Washington to see the President. It is the pride of the Berthold Indians that they never have murdered a white man, and for

their steadfast friendship they have been nearly decimated by the Sioux who have made continual war upon them as the white man's dogs.[7]

Nor were Sioux raids directed solely against those tribes allied with the whites or the exposed frontier settlements, for the bold warriors were equally willing to take on regular army troops. Fort Fetterman, in Wyoming, and Fort Abraham Lincoln, on the Missouri River, were regular targets for Sioux raiders, with some of the Indian parties numbering in the hundreds. Despite their formidable size, the military escorts for the Northern Pacific Railroad survey parties were not immune from attack by the Sioux either. Major Eugene Baker, with four companies of cavalry and five infantry companies, was surprised by the Sioux on August 14, 1872, while escorting surveyors near Pryor's Creek, Montana. Although the Indians were driven off, the fight so unnerved the surveyors that they halted their work. The following year the same pattern was followed as Sioux warriors twice battled with survey escort troops under Lieutenant Colonel Custer on the tributaries of the Yellowstone River. Custer estimated that he fought nearly a thousand warriors on the Yellowstone in August 1873, but others put the figure at nearer five hundred. Whichever figure was correct, it was clear that Sioux resistance was not limited to a few nonreservation malcontents.[8]

Full-scale war might well have come to the northern plains in 1873, had not the collapse of the Northern Pacific Railroad momentarily put the Sioux hunting ground beyond the white man's grasp. Nevertheless, the secretary of the interior requested that Sheridan arrest the Sioux leaders who battled Custer, which was tantamount to a declaration of war. Sheridan was quick to admit that 1873 had seen a decided rise in Indian raids: "There has been more people killed by Indians during the last twelve months in my command than for any period since 1867," he confessed in May 1873—but he still declined to move against the Sioux. He was confident that even if it were possible to distinguish which bands had been engaged in the battles, which was doubtful, as soon as his troops crossed the North Platte River they "will have to fight all the Sioux, guilty or not." If the secretary of the interior wished to be responsible for a general Indian war, the troops could proceed, but otherwise Sheridan desired to let matters rest. The secretary declined war.[9]

Sherman agreed with Sheridan that the winter of 1873 was no

time for a war, for there were simply not enough available troops to tackle the Sioux. "I suppose we had better let things take their natural course until the mass of Indians commit some act that will warrant a final war," Sherman concluded, "or until they subside into the condition of the Pawnees and Santee Sioux, about the highest state of civilization of which they seem capable."[10]

Despite the reluctance of both the Department of the Interior and military authorities to initiate war with the Sioux, it soon became apparent that some military action was essential. By the winter of 1873–74 the agencies for Red Cloud and Spotted Tail were near anarchy. An always-tense situation had become more difficult with the arrival of hundreds of nonreservation Indians from the north, demanding rations with liberal threats of violence if they did not get them. The chief clerk at Red Cloud Agency was murdered on February 9, and on the same day a lieutenant and corporal from Fort Laramie were killed. The Indians at Spotted Tail Agency assumed control of the beef issue and threatened to kill their agent if he intervened. The agents called on the military for protection.[11]

Word of the crisis at the agencies reached Sheridan in New York. He hurried back to his headquarters, wiring Sherman, "The trouble with the Sioux which for sometime past we have been trying to avoid seems now beyond any peaceable solution."[12] Although Sheridan had already declined a request from the Indian Bureau to establish military posts near the agency, he now had no choice but to acquiesce.

On February 18, he ordered General Ord, commanding the Department of the Platte, to dispatch Colonel (Brevet Major General) John E. Smith, Fourteenth Infantry, from Fort Laramie with enough troops to establish order at the two agencies. Smith was to inform the Sioux that the government would punish all who refused to obey. Sheridan hoped to avoid war, but if Smith had cause to believe the Indians planned to attack, Sheridan wanted him to "strike the first blow, always saving women and children."[13]

Fearing that Smith's expedition might lead to war, Sheridan and James Forsyth departed for Fort Laramie on February 19, picking up Ord in Omaha. Reaching the fort on February 22, the generals conferred briefly with Smith. The colonel convinced Sheridan that the agency Indians were unlikely to resist the one thousand men he planned to march against them. His main problem was not the Sioux,

Sioux Leaders

Sitting Bull, Hunkpapa. (*Custer Battle-field National Monument, National Park Service*)

Red Cloud, Oglala. (*Bureau of American Ethnology, Smithsonian Institution*)

but rather the weather, for temperatures of thirty-four degrees below zero and deep snow made his 125-mile march hazardous.[14]

Reassured by Colonel Smith that full-scale war was not imminent, Sheridan returned to Chicago after only a day's visit. James Forsyth stayed at the fort to accompany the expedition and prepare a full report on the agency situation. Smith departed Fort Laramie on March 1, 1874, and when his cavalry approached the agencies five days later, the malcontents and troublemakers among the Sioux fled north. The rest of the Indians remained sullen but the troops encountered no opposition to their occupation of the two agencies.[15]

Sheridan, back in Chicago, wrote Sherman a detailed account of the troubles at the agencies, including such information as he gathered on his brief trip west. The Indians were traveling back and forth the thirty-five miles between the two agencies, drawing rations at both places. Sheridan estimated that the beef issue at Red Cloud Agency was running more than twelve hundred cattle per month, with another nine hundred cattle issued at Spotted Tail Agency, which was thought to be between one-third and one-half too much. An effort on the part of the agents to take a census of their wards—and the fierce resistance of the Indians to such a count—was what had led to the calling out of Smith's troops.

What worried Sheridan most was that the exaggerated beef issue at the agencies had provided the Indians with substantial amounts of cash. They were allowed to sell their beef hides each month at the agency for $2.50 each, the proceeds of which Sheridan felt "were mostly invested in powder and the possibility is that when the spring opens we will have lively times from raiding parties." He was convinced that "the majority of the Sioux bands have been preparing for hostilities by the purchase of arms and ammunition for some two years back, and as they have been accumulating they have been growing more insolent and exacting."[16]

Sheridan hoped Smith's occupation of the agencies would quiet the situation enough to prevent an outbreak. Even if war came, he felt it would "be simply the pursuit of small raiding parties, since no large force of Indians could "be kept together for want of the necessary commissariat."[17] This fatal misconception, shared by all of Sheridan's officers, would eventually have tragic consequences.

Forsyth's report on the agencies confirmed Sheridan's opinions. Sheridan reiterated his conviction that the agencies were not on the Sioux Reservation at all, but in Nebraska, and that the Indian Bureau should relocate them back to the Missouri River. If they were not to be moved, Sheridan requested funds to construct two posts to guard them in their present location.[18]

The Indian Bureau was unwilling, or unable, to move the agencies and was little disposed to cooperate with the military authorities. Despite the fact that the Indian Bureau had called for the troops in the first place, Secretary of the Interior Columbus Delano now wrote to Belknap requesting that the army display forbearance. "While I have no desire or design to dictate the movements of the Army," Delano wrote, "I shall exceedingly regret the occurance [*sic*] of hostilities with the Sioux, and if they do occur I trust that your department will be able to show clearly that they did not result from this effort to protect Red Cloud's and Spotted Tail's agencies."[19]

Sheridan and Sherman had come to expect such behavior from the Department of the Interior, but it continued to anger them. "That letter of the Secretary of the Interior was meant to throw on us the blame in case of an Indian War," Sherman grumbled to Sheridan. "Everybody, even Mr. Delano, would be made happy if the troops should kill a goodly proportion of those Sioux, but they want to keep the record to prove that they didn't do it. We can afford to be frank and honest," he concluded, "for sooner or later these Sioux have to be wiped out or made to stay just where they are put."[20]

To help ensure that the Sioux stayed put, two posts were constructed near their agencies. Colonel Smith built Camp Robinson on the bank of White River about a mile and a half from Red Cloud Agency, and Camp Sheridan was established the following September about a quarter of a mile from Spotted Tail Agency. These posts would prove invaluable in the coming conflict.[21]

The crisis at the agencies convinced Sheridan that it was time to put into operation a general plan to check Sioux power and protect the white settlers and friendly tribes. Sheridan concluded that "it would be the best policy for the Government to surround this [Sioux] Reservation by large military posts to ultimately keep the Indians within its boundary and white people from encroaching on its limits." In case of a general Indian war, such posts would enable Sheridan to "make it a little hot for their villages and stock if these Indians attempted to raid on the settlements south."[22]

Forts Lincoln and Rice to the north of the reservation, Forts Sully and Randall to the east, and Camp Robinson to the south had the Sioux fairly well encircled by the spring of 1874, but a post was still needed on the western edge of the reservation. Sheridan hoped to fill this gap by the construction of one or two small posts in the Yellowstone Valley, in the heart of the favorite country of the nonreservation Sioux, and of a substantial fort in the Black Hills of Dakota.[23]

Sheridan presented his proposal to Grant, Belknap, Delano, and Sherman in a Washington meeting in the fall of 1873. Getting a favorable response, he set about planning a military reconnaissance of the Black Hills. Although he had originally planned to start the expedition from Fort Laramie, Smith's expedition to the agencies had changed his mind. The sullen mood of Red Cloud's people made it unwise to march another large body of troops near their agency. Turning his attention to Fort Abraham Lincoln, Sheridan selected Custer to lead the expedition and sent him off to the Black Hills in July 1874. The path that Custer's thousand men pressed into the hard Dakota sod was thereafter known as the Thieves' Road by the angry Sioux. The gold that Custer's prospectors discovered set off a chain of events leading to the greatest Indian war of Sheridan's career.[24]

Sheridan had a long-standing interest in the Black Hills, having first heard of them while a lieutenant in Oregon from the noted Jesuit missionary Father Pierre Jean De Smet. The priest told Sheridan that Sioux Indians had shown him gold nuggets taken from the tributaries of the Yellowstone River, and upon his declaration of the gold's value, the warriors declared that a mountain of it existed in the Black Hills. Sheridan had long discounted the mountain-of-gold story as a humbug, although he was convinced that gold in paying quantities could be found in the tributaries of the Yellowstone, in the Wind River Mountains, and perhaps even in the Black Hills. Interest in the Black Hills had always been high and was fueled by the fact that, since the hills were a part of the Sioux reservation, whites were prohibited. The financial panic of 1873 had resulted in increased interest in potential Black Hills gold. While Fort Meade was finally built in 1878 near the site selected by Custer in 1874, most interested spectators, both red and white, viewed the fort issue as a red herring calculated to hide the real reason for the reconnaissance: a gigantic prospecting expedition.[25]

Sheridan, however, was not sanguine "of the existence of gold in great quantities." He reminded the public that even if the gold existed, the treaty of 1868 "virtually deeds this portion of the Black Hills to the Sioux Indians." This was, however, no gallant defense of Sioux property rights, for in a letter transmitted to Sherman for release to the press, Sheridan painted a glowing picture of the Yellowstone Basin to the west of the Black Hills. Gold was to be found in all the tributaries of the Yellowstone River, he declared, and the Indians had no claim on this region except the right to hunt. Increased white settlement, and the resulting destruction of game, would take care of that Indian right. Despite this promotion of the Yellowstone country, Sheridan was mindful of the uses of the Black Hills, confiding to Congressman Henry Banning that the hills, "if properly dealt with, will greatly relieve the country of much of our idle population."[26]

Sheridan did not oppose white settlement in the Black Hills, except to the extent that he was required by law and duty to prevent trespass on the Sioux reservation, but he was even more eager for whites to move into northern Wyoming and southeastern Montana. This latter region posed a greater problem for him because the Sioux retained the right to hunt there. It was imperative to extinguish this hunting right, essentially the right to retain a nomadic life, and Sheridan saw a way to do so through the promotion of western lands. As these lands filled with whites, the politicians would be made to listen, the game killed off, and the Indian right to hunt nullified.

The western press broadcast the news of Black Hills gold in the best boomer tradition, while western businessmen seized upon the discovery as a grand opportunity to rejuvenate an economy slumped in depression. Parties began to organize in several western cities to invade the Sioux reservation; one company even opened an office in Chicago. Custer had hardly settled back into his Fort Lincoln headquarters before gold mining parties from Sioux City and Yankton were attempting to hire the services of his top scout, Charley Reynolds. Although Reynolds declined to lead such an illegal enterprise, Custer reported the miners ready "to start to the Black Hills at an early date unless prevented by the military authorities."[27]

Sheridan moved quickly to halt an invasion of the Black Hills. "Should companies now organizing at Sioux City and Yankton trespass on the Sioux Indian Reservation," he wrote Department of Dakota commander Terry on September 3, 1874, "you are hereby directed to use the force at your command to burn the wagon trains, destroy the outfit and arrest the leaders, confining them at the nearest military post." But Sheridan's heart was not in the order, for he undercut its moral authority by closing with the remark that should Congress extinguish the Sioux claim to the region, he would "give cordial support to the settlement of the Black Hills."[28]

Despite the efforts of army patrols to close off the Black Hills, a party from Sioux City spent the winter searching for gold along French Creek. Word soon reached Yankton that the party had found gold, and this led to increased agitation for opening up the hills. Sheridan, outraged at the boldness of the miners, disregarded Sherman's advice and sent detachments from Fort Randall and Camp Robinson to arrest them. On both occasions the soldiers were forced back by bad weather, so that it was April before a troop of the Second Cavalry from Fort Laramie finally escorted the intruders off the reservation. Far from dampening the spirit of the western boomers, the arrest of the miners only added to the frenzy. Their tales of gold from the grass roots to the bedrock received wide circulation.[29]

As spring approached, it became clear that the army had not dented the enthusiasm of the miners intent on invading the hills. So many parties were requesting special group ticket arrangements from the Union Pacific Railroad in order to travel to within striking distance of the Black Hills that the chief ticket agent asked Sheridan's office whether it would be all right to accept their business. The commandant at Fort Randall pleaded for reinforcements in March, assuring his superiors "that all the vagrant population of this frontier will endeavor early in the season, to go into the Sioux reservation." The instigators of this lawless situation he labeled as the "railroad and newspaper people, merchants and hotel people, farmers and freighters of this frontier."[30]

General Terry, who had helped negotiate the 1868 Sioux treaty, was deeply troubled. "At the present time when large numbers are out of employment, men are easily attracted to any scheme of adventure which promises profit," he warned division headquarters, "and I am impressed with the belief that unless the most active preventative measures be taken the whole of the hill country will be over-run by miners as soon as the season will permit it to be entered with safety." Terry's sympathy was with the Sioux, and he pleaded with Sheridan to uphold "the national good faith and honor." Terry asked for more troops with which to patrol the hills.[31]

Sheridan reiterated his order to keep out the miners to his department commanders. He wrote Sherman on March 25, 1875, that he felt "quite confident of our ability to prevent the intended trespass on the rights of the Indians; and cavalry and infantry in the Department of Dakota are being moved at the present time to the most available points, to carry out my directions of September 3rd of last year."[32]

Sheridan was wrong, for the army could not keep the miners out. By late summer General Crook estimated that twelve hundred men and slipped into the hills. Realizing that it was impossible to keep whites from overrunning the hills, the government decided to purchase them. In order to fix a price on the region, the Department of the Interior ordered geologist Walter P. Jenney to survey the Black Hills during the summer of 1875. Jenney left Fort Laramie on May 24, escorted by four hundred troopers under the command of Lieutenant Colonel (Brevet Colonel) Richard I. Dodge and guided by Sheridan's old friend, California Joe Milner. Jenney's expedition discovered parties of miners panning the surface dirt with considerable success. The miners—one officer characterized them as not being "visionary enthusiasts," but rather hardened professionals who had worked gold rushes in New Zealand, Australia, California, and Colorado—claimed that the placers would pay fifty to seventy-five dollars per day to the hand. The main purpose of the expedition, "the discovery of gold in paying quantities," was quickly accomplished. In his final report Jenney was not overly optimistic about placer mining in the hills, correctly predicting that it would prove difficult to extract the gold. Still, he had confirmed the existence of gold, and the Black Hills fever continued unabated.[33]

The Jenney expedition frustrated Sheridan. He protested the government's dual policy: "To expect me to keep miners out of the Black Hills, while the Indian Bureau, by this examination, is affording an opportunity for skilful and practical miners to ascertain the minerals in it, and newspaper correspondents to publish it to the world, is putting on me a duty which my best skill and most conscientious desire to perform it, with the means I have at hand, will make a failure of." Sheridan recommended that Jenney be recalled or the army's orders changed.[34]

The authorities in Washington seemed unsure of their own policy and for two weeks in early July simply ignored Sheridan. Furious, Sheridan asked Sherman whether Jenney's expedition had led to an alteration of government policy. "It is a little chafing to be obliged to submit to such a measley condition of affairs, and I wish you would help me out," protested Sheridan. Sherman, hardly in any better position to unravel the puzzle of the government's policy than Sheridan, suggested that the order to expel the trespassers still stood, but that Sheridan might go lightly on its enforcement until a new agreement could be reached with the Sioux.[35]

Sherman was helpless to assist Sheridan at this critical moment, because he had essentially abdicated his influence as commanding general by moving his headquarters to Saint Louis. At the same time that the conflict on the northern plains was heating up, so was the long-simmering feud between Sherman and Secretary of War William W. Belknap. Not only did their hostility inhibit the ability of the army to act during the Black Hills crisis, it also greatly influenced Sheridan's eventual performance as commanding general.

When Sherman assumed command of the army in March 1869, his initial commission contained an order directing the chiefs of all staff corps, departments, and bureaus to report to and act under the orders of the army commander. All orders from the president and secretary of war were also to be issued through the commanding general's office. The order stood for less than a month. Secretary of War John A. Rawlins, Grant's wartime chief of staff and close personal friend, objected on the grounds that the order compromised the principle of civilian control of the military. The order was rescinded by the president over Sherman's objection.[36]

In essence the commanding general was reduced to a figurehead, while the adjutant general, acting under the authority of the secretary of war, became the de facto army commander. The controversy was perennial, and the bitterness between commanding general and secretary of war traditional. Congress had created the position of general in chief of the army, later called commanding general, in 1821. The position did not achieve its full horizons, or enter into heated controversy, until occupied by Winfield Scott in 1841. General Scott argued bitterly with various secretaries, most especially Jefferson Davis, and removed army headquarters from Washington to New York to avoid contact with the politicians. The problem had been somewhat rectified by the close working relationship between Secretary of War Edwin Stanton and General Grant during the later years of the Civil War. Sherman had anticipated that Grant's personal experience with the problem of divided authority would result in a decision favorable to the army, but his hopes were dashed in 1869. The decision in favor of the secretary of war's controlling the army was, despite the fact that it was made by Grant out of personal favoritism, the proper one in constitutional terms. The fact was that the commanding general had no vital responsibilities in time of peace.[37]

When Rawlins, long in ill health, died, Sherman maneuvered to have Belknap appointed secretary of war. Sherman and Belknap had been warm friends. Sherman had secured a brigadier's star for the Iowa volunteer officer in 1864, and Belknap commanded a division in the Georgia campaign and March to the Sea. Belknap displayed little gratitude to his sponsor. The new secretary blatantly undercut Sherman's relationship with Grant, entrenched himself with War Department bureaucrats, and worked through the army staff bureaus to bypass Sherman in issuing orders. So successful was Belknap at this devious game that Sherman's position was soon but an ornamental sinecure.

"My office has been by law stript of all the influence and prestige it possessed under Grant," Sherman complained in 1871. "The old regulations of 1853, made by Jeff Davis in hostility to General Scott, are now strictly construed and enforced; and in these regulations the War Department is everything, and the name of General, Lieutenant-General, or Commander-in-Chief even, does not appear in the book. Consequently, orders go to parts of the army supposed to be under my command, of which I know nothing till I read them in the newspapers."[38] Sherman confessed to Sheridan that he was unable to stop Belknap's aggrandizement of power, for "little by little the Secretary of War has regained the actual command of the army. Even appointing *post* commanders. The staff depts. are utterly independent of the General of the Army."[39]

As early as 1871 Sherman had thought of moving his headquarters to Saint Louis, just as Scott had removed to New York, to avoid the daily humiliation of dealing with Belknap. Finally, on May 8, 1874, his patience gave out, and he applied for permission to move. His request was granted with unseemly haste.[40]

Sheridan thought Sherman's move ill advised. "I assure you, my dear General, you have the confidence of the people and the Army, in the stability and steadiness which they have always attached to your name," Sheridan wrote Sherman upon learning of the move. "You bring a condition on the Army which will ruin it forever, by establishing a precedent which places its General-in-Chief in retirement for all time to come. You endanger its very existence by putting its command absolutely in the hands of the Secretary of War, whose office lasts for only four years, and who can compromise our integrity by attempting to use us for personal or political purposes." Sheridan declared there to be no officer in the army who would sustain Sherman's course, and reminded his friend that even as general of the army he was not "at liberty to break us down because you have been or may be subjected to annoyances at Washington."[41]

Sherman appreciated Sheridan's frankness. "No one has a better right to offer advice, and there is no one whose advice I would sooner accept in cases of doubt," he replied. Still, he would not alter his decision. All attempts to have Grant or Belknap define his duties had been snubbed. "Could I be of any service to the Army here, I would make any personal sacrifice," declared Sherman, "but without some recognition on the part of the President it is impossible. What can we expect when a civilian becomes President?"[42]

Sherman felt that he could fulfill his minimal duties in Saint Louis as well as Washington, while at the same time enjoying more congenial and less expensive surroundings. He assured Sheridan that the move would not lessen the authority of division commanders. "I do not propose to meddle or interfere with the clear well defined command of yourself, Schofield & McDowell," he promised, "but to sustain you all I can: which will be to let you alone."[43]

The Sherman-Belknap feud left Sheridan in a difficult position. He liked Belknap and worked well with the secretary. Their close working relationship had been one of the irritations that caused Sherman's departure. Sheridan was quick to take offense when Sherman's friends Ord and Grierson communicated directly with the commanding general without going through division headquarters. He gave little thought, however, to the damage he had done his superior by secretly working with Belknap to send Mackenzie across the Mexican border the previous year. Now, with Sherman out of Washington and the War Department silent on the Black Hills, Sheridan had to wait and see whether a new agreement could be reached with the Sioux.

There was to be no new agreement. A formal commission headed by Iowa Senator William B. Allison met in council with the Sioux on the White River, some eight miles from Red Cloud Agency. The Sioux, fiercely divided into factions for and against selling the hills, could not reach agreement, and the council ended on September

General William Tecumseh Sherman's keen mind and force of character gave a steady hand of direction to the Old Army. If Sheridan was the heart of the army, Sherman was its very soul. (*U.S. Signal Corps photo no. B-2860, Brady Collection, National Archives*)

29, 1875. The commissioners then recommended that Congress set a fixed price on the Black Hills and have the government force it on the Indians.[44]

The failure of the Allison commission led to an important conference in Washington on November 3, 1875. Sheridan was honeymooning in San Francisco when he received orders to report for a high-level White House meeting on the Sioux question. Hurrying eastward, he picked up George Crook in Omaha. In anticipation of war on the northern plains, Sheridan had transferred Ord to Texas and appointed Crook commander of the Department of the Platte in April. Sherman was conspicuously absent from the meeting, for he was now as often ignored as consulted, especially if Belknap had his way. Secretary of the Interior Delano was also absent, for he had resigned on October 1, 1875, after charges of corruption had tainted his administration of the Indian Bureau. He had been replaced by Zachariah Chandler, a blustering ex-senator and Michigan political hack, who was considerably more willing than his predecessor to give the military control over the Indians. Commissioner of Indian Affairs Edward Smith, implicated in the scandal that claimed Delano and soon to resign, was present as well.[45]

The meeting gave Sheridan all he hoped for. The distasteful and futile duty of guarding the Black Hills from white miners was to end. The president's order to protect the integrity of the Sioux reservation would stand, but the army was no longer to enforce it, thus allowing the whites to enter with impunity. Since it was clear that the effort to purchase the Black Hills had been frustrated by the influence of nonreservation Sioux from the Yellowstone River and Big Horn regions, it was decided to force them onto the reservation, where they could be controlled. If these hostile bands, led by such chiefs as Sitting Bull, Crazy Horse, and Gall, would not report to their agencies, then Sheridan was to launch a winter campaign against them.

Sheridan worried a bit about General Terry's scruples concerning Sioux treaty rights. In a letter marked "confidential" he made it clear to Terry that this reversal of military policy was a presidential decision. "The President decided that while the orders heretofore issued forbidding the occupation of the Black Hills country, by miners, should not be rescinded," Sheridan wrote on November 9, "still no further resistance by the military should be made to the miners going in; it being his belief that such resistance only increased their desire and complicated the troubles." Terry was ordered to "quietly cause the troops in your Department to assume such attitude as will meet the views of the President in this respect."[46]

Six days after the White House conference, Indian Bureau Inspector Erwin C. Watkins reported to his superiors on "Sitting Bull's band and other bands of the Sioux Nation, under chiefs or 'head-men' of less note, but no less untamable and hostile." These Indians, Watkins declared, were in possession of "the best hunting-ground in the United States" and as a result had "never accepted aid or been brought under control." From their Powder River and Yellowstone Valley haunts these bands, numbering "but a few hundred warriors" according to Watkins, raided the white settlements and the villages of the friendly bands with impunity. Their success led Watkins to fear the danger of "some of the young warriors from friendly tribes falling off and joining with these hostile bands, until, with these accessions, they would be somewhat formidable." Since all peaceful attempts to reason with these "wild and untamable" Indians had failed, Watkins declared that the government owed it to "civilization and the common cause of humanity" to "send troops against them in the winter—the sooner the better—and whip them into subjection."[47]

Commissioner of Indian Affairs Smith passed the Watkins report on to Secretary of the Interior Chandler, with the recommendation that it be referred to "Lieutenant-General Sheridan, who is personally conversant with the situation on the Upper Missouri, and with the relations of Sitting Bull's band to the other Sioux tribes." Chandler then sent instructions to the Indian agents at all the Sioux agencies "to notify Sitting Bull's band, and other wild and lawless bands of Sioux Indians residing without the bounds of their reservation," to report to their agencies before January 31 or be forced there by the army.[48] It had taken exactly one month for the cogs of the federal bureaucracy to produce an official justification for a war on the nonreservation Sioux and then put it through proper channels. Thus was implemented the decision reached at the White House on November 3.

Sheridan began his preparations for a winter campaign immediately after the Washington meeting. He and Crook proceeded to Camp Supply a few days after the conference, supposedly for a turkey hunt, but actually to check on the temper of the southern tribes and confer with Ben Clark. There was no other man on the plains whom Sheridan trusted more implicitly or found more reliable than the unassuming, thirty-four-year-old Clark. He had served the government since 1857, when he had marched west against the Mormons with Colonel Albert Sidney Johnston during the Utah War. Clark first came to Sheridan's attention during the Cheyenne War, when he had served

Sully and Custer as chief of scouts. Sheridan appointed him as post guide and interpreter at Camp Supply in 1869, and he continued in that capacity except for a stint as Miles's chief of scouts during the Red River War. Clark, whom Sheridan described as "the most reliable and accomplished man of his class on the plains," was a master of Indian sign language and was fluent in the Cheyenne tongue. Sheridan now confessed to his favorite scout that he anticipated war with the Sioux and wanted him to go north and scout for Crook. Although Clark protested that he was neither a good Sioux interpreter nor acquainted with the Big Horn country, the general was not to be dissuaded. Sheridan told Clark to be ready to head north and, true to his word, ordered him to join Crook on February 8, 1876.[49]

Sheridan's plan of campaign was a familiar one: take advantage of the winter weather, converge columns into the hostiles' country, and repeat the success of 1868 and 1874. Scouts, dispatched in December, had located Sitting Bull's people on the Little Missouri River, and Custer was to march west from Fort Abraham Lincoln with the Seventh Cavalry and strike them. Colonel John Gibbon would march east from Forts Shaw and Ellis to scour the Yellowstone Valley, while Crook would move north from Fort Fetterman toward the headwaters of the Powder River. Sheridan did not plan for troops from Terry's Department of Dakota and Crook's Department of the Platte to work in concert, although he gave his commanders latitude to use their own discretion.

His main concern was that the Department of the Interior would dally with notifying the Sioux to report to their agencies, an action which he felt would "be regarded as a good joke by the Indians." The general feared that he would not be able to get his columns off early enough to take advantage of the winter weather, and worried, "Unless [the Sioux] are caught before early spring, they can not be caught at all."[50]

CHAPTER 14

The Great Sioux War: "We Ought Not to Allow Savages to Beat Us"

On February 7, 1876, Sheridan received authorization from the secretary of the interior to proceed against the nonreservation Sioux. He promptly passed the word along to Terry and Crook. Terry, however, responded that he could not get Custer's column off before spring. He had learned that Sitting Bull's band, estimated at thirty or forty lodges, had moved some two hundred miles west of the Little Missouri. The weather had turned increasingly treacherous, with deep snows making transportation impossible. This frustrating delay led Sheridan to renew his effort to have Congress appropriate funds for the construction of forts on Montana's Tongue and Big Horn rivers. These sites, selected by James Forsyth and Fred Grant during their 1875 reconnaissance of the Yellowstone River, would give the troops supply bases in the heart of the favorite Sioux hunting grounds.[1]

Colonel John Gibbon's Montana Column, consisting of six companies of his own Seventh Infantry, four companies of the Second Cavalry, and twenty-five Crow Indian scouts, got under way on March 17. They struggled through deep snow from Fort Ellis down the Yellowstone River, hoping to block the Sioux from moving north to hunt buffalo. Establishing a supply depot at the junction of the Big Horn and Yellowstone rivers, Gibbon sent scouting patrols up the Yellowstone's tributaries but found no Indians.[2]

George Crook departed Fort Fetterman, Wyoming, on March 1, with a formidable force of ten cavalry companies and two infantry companies, almost nine hundred strong. Fierce storms and subzero temperatures buffeted the soldiers before they reached the vicinity of the Powder River on March 16. Scouts reported a village of 105 lodges camped in the heavily timbered bottomlands some miles north of the mouth of the Little Powder River. Crook dispatched Colonel Joseph Reynolds with three hundred men to strike the Indians, while he remained with the pack train.

This was Reynolds's opportunity to retrieve his reputation, sullied by his mishandling of the Department of Texas and his 1871 confrontation with Colonel Mackenzie, but he bungled it. Although Reynolds's troopers easily carried the village in a dawn attack on March 17, driving out the Cheyenne and Oglala Sioux inhabitants and capturing a large pony herd, a bold counterattack by the Indians drove the soldiers from the village. Reynolds lost his nerve and, with but four dead and six wounded, hurried back to rejoin Crook, losing the Indian pony herd on the way. A potential victory had turned into a humiliating defeat. Crook, enraged, filed court-martial charges against Reynolds as soon as the expedition reached Fort Fetterman.[3]

Reynolds's failure effectively ended the winter campaign. Sheridan was livid. He agreed with Crook's court-martial charges, finding it amazing that so few warriors, estimated at between one and two hundred, could demoralize a force three or four times their size. Reynolds's regiment, the Third Cavalry, was notorious for its division into bitter cliques, and Sheridan correctly surmised that these old animosities played a major role in the defeat. "There were too many giving orders," he complained. "There was too great a desire to receive orders, there was too much of a desire to be supported when there was no necessity for support. The affair is shamefully disgraceful."[4]

The failure of Crook's campaign made a summer expedition essential. Sheridan planned to repeat his winter strategy with Custer, sweeping west from Fort Abraham Lincoln, pushing the hostiles toward the Big Horn Valley where Crook, again moving north from Fort Fetterman, could force them back onto Custer. Gibbon, already in the field, would continue his movement down the Yellowstone River, blocking escape to the north. Sheridan also hoped for authority to assume control of the Indian agencies as he had done in the south.

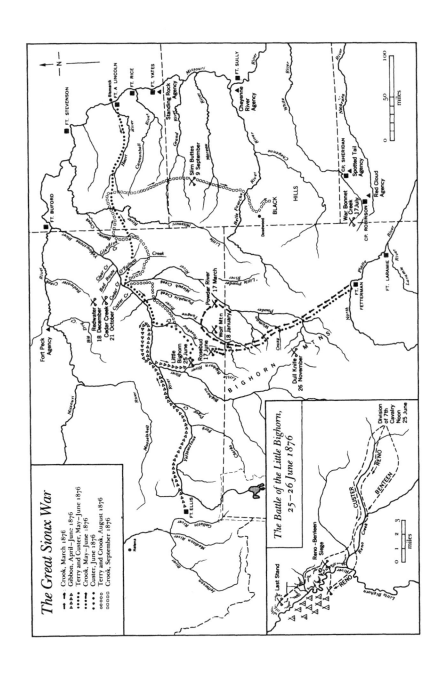

The Great Sioux War

Crook, March 1876
Gibbon, April–June 1876
Terry and Custer, May–June 1876
Crook, May–June 1876
Custer, June 1876
Terry and Crook, August 1876
Crook, September 1876

The Battle of the Little Bighorn,
25–26 June 1876

This would prevent any hostiles from entering the reservation except by unconditional surrender, while at the same time preventing the agency Sioux from aiding their brethren with supplies or reinforcements.[5]

Sheridan left the actual organization and field strategy of the expedition to his department commanders, allowing them wide discretionary powers. "I have given no instruction to Gens. Crook or Terry," he explained to Sherman in describing his plan, "as I think it would be unwise to make any combination in such a country as they will have to operate in." Once more he stated his misapprehension of Indian strength: "As hostile Indians, in any great numbers, cannot keep the field as a body for a week or at most ten days, I therefore consider—and so do Terry and Crook—that each column will be able to take care of itself, and of chastising the Indians should it have the opportunity."[6]

Evidence mounted of a large concentration of hostiles. Terry's scouts on the Little Missouri estimated Sitting Bull's strength to have swelled to fifteen hundred lodges by May. Disturbing reports from Fort Laramie declared fourteen hundred warriors to have left Red Cloud and Spotted Tail agencies for the Powder River. But Sheridan, not easily impressed by numbers, held to his conviction that the Indians could not unite long enough to threaten any of his columns.[7]

Sherman approved Sheridan's plan, although his high opinion of Crook's ability led him to prefer that that officer assume full command of all the troops if the opportunity arose. Sherman urged Sheridan to let his department commanders handle the Sioux, since more pressing matters in the East required the lieutenant general's attention. "Now as to yourself," Sherman wrote Sheridan as the summer campaign was being planned, "of course we all recognize the fact that you are the man to deal with Indians, but the South may become again the theatre of trouble, and here you are equally necessary, as illustrated by having the Gulf Dept. added to your vast area of command." Sheridan needed to stick close to his headquarters, leaving Crook and Terry "to finish this Sioux business which is about the last of the Indians."[8]

Frustrating delays became a trademark of the campaign from its inception; as summer approached, they continued. This time the blame lay with politics rather than weather. Lieutenant Colonel Custer, the commander of the Dakota Column from Fort Abraham Lincoln, had spent much of the winter on leave in the East, managing to sink up to his neck in the political quagmire engulfing the Grant administration. While in New York City, Custer gave a candid report of irregularities in the administration of army post sutlerships to his friend James Gordon Bennett, flamboyant publisher of the *New York Herald*. On February 10, 1876, Bennett's newspaper inaugurated a protracted exposé of the War Department, accusing Secretary of War Belknap of selling post traderships on the frontier and implicating Orvil Grant, the president's brother, along with him.[9]

Charges of fraud and extortion in the administration of army post traderships were hardly new. Colonel Hazen had exposed irregularities in the Fort Sill trader's office back in 1872. Hazen testified before the House Military Affairs Committee, but nothing came of the investigation. The *New York Herald* articles inspired a new investigation, and with the Democrats now in the majority in the House of Representatives it promised to be considerably more thorough.

The House Committee on Expenditures in the War Department, chaired by Pennsylvania Democrat Hiester Clymer, soon gathered enough evidence to prove that Belknap had accepted cash payments of over twenty thousand dollars between 1871 and 1876 in exchange for the appointment of John Evans as post trader at Fort Sill. Belknap, informed of the committee's evidence on March 1, 1876, resigned his office the next day.[10]

The Democrats, however, were far from finished. Clymer's committee, after presenting its findings to the House, was instructed to continue its investigation of malfeasance in the War Department while the Judiciary Committee began impeachment proceedings against Belknap (an action the secretary hoped to prevent by resigning). Since Custer's views on Belknap were well known, he was called to testify before both committees. Busy preparing his regiment to take the field by mid-April, he attempted to evade the summons by offering to submit his testimony in writing. Clymer, however, would not relent, and the dejected officer was soon on an eastbound train for Washington.[11]

Custer was only one of several army officers who testified for the Clymer committee. Before Custer's March 29 and April 4 appearances before the committee, Colonel Hazen testified by letter—he was in Mexico—on his previous charges regarding the Fort Sill trader. Lieutenant Colonel (Brevet Major General) Alexander McCook, of Sher-

William W. Belknap, secretary of war from 1869 to 1876, repeatedly abused his high office and betrayed the trust of his
friends Grant and Sheridan. Nevertheless, they loyally stood by
him. (*U.S. Signal Corps photo no. 111-sc-94177, National Archives*)

man's staff, and Lieutenant Robert Carter, Fourth Cavalry, testified on the 1871 Mackenzie-Reynolds confrontation in Texas, insinuating that Reynolds's malfeasance had been covered up by Belknap.[12]

Sheridan, closely following the investigation, read newspaper accounts of Custer's testimony with alarm. Much of his friend's testimony was hearsay, and some of it was exceedingly reckless. Custer portrayed the post traders on the Missouri River as parasites leeching off the officers and enlisted men of the army with exorbitant prices, while protected in their monopoly by Belknap, who was their silent partner. Custer claimed that he attempted to put an end to such practices, only to be rebuffed by Belknap. Once, when refusing a shipment of corn in sacks branded with the name of the Indian Bureau, fearing that the goods were being illegally sold to the troops instead of going to the starving Indians, he had been forced by Belknap to take the corn. Officers who had protested the high prices and corrupt practices of the traders were silenced by a gag rule from Belknap's office.

Particularly galling to Sheridan was Custer's charge that Colonel Hazen, one officer who would not submit to Belknap's censorship, had been exiled to the frontier's worst post as a result. Hazen, so long the bitter professional enemy of both Sheridan and Custer, suddenly became "one of the most meritorious officers in the service." With a self-serving flourish, Custer declared that he ceased all communication with Belknap beyond what was demanded by army rules, and avoided socializing with him during a September 1875 visit to Fort Lincoln. After recklessly repeating some rumors implicating Orvil Grant in the post trader scandal, Custer ended his testimony with an emphatic assertion that no brass buttons would be tarnished by the investigation.[13]

Sheridan was placed in an exceedingly disagreeable position by Custer's testimony. He had always championed Custer, but in attacking Belknap, and thus indirectly Grant, his protégé had gone too far. Sheridan agreed with Grant that the House investigations were crude election-year power plays and that Custer was helping the Democrats besmirch the president. In a tug-of-war for Sheridan's loyalty between Custer and Grant, there was not the slightest doubt of whom the general would support.

Sheridan wrote the War Department contradicting those portions of Custer's testimony referring to the corn transaction at Fort Lincoln and the transfer of Colonel Hazen to Fort Buford. "These papers are not intended to do any harm to Col. Custer," Sheridan added, unwilling to completely undercut his friend, "but to correct the errors he seems to have committed in his testimony published to the country."[14]

Another letter contradicting more of Custer's testimony was written by Sheridan's military secretary, James Forsyth. He had been with Belknap on the September 1875 visit to Fort Lincoln. Forsyth described Custer's behavior toward the secretary as being far from hostile. Belknap had the letter, with Forsyth's permission, widely published in the national press in an unsuccessful attempt to discredit Custer.[15]

Forsyth, in a private letter, assured Belknap that none of the army officers he knew approved of Custer's testimony, which he characterized as "nothing but hearsay—which is largely made up of frontier gossip and stories." Forsyth saw political ambition behind the attacks on Belknap: "The fact of the matter is that both Hazen, and Custer, are now working to make capital with the Democratic party—*they want stars.* As for McCook he is a damn fool who thinks too little and talks too much, and has but just recovered his mind which he lost when he ran away from Braxton Bragg and his own army corps at Chickamauga *more than a dozen years ago.*"[16]

This was not the first time Sheridan hastened to rescue Grant from scandal. When Orville Babcock, Grant's private secretary as well as a major in the army, was accused of taking bribes from the Saint Louis whiskey ring, Sheridan assisted in a scheme hatched by Grant and Belknap to save their friend from civil prosecution. Sheridan, like Grant, saw anti-Republican conspiracies behind the charges against Babcock and chose to ignore the mass of evidence against his wartime friend. In order to head off a civil trial and obtain the evidence held by prosecutors in Saint Louis, Babcock was to be investigated by a court of inquiry headed by Sheridan. There is little doubt that Sheridan's court intended to whitewash Babcock and end the scandal quickly. But when the court convened in Chicago on December 9, 1875, they had no evidence, for the Saint Louis prosecutors wisely held on to their treasured documents. Unable to act without the evidence, Sheridan dropped the case. Babcock eventually won acquittal in civil court, but his days as Grant's secretary were over.[17]

Although he had lost Sheridan's protection, Custer's testimony won him General Sherman's support. The new secretary of war, Alphonso Taft, recalled Sherman to Washington in March. Sherman took no personal part in Belknap's downfall—he was truly above such strife—but Colonel Hazen, the general's warm friend, and Lieutenant Colonel McCook, his aide-de-camp, had gladly played leading roles as his unsolicited surrogates. Sherman now befriended Custer, dining often with him and personally taking him to meet the new secretary of war. Sherman also obliged Custer by ordering three companies of the Seventh Cavalry to Dakota from the South and by intervening with the Belknap impeachment prosecutors to have the anxious cavalryman released from his summons so he might rejoin his regiment, then awaiting him to take the field.[18]

Custer was certain that with Sherman's support he could avoid testifying and would soon be in more congenial haunts on the plains. He had not, however, reckoned on the power of the vindictive Belknap. James Forsyth, Belknap's informant in Sheridan's headquarters, warned the former secretary on April 10 that Custer would soon be on his way west to rejoin the Dakota Column. Even though Sheridan heartily disapproved of Custer's testimony, he remained eager to have his experienced and trusted lieutenant lead the expedition. Forsyth assured Belknap, "There is no use of asking who will go in command of any troops, or expedition sent against the Indians in Dakota—for if Custer is available *he is certain to have the command.*" Forsyth warned Belknap: "If you are going to want him you had better make your application at once and have the War Department telegraph and call Custer back."[19]

Secretary of War Taft, at Sherman's behest, agreed to intervene with the impeachment committee on Custer's behalf, but when he brought up the issue with Grant, the president not only forbade him to contact the committee but ordered him to strip Custer of the command of the Dakota Column. The secretary complied, telling Sheridan on April 28 to find another officer to lead the expedition. Sheridan consulted with Terry on alternatives to Custer, but with no acceptable officers available, he ordered the department commander to take personal command of the expedition.[20]

Sheridan and Sherman were helpless to save Custer from the president's spite. Sherman did manage to persuade Grant at least to allow the humiliated officer to sit out his detention with his wife at Fort Lincoln.[21] Custer stopped off at Department of Dakota headquarters in Saint Paul to enlist Terry's support in petitioning the president to reconsider. Custer composed a simple but moving letter to the president that concluded with words certain to win Grant's sympathy: "I appeal to you as a soldier to spare me the humiliation of seeing my regiment march to meet the enemy and I to not share its dangers." Terry endorsed it with a short statement on how valuable Custer's services would be on the expedition.[22]

Sheridan forwarded the telegram from his headquarters with an endorsement calculated to appease the president while securing the requested boon:

> The following dispatch from General Terry is respectfully forwarded. I am sorry Lieutenant Colonel Custer did not manifest as much interest by staying at his post to organize and get ready his regiment and the expedition as he does now to accompany it. On previous occasion, in eighteen sixty-eight (1868), I asked executive clemency for Colonel Custer to enable him to accompany his regiment against the Indians and I sincerely hope if granted this time it will have sufficient effect to prevent him from again attempting to throw discredit on his profession and his brother officers.[23]

Grant relented, and on May 8, 1876, Sherman telegraphed Terry permission for Custer to go in command of the Seventh Cavalry. Custer had played a dangerous political game, Sherman lamented to Terry, and had "compromised his best friends here, and almost deprived us of the ability to serve him."[24]

With Custer finally back at the head of the Seventh, General Terry was prepared to depart Fort Lincoln on May 17. His column numbered almost a thousand men, with twelve companies of the Seventh Cavalry, forty Arikara scouts, and three infantry companies to guard the 150-wagon supply train. Despite such impressive strength, Terry was worried. Disturbing reports that fifteen hundred Sioux lodges were in western Dakota made him fear that he might not have enough troops. He ordered Gibbon to push farther east to meet the Dakota Column. He wired Sheridan to speed up Crook's departure from Fort Fetterman.

Sheridan was not concerned. "I will hurry up Crook, but you must rely on the ability of your own column for your best success," the lieutenant general replied, hoping to calm Terry. "I believe it to be fully equal to all the Sioux which can be brought against it, and only hope they will hold fast to meet it." Sheridan urged Terry not to fret about rumors of Sioux strength, assuring him of "the impossibility of any large number of Indians keeping together as a hostile body for even one week."[25]

Crook finally led his column north from Fort Fetterman on May 29. With ten companies of the Third Cavalry and five of the Second commanded by Lieutenant Colonel William B. Royall, a veteran of Sheridan's 1868 campaign, and two companies of the Fourth Infantry and three of the Ninth commanded by Major (Brevet Brigadier General) Alexander Chambers, the column numbered over a thousand men. Crook had hoped to augment his force with Sioux and Cheyenne warriors from the White River agencies, thereby repeating the tactic of turning the tribes against themselves that he had successfully used in Arizona. Red Cloud and his warriors, however, had refused to join with Crook when he visited their agency on May 15, presenting a remarkably defiant attitude for supposedly peaceful Indians. In fact, Crook learned that many of Red Cloud's young men had gone north to join the hostiles. His effort to recruit allies from among other tribes met with more success, 176 Crows and 86 Shoshones joining his column on June 14.[26]

Crook's account of his visit to the agencies led Sheridan, on June 2, to transfer Lieutenant Colonel Eugene Carr and eight companies of the Fifth Cavalry, then scattered about General Pope's department, to Wyoming. Sheridan's initial plan was to have the Fifth guard the White River agencies from Camps Robinson and Sheridan, but he decided to hold off issuing final orders until he could inspect the agencies in person. After a hurried appearance at an Army of the Potomac reunion, Sheridan headed west.[27]

Sheridan, accompanied by his adjutant, Colonel (Brevet Major General) James B. Fry, and James Forsyth, reached Fort Laramie on the evening of June 14, at about the same time that Carr marched into the post with the Fifth. With Carr was Sheridan's old friend Bill Cody, back with his regiment as chief of scouts after four triumphant seasons before the eastern footlights. Sheridan, delighted to see his famous friend, enlisted Cody to accompany him to the agencies. With a troop of the Fifth as escort, Sheridan, Fry, Forsyth, and Cody departed for Camp Robinson the morning of June 15. Sheridan found it quiet along the White River, which confirmed his suspicion that the reports of Indians leaving the agencies were exaggerated. Ben Clark, now back in the Indian Territory, had reported that many of the Cheyennes had come south, and Sheridan felt this explained the exodus from the northern agencies. After arranging for the troops at Camp Robinson to patrol the nearby roads, Sheridan returned to Fort Laramie, reaching the post on June 18.[28]

Convinced that there would be no trouble at the agencies, Sheridan ordered the Fifth north to the Powder River trail, which led from Red Cloud Agency to the Powder and Yellowstone rivers. Carr was to travel light—Sheridan anticipated the regiment being out no longer than six weeks—and scout westward along the trail in order to block the retreat of Indians fleeing toward the White River agencies. Carr should also keep an eye toward the agencies to stop any reinforcements from reaching the hostiles. Sheridan hoped that this scout by the Fifth Cavalry might "stir things up and prove advantageous in the settlement of the Indian question."[29]

No sooner had Sheridan settled back into his Chicago office than he learned that affairs had been stirred up but not as he had hoped. On June 17, Crook's column was attacked by a large force of Sioux and Cheyennes under Crazy Horse on Montana's Rosebud River. The Indians, well organized and fighting on favorable terrain, battled Crook for six hours before withdrawing. Crook reported ten killed and twenty-one wounded to Sheridan, but his chief of scouts, Frank Grouard, later put the figures at twenty-eight killed and fifty-six wounded. Crook claimed victory since he held the battlefield, but his immediate retreat to his supply base on Goose Creek, where he hunkered down to await reinforcements, told the true story.[30]

Sheridan knew his friend had been beaten, diplomatically commenting that "the victory was barren of results, however, as on account of his wounded and a lack of rations for his troops, General Crook was unable to pursue the enemy."[31] He ordered four companies from Fort

Douglas and another from Fort Sanders to reinforce Crook at Fort Fetterman. Carr was ordered to halt his troops where the Powder River trail crossed the South Cheyenne River, directly to the west of the Black Hills, and await developments. Crook's report of the Rosebud fight was forwarded to Terry. "I presume that long before this reaches you," Sheridan prophetically commented, "you will have encountered the Indians who fought Crook."[32]

In a surprising move, Sheridan now changed the field commander of the Fifth Cavalry. He had fretted for some time over the retirement of the Fifth's colonel, William Emory, sending daily telegrams to Sherman inquiring if the retirement papers had been processed. When it became apparent that Emory would retire as of July 1, Sheridan ordered Lieutenant Colonel Wesley Merritt to proceed to the Powder River trail and assume command of the Fifth Cavalry and the District of the Black Hills. Leaving Chicago on June 23, Merritt reached the Fifth's camp on July 1, the day his promotion to colonel became effective.[33]

Merritt's promotion came strictly in line with military rules of seniority, but his hasty assumption of command while the regiment was in the field was a hard blow to Lieutenant Colonel Carr. "It is, of course, an humiliation to me to have him come in and take command," Carr lamented. "It seems curious that the Government should find it necessary to spend large amounts of money and some blood to teach Terry, Crook and Merritt how to fight these Prairie Indians when there are others who know better how to do it."[34]

Sheridan was eager to get Merritt into the field so that he might have a chance at some glory in this last great Indian war. Merritt had commanded Sheridan's cavalry in the Shenandoah and Appomattox campaigns, and there were few officers the general placed more faith in. As lieutenant colonel of the Ninth Cavalry after the war, Merritt had no opportunity to distinguish himself as did his Civil War rivals Crook, Custer, and Mackenzie. Anxious to transfer out of the black regiment, he had been obliged by Sheridan in 1875 with an appointment as special cavalry inspector on the division staff. Although the appointment was supposed to run for only four months, Sheridan used his influence to keep Merritt in Chicago until some choice opportunity for him should arise. That opportunity had come, and Merritt, completely inexperienced in Indian warfare, replaced the seasoned, effective Indian fighter Eugene Carr.[35]

Merritt was instructed to hold the Fifth in readiness on the South Cheyenne River until Terry was heard from. No word had come from the Dakota Column since June 20, when Terry reported joining Gibbon on the Yellowstone River, having found no Indians east of Powder River. Sheridan doubted whether much would come in from Terry for some time, since the telegraph line from Fort Ellis had been out of commission since May 16. Nor could he wait around his headquarters for word, since his attendance was required at the Centennial Exposition in Philadelphia.[36]

On Independence Day a dispatch from Terry was finally received at headquarters and immediately forwarded to Sheridan at the Continental Hotel in Philadelphia. As of June 21, Terry's column had yet to make contact with the enemy, although fresh traces of a large camp had been discovered some twenty to thirty miles up the Rosebud River. Terry had put his troops in motion, with Gibbon moving up the Big Horn River to the Little Big Horn River, while Custer, with his whole regiment, was sent up the Rosebud to approach the Little Big Horn from the southeast. "I hope that one of the two columns will find the Indians," Terry concluded. "I go personally with Gibbon."[37]

On July 4, an Associated Press wire story originating in Salt Lake City claimed that one of Terry's columns had indeed found the Indians, and as a result Custer and every man of five companies of the Seventh were killed. In Philadelphia, Sheridan and Sherman responded as one. The story was preposterous they claimed, such wild rumors being common on the frontier. There had been no official report of a battle, and when Sheridan wired his Chicago headquarters for information on Terry's column, he found that nothing had been received.[38]

The next day, however, a confidential report from Terry was received in Chicago and forwarded to Sheridan. The newspaper reports were true: Custer had met disaster on the Little Big Horn. Sheridan was stricken, for despite Custer's flaws, he remained a close friend. The general's grief was mixed with anger over Terry's message. Instead of a report on the battle with a list of casualties, it was a defense of Terry's conduct of the campaign. Terry claimed that Custer had disobeyed orders by not making a wide sweep south of the Little Big Horn. He was supposed to block the Indian escape route into Wyoming, and then unite with Terry and Gibbon on June 26. Instead, Custer had forced-marched his men, following a previously discovered Indian trail leading directly to the Little Big Horn. There he had rashly divided his regiment into three attack columns and plunged into the Sioux. "I do not tell you this to cast any reflection upon Custer," Terry declared, "for whatever errors he may have committed he has paid the penalty, and you cannot regret this loss more than I do, but I feel that our plan must have been successful had it been carried out, and I desire you to know the facts."[39]

This hardly squared with Terry's earlier dispatch, in which he had portrayed Gibbon and Custer as marching independently in search of the Indians. The strategy Terry had worked out with Gibbon, Custer, and Major James Brisbin in a June 21 council of war had been one to find the Indians, not entrap them as he now insinuated. His written orders to Custer had given the cavalryman latitude of action, although Terry had made it clear that Custer was not to follow the Indian trail west from the Rosebud until he had scouted farther south.

Custer, not a man easily diverted from a hot trail, was not eager to share the glory of defeating the Sioux with Terry and Gibbon. No sooner had permission to accompany the expedition been received back in May, after Terry and Sheridan had intervened with Grant, than Custer confided to a friend his intention "to cut loose from and make my operations independent of, General Terry during the summer."[40] Now he had his chance; the seeds of disaster planted during the political battle with Belknap bore deadly fruit.

Custer, with a force of over six hundred men, reached the Indian trail turning west from the Rosebud on June 24 and followed it. At dawn the next morning his scouts located an Indian village in the Little Big Horn Valley, little more than fifteen miles from where the exhausted Seventh had made camp. At the same time, Custer learned that the regiment had been spotted by enemy scouts. With no idea of the size of the force to his front, Custer decided to attack.

Captain Frederick Benteen was sent off to the south with 125 men to prevent any Indian movement in that direction. Leaving one company to guard his pack train, Custer dispatched Major Marcus

Reno with three companies to attack the still-unseen village while he took five companies to the north to move in from another direction.

Contrary to the expectation of Sheridan, Terry, Crook, and Custer, the Indians did not run. The great village held between one and two thousand warriors, no one knows for sure how many, including Hunkpapas under Sitting Bull and Gall, Oglalas under Crazy Horse (fresh from whipping Crook on the Rosebud), Miniconjous, Northern and Southern Cheyennes, as well as smaller groups of Sans Arcs, Blackfeet, Brulés, Santees, Yanktonais, and Northern Arapahos. However many warriors were concentrated in the six great tribal circles encamped on the Little Big Horn, it was enough.[41]

Reno was repulsed from his attack on the southern end of the village, losing nearly half his command in a wild retreat to the high bluffs above the river. Custer, after sending a messenger galloping back to order Benteen to rejoin the regiment, hurried across broken country toward the other end of the village. Warriors swarmed across the river to meet him, encircled his 215 men, and wiped them out within an hour. Benteen joined Reno on the bluffs, where they stood off the warriors until the Indians triumphantly withdrew late on June 26, signaling the arrival of Terry and Gibbon the next morning. The Seventh was shattered, with 263 killed and another 59 wounded.[42]

Blame for the disaster was laid squarely on Custer by most of the press. Terry's confidential report to Sheridan quickly found its way into print when General Sherman, thinking him a government messenger, mistakenly handed it to a reporter for the *Philadelphia Inquirer*. Much to Sheridan's consternation, Major Reno's official report of the battle, also condemning Custer, was published in the newspapers before it reached his desk. Most of the early press accounts agreed with the estimate of Custer given by one of Sheridan's military companions at the Philadelphia Exposition: "The truth about Custer is that he was a pet soldier who had risen not above his merit but higher than men of equal merit. He fought with Phil Sheridan and through the patronage of Sheridan he rose, but while Sheridan liked his valor and his dash he never trusted his judgement. . . . We all think, much as we lament Custer . . . that he sacrificed the Seventh cavalry to ambition and wounded vanity."[43]

Sheridan, not as harsh on Custer as most, was willing to admit

A. R. Waud's *Custer's Last Fight* was an illustration in Frederick Whittaker's 1876 biography, *A Complete Life of General George A. Custer*, and thus ranks among the earliest of some two thousand artistic renderings of the most famous moment in the long struggle between whites and Indians for possession of the continent. It helped create a heroic image that quickly became enshrined in national myth. (*Author's Collection*)

that "it was an unnecessary sacrifice due to misapprehension and superabundant courage—the latter extraordinarily developed in Custer." He had often warned Custer to be more prudent, but his friend considered his regiment invincible and himself to have a charmed life. As he thought of all the officers and men who perished with Custer, many of whom he knew well, Sheridan was sickened.[44]

There was little time, however, for mourning the dead. From Philadelphia he ordered six companies of the Twenty-second Infantry, under Lieutenant Colonel (Brevet Major General) Elwell S. Otis, from posts along the Great Lakes to Dakota, and instructed Colonel Miles to bring up six companies of his Fifth Infantry from the Department of the Missouri and reinforce Terry. Merritt was ordered to Fort Laramie or Camp Robinson to stand in readiness to join Crook.

On July 7, Sheridan wrote Sherman, who had returned to Washington the previous day, reiterating his request for funds to build two posts on the Tongue and Big Horn rivers. "Terry and Crook are all right," Sheridan assured Sherman. "There is nothing to be regretted but the loss of poor Custer and the officers and men with him. Terry's column was sufficiently strong to have handled the Indians, if Custer had waited for the junction." With reinforcements Terry would be again strong enough to give the Sioux a fight, and Sheridan did not want his superiors to be alarmed. He was leaving for Chicago on the night express: "As soon as I get home I will take the campaign fully in hand, and will push it to a successful termination sending every man that can be spared."[45]

There was a quick response to Sheridan's long-standing request for forts, men, and control over the Sioux agencies. In July Congress authorized the construction of the two posts on the Yellowstone's tributaries, and in August authorized the enlistment of twenty-five hundred cavalry privates. Late in July the secretary of the interior turned control of all the Sioux agencies over to Sheridan. Custer's defeat had worked wonders, but at a terrible price.[46]

Merritt, after skirmishing with a party of Cheyennes twenty-five miles northwest of Red Cloud Agency at War Bonnet Creek on July 17 and driving them back to the agency, moved north and joined Crook at Goose Creek on August 3. Crook now had over two thousand men; twenty-five companies of cavalry under the overall command of Merritt, ten companies of infantry commanded by Major Chambers, and over three hundred Shoshone, Ute, and Crow auxiliaries. The bold, innovative campaigner who had once held his superiors' esteem as the army's premier Indian fighter now grew timid after two defeats at the hands of the hostiles. The slaughter of the Seventh compounded the problem, justifying in Crook's nervous mind the need for extreme caution. On August 5, with his reinforcements in place, Crook finally felt strong enough to march north to join Terry on the Yellowstone.[47]

Terry gathered his reinforcements together at the juncture of the Rosebud and Yellowstone rivers. While encamped there he conferred at length with James Forsyth, sent out by Sheridan on July 15 to get details on the campaign and advise Terry on where to build the two new posts. Forsyth stayed with Terry for almost a month. Otis's six companies of the Twenty-second Infantry arrived there by steamer on August 1, followed the next day by Miles with six companies of the Fifth Infantry.

Miles was not impressed by what he found. Noting that Terry "does not seem very enthusiastic or to have much heart in the enterprise," Miles could not recall ever seeing a "command so completely stampeded as this—either in the volunteer or regular service." He fretted over every summer day lost in the camp on the Yellowstone. "The more I see of movements here the more admiration I have for Custer," Miles wrote his wife on August 7, "and I am satisfied his like will not be found very soon again."[48]

On August 8, Terry felt confident enough to lead his seventeen hundred men up the Rosebud. The infantry companies were placed under the command of Colonel Gibbon, which did nothing to improve Miles's distemper, while Major Brisbin commanded the combined troops of Second and Seventh Cavalry. Fifty Crow scouts accompanied the soldiers. Crook's column was met two days later, and the combined commands turned eastward to follow an Indian trail. Colonel Miles, anxious for any kind of independent command, suggested that he take his regiment back to the Yellowstone River to patrol the fords and prevent any Indians from escaping to the north, and Terry relented. Even with Miles's departure, the combined force was the largest yet assembled on the plains.[49]

The slaughter of the Seventh had changed Sheridan's mind on the wisdom of Terry's and Crook's joining forces. He had written both of them in July suggesting such a combination, making it clear that Terry would command because of seniority. He had also attempted to reinvigorate them, correctly surmising that the fights on the Rosebud and Little Big Horn had shaken their confidence. He emphasized to each his confidence in their ultimate success. Sheridan felt his hands tied in going much further, for he could hardly undercut the position of his department commanders by taking charge himself. Events in the East, with the tense presidential election battle brewing, would hardly allow him to do so even if he wished.[50]

"Genls. Crook and Terry have now with them or ordered to them all the men that can be spared from this division," Sheridan reported to Sherman. "Either column will, I hope be strong enough to defeat the enemy, and·if there are any doubts in the minds of the officers commanding they will surely unite." Although it was hardly necessary, something inside compelled Sheridan to make excuses to Sherman for why he had not taken firmer control. "As I have reason to believe both commanders had a full knowledge of each other's intentions before starting out," Sheridan explained, "and have opened communication with each other since, I deem it the best judgement to give no positive orders."[51]

Sheridan was in for more disappointment from his field commanders. The vast column, so large and ponderous that it never had a chance of surprising or overtaking any Indians, muscled its way through frigid rains and mud, taking a full week to reach the mouth of the Powder River. Boats brought in critical supplies, for the last few days of the march had become a battle with mud, scurvy, hunger, and bad tempers. Not only did Terry's army have no chance of catching Indians, it was so large that it was all but impossible to supply for even a week. "It has reached beyond a joke that we should be kept out and exposed because two fools do not know their business," noted Eugene Carr in disgust. "I would leave the expedition today, if I could." Some did leave. Scout Cody decided to return to the stage, where the opportunities for glory loomed larger. Chief Washakie, who had also seen enough of Crook's and Terry's brand of campaigning, took his Shoshones home. Most of the newspaper correspondents left as well.[52]

Terry and Crook wisely decided to part. This was especially gratifying to Crook, who had been most unhappy in a subordinate role. Terry temporarily encamped his forces on the Yellowstone, at the mouth of Glendive Creek, and began stockpiling supplies to enable Colonel Miles to establish a cantonment at the juncture of the Tongue River and remain there all winter. Busy with this task, and not planning any more operations against the Sioux, he ordered Gibbon's command back to Forts Shaw and Ellis.[53]

Sheridan's hope of building two posts on the Tongue and Big Horn rivers had been frustrated by Congress's tardy appropriation and the falling waters of the Yellowstone. With the river too low to move building materials and supplies upriver, the forts would have to wait until spring. Sheridan felt it imperative, however, to occupy the Sioux hunting grounds and so assigned Miles, with twelve infantry companies, to build a cantonment on the Tongue River to prevent the Sioux from returning to the region.[54]

The Tongue River cantonment was part of a new strategy that Sheridan developed in Chicago while Terry and Crook were blundering ponderously across the Montana prairie. He had already given up hope that the forces in the field would bring the Sioux to combat. "I have never looked on any decisive battle with these Indians as a settlement of the trouble," Sheridan explained to Sherman in outlining his strategy for the fall and winter. "Indians do not fight such battles; they only fight boldly when they have the advantage, as in the Custer case, or to cover the movement of their women and children as in the case of Crook on June 17, but Indians have scarcely ever been severely punished unless by their own mode of warfare or tactics and stealing on them."[55]

Sheridan saw but one solution to the Sioux problem, and it was the same remedy he had been advocating for two years: "the occupation of the game country of the Yellowstone valley and the control of the Agencies from whence most of the hostiles come." By his placing troops in the Sioux hunting grounds, the Indians could be continually harrassed and forced by fear and hunger to come into the agencies. With the agencies under military control, they would find a hostile reception and be disarmed, dismounted, and punished. It was essentially a repetition of the harsh policy successfully used against the southern tribes in the Red River War.[56]

Miles's temporary cantonment would be replaced in the summer of 1877 by the construction of two permanent posts, Fort Custer, on the Big Horn River, and Fort Keogh on the Tongue River. Sheridan also desired that the Big Horn country be occupied and to that end established a cantonment on the Powder River about three miles above old Fort Reno, abandoned as a result of the 1868 Sioux treaty. The cantonment, established in October 1876, became a permanent post, Fort McKinney, in 1877. The construction of these posts gave Sheridan control of all the country west of the Black Hills to the Big Horn River, and south of the Yellowstone River to the Wind River Mountains. Thus the vast unceded Sioux hunting region was at last denied to the Indians and thrown open to the whites.[57]

Occupation of the Big Horn and Yellowstone regions denied the Sioux a place of refuge when Sheridan sprang the second half of his strategy—the disarming and dismounting of the Indians. To ensure that the Indians would not scatter upon learning of his plan, Sheridan anticipated waiting until late fall to initiate action so that the weather would inhibit any movement. Sheridan knew "the very man" to tackle the delicate job of disarming the proud and still powerful

Oglalas at Red Cloud Agency—Colonel Ranald Mackenzie. Over the protest of General Pope, Mackenzie and six companies of the Fourth Cavalry were ordered north from Fort Sill.[58]

Mackenzie, given command of the District of the Black Hills and Camp Robinson, reached his new post on August 17. His cavalry companies were reinforced by two companies of the Second Cavalry and by Frank and Luther North with fifty Pawnee scouts. Sheridan, never an advocate of the use of Indian auxiliaries, had nevertheless called Frank North to Chicago and recruited him and his brother to raise one hundred Pawnee scouts for use against the Sioux. Mackenzie was thankful for all the men he could get, for he was not pleased with the temper of the friendlies at Red Cloud Agency. He found less than half the Indians at the agency that the Indian Bureau had reported during the summer. Red Cloud and Red Leaf were encamped some thirty miles from the agency with over two hundred warriors and their families, defiantly refusing to report in. This situation was intolerable, for without close military supervision the hostile and agency Sioux easily intermixed.[59]

Sheridan decided to travel to Fort Laramie and confer with Crook and Mackenzie on the situation. He was accompanied on his journey west by two high-ranking officers of the Japanese army, neither of whom spoke English or had an interpreter. As part of a commission examining American military institutions, they were eager to observe methods of Indian warfare. Sheridan's entourage arrived at Fort Laramie on September 16 to find that Crook had been delayed. Settling in to wait, Sheridan charmed the garrison ladies with his modest, unassuming manner and cordial interest in their affairs. "Fishing was his principal pastime," recalled one officer's wife. "General Sheridan proved himself a No. 1 sportsman in addition to his other accomplishments."[60]

Crook was in the Black Hills when he finally received Sheridan's order to hurry to Fort Laramie for a conference. Since leaving Terry on the Powder River, he had marched his column eastward across Montana and Dakota to the headwaters of Heart River and then turned south toward the Black Hills. Drenching rains and short rations won the names Mud March and Horsemeat March for Crook's search for the hostiles. The only Indians encountered consisted of thirty-seven Sioux lodges near Slim Buttes, north of the Black Hills, surprised

Despite the bungling and mixed results of the Great Sioux War, it was soon enveloped in a romantic haze that obscured historical reality. No one contributed more to this than Sheridan's old friend Buffalo Bill Cody. His Wild West extravaganza, founded in 1883, exploited the romantic possibilities of the vanishing frontier to create a grand epic of triumphal conquest. The promotional flyer for the 1899 season commented on the 1898 exploits of Theodore Roosevelt's Rough Riders in Cuba while reminding patrons of the "Historic Rough Riders of the Sixties"—Sheridan, Cody, and Custer. (*Courtesy of the Buffalo Bill Historical Center, Cody, Wyoming*)

324

by Captain Anson Mills in a dawn attack on September 9. Mills, with a detachment of the Third Cavalry, captured the village and held it for several hours until reinforced by Crook in the afternoon. A sizable band of Sioux had then skirmished with Crook's column for another day before withdrawing. The fight at Slim Buttes had not amounted to much. Only a handful of Indians were killed, and Crook neglected to press after the Sioux who attacked his column—even though they were the very Indians he had been searching for. The truth was that Crook had so overtaxed his men, who were literally·starving because he had neglected to procure enough supplies, that when he finally found the hostiles, he could not pursue them.[61]

At Fort Laramie, on September 21, Sheridan explained his plan for occupying the Sioux hunting grounds and controlling the agencies. Crook had hoped to operate out of the Black Hills during the winter, but Sheridan vetoed the plan, ordering him instead to establish a cantonment near old Fort Reno to control the country between the Black Hills and Big Horn Mountains. The Seventh Cavalry would soon occupy the Missouri River agencies, disarming and dismounting all the natives, Sheridan told his two subordinates, and Crook and Mackenzie were to occupy the White River agencies. Mackenzie was to begin by taking the recalcitrant Red Cloud and Red Leaf bands back to Red Cloud Agency, disarming and dismounting all the Sioux as punishment for their defiance of government authority. All hostiles who came in to surrender were to be disarmed and dismounted as well, with the disposition of the leading warriors to be decided upon later. Indian ponies would be sold and proceeds used to purchase cattle for the tribes. Satisfied that Crook clearly understood his views, Sheridan departed for Chicago the next day.[62]

On October 23, Mackenzie surrounded the villages of Red Cloud and Red Leaf and compelled them to surrender without a fight. These bands had never been hostile, but they had chosen a poor time to assert their right to camp where they wished. Instead of disarming and dismounting all the Sioux, as Sheridan wished, Crook stopped with the bands of Red Cloud and Red Leaf. He not only left the rest of the Sioux armed, he enrolled five hundred of them as scouts for a winter campaign against Crazy Horse.[63] Sheridan warmly approved Mackenzie's quick work with the bands of Red Cloud and Red Leaf, but angrily condemned Crook's disobedience in not continuing the disarmament.

"His neglect to disarm and dismount other bands at the Agency is disapproved," Sheridan told the secretary of war, "and all the theories in this report seem to be given as a plea for not having performed what he promised and what was expected of him, and which could have been good policy and true humanity."[64]

Crook, however, was convinced that his summer campaign had failed for lack of Indian scouts who knew the country. The Sioux, he felt, would remedy that situation. On November 14, Crook headed north with another vast column numbering over two thousand men. After camping at the newly established cantonment near old Fort Reno, Crook dispatched Mackenzie with ten companies of cavalry and the Indian scouts to search for a rumored Cheyenne village in the Big Horn Mountains. On November 25, Mackenzie scored a smashing victory over the Cheyennes of Dull Knife and Little Wolf, destroying their two hundred lodges on the Red Fork of the Powder River, capturing seven hundred ponies, and killing at least forty warriors. After this promising start, however, the campaign proved fruitless, and Crook returned to winter quarters in December.[65]

On the Yellowstone, Colonel Miles kept up a determined winter campaign with only five hundred men, using the Tongue River cantonment as a base camp. His troops chased Sitting Bull's band over a good portion of Montana, sometimes skirmishing but mostly harrassing, until that chief fled across the border into Canada. Miles also battled the Sioux and Cheyennes under Crazy Horse, who had eluded Crook, and defeated that bold chief at Wolf Mountain on January 8, 1877. Miles's determined marches made it unhealthy to remain in the favored Montana river valleys, and most of the Sioux and Cheyennes drifted into the agencies to surrender. On May 6, 1877, Crazy Horse surrendered at Red Cloud Agency and, with Sitting Bull in Canada, the Sioux war came to an end. The war, as Sheridan had predicted, had fizzled out.[66]

With the bright exceptions of Miles and Mackenzie, the war had enhanced no military reputations and had tarnished several. General Crook, in particular, had come up short in every instance. Sherman blamed Crook for the Custer debacle, feeling that his retreat from the Rosebud had been inexcusable. "Surely in Grand Strategy we ought not to allow savages to beat us," he declared, "but in this instance they did."[67]

Sheridan agreed. "The fact of the case is, the operations of Gens. Terry and Crook will not bear criticism," he confessed to Sherman, "and my only thought has been to let them sleep. I approved what was done, for the sake of the troops, but in doing so, I was not approving much, as you well know."[68]

Sheridan now doubted not only Crook's ability but also his loyalty. In January 1877 newspaper articles appeared blaming the campaign's failures on Sheridan's faulty strategy and Merritt's slowness in reinforcing Crook. Convinced that these articles originated at Crook's headquarters, Sheridan dashed off an angry letter to Crook, defending Merritt and warning his old friend not to engage in "ignorant criticisms of [his] superiors, in the newspapers."[69]

Sheridan deserved criticism for his handling of the Great Sioux War. By 1875 he was so wedded to his converging columns, winter campaign strategy that he refused to consider alternatives. Blinded by the victories of 1868–69 and 1874–75 on the southern plains, he put into operation a strategy that was not practical during the winter season on the northern plains. His logistical problems—enormous on the southern plains—were insurmountable in the north.

Of course, Sheridan had hoped to overcome the twin problems of supply and long-term exposure by constructing forts on the Tongue and Big Horn rivers. These posts would have allowed his troops to occupy the country of the hostiles and thus avoid the long, debilitating marches that proved so disastrous to the campaign. Congress, by refusing to appropriate funds for the forts until after Custer's defeat, forced Sheridan to send his columns on extended marches across rough country. Once the posts were built, the Indians were deprived of their best hunting grounds and quickly defeated.

The politicization of the army during this period also contributed to the campaign's problems. Sheridan was distracted throughout the Indian conflict by the Belknap scandal, the Louisiana crisis, and the election crisis. Instead of attending to their legitimate military duties, both Sheridan and Sherman busied themselves with political games. Sherman, of course, stormed off in a huff to Saint Louis, abdicating his responsibilities and avoiding a serious role in the conspiracy to seize the Black Hills and conquer the Sioux. He made no effort, however, to dissuade Hazen, McCook, and Custer from continuing his battle with Belknap.

Grant's vindictive demotion of Custer put the Dakota Column in the hands of the inexperienced Terry. It also put the proud Custer in an even rasher mood than usual and undoubtedly contributed to his decision to push to the Little Big Horn ahead of Terry and Gibbon.

Although Custer's testimony against Belknap was self-serving, it was essentially true. Custer's readiness to unmask the thieving secretary of war was a courageous act. The quickness with which Sheridan rushed to assist both Belknap and Babcock reflected poorly on him. By attempting to prop up these political leeches he sullied himself and the army. As with his defense of Baker's Piegan massacre, Sheridan once again put loyalty above integrity. By supporting Grant and his crooked cronies, Sheridan undercut Custer when he should have protected his protégé.

Sheridan's most grievous error, however, was his refusal to recognize the ability of the hostiles to muster large numbers of warriors or to comprehend their willingness to stand and fight. No amount of evidence could dissuade him from his conviction that large numbers of Indians could not combine against his troops. A one-day visit to the agencies was enough to assure him that scouting reports were all false. His worry was that the troops might not find the Indians, not that they could be defeated if they did find them.

In fact, the Great Sioux War was the only conventional war the army ever fought against the trans-Mississippi Indians. It was the type of conflict these Civil War veterans were supposedly used to, where large, massed bodies of troops maneuvered for control of battlefields. Reynolds, Crook, and Custer were simply outmaneuvered and defeated in quite conventional battles. It was only when the military could return to the harassing tactics employed so successfully in the Red River War that the Indians were defeated by starvation and exhaustion.

In June 1877 Sheridan decided to make a personal reconnaissance of the seat of war, accompanied by both Forsyths, General Crook, Lieutenant John Bourke, and several other officers. After traveling by rail to the Green River station of the Union Pacific, the party struck north across the majestic Wind River Mountains, turning northeast on the Tongue River Trail across Wyoming's Big Horn Mountains. While in the Big Horns a zoologist with the party discovered a new species of mountain butterfly, thoughtfully naming it the *Theela sheridani* in honor of the general. After reaching the eastern base of the Big Horns, Sheridan proceeded north along the Little Big Horn valley, where only the year before Custer had fought his last battle.

Sheridan spent most of July 21 studying the Custer battlefield. Just the previous month Mike Sheridan, with Troop I, Seventh Cavalry, had visited the battlefield to remove the remains of Custer and his officers for reburial by their relatives. Mike had carefully marked the burial sites of the enlisted men with stakes, reinterring many of the troopers whose remains had been exposed by weather, animals, and souvenir hunters.[70]

Just in case his brother's party had missed any bones, the general now ordered Sandy Forsyth, with seventy men and several Sioux guides, to scour the surrounding countryside. While this search was on, Sheridan inspected the sprawling battleground. Fascinated by Custer's defeat, he carefully reconstructed the battle. His conviction that, had Custer held together his regiment, he could have defeated the Indians or at least defended himself, was further reinforced. It had been a terrible sacrifice, but not a useless one in Sheridan's mind.[71]

As he surveyed the valley of the Little Big Horn, soaked rich with the blood of his friends, he could see its potential riches. These rolling hills and broad plains would one day support a great cattle empire that would feed millions. "The cattle-range here for hundreds of miles is superb," he declared, with "grass nearly high enough to tie the tops from each side across a horse's back."[72]

His brief visit to the battlefield convinced him of the necessity of having the site declared a national cemetery. Only in this way could the graves be properly secured and cared for. Upon his return to Chicago he successfully pressed his wish on the government, and the battlefield was designated a national cemetery in 1879.

On July 22, Sheridan's party pushed on to the confluence of the Big Horn and Little Big Horn rivers where the cantonment of the Eleventh Infantry, soon to be Fort Custer, was located. Sheridan traveled by steamboat down the Big Horn and Yellowstone rivers to the mouth of Tongue River, where the second post, to be named Fort Keogh, was under construction. The river valleys of the Big Horn and Yellowstone, Sheridan felt, held rich prospects for the American farmer. As Sheridan continued his journey down the Yellowstone and

Missouri to Bismarck, and then by rail back to Chicago, he could take satisfaction that the Yellowstone country had proved worthy of his efforts to explore it and open it up to white settlement.

The nomadic tribes who once roamed across vast expanses of virgin land were now concentrated on reservations, guarded by Sheridan's troops, and everywhere the general looked, he saw settlers moving in to take up this newly won empire. "This population, numbering probably two millions of men," noted Sheridan with pride, "engaged in mining, grazing, and agricultural pursuits, pays taxes, builds farmhouses, and constructs fences, plows up the ground, erects school-houses, and founds villages, towns, etc., and the millions obtained by the sweat of their brow add so much more to the trade, commerce, and prosperity of the world"[73] "This was the country of the buffalo and hostile Sioux only last year," he wrote in his report of the reconnaissance. "There are no signs of either now; but in their places we found prospectors, emigrants, and tramps." Civilization marched on, and Sheridan saw himself as its instrument.[74]

CHAPTER 15

The Closing Military Frontier

As Sheridan had predicted, the subjugation of the Sioux cleared the western plains of the last major obstacle to national expansion. Not that the Indian wars were over. There would be other campaigns, against the Nez Perces in 1877, the Northern Cheyennes in 1878, the Utes in 1879, and Victorio's New Mexico Apaches throughout 1877–80, but these were against a foe clearly on the defensive and usually unable to muster much strength. Sheridan's new Indian strategy was one of watchful waiting. Instead of marching into strange country against a foe of unknown size, the soldiers now ringed the reservations with their forts, guarding against the outbreak of the malcontented. By the fall of 1879 Sheridan could report, "There has been no general combination of hostile Indians in this military division during the past year, and I doubt that such combinations can ever exist again."[1]

While the nomadic tribes had been able to surmount the Rocky Mountains and ford the swollen waters of the great rivers of the West, they found it more difficult to deal with the unnatural obstacles placed by the encroaching white civilization. Sprawling towns now occupied the rich valleys of the Arkansas, Smokey Hill, Platte, Yellowstone, and Black Hills. White farmers swarmed over the land like locusts, consuming acres like that winged visitor, but unlike him, not moving on. The steel bands of the Union Pacific, the Kansas Pacific, the Atchison, Topeka and Santa Fe, and the Northern Pacific railroads could not have better divided the land and prevented the natives from roaming had the rails been fifty feet high. The great lines and their branches were vital arteries of civilization to whites, but to Indians they were like a spider's enveloping web. Little wonder that the Cheyennes used the same word for spider and white man. The Indians were not swept asunder by a tide of white settlement advancing from east to west. They were rather crushed between the dual movement of settlers pushing in from both the east and the west.

Sheridan recognized these enveloping factors, and welcomed them. He felt them to be the natural and glorious result of his long labor on the frontier. The settlements and railroads had "thrown too many obstacles in the way for Indian runners to communicate intelligence among the various tribes." Population growth spelled doom for the natives' commissary, for "the great southern buffalo herds, together with the elk, antelope, and deer, upon which they depended to subsist their warriors, are now nearly gone." Sheridan was convinced that "Indian troubles that will hereafter occur will be those which arise upon the different Indian reservations, or from attempts made to reduce the number and size of these reservations, by the concentration of the Indian tribes." His assumption proved correct.[2]

Sheridan's guardians of this rapidly closing frontier were stretched in a thin blue line across the West. He could muster but one man for every 75 square miles of territory in the Departments of the Missouri, the Platte, and Dakota and one to every 120 square miles in the Department of Texas. Infantry companies averaged but forty men, while the cavalry and artillery did only slightly better with sixty and fifty men, respectively. Sheridan was quick to complain that three or four of his companies were "expected to hold and guard, against one of the most acute and wary foes in the world, a space of country that in any other land would be held by a brigade."[3]

With his troops scattered across the frontier at small posts, Sheridan found it difficult to prosecute the few Indian campaigns he faced after 1877. The cost of mobilizing forces at any one place was high, and the time lost in concentrating troops gave the Indians a brief advantage. These problems were especially telling in the characteristic type of campaign fought after 1877, the pursuit of Indian fugitives over large expanses of territory.

The seventeen-hundred-mile flight to Canada of Chief Joseph's Nez Perce band, some eight hundred strong, across parts of Oregon, Idaho, Wyoming, and Montana was a case in point. For almost four months they eluded or outfought all the troops the army sent against them, at the same time mauling the reputations of General Oliver O. Howard and Colonels John Gibbon and Samuel D. Sturgis, before finally surrendering to exhaustion, hunger, and Colonel Nelson Miles on October 5, 1877, at Montana's Bear Paw Mountains. Since Joseph led his people from the Division of the Pacific into the Division of the Missouri, he caused a jurisdictional squabble between the various military commands. Sherman gave his old friend Howard, commander of the Department of the Columbia, permission to ignore division lines in his pursuit of the Indians. All might have been well, except that Colonel Miles, of Sheridan's command, swooped in to bag the Nez Perces before the faltering Howard could catch them. A heated debate followed over who deserved the dubious honor of capturing the heroic band. Miles claimed all the credit for his command, despite the fact that Howard was present at the surrender. Howard responded by authorizing a press release which declared that Sheridan supported his claims to credit over the boasts of Miles. This was far from the truth, and Sheridan called Howard into his Chicago office for a severe dressing down. The acrimony continued for some time, with General Terry stepping in to attack Howard for daring to issue orders to Department of Dakota troops after Joseph's surrender. Sherman, exasperated, finally silenced all the parties.[4]

Sheridan took a keen interest in the disposition of the captured Nez Perces. Miles had promised Joseph that if he would surrender, his people could return to the Lapwai reservation in Idaho, but he had exceeded his authority. Sheridan was determined that the Indians should be punished, for he visualized an Indian domino theory if they were not. Sheridan worried that since the Nez Perces had made war on the federal government, killing its soldiers, they would be regarded as heroes by the other tribes. "If they can do all this, and then be returned to their old haunts . . . the effect on other Indians in that region will be bad and damaging," Sheridan protested. "It may induce them to engage in a like enterprise. It is a common saying now among Indians, and there is much reason in it, that Indians never get enough to eat or much consideration and kindness from the Government except after having made war upon its citizens and soldiers." Sheridan recommended that the Nez Perces be banished to the Indian Territory, and he prevailed.[5]

A repetition of the flight of the Nez Perces occurred in the fall of

1878, when more than three hundred Northern Cheyennes fled their Indian Territory reservation to return to their former home in the north. These were the people of Dull Knife and Little Wolf, defeated by Mackenzie in November 1876, who had surrendered at Camp Robinson in April 1877. At Sheridan's behest, Crook and Mackenzie, aided by Indian Bureau officials, had persuaded the Northern Cheyennes to join their southern cousins at the Cheyenne agency in Indian Territory.[6]

Sheridan held a personal vendetta against the Cheyennes and was determined to rid the northern plains of them. He respected them above all other tribes as fighters, holding them, and not the Sioux of Sitting Bull and Crazy Horse, responsible for playing the major role in defeating Custer. He knew more about the Cheyennes than any other tribe, partly through the tutoring of Ben Clark. He had Clark prepare a Cheyenne dictionary and grammar of the language for him and encouraged bright young officers like Hugh Scott and William P. Clark to study the tribe. This interest, however, did not translate into compassion. Fearful of Cheyenne battle prowess, Sheridan worried about the impact of their independent spirit on other tribes. Neutralizing the Cheyennes became such an obsession with him that even the intervention of Ben Clark could not change his mind. While he opposed the movement of other northern tribes to the Indian Territory, Sheridan was adamant that the Cheyennes should go.[7]

When Dull Knife and Little Wolf led their people from the southern reservation on September 9, 1878, Sheridan was informed by Ben Clark that the Indians had good reason to flee. Clark, who was working as Indian interpreter at Fort Reno, a post established in 1874 about a mile from the Cheyenne-Arapaho agency, reported the Northern Cheyennes starving and wracked by diseases. Colonel Mackenzie, back at Fort Sill, had warned of a possible outbreak as early as November 1877, blaming insufficient Indian Bureau rations for Cheyenne dissatisfaction. Sheridan was quick to concede that the outbreak had been caused by "insufficiency of food and irregularity in its supply," but that factor did not lead him to side with the unfortunate Cheyennes. Instead he ordered out all the troops he could spare, instructing Crook "to spare no measures" in killing or capturing the Indians.[8]

The Cheyennes managed to elude troops from both the Department of the Missouri and the Department of the Platte, fleeing northward through Kansas and Nebraska. They skirmished with the soldiers on occasion, and some warriors disobeyed Little Wolf's orders and raided the settlements, but the flight was generally bloodless. Splitting into two bands after crossing the Platte, Dull Knife's followers surrendered at Fort (formerly Camp) Robinson on October 23, 1878, while Little Wolf led the rest of the Cheyennes toward Montana. Dull Knife's people, 149 in all with but 46 warriors, were held at Fort Robinson until the government could decide on their disposition. They informed the post commander, Captain Henry Wessells, Third Cavalry, that they would rather die then return to the hated Indian Territory. Many of the officers at Fort Robinson sympathized with the Cheyennes and made their feelings public. General Crook also spoke out in opposition to returning the Cheyennes south. All these statements added to a wave of national concern for the plight of Dull Knife's homeless people.[9]

Sheridan was unmoved. At the very time that Little Wolf and Dull Knife were moving north, and with full knowledge of the sad treatment the Northern Cheyennes had received in Indian Territory, Sheridan had ordered Ben Clark and a detachment of the Fourth Cavalry to escort Little Chief's band of Northern Cheyennes to the southern reservation. Little Chief's people, some of whom had scouted for Colonel Miles against the Sioux and Nez Perces, passed within a few miles of their fugitive relatives during the journey but did not make contact. Sheridan now worried that "the remaining Cheyennes in the Indian Territory will go north, if these Indians are allowed to go free!"[10]

Sheridan was especially disturbed by the military officers in Crook's department who were speaking up for the Cheyennes. "I sympathize as much with Indians as any one," he declared, "but I think for officers to encourage Indians in opposition to the policy of the Government a matter of doubtful propriety. The condition of these Indians is pitiable, but it is my opinion that, unless they are sent back to where they came from, the whole reservation system will receive a shock which will endanger its stability." Sheridan wanted the Cheyennes returned south immediately, with the leaders of the band imprisoned in Florida. He ordered Crook to move them south as soon as possible.[11]

Captain Wessells was determined to comply with Sheridan's

wishes. The Indians were just as determined to remain in the north. To force them to agree to return to the Indian Territory, Wessells ordered the Cheyennes—men, women, and children—locked in a barracks building and denied them heat, food, and water. On January 9, 1879, after enduring nearly a week of this torture, they made a desperate break. Using a dozen guns that had been hidden among the women, they shot their guards and escaped into the bitterly cold darkness. Many were killed in the breakout, and in the dozen days that followed the soldiers relentlessly tracked down the pitiful remnant. Sixty-four men, women, and children were slain, and seventy-eight recaptured. Eleven soldiers had been killed in the unequal contest, with ten others, including Captain Wessells, wounded. The American people were outraged over the Fort Robinson slaughter, for only the coldest of hearts would not have warmed to the tragedy of Dull Knife's people.[12]

Sheridan defended his soldiers. "I am quite convinced," he asserted, "there was no unnecessary cruelty at Fort Robinson, on the contrary, the officers were governed by the highest sentiments of humanity throughout."[13] While this was an overstatement, especially in light of Wessells's harsh starvation tactic, it was somewhat supported by numerous humanitarian acts on the part of the soldiers at Fort Robinson, few of whom took any pleasure in hunting down the Cheyennes. As usual, Sheridan pushed his point too far, for his rhetoric was ever unrestrained. "It is enough for me to say," he lied, "that the 'poor Indian' fully sustained his cruel nature by making a breastwork of his women and children in resistance to the orders which sent him back to his agency." He again presented a litany of atrocity stories concerning the Cheyennes—murdered farmers, raped women, brutalized children.[14]

This time the public would not listen. Not even Sheridan could convince them that this pitiful band of wandering Cheyennes were cruel savages bent on rape and plunder. Sheridan's repeated request that the remaining Cheyennes be returned to Indian Territory was ignored. Dull Knife and the remainder of his band were allowed to settle with the Sioux at Pine Ridge Agency in southwestern Dakota. Little Wolf had surrendered his 126 followers to Lieutenant William P. Clark on March 27, 1879, in southeastern Montana. They were allowed to encamp at Fort Keogh, where many of the warriors signed on as scouts for Colonel Miles. Through the intervention of Miles and others, a reservation was set aside in 1884 for the Northern Cheyennes, and the people of Dull Knife and Little Wolf were allowed to make their homes amidst the rich Tongue River region that had once been a favorite hunting ground.[15]

Sheridan, noting the decision to allow the Cheyennes to remain in the north and not willing to concede an error of judgment, grumbled that he was glad to see the question settled. He insisted, "It is a mistake to say that the Northern Cheyennes were treated with injustice, but is is no mistake to say that they were treated in a bungling and impolitic manner."[16]

Writing confidentially to Sherman, Sheridan blamed the tragedy on Crook. He accused Crook of not taking the necessary precautions in light of the Cheyennes' determination not to return south. Sheridan branded the Fort Robinson affair as just another in an increasingly long list of Crook's failures.[17]

Publicly, however, Sheridan cast the blame for such tragedies on the Indian Bureau. He regarded the Northern Cheyenne outbreak as avoidable; its cause lay in Indian Bureau mismanagement. Since his days as a young officer in the Pacific Northwest he had observed Indian Bureau corruption and bungling. Never shy about criticizing Indian agents and traders, the Fort Robinson tragedy again stirred him to the attack. He was convinced more than ever "that it is not the Government which is managing the Indians, it is the contractors, traders and supply interests." These predatory harpies, aided and abetted by corrupt Indian Bureau employees, he held responsible for driving the Northern Cheyennes from the Indian Territory.[18] He was weary of charges that the army sought Indian conflicts for glory and then prosecuted them with uncivilized cruelty, while the true instigator of war, the Indian Bureau, escaped criticism by posing as the Indian's champion.

In his annual report for 1878, Sheridan lashed out at the "wretched mismanagement" of the Indian Bureau. He noted that through corruption and waste it repeatedly squandered appropriations so that it never provided enough rations to supply the tribes properly. The result was that "hunger has made the Indians in some cases desperate, and almost any race of men will fight rather than starve." Incompetence was partly to blame for this long-standing and intolerable situation, but Sheridan accused government contractors and traders, working in collusion with corrupt Indian Bureau agents,

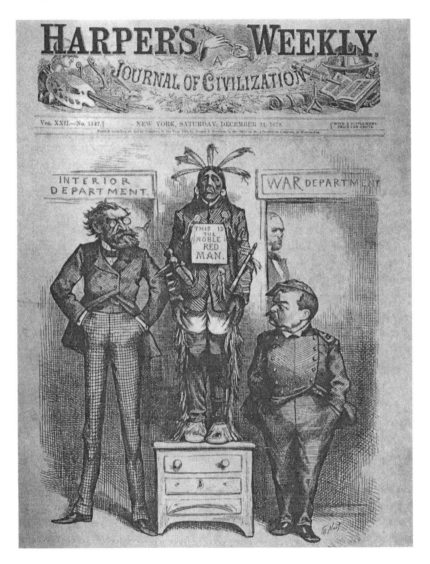

Cartoonist Thomas Nast wryly commented on the feud between Sheridan and Schurz on the cover of the December 21, 1878, issue of *Harper's Weekly*. In "The New Indian War" the subject of their debate is, in typical Nast style, depicted in an unflattering light between them while General Sherman offers his friend Sheridan moral support from the War Department doorway. In a jab at Schurz's foreign birth a German helmet appears over his shoulder. (*Author's Collection*)

338

of being the real cause of mismanagement. "There does not seem to be now, and there never has been," he declared, "much steadiness in the management of the Indians, and if it were not for the results which so severely involve the military, this would be none of my business." But, Sheridan asserted, he was compelled to indict the Indian Bureau because its poor management had repeatedly driven the tribes to war.[19]

Secretary of the Interior Carl Schurz returned Sheridan's fire in kind. In a letter to the secretary of war he demanded to know upon what evidence Sheridan based his charges of corruption. He felt that such serious charges, if based merely on hearsay, should be retracted. As he had so eloquently done when Sheridan's troops evicted the Democrats from the Louisiana legislature in 1875, Schurz again reminded the general of the superiority of the civilian government over the military establishment.[20]

Sheridan had never liked Schurz, who as a leader of the Liberal Republicans had been a thorn to President Grant, and the letter infuriated him. "It is not necessary to remind me of the superiority of the civil to the military in this country," he angrily wrote Sherman in response to Schurz. "I drank that in my milk from the time I was born. I did not have to learn it, and such talk is a poor cloak for the bad management of Indian affairs which is wasting our appropriations; and this is a professional question I have a right to complain of and report."[21] Calming down, he thought of better ways to beat Schurz and deleted the rhetoric. In its place came a list of examples of Indian Bureau ineptitude and corruption of which he had personal knowledge. He also wrote his department commanders for information "relative to abuses or corruption on the part of the Indian Agents."[22]

Sheridan prepared a supplemental annual report for Sherman, comprising over twenty tightly printed pages "replete with instances of rascalities and irregularities at a great majority of the agencies in the Military Division of the Missouri, [which] throw a flood of light on the mismanagement of affairs in the Indian service."[23] Schurz had demanded evidence, and Sheridan gave it to him. The fact of Indian Bureau corruption, however, came as a surpise to no one. Schurz had himself appointed a special board of inquiry in 1877, which had reported widespread dishonesty. Schurz was dedicated to purging the bureau of corrupt employees, but he did not want Sheridan's help.[24]

"Old Schurz, just as you and I expected, played the adroit in the correspondence," Sheridan noted to Sherman after the controversy had blown over, "but he had not made much by it. I made no attack on him, but on the system, and the evidence furnished will have its effect."[25] Sheridan's charges, however, had no real effect. The real issue behind the argument with Schurz was the transfer of Indian affairs to the War Department, for Congress was again considering a bill to accomplish that goal. Schurz was in agreement with Sheridan on the urgent need for reform, but he was adamant that any housecleaning be done by civilians and not the military. His energetic efforts at reforming the Indian Bureau and his stern rebuttal of Sheridan's charges gave Schurz enough prestige to withstand this last major push for transfer and hold Indian control within the Department of the Interior.[26]

Sheridan's 1878 attack on the Indian Bureau, however, was not solely motivated by his desire to secure passage of a transfer bill or to shift blame for the Fort Robinson tragedy. After the defeat of the plains tribes, Sheridan was more willing to act as their advocate. The incursions of whites into the Indian Territory especially concerned him. He repeatedly urged "Congressional action to keep out intruders from the Indian Territory," claiming that had "it not been for the military, the territory of Oklahoma would have now been covered with settlements."[27]

There was a concerted effort by squatters to occupy portions of the Indian Territory in 1879. Sheridan responded by ordering four companies of the Fourth Cavalry and four companies of the Twenty-second Infantry to the Indian Territory to reinforce the troops guarding the borders. By stationing companies at key points along the border, such as Coffeyville, Wichita, Baxter Springs, Arkansas City, and Vinita, he hoped to stop boomer parties before they could get started. Other soldiers from Indian Territory military posts patrolled the borders of Kansas and Missouri in search of intruders. "There is not the slightest doubt of our ability to keep squatters out," Sheridan assured his superiors. "Squatters are easily turned back. They have families and intend to have fixed habitations. It is the adventurers after gold and silver with no families and but little impediments who have heretofore given us trouble." Sheridan promised to watch the situation closely and "not allow our vigilance to relax."[28]

With Indian power broken and the natives concentrated on reservations, Sheridan determined to study Indian culture before it vanished altogether. In particular, he turned to two brilliant young officers to carry out this scientific work: William Philo Clark and John G. Bourke, both of Crook's staff.

Bourke, an 1869 graduate of West Point who had fought as an enlisted man at Stones River, Chickamauga, and Chattanooga, had served on Crook's staff since September 1871. Bourke saw hard fighting against the Apaches in Arizona and in the Great Sioux War, but emerged from these conflicts with a deepening respect for Indian culture. His service with Crook's Apache scouts had been instrumental in transforming Bourke from a racist Indian-hater to an enlightened ethnocentrist with true respect for the diverse and rich Indian cultures.[29]

In the summer of 1881 Bourke submitted "Memoranda for Use Obtaining Information concerning the Indian Tribes" to Sheridan, and in response the general assigned the lieutenant to duty as an ethnologist for the army. Sheridan wished Bourke to concentrate his studies on those tribes south of the Union Pacific line, but gave him latitude otherwise. "Take your time," he told Bourke. "I want you to make a success of this and I'll back you up in every possible way."[30]

By September 1881 Bourke had a detailed report on the snake dance of the Moquis Indians of Arizona in Sheridan's hands. Delighted, the lieutenant general published portions of the report in the *Chicago Times*.[31] It was the beginning of important work for Bourke that eventually led to a series of ethnological publications, election to the American Association for the Advancement of Science, and an international reputation as a scholar.

Sheridan selected Captain William P. Clark to study the tribes on the northern plains. There was scarcely a young officer in the service who was more accomplished or better known than Clark. After graduating from West Point in 1868, he joined the Second Cavalry, coming to the attention of General Crook during the Great Sioux War and joining his staff. Crook detailed Clark to command a force of three hundred Indian scouts from various tribes. White Hat, as the scouts called their leader, saw hard service under both Crook and Miles, personally accepting the surrenders of Crazy Horse in 1877 and Little

Wolf in 1879 and leading the last strike against Sitting Bull at Milk River, Montana, on July 17, 1879. [32]

Clark's fairness and essential decency won him the admiration of Indians both hostile and friendly. After the surrender of Crazy Horse he served for a year at Red Cloud and Spotted Tail agencies, using every opportunity to study carefully Sioux, Cheyenne, and Arapaho festivals, funerals, and ceremonies. His service with mixed bands of scouts—Pawnee, Shoshone, Crow, Arapaho, Cheyenne, and Sioux—led him to master the complex intertribal sign language. This proficiency with sign language and his ability as an interpreter resulted in an occasional assignment of bringing delegations to Washington.

In 1881 Sheridan ordered Clark to prepare a study of Indian sign language, supplemented with remarks on native habits, manners, and customs. Sheridan authorized Clark to visit tribes in the Indian Territory, Minnesota, Dakota, Montana, Nebraska, Utah, Wyoming, Idaho, and Canada. It took Clark four years of intensive study and writing to produce his brilliant work, *The Indian Sign Language*, which Sheridan had published in 1885. [33]

Clark did not live to see his book published. Upon Sheridan's promotion to command the army, he selected Clark for his staff. But the thirty-nine-year-old officer was stricken with peritonitis and died suddenly on September 22, 1884, in Washington, D.C. His death was a hard blow to Sheridan and a grievous loss to the army. [34]

The melancholy irony of Sheridan's sponsorship of the ethnographic scholarship of Clark and Bourke is that, once he had destroyed the Indians' old way of life, he wished to preserve some remnant as an exhibit for a curious posterity. Confident that the Indian was now a harmless "vanishing race," Sheridan rushed to save some bits and pieces of their history before they faded away as an identifiable people. While his eagerness to see Indian lifeways recorded resulted in some valuable anthropological studies, it nevertheless stemmed from ethnocentric arrogance.

At the same time that he was sponsoring the studies of Clark and Bourke, Sheridan was advocating the dissolution of the reservation system. For once the general was in agreement with the eastern humanitarians with whom he had so often battled. He strongly advocated the adoption of a land-in-severalty program for the tribes. This was the same concept that the reformers viewed as a panacea for the Indian problem.

Carl Schurz had proposed a severalty plan in his 1879 report as secretary of the interior, building on ideas that had been bandied about since the Civil War. With Schurz's backing, a movement to enact severalty legislation was organized. Texas Senator Richard Coke and Massachusetts Senator Henry L. Dawes, each at times chairman of the Committee on Indian Affairs, championed the cause of the allotment of land in severalty in Congress. Sheridan placed the influence of his position as lieutenant general behind the plan.

The concept of land in severalty had long appealed to Sheridan. He had recommended its adoption some twenty years before he came out forcefully in support of the severalty plan proposed by the 1885 Lake Mohonk Congress of Indian reformers. Although in general agreement with the reformers' land allotment proposals, he differed on specifics. In 1885 press releases, and again in his 1886 annual report, he recommended that 320 acres of land be set aside for each Indian family, with all surplus reservation land purchased by the government at $1.25 an acre. The funds from this purchase could be invested in bonds and the interest used for annual cash payments to each family and for the purchase of houses, schools, and agricultural equipment. When the Indians reached an adequate state of "civilization and intelligence," the principal derived from the sale of their lands could be returned to them.[35]

Unlike the humanitarian reformers, however, Sheridan did not advocate this policy solely out of concern for the Indians' welfare. He saw it as a cost-effective way to break up tribal organization, alleviate the federal government of the expense of much of the Indian service bureacracy, and release the military from the unpopular duty of guarding the reservations from white intruders, while opening nearly 170,000 square miles of new lands to his adopted constituency, the western promoters and settlers.[36]

He recognized the inequities that would result in the relocating of Indian families on some 26,000 square miles of land and the sale of the remainging 170,000 square miles. Some of this land was already worth $8.00 to $10.00 dollars an acre, but he was not bothered by the government paying only $1.25 an acre for it. This bargain would help offset the long-standing financial investment made in the Indians. Sheridan viewed these lands as unproductive in Indian hands and was anxious to transfer ownership to those whom he felt better able to exploit the potential of the western soil. He did, however, advocate the gradual implementation of any severalty plan so as to lessen its impact on the Indians.[37]

On February 8, 1887, President Cleveland signed into law the Dawes General Allotment Act, which gave to the Indians individual land ownership and opened up surplus reservation lands to eventual white settlement. Instead of the half-section of land advocated by Sheridan, each head of an Indian household would receive a quarter-section (160 acres), with smaller sections going to single persons and dependents. The allotments would be held in trust by the government for twenty-five years. The exultation of the friends of the Indian over passage of the Dawes Act was shared by land-hungry westerners. Within fifteen years of the enactment of the allotment act, the total acreage held by the Indians was cut in half.[38]

The enactment of this reformist-backed legislation dispossessed the Indians at a far more rapid rate than had any of Sheridan's military campaigns. His pragmatic alliance with his old adversaries, the humanitarians, enabled Sheridan finally to achieve his goal of extinguishing Indian title to the best western lands so that they could be opened to commercial interests and white settlers. The fact that the leading reformers enthusiastically participated in this well-intentioned land swindle, believing it would americanize the Indians, confirms that Sheridan's long-standing contempt for the humanitarians was not necessarily misplaced.

When history connects Phil Sheridan with the Indians and the last frontier, it is not as the protector of the Indian Territory, the sponsor of ethnographic scholarship, or an advocate of the Dawes Act. Inexorably the name is joined with that brutal "only good Indian is a dead Indian" statement whenever it is linked to the frontier. Usually, however, despite his long years of frontier service, Sheridan's name is not identified with the West at all.

The Indian wars never allowed Sheridan an opportunity to display his impressive talents as a tactical field commander and were thus anticlimactic to his Civil War career. Sheridan's Civil War achievements were, of course, so dramatic and important that the small-scale

Indian conflicts paled in comparison. Furthermore, Sheridan often stepped aside in the West so as to give his subordinates their chance of the limelight or in order not to compromise their independent commands. This was clearly the case in 1868–69 and again in 1876–77. Thus younger officers like Mackenzie, Miles, Carr, and Custer made reputations as Indian fighters that far overshadowed their impressive Civil War records. Sheridan, despite the fact that he took an active part in some campaigns and planned the overall strategy for most of them, never became identified as an Indian fighter.

Yet Sheridan was the nation's chief Indian fighter from 1867 until he assumed overall command of the army in 1883. He commanded a larger frontier region for a longer period of time than any other soldier in the history of the Republic. Under his immediate command the final and greatest Indian campaigns of the century were planned and executed. Between 1867 and 1884 the troops under Sheridan's command fought 619 engagements with the natives, with a loss of 565 officers and men killed and another 691 wounded.[39] By 1880 Sheridan had completed the subjugation of the American natives that had been put in motion almost four centuries before when Columbus reached the New World.

With serious Indian resistance over by 1880, Sheridan was further reduced to the position of administrator, a role which he was poorly fitted by inclination or temperament to occupy. Thus he naturally looked forward with considerable anticipation to Sherman's retirement so that his duties might be enlarged.

CHAPTER 16

Four Stars

William Tecumseh Sherman retired on February 4, 1884, upon reaching the age of sixty-four. It was suggested by many that an exception to the compulsory retirement law, passed with Sherman's staunch support in 1882, could be arranged, but the commanding general declined all such offers. He decided to vacate his position on November 1, 1883, in order to give Sheridan time to get his new office in order before Congress convened. Although able to turn over the position of commanding general to his friend, Sherman could not pass on his rank of full general, for by law the four stars retired with him.[1]

Sherman had long contemplated retirement. "Sheridan is 10 years my junior in years and I have had supreme command for 10 years and it is but fair he should have his chance," he wrote his wife in 1879. "He don't ask for it or want it, but there is such a principle as 'turn about fair play.' "[2] In April 1880 Sherman had assured Sheridan that he was convinced that "all Army officers should have in mind the rights of Juniors to promotion and command—and all should at the age of 62 be ready to retire gracefully and not wait to be kicked out."[3] Sherman's hope for early retirement, however, was frustrated by the pressing need to serve long enough to secure a full pension.

In his last days in command Sherman had the satisfaction of observing his old adversaries, the staff and bureau officers, wringing their hands over his departure. "Now that I am off," he chortled to his wife, "many of the Staff who thought me partial to the Line call with strong expressions of regret at my departure, for they realize that I have saved them many a lick against which Sheridan cannot parry."[4]

346

He was pleased with the status of the army that he was transferring to Sheridan, feeling it to be "in reasonably good condition, considering the fact that peace and politics are always more damaging than war."[5]

While delighted at the prospect of commanding the army, Sheridan was nevertheless saddened to be leaving Chicago. His warm attachment to the city was heartfelt; he could never bring himself to sell his Michigan Avenue home. This was the city of his marriage and the birthplace of his children. Above all other places, he thought of Chicago as home.

"I have seen the city in its magnificent boyhood," he told a distinguished group of Chicago civic and business leaders who gathered at the Commercial Club for a farewell banquet. "I have seen it burn down, and I have seen it grow up into vigorous manhood. I have seen, not many years ago, the whole northwestern country covered with Indians and buffalo, and I have lived to see it covered with cities . . . which are sending their products to Chicago, the distributing point for the great Northwest." The conquest of this last frontier, the general declared, had been "fostered and encouraged by the citizens of Chicago in the true spirit of enterprise."[6]

To the leading citizens of Chicago, Phil Sheridan had indeed been a good friend. His services to his adopted city during the great fire, the 1877 labor disputes, and as an unofficial agent for their expanding commercial empire were of incalculable value. They honored him with receptions and banquets and presented him with the deed to a new home in Washington as a token of their esteem and in acknowledgment of his services to them. The roomy home at the corner of Rhode Island and Seventeenth Street was purchased out of a forty-four-thousand-dollar fund raised by a committee of thirty-one Chicago businessmen that included Anson Stager, Marshall Field, George M. Pullman, Philip D. Armour, Levi Leiter, Jospeh Medill, and Potter Palmer.[7]

At ten o'clock on Thursday morning, November 1, Sheridan joined Sherman in the commanding general's Washington office. The outgoing and incoming army chiefs spent much of the morning discussing the affairs of the office. In another room their respective staffs went over the routine business of army headquarters and compared notes on which politicians were either hostile or favorably inclined toward the military.

347

Lieutenant General Philip H. Sheridan and Staff, 1888, by Henry Alexander Ogden. The artist was commissioned by the Quartermaster General to produce a series of forty-four paintings illustrating army uniforms from 1776 to 1888. His painting of Sheridan depicts the general in full dress uniform, wearing a chapeau decorated with black ostrich feathers and patterned on one worn by General Sherman. To the rear and right is Colonel Michael Sheridan, the general's brother. The officer saluting is in the Light Artillery, as indicated by the red piping on his saddle cloth. Behind the general is a helmeted cavalry officer and an officer of the Staff Corps.

Major Mike Sheridan headed up the new commanding general's staff as military secretary with the rank of lieutenant colonel. Captain James F. Gregory, of the engineers, and Captain William J. Volkmar, Fifth Cavalry, both of whom had served on the Division of the Missouri staff since 1881, were appointed aides-de-camp with the rank of lieutenant colonel.

At noon Sherman issued a formal order relinquishing command of the army, and Sheridan did the same for the Division of the Missouri. Sheridan's West Point classmate, John Schofield, now assumed command of the division. There was the obligatory call on the president and then a reception at army headquarters. The retiring general was at ease and in good spirits, but his uncomfortable successor seemed to wish that formal receptions could be forbidden by military law.[8]

The *Army and Navy Register* lamented Sherman's departure, characterizing him as "the most wonderful man of the age."[9] Many agreed that the statement was no exaggeration. It was indeed a sad day when William T. Sherman stepped down from command of the army he had so indelibly stamped his strong character upon. His wisdom and steady hand would be sorely missed. Sheridan may have been the heart of the old army, but Sherman was its very soul.

One of Sheridan's first actions as commanding general was to attempt to solve the problem of command that had bedeviled the army for so many years. He boldly announced to friends that he intended to regain the ground lost in the past when "Sherman threw up the sponge." Determined to assume control of all the army, he did not intend the staff bureau chiefs to enjoy the power they had known for so long. Sheridan's effort to limit the bureau chiefs to what he interpreted as their proper prerogatives, the fiscal administration of the army, and his attempt to establish his authority over them by issuing them orders without the prior approval of the secretary of war, led to immediate conflict.

Secretary of War Robert T. Lincoln responded in a kind but firm letter defining his interpretation of the relationship of the staff bureau chiefs to the secretary of war and commanding general. Although this interpretation was in direct contradiction of Sheridan's position, the general suddenly declined to press the fight, refusing even to reply to Lincoln's letter. The bureau chiefs were thus assured their independence. To add to Sheridan's humiliation, whenever the secretary of war was out of the capital, the senior bureau chief temporarily assumed that office. "But the loyal, subordinate soldier," gloomily noted Major General Schofield, "who had commanded great armies and achieved magnificent victories in the field while those bureau chiefs were purveying powder and balls, or pork and beans, submitted even to that without a murmur, for a great lawyer had told him such was the law, and how could he know better."[10]

As might be expected, considering Sheridan's well-known political prejudices, the situation deteriorated even more when a Democratic administration assumed power in 1885. President Grover Cleveland's secretary of war, Massachusetts jurist William C. Endicott, immediately asserted his complete authority, as well as that of the bureau chiefs, over army command and administration. Just in case anyone had forgotten the proper distribution of authority, Endicott printed copies of Secretary of War Lincoln's letter rebuking Sheridan and sent them to all army generals.

When a railroad magnate complained that Sheridan was marching troops from post to post during transfers instead of sending them by rail, Endicott demanded an explanation from the commanding general. Sheridan's sensible response, that troops should always march when practical since it provided an opportunity for field practice, was not satisfactory to the secretary. In response Endicott forbade Sheridan even to transfer troops without his prior approval. This sort of bickering continued unabated until June 1887, when a complete rift occurred. Sheridan vigorously protested Endicott's order directing the return of captured Confederate flags to the states from which they had been taken. The intense backlash from the Grand Army of the Republic and northern politicians when the order was announced vindicated Sheridan's opposition and led President Cleveland to rescind the order. This skirmish gave Sheridan his only victory over Endicott. Watching the sad spectacle from afar, Sherman mused that he was "perfectly content to have retired when I did, as the present *régime* makes Sheridan's command of the army a farce."[11]

Although Sheridan did not skulk away with his headquarters to another city, as Scott and Sherman had done, he was left as powerless as if he had. He might well enjoy the high honor of his sinecure, going to his office in the old State-War-Navy Building each day to read in the newspapers what orders had been issued over his name by some staff bureau chief, but it was a command without real power. It is a terrible thing to reach the pinnacle of power and professional achievement, only to find it devoid of authority. The anomaly was that the position of commanding general of the army had, especially in time of peace, fewer important powers and duties than those possessed by staff bureau officers and division and department commanders. The actual administration of the army was performed by the various staff bureau officers who answered directly to the secretary of war. The commanding general was, in essence, an advisor to the secretary of war.[12] Still, Sheridan was not without influence, and his years as commanding general were marked by some modest achievements.

With the Indian threat over, Sheridan busied himself consolidating army posts in order to garrison large numbers of troops near major cities and railway centers, while abandoning scattered frontier outposts. This was in recognition of the role the army might be called on to play in future labor disturbances. Such a concentration also resulted in greater economy of supply and improved training opportunities. Several key forts were enlarged under this policy, with troops transferred to them as frontier posts were abandoned. Most notable as points of troop concentration were Fort Logan, at Denver; Fort McPherson, at Atlanta; Fort Niagara, near Buffalo, New York; Fort Riley, in Kansas; Fort Sam Houston, at San Antonio; Fort Sheridan, near Chicago; and Fort Snelling, near Minneapolis.[13]

The lieutenant general took particular pride in Fort Sheridan. His friends at the Chicago Commercial Club purchased a 635-acre tract of land twenty-four miles north of the city in 1886, in the wake of the Haymarket tragedy, and donated it to the federal government as a site for a fort. Through the efforts of Senator John Logan, Congress accepted the gift, and President Cleveland directed that the new fort be named in honor of the commanding general. At the time of Sheridan's death construction was under way, but only two companies of infantry garrisoned the handsome military reservation bordering Lake Michigan. Still, Chicago's nervous men of property could slumber more peacefully at night, warmed by the knowledge that Sheridan's Boys were but a few miles to the north, ready to march against the laboring classes should they forget their proper station in life.[14]

There was some public agitation to abandon Fort Riley, Kansas, and turn the military reservation over to civilian interests. Working closely with General Schofield and Kansas Senator Preston Plumb, Sheridan blocked the schemes and secured congressional approval for the enlargement of Fort Riley to facilitate the establishment of schools of cavalry and light artillery. Sheridan realized that technological improvements had revolutionized warfare. The introduction of magazine rifles, breech-loading steel field pieces, and improved explosives would end mobility on the battlefield as armies entrenched to avoid the rapid, accurate firepower of their enemies. Sheridan correctly foresaw the dawning of an age of prolonged, total wars. He incorrectly felt, however, that cavalry would prove indispensible in future wars for commerce raiding. In Fort Riley he envisioned the perfect place not only to train cavalry and light artillery officers for future wars but also to breed cavalry mounts as the Europeans did. In response Congress authorized a "school of instruction" for cavalry and light artillery at Fort Riley in 1887. Sheridan's dream, however, did not become a reality until 1892. This impressive step toward professionalism was, of course, several decades too late. By 1887 cavalry was well down the trail to obsolescence.[15]

In this period of technological transition, ordnance became one of Sheridan's more pressing concerns. The breech-loading Springfield rifle, adopted by the army in 1873, was as good a single-shot, black-powder weapon as then existed, but it was hardly a match for the new magazine rifles carried by European armies. In response to calls by Sheridan and others for the adoption of a magazine rifle, the administration appointed a board of officers to study the respective merits of various American-made rifles. But progress was so slow that in 1887 Sheridan recommended that the government adopt a European magazine rifle "rather than adhere longer to our present single loader, effective, even, as its fire can sometimes be made."[16] In 1893 the army adopted the Krag-Jorgensen, a Danish rifle with a box magazine of five rounds that used smokeless powder, and began production at the Springfield armory.[17]

Sheridan also lobbied for the establishment of a modern system of seacoast fortifications. The antique coastal fortifications then in existence were more picturesque than useful, belonging more to the realm of historical societies than militarists. The Civil War had already proven the obsolescence of masonry forts. What was needed were earth-covered concrete bunkers, shielded by armor plate, and armed with breech-loading, heavy-rifled artillery. Sheridan's recommendations contributed to the creation of the Endicott Board in 1885, which made wide-ranging proposals for coastal fortifications, and the Army Board of Ordnance and Fortification in 1888, which attempted to make the necessary emplacements. Sheridan proved an able voice for national preparedness and for the need to keep pace with rapid changes in international military technology.[18]

Sheridan's brief tenure as commanding general was marked by a number of important command changes. Schofield, commanding the now-quiet Division of the Missouri, had Terry in the Department of Dakota, Howard in the Department of the Platte, and Stanley taking command in Texas. Augur commanded the Department of the Missouri until his retirement from the army on July 10, 1885. He was replaced by Miles. Pope took command of the Division of the Pacific in 1883, remaining there until his retirement in 1886. Howard, promoted to major general, succeeded Pope in that division, with his Department of the Platte position going to Crook. Hancock remained in command of the Division of the Atlantic until his death in February 1886. Sheridan then assigned Schofield to the Atlantic and moved Terry, promoted to major general, up to command the Division of the Missouri.[19]

Sheridan worked assiduously to secure promotion for Mackenzie, but found it difficult because of the colonel's relative youth and lack of political connections. "There is no one who has had the opportunity of judging of the services of officers since the war as myself," Sheridan assured Secretary of War Lincoln in 1881, "and I am of the belief that those of the greatest value to the Government have been rendered by Colonel R. S. Mackenzie."[20] Sheridan, with the timely assistance of Grant, finally prevailed, and Mackenzie was promoted to brigadier general in October 1882. For Mackenzie, however, the star came too late. His health had been shattered by long years of campaigning on the most distant frontiers, and, after but a month in command of the Department of Texas, his mind snapped. His behavior became increasingly erratic, and although never before a drinker, he suddenly became a hopeless alcoholic.[21]

Mackenzie's sister pleaded with Sheridan to place her brother in an asylum. Mackenzie had taken to ranting that the army needed urgent reorganization and that he and Sheridan were just the men to do it. Sheridan, learning of this, ordered Mackenzie to Washington for a conference on that subject in late December 1883. Instead of Washington, however, Mackenzie was tricked into going to New York City, where he was placed in the Bloomingdale Asylum. After consulting with Mackenzie's Texas doctors, Sheridan had recommended the commitment of his favorite field officer. A retiring board, convened in March 1884, concluded that the hopelessly insane officer should receive a disability retirement. Hidden away and forgotten, Mackenzie died five years later at the age of forty-eight.[22]

One benefit of the light duties attached to the commanding general's office was that Sheridan could continue to pay close attention to affairs in the West. He often traveled west on inspection tours, good excuses for fishing and hunting jaunts as well.

His keen interest in the Yellowstone country never slackened. In each of the three summers before he moved to Washington he had made extensive tours of the park. What he saw in 1882 deeply troubled him.

Sheridan's 1882 Yellowstone expedition was no small affair, consisting of 129 soldiers, scouts, and civilians. Along with Mike Sheridan, W. P. Clark, and James Gregory of his staff, the general invited several friends, including William Strong and Anson Stager of Chicago. Secretary of War Lincoln had planned to go but was forced to cancel at the last minute. To handle the 261 horses and mules, Sheridan secured the services of Crook's famous packmaster, Thomas Moore. This party cut the first trail along the Snake River from Jackson Hole to the thumb of Lake Yellowstone. Thereafter known as Sheridan Trail, it was the main southern entry route to the park until a road was completed in 1895.[23]

Sheridan was enraged to learn of the slaughter of the park's wildlife by hide hunters. He was told that over four thousand elk had been killed in one winter for their hides. The tiny civilian park staff could not hope to stop the well-organized poachers and had proven equally unsuccessful in halting vandalism of the park's natural wonders.[24]

Upon reaching the line of the Northern Pacific Railroad, Sheridan made an even more disturbing discovery. The so-called Yellowstone Park Improvement Company, affiliated with the Northern Pacific Railroad, had been granted monopoly rights to develop the park. This company had secured rights to forty-four hundred acres within the park, including Old Faithful, Mammoth Hot Springs, Lake Yellowstone, and the Grand Canyon of the Yellowstone. Their monopoly included all transportation rights, including boating, rights to all arable land, retail rights, and the use of such timber and coal from the park as they might need. The Department of the Interior granted this monopoly to the minions of the Northern Pacific for an annual rent of but two dollars an acre.[25]

Sheridan vigorously opposed this leasing of the national trust. "The improvements in the park should be national, the control of it in the hands of an officer of the government," he declared in his report of the 1882 expedition. If the Department of the Interior could not protect the park, then he would. "I will engage to keep out skin hunters and all other hunters," he told the administration, "by use of troops from Fort Washakie on the south, Custer on the east, and Ellis on the north, and, if necessary, I can keep sufficient troops in the park to accomplish this object, and give a place of refuge and safety for our noble game."[26]

Sheridan also put forward a bold plan to expand the park. He wanted the eastern boundary extended forty miles and the southern boundary dropped ten miles to the forty-fourth parallel. This annexation would increase the size of the park by over three thousand square miles and incorporate vital game habitat within its boundaries. Sheridan's proposal, eventually labeled the Greater Yellowstone Movement by writer Emerson Hough, gained many influential friends, including the American Forestry Association. Most residents of the neighboring territories, however, tended to agree with a typically provincial Montana editor who characterized Yellowstone Park as "too huge a joke for them to comprehend."[27]

Sheridan realized that he needed strong allies in order to block the monopolists, expand the park, and transfer its control to the military. He appealed "to all the sportsmen in the country, and to the different sportsmen's clubs," to lobby Congress on behalf of his plan. In response, George Bird Grinnell, editor in chief of *Forest and Stream*, enlisted his journal in Sheridan's crusade. Sheridan had sponsored Grinnell with Custer's Black Hills expedition, and the famed naturalist now had the pleasant opportunity of repaying an old debt while continuing his long-standing conservation work.[28]

355

Grinnell was not the only acquaintance from the past who rallied to Sheridan's banner. Buffalo Bill Cody took time out from organizing his Wild West Show to write a letter in support of Sheridan's call for conservation. Times had changed, Bill declared, and the slaughter of game that had won him a name "does not find favor in the West as it did a decade or so ago."[29] Sheridan's former military aide John Schuyler Crosby, now territorial governor of Montana, also entered the fray as an ardent ally of his old commander.

Sheridan's most important ally, however, was Missouri Senator George Graham Vest, chairman of the Senate Committee on Territories. Soon after his return from the park Sheridan sent the senator a copy of his report and a map showing the proposed boundary lines. He pleaded with Vest to champion Yellowstone's cause, for with the settlement of the Big Horn country the park and its surrounding lands had become the last refuge for many western animals. "The suggestions made in my report are the only things left for us to do to save this noble game," Sheridan assured Vest.[30]

Senator Vest introduced a bill on January 3, 1883, that incorporated Sheridan's proposals. The bill called for the enlargement of the park, protected most of the wildlife, gave park regulations the force of law, prohibited the granting of monopoly rights, increased appropriations for park administration, and authorized the use of troops to manage the park. Secretary of the Interior Henry M. Teller, in response to the bill and under intense public pressure, prohibited the killing of game within the park's boundaries. Vest's bill, however, failed to pass.

Undeterred, Vest next attached a rider to the Sundry Civil Appropriations bill forbidding the secretary of the interior to grant monopolies within the park. This rider was further amended to authorize the detailing of troops to protect the park, and as such became law on March 3, 1883. The Yellowstone Park Improvement Company still obtained leases to key areas within the park, but for only a ten-year period and on a total of but ten acres of land. Most important, however, the bill set in place the machinery for military guardianship of the park.[31]

Although delighted with Vest's partial victory, nothing less than his park expansion plan could satisfy Sheridan. To that end, and in

The presidential party pauses during a picnic in Yellowstone for photographer Frank Jay Haynes. Left to right: Lieutenant Colonel James F. Gregory; John Schuyler Crosby, Sheridan's former aide and now Montana territorial governor; Sheridan; Secretary of War Robert Todd Lincoln; President Chester A. Arthur; Captain William Philo Clark; Missouri Senator George Vest; Lieutenant Colonel Michael V. Sheridan; Judge Daniel G. Rollins, surrogate of New York; and Anson Stager, president of Western Union. (*DeGolyer Library, Southern Methodist University*)

order better to publicize the park, he organized a presidential excursion to Yellowstone for the summer of 1883.[32]

Sheridan's party would be the most distinguished ever to travel to Yellowstone. The general and President Chester A. Arthur would be accompanied by Secretary of War Lincoln; Senator Vest; Montana Governor Crosby; Daniel G. Rollins, surrogate of New York and a friend of the president; George Vest, Jr., the senator's son; Anson Stager; and photographer Frank Jay Haynes. Members of Sheridan's staff—Clark, Gregory, and Mike Sheridan—and a military physician, W. H. Forwood, completed the party. Troop G, Fifth Cavalry, would provide the seventy-five-man escort. This company had been hand-picked by Sheridan because its commander, Captain Edward M. Hayes, had given excellent service as quartermaster on the great buffalo hunts in 1871 and 1872. Packmaster Thomas Moore once again took charge of Sheridan's pack train.[33]

Departing Chicago on August 2, the party traveled over the Union Pacific to Green River, Wyoming, and then moved north by spring wagon to old Camp Brown, renamed Fort Washakie in 1878 in honor of the army's great Shoshone ally.

The president spent a day at Fort Washakie enjoying the nearby hot springs and meeting Shoshone and Arapaho chiefs from the Wind River Reservation. Once more Sheridan planned a grand Wild West Show for his guests. Over five hundred Indians galloped into camp on August 8, well mounted on sleek ponies, gaudily painted, and dressed in their finest beadwork. Captain Hayes's troop and a band of warriors staged a parade and mock battle.

These scenes of savage splendor delighted the distinguished tourists, at least until the speeches began. As the politicians and chiefs droned on, many of the waiting warriors opened brightly colored umbrellas to shield themselves from the mid-day sun, destroying their savage mystique and reminding the whites that it was all a show after all. Washakie, the army's loyal ally in nearly every campaign on the northern plains, now in his fourth decade as chief of the Shoshones, reaffirmed his friendship but also gently urged the president to allow his people to enjoy the fruits of capitalism by trading their goods to others besides the Indian Bureau store on their reservation.[34]

Sheridan, eager for the president to enjoy a relaxing holiday, was glad to be off the next day and avoid any more exposure to Shoshone grievances. Conservation of the land, not its natives, was the goal of this expedition. There was scenery aplenty for all, as Sheridan guided his party, all on horseback, up the Wind River to the mountains of that name, across the divide to the Snake River, and then to the magnificent Teton Basin. The incomparable Grand Tetons had the desired effect on the president. "It was the universal sentiment of the party that that sight alone would have fully repaid all the toils and perils of the march," Mike noted in his Associated Press dispatch.[35] Sheridan's scheme to let the land win his guests over to the cause of conservation was working.

358

They spent several days hunting and fishing in the shadow of the Tetons before moving north along the Snake River, following the Sheridan Trail, toward the national park. Sheridan allowed his guests to fish to their hearts' content—Arthur and Vest hooked 105 pounds in a single day—but he strictly limited hunting. In the spirit of conservation Sheridan allowed the killing of only such game as was necessary for food, and once within the park forbade all hunting.

Sheridan led his party into the park on August 23, camping near Old Faithful the following day. The weary tourists, having covered 230 miles on horseback since leaving Fort Washakie, spent an extra day taking in the wonders of the Upper Geyser Basin.

Like the Indians, trappers, explorers, and soldiers before them, and like countless tourists since, Sheridan's party spent over a week observing the marvels of the national treasure that is Yellowstone. On August 31, they reached the park superintendent's headquarters at Mammoth Hot Springs, concluding a twenty-five day journey of 350 miles. Arthur left the next day by wagon for Livingston, Montana, and the Northern Pacific Railroad, where a private car awaited. On August 3 he joined General Grant and other dignitaries at Saint Paul to mark the completion of the transcontinental Northern Pacific.

Sheridan, physically drained and in ill health as a result of the trip, was nevertheless well pleased with his expedition. He had secured the good will of his influential guests toward the park and, perhaps more important, had focused attention on Yellowstone for an extended period of time. He believed that if the people were made aware of Yellowstone's wonders, they would compel their representatives to preserve the park, safeguarding it from speculators and monopolists.[36]

The interest engendered by the presidential visit gave Senator Vest enough political clout to block attempts by the Northern Pacific to run a spur line into the park. He also quashed proposals by other legislators to return the park to the public domain. He was, however, unable to gather enough support to appropriate adequate funds to administer the park. Scandals in the administration of the park led Congress to cut off all funding in 1886, which deed forced the secretary of the interior to call upon the army to administer the park as stipulated in the act of March 1883.[37]

Sheridan's plan for the transfer of control of the park to the Department of War had come to fruition. Now he would make sure that the land and the animals were protected. In August 1886 the general had the pleasure of ordering Captain Moses Harris, with M Troop, First Cavalry, to proceed from Fort Custer to Yellowstone National Park and take control of the place. On August 20, 1886, Captain Harris assumed control of Yellowstone, inaugurating thirty-two years of military administration of the park. As one historian put it, the result was that "the cavalry saved these parks, and in so doing, saved the National Park idea."[38]

Sheridan's dream of a Greater Yellowstone also met with success, although more limited. Efforts to have Congress increase the park's size got nowhere, but in 1891 the conservationists got congressional authorization for the president to designate national forest reserves by executive order. As a result Benjamin Harrison in 1891, Grover Cleveland in 1896, and Theodore Roosevelt in 1902 set aside vast areas abutting Yellowstone National Park as protected forest reserves. These forest reserves included most of the land that Sheridan had proposed for park expansion in 1882. While the park was not enlarged as the general had hoped, his plan had still resulted in the creation of a system of protected national forests.[39]

When Phil Sheridan rode to the rescue of Yellowstone National Park, he left as great a legacy to his nation as had his more famous ride from Winchester eighteen years before. By blocking the exploitive schemes of the capitalists, by assuring competent military protection for the park, and by initiating a crusade for a Greater Yellowstone, the general secured a national treasure for posterity. In Sheridan's rather melancholy last years his crusade for Yellowstone represented his finest hour and greatest achievement.

At the same time that he was working to save Yellowstone, Sheridan had another opportunity to ride to the rescue. Once more he clashed with western capitalists, but this time in defense of his old enemies, the Cheyenne and Arapaho Indians.

For years Sheridan had employed his troops to keep boomers out of the Indian Territory. Although his efforts met with considerable success, whites had nevertheless managed to secure de facto control over large sections of the Indian Territory. In 1882 a consortium of cattlemen, encouraged and assisted by Indian agent John D. Miles, had reached agreement with the chiefs of the Cheyennes and Arapahos to lease grazing rights to 2,400,000 acres of reservation land at two cents an acre. This came to an annual payment of ten dollars for each tribal member. Other agreements followed, until almost all of the reservation was leased out to cattle interests. The secretary of the interior, Henry M. Teller, refused to approve the leases, but he also refused to interfere with the right of the Indians to make such business arrangements. Thus Teller assented to the extension of grazing permits on the reservation, but nothing else. Similar grazing agreements were soon negotiated with other tribes throughout the Indian Territory.[40]

Within a few years this policy, which saw 220,000 cattle grazing on the Cheyenne-Arapaho Reservation by 1885, came under severe criticism. Three important Cheyenne chiefs, Stone Calf, White Shield, and Little Robe, had opposed the leases from the beginning and, with seven hundred followers, refused to accept any payments from the cattlemen. Agent Miles, who had staked his reputation on the success of the leasing system, resigned in March 1884, turning over his agency to D. B. Dyer. The new agent found the situation tense and feared an outbreak. Discontented bands raided the cattle herds on occasion, and there were armed clashes between the Texas cowboys and the Indians. Dyer branded Chiefs Little Robe and Stone Calf, both well known to Sheridan, as leaders of outlaw bands and labeled Amos Chapman, an old scout for Sheridan who was married to Stone Calf's daughter, as conspiring with the malcontents to cause trouble. Dyer wanted troops sent in to protect those Indians who supported the leases from the intimidation of Stone Calf, Little Robe, White Shield, and their Dog Soldier followers.[41]

President Grover Cleveland called Sheridan to the White House in July 1885 for an interview on the Cheyenne-Arapaho troubles, and after a lengthy discussion asked him to proceed to the reservation and investigate the situation. Accompanied by Mike Sheridan, the lieutenant general left Washington for Chicago to confer with Division of the Missouri commander Schofield. The western press was full of wild rumors of an Indian outbreak; so, to reassure the nervous settlers, Sheridan ordered Schofield to send several companies to reinforce troops in southern Kansas and Indian Territory. Brigadier General Nelson Miles, who had assumed command of the Department of the Missouri that month, joined Sheridan in Chicago. Miles had finally won his star in 1880 when lame-duck President Rutherford B. Hayes forced General Ord to retire to create a brigadier's berth for his fellow Ohioan.

Sheridan and Miles reached the agency on July 15 and called on the dissatisfied Cheyennes to come in for a council. Stone Calf forcefully presented the dissidents' position and was supported by Little Robe, White Shield, White Horse, and others. They declared their peaceful intentions, branding as ludicrous rumors of an outbreak, but they were adamant in demanding that the cattlemen be forced off their reservation. Sheridan heard a familiar list of grievances—short rations, white horse thieves, corrupt officials. On July 19 Sheridan met with chiefs who had initially agreed to the cattle leases. He found them equally unhappy with the arrangement, for clearly the leases caused more trouble than they were worth. Some chiefs claimed that they had only signed the agreement in the first place because of pressure applied by agent John Miles.[42] Many of these Indians were well known to Sheridan from the 1868 and 1874 wars, and he believed what they said.

Sheridan found the Indians divided into factions either willingly supporting the leases, supporting the leases because of pressure from the Indian agent, or opposing the leases. Although difficult to discern the true level of support for the leasing program, it was clear that by bringing whites onto the reservation the leasing policy encouraged racial tension and conflict.[43]

He also heard from representatives of the cattlemen. They portrayed the protesting Cheyennes as consistent troublemakers who opposed every progressive step taken by the government. Sheridan knew better, for Little Robe in particular had been a voice for accommodation among the Cheyennes since 1869. The cattlemen's picture of a hostile minority of Cheyennes dictating policy to the rest of the tribe did not square with what Sheridan had seen during his visit.[44]

Sheridan and Miles spent a week on the reservation, using nearby Fort Reno as their headquarters. After hearing from representatives of all the parties, Sheridan recommended to President Cleveland that the cattlemen be immediately ordered off the Cheyenne-Arapaho Reservation and that agent Dyer be replaced by Captain Jesse M. Lee, Ninth Infantry.[45]

On July 23, 1885, Cleveland ordered all the cattle cleared from the reservation within forty days. Agent Dyer was removed at the same

362

time, Captain Lee taking charge of the agency. Intense pressure was placed on Cleveland to delay his order for a year so that the cattlemen would not have to take a severe loss by dumping their herds on the market at one time. The president wired Sheridan at Fort Reno on July 25 to seek his advice. The general replied that forty days was more than enough time to remove the herds. Sheridan was willing to give the cattlemen an additional twenty days, but a year was out of the question. "I have assured the Indians you would right their wrongs," he told Cleveland, "and you have done so by your proclamation and changing their agent. They are now satisfied and if the conditions involved by these acts are carried out will remain peaceful and contented."[46]

Cleveland held firm, and the cattlemen grudgingly departed the reservation. They blamed Sheridan for their misfortune. One cattleman grumbled that while Sheridan might be a good soldier, he was certainly "never accused of being a statesman." The cattle were moved onto the already overcrowded ranges of the Texas Panhandle, Colorado, and western Kansas, just in time to face the ghastly winter of 1885–86, where 85 percent of them perished.[47] The eastern and western capitalists who bankrolled the herds suffered terrible losses. That was unfortunate, but the integrity of the Cheyenne-Arapaho Reservation had been preserved. Sheridan had correctly perceived that the cattle interests were exploiting the Indians, and he promptly acted to end that intolerable situation, whatever might be the consequences for the capitalists. In doing so he demonstrated that he could be as strong a defender of the Indians as he had earlier been an advocate of relentless war upon them.

This defense of the Indians was no sign that age had mellowed the general. When confronted with an Apache outbreak in the Southwest at about the same time as the Indian Territory crisis, he proved as relentlessly ruthless toward the natives as ever, seeking to punish the innocent along with the guilty. As a result Sheridan's long friendship with George Crook, increasingly strained over the years, finally disintegrated.

Crook had been reassigned to command the Department of Arizona in September 1882, after a group of Chiricahua Apaches broke from their reservation and fled to Mexico. The Southwest was on edge and other Apache bands were in a dangerous state of unrest. Crook had promptly quieted the reservation Apaches, at the same time raising several companies of Apache scouts to track down their own people. Bold and innovative once again, he had penetrated deep into Mexico's Sierra Madre, using his Apache scouts extensively, and compelled the Chiricahuas to return north to their reservation.[48]

In May 1885, however, forty-two Apache warriors, accompanied by ninety-two women and children, again fled the reservation and crossed into Mexico. This time the Apaches, under Geronimo, managed to elude the troopers and Indian scouts that Crook sent into the Sierra Madre after them. A small raiding party of these Apaches, led by the warrior Ulzana, swept across southern Arizona and New Mexico in November, killing thirty-eight people before scampering untouched back into Mexico.

Ulzana's raid was particularly embarrassing to Sheridan, since he had just penned a vigorous defense of Crook's Arizona operations a few days before the Apaches struck. The intense criticism of Crook, especially from southwestern commercial interests whose business was being disrupted, had been answered by Sheridan in his annual report. He pleaded with the citizens of Arizona to be patient and to "bear in mind that General Crook is the best man we have to deal with these hostile Indians." Sheridan assured the westerners that Crook was dedicated to the "welfare of the people in that section as regards life, property, and business interests."[49]

The raid brought Sheridan west. He had decided that the only way to secure peace in the Southwest was to remove the Chiricahua and Warm Springs Apaches out of the region. Secretary of War Endicott agreed to go along with this plan, but wanted Sheridan to inspect the area and confer with Crook before taking any action. The general stopped first in Santa Fe for a brief conference with Colonel Luther P. Bradley, commander of the District of New Mexico. Accompanied by Bradley, he then hurried on to Fort Bowie to meet Crook.

Reaching Fort Bowie on November 29, Sheridan found Crook about to dispatch a force of two hundred Apache scouts under Captain Emmet Crawford off to Mexico in search of Geronimo. Many of these scouts were Chiricahuas. Crook adamantly opposed the removal plan. To buttress his position he called in Captain Crawford to give his view of the situation. Crawford's confidence in his Indian scouts was unshakable, but he did not see how he could ask them to fight Geronimo while their own families were being banished from their homeland.

Noted military artist R. F. Zogbaum created this illustration, entitled "Sheridan on the Plains," to accompany an August 8, 1885, *Harper's Weekly* story on the Cheyenne-Arapaho Reservation troubles. Sheridan sided with the Indians against their agent and forced an end to the leasing of reservation land to cattle interests. In doing so he demonstrated that he could be as strong a defender of the Indians as he had earlier been an advocate of relentless war upon them. (*Author's Collection*)

Crawford had a reputation as a cool-headed, steady officer, and Sheridan valued his opinion. The general, reluctant to undercut his officers in the field, relented. He was, however, undeterred in his determination to move the Apaches east, but agreed to await a more opportune time. Better to unify operations against the hostiles, he enlarged Crook's command by transferring Bradley's District of New Mexico out of the Department of the Missouri and into the Department of Arizona.[50]

Although willing to give Crook another chance at the Apaches, Sheridan was far from satisfied with the situation. He was particularly displeased that Crook's Indian scout program had blocked his plan to move the Apaches. He looked unfavorably on the use of Indian auxiliaries in the first place. The Indians made poor allies, since they did "not possess stability or tenacity of purpose," Sheridan declared, adding that it would be unwise to recruit a military force from "a race so distinctive from that governing this country."[51] With the memory of recent army strength reductions still fresh, he undoubtedly worried about the dangerous precedent of using inexpensive native mercenaries in place of regular troops.

Crawford's campaign almost succeeded. On January 10, 1886, his scouts surprised Geronimo's band, capturing their camp and herd. Geronimo asked for a truce and offered to open negotiations with Crawford the next day, but before they could meet, a band of Mexican militiamen stumbled onto the scene. The militiamen blamed the Apache army scouts for depredations in northern Mexico, and they wasted no time in attacking Crawford's command. After Crawford was mortally wounded, his second in command, Lieutenant Marion P. Maus, ordered a withdrawal. Once safely away from the Mexicans, who had lost all their officers in the fight and did not pursue, Maus reopened negotiations with Geronimo, who had been watching the battle with considerable pleasure. Geronimo was far from beaten, but he did agree to meet with Crook near the international line to discuss returning to the reservation.[52]

On March 25, 1886, Crook and Geronimo met some twelve miles south of the international line at Cañon de los Embudos. Crook promised the Apaches that while they would be detained in the East for a couple of years, they could eventually settle back on their Arizona reservation. After much discussion the Apaches agreed to come back across the border. Crook hastened to Fort Bowie to telegraph the news of Geronimo's surrender to Sheridan, while his officers and a detachment of Apache scouts escorted the Indians north.[53]

Cleveland disapproved the surrender terms. Sheridan, who influenced the president in his course, declared unconditional surrender to be the only terms possible. Crook was to safeguard against the escape of the hostiles, inform them that only unconditional surrender was possible, and then annihilate them if they balked at this new situation. Once more, Sheridan's pragmatism clashed with Crook's integrity. This undermining of Crook's position did not matter anyway, since Geronimo and a small band slipped away from their guards and escaped into Mexico again. Upon learning of this, Sheridan was furious. "I feel ashamed of the whole business," he at first wrote Crook, but thinking better of it crossed out the line and continued that the news "has occassioned great disappointment. It seems strange that Geronimo and party could have escaped without the knowledge of the scouts."[54]

Crook vigorously defended the loyalty of his Indian auxiliaries, but it was clear to him that he had lost Sheridan's confidence. "I believe that the plan upon which I have conducted operations is the one most likely to prove successful in the end," he wrote Sheridan on April 1. "It may be, however, that I am too much wedded to my own views in this matter, and as I have spent nearly eight years of the hardest work of my life in this department, I respectfully request that I may now be relieved from its command."[55] Sheridan immediately granted Crook's request.

Nelson Miles replaced Crook, who returned to the Department of the Platte. Sheridan impressed on Miles "the necessity of making active and prominent use of the Regular troops of your command." Miles set out against the Apaches with characteristic vigor. At first he adopted a campaign strategy suggested by Sheridan: the occupation of key water holes and passes by infantry while cavalry searched for the hostiles. Quite a few horses were worn out in fruitless pursuits, while Geronimo's tiny band seemed to raid at will. Miles soon came to rely on Crook's Apache scouts, keeping their profile low, to guide his troops after the hostiles. In August 1886 the scouts led Lieutenant Charles B. Gatewood, a Crook protégé, to Geronimo's Mexican camp, and that bold officer persuaded the Apaches to surrender.[56]

367

Sheridan was delighted. He hoped to turn Geronimo over to local civil authorities, as had been done in 1871 with Satanta. The general was confident that Geronimo would hang. This desire was frustrated by Miles, who hurriedly shipped the hostiles to Florida before his superiors or the Arizona legal system might act. Miles and Gatewood had promised Geronimo that he would not be executed and could join his people in Florida.

Sheridan had to be satisfied with imprisoning the famed Apache at Fort Pickens, Florida. "If he cannot be dealt with summarily," the general grumbled, "the Dry Tortugas would be a good reservation for him."[57] At Sheridan's behest all of the Chiricahuas, including the loyal army scouts, had been removed to Fort Marion, Florida. Sheridan agreed with many of his officers in Arizona that the reservation Chiricahuas had supplied arms and supplies to the hostiles. The wisdom of this removal, despite its debatable morality, was proven when Gatewood used it to shake Geronimo's confidence and convince·him to surrender. General Crook, however, was enraged, especially over the treatment of his former scouts. Until his death in 1890, Crook campaigned alongside various Indian rights groups to secure the return of the Chiricahuas to Arizona. He never forgave Sheridan, and their long but stormy friendship came to a sad close.[58]

The break with Crook added to the growing melancholy of Sheridan's last years. The unwelcome inactivity forced by his loss in the power struggle with the secretary of war led him to be more reflective, withdrawing from society and seeking comfort with his family.

This withdrawal became especially pronounced after the critical illness of his wife, Irene, in late February 1886. For several days the physicians doubted her ability to recover from severe peritonitis. The general's gloom was compounded by the fact that William P. Clark, about his wife's age, had recently died of the same illness. By the first week of March, however, the crisis passed, although Irene's recovery took several more weeks.[59] While stricken with worry over Irene, Sheridan had confronted Crook's surrender terms to Geronimo. His grief may well have influenced his judgment.

Sheridan spent much of his time at his roomy home at Rhode Island Avenue and Seventeenth Street in Washington. He gloried in his children—the eldest a girl, named Mary after his mother; then twin

Sheridan rented a cottage at the quiet seaside resort of Nonquitt, Massachusetts, seven miles below New Bedford, in the summer of 1887 and liked the area so much that he purchased a lot and had a handsome cottage constructed there. He occupied this new home only once, while on his deathbed. The Sheridan family was photographed during their 1887 visit to Nonquitt. Left to right, top: Mrs. Michael V. Sheridan, Michael V. Sheridan, Mrs. Philip Sheridan, General Sheridan. Bottom: Irene, Philip, Jr., Louise, and Mary Sheridan. (*National Archives*)

girls, Irene and Louise; and the youngest, a son, Philip Henry, Jr. The children were well known for their brightness, gentility, and devotion to the Catholic faith. Their mother was extremely devout, and she took great interest in their religious instruction. In addition the family circle included brother Mike and his wife, who lived but a short distance from the general.[60]

When seen in public Sheridan was more often than not in civilian clothes. The years had not been kind, for his oddly shaped figure had grown increasingly portly and his face more reddened and fleshy. His hair had long since turned iron gray. The *New York World* described this unimposing figure to its readers: "He wore upon the back of his round, bullet head an old fashioned silk hat about two sizes too small. He wore a short, light, yellow-gray overcoat which had only two buttons and they were ready to fly off from the undue strain of Sheridan's round figure. The trousers were a gray plaid and fitted very snugly to the General's fat legs."[61]

There was talk in the eighties of Sheridan running for president, but his identification as a Roman Catholic made his nomination highly unlikely. He had no desire to run for political office, candidly admitting his ambition to be remembered in history as a patriot soldier. When at the 1880 Republican National Convention a delegate from Wyoming Territory had cast his ballot for Sheridan, the general, a guest on the chairman's platform, had jumped to the front of the stage to declare: "I am very much obliged to the delegate from Wyoming for mentioning my name in this convention, but there is no way in which I could accept a nomination from this convention, if it were possible, unless I should be permitted to turn it over to my best friend." He meant Grant, of course. The chairman thanked Sheridan for his sentiments and reminded the convention that no one save the general would be allowed to so interrupt parliamentary order.[62]

Nevertheless, as the idol of the Grand Army of the Republic and other veterans' organizations, Sheridan had an automatic constituency that made him particularly attractive to professional politicians. Their blandishments did not sway him. He had seen what politics had done to "the old man," as he called Grant, and he did not wish to chance such a fate. "I have led forlorn hopes enough in the Army," he declared in March 1888. "This being pulled and hauled by politicians does not suit a soldier."[63]

Another reason to decline politics was the precarious state of his health. When Daniel Butterfield suggested that he run for president, the general admitted: "It would be very foolish in me, and aside from that it would kill me in sixty days. I know myself and my nature and the situation well enough to know that."[64]

Sheridan had felt his health slipping for several years. First he began to tire easily, and then he had trouble digesting food. Finally, in November 1887, his physician, Major Robert M. O'Reilly, diagnosed heart disease of the mitral and aortic valves. At first he discounted O'Reilly's diagnosis, but an examination by specialists in New York City confirmed the fateful news.

He had been working on his memoirs for a year, and this medical news caused him to redouble his efforts. He hated the manual labor of writing, but now passionately stuck to a daily routine. Most of this work he completed in his home study, in surroundings congenial to the task. He worked over a small mahogany library table, writing with steel ink pens on a thick tablet of unruled paper. His desk faced a broad window that looked out onto the street, but his gaze and thoughts must have turned inward. The red silk-papered walls were covered with portraits of Grant, Sherman, and Custer, alongside framed copies of his commissions. Mementos and curios of a busy life—medals, swords, guns, books, a vast coin collection—surrounded him as he pieced together his personal story. He had hoped to take the memoirs up to his appointment as commanding general, but his health forced him to end the manuscript with the Franco-Prussian War. On March 23, 1888, he sent it to his publisher, Charles L. Webster and Company of New York. He was proud of his work, declaring it to be "about all I have to leave my family."[65]

Completion of the manuscript came none too soon. He had just returned from Chicago, where he had inspected the site for Fort Sheridan, when he collapsed from a severe heart attack on May 22, 1888. This news was kept from the public to save his mother, herself in grave health, from alarm.[66]

He recovered enough on the next day to dictate his will. One-third of his real estate and personal property was to go to Irene, with the rest left in trust for the education of their children. He was not a wealthy man. The estate consisted of real estate in Washington, Chicago, and Nonquitt, Massachusetts; $2,721 in cash; $8,000 in stock; $5,000 in swords; $3,000 in furnishings; and a $600 horse-and-carriage outfit.[67]

On May 26 a string of heart attacks of increasing seriousness racked him. At one point his heart ceased functioning, but the doctors managed to revive him with stimulants. "I nearly got away from you that time, doctor," Sheridan feebly joked. Dr. O'Reilly now stayed by the general's bedside, and a priest was called in to administer the last rites. This time the news could not be suppressed.[68]

The announcement of Sheridan's grave condition led Congress to revive the grade of general of the army, allowed to lapse upon Sherman's retirement, and President Cleveland promptly signed the commission. Sheridan now joined Washington, Grant, and Sherman in holding that rank. The commission was carried to his bedside by a delegation of senators, and it was from there that the new four-star general issued his first and final order on June 1—the appointment of Major Mike Sheridan, Captain Sanford C. Kellog, and Captain Stanhope Blunt as colonels and aides-de-camp on his staff.[69]

The promotion so buoyed his spirits that he began to regain strength. There was brief hope of recovery—he was, after all, only fifty-seven—but the once-robust body, now frail and emaciated, was far too wasted. Another string of heart attacks was followed by liver failure, and even the most optimistic of his friends despaired of hope. The national press began a deathwatch of daily bulletins on his condition similar to the coverage, three years before, of Grant's illness and death.

In hopes that a cooler climate might improve their patient's condition, Sheridan's doctors agreed to his request to be moved to his seaside cottage at Nonquitt, Massachusetts. Taken aboard the naval steamship *Swatara*, he arrived at Nonquitt on July 8. Looking over the lovely summer sea of Buzzard's Bay, some seven miles below New Bedford, Sheridan calmly awaited death throughout the month of July. He did not have the comfort of religious faith, despite his nominal adherence to Catholicism. "If I only had the simple faith of my wife," he lamented. "But I have not. To me the future seems oblivion."[70]

Death had surrounded Phil Sheridan all of his adult life. He had faced it many times before. He was not afraid when it came for him at 10:30 on the Sabbath evening of August 5, 1888.

An honor guard brought him back to Washington by train, and he lay in state at Saint Matthew's Church until the funeral mass on August 11. Congress was not in session, and the executive departments closed on that day so that the nation's political and military leaders could attend. What would have touched Sheridan most, however, was the reunion of his old staff, long since scattered: James and Sandy Forsyth, John Schuyler Crosby, Fred Grant, James Gregory. Mike was there, of course, just as he had always been at his brother's side; now he stood with the grieving widow. Sherman, resplendent in the dress uniform of the general of the army, led the pallbearers.

Cardinal Gibbons delivered a moving funeral oration. He be-

William T. Sherman doffs his hat as Sheridan's casket is removed from Saint Matthew's Church and placed on a caisson to be carried to Arlington Cemetery. Sheridan's horse, boots reversed in the stirrups, stands ready to begin the sad procession. (*National Archives*)

gan: "And Jonathan and Simon took Judas their brother, and buried him in the sepulchre of their fathers, in the city of Modin. And all the people of Israel bewailed him with great lamentation; and they mourned for him many days, and said: How is the mighty fallen that saved the people of Israel."[71]

They took him to Arlington Cemetery, as he had requested, and laid him to rest on a high, green knoll looking eastward over the city of Washington. It was a bright, cloudless day, and the sunlight gleamed off the upraised rifles of the infantry squad that fired a final salute. As the sharp crack of the volleys echoed across the cemetery grounds, bugler Charles Kimball, who had campaigned with Sheridan, raised a trumpet to his lips and sounded the plaintive wail of taps.

Slowly the crowd melted away, leaving a solitary figure at graveside. Sherman, ramrod straight in his sixty-eighth year, the last of the great captains who had saved the Union, stood beside the open

373

grave and wept. At last he turned, walking down the grassy knoll, past the white markers aligned in orderly ranks spreading out from the base, and away from the final encampment of Phil Sheridan and his army.

NOTES

CHAPTER 1

1. *Army and Navy Journal* 13, (March 11, 1876), 506; Allan Nevins and Milton Halsey Thomas, eds., *The Diary of George Templeton Strong*, 4 vols. (New York, Macmillan, 1952), 4:165; H. C. Greiner, *General Phil Sheridan as I Knew Him, Playmate-Comrade-Friend*, 413.

2. Philip H. Sheridan to S. Cooper, July 13, 1853, Sheridan to S. Thomas, August 3, 1861, Sheridan to L. Thomas, September 30, 1862, Box 1, Philip H. Sheridan Papers; *Personal Memoirs of P. H. Sheridan, General, United States Army* 1:2; and *Unveiling of the Equestrian Statue of General Philip H. Sheridan, Capitol Park, Albany, New York, October 7, 1916*, 29–30. Sheridan's relatives supposedly admitted in 1905 that he was "born on the ocean, when his parents were coming from Ireland" and that it had been kept secret to allow him to run for the presidency. However, since it seems unlikely that Lieutenant Sheridan had such lofty ambitions in 1853, and it is beyond doubt that he rejected the office later in life, the story seems apocryphal. Richard O'Connor, *Sheridan the Inevitable*, 361.

3. Greiner, *Phil Sheridan*, 16, 26.

4. Sheridan, *Personal Memoirs* 1:4–5; Greiner, *Phil Sheridan*, 47, 353.

5. David S. Stanley, *Personal Memoirs of Major-General D. S. Stanley, U.S.A.*, 17–18; O'Connor, *Sheridan*, 29–30. See also John L. Hathaway, "Recollections of Sheridan as a Cadet," in *War Papers Read before the Commandery of the State of Wisconsin, Military Order of Loyal Legion of the United States* 1:270–74.

6. Sheridan to "Sister," February 17, 1849, Philip H. Sheridan File, no. 1612, United States Military Academy Archives.

7. Ibid.

8. Official Register of the Officers and Cadets of the U.S. Military Academy, West Point, New York, June 1849, June 1850, June 1851, June 1852, June 1853.

9. Sheridan, *Personal Memoirs* 1:9, O'Connor, *Sheridan*, 33–37.

10. Sheridan, *Personal Memoirs* 1:11–13.

11. Official Register of the Officers and Cadets of the U.S. Military Academy, West Point, New York, June, 1853; Sheridan, *Personal Memoirs* 1:13–14.

12. Sheridan, *Personal Memoirs* 1:31–34.

13. Martin F. Schmitt, ed., *General George Crook: His Autobiography*, 6–10; Sheridan, *Personal Memoirs* 1:35–36. See also Turner F. Levens, "When Sheridan Was in Oregon," *Washington Historical Quarterly* 16 (July 1925): 163–85; and Leslie M. Scott, "Military Beginnings of the Salmon River Highway," *Oregon Historical Quarterly* 35 (September 1934): 228–34.

14. Robert M. Utley, *Frontiersmen in Blue: The United States Army and the Indian, 1848–1865*, 178–81, 193. For background on the northwestern Indian conflicts, see Robert Carlton Clark, "Military History of Oregon, 1849–59," *Oregon Historical Quarterly* 36 (March 1935): 14–59; William N. Bischoff, "The Yakima Campaign of 1856," *Mid-America* 31 (April 1949):163–208; Francis Fuller Victor, *The Early Indian Wars of Oregon, Compiled from the Oregon Archives and Other Original Sources, with Muster Rolls*; J. P. Dunn, *Massacres of the Mountains: A History of the Indian Wars of the Far West, 1815–1875*, 167–90; Utley, *Frontiersmen in Blue*, 175–210; H. Dean Guie, *Bugles in the Valley: Garnett's Fort Simcoe*.

15. Schmitt, ed., *Crook Autobiography*, 16; Sheridan, *Personal Memoirs* 1:44–45, 70.

16. Sheridan, *Personal Memoirs* 1:56, 58, 68–69; Utley, *Frontiersmen in Blue*, 189–90; Guie, *Bugles in the Valley*, 15–21.

17. Sheridan, *Personal Memoirs* 1:70–81; Utley, *Frontiersmen in Blue*, 195; Dunn, *Massacres of the Mountains*, 185–86. For his actions at the Cascades Sheridan was commended in general orders signed by General Winfield Scott. Sheridan, *Personal Memoirs* 1:90.

18. Lavens, "When Sheridan Was in Oregon," 167–68, 170–71; Sheridan, *Personal Memoirs* 1:83–84, 89.

19. Sheridan, *Personal Memoirs* 1:85–89.

20. Ibid., 91–120; Fred Lockley, "Reminiscences of Mrs. Frank Collins, Nee Martha Elizabeth Gilliam," *Quarterly of the Oregon Historical Society* 17 (December 1916): 367–68; Grace E. Cooper, "Benton County Pioneer-Historical Society," *Oregon Historical Quarterly* 57 (March 1956): 83–93; and *Oregonian*, January 2, 1938. Frances visited Sheridan in Washington, D.C., after the Civil War, but then returned to Oregon, where she married a Hudson's Bay Company trapper and moved to Canada. Such liaisons were common in the Northwest, but Sheridan never mentioned it. Upon Grant's election to the presidency and Sherman's promotion, Sheridan begged the president not to transfer him to the Northwest. "I don't wish to go to the Pacific coast for many reasons some of which are personal," he wrote Grant. "It would disappoint me greatly to go there." Sheridan to Grant, January 19, 1869, Box 39, Sheridan Papers.

21. Sheridan, *Personal Memoirs* 1:106–20.

22. Ibid., 121–23.

23. Whitelaw Reid, *Ohio in the War: Her Statesmen, Her Generals, and Soldiers* 1:500.

24. Ibid., 501.

25. Sheridan to Samuel R. Curtis, March 5, 1862, Box 1, Sheridan Papers.

26. W. S. Rosecrans, C. C. Sullivan, G. Granger, W. L. Elliott, and A. Asboth to Henry Halleck, July 30, 1862, and G. Granger and H. G. Wright to Halleck, September 12, 1862, Box 1, Sheridan Papers.

27. Sheridan's Civil War campaigns are covered in great detail elsewhere. Besides the memoirs of Sheridan and Grant, the following should be consulted: Joseph Hergesheimer, *Sheridan: A Military Narrative*; Edward J. Stackpole, *Sheridan in the Shenandoah: Jubal Early's Nemesis*; George E. Pond, *The Shenandoah Valley in 1864*; Sanford C. Kellogg, *The Shenandoah Valley and Virginia, 1861 to 1865: A War Study*; [Frederic Cushman Newhall], *With General Sheridan in Lee's Last Campaign, by a Staff Officer*; Henry Edward Tremain, *Last Hours of Sheridan's Cavalry: A Reprint of War Memoranda*; E. R. Hagemann, ed., *Fighting Rebels and Redskins: Experiences in Army Life of Colonel George B. Sanford, 1861–1892*, 221–339; Fletcher Pratt, *Eleven Generals: Studies in American Command*, 113–69; Edwin B. Parsons, "Sheridan," in *War Papers Read before the Commandery of Wisconsin*, 275–84; Charles C. MacConnell, "Service with Sheridan," in *War Papers Read before the Commandery of Wisconsin*, 285–93; James B. Black, "General Philip Henry Sheridan," in *War Papers Read before the Indiana Commandery, Military Order of the Loyal Legion of the United States*, 42–72; James Harrison Wilson, *Under the Old Flag: Recollections of Military Operations in the War for the Union, the Spanish War, the Boxer Rebellion, Etc.*, 2 vols.; Stephen Z. Starr, *The Union Cavalry in the Civil War*, 2 vols.; Roger Thomas Zeimet, "Philip H. Sheridan and the Civil War in the West"; Robert Underwood Johnson and Clarence Clough Buel, eds., *Battles and Leaders of the Civil War: The Way to Appomattox* 4:188–94, 233–39, 500–530, 708–24; Louis H. Carpenter, "Sheridan's Expedition around Richmond, May 9–25, 1864," *Journal of the United States Cavalry Association* 1 (November 1888): 300–324; Moses Harris, "With the Reserve Brigade—From Winchester to Appomattox," *Journal of the United States Cavalry Association* 4 (March 1891): 3–26; John G. Yenchar, "General Philip H. Sheridan," *Cavalry Journal* 46 (November-December 1937): 499–502; Reid, *Ohio in the War* 1:495–560.

28. Reid, *Ohio in the War* 1:505–6. Father Tracy was the priest assigned to Rosecrans's headquarters.

29. Ibid., 1:509–11; Sheridan, *Personal Memoirs* 1:308–18; O'Connor, *Sheridan*, 133–39.

30. Bruce Catton, *Grant Takes Command* (Boston, Little, Brown, 1968), 90.

31. Stackpole, *Sheridan in the Shenandoah*, 269–70, 358; and O'Connor, *Sheridan*, 213.

32. Sheridan, *Personal Memoirs* 2:119.

33. Hagemann, ed., *Fighting Rebels*, 269. A discussion of the Clausewitzian "strategy of annihilation" pursued by Grant, Sherman, and Sheridan is

in Russell F. Weigley, *The American Way of War: A History of United States Military Strategy and Policy,* 128–52.

34. Russell F. Weigley, *Towards an American Army: Military Thought from Washington to Marshall,* 88; Sheridan, *Personal Memoirs* 1:487–88.

35. *The War of the Rebellion: A Compilation of the Official Records of The Union and Confederate Armies,* 70 vols. (Washington, D.C., 1881–1901), ser. 1, 43, pt. 2, pp. 671–72; Virgil Carrington Jones, *Ranger Mosby,* 199–241; Sheridan, *Personal Memoirs* 2:99–100.

36. Sheridan, *Personal Memoirs* 1:241; "General Sheridan's address to the graduates of Westpoint, Class of 1878," Box 109, Sheridan Papers.

37. Sheridan, *Personal Memoirs* 1:154; O'Connor, *Sheridan,* 170.

38. Greiner, *Phil Sheridan,* 409–10.

39. Theodore R. Davis, "General Sheridan's Personality," *Cosmopolitan* 13 (June 1892): 210.

40. Hagemann, ed., *Fighting Rebels,* 312; Sheridan, *Personal Memoirs* 2:112, 165–70; Francis B. Heitman, *Historical Register and Dictionary of the United States Army, from Its Organization, September 29, 1789, to March 2, 1903* 1:965; O'Connor, *Sheridan,* 255.

41. Both men devoted portions of their memoirs to the controversy. W. B. Hazen, *A Narrative of Military Service,* 173–235; and Sheridan, *Personal Memoirs* 1:320–24.

42. M. A. DeWolfe Howe, ed., *Home Letters of General Sherman,* 314.

43. Adam Badeau, *Grant in Peace: From Appomattox to Mount McGregor: A Personal Memoir,* 95–99; George F. Hoar, *Autobiography of Seventy Years* 1:209.

44. Sheridan, *Personal Memoirs* 2:208–11; Badeau, *Grant in Peace,* 180–82.

45. Sheridan, *Personal Memoirs* 2:214–28; Badeau, *Grant in Peace,* 180–89. For a brief overview of this affair, see Clarence C. Clendenen, *Blood on the Border: The United States Army and the Mexican Irregulars,* 45–59.

46. Sheridan, *Personal Memoirs* 2:227–28.

47. Ibid., 231–33.

48. *Army and Navy Register* 4 (November 3, 1883): 8–9.

49. James E. Sefton, *The United States Army and Reconstruction 1865–1877,* 88. Details of the New Orleans police riot are in Michael Les Benedict, *A Compromise of Principle: Congressional Republicans and Reconstruction, 1863–1869* (New York, W. W. Norton, 1974), 204–6; Eric L. McKitrick, *Andrew Johnson and Reconstruction,* 424–27; Sheridan, *Personal Memoirs* 2:234–40; *Report of the Select Committee on the New Orleans Riots* (Washington, 1867). For a rather twisted, anti-Unionist account of the riot, see Willie Malvin Caskey, *Secession and Restoration of Louisiana* (University, La., Louisiana State University Press, 1938), 211–31.

50. McKitrick, *Johnson and Reconstruction,* 426–27; Sheridan, *Personal Memoirs* 2:121, 235–37, 279–80.

51. Sheridan, *Personal Memoirs* 2:262.

52. *House Reports*, 39th Cong., 1st sess., no. 30, pt. 4, p. 123.

53. Badeau, *Grant in Peace*, 101; O'Connor, *Sheridan*, 291. Grant played a rather Machiavellian role in the Reconstruction battle between Johnson and Congress until the fall of 1867, when he finally made his position clear. See Martin E. Mantell, *Johnson, Grant, and the Politics of Reconstruction*, 27–70; Benedict, *Compromise of Principle*, 265–70; William S. McFeely, *Grant: A Biography*, 259–63.

54. Sheridan, *Personal Memoirs* 2:253; Badeau, *Grant in Peace*, 102–3. For much of the private correspondence between Grant and Sheridan, see Badeau, *Grant in Peace*. For the official correspondence, see *Senate Exec. Docs.*, 40th Cong., 1st sess., no. 14, pp. 192–287.

55. *Senate Exec. Docs.*, 40th Cong., 1st sess., no. 14, pp. 236–37; Sheridan, *Personal Memoirs* 2:257–60.

56. Andrew Johnson to U. S. Grant, August 19,1867, Box 6, Sheridan Papers.

57. Carl Coke Rister, *Border Command: General Phil Sheridan in the West*, 32. See also William L. Richter, "Tyrant and Reformer: General Griffin Reconstructs Texas, 1865–66," *Prologue* 10 (Winter 1978): 225–41.

58. McFeely, *Grant*, 262; Badeau, *Grant in Peace*, 104–5.

59. Johnson to Grant, August 19, 1867, Box 6, Sheridan Papers; Badeau, *Grant in Peace*, 104–5. See also Joseph G. Dawson III, "General Phil Sheridan and Military Reconstruction in Louisiana," *Civil War History* 24 (June 1978): 133–51; and, Joseph G. Dawson III, *Army Generals and Reconstruction: Louisiana, 1862–1877*, 24–62.

CHAPTER 2

1. William T. Sherman to Ellen Sherman, January 17, 1868, Sherman Family Papers; and February 29, 1868, Albert Barnitz Diary, Albert and Jennie Barnitz Diaries and Letters. Portions of the Barnitz Diaries and Letters have been published in Robert M. Utley, ed., *Life in Custer's Cavalry: Diaries and Letters of Albert and Jennie Barnitz 1867–1868*.

2. *Annual Report of the Secretary of War [1868]*, 2 vols. (Washington, 1869), 1:736–37.

3. Ibid., 16.

4. In May 1868, Colonel William Hoffman was replaced by Major Thomas C. English, Fifth Infantry, as commander of the district. Ibid., 17.

5. Ibid. For the size and location of the various forts, see Philip H. Sheridan, *Outline Description of the Military Posts in the Division of the Missouri*, 116–79.

6. For the Pawnee Fork episode, see Theodore R. Davis, "A Summer on the Plains," *Harper's New Monthly Magazine* 36 (February 1868): 294–96; George Armstrong Custer, *My Life on the Plains; or, Personal Experiences with*

Indians, ed. Edgar I. Stewart, 29–33; Ed Guerrier, Field Notes, unclassified envelope 3, Walter Camp Mss.; David Dixon, "A Scout with Custer: Edmund Guerrier on the Hancock Expedition of 1867," *Kansas History* 4 (Autumn 1981): 155–65.

7. Sheridan to Elizabeth Custer, April 10, 1865, "Correspondence, Other Sources," Elizabeth B. Custer Collection; Marguerite Merington, ed., *The Custer Story: The Life and Intimate Letters of General George A. Custer and His Wife Elizabeth*, 85, 159; H. C. Greiner, *General Phil Sheridan as I Knew Him, Playmate-Comrade-Friend*, 357–58. See also Jay Monaghan, *Custer: The Life of General George Armstrong Custer*, for a generally favorable interpretation; and Frederic F. Van de Water, *Glory-Hunter: A Life of General Custer*, for a negative portrait of Custer. For Sheridan's recommendation for Custer's promotion to colonel, see Sheridan to E. M. Stanton, April 6, 1866, "Correspondence, Other Sources," Custer Collection.

8. [Frederic Cushman Newhall], *With Sheridan in Lee's Last Campaign, by a Staff Officer*, 211–12; May 17, 1867, Albert Barnitz Diary, and Albert Barnitz to Jennie Barnitz, May 15, 1867, Barnitz Diaries and Letters.

9. *House Exec. Docs.*, 41st Cong., 2d sess., no. 240, pp. 68–75. Custer was outraged by Hancock's behavior throughout this campaign. A better account of the expedition than the one in Custer's *My Life on the Plains* can be found in Brian W. Dippie, ed., *Nomad: George A. Custer in Turf, Field, and Farm*, 20–39.

10. [Henry M. Stanley], "A British Journalist Reports the Medicine Lodge Peace Councils of 1867," *Kansas Historical Quarterly* 33 (Autumn 1967): 271–73. A useful source on the campaign is Henry M. Stanley, *My Early Travels and Adventures in America and Asia* 1:1–215.

11. Merington, ed., *Custer Story*, 211. For accounts of Custer's campaign, see Minnie Dubbs Millbrook, "The West Breaks in General Custer," *Kansas Historical Quarterly* 36 (Summer 1970): 113–48; Davis, "Summer on the Plains," 298–307; Custer, *My Life on the Plains*, 53–123; James M. Bell, "Reminiscences," *Journal of the United States Cavalry Association* 10 (December 1897): 434–45.

For the court-martial, see Lawrence A. Frost, *The Court-Martial of General George Armstrong Custer*. Sheridan, upon assuming command of the department, turned over his quarters at Fort Leavenworth to the Custers. He promised Custer that he would investigate the case, for he "had no reason to suppose any such punishment would be awarded" (p. 256).

12. For details of the Hancock campaign, see Lonnie J. White, "The Hancock and Custer Expeditions of 1867," *Journal of the West* 5 (July 1966): 355–78; Robert M. Utley, *Frontier Regulars: The United States Army and the Indian, 1866–1891*, 114–20; William H. Leckie, *The Military Conquest of the Southern Plains*, 38–56; *Harper's Weekly* 11 (May 11, 1867): 301–2, (June 29, 1867): 406–7, (August 3, 1867): 481, 484, (August 17, 1867): 513–14.

13. For the Peace Commission and the Medicine Lodge treaties, see [Stanley], "British Journalist," 249–320; Douglas C. Jones, *The Treaty of Medi-*

cine Lodge: The Story of the Great Treaty Council as Told by Eyewitnesses; Donald J. Berthrong, *The Southern Cheyennes*, 289–99; Charles J. Kappler, *Indian Affairs: Laws and Treaties*, 2 vols. (Washington, 1904), 2:977–89; E. S. Godfrey, "Reminiscences of the Medicine Lodge Peace Treaties," *Cavalry Journal* 37 (January 1928): 112–15.

14. [Stanley], "British Journalist," 315; Stan Hoig, *The Battle of the Washita: The Sheridan-Custer Indian Campaign of 1867–69*, 37; Jones, *Treaty of Medicine Lodge*, 199–202; and October 28, 1867, Albert Barnitz Diary, Barnitz Diaries and Letters.

15. Leckie, *Conquest*, 67.

16. William T. Sherman to Ellen Sherman, July 15, 1868, Sherman Family Papers.

17. *Personal Memoirs of P. H. Sheridan, General, United States Army* 2:284–86; George E. Hyde, *Life of George Bent: Written from His Letters*, ed. Savoie Lottinville, 290. George Bent was Sheridan's interpreter at the council.

18. De B. Randolph Keim, *Sheridan's Troopers on the Borders: A Winter Campaign on the Plains*, 58.

19. Sheridan, *Personal Memoirs* 2:299.

20. Ibid., 286–87; Robert Lynam, ed., *The Beecher Island Annual: Sixty-second Anniversary of the Battle of Beecher Island, Sept. 17, 18, 1868*, 57–58; Custer, *My Life on the Plains*, 145; John S. Gray, "New Light on Will Comstock, Kansas Scout," in *Custer and His Times*, ed. Paul A. Hutton (El Paso, Tex., Little Big Horn Associates, 1981), 183–207.

21. Utley, *Frontier Regulars*, 138; Berthrong, *Southern Cheyennes*, 303–5; Philip H. Sheridan, "Report, In the field, Fort Hays, Sept. 26, 1868," Box 83, Sheridan Papers.

22. For Abner Grover's account, see Sheridan, *Personal Memoirs* 2:292–94. George Bent claims that no treachery was involved and that the scouts were intercepted by warriors returning to the village and a fight ensued. Bent also declares the affair took place near the Dog Soldier's camp, not Turkey Leg's village. Hyde, *George Bent*, 294–95. Also see Gray, "Will Comstock," 204–6.

23. Sheridan, "Report, Sept. 26, 1868," Box 83, Sheridan Papers.

24. Grenville M. Dodge, *Paper Read Before the Society of the Army of the Tennessee at Its Twenty-first Annual Reunion at Toledo, O., Sept. 15, 1888*, 48–49.

25. Grenville M. Dodge, *Personal Recollections of President Abraham Lincoln, General Ulysses S. Grant, and General William T. Sherman*, 187–88; Stanley P. Hirshson, *Grenville M. Dodge: Soldier, Politician, Railroad Pioneer*, 162.

Other transportation companies were also well disposed toward influential military officers, and besides his many railroad passes, Sheridan had a lifetime pass on the Wells Fargo Stage line. W. H. Cottrell to Sheridan, November 23, 1868, Box 16, Division of the Missouri, Special File, RG 393, Records of United States Army. Also see Sheridan to Ben Holladay, August 15, 1875, Division of the Missouri, Letters Sent, ibid.

26. Dodge, *Personal Recollections*, 195. See also *Annual Report of the Secretary of War [1867]*, 2 vols. (Washington, 1868), 1:36.

27. Sheridan, "Report, Sept. 26, 1868," Box 83, Sheridan Papers. See also Thomas D. Isern, "The Controversial Career of Edward W. Wynkoop," *Colorado Magazine* 56 (Winter-Spring 1979): 1–18.

28. Sheridan, "Report, Sept. 26, 1868," Box 83, Sheridan Papers; "Report of Lieutenant General W. T. Sherman," in *Annual Report of the Secretary of War [1868]* 1:4.

29. W. T. Sherman to John Sherman, September 23, 1868, in *The Sherman Letters: Correspondence between General and Senator Sherman from 1837 to 1891*, ed. Rachel Sherman Thorndike, 231.

30. *Annual Report of the Secretary of War [1868]* 1:8–9.

31. Quoted in *The Hazen Court-Martial: The Responsibility of the Disaster to the Lady Franklin Bay Polar Expedition Definitely Established with Proposed Reforms in the Law and Practice of Courts-Martial*, ed. T. J. Mackey, 58. See also Marvin E. Kroeker, *Great Plains Command: William B. Hazen in the Frontier West*; Edgar I. Stewart, ed., *Penny-an-Acre Empire in the West*, 3–22.

32. "Inspection by Generals Rusling and Hazen,"*House Exec. Docs.*, 39th Cong., 2d sess., no. 45, p. 5.

33. *Army and Navy Journal*, January 22, 1887.

34. William B. Hazen to James Garfield, July 23, 1871, James A. Garfield Papers.

35. *Annual Report of the Secretary of War [1868]*, 1:17; G. A. Forsyth, "A Frontier Fight," *Harper's New Monthly Magazine* 91 (June 1895): 42.

36. George Forsyth, who also held the brevet of brigadier general of volunteers from the Civil War, eventually wrote two books which reveal much concerning his character and times. *Thrilling Days in Army Life* relates four episodes from his career, including Sheridan's ride and the Arickaree fight. *The Story of the Soldier*, while intended as a general history of the American army, contains several autobiographical segments. For additional biographical information, see Francis B. Heitman, *Historical Register and Dictionary of the United States Army, from Its Organization, September 29, 1789, to March 2, 1903* 1:420; Lynam, ed., *Beecher Island Annual*, 54–56.

37. George A. Armes, *Ups and Downs of an Army Officer*, 273; Forsyth, "A Frontier Fight," 34–44; Sig Schlesinger, "Scout Schlesinger's Story," in *Beecher Island Annual*, ed. Lynam, 77.

38. Forsyth, "A Frontier Fight," 45; John Hurst, "Scout John Hurst's Story of the Fight," in *Beecher Island Annual*, ed. Lynam, 69.

39. Interview with Chalmers Smith, January 18, 1913, Field Notes, unclassified envelope 64, Camp Mss.

40. Forsyth's published versions of the fight, called the Battle of Beecher's Island in honor of the lieutenant, are highly romanticized. A more accurate version, brief but without embellishment, is contained in Forsyth's often-reprinted second message requesting help. G. A. Forsyth to H. C. Bank-

head, September 19, 1868, Box 6, Sheridan Papers. An account by Major James S. Brisbin, Second Cavalry, who was part of the second relief column to reach Forsyth, is in Harry H. Anderson, "Stand at the Arickaree," *Colorado Magazine* 41 (Fall 1964): 336–42. Narratives by participants include: John Hurst, "The Beecher Island Fight," *Collections of the Kansas State Historical Society* 15 (1919–22): 530–38; Merrill J. Mattes, "The Beecher Island Battlefield Diary of Sigmund Schlesinger," *Colorado Magazine* 29 (July 1952): 161–69; Sigmund Schlesinger, "The Beecher Island Fight," *Collections of the Kansas State Historical Society* 15 (1919–22):528–47; interview with Chalmers Smith, January 18, 1913, and interview with Mr. [James J.] Peate, January 18, 1913, Field Notes, unclassified envelope 64, Camp Mss.; and the narratives in *Beecher Island Annual*, ed. Lynam. See also Lonnie J. White, "The Battle of Beecher Island: The Scouts Hold Fast on the Arickaree," *Journal of the West* 5 (January 1966): 1–24; Hyde, *Life of George Bent*, 297–308; George Bird Grinnell, *The Fighting Cheyennes*, 277–92.

41. White, "Battle of Beecher Island," 79, 82; William H. Leckie, *The Buffalo Soldiers: A Narrative of the Negro Cavalry in the West*, 36.

42. Sheridan later attempted to secure military pensions for the wounded scouts. Sheridan to Secretary of War, November 4, 1872, Box 8, Sheridan Papers.

43. *Annual Report of the Secretary of War [1868]* 1:18; Lonnie J. White, "General Sully's Expedition to the North Canadian, 1868," *Journal of the West* 11 (January 1972): 85.

44. Albert Barnitz to Jennie Barnitz, November 11, 1868, Barnitz Diaries and Letters. Also see Langdon Sully, *No Tears for the General: The Life of Alfred Sully, 1821–1879*.

45. Albert Barnitz to Jennie Barnitz, September 16, 1868, Barnitz Diaries and Letters. See also Melbourne C. Chandler, *Of Garry Owen in Glory: The History of the Seventh United States Cavalry Regiment*, 10–11, 26–27.

46. Interview with General J. M. Bell, Field Notes, Topics A–L, folder 1, Box 2, Camp Mss.; E. S. Godfrey, "Some Reminiscences, Including an Account of General Sully's Expedition against the Southern Plains Indians," *Cavalry Journal* 36 (July 1927): 421–23.

47. Albert Barnitz to Jennie Barnitz, September 22, 1868, Barnitz Diaries and Letters. For a good general account of the campaign see White, "Sully's Expedition," 75–98.

48. "Tabular Statement of murders, outrages, robberies and depredations committed by Indians in Department of Missouri and Northern Texas, 1868," Box 68, Sheridan Papers; "List of murders, outrages, and depredations committed by Indians from 3rd August to 24th October, 1868, officially reported to Headquarters Department of the Missouri, in the field," ibid.; Philip H. Sheridan, *Record of Engagements with Hostile Indians within the Military Division of the Missouri, from 1868 to 1882, Lieutenant-General P. H. Sheridan, Commanding* 7–12.

49. *Annual Report of the Secretary of War [1868]* 1:18–19.

50. Sheridan to Adjutant General, December 17, 1881, Box 30, Sheridan Papers.

51. For a biography of Carr, see James T. King, *War Eagle: A Life of General Eugene A. Carr*; George F. Price, *Across the Continent with the Fifth Cavalry*, 259–65; Ezra J. Warner, *Generals in Blue: Lives of the Union Commanders*, 70–71.

52. King, *War Eagle*, 81–85. For the Indian side of this skirmish, see Hyde, *Life of George Bent*, 309–11; Grinnell, *Fighting Cheyennes*, 292–97. Abner "Sharp" Grover, who had now survived three close encounters with the Indians within that many months, was soon after killed in a saloon brawl. Interview with Howard Morton, Field Notes, unclassified envelope 64, Camp Mss.

53. Sheridan to Carr, October 21, 1868, Box 6, Sheridan Papers; King, *War Eagle*, 86–87; Price, *Across the Continent*, 132–33.

54. Albert Barnitz to Jennie Barnitz, October 18, 1868, Barnitz Diaries and Letters; Sheridan to Custer, September 24, 1868, "Correspondence, Other Sources," Custer Collection; and Custer, *My Life on the Plains*, 183. See also James Forsyth to Sheridan, October 7, 1868, Box 6, Sheridan Papers; Elizabeth Custer, *Following the Guidon*, 11–12.

55. Custer to Sheridan, October 28, 1868, Box 6, Sheridan Papers; Custer, *My Life on the Plains*, 199–204; Chandler, *Of Garry Owen in Glory*, 12–13.

56. W. T. Harrington to Sheridan, November 8, 1868, Box 16, Division of the Missouri, Special File, RG 393, Records of United States Army.

57. Sherman to Sheridan, October 15, 1868, *Sen. Exec. Docs.*, 40th Cong., 3d sess., no. 18, pt. 1, p. 5.

58. *Annual Report of the Secretary of War [1869]* 2 vols. (Washington, 1870), 1:44–45. Further vital information regarding the location of the Indians was sent to Sheridan at Fort Hays in mid-September by Colonel Hazen. This information was carried by William "Buffalo Bill" Cody, whose brave services as a dispatch rider during this critical period led Sheridan to appoint him chief of scouts for the Fifth Cavalry. Sheridan, *Personal Memoirs* 2:301; Don Russell, *The Lives and Legends of Buffalo Bill*, 103–4.

59. *Annual Report of the Secretary of War [1869]* 1:44–46; Sheridan, *Personal Memoirs* 2:307–10. For the organization of the New Mexico column, see Carl Coke Rister, ed., "Colonel A. W. Evans' Christmas Day Indian Fight (1868)," *Chronicles of Oklahoma* 16 (September 1938): 281–92. For Carr's column, see King, *War Eagle*, 86–88; Morris F. Taylor, "The Carr-Penrose Expedition: General Sheridan's Winter Campaign, 1868–1869," *Chronicles of Oklahoma* 51 (Summer 1973): 159–76. For the story of the Nineteenth Kansas, consult Mark A. Plummer, *Frontier Governor: Samuel J. Crawford of Kansas*, 125–33; Lonnie J. White, "Winter Campaigning with Sheridan and Custer: The Expedition of the Nineteenth Kansas Volunteer Cavalry," *Journal of the West* 6 (January 1967): 68–98; James Albert Hadley, "The Nineteenth Kansas Cavalry and the Conquest of the Plains Indians," *Transactions of the Kansas State*

Historical Society 10 (1907–1908): 428–56; Horace L. Moore, "The Nineteenth Kansas Cavalry," *Transactions of the Kansas State Historical Society* 6 (1897–1900): 35–52.

Sheridan also secured the services of Ute and Osage Indians to act as scouts, promising them booty as well as pay. Keim, *Sheridan's Troopers*, 63–64.

60. Sheridan, *Personal Memoirs* 2:307; Custer to Sheridan, October 28, 1868, Box 6, Sheridan Papers.

61. Sheridan, *Personal Memoirs* 2:307–8.

62. Ibid., 310–11; Keim, *Sheridan's Troopers*, 88–90.

CHAPTER 3

1. *House Exec. Docs.*, 41st Cong., 2d sess., no. 240, pp. 150–51; E. W. Wynkoop to N. G. Taylor, November 29, 1868, ibid., 4–5; Stan Hoig, *Battle of the Washita: The Sheridan-Custer Indian Campaign of 1867–69*, 88; William H. Leckie, *The Military Conquest of the Southern Plains*, 22–23.

2. *Sen. Exec. Docs.*, 40th Cong., 3d sess., no. 18, pt. 1, p. 25; Marvin E. Kroeker, *Great Plains Command: William B. Hazen in the Frontier West*, 78–79.

3. *Sen. Exec. Docs.*, 40th Cong., 3d sess., no. 18, pt. 1, p. 22.

4. For Hazen's reasoning, see his November 22, 1868, report to Sherman, in ibid., 22–24.

5. Ibid., 23

6. Ibid., 24–25, 42.

7. Ibid., 41–42; Hoig, *Battle of the Washita*, 96–97.

8. *Sen. Exec. Docs.*, 40th Cong., 3d sess., no. 18, pt. 1, pp. 25, 42; Kroeker, *Great Plains Command*, 82–84.

9. *Personal Memoirs of P. H. Sheridan, General, United States Army* 2:311; De B. Randolph Keim, *Sheridan's Troopers on the Border: A Winter Campaign on the Plains*, 88–93.

10. Keim, *Sheridan's Troopers*, 95–96, 98.

11. Ibid., 97–99; Sheridan, *Personal Memoirs* 2:311.

12. November 19, 21, 23, 1868, Albert Barnitz Diary, Barnitz Diaries and Letters; George Armstrong Custer, *My Life on the Plains; or, Personal Experiences with Indians*, 211–13; E. S. Godfrey, "Some Reminiscences, Including the Washita Battle, November 27, 1868," *Cavalry Journal* 37 (October 1928): 487.

13. November 21, 1868, Albert Barnitz Diary, and Albert Barnitz to Jennie Barnitz, November 21, 1868, Barnitz Diaries and Letters.

14. Keim, *Sheridan's Troopers*, 102; Elizabeth B. Custer, *Following the Guidon*, 17; John M. Carroll, ed., *The Benteen-Goldin Letters on Custer and His Last Battle*, 264; November 10, 1868, Albert Barnitz Diary, Barnitz Diaries and Letters; E. S. Godfrey to John Neihardt, February 23, 1924, John G. Neihardt Papers.

15. Custer, *My Life on the Plains*, 214–15; Keim, *Sheridan's Troopers*, 102–3.

16. Keim, *Sheridan's Troopers*, 103; J. Schuyler Crosby to Custer, November 22, 1868, "Correspondence, Other Sources," Custer Collection.

17. J. Schuyler Crosby to Custer, November 22, 1868, "Correspondence, Other Sources," Custer Collection; Custer, *My Life on the Plains*, 216–17; Marguerite Merington, ed., *The Custer Story: The Life and Intimate Letters of General George A. Custer and His Wife Elizabeth*, 218–19; Godfrey, "Washita Battle," 488.

18. Keim, *Sheridan's Troopers*, 105–6.

19. For the march of the Nineteenth Kansas Volunteer Cavalry, see Lonnie J. White, "Winter Campaigning with Sheridan and Custer: The Expedition of the Nineteenth Kansas Volunteer Cavalry," *Journal of the West* 6 (January 1967): 69–98; Mark A. Plummer, *Frontier Governor: Samuel J. Crawford of Kansas*, 128–31; Lonnie J. White, ed., "The Nineteenth Kansas Cavalry in the Indian Territory, 1868–1869; Eyewitness Accounts of Sheridan's Winter Campaign," *Red River Valley Historical Review* 3 (Spring 1978): 166–71; David L. Spotts, *Campaigning with Custer and the Nineteenth Kansas Volunteer Cavalry on the Washita Campaign, 1868–'69*, ed. E. A. Brininstool, 45–65.

20. White, "Winter Campaigning with Sheridan and Custer," 76–77; Keim, *Sheridan's Troopers*, 106–7, 125–26.

21. Sheridan, *Personal Memoirs* 2:321–22. In his memoirs Sheridan claimed that the volunteers had lost 700 of their horses in the march and could only be used as infantry thereafter. Sheridan was, however, confused on his figures, for the volunteers had 700 disabled horses in the entire campaign, not just in the first march. In February 1869 the Kansans were all dismounted and their remaining horses turned over to the Seventh Cavalry. At that time, after two more marches, they still had 550 horses left, although most were quite weak. Henry Alvord to Benjamin H. Grierson, February 2, 1869, Benjamin H. Grierson Papers, Newberry Library. Also see White, "Winter Campaigning with Sheridan and Custer," 79; Spotts, *Campaigning with Custer*, 57.

22. Sheridan, *Personal Memoirs* 2:321; Plummer, *Frontier Governor*, 130–31; James Albert Hadley, "The Nineteenth Kansas Cavalry and the Conquest of the Plains Indians," *Transactions of the Kansas State Historical Society* 10 (1907–1908): 435.

23. Robert C. Carriker, *Fort Supply, Indian Territory: Frontier Outpost on the Plains*, 20–21.

24. Keim, *Sheridan's Troopers*, 107–9.

25. Ibid., 111, 139–40.

26. Custer, *My Life on the Plains*, 193; Ben Clark, Field Notes, folder 4, Box 2, Camp Mss. For a biography of this colorful character, see Joe E. Milner and Earle R. Forrest, *California Joe, Noted Scout and Indian Fighter* (Caldwell, Idaho, Caxton, 1935).

27. "Report of Lieutenant Colonel G. A. Custer, 7th Cavalry, Brevet

Major General, U.S.A., of the attack on Black Kettle's Camp," November 28, 1868, Box 83, Sheridan Papers.

28. Ibid.

29. Ibid. Custer also reported the murders of a white woman and a young boy held captive by the Indians and the rescue of two other white children. No further mention was ever made of the dead woman or two rescued children in the military reports of Custer and Sheridan (although Sheridan repeated Custer's claims in his first report to Sherman on the battle, dated November 29), or in the memoirs of Custer, Sheridan, or Keim.

Much was subsequently made of the murder of the young boy, who was supposedly disembowled by a crazed Indian woman as the troops tried to rescue him. This murder was used by Sheridan, Custer, and others to point up the savage nature of their enemy, as an excuse for the killing of Indian women, and as proof positive that Black Kettle's people had been warring on the white settlements. Scout Ben Clark, however, who was an eyewitness to this incident, declared that the child was a fair-skinned Cheyenne whose mother stabbed him and then herself to prevent capture. Battle of Washita, Ben Clark interview, Field Notes, folder 11, Box 1, Camp Mss.; Blaine Burkey, *Custer, Come at Once! The Fort Hays Years of George and Elizabeth Custer, 1867–1870*, 68.

30. "Report of Lieutenant Colonel G. A. Custer," November 28, 1868, Box 83, Sheridan Papers. Custer's report of Indian casualties, which he claimed to be the result of a careful body count, has often been disputed. Cheyenne sources report so few casualties that they tend to discredit themselves. Considering the surprise nature of the attack, the duration of the battle, and the size of the village, it seems probable that Indian losses were heavy. George Bent, however, declared that but eleven Cheyenne warriors, two Arapaho warriors, twelve women, and six children were killed at Washita (George E. Hyde, *Life of George Bent: Written from His Letters*, 322). A similar accounting (thirteen men, sixteen women, and nine children), was given by Little Robe in an interview with Vincent Coyler in April 1869 ("Report of the Commissioner of Indian Affairs," *Report of the Secretary of the Interior* [Washington, 1869], 525). Kiowa chief Black Eagle gave almost the same casualty report to Hazen at Fort Cobb a few days after the battle. A much higher Indian loss was reported to former agent Wynkoop on December 14, 1868, by James S. Morrison, who had been in his employ. Writing from Fort Dodge, Morrison stated that two of Custer's scouts (John Poysell and Jack Fitzpatrick) told him that not over twenty warriors had been slain, but that about forty women and children had fallen. Captain Henry Alvord, who as Hazen's assistant had developed a good rapport with the Indians, reported on December 7, 1868, that his sources indicated a tally of eighty dead warriors (*House Exec. Docs.*, 41st Cong., 2d sess., no. 240, pp. 11, 147–48, 151–52).

These contradictory accounts make it impossible to come to any positive conclusions regarding Indian casualties. Custer, like many of his contemporaries, was not above exaggerating enemy losses in his battle reports in order to inflate the importance of his victory. In fact, he later claimed that his initial count was too low and that Indian captives had informed him of 140 dead at Washita. There is no reason, however, to assume Indian accounts to be more reliable. In the confusion after the battle the Indians had no way of reaching an accurate account of casualties. For example, early Indian accounts listed 37 women and children captured, while 57 was the true figure.

But this does not mean that Custer's figure of 103 should be allowed to stand. If we accept the general estimate that each Cheyenne lodge held 7 persons, and that 2 of these were males of fighting age (anywhere from a young teenager to an elderly man), the Custer figure becomes highly suspect. Custer reported destroying fifty lodges. Thus to accept his 103 dead warriors figure is to believe that every male who could shoulder a weapon in Black Kettle's camp was killed. Even taking into consideration warriors from the other villages killed later in the day, this is an astonishingly high figure. It is not impossible, but it will satisfy only the more credulous. It should be noted, however, that Custer never disclosed the number of women and children killed, even though he admitted some were accidently slain. Again, considering the nature of the dawn surprise attack, it seems probable that many noncombatants fell in the confusion. Scout Ben Clark later reported that many women and children were purposefully killed before Custer learned of the slaughter and stopped it. Thus, Custer's 103 figure may well be reasonably accurate, if we assume it to be all the Indians—men, women, and children—killed in the battle. Ben Clark, Field Notes, folder 4, Box 2, Camp Mss. See also Hoig, *Battle of the Washita*, 140, 200–201; *House Exec. Docs.*, 41st Cong., 2d sess., no. 240, p. 161.

31. Sheridan to Sherman, November 29, 1868, Division of the Missouri, Letters Sent, RG 393, Records of United States Army. For Custer on Sheridan, see Custer, *Following the Guidon*, 57; Jay Monaghan, *Custer: The Life of General George Armstrong Custer*, 323.

32. Sherman to E. D. Townsend, December 2, 1868, Division of the Missouri, Letters Sent, RG 393, Records of United States Army.

33. Sherman to Commanding Officer, Fort Hays, December 2, 1868, ibid.

34. For accounts of the review at Camp Supply, see Spotts, *Campaigning with Custer*, 65–66; Keim, *Sheridan's Troopers*, 121–23; Custer, *My Life on the Plains*, 267–69; Sheridan, *Personal Memoirs* 2:319–20; Godfrey, "Washita Battle," 499.

35. *Sen. Exec. Docs.*, 40th Cong., 3d sess., no. 18, pt. 1, pp. 34, 43.

36. Sheridan, *Personal Memoirs*, 2:320; Hoig, *Battle of the Washita*, 137, 141–42; Godfrey, "Washita Battle," 495–96.

37. Sheridan, *Personal Memoirs* 2:320.

38. Sherman to Commanding Officer, Fort Hays, December 2, 1868, Division of the Missouri, Letters Sent, RG 393, Records of United States Army; Custer, *My Life on the Plains*, 271.

39. Keim, *Sheridan's Troopers*, 123–24.

40. Ibid., 124; and *Sen. Exec. Docs.*, 40th Cong., 3d sess., no. 18, pt. 1, pp. 34–35. Mah-wis-sa was not completely truthful in her story to Sheridan, or was not understood correctly. The war party that made the trail Custer followed did not belong only to Black Kettle's village. The party had in fact divided at the Canadian River, with some going to Black Kettle's camp and others to the villages farther downstream. A Kiowa war party, returning from raiding the Utes, also passed through Black Kettle's village the night before the battle. George Bent claimed that the Cheyennes from the war party were just visiting at Black Kettle's village and were not of his band. Hyde, *Life of George Bent*, 315; George Bird Grinnell, *The Fighting Cheyennes*, 301; *House Exec. Docs.*, 41st Cong., 2d sess., no. 240. p. 147.

41. Custer, *My Life on the Plains*, 254.

42. Ben Clark, Field Notes, folder 4, Box 2, Camp Mss.; Carroll, ed., *Benteen-Goldin Letters*, 271. Further evidence of the relationship between army officers and the female captives is found in a letter from Captain Myles Keogh, Seventh Cavalry, to his brother. "We have knocked the Indians up a cocked hat, yet they are still on the war path. We have here [Fort Hays] about ninety squaws—from our last fight—some of them are very pretty. I have one that is quite intelligent. It is usual for officers to have two or three lounging around." Myles Keogh to Tom Keogh, May 9, 1869, MS 3885, Manuscript Archives, National Library, Dublin, Ireland.

43. Carriker, *Fort Supply*, 19–20.

44. Sheridan to Sherman, November 30, 1881, Box 30, Sheridan Papers; Carriker, *Fort Supply*, 26; Keim, *Sheridan's Troopers*, 127.

45. For the organization of the expedition, see Custer, *My Life on the Plains*, 279, 281–82; Keim, *Sheridan's Troopers*, 128.

Custer, in his memoirs, claims sole command of the expedition, describing Sheridan as a "passenger." As subsequent events proved, the department commander was hardly just a "passenger" on the expedition. Rather, he exercised complete control at all times of potential conflict, but tended to leave routine command duties to Custer. Sheridan, *Personal Memoirs* 2:323–47; Keim, *Sheridan's Troopers*, 128–60.

Mo-nah-se-tah, the daughter of Little Rock, a distinguished Cheyenne killed at the Washita, figures prominently in Custer's memoirs and in Elizabeth Custer's *Following the Guidon* as an attractive and able intermediary with the hostiles. Although Mo-nah-se-tah was six or seven months pregnant at the time of the battle, Cheyenne oral tradition, as independently reported by Thomas Marquis, Mari Sandoz, Charles Brill, and David Miller, contends that she was Custer's mistress. This is corroborated by Ben Clark (who did not identify the woman) and Captain Frederick Benteen and appears to have been fairly common camp gossip in military circles. The fact that more was not made of it during the period by other officers probably reflects a gentlemen's agreement to keep quiet on a not uncommon practice of the frontier military. Thomas B. Marquis, *Custer on the Little Bighorn* (Lodi, Calif., Kain Publishing Co., 1969), 35,

43; Mari Sandoz, *Cheyenne Autumn* (New York, Hastings House, 1953), xvii; Charles J. Brill, *Conquest of the Southern Plains: Uncensored Narrative of the Battle of the Washita and Custer's Southern Campaign*, 22, 45–46; David Humphreys Miller, *Custer's Fall: The Indian Side of the Story* (New York, 1957), 67–68, 237; Carroll, ed., *Benteen-Goldin Letters*, 271; Ben Clark, Field Notes, folder 4, Box 2, Camp Mss.

CHAPTER 4

1. This account of the Indian council was reported to Captain Henry Alvord by Black Eagle, Kicking Bird, and Little Heart. *House Exec. Docs.*, 41st Cong., 2d sess., no. 240, pp. 151–53. Also see W. S. Nye, *Carbine and Lance: The Story of Old Fort Sill*, 58, 72.

2. De B. Randolph Keim, *Sheridan's Troopers on the Border: A Winter Campaign on the Plains*, 130–31.

3. The Sheridan-Custer column moved almost parallel, but east, of the route Custer had followed in November. For details of the march, see *Personal Memoirs of P. H. Sheridan, General, United States Army* 2:323–28; Keim, *Sheridan's Troopers*, 128–40; David L. Spotts, *Campaigning with Custer and the Nineteenth Kansas Volunteer Cavalry on the Washita Campaign, 1868–'69*, 72–74.

4. For Custer's report on finding Major Elliott's party, see *House Exec. Docs.*, 41st Cong., 2d sess., no. 240, pp. 156–57. Also see Keim, *Sheridan's Troopers*, 144–50; Sheridan, *Personal Memoirs* 2:328–30.

5. Sheridan, *Personal Memoirs* 2:328–30.

6. Lonnie J. White, ed., "The Nineteenth Kansas Cavalry in the Indian Territory, 1868–1869: Eyewitness Accounts of Sheridan's Winter Campaign," *Red River Valley Historical Review* 3 (Spring 1978): 174; Nye, *Carbine and Lance*, 71; Keim, *Sheridan's Troopers*, 150; Sheridan, *Personal Memoirs* 2:331.

7. Keim, *Sheridan's Troopers*, 151; Custer's report in *House Exec. Docs.*, 41st Cong., 2d sess., no. 240, p. 157. Also see George Armstrong Custer, *My Life on the Plains; or, Personal Experiences with Indians*, 293.

8. Sheridan, *Personal Memoirs* 2:331–32; Keim, *Sheridan's Troopers*, 152–53.

9. Custer, *My Life on the Plains*, 291–92; Sheridan, *Personal Memoirs* 2:333–34; *House Exec. Docs.*, 41st Cong., 2d sess., no. 240, p. 158.

10. "Report of Lieutenant General Sheridan," *Report of the Secretary of War [1869]*, 2 vols. (Washington, 1869), 1:49; Sheridan to Adjutant General, June 19, 1872, Box 7, Sheridan Papers; *Sen. Exec. Docs.*, 40th Cong., 3d sess., no. 18, pt. 1, p. 43.

11. Custer, *My Life on the Plains*, 291.

12. Hazen remained publicly silent concerning the true situation despite the aspersions cast on him in the official reports of Sheridan and Custer. However, when Custer took a few more cheap shots in a February 1874 *Galaxy*

magazine article on the campaign (later republished as part of *My Life on the Plains*), Hazen published a rebuttal. Entitled *Some Corrections of "Life on the Plains"* (Saint Paul, Minn., 1875), it presented Hazen's side of the affair and also printed affidavits from Captain Alvord, interpreter Philip McCusker, and others who were on the scene in 1868–69 and knew the true situation. This pamphlet is conveniently reprinted as an appendix to the University of Oklahoma Press edition of Custer, *My Life on the Plains*, 383–407.

13. Keim, *Sheridan's Troopers*, 156; Custer, *My Life on the Plains*, 292.

14. Spotts, *Campaigning With Custer*, 81; Keim, *Sheridan's Troopers*, 156–57; Custer, *My Life on the Plains*, 293–94; Sheridan, *Personal Memoirs* 2:334.

15. Custer, *My Life on the Plains*, 294; Keim, *Sheridan's Troopers*, 157; Nye, *Cabine and Lance*, 74.

16. Sheridan, Custer, and Keim each gave a somewhat different version of Satanta's attempted escape. Sheridan, *Personal Memoirs* 2:334–35; Custer, *My Life on the Plains*, 298–99; Keim, *Sheridan's Troopers*, 157. Also see Spotts, *Campaigning With Custer*, 80.

17. Hazen, "Some Corrections," in *My Life on the Plains*, by Custer, 383, 391.

18. Ibid., 398.

19. Keim, *Sheridan's Troopers*, 161, 165–66; Spotts, *Campaigning with Custer*, 84, 86–87; Sheridan, *Personal Memoirs* 2:339.

20. *House Exec. Docs.*, 41st Cong., 2d sess., no. 240, p. 154.

21. Ibid.; Custer, *My Life on the Plains*, 304–5.

22. Horace L. Moore, "The Nineteenth Kansas Cavalry," *Transactions of the Kansas State Historical Society* 6 (1897–1900): 35–52; White, ed., "Nineteenth Kansas Cavalry," 174.

23. *Report of the Secretary of War [1869]* 1:49; Custer, *My Life on the Plains*, 308–10; Keim, *Sheridan's Troopers*, 163–65; Sheridan, *Personal Memoirs* 2:335–36.

24. *House Exec. Docs.*, 41st Cong., 2d sess., no. 240, pp. 151–52; Robert Utley, *Frontier Regulars: The United States Army and the Indians, 1866–1891*, 154–55; Nye, *Carbine and Lance*, 58.

25. Custer, *My Life on the Plains*, 311–13; Sheridan, *Personal Memoirs* 2:337–38.

26. Keim, *Sheridan's Troopers*, 164–65.

27. Ibid., 171–72; Spotts, *Campaigning with Custer*, 88.

28. Major Andrew Evans's report of his march and battle is reprinted in "Colonel A. W. Evans' Christmas Day Indian Fight (1868)," ed. Carl Coke Rister, *Chronicles of Oklahoma* 16 (September 1938): 275–301; see 292–93. John F. Finerty, *War-Path and Bivouac; or, The Conquest of the Sioux*, 34; Nye, *Carbine and Lance*, 78–79.

29. Rister, ed., "Christmas Day Indian Fight," 294.

30. Ibid., 296. Indian accounts listed only one man killed, the Comanche war chief, Arrow Point. Nye, *Carbine and Lance*. 80.

31. *Sen. Exec. Docs.*, 40th Cong., 3d sess., no. 18, pt. 2, p. 1; Rister, ed., "Christmas Day Indian Fight," 299.

32. *Sen. Exec. Docs.*, 40th Cong., 3d sess., no. 18, pt. 2, pp. 1–2.

33. Carl Coke Rister, *Border Command: General Phil Sheridan in the West,* 137–38; Donald J. Berthrong, *The Southern Cheyennes,* 333–34.

34. Marguerite Merington, ed., *The Custer Story: The Life and Intimate Letters of General George A. Custer and His Wife Elizabeth,* 228; *Sen. Exec. Docs.*, 40th Cong., 3d sess., no. 18, pt. 2, pp. 1–2.

CHAPTER 5

1. *House Exec. Docs.*, 41st Cong., 2d sess., no. 240, pp. 5–11; "Report of the Commissioner of Indian Affairs," *Report of the Secretary of the Interior[1868]* (Washington, 1868), 834; *New York Times,* December 24, 1868.

2. Marvin H. Garfield, "Defense of the Kansas Frontier, 1868–1869," *Kansas Historical Quarterly* 1 (November 1932): 466; *House Exec. Docs.*, 41st Cong., 2d sess., no. 240, pp. 10–11.

3. *New York Times,* February 14, 1869; W. A. Graham, *The Custer Myth: A Source Book of Custeriana,* 212–13.

4. John M. Carroll, ed., *The Benteen-Goldin Letters on Custer and His Last Battle,* 280–81.

5. Grierson to "Father" Kirk, April 6, 1869, Grierson Papers, Newberry Library.

6. *House Exec. Docs.*, 41st Cong., 2d sess., no. 240, p. 166; *Report of the Secretary of War [1869]* 1:47.

7. *Sen. Exec. Docs.*, 40th Cong., 3d sess., no. 18, pt. 3, p. 1.

8. *House Exec. Docs.*, 41st Cong., 2d sess., no. 240, p. 167.

9. *Report of the Secretary of War [1869]* 1:47–48.

10. Sherman to Sheridan, January 19, 1869, and Sherman to Sheridan, Hazen, and Grierson, December 23, 1868, Division of the Missouri, Letters Sent, RG 393, Records of United States Army.

11. *Army and Navy Journal* 12 (January 2, 1875): 327.

12. W. S. Nye, *Carbine and Lance: The Story of Old Fort Sill,* 75–78, 84. For an account of Colonel Grierson's survey of the Medicine Bluff region, see De B. Randolph Keim, *Sheridan's Troopers on the Border: A Winter Campaign on the Plains,* 231–51.

13. Philip H. Sheridan, *Outline Descriptions of the Posts in the Military Division of the Missouri,* 174–77; David L. Spotts, *Campaigning with Custer and the Nineteenth Kansas Volunteer Cavalry on the Washita Campaign, 1868–'69,* 96–102; Keim, *Sheridan's Troopers on the Border,* 255–56; Marguerite Merington, ed., *The Custer Story: The Life and Intimate Letters of General George A. Custer and His Wife Elizabeth,* 226.

14. Nye, *Carbine and Lance,* 84–86; William H. Leckie, *The Buffalo Sol-*

diers: A Narrative of the Negro Cavalry in the West, 47–49; *Personal Memoirs of P. H. Sheridan, General, United States Army* 2:338–39.

15. Nye, *Carbine and Lance,* 86; Marvin E. Kroeker, *Great Plains Command: William B. Hazen in the Frontier West,* 82, 86.

16. "Memoranda on Indians," Henry E. Alvord, February 5, 1869, Grierson Papers, Newberry Library.

17. Ibid.

18. Ibid.; Sheridan, *Personal Memoirs* 2:338, 342–43.

19. George Armstrong Custer, *My Life on the Plains; or, Personal Experiences with Indians,* 316–18; Sheridan, *Personal Memoirs* 2:343; Elizabeth B. Custer, *Following the Guidon,* 49.

20. Custer, *Following the Guidon,* 49; Melbourne C. Chandler, *Of Garry Owen in Glory: The History of the Seventh United States Cavalry Regiment,* 28.

21. Custer, *My Life on the Plains,* 319–37; Merington, ed., *The Custer Story,* 225; Chandler, *Of Garry Owen in Glory,* 29.

22. Alvord to Grierson, January 30, February 2, 1869, Grierson Papers, Newberry Library.

23. Alvord to Grierson, February 9, 1869, ibid.; Custer, *Following the Guidon,* 50; Custer, *My Life on the Plains,* 338–43; Chandler, *Of Garry Owen in Glory,* 29; Sheridan, *Personal Memoirs* 2:343–44.

24. Keim, *Sheridan's Troopers,* 272–73; Alvord to Grierson, February 9, 1869, Grierson Papers, Newberry Library.

25. Merington, ed., *The Custer Story,* 228; Keim, *Sheridan's Troopers,* 273. See also *House Exec. Docs.,* 41st Cong., 2d sess., no. 240, pp. 150–51.

26. Alvord to Grierson, February 9, 1869, Grierson Papers, Newberry Library.

27. Sheridan, *Personal Memoirs* 2:340–41; Merington, ed., *The Custer Story,* 227; Keim, *Sheridan's Troopers,* 256; Alvord to Grierson, January 30, 1869, and Alvord to Samuel Woodward, February 5, February 6, 1869, Grierson Papers, Newberry Library.

28. Sheridan, *Personal Memoirs* 2:342.

29. Alvord to Grierson, February 2, 1869, and Alvord to Woodward, February 5, 1869, Grierson Papers, Newberry Library; Lonnie J. White, "Winter Campaigning with Sheridan and Custer: The Expedition of the Nineteenth Kansas Volunteer Cavalry," *Journal of the West* 6 (January 1967): 69–98.

30. Alvord to Grierson, February 9, 1869, Grierson Papers, Newberry Library.

31. Nye, *Carbine and Lance,* 92–93; Custer, *My Life on the Plains,* 344.

32. Keim, *Sheridan's Troopers,* 275–76.

33. Sherman to Sheridan, January 18, 1869, Division of the Missouri, Letters Sent, RG 393, Records of United States Army; Hazen to Sheridan, March 18, 1869, Box 6, Sheridan Papers; Leckie, *Buffalo Soldiers,* 47.

34. Sheridan to Grierson, February 23, 1869, Grierson Papers, Newberry Library.

35. Sheridan, *Personal Memoirs* 2:344–45; Custer, *My Life on the Plains,* 343.

36. Morris F. Taylor, "The Carr-Penrose Expedition: General Sheridan's Winter Campaign, 1868–1869," *Chronicles of Oklahoma* 51 (Summer 1973): 159–76; George A. Armes, *Ups and Downs of an Army Officer,* 278–84; James T. King, *War Eagle: A Life of General Eugene A. Carr,* 87–90.

37. King, *War Eagle,* 90–92; Joseph G. Rosa, *They Called Him Wild Bill: The Life and Adventures of James Butler Hickok,* 124–25; Don Russell, *The Lives and Legends of Buffalo Bill,* 112; George F. Price, *Across the Continent with the Fifth Cavalry,* 133.

38. Keim, *Sheridan's Troopers,* 298–99; Spotts, *Campaigning with Custer,* 104, 125; Ben Clark, Field Notes, folder 4, Box 2, Camp Mss.

39. Merington, ed., *The Custer Story,* 228.

40. Custer, *Following the Guidon,* 56–57; Custer, *My Life on the Plains,* 345–76; Spotts, *Campaigning with Custer,* 136–72; Lonnie J. White, ed., "The Nineteenth Kansas Cavalry in the Indian Territory, 1868–1869: Eyewitness Accounts of Sheridan's Winter Campaign," *Red River Valley Historical Review* 3 (Spring 1978): 164–85.

41. Grierson to Assistant Adjutant General, April 10, 1869, Grierson Papers, Newberry Library; Donald J. Berthrong, *The Southern Cheyennes,* 338–40.

42. Berthrong, *Southern Cheyennes,* 339–40.

43. King, *War Eagle,* 95–102; George F. Hyde, *Life of George Bent: Written from His Letters,* 328–29.

44. King, *War Eagle,* 112–16; Price, *Across the Continent with the Fifth,* 138–41; Russell, *Buffalo Bill,* 129–48; George Bird Grinnell, *The Fighting Cheyennes,* 310–18; Hyde, *Life of George Bent,* 331–35.

45. Berthrong, *Southern Cheyennes,* 344, 348–49; Robert M. Utley, *Frontier Regulars: The United States Army and the Indian, 1866–1841,* 157.

46. Surgeon Morris Asch's report on the health of the troops is in *Sen. Exec. Docs.,* 40th Cong., 3d sess., no. 40, pp. 10–11. For stock losses, see Alvord to Grierson, February 2, 1869, and Alvord to Woodward, February 5, 1869, Grierson Papers, Newberry Library; Carl Coke Rister, ed., "Colonel A. W. Evans' Christmas Day Indian Fight (1868)," *Chronicles of Oklahoma* 16 (September 1938): 299–300; Chandler, *Of Garry Owen in Glory,* 29.

47. Merington, ed., *The Custer Story,* 228; H. C. Greiner, *Phil Sheridan as I Knew Him, Playmate-Comrade-Friend,* 412–13; Keim, *Sheridan's Troopers,* 307.

CHAPTER 6

1. Rachel Sherman Thorndike, ed., *The Sherman Letters: Correspondence between General and Senator Sherman from 1837 to 1891,* 324–25.

2. Richard O'Connor, *Thomas: Rock of Chickamauga* (New York, Prentice, Hall, 1948), 358; Lloyd Lewis, *Sherman: Fighting Prophet*, 602.

3. A. Baird to Sheridan, April 13, 1869, Box 6, Sheridan Papers; George Meade, *The Life and Letters of George Gordon Meade: Major-General, United States Army* 2:299–300; Freeman Cleaves, *Meade of Gettysburg* (Norman: University of Oklahoma Press, 1960), 247–48; *Memoirs of Gen. W. T. Sherman, Written by Himself* 2:439–40.

4. Sheridan to Grant, January 19, 1869, Box 39, Sheridan Papers; *Personal Memoirs of P. H. Sheridan, General, United States Army* 2:347.

5. *Report of the Secretary of War [1869]*, 1:36; Philip H. Sheridan, *Outline Descriptions of the Posts in the Military Division of the Missouri*, 3–4; *Record of Engagements with Hostile Indians within the Military Division of the Missouri, from 1868 to 1882, Lieutenant-General P. H. Sheridan, Commanding*, 4–6.

6. Sheridan, *Record of Engagements*, 6. During Sheridan's tenure the largest number of troops under his command was 16,925 in 1873; the smallest number was 11,666 in 1871. This is only paper strength, so the actual numbers were probably smaller.

7. John M. Schofield, *Forty-six Years in the Army*, 438; Ezra J. Warner, *Generals in Blue: Lives of the Union Commanders*, 425–26; James L. McDonough, *Schofield: Union General in the Civil War and Reconstruction*.

8. Warner, *Generals in Blue*, 376–80; *Webster's American Military Biographies* (Springfield, Mass.: G. & C. Merriam Co., 1978), 327–30. For John Pope's career in the West, see Richard N. Ellis, *General Pope and U.S. Indian Policy*.

9. Sheridan to Sherman, December 24, 1878, Box 19; Sheridan to Secretary of War, May 16, 1876, Box 15, Sheridan Papers. Also see Sheridan to Sherman, December 24, 1872, Box 8; Sheridan to Pope, August 21, 1874, Box 11; Sheridan to Sherman, September 7, 1874, Box 11, Sheridan Papers.

10. See Alfred H. Terry to Sheridan, May 1, 1880, Box 26; Sheridan to Robert Lincoln, September 25, 1883, Box 34; Sheridan to Pope, December 19, 1872, Box 8, Sheridan Papers.

11. Sheridan to Sherman, April ——, 1878, Box 19, Sheridan Papers.

12. Robert Edgar Riegel, *The Story of the Western Railroads: From 1852 through the Reign of the Giants* (Lincoln: University of Nebraska Press, 1964), 114–18.

13. *Report of the Secretary of War [1869]* 1:70–75. Also see Richard White, "The Winning of the West: The Expansion of the Western Sioux in the Eighteenth and Nineteenth Centuries," *Journal of American History* 65 (September 1978): 319–43.

14. *Report of the Secretary of War [1869]* 1:36–37; Sherman to Sheridan, April 30, 1870, Box 39; Sheridan to Edward O. C. Ord, January 29, 1872, Box 7; Sherman to Sheridan, March 7, 1870, Box 91, Sheridan Papers. See also Thorndike, ed., *Sherman Letters*, 288.

15. Christopher C. Augur to John Taffe, January 23, 1871, Bureau of Indian Affairs, Letters Received, Wyoming Territory, 1869–1880 (microfilm M234, reel 953), Record Group 75, National Archives. Also see Warner, *Generals in Blue,* 12; Francis B. Heitman, *Historical Register and Dictionary of the United States Army, from Its Organization, September 29, 1789, to March 2, 1903* 1:175.

16. Robert M. Utley, *Frontier Regulars: The United States Army and the Indian, 1866–1891,* 366th n; Lewis, *Sherman,* 58, 75, 80; Sheridan, *Personal Memoirs* 1:68–80, 2:190–93, 200–1; Warner, *Generals in Blue,* 349–50; *Webster's American Military Biographies,* 303; Bernarr Cresap, *Appomattox Commander: The Story of General E. O. C. Ord.*

17. Sheridan to Sherman, December 18, 1879, Box 25; Sheridan to Sherman, September 25, 1872, Box 7; Sheridan to Sherman, March 4, 1874, and Sheridan to Secretary of War, October 28, 1873, Box 10; Sheridan to Ord, April 18, 1874, Box 11; Sherman to Sheridan, April 22, 1874, July 14, 1875, Box 39, Sheridan Papers; Sheridan to Ord, February 3, 1876, Division of the Missouri, Letters Sent, RG 393, Records of United States Army.

18. Sherman to Sheridan, November 29, 1877, Box 39; Sherman to Sheridan, December 18, 1879, Box 25, Sheridan Papers; Utley, *Frontier Regulars,* 353–56; Cresap, *Appomattox Commander,* 315–16, 321–25.

19. Warner, *Generals in Blue,* 102–4; Heitman, *Historical Register* 1:340; *Webster's American Military Biographies,* 86–87; Martin F. Schmitt, ed., *General George Crook: His Autobiography,* 83–85.

20. Sheridan, *Personal Memoirs* 1:474; Warner, *Generals in Blue,* 103; Schmitt, ed., *Crook Autobiography,* 89–124.

21. C. R. Williams, ed., *Diary and Letters of Rutherford Birchard Hayes* 5:514; Sheridan, *Personal Memoirs* 2:33–42; Schmitt, ed., *Crook Autobiography,* 126–27. See also Henry A. Du Pont, *The Campaign of 1864 in the Valley of Virginia and the Expedition to Lynchburg,* 134; Edward J. Stackpole, *Sheridan in the Shenandoah: Jubal Early's Nemesis,* 246–57.

22. Schmitt, ed., *Crook Autobiography,* 134.

23. Ibid.; O'Connor, *Sheridan,* 220–31; Stackpole, *Sheridan in the Shenandoah,* 295–98.

24. Schmitt, ed., *Crook Autobiography,* 134.

25. Ibid., 135–36, 141, 303–5; Warner, *Generals in Blue,* 103.

26. Heitman, *Historical Register* 1:340; Schmitt, ed., *Crook Autobiography,* 142–59; Utley, *Frontier Regulars,* 177–81.

27. Crook quoted in James T. King, "George Crook: Indian Fighter and Humanitarian," *Arizona and the West* 9 (Winter 1967): 339. Also see Schmitt, ed., *Crook Autobiography,* 160–83; John G. Bourke, *On the Border with Crook,* 176–229; Utley, *Frontier Regulars,* 192–98.

28. Bourke, *With Crook,* 108; Utley, *Frontier Regulars,* 179–80, 198; John F. Finerty, *War-Path and Bivouac; or, The Conquest of the Sioux,* 316–17; Frazier Hunt and Robert Hunt, *I Fought With Custer: The Story of Sergeant Windolph,* 198.

29. Sheridan to August Kautz, October 25, 1876, Sheridan to Secretary of War, November 6, 1876, Sheridan to Sherman, February 9, 1877, Box 16; Sherman to Sheridan, February 17, 1877, Box 39, Sheridan Papers. Also see James T. King, "Needed: A Re-evaluation of General George Crook," *Nebraska History* 45 (September 1964): 223–35.

30. King, "George Crook," 342; Bourke, *With Crook*, 225, 215–29; Francis Paul Prucha, *American Indian Policy in Crisis: Christian Reformers and the Indian, 1865–1900*, 99–100. Also see Thomas C. Leonard, "Red, White, and the Army Blue: Empathy and Anger in the American West," *American Quarterly* 26 (May 1974): 181, 183–88.

31. Bourke, *With Crook*, 486; Richard N. Ellis, "The Humanitarian Generals," *Western Historical Quarterly* 3 (April 1972): 171–73; King, "George Crook," 342–47; Schmitt, ed., *Crook Autobiography*, 221–26, 260–71, 289–300; Indian Rights Association, *Annual Reports, 1883–1885*, 15; James T. King, "A Better Way: General George Crook and the Ponca Indians," *Nebraska History* 50 (Fall 1969): 239–56.

32. Sheridan to Sherman, January 22, 1879, Box 21, Sheridan Papers.

33. Bourke, *With Crook*, 109; Du Pont, *Campaign of 1864*, p. 135.

34. Sherman to Sheridan, November 13, 1880, Box 39, Sheridan Papers; Sheridan, *Personal Memoirs* 2:275; James E. Sefton, *The United States Army and Reconstruction, 1865–1877*, 156–57; Marguerite Merington, ed., *The Custer Story: The Life and Intimate Letters of General George A. Custer and His Wife Elizabeth*, 211; Lawrence A. Frost, *The Court-Martial of General George Armstrong Custer*, 254–56, 266.

35. Warner, *Generals in Blue*, 497–98; *Webster's American Military Biographies*, 433; John W. Bailey, *Pacifying the Plains: General Alfred Terry and the Decline of the Sioux*.

36. Baird to Sheridan, April 13, 1869, Box 6; Sherman to Sheridan, November 16, 1872, Box 39, Sheridan Papers; Schofield, *Forty-six Years in the Army*, 446–47, 535.

37. Utley, *Frontier Regulars* 94, 120–22, 132–39.

38. General Harney gave an account of the Missouri River agencies in a November 23, 1868, letter to Sherman reprinted in *Sen. Exec. Docs.*, 40th Cong., 3d sess., no. 11, pp. 2–6. Also see James C. Olson, *Red Cloud and the Sioux Problem*, 83–155; Utley, *Frontier Regulars*, 237–42.

39. Wayne Gard, *The Great Buffalo Hunt*, 5–6, 256–72.

40. Reigel, *Story of the Western Railroads*, 120–28; Robert G. Athearn, *Forts of the Upper Missouri*, 277–79.

41. Athearn, *Forts of the Upper Missouri*, 293, 260–92; *Report of the Secretary of War [1869]* 1:37; *Report of the Secretary of War [1871]*, 2 vols. (Washington, 1871), 1:22; Sheridan to Sherman, June 11, 1873, and Sheridan to William Whipple, June 21, 1873, Division of the Missouri, Letters Sent, RG 393, Records of United States Army. Also see Ray H. Mattison, "The Army Post of the Northern Plains, 1865–1885," *Nebraska History* 35 (March 1954): 17–43.

42. Warner, *Generals in Blue*, 397–98; Brigadier General Augur was assigned to command the Department of Texas as of November 1, 1871, but did not assume command until January 29, 1872. Raphael P. Thain, *Notes Illustrating the Military Geography of the United States, 1813–1880*, 99–100.

43. Sheridan, *Record of Engagements with Hostile Indians*, 4; idem, *Outline of Posts*, 181; Utley, *Frontier Regulars*, 209.

44. *Sen. Exec. Docs.*, 40th Cong., 3d sess., no. 40, pp. 12–17; Sheridan, *Outline of Posts*, 185–94; Utley, *Frontier Regulars*, 344–46.

45. Sheridan, *Outline of Posts*, 194–209; Utley, *Frontier Regulars*, 207–11.

46. In 1874 Ord was the oldest at fifty-six, and Schofield was the youngest at forty-three, with most of the other officers being in their early fifties.

47. The age range of Sheridan's colonels in 1874 went from Ranald Mackenzie, Fourth Cavalry, at thirty-four, to John E. Smith, Fourteenth Infantry, at fifty-eight. Nine of the colonels were in their fifties in 1874, five were in their forties, and two were in their thirties. This age range would vary only slightly from year to year as officers returned from detached duty or were transferred into the division. Data compiled from Heitman, *Historical Register*, vol. 1; Warner, *Generals in Blue*; *Webster's American Military Biographies*; and *Report of the Secretary of War [1874]*, 2 vols. (Washington, 1874), 1:70–75. Also see Arthur P. Wade, "Roads to the Top—An Analysis of General-Officer Selection in the United States Army, 1789–1898," *Military Affairs* 30 (December 1976): 157–63.

48. Sheridan to Robert Lincoln, December 8, 1881, Box 30, Sheridan Papers.

49. W. T. Sherman to Ellen Sherman, September 16, 1883, Sherman Family Papers.

50. Albert Barnitz to Jennie Barnitz, July 15, 1868, Barnitz Diaries and Letters; Virginia Weisel Johnson, *The Unregimented General: A Biography of Nelson A. Miles*, 44; Russell F. Weigley, *History of the United States Army*, 270–71; *Army and Navy Journal* 13 (April 1, 1876): 546; John M. Carroll, ed., *The Benteen-Goldin Letters on Custer and His Last Battle*, 278–79.

51. "General Sheridan's address to the graduates of Westpoint, Class of 1878," Box 109, Sheridan Papers; *Philadelphia Press*, August 11, 1888.

52. In 1875 the army consisted of 2,395 officers; 37 percent were West Pointers, 57 percent were civil appointees, and 9 percent were raised from the ranks. Of those officers cashiered, deserted, or dismissed between 1862 and 1875 the proportions were: civil appointments, 88 percent; from the ranks, 9 percent; and West Point, 3 percent. *Army and Navy Journal* 13 (December 4, 1875): 271. Data on officers compiled from Heitman, *Historical Register*, vol. 1; Warner, *Generals in Blue*; *Webster's American Military Biographies*; *Report of the Secretary of War [1874]* 1:70–75. Also see Wade, "Roads to the Top," 161–62; Utley, *Frontier Regulars*, 15, 18–20.

53. Sherman to Sheridan, September 26, December 2, 1872, and De-

cember 20, 1869, Box 39, Sheridan Papers; W. T. Sherman to Ellen Sherman, January 11, 1879, Sherman Family Papers; Johnson, *Unregimented General*, 89.

54. Jay Monaghan, *Custer: The Life of General George Armstrong Custer*, 267, 336, 371.

55. John A. Carpenter, *Sword and Olive Branch: Oliver Otis Howard*, 245, 277; Don E. Alberts, *Brandy Station to Manila Bay: A Biography of General Wesley Merritt*, 214–16.

56. Sherman to Sheridan, July 25, 1879, Box 39, Sheridan Papers; Johnson, *Unregimented General*, 37, 43–44, 154–55, 192–93, 214–15.

57. Custer to Merritt, November 15, 1875, Box 14, Sheridan Papers.

58. Lewis, *Sherman*, 607; Heitman, *Historical Register* 1:470.

59. Russell F. Weigley, *Quartermaster General of the Union Army: A Biography of M. C. Meigs*, 356–57; Wade, "Roads to the Top," 162.

60. Sherman to Sheridan, November 13, 1880, Box 39, Sheridan Papers; Weigley, *Quartermaster General*, 357.

61. *Army and Navy Journal* 13 (March 11, 1876) 506.

62. "Address by General Charles King," in *The Papers of the Order of Indian Wars*, ed. John M. Carroll, 46. For a discussion of Charles King and the heroic self-image of the frontier soldiers, see Oliver Knight, *Life and Manners in the Frontier Army*.

63. *Army and Navy Journal* 13 (August 21, 1875): 24.

64. Sheridan to William Belknap, November 8, 1874, Box 11; Sheridan to Q. A. Gillmore, February 28, 1875, Box 13, Sheridan Papers. The young officer, the son of a general, was reappointed to another regiment four months after his resignation.

65. Merington, ed., *Custer Story*, 159. For the role of women on the military frontier, see Patricia Y. Stallard, *Glittering Misery: Dependents of the Indian Fighting Army*; Sandra L. Myres, "Romance and Reality on the American Frontier: Views of Army Wives," *Western Historical Quarterly* 13 (October 1982), 409–27.

66. Sheridan to Sherman, November 30,1872, Box 8, Sheridan Papers. The woman, Mary Jordan, was never found, and it was assumed that her Cheyenne captors killed her. She was probably killed before Sheridan opposed her ransoming. See Minnie Dubbs Millbrook, "The Jordan Massacre," *Kansas History* 2 (Winter 1979): 218–30.

67. *Sheridan's Veterans: A Souvenir of Their Two Campaigns in the Shenandoah Valley: The One, of War, in 1864, the Other, of Peace, in 1883*, 13; Jennie Barnitz Diary, April 22, 1868, Barnitz Diaries and Letters.

68. Sheridan to Benjamin Alvord, March 15, 1873, Box 9, Sheridan Papers.

69. Custer, *My Life on the Plains*, 22. Also see Robert M. Utley, *The Contribution of the Frontier to the American Military Tradition*, 5–7.

70. Carroll, ed., *Order of the Indian Wars*, 56. Also see Richard N. Ellis,

"The Humanitarian Soldiers," *Journal of Arizona History* 10 (Summer 1969): 53–66.

71. Richard Robins, comp., *Toasts and Responses at Banquets Given Lieut.-Gen. P. H. Sheridan, United States Army, "Commander," by the Military Order of the Loyal Legion of the United States, Commandery of the State of Illinois, March 6, 1882–3*, 27, 53; *Sheridan's Veterans*, 27; *Proceedings of the Senate and Assembly of the State of New York, on the Life and Services of Gen. Philip H. Sheridan, Held at the Capitol, April 9, 1889*, 35; Sheridan, *Personal Memoirs* 2:447–51.

72. Frank A. Burr and Richard J. Hinton, *The Life of Gen. Philip H. Sheridan: Its Romance and Reality*, 436.

73. *Proceedings of the Senate and Assembly of New York*, 43–44.

74. Burr and Hinton, *Life of Sheridan*, 435; Wallace Evan Davies, *Patriotism on Parade: The Story of Veterans' and Heriditary Organizations in America, 1783–1900* (Cambridge, Mass., Harvard University Press, 1955), 249–50.

75. Sheridan to Sherman, January 3, 1879, Box 21, Sheridan Papers; Marvin E. Kroeker, *Great Plains Command: William B. Hazen in the Frontier West*, 39–40, 154–62. Despite Sheridan's opposition, a court-martial was ordered in 1879. Stanley, unsuccessful for so long, managed to bring matters to a climax by charging Hazen with perjury in the Belknap impeachment trial. He was aided in these new charges by former Secretary of War Belknap, now working in an Iowa law firm. Hazen demanded that Stanley be court-martialed for slandering a fellow officer. In the resulting trial, Sheridan testified for Stanley and against Hazen on the question of Missionary Ridge, but Stanley was quite properly found guilty of "conduct to the prejudice of good order and military discipline."

76. Sheridan to Adjutant General, August 24, 1872, Box 7, Sheridan Papers. Also see Kroeker, *Great Plains Command*, 112–14.

77. Sheridan to Sherman, March 4, 1874, Box 10, Sheridan Papers.

78. O'Connor, *Sheridan*, 317; Sheridan, *Personal Memoirs*, 2:43–45.

79. Warner, *Generals in Blue*, 541–42.

80. O'Connor, *Sheridan*, 347–48; Asa Bird Gardner, *Argument on Behalf of Lieut. Gen. Philip H. Sheridan, U.S.A., Respondent, by Asa Bird Gardner, LL.D., Judge-Advocate, U.S.A., of Counsel, before the Court of Inquiry Convened by the President of the United States in the Case of Lieut. Col. and Bvt. Major-General Gouverneur K. Warren, Corps of Engineers, formerly Major-General Commanding the 5th Army Corps, Applicant.*

81. William Addleman Ganoe, *The History of the United States Army*, 298–354.

CHAPTER 7

1. W. E. Strong, *A Trip to the Yellowstone National Park in July, August, and September, 1875*, 4; Frank A. Burr and Richard J. Hinton, *The Life of Gen. Philip*

H. Sheridan: Its Romance and Reality, 366–67; Ezra J. Warner, *Generals in Blue: Lives of the Union Commanders*, 156–67; Francis B. Heitman, *Historical Register and Dictionary of the United States Army, from Its Organization, September 29, 1789, to March 2, 1903* 1:430.

2. Sheridan to Townsend, March 13, 1869, Box 6, Sheridan Papers; *Report of the Secretary of War [1869]* 1:38–39; Allen Johnson and Dumas Malone, eds., *Dictionary of American Biography*, 11 vols. (New York, 1957), 2:568; Heitman, *Historical Register* 1:430, 881; *Army and Navy Register* 58 (September 18, 1915): 356.

3. George Forsyth to Townsend, April 13, 1874; George Forsyth to Daniel Drennan, April 13, December 17, 1874, Box 45, Sheridan Papers. The daily paperwork of the division is well documented in the Forsyth Letterbooks (ibid). Also see Sheridan to Chief Clerk, War Department, December 4, 1879, Division of the Missouri, Letters Sent, RG 393, Records of United States Army.

4. H. C. Greiner, *Phil Sheridan as I Knew Him, Playmate-Comrade-Friend*, 376–79. The Forsyth Letterbooks, Box 45, Sheridan Papers, are full of correspondence regarding Civil War veterans.

5. George Forsyth to D. H. Brotherton, May 20, 1870, Box 45, Sheridan Papers. For Sheridan's policy on endorsements and recommendations, see also George Forsyth to Custer, February 21, 26, 1873, George Forsyth to Major Kiddoo, May 19, 1872, George Forsyth to W. T. Wilson, September 8, 1874, and James Forsyth to Ranald Mackenzie, March 10, 1876, Box 45, Sheridan Papers.

6. Records diagrams, Box 11, Daniel O. Drennan Papers.

7. Sheridan to Sherman, May 22, 1878, Box 19, Sheridan Papers.

8. Sheridan to Hancock, March 2, 1872, Box 7, Sheridan Papers.

9. Sheridan to Townsend, December 16, 1872, Box 8, Sheridan Papers.

10. Sheridan endorsement, March 13, 1873, Box 9; Sheridan to Sherman, October 23, 1871, Box 6, ibid.

11. Sheridan to Martin Maginnis, June 9, 1874, Division of the Missouri, Letters Sent, RG 393, Records of United States Army; Sheridan to Secretary of War, February 26, 1879, Box 21, Sheridan Papers.

12. Sheridan to Secretary of War, September 22, 1873, Box 19, Sheridan Papers.

13. Sheridan to Townsend, September 28, 1872, Box 7, ibid.; Sheridan to Sherman, May 1, 1874, Division of the Missouri, Letters Sent, RG 393, Records of United States Army. Also see Sheridan to Terry, June 10, 26, 1873, Sheridan to Whipple, July 27, 1873, Division of the Missouri, Letters Sent, RG 393, Records of United States Army; Philip H. Sheridan, *Outline Description of the Posts in the Military Division of the Missouri*.

14. Sheridan to Secretary of War, October 28, 1873, Box 10, Sheridan Papers.

15. Sheridan to Townsend, December 16, 1872, and Sheridan to Secre-

tary of War, December 16, 1872, Box 8; Sheridan to Secretary of War, September 23, 1873, Box 10; Sheridan to Townsend, January 24, 1876, Box 14, Sheridan Papers.

16. Sheridan to Maginnis, February 26, 1876, Box 14, ibid. Also see Sheridan's annual reports for 1875 and 1876, Box 85, ibid.

17. *Report of the Secretary of War [1885]*, 4 vols. (Washington, 1885), 1:64–65; *Report of the Secretary of War [1887]*, 4 vols. (Washington, 1887), 1:77–78; Donald Nevius Bigelow, *William Conant Church and The Army and Navy Journal*, 184–86; Lee Kennett and James LaVerne Anderson, *The Gun in America: The Origins of a National Dilemma* (Westport, Conn., Greenword, 1975), 138–39; *Report of the Secretary of War [1882]*, 4 vols. (Washington, 1882), 1:80; Sheridan to Sherman, October 23, 1881, Box 29, Sheridan Papers. Also see Douglas C. McChristian, *An Army of Marksmen: The Development of United States Army Marksmanship in the Nineteenth Century*, 41–81.

18. Sheridan to Secretary of War, April 21, 1876, Box 14, Sheridan Papers.

19. Sheridan letter of introduction, July 20, 1875, Box 13; George Forsyth to Sheridan, September 15, 1876, Box 15, Sheridan Papers; Stephen E. Ambrose, *Upton and the Army*, 16–53, 87–111; Russell F. Weigley, *Towards an American Army: Military Thought from Washington to Marshall*, 100–26.

20. Sherman to Sheridan, July 13, 31, November 22, 1881, Box 39; Sheridan to Sherman, October 23, 1881, Box 29, Sheridan Papers; Timothy K. Nenninger, *The Leavenworth Schools and the Old Army: Education, Professionalism, and the Officer Corps of the United States Army, 1881–1918*, 21–33; Russell F. Weigley, *History of the United States Army*, 273–74.

21. Sherman to Sheridan, July 31, 1881, Box 39, Sheridan Papers.

22. Ambrose, *Upton and the Army*, 106–7; James A. Garfield, "The Army of the United States," *North American Review* 261 (March-April 1878): 210.

23. Gilbert C. Fite, *The Farmer's Frontier, 1865–1900*, 61; Sherman to Sheridan, May 24, 1875, Box 39, Sheridan Papers.

24. Gilbert C. Fite, "The United States Army and Relief to Pioneer Settlers, 1874–1875," *Journal of the West* 6 (January 1967): 100–3.

25. *Sen. Exec. Docs.*, 43d Cong., 2d sess., no. 5, pp. 4–5.

26. Fite, "Army and Relief," 104–5; *Army and Navy Journal* 12 (February 6, 1875): 404, (March 6, 1875): 468, (April 3, 1875): 532. The War Department, in a remarkable public-works type of program, ordered that destitute local settlers be employed to construct Fort Hartsuff, on Nebraska's Loup River. Richard Guentzel, "The Department of the Platte and Western Settlement, 1866–1877," *Nebraska History* 56 (Fall 1975): 408. See also Robert N. Manley, "In the Wake of the Grasshoppers: Public Relief in Nebraska, 1874–1875," *Nebraska History* 44 (December 1963): 255–75.

27. *Personal Memoirs of P. H. Sheridan, General, United States Army* 2:349–50.

28. *Sen. Exec. Docs.*, 41st Cong., 3d sess., no. 51, pp. 1–40; H. Duane

Hampton, *How the U.S. Cavalry Saved Our National Parks*, 24–27; Merrill D. Beal, *The Story of Man in Yellowstone*, 116–35; Aubrey L. Haines, *The Yellowstone Story: A History of Our First National Park 1:105–41;* Orrin H. Bonney and Lorraine Bonney, *Battle Drums and Geysers: The Life and Journals of Lt. Gustavus Cheyney Doane, Soldier and Explorer of the Yellowstone and Snake River Regions,* 215–388; W. Turrentine Jackson, "The Washburn-Doane Expedition of 1870," *Montana: The Magazine of Western History* 7 (July 1957): 36–51.

29. Haines, *Yellowstone Story* 1:142–44; William H. Goetzmann, *Exploration and Empire: The Explorer and the Scientist in the Winning of the American West,* 406–9.

30. *Sen. Exec. Docs.*, 42d Cong., 2d sess., no. 66, pp. 3–43; Haines, *Yellowstone Story* 1:142–53.

31. Sheridan to William Whipple, May 16, 1874, Division of the Missouri, Letters Sent, RG 393, Records of United States Army; Haines, *Yellowstone Story* 1:201–3; Goetzmann, *Exploration and Empire*, 409–12.

32. Haines, *Yellowstone Story* 1:204; John F. Reiger, ed., *The Passing of the Great West: Selected Papers of George Bird Grinnell,* 108–21; Bonney, *Battle Drums and Geysers*, 433–578; Thomas B. Marquis, *Custer, Cavalry, and Crows: The Story of William White*, ed. John A. Popovich, 101–14.

33. Sheridan to George Forsyth, March 20, 1873, Box 9, Sheridan Papers; Sheridan to Terry, May 20, 1873; Sheridan to Sherman, May 20, 1873, Division of the Missouri, Letters Sent, RG 393, Records of United States Army; Mark H. Brown, *The Plainsmen of the Yellowstone: A History of the Yellowstone Basin*, 203; Luther S. Kelly, *"Yellowstone Kelly": The Memoirs of Luther S. Kelly*, ed. M. M. Quaife, 98–102.

34. Sheridan to ———, July 13, 1874, Box 11; James Forsyth to Sheridan, June 22, 1875, Box 45, Sheridan Papers; James W. Forsyth and F. D. Grant, *Report of an Expedition up the Yellowstone River, Made in 1875. . . .*

35. *Report of the Secretary of War [1874]* 1:24; R. C. Drum to Terry, May 15, 1874, Division of the Missouri, Letters Sent, RG 393, Records of United States Army; Sheridan to Sherman, May 1, 1874, Box 11, Sheridan Papers; Donald Jackson, *Custer's Gold: The United States Cavalry Expedition of 1874,* 15–25.

36. Jackson, *Custer's Gold*, 49–60; Reiger, *Passing of the Great West*, 80–81; Marguerite Merington, ed., *The Custer Story: The Life and Intimate Letters of General George A. Custer and His Wife Elizabeth*, 52.

37. Sheridan to Ord, June 2, 1873, Box 9, Sheridan Papers; Goetzmann, *Exploration and Empire*, 425–29; Reiger, *Passing of the Great West*, 33–38; Don Russell, *The Lives and Legends of Buffalo Bill*, 166–68; Anson Mills, *My Story*, 148–49; Merrill J. Mattes, *Indians, Infants, and Infantry: Andrew and Elizabeth Burt on the Frontier*, 193–97. Also see Charles Schuchert and Clara Mae LeVene, *O. C. Marsh: Pioneer in Paleontology* (New Haven, Conn.: Yale University Press, 1940), 94–168; C. W. Betts, "The Yale College Expedition of 1870," *Harper's New Monthly Magazine* 43 (October 1871): 663–71.

38. Sheridan to Belknap, May 25, 1873, Box 9, Sheridan Papers; Goetz-mann, *Exploration and Empire*, 415; James B. Fry to Sheridan, May 12, 1873; Sheridan to Belknap, May 19, 1873, Division of the Missouri, Letters Sent, RG 393, Records of United States Army.

39. Goetzmann, *Exploration and Empire*, 429.

40. Jackson, *Custer's Gold*, 85–91.

41. Herbert Krause and Gary D. Olson, *Prelude to Glory: A Newspaper Accounting of Custer's 1874 Expedition to the Black Hills*, 231, 233, 245.

42. George Forsyth to Sheridan, August 2, 1874; George Forsyth to R. C. Drum, October 12, 1874, Box 45, Sheridan Papers; Sheridan to Sherman, March 3, 1875, Division of the Missouri, Letters Sent, RG393, Records of United States Army; *Army and Navy Journal* 12 (April 3, 1875):533. George Forsyth's journal of the Black Hills expedition is in Box 45, Sheridan Papers.

43. This alliance was sometimes based on more than just a mutual interest in white settlement. See Richard Slotkin," '. . . & Then the Mare Will Go!': An 1875 Black Hills Scheme by Custer, Holladay, and Buford," *Journal of the West* 15 (July 1976): 60–77.

44. Edgar I. Stewart, ed., *Penny-an-Acre Empire in the West*, 182, 139–83; Marvin E. Kroeker, *Great Plains Command: William B. Hazen in the Frontier West*, 120–42; David M. Emmons, *Garden in the Grasslands: Boomer Literature of the Central Great Plains*, 163–64.

45. Stewart, ed., *Penny-an-Acre Empire*, 162.

46. Thomas Rosser to Custer, February 16, 1874; A. B. Nettleton to Custer, March 19, 1874, Correspondence, Other Sources, Custer Collection; Stewart, ed., *Penny-an-Acre Empire*, 47–54, 71–113.

It is interesting to note that while Rosser, who as a Confederate cavalry general had battled Custer and Sheridan repeatedly, remained close friends with Custer, he never got over his Civil War hatred of Sheridan. This did not, however, inhibit Rosser's ability to work closely with Sheridan on matters concerning the Northern Pacific Railroad. Just after Sheridan's death, Rosser wrote this characterization of the general: "Gen. Sheridan is now dead—Peace to his ashes—but as I disliked him very much, I fear that I failed to see any high military virtues in him. To me he always appeared vulgar and coarse. I often met him while I was connected with the Northern Pacific Railroad, and I saw that he was very intemperate and barbarously profane and was neither great nor good." Thomas L. Rosser to Edgar F. Gladwin, September 3, 1888, Thomas L. Rosser Collection.

47. Sherman to Sheridan, September 26, October 7, 1872, Box 39, Sheridan Papers.

48. Robert Vaughn, *Then and Now; or, Thirty-six Years in the Rockies*, 332–33. See also Robert G. Athearn, *William Tecumseh Sherman and the Settlement of the West*, 330–34.

49. Sheridan to George W. Cass, January 27, 1873, Division of the Missouri, Letters Sent, RG 393, Records of United States Army. Also see

Sheridan to W. Milnor Roberts, June 21, 1872, and Sheridan to Cass, February 24, 1873, ibid.

50. On forts and the railroad, see Sheridan to Hancock, January 31, April 6, 1872, Box 7, Sheridan Papers; Sheridan to Roberts, June 21, 1872, Division of the Missouri, Letters Sent, RG 393, Records of United States Army.

51. For troop changes to accommodate the railroad, see Sheridan to Hancock, June 29, 1872; Sheridan to Irvin McDowell, June 30, 1872; Sheridan to Cass, February 24, 1873, Division of the Missouri, Letters Sent, RG 393, Records of United States Army. Also see Sheridan to Townsend, March 25, April 7, 1872, Box 7, Sheridan Papers.

52. Fry to Hancock, June 29, 1872; Sheridan to Cass, February 24, 1873, Division of the Missouri, Letters Sent, RG 393, Records of United States Army; Sheridan to Roberts, June 21, 1872, Box 7, Sheridan Papers; Goetzmann, *Exploration and Empire*, 412–13; Brown, *Plainsmen of the Yellowstone*, 196–203.

53. Fry to Sheridan, April 19, 1873; Sheridan to Terry, March 21, 1873; Sheridan to W. D. Whipple, March 26, 1873; Sheridan to Cass, March 21, 1873, Division of the Missouri, Letters Sent, RG 393, Records of United States Army. See also D. S. Stanley, *Report of the Yellowstone Expedition of 1873*.

54. Rosser to George Forsyth, November 13, 1874, Division of the Missouri, Special File, Box 16, RG 393, Records of United States Army. See also James Forsyth to W. H. Lewis, November 3, 1876; George Forsyth to Rosser, November 9, 1874, Box 45, Sheridan Papers; Rosser to Sheridan, August 27, 1877, Division of the Missouri, Special File, Box 16, RG 393, Records of United States Army.

55. For a listing of Sheridan's railroad passes see the Forsyth Letterbooks for January 1874, Box 45, Sheridan Papers. Also see Sheridan to Hancock, August 26, 1872, Box 7; James Forsyth to G. G. Sanborn, August 29, September 29, 1876, Box 45, Sheridan Papers.

Sheridan was quick to return the courtesies extended by the railroads by offering military escorts and camp equipment to railroad managers traveling on the frontier, even if their trip was purely for pleasure. See Sheridan to Frank Thomson (General Manager, Pennsylvania R.R.), May 10, 1879, Box 23; Sheridan to Terry, May 10, 1879, Box 23; Sheridan to Commanding Officer, Fort Ellis, May 8, 1880, Box 26, Sheridan Papers (concerning an escort for Jay Cooke and friends).

56. Sheridan to Sidney Dillon, May 23, 1877, Box 17, Sheridan Papers.

57. Sheridan to Jay Gould, April 24, 1879, Box 22, Sheridan Papers. For other examples, see Sheridan to William Dodge, March 21, 1873, Division of the Missouri, Letters Sent, RG 393, Records of United States Army; Sheridan to Strong, April 24, 1879, Box 22, Sheridan Papers.

58. *Proceedings of the State and Assembly of New York, on the Life and Services of Gen. Philip H. Sheridan, Held at the Capitol, April 9, 1889*, 53, 63.

59. Sheridan to Townsend, May 21, 1872; Sheridan to Levi Parsons, May 20, 1872, Box 7, Sheridan Papers.

60. Sheridan to Secretary of War, December 9, 1872, Box 8, Sheridan Papers.

61. Sheridan to Secretary of War, November 17, 1872, Box 8, Sheridan Papers. When the Saint Paul, Minneapolis and Manitoba Railroad obtained a right-of-way through a northern Montana Indian reservation, Sheridan protested so vigorously that the president vetoed the bill granting the right-of-way. *Army and Navy Register* 7 (July 10, 1886): 432.

62. *Report of the Secretary of War [1880]*, 4 vols. (Washington, 1880), 1:53, 56.

63. Eugene F. Ware, *The Indian War of 1864* (Lincoln: University of Nebraska Press, 1963), 405.

64. Robert G. Athearn, *Union Pacific Country* (Lincoln: University of Nebraska Press, 1976), 209–10; O. M. Poe, "Report on Transcontinental Railways, 1883," in *Report of the Secretary of War [1883]*, 4 vols. (Washington, 1883), 1:253–317 (comparative freight rates are discussed on pp. 300–302).

65. *Report of the Secretary of War [1882]* 1:80; Athearn, *Union Pacific Country*, 199–212.

66. Frederick T. Wilson, *Federal Aid in Domestic Disturbances, 1787–1903*, 331, 189–205. Also see Jerry M. Cooper, "The Army as Strikebreakers—The Railroad Strikes of 1877 and 1894," *Labor History* 18 (Spring 1977): 179–96; Barton C. Hacker, "The United States Army as a National Police Force: The Federal Policing of Labor Disputes, 1877–1898," *Military Affairs* 33 (April 1969): 255–64; Thomas A. Scott, "The Recent Strikes," *North American Review* 258 (September-October 1877): 351–62; Robert V. Bruce, *1877: Year of Violence*; Philip S. Foner, *The Great Labor Uprising of 1877*; Jerry M. Cooper, *The Army and Civil Disorder: Federal Military Intervention in Labor Disputes, 1877–1900*, 43–98; Richard Schneirov, "Chicago's Great Upheaval of 1877," *Chicago History* 9 (Spring 1980): 3–17.

67. *Annual Report of the Secretary of War [1877]*, 2 vols. (Washington, 1877), 1:56; Philip H. Sheridan and Michael V. Sheridan, *Personal Memoirs of Philip Henry Sheridan, General, United States Army: New and Enlarged Edition, with an Account of His Life from 1871 to His Death, in 1888* 2:527.

68. Wilson, *Federal Aid*, 330; Bruce, *1877*, 240–53; Foner, *Great Labor Uprising*, 149–56.

69. Foner, *Great Labor Uprising*, 156; *Report of the Secretary of War [1877]* 1:56; Bruce, *1877*, 251–53; Wilson, *Federal Aid*, 201.

70. Cooper, "Army as Strikebreakers," 183; Bruce, *1877*, 255–60, 274–76, 281–82; Wilson, *Federal Aid*, 202–3, 333; Foner, *Great Labor Uprising*, 157–87.

71. Cooper, "Army as Strikebreakers," 194–95. The *Army and Navy Journal* 15 (August 18, 1877): 24, editorialized that "those who oppose the Army and ask for its reduction are the same who encourage the rioters to their

work," and called for expansion of the army. The *New York Times* agreed, calling the army "the bulwark of law and order" (July 28, 1877).

72. George F. Price, *The Necessity for Closer Relations between the Army and the People, and the Best Method to Accomplish the Result,* 17–18, 21.

73. Sheridan to Townsend, May 9, 1878, Box 19, Sheridan Papers. One of the reasons for the establishment of Fort Sheridan, just north of Chicago, was fear of labor unrest.

74. *Report of the Secretary of War [1884],* 4 vols. (Washington, 1884), 1:49.

75. Burr and Hinton, *Life of Sheridan,* 358.

CHAPTER 8

1. Philip Sheridan and Michael V. Sheridan, *Personal Memoirs of Philip Henry Sheridan, General, United States Army: New and Enlarged Edition, with an Account of His Life from 1871 to His Death, in 1888* 2:464–65; Edward S. Ellis, *The History of Our Country: From the Discovery of America to the Present Time,* 8 vols. (Cincinnati, 1900), 6:1483.

2. Sheridan to Secretary of War, May 27, 1873, Box 9, Sheridan Papers.

3. Sheridan to J. T. Averill, January 28, 1874, Box 10, ibid.

4. "Indian Affairs," Daniel Drennan memoirs, Box 110, ibid.

5. Sheridan to War Department, July 11, 1872, Box 7, ibid.

6. Sheridan to War Department, November 7, 1872, Box 8, ibid.

7. Sheridan to Averill, January 28, 1874, Box 10, ibid.

8. For Sheridan's testimony before Congress on transfer, see *Army and Navy Journal* 13 (February 26, 1876): 469. For background on the transfer controversy see Robert Winston Mardock, *The Reformers and the American Indian,* 42–46, 139–41, 159–67; Francis Paul Prucha, *American Indian Policy in Crisis: Chistian Reformers and the Indian, 1865–1900,* 72–102; Robert M. Utley, *Frontier Regulars: The United States Army and the Indian, 1866–1891,* 188–92; Donald J. D'Elia, "The Argument over Civilian or Military Indian Control, 1865–1880," *Historian* 24 (February 1962): 207–25.

9. *Annual Report of the Secretary of War for the Year 1878,* 2 vols. (Washington, 1878), 1:36.

10. Ibid., 36–38.

11. *Annual Report of the Secretary of War for the Year 1879,* 4 vols. (Washington, 1879), 1:45.

12. *Report of the Secretary of War 1878* 1:36–38.

13. Sheridan to Sherman, March 18, 1870, Box 91, Sheridan Papers.

14. For the invasion of the Ute reservation, see Sheridan to Pope, February 21, 1873, and Sheridan to Whipple, February 27, 1873, Box 8, ibid. For the squatter problem in the Indian Territory, see Sheridan to Sherman,

May 11, 1879, Box 23; Sheridan to Adjutant General, July 28, 1879, Box 24, ibid.

15. Sheridan to War Department and Indian Bureau, June 27, 1872, Box 7, ibid.

16. Carolyn Thomas Foreman, "General Benjamin Henry Grierson," *Chronicles of Oklahoma* 24 (Summer 1946): 205.

17. Sheridan to Sherman, May 9, 1873, Division of the Missouri, Letters Sent, RG 393, Records of United States Army; Sheridan to Sherman, March 18, 1870, Box 91, Sheridan Papers.

18. Sheridan to Sherman, March 18, 1870, Box 91, Sheridan Papers.

19. Ibid.

20. *Platte Journal* (Columbus, Nebr.), June 29, 1870; *Chicago Tribune*, April 25, 1870.

21. Prucha, *American Indian Policy in Crisis*, 50.

22. "Report of General James A. Hardie, Inspr. Genl. M.D. Mo. & enclosures," January 29, 1870, Box 91, Sheridan Papers; Robert J. Ege, *"Tell Baker to Strike Them Hard!": Incident on the Marias, 23 Jan. 1870*, 1–33; J. P. Dunn, Jr., *Massacres of the Mountains: A History of the Indian Wars of the Far West, 1815–1875*, 444–47; Wesley C. Wilson, "The U.S. Army and the Piegans: The Baker Massacre on the Marias, 1870," *North Dakota History* 32 (January 1965): 47–48; Paul A. Hutton, "Phil Sheridan's Pyrrhic Victory: The Piegan Massacre, Army Politics, and the Transfer Debate," *Montana: The Magazine of Western History* 32 (Spring 1982): 32–43; John C. Ewers, *The Blackfeet: Raiders of the Northwestern Plains*, 236–53.

23. Sherman to Sheridan, December 20, 1869, Box 39, Sheridan Papers.

24. Ezra J. Warner, *Generals in Blue: Lives of the Union Commanders*, 121–22. Colonel de Trobriand's western career, with but a brief mention of the Piegan troubles, is covered in Milo Milton Quaife, ed., *Army Life in Dakota: Selections from the Journal of Philippe Régis Denis de Keredern de Trobriand*, trans. George Francis Will. Also see Lucille M. Kane, ed. and trans., *Military Life in Dakota: The Journal of Philippe Régis de Trobriand*.

25. Sheridan to Sherman, February 28, 1870, Box 91; "Report of General Hardie," January 29, 1870, Sheridan Papers.

26. Sherman to Sheridan, December 20, 1869, Box 39, ibid.

27. Sheridan to Hancock, November 15, 1869, Box 91, ibid.

28. "Report of General Hardie," January 29, 1870, ibid.

29. Ibid.

30. Ibid.

31. Ege, *Strike Them Hard*, 37–45; Orrin H. Bonney and Lorraine Bonney, *Battle Drums and Geysers: The Life and Journals of Lt. Gustavus Cheyney Doane, Soldier and Explorer of the Yellowstone and Snake River Regions*, 22–25; Dunn. *Massacres of the Mountains*, 448–51; Ewers, *Blackfeet*, 249–51; Hutton, "Phil Sheridan's Pyrrhic Victory," 38–39.

32. Ege, *Strike Them Hard*, 45–57; Wilson, "U.S. Army and the Piegans," 49–52. For an Indian account, see James Willard Schultz, *Blackfeet and Buffalo: Memories of Life among the Indians*, ed. Keith C. Seele (Norman: University of Oklahoma Press, 1962), 282–305. Also see Thomas B. Marquis, *Custer, Cavalry, and Crows: The Story of William White*, ed. John A. Popovich, 31–34.

33. Sheridan to Sherman, January 29, 1870, Box 91; Sherman to Sheridan, January 29, 1870, Sheridan Papers.

34. Mardock, *Reformers and the Indian*, 67–68; Robert G. Athearn, *William Tecumseh Sherman and the Settlement of the West*, 278–79.

35. Sheridan to Sherman, February 28, 1870, Box 91, Sheridan Papers.

36. Ibid.

37. Prucha, *American Indian Policy in Crisis*, 27, 50, 52–53.

38. Mardock, *Reformers and the Indian*, 70.

39. Sherman to Sheridan, March 5, 7, 1870, Box 91, Sheridan Papers; see also Sheridan to Sherman, February 28, 1870. In September 1870 Sully was removed from his position as Montana Indian superintendant and transferred to Reconstruction duty in Louisiana. Late in 1873 he was ordered to take command at Fort Vancouver, Washington, and remained there until his death in April 1879. Sheridan and Sherman were limited by Sully's rank and reputation from doing much more than shunting him aside and attempting to keep him out of Indian affairs. Langdon Sully, *No Tears for the General: The Life of Alfred Sully, 1821–1879*, 218–19, 234.

40. Sherman to Sheridan, March 12, 1870, Box 91, Sheridan Papers.

41. Sheridan to Sherman, March 27, 1870, enclosing Baker to Sheridan, March 23, 1870, ibid.

42. *New York Times*, February 24, March 10, 12, 1870.

43. Mardock, *Reformers and the Indian*, 71–72, 73.

44. Ibid., 71, 73.

45. Ibid., 73.

46. Ege, *Strike Them Hard*, 51–52.

47. Athearn, *Sherman and the West*, 281.

48. Prucha, *American Indian Policy in Crisis*, 48–52; Utley, *Frontier Regulars*, 188–92; Clyde A. Milner II, *With Good Intentions: Quaker Work among the Pawnees, Otos, and Omahas in the 1870s*, 1–26.

49. James H. Bradley, *The March of the Montana Column: A Prelude to the Custer Disaster*, 55–63.

CHAPTER 9

1. *Personal Memoirs of P. H. Sheridan, General, United States Army* 2:359. For Grant's opinion of Napoleon III, see Adam Badeau, *Grant in Peace: From Appomattox to Mount McGregor: A Personal Memoir*, 188–89.

2. Moritz Busch, *Bismarck: Some Secret Pages of His History* 2:67–68.

3. Ibid., 71–72, 74.

4. "Sheridan at the Battle of Gravelotte," *Army and Navy Register* 4 (August 4, 1883): 4; Sheridan, *Personal Memoirs* 2:370–77.

5. Sheridan, *Personal Memoirs* 2:422–23.

6. Richard Robins, comp., *Toasts and Responses at Banquets Given Lieut.-Gen. P. H. Sheridan, United States Army, "Commander," by the Military Order of the Loyal Legion of the United States, Commandery of the State of Illinois, March 6, 1882–3*, 74; Sheridan, *Personal Memoirs* 2:381–83; Busch, *Bismarck*, 2:72.

7. Busch, *Bismarck*, 2:127–28.

8. Ibid., 128.

9. Michael Howard, *The Franco-Prussian War: The German Invasion of France, 1870–1871* (London, Rupert Hart-Davis, 1961), 380.

10. Sheridan, *Personal Memoirs* 2: 432–36.

11. Ibid., 446–47.

12. Sherman to Sheridan, April 1, 1871, Box 39, Sheridan Papers.

13. Sheridan to Grant, September 13, 1870, Box 83, ibid.

14. Frank A. Burr and Richard J. Hinton, *The Life of Gen. Philip H. Sheridan: Its Romance and Reality*, 355.

15. Marguerite Merington, ed., *The Custer Story: The Life and Intimate Letters of General George A. Custer and His Wife Elizabeth*, 239.

16. Sheridan, *Personal Memoirs* 2:362–453. Also see Philip H. Sheridan, "From Gravelotte to Sedan," *Scribner's Magazine* 4 (November 1888): 515–35, for an illustrated excerpt from the memoirs.

17. Henry Eugene Davies, *Ten Days on the Plains*, 15–16.

18. James T. King, *War Eagle: A Life of General Eugene A. Carr*, 125–26; Don Russell, *The Lives and Legends of Buffalo Bill*, 170–73.

19. Davies, *Ten Days*, 29.

20. *The Life of Hon. William F. Cody, Known as Buffalo Bill, the Famous Hunter, Scout, and Guide: An Autobiography*, 282.

21. Russell, *Buffalo Bill*, 173; Davies, *Ten Days*, 25, 46, 61–62.

22. Davies, *Ten Days*, 66.

23. Sherman to Sheridan, September 16, October 16, 1871, Box 39, Sheridan Papers.

24. Mabel McIlvaine, comp., *Reminiscences of Chicago during the Great Fire*, xxiii; Philip H. Sheridan and Michael V. Sheridan, *Personal Memoirs of Philip Henry Sheridan, General, United States Army: New and Enlarged Edition, with an Account of His Life from 1871 to His Death, in 1888* 2:471–72; Robert H. Woody, ed., "A Description of the Chicago Fire of 1871," *Mississippi Valley Historical Review* 33 (March 1947): 612.

25. Sheridan to William W. Belknap, October 9, 1871, Philip H. Sheridan Collection; Sheridan to Belknap, October 12, 1871, Division of the Missouri, Letters Sent, RG 393, Records of United States Army; George Forsyth to Pope, October 23, 1871, Box 45, Sheridan Papers; H. C. Greiner, *General Phil Sheridan as I Knew Him, Playmate-Comrade-Friend*, 402. The loss of his personal

and professional papers was especially grievous to Sheridan, and much effort was expended in duplicating these records. Corporal Drennan and Private Jesse M. Clark spent several months in the War Department archives making copies of all pertinent letters, endorsements, and reports. A long list of officers were also requested to send copies of letters and reports to Sheridan, as was the adjutant general's office. George Forsyth to Adjutant General, October 30, 1871, Box 45; George Forsyth to Townsend, July 9, 1872, Sheridan Papers. A list of officers written to for copies of correspondence is in Box 7, Sheridan Papers.

26. Sheridan and Sheridan, *Memoirs* 2:472–73.

27. Sheridan to H. W. Halleck, October 12, 1871; Sheridan to Francis T. Sherman, October 11, 1871; Sheridan to Adjutant General, October 25, 1871, Division of the Missouri, Letters Sent, RG 393, Records of United States Army; Sheridan to G. D. Ruggles, October 9, 1871, Sheridan Collection; James B. Fry to Francis T. Sherman, October 11, 1871, folder 1, James F. Aldrich Collection. The muster rolls, orders, and reports of the First Regiment of Chicago Volunteers, or Sheridan's Guards, are in the Chicago Fire Guards Collection.

28. Sheridan to Grant, October 11, 1871, Division of the Missouri, Letters Sent, RG 393, Records of United States Army; Sheridan and Sheridan, *Memoirs* 2:473; Sheridan to Military Storekeeper, Jeffersonville, Indiana, October 9, 1871; Sheridan to Col. Penrose, October 9, 1871, Sheridan Collection.

29. Sherman to Sheridan, October 16, 1871, Box 39, Sheridan Papers.

30. Sheridan and Sheridan, *Memoirs* 2:475–76.

31. McIlvaine, *Chicago during the Fire*, 90–91.

32. Burr and Hinton, *Life of Sheridan*, 357.

33. John M. Palmer to R. B. Mason, October 21, 1871; Mason to Sheridan, November 22, 1871; Sheridan to Belknap, November 18, 1871, Box 6, Sheridan Papers.

34. Roscoe Conkling to Sheridan, November 11, 1871, ibid.

35. Sheridan and Sheridan, *Memoirs* 2:480–83; Richard O'Connor, *Sheridan the Inevitable*, 314–15.

36. Sheridan to Belknap, November 18, 1871, Box 6, Sheridan Papers.

37. Sherman to Sheridan, October 16, 1871, Box 39, ibid.

38. For an overview of the grand duke's visit, see William F. Zornow, "When the Czar and Grant Were Friends," *Mid-America* 43 (July 1961): 164–81. For a contemporary account, compiled from newspaper clippings, see *His Imperial Highness the Grand Duke Alexis in the United States of America during the Winter of 1871–72* (Cambridge, Mass., 1872), reprinted as *The Grand Duke Alexis in the United States* (New York, Interland Publishing, 1972).

39. Sheridan and Sheridan, *Memoirs* 2:485–86; Russell, *Buffalo Bill*, 175.

40. Russell, *Buffalo Bill*, 175; Cody, *Life of Hon. William F. Cody*, 295–98.

41. *Grand Duke Alexis in the United States*, 152–57.

42. For details of the hunt, see ibid., 157–59; Cody, *Life of Hon. William*

F. Cody, 295–305; Russell, *Buffalo Bill*, 174–84; Sheridan and Sheridan, *Memoirs* 2:484–93; James Albert Hadley, "A Royal Buffalo Hunt," *Transactions of the Kansas State Historical Society* 10 (1907–1908): 564–80; John I. White, "Red Carpet for a Romanoff," *American West* 9 (January 1972): 5–9; Marshall Sprague, *A Gallery of Dudes*, 95–117.

43. Cody, *Life of Hon. William F. Cody*, 305–08.

44. Ibid., 312; Russell, *Buffalo Bill*, 180–84.

45. Hadley, "A Royal Buffalo Hunt," 577–78.

46. Sheridan to Belknap, January 27, 1872, Box 7; Sheridan to Simon Cameron, June 22, 1873, Box 9; Count Henry d'Offenberg to Sheridan, June 27, 1873, Box 9, Sheridan Papers.

47. A. M. Gibson, *The Kickapoos: Lords of the Middle Border*, 179–207.

48. Augur to Sheridan, June 4, 1873, Division of the Missouri, Special File, Box 13, RG 393, Records of United States Army; Gibson, *Kickapoos*, 208–35.

49. Sheridan to Sherman, July 2, 1878, Box 19, Sheridan Papers.

50. R. G. Carter, *On the Border with Mackenzie; or, Winning West Texas from the Comanches*, 419.

51. Sheridan, *Personal Memoirs* 2:89.

52. *Personal Memoirs of U. S. Grant* 2:541. For Mackenzie's Civil War career, see Ezra J. Warner, *Generals in Blue: Lives of the Union Commanders*, 301–3; Francis B. Heitman, *Historical Register and Dictionary of the United States Army, from Its Organization, September 29, 1789, to March 2, 1903* 1:672; Sheridan, *Personal Memoirs* 2:89, 155, 158, 162, 175, 187–88, 192; Ernest Wallace, *Ranald S. Mackenzie on the Texas Frontier*, 7–11; Ernest Wallace, ed., *Ranald S. Mackenzie's Official Correspondence Relating to Texas*, vol. 1; J. Evetts Haley, *Men of Fiber* (El Paso, Tex., Carl Hertzog, 1963), 20–24.

53. Robert M. Utley, *Frontier Regulars: The United States Army and the Indian, 1866–1891*, 209–12; Wallace, *Mackenzie*, 19–89; Carter, *On the Border with Mackenzie*, 421.

54. Pope to Sheridan, July 25, 1876, Division of the Missouri, Special File, Box 16, RG 393, Records of United States Army.

55. Sheridan to Robert Lincoln, December 8, 1881, Box 30, Sheridan Papers. Also see Edward S. Wallace, "General Ranald Slidell Mackenzie: Indian Fighting Cavalryman," *Southwestern Historical Quarterly* 56 (January 1953): 378–96.

56. Sheridan to Belknap, February 24, 1873, Box 8, Sheridan Papers.

57. Carter, *On the Border with Mackenzie*, 416–17.

58. Ibid., 422–23. R. G. Carter, who was Mackenzie's acting adjutant at the time, was not present at the meeting but was given a detailed version several days afterward by the colonel. Carter was sworn to secrecy by Mackenzie and was the only officer in the regiment to know of the planned border crossing until it occurred (ibid., 423–24). Although Sheridan could not order Mackenzie to violate international law by crossing the border, there is no doubt that he

meant for the colonel to go over. He would later tell a friend in Chicago "that Mackenzie was going over," several days before the raid occurred. Sheridan to Augur, May 27, 1873, Division of the Missouri, Letters Sent, RG 393, Records of United States Army.

59. Carter, *On the Border with Mackenzie*, 428–60; Wallace, *Mackenzie*, 97–104; Gibson, *Kickapoos*, 239–44; Ernest Wallace and Adrian S. Anderson, "R. S. Mackenzie and the Kickapoos: The Raid into Mexico in 1873," *Arizona and the West* 7 (Summer 1965): 105–26. For Mackenzie's report, see Wallace, ed., *Mackenzie's Official Correspondence*, 1: 167–71.

60. Wallace, ed., *Mackenzie's Official Correspondence* 1:166.

61. Sheridan to Augur, May 27, 1873, Division of the Missouri, Letters Sent, RG 393, Records of United States Army.

62. Sheridan to Belknap, May 28, 1873, Box 9, Sheridan Papers; Sheridan to Belknap, May 27, 1873, Division of the Missouri, Letters Sent, RG 393, Records of United States Army.

63. Sheridan to Sherman, June 5, 1873, Box 9, Sheridan Papers.

64. Sherman to Sheridan, June 3, 1873, Box 39, ibid.

65. Utley, *Frontier Regulars*, 286.

66. Belknap to Sheridan, May 31, 1873, Box 9, Sheridan Papers.

67. Wallace and Anderson, "Mackenzie and the Kickapoos," 120–22. The Texas legislative resolution is reprinted in Wallace, ed., *Mackenzie's Official Correspondence* 1:189–90.

68. Sheridan to Augur, June 16, 1873, Division of the Missouri, Letters Sent, RG 393, Records of United States Army. See also Sheridan to Sherman, June 10, 14, 1873; Sheridan to Augur, June 14, 1873, ibid.; Gibson, *Kickapoos*, 245–48.

69. Gibson, *Kickapoos*, 249–52.

CHAPTER 10

1. George A. Armes, *Ups and Downs of an Army Officer*, 2.

2. Sherman to Hancock, January 24, 1867, Grierson Papers, Newberry Library; Ezra J. Warner, *Generals in Blue: Lives of the Union Commanders*, 189–90, William H. Leckie, *The Buffalo Soldiers: A Narrative of the Negro Cavalry in the West*, 7–8. Also see Carolyn Thomas Foreman, "General Benjamin Henry Grierson, *Chronicles of Oklahoma* 24 (Summer 1946): 195–218; Frank M. Temple, "Colonel Grierson in the Southwest," *Panhandle-Plains Historical Review* 30 (1957): 27–54; and *Brief Record of General Grierson's Services during and since the War, with Special Testimonials and Recommendations from General Officers, Senators, Representatives, and Other Officials, 1861 to 1882* (n.p., n.d.).

3. Grierson to Alice Grierson, November 18, 1871, Benjamin H. Grierson Papers, Illinois State Historical Society.

4. Leckie, *Buffalo Soldiers*, 14–15.

5. Grierson to Alice Grierson, December 21, 1868, Grierson Papers, Newberry Library.

6. Grierson to Alice Grierson, June 21, 1875, Grierson Papers, Illinois State Historical Society.

7. Ibid.

8. Anson Mills, *My Story*, ed. C. H. Clandy, 182.

9. Grierson to Alice Grierson, April 6, 1869; Grierson to Felix Brunot, August ———, 1869; Alvord to Grierson, April 24, 1869; Grierson to John Grierson, February 23, 1870; Grierson to Alice Grierson, April 2, 1869, Grierson Papers, Newberry Library.

10. Grierson to Lawrie Tatum, September 30, 1869, Grierson Papers, ibid.

11. Foreman, "General Grierson,"205–6; Lawrie Tatum, *Our Red Brothers and the Peace Policy of President Ulysses S. Grant*, 30–31.

12. Grierson to Lawrie Tatum, September 30, 1869, Grierson Papers, Newberry Library.

13. Grierson to Brunot, November 22, 1872, ibid.

14. Brunot to Grierson, June 18, May 12, 1870; Grierson to Tatum, September 30, 1869, ibid.

15. For an account of Kiowa and Comanche raids in the 1869–71 period, see Rupert Norval Richardson, *The Comanche Barrier to South Plains Settlement: A Century and a Half of Savage Resistance to the Advancing White Frontier* (Glendale, Calif., Arthur H. Clark 1933), 335–47; William H. Leckie, *The Military Conquest of the Southern Plains*, 136–45; W. S. Nye, *Carbine and Lance: The Story of Old Fort Sill*, 106–32.

16. Tatum, *Our Red Brothers*, 35.

17. Foreman, "General Grierson," 305–6; Nye, *Carbine and Lance*, 117.

18. Leckie, *Military Conquest*, 146.

19. Temple, "Colonel Grierson," 34; Nye, *Carbine and Lance*, 114; Leckie, *Buffalo Soldiers*, 54.

20. Nye, *Carbine and Lance*, 114–15, 134.

21. Robert G. Athearn, *William Tecumseh Sherman and the Settlement of the West*, 289–90; Leckie, *Military Conquest*, 147.

22. Nye, *Carbine and Lance*, 124; R. G. Carter, *On the Border with Mackenzie; or, Winning West Texas from the Comanches*, 76–78.

23. Nye, *Carbine and Lance*, 126–32; Carter, *On the Border with Mackenzie*, 80–82.

24. Carter, *On the Border with Mackenzie*, 83–84; Tatum, *Our Red Brothers*, 114; Athearn, *Sherman and the Settlement of the West*, 290–92.

25. Tatum, *Our Red Brothers*, 116–17.

26. The dramatic arrest of the Kiowas is covered in Richard Henry Pratt, *Battlefield and Classroom: Four Decades with the American Indian, 1867–1904*, ed. Robert M. Utley, 43–46; Nye, *Carbine and Lance*, 136–43; Carter, *On the Border with Mackenzie*, 85–89; Leckie, *Buffalo Soldiers*, 59–62. Reports on the

arrest and transport of the Kiowas to Texas are reprinted in Ernest Wallace, ed., *Ranald Mackenzie's Official Correspondence relating to Texas* 1:27–31.

27. Sherman to Grierson, June 23, 1871, Grierson Papers, Newberry Library.

28. Carter, *On the Border with Mackenzie*, 99–103; Mildred P. Mayhall, *The Kiowas*, 235–36; J'Nell Pate, "Indians on Trial in a White Man's Court," *Great Plains Journal* 14 (Fall 1974): 56–71. Also see Carl Coke Rister, "The Significance of the Jacksboro Indian Affair of 1871," *Southwestern Historical Quarterly* 29 (January 1926): 181–200.

29. Sherman to Sheridan, April 1, 1871, Box 39, Sheridan Papers; Raphael Thian, *Notes Illustrating the Military Geography of the United States, 1813–1880*, 99–100.

30. Ernest Wallace, *Ranald S. Mackenzie on the Texas Frontier*, 39–40, 62–64; *Army and Navy Journal* 13 (April 1, 1876): 551; Wallace, ed., *Mackenzie's Official Correspondence* 1:44.

31. Grierson to Alice Grierson, November 25, 1871, Grierson Papers, Illinois State Historical Society; L. H. Carpenter to Grierson, June 27, 1872, Grierson Papers, Newberry Library.

32. Carter, *On the Border with Mackenzie*, 123–24, 129.

33. Wallace, *Mackenzie* 42–43; Leckie, *Buffalo Soldiers*, 64.

34. Sheridan to Augur, May 28, 1872, Box 7, Sheridan Papers.

35. William H. Beck to Grierson, September 21, 1873, July 23, 1874; Carpenter to Grierson, June 27, 1872, Grierson Papers, Newberry Library; Leckie, *Buffalo Soldiers*, 68–69; Homer K. Davidson, *Black Jack Davidson: A Cavalry Commander on the Western Frontier*, 169–72.

36. Grierson to Alice Grierson, June 21, 1875, Grierson Papers, Illinois State Historical Society.

37. Sheridan to Pope, September 2, 1874, Box 11, Sheridan Papers.

38. Sheridan to Belknap, July 21, November 8, 1874, Box 11; Sheridan to Q. A. Gillmore, February 28, 1875, Box 13, ibid.

39. Sheridan to Belknap, July 28, 1874, Box 11, ibid.

40. Wallace, *Mackenzie*, 45–56; Leckie, *Conquest*, 158–61.

41. Nye, *Carbine and Lance*, 152–55; Leckie, *Conquest*, 161–63.

42. Alvord to Grierson, June 9, 1872, Grierson Papers, Newberry Library.

43. Sheridan to Adjutant General, June 19, 1872, Box 7, Sheridan Papers.

44. Nye, *Carbine and Lance*, 157.

45. Tatum, *Our Red Brothers*, 125–26; Nye, *Carbine and Lance*, 155–57; Leckie, *Conquest*, 163–65.

46. Tatum, *Our Red Brothers*, 125–26; Nye, *Carbine and Lance*, 154–55.

47. Sheridan to War Department, July 11, 1872, Box 7, Sheridan Papers.

48. Sheridan to War Department, July 8, 1872, ibid.

49. Wallace, *Mackenzie*, 78–87; Tatum, *Our Red Brothers*, 133–44; Leckie, *Conquest*, 165–73; Wallace, ed., *Mackenzie's Official Correspondence* 1:141–45, 149–55.

50. Sheridan to Edmund J. Davis, April 26, 1872, Box 7, Sheridan Papers.

51. Pate, "Indians on Trial," 66–67; Mayhall, *Kiowas*, 240–43.

52. Tatum, *Our Red Brothers*, 160.

CHAPTER 11

1. Donald J. Berthrong, *The Southern Cheyennes*, 379–87; James L. Haley, *The Buffalo War: The History of the Red River Indian Uprising of 1874*, 21–58.

2. The fight at Adobe Walls, generally regarded as the opening of the Red River War, is covered in detail in Haley, *Buffalo War*, 59–78; Wayne Gard, *The Great Buffalo Hunt*, 166–81; J'Nell Pate, "The Battles of Adobe Walls," *Great Plains Journal* 16 (Fall 1976): 2–44.

3. Haley, *Buffalo War*, 77, 101–2.

4. Sheridan to Adjutant General, October 13, 1881, Box 29, Sheridan Papers. See also Sherman to Sheridan, May 2, 1873, Box 39, ibid.; Frank Gilbert Roe, *The North American Buffalo: A Critical Study of the Species in Its Wild State* (Toronto, University of Toronto Press, 1951), 416–46, 804–16; Gard, *Great Buffalo Hunt*, 206–16. John R. Cook, himself a buffalo hunter in the 1870s, left an account of an 1875 message from Sheridan to the Texas state legislature that is often quoted as an example of the military's attitude toward the destruction of the great buffalo herds. The legislature was considering a bill to protect the buffalo, which Sheridan protested. Instead of outlawing the slaughter, declared Sheridan, the legislature would strike a medal, with a dead buffalo pictured on one side and a discouraged Indian on the other, and bestow it upon the hunters. John R. Cook, *The Border and the Buffalo: An Untold Story of the Southwest Plains*, 163–64.

5. Sheridan to Sherman, July 18, 1874; Sheridan to Sherman, July 16, 1874; Sheridan to Pope, July 18, 24, 1874, Division of the Missouri, Letters Sent, RG 393, Records of United States Army; Sherman to Sheridan, July 23, 1874, Box 39, Sheridan Papers; Richard N. Ellis, *General Pope and U.S. Indian Policy*, 183–85.

6. Sheridan to Sherman, July 29, 1874, Box 11, Sheridan Papers; Sheridan to Sherman, July 16, 1874, Division of the Missouri, Letters Sent, RG 393, Records of United States Army; Sheridan to Sherman, August 1, September 12, 1874, Box 39, Sheridan Papers.

7. Sherida to Pope, August 21, 1874, Division of the Missouri, Letters Sent, RG 393, Records of United States Army.

8. Ibid.

9. Sherman to Sheridan, September 12, 1874, Box 39; Sheridan to Sherman, September 7, 1874, Box 11, Sheridan Papers.

10. Sheridan to Sherman, July 18, 1874; Sheridan to Pope, July 21, 1874, enclosing Sherman to Sheridan, July 20, 1874, Division of the Missouri, Letters Sent, RG 393, Records of United States Army.

11. Sherman to Sheridan, July 23, 1874, Box 39, Sheridan Papers; Sheridan to Sherman, August 13, 1874, Division of the Missouri, Letters Sent, RG 393, Records of United States Army.

12. Sheridan to Pope, July 21, 24, 1874, Division of the Missouri, Letters Sent, RG 393, Records of United States Army; Robert M. Utley, *Frontier Regulars; The United States Army and the Indian, 1866–1891*, 220; Haley, *Buffalo War*, 104–6; *Report of the Secretary of War [1874]* 1:25.

13. Sheridan to Augur, July 21, 1874; Sheridan to Pope, August 13, 1874, Division of the Missouri, Letters Sent, RG 393, Records of United States Army; *Report of the Secretary of War [1874]*, 1:27.

14. Sheridan to Pope, July 21, August 13, 1874, Division of the Missouri, Letters Sent, RG 393, Records of United States Army; Also see Ernest Wallace, ed., *Ranald S. Mackenzie's Official Correspondence relating to Texas* 2:77–78.

15. Sheridan to R. Williams, October 5, 6, 1874; Sheridan to Pope, August 13, 1874; Sheridan to George Russell, August 13, 1874, Division of the Missouri, Letters Sent, RG 393, Records of United States Army.

16. Sheridan to Pope, July 24, 1874, ibid.

17. Sheridan to Pope, August 13, 1874, ibid.; *Personal Recollections and Observations of General Nelson A. Miles*, 163–64, 168.

18. W. S. Nye, *Carbine and Lance: The Story of Old Fort Sill*, 206–10; Haley, *Buffalo War*, 114–23; Ellis, *General Pope*, 187.

19. Virginia Weisel Johnson, *The Unregimented General: A Biography of Nelson A. Miles*, 59. The story of Miles's campaign is covered in detail in Miles, *Personal Recollections*, 156–74; William H. Leckie, *The Military Conquest of the Southern Plains*, 208–16; Nye, *Carbine and Lance*, 213–21; Robert C. Carriker, *Fort Supply Indian Territory: Frontier Outpost on the Plains*, 93–102; Haley, *Buffalo War*, 125–67

20. Sheridan to R. Williams, October 6, 1874, Box 11, Sheridan Papers.

21. *Report of the Secretary of War [1874]* 1:26.

22. Sheridan to Belknap, November 8, 1874, Box 11, Sheridan Papers. For Davidson's campaign, see Joseph A. Stout, Jr., "Davidson's Campaign," *Red River Valley Historical Review* 3 (Spring 1978): 194–201.

23. Richard Henry Pratt, *Battlefield and Classroom: Four Decades with the American Indian, 1867–1904*, 70–72.

24. Sheridan to Sherman, October 25, 1874; Sheridan to Davidson, October 25, 1874, Division of the Missouri, Letters Sent, RG 393, Records of United States Army. For Mackenzie's campaign, see Ernest Wallace, *Ranald Mackenzie on the Texas Frontier*, 128–49; R. G. Carter, *On the Border with Macken-*

zie; or, Winning West Texas from the Comanches, 475–96; Haley, *Buffalo War*, 172–83; Wallace, ed., *Mackenzie's Official Correspondence* 2:112–24. Also see W. A. Thompson, "Scouting with Mackenzie," *Journal of the United States Cavalry Association* 10 (December 1897); 429–33.

25. Sherman to Sheridan, October 30, 1874; Box 39; Sherman to Sheridan, September 12, 1874, Box 39, Sheridan Papers.

26. Sheridan to Columbus Delano, November 14, 1874, Box 11, ibid.; Ben Clark, Field Notes, folder 4, Box 2, Camp Mss.

27. Sheridan to Belknap, October 5, 1874; Belknap to Sheridan, October 6, 1874, Division of the Missouri, Special File, Box 5, RG 393, Records of United States Army.

28. Sheridan to Pope, December 3, 1874; Sheridan to Augur, December 4, 15, 1874, Letters Sent; Augur to Sheridan, December 10, 1874, Division of the Missouri, Special File, Box 5, RG 393, Records of United States Army.

29. Sheridan to Richard Coke, October 30, 1874; James Forsyth to C. H. Carlton, October 30, 1874, Division of the Missouri, Letters Sent, RG 393, Records of United States Army; Sheridan to Delano, November 14, 1874, Box 11, Sheridan Papers; J'Nell Pate, "Indians on Trial in a White Man's Court," *Great Plains Journal* 16 (Fall 1976): 68. For a brief account of Satanta's career, see Donald Worcester, "Satanta," in *American Indian Leaders: Studies in Diversity*, ed. R. David Edmunds, 107–30.

30. *Report of the Secretary of War [1874]* 1:26.

31. Berthrong, *Southern Cheyennes*, 394.

32. Sheridan to Miles, October 30, 1874; Sheridan to J. Taylor, October 25, 1874, Division of the Missouri, Letters Sent, RG 393, Records of United States Army.

33. Sheridan to George Forsyth, November 18, 1874; Sheridan to Augur, November 18, 1874; Sheridan to Whipple, January 23, 1875; Sheridan to Richard Coke, December 16, 1874, March 25, 1875, ibid.; George Forsyth to Sheridan, December 1, 1874, Box 45, Sheridan Papers; Philip H. Sheridan, *Outline Descriptions of the Posts in the Military Division of the Missouri*, 178–79. Also see John Q. Anderson, "Fort Elliott, Texas: Last Guard of the Plains Indians," *Texas Military History* 2 (November 1962): 243–54.

34. George Forsyth to Sheridan, December 1, 1874, Box 45, Sheridan Papers; Miles, *Personal Recollections*, 172–81; Haley, *Buffalo War*, 186–205; Berthrong, *Southern Cheyennes*, 393–405; Leckie, *Conquest*, 226–30; Jerry L. Rogers, "The Indian Territory Expedition: Winter Campaigns, 1874–1875," *Texas Military History* 8, no. 4 (1970): 233–50.

35. William H. Leckie, "Buell's Campaign," *Red River Valley Historical Review* 3 (Spring 1978): 186–93; Wallace, *Mackenzie*, 150–66; Nye, *Carbine and Lance*, 225–35; Wallace, ed., *Mackenzie's Official Correspondence* 2:136–42, 154–58, 187–92.

36. Berthrong, *Southern Cheyennes*, 401–4.

37. Pratt, *Battlefield and Classroom*, 107; Haley, *Buffalo War*, 213–14;

Nye, *Carbine and Lance*, 231; Arrell Morgan Gibson, "The St. Augustine Prisoners," *Red River Valley Historical Review* 3 (Spring 1978): 259–70.

38. Sheridan to Belknap, April 30, 1875, Special File, Box 5; Sheridan to Pratt, July 18, 1875; Sheridan to A. A. Humphreys, July 17, 1875, Division of the Missouri, Letters Sent, RG 393, Records of United States Army; Pratt, *Battlefield and Classroom*, 106–11. For biographical data on Pratt, see the introduction to *Battlefield and Classroom* by Robert M. Utley, ix–xviii; Elaine Goodale Eastman, *Pratt: The Red Man's Moses* (Norman: University of Oklahoma Press, 1935).

39. Sherman to Sheridan, November 12, 1875, Box 39, Sheridan Papers. For the sale of Indian horses to purchase sheep, an experiment which ended in failure, see Sheridan to Pope, August 14, 1875; Sheridan to Benjamin Corven, August 10, 1875; Sheridan to R. Williams, August 14, 1875, Division of the Missouri, Letters Sent, RG 393, Records of United States Army; Wallace, *Mackenzie*, 171.

40. Sheridan to Whipple, November 23, 1875, Box 85, Sheridan Papers; Adjutant General's Office, *Chronological List of Actions, &c., with Indians from January 15, 1837 to January, 1891*, 57–59.

CHAPTER 12

1. Ella Lonn, *Reconstruction in Louisiana after 1868*, 206–91; Joe Gray Taylor, *Louisiana Reconstructed, 1863–1877*, 253–304; James E. Sefton, *The United States Army and Reconstruction, 1865–1877*, 239–40; Joseph G. Dawson III, *Army Generals and Reconstruction: Louisiana, 1862–1877*, 113–19.

2. For Grant's mind-set on Louisiana affairs, see William B. Hesseltine, *Ulysses S. Grant, Politician*, 345–50.

3. Sefton, *Army and Reconstruction*, 240; Richard O'Connor, *Sheridan the Inevitable*, 328–29; *Senate Exec. Docs.*, 43d Cong., 2d sess., no. 13, pp. 19–20.

4. Rachel Sherman Thorndike, ed., *The Sherman Letters: Correspondence between General and Senator Sherman from 1837 to 1891*, 342; Sherman to Sheridan, January 2, 1875, Box 39, Sheridan Papers; Sheridan to Sherman, January 12, 1875, Division of the Missouri, Letters Sent, RG 393, Records of United States Army.

5. Lonn, *Reconstruction in Louisiana*, 292.
6. Sheridan to Belknap, January 2, 1875, Box 12, Sheridan Papers.
7. Sheridan to Belknap, February 9, 1875, Box 13, ibid.
8. Sheridan to Belknap, January 2, 1875, Box 12; Sheridan to Belknap, February 9, 24, 1875, Box 13, ibid.
9. Taylor, *Louisiana Reconstructed*, 204–5; Lonn, *Reconstruction in Louisiana*, 295–97; Philip H. Sheridan and Michael V. Sheridan, *Personal Memoirs of Philip Henry Sheridan, General, United States Army: New and Enlarged*

Edition, with an Account of His Life from 1871 to His Death, in 1888 2:519–21;
Dawson, *Army Generals*, 203–5.

10. Taylor, *Louisiana Reconstructed*, 205; Sheridan and Sheridan,
Memoirs 2:521; Sefton, *Army and Reconstruction*, 241.

11. Sheridan to Belknap, January 4, 1875, Division of the Missouri,
Letters Sent, RG 393, Records of United States Army. Also see Sheridan and
Sheridan, *Memoirs* 2:522–33.

12. Sheridan to Belknap, January 5, 1875, Division of the Missouri,
Letters Sent, RG 393, Records of United States Army. For background on the
White League, see Taylor, *Louisiana Reconstructed*, 279–99. Sheridan borrowed
the word "banditti" from the attorney general's characterization of the insur-
gent Modoc Indians in 1873. Sheridan to Belknap, January 9, 1875, Box 12,
Sheridan Papers.

13. William S. McFeely, *Grant: a Biography*, 370–72; Robert M. Utley,
Frontier Regulars: The United States Army and the Indian, 1848–1865, 205–6.

14. George F. Hoar, *Autobiography of Seventy Years* 1:208.

15. Lonn, *Reconstruction in Louisiana*, 301–3; Dawson, *Army Generals*,
208.

16. O'Connor, *Sheridan*, 330; James Ford Rhodes, *History of the United
States from the Compromise of 1850*, 8 vols. (New York, 1900–1919), 6:122.

17. *Congressional Record*, 43d Cong., 2d sess., 331.

18. Ibid., 367–71.

19. Harry James Brown and Frederick D. Williams, eds., *The Diary of
James A. Garfield* 3:4, 6; Lonn, *Reconstruction in Louisiana*, 304.

20. Allan Nevins, *Hamilton Fish: The Inner History of the Grant Administration*, 753; Fred Grant to Sheridan, January 14, 1875, Box 12, Sheridan Papers;
Hesseltine, *Grant*, 353; Brown and Williams, eds., *Garfield Diary* 3:7. Sheridan
would have been shocked to discover that even his old friend Custer opposed
his Louisiana policies. Writing in confidence to a personal friend, Custer
delcared, "My blood boils within me with indignation when I think of the
unjust course now being pursued towards our brethren of the south. . . . There
is not a citizen in Louisiana . . . who more heartily disapproves of the recent
course of the Administration than I do." Custer to Lawrence Barrett, February
18, 1875, Graff Collection, Newberry Library, Chicago.

21. Sheridan to Belknap, January 6, 1875 Box 12; Belknap to Sheridan,
January 6, 1875, Box 10, Sheridan Papers.

22. Hoar, *Autobiography of Seventy Years* 1:208.

23. Lonn, *Reconstruction in Louisiana*, 300; *Proceedings of the State and
Assembly of the State of New York, on the Life and Services of Gen. Philip H. Sheridan,
Held at the Capitol, April 9, 1889*, 47.

24. Sheridan to Belknap, January 10, 1875, Box 12, Sheridan Papers.

25. Rhodes, *History of the United States* 7:125. Lawrence Barrett related
this incident to James Ford Rhodes.

26. James D. Richardson, *A Compilation of the Messages and Papers of the Presidents, 1789–1897*, 10 vols. (n.p., 1900), 7:311–12.

27. Ibid., 312.

28. Ibid., 312, 314.

29. Hesseltine, *Grant*, 354.

30. Rhodes, *History of the United States* 7:126. This was the second committee to visit New Orleans, The first had delivered a report on January 15 so critical of the Kellogg government that it proved embarrassing to the administration and the Republican Party. Thus a second committee was sent in hopes of obtaining a more agreeable final report.

31. Hoar, *Autobiography of Seventy Years*, 243–44; Hesseltine, *Grant*, 355–56; Taylor, *Louisiana Reconstructed*, 308–10; Lonn, *Reconstruction in Louisiana*, 339–79.

32. Sheridan to Orville Babcock, January 24, 1875, Box 12, Sheridan Papers.

33. Sheridan to Belknap, February 24, 1875, Box 13, Sheridan Papers.

34. Belknap to Sheridan, March 3, 1875, Box 13; Sheridan to Belknap, March 4, 1875, ibid. Also see Dawson, *Army Generals*, 212–15.

35. George Forsyth to Sheridan, March 28, 1875, Box 13, Sheridan Papers. For Sheridan's dedication to the cause of black suffrage, see Sheridan and Sheridan, *Memoirs* 2:523.

36. Hesseltine, *Grant*, 358.

37. Frank A. Burr and Richard J. Hinton, *The Life of Gen. Philip H. Sheridan: Its Romance and Reality*, 371–72.

38. Sherman to Sheridan, May 5, 1875, Box 39, Sheridan Papers.

39. *Army and Navy Journal* 12 (June 12, 1875): 701; O'Connor, *Sheridan*, 333–35; Burr and Hinton, *Life of Sheridan*, 373.

40. O'Connor, *Sheridan*, 334; Dawson, *Army Generals*, 222.

41. *Harper's Weekly* 19 (June 5, 1875); Albert Bigelow Paine, *Th. Nast: His Period and His Pictures*, 310–11.

42. Grierson to Alice Grierson, June 12, 1875, Grierson Papers, Illinois State Historical Society.

43. Vol. 29, p. 10, John G. Bourke Diaries; E. R. Hagemann, ed., *Fighting Rebels and Redskins: Experiences in Army Life of Colonel George B. Sanford, 1861–1892*, 269–70.

44. Sherman to Sheridan, July 18, 24, 1875, Box 39, Sheridan Papers.

45. Hesseltine, *Grant*, 418–19.

46. Ibid., 414. Also see McFeely, *Grant*, 446–48.

47. Sheridan and Sheridan, *Memoirs* 2:524–25; Dawson, *Army Generals*, 231, 237–39.

48. *Sen, Exec. Docs.*, 40th Cong., 1st sess., no. 14, p. 213.

49. Hesseltine, *Grant*, 415; Taylor, *Louisiana Reconstructed*, 492–93; Lonn, *Reconstruction in Louisiana*, 457–60; Paul L. Haworth, *The Hayes-Tilden Election*, 111–14.

50. Dawson, *Army Generals*, 240.

51. Haworth, *Hayes-Tilden*, 168–71, 187–88; Hoar, *Autobiography of Seventy Years* 1:369–70.

52. Sherman to Sheridan, November 8, 1876, Box 39, Sheridan Papers.

53. Sherman to Ellen Sherman, November 12, 1877, Sherman Family Papers.

54. Sheridan and Sheridan, *Memoirs* 2:580–81.

55. Sherman to Sheridan, December 11, 1876, Box 39, Sheridan Papers.

56. Ibid.

57. Ibid.; Sherman to Sheridan, December 21, 1876, ibid.

58. Hesseltine, *Grant*, 420–21; Haworth, *Hayes-Tilden*, 220–304; C. Vann Woodward, *Reunion and Reaction: The Compromise of 1877 and the End of Reconstruction* (Boston, Little, Brown, 1951).

59. Sherman to Sheridan, January 29, 1877, Box 39, Sheridan Papers.

60. Thorndike, ed., *Sherman Letters*, 343–44.

CHAPTER 13

1. Sheridan memorandum, December 7, 1872, Box 8, Sheridan Papers.

2. Sherman to Sheridan, June 13, 1870, Box 39, Sheridan Papers;

3. Sherman to Sheridan, May 2, 1873, Box 39, Sheridan Papers; Sheridan to Sherman, March 25, 1875, Division of the Missouri, Letters Sent, RG 393, Records of United States Army.

4. Augur to Hartsuff, March 12, 1870, Box 6, Sheridan Papers.

5. Sheridan to Sherman, April 14, 15, 1874, Box 11, ibid.

6. Sheridan to Sherman, June 11, 21, August 8, 1873, Box 9; Sheridan to War Department, May 27, 1873, Box 9, ibid.; Mark H. Brown, *The Plainsmen of the Yellowstone: A History of the Yellowstone Basin*, 197–209; Philip H. Sheridan, *Record of Engagements with Hostile Indians within the Military Division of the Missouri, from 1868 to 1882, Lieutenant-General P. H. Sheridan, Commanding*, 32–37.

7. Sheridan to Commissioner of Indian Affairs, December 6, 1872, Box 8, Sheridan Papers.

8. Sheridan to Sherman, June 11, 21, and August 8, 1873; Sheridan to War Department, May 27, 1873, Box 9, Sheridan Papers; Brown, *Plainsmen of the Yellowstone*, 197–209; Robert M. Utley, *Frontier Regulars: The United States Army and the Indian, 1866–1891*, 242–43; Sheridan, *Record of Engagements*, 32–37.

9. Sheridan to War Department, May 27, 1873, Box 9; Sheridan to Sherman, October 30, 1873, Box 10, Sheridan Papers.

10. Sherman to Sheridan, November 3, 1873, Box 39, ibid.

11. Olson, *Red Cloud*, 162–64.

12. Ibid., 164.

13. Sheridan to Ord, February 18, 1874, Division of the Missouri, Letters Sent, RG 393, Records of United States Army.

14. Sheridan to Sherman, February 18, 23, March 1, 1874; Sheridan to John E. Smith, February 21, 1874, ibid.

15. Sheridan to Sherman, February 26, March 2, 1874, ibid.; Sheridan to Sherman, March 4, 1874, Box 10, Sheridan Papers; George E. Hyde, *Red Cloud's Folk: A History of the Oglala Sioux Indians*, 213–14.

16. Sheridan to Sherman, March 3, 1874, Box 10, Sheridan Papers.

17. Ibid.

18. Sheridan to Sherman, March 31, 1874, ibid.

19. Olson, *Red Cloud*, 165.

20. Sherman to Sheridan, March 6, 1874, Box 39, Sheridan Papers.

21. Philip H. Sheridan, *Outline Descriptions of the Posts in the Military Division of the Missouri*, 111–14.

22. Sheridan to Wheeler, November 24, 1874, Box 11, Sheridan Papers.

23. Ibid.

24. Ibid.; *Report of the Secretary of War [1874]* 1:24. Sheridan disagreed with those who saw a direct cause-and-effect relationship between his decision to send Custer into the Black Hills and the Sioux War. "It is nonsense to suppose that the Indians now hostile are so from the Black Hills invasion," he wrote. "They wanted to fight, and have been preparing for it for years back. It is their profession, their glory and the only thing that stirs them up from absolute idleness." Sheridan to Sherman, July 18, 1876, Box 15, Sheridan Papers. President Grant and General Crook agreed with Sheridan that the discovery of gold in the Black Hills did not cause war with the Sioux. See also Edgar I. Stewart, *Custer's Luck*, 70–72; Mark H. Brown, "Muddled Men Have Muddied the Yellowstone's True Colors," *Montana: The Magazine of Western History* 11 (January 1961): 28–37.

25. Sheridan to Whipple, May 25, 1874; Sheridan to Sherman, March 25, 1875, Division of the Missouri, Letters Sent, RG 393, Records of United States Army; Sheridan to Wheeler, November 24, 1874, Box 11, Sheridan Papers.

26. Sheridan to Henry Banning, February 28, 1876, Box 14, Sheridan Papers; Sheridan to Sherman, March 3, 1875, Division of the Missouri, Letters Sent, RG 393, Records of United States Army; *Army and Navy Journal* 12 (April 3, 1875): 533.

27. Custer to Terry, September 2, 1874, Division of the Missouri, Special File, Box 1, RG 393, Records of United States Army; Watson Parker, *Gold in the Black Hills*, 28–29.

28. Sheridan to Terry, September 3, 1874, Division of the Missouri, Special File, Box 1, RG 393, Records of United States Army.

29. Parker, *Gold in the Black Hills*, 34–36; Donald Jackson, *Custer's Gold: The United States Cavalry Expedition of 1874*, 111–13. Also see Rodman Wilson

Paul, *Mining Frontiers of the Far West, 1848–1880* (New York, Holt, Rinehart and Winston, 1963), 176–78; Watson Parker, "The Majors and the Miners: The Role of the U.S. Army in the Black Hills Gold Rush," *Journal of the West* 11 (January 1972): 99–113.

30. Pinkney Lugenbel to Terry, March 5, 1875, Division of the Missouri, Special File, Box 1; Drum to Sheridan, March 12, 1875, Division of the Missouri, Letters Sent, RG 393, Records of United States Army.

31. Terry to Assistant Adjutant General, Division of the Missouri, March 9, 1875, Division of the Missouri, Special File, Box 1, RG 393, Records of United States Army. Also see John W. Bailey, *Pacifying the Plains: General Alfred Terry and the Decline of the Sioux, 1866–1890*, 91–109.

32. Sheridan to Sherman, March 25, 1875; Sheridan to Whipple, March 25, 1875, Division of the Missouri, Letters Sent, RG 393, Records of United States Army.

33. John G. Bourke to Crook, June 15, 1875, Box 13, Sheridan Papers; Merrill J. Mattes, *Indians, Infants, and Infantry: Andrew and Elizabeth Burt on the Frontier*, 200–204; Parker, *Gold in the Black Hills*, 63–65; Olson, *Red Cloud*, 200; May 12–June 22, 1875, John G. Bourke Diaries, vol. 121.

34. Sheridan to Sherman, July 3, 1875, Division of the Missouri, Letters Sent, RG 393, Records of United States Army.

35. Sheridan to Sherman, July 12, 1875, Letters Sent; Sherman to Sheridan July 12, 1875, Special File, Box 1; Sheridan to Crook, July 10, 1875, Letters Sent; Drum to Crook, July 13, 14, 1875, Letters Sent; Drum to Terry, July 14, 1875, Letters Sent, ibid.

36. Sherman to Sheridan, April 10, 1869, Box 39, Sheridan Papers; Lloyd Lewis, *Sherman: Fighting Prophet*, 601–2.

37. Russell F. Weigley, *History of the United States Army*, 192–94, 285–86; William Harding Carter, *The American Army*, 188–92.

38. Rachel Sherman Thorndike, ed., *The Sherman Letters: Correspondence between General and Senator Sherman from 1837 to 1891*, 331; Sherman to Sheridan, December 10, 1869, Box 39, Sheridan Papers; Sherman to Ellen Sherman, October 4, 1875, Sherman Family Papers.

39. Sherman to Sheridan, April 1, 1871, Box 39, Sheridan Papers. See also Sherman to Sheridan, October 7, 1872, ibid.; Robert G. Athearn, *William Tecumseh Sherman and the Settlement of the West*, 257–68; Thorndike, ed., *Sherman Letters*, 346–49.

40. Athearn, *Sherman and the Settlement of the West*, 263; Lewis, *Sherman*, 615.

41. Sheridan to Sherman, May 26, 1874, Box 11, Sheridan Papers.

42. Sherman to Sheridan, June 4, 1874, Box 39, ibid.

43. Ibid. Also see *Memoirs of W. T. Sherman, Written by Himself* 2:442–54.

44. Olson, *Red Cloud*, 201–13; Hyde, *Red Cloud's Folk*, 240–48; John G. Bourke, *On the Border with Crook*, 243–44.

45. It had been Sheridan's friend, Professor O. C. Marsh of Yale, whose

charges of corruption in the Indian Bureau's handling of the Red Cloud Agency had led to a congressional investigation and the eventual resignation of Delano and Smith. Although it is unlikely that he meant it as such, Marsh handsomely repaid Sheridan's favors in providing him military escorts by the blow he struck at the general's Indian Bureau enemies. See Olson, *Red Cloud*, 179–84, 189–98; Hyde, *Red Cloud's Folk*, 224–28, 231–39; Allan Nevins, *Hamilton Fish: The Inner History of the Grant Administration*, 776–77.

46. Sheridan to Terry, November 9, 1875; Sheridan to Sherman, November 13, 1875; Sherman to Sheridan, November 20, 1875, Box 39, Sheridan Papers. John S. Gray, *Centennial Campaign: The Sioux War of 1876*, 25–27; George W. Manypenny, *Our Indian Wards*, 301–8.

47. Watkins's report, and most other serial set documents relating to the Sioux War, are conveniently reprinted in John M. Carroll, ed., *General Custer and the Battle of the Little Big Horn: The Federal View*, 5–7. Watkins's report is so reflective of Sheridan's views that it might as well have been written by one of the general's staff officers, and it is interesting to note that during the Civil War Watkins had served as an adjutant in one of Sheridan's cavalry units. Gray, *Centennial Campaign*, 28; Francis B. Heitman, *Historical Register and Dictionary of the United States Army, from Its Organization, September 29, 1789, to March 2, 1903* 1:1008.

48. Carroll, ed., *Federal View*, 7–8.

49. Ben Clark, Field Notes, folder 4, Box 2, Camp Mss.; Sheridan to Crook, February 8, 1876; Sheridan to Pope, February 8, 1876, Division of the Missouri, Letters Sent, RG 393, Records of United States Army. For biographical data on Clark, see Hugh Lenox Scott, *Some Memories of a Soldier*, 176–79; J. W. Vaughn, *The Reynolds Campaign on Powder River*, 40–41; Sheridan, *Personal Memoirs of P. H. Sheridan, General, United States Army* 2:324; William E. Strong, *Canadian River Hunt*, xii, 10–11; March 3, 1876, Bourke Diaries 3:38–39.

50. Sheridan to Secretary of the Interior, February 4, 1876, Box 91; Sheridan to Terry, February 8, 1876, Box 14, Sheridan Papers; *Report of the Secretary of War [1876]* 4 vols. (Washington, 1876), 1:440–41.

CHAPTER 14

1. Drum to Terry, February 8, 1876; Drum to Crook, February 8, 1876; Sheridan to Terry, February 9, 1876, Division of the Missouri, Letters Sent, RG 393, Records of United States Army; Sheridan to Maginnis, February 26, 1876, Box 14, Sheridan Papers.

2. Detailed coverage of Gibbon's movement is provided by several good memoirs. See James H. Bradley, *The March of the Montana Column: A Prelude to the Custer Disaster*, 7–68; John Gibbon, *Gibbon on the Sioux Campaign of 1876*, 4–17; John F. McBlain, "With Gibbon on the Sioux Campaign of 1876,"

Journal of the United States Cavalry Association 9 (June 1896): 139–48; George A. Schneider, ed., *The Freeman Journal: The Infantry in the Sioux Campaign of 1876*.

3. J. W. Vaughn, *The Reynolds Campaign on Powder River, 43–165;* John G. Bourke, *On the Border with Crook*, 256–82.

4. Sheridan to Department of War, May 17, 1876, Box 15, Sheridan Papers; Sherman to Sheridan, May 22, 1876, Division of the Missouri, Letters Sent, RG 393, Records of United States Army. Reynolds was court-martialed in January 1877 and convicted. His sentence of suspension of rank and command for one year was remitted by President Grant. Reynolds retired in June 1877. Vaughn, *Reynolds Campaign*, 166–90.

5. Sheridan to Sherman, May 29, 1876, Box 15, Sheridan Papers; Sheridan to Crook, May 29, 1876, Division of the Missouri, Letters Sent, RG 393, Records of United States Army.

6. Sheridan to Sherman, May 29, 1876, Box 15, Sheridan Papers.

7. Sheridan to Crook, May 16, 1876; Sheridan to Townsend, May 13, 1876, Division of the Missouri, Letters Sent, RG 393, Records of United States Army.

8. Sherman to Sheridan, April 1, 1876, Box 39, Sheridan Papers.

9. Edgar I. Stewart, *Custer's Luck*, 120–21; Allan Nevins, *Hamilton Fish: The Inner History of the Grant Administration*, 804.

10. Marvin E. Kroeker, *Great Plains Command: William B. Hazen in the Frontier West*, 105–12; Nevins, *Hamilton Fish*, 805–7; William B. Hesseltine, *Ulysses S. Grant, Politician*, 395–96.

11. Stewart, *Custer's Luck*, 123–24; Jay Monaghan, *Custer: The Life of General George Armstrong Custer*, 364–65; John S. Gray, *Centennial Campaign: The Sioux War of 1876*, 62.

12. *Army and Navy Journal* 12 (April 1, 1876): 551; Kroeker, *Great Plains Command*, 145–47.

13. *Army and Navy Journal* 12 (April 1, 1876): 551; Stewart, *Custer's Luck*, 125–31; Kroeker, *Great Plains Command*, 148.

14. Sheridan to Townsend, April 27, 1876, Box 14, Sheridan Papers.

15. James Forsyth to Belknap, April 5, 1876, Box 45, Sheridan Papers. Custer clearly erred in his testimony concerning the visit, slanting it to place himself in the best possible light while discrediting Belknap. This portion of Custer's testimony does not hold up. Support of the Forsyth-Belknap version of the visit is in William E. Strong, *A Trip to the Yellowstone National Park in July, August, and September, 1875*, 158–60.

16. James Forsyth to Belknap, April 5, 1876, Box 45, Sheridan Papers.

17. Hesseltine, *Grant*, 381, 380–88; William S. McFeely, *Grant: A Biography* 407–16; Nevins, *Hamilton Fish*, 790–804.

18. Rachel Sherman Thorndike, ed., *The Sherman Letters: Correspondence between General and Senator Sherman from 1837 to 1891*, 348–49; Marguerite Merington, ed., *The Custer Story: The Life and Intimate Letters of General George A.*

Custer and His Wife Elizabeth, 281–82, 290–93. The appointment of post sutlers had been a major point of argument between Sherman and Belknap.

19. James Forsyth to Belknap, April 10, 1876, Box 45, Sheridan Papers. Belknap and his partisans were collecting material to build a perjury case against Custer and thus discredit his committee testimony before it was used at the impeachment trial. While Custer had slanted his testimony somewhat, he had not perjured himself, and Belknap's effort proved fruitless. Belknap's impeachment trial ended on August 1, 1876, in acquittal. It was almost a strict party vote, with most of those who voted for acquittal claiming that they had done so because Belknap's resignation had ended Senate jurisdiction over the case.

20. Sheridan to Terry, April 28, 29, 1876; Sheridan to Sherman, April 29, May 1, 1876, Division of the Missouri, Letters Sent, RG 393, Records of United States Army.

21. Sheridan to Sherman, May 2, 4, 1876; Drum to Terry, May 5, 1876, Missouri, Letters Sent, RG 393, Records of United States Army.

22. Custer to Grant, May 6, 1876, and Terry to Grant, May 6, 1876, enclosed in Sheridan to Townsend, May 7, 1876, ibid.; John W. Bailey, *Pacifying the Plains: General Alfred Terry and the Decline of the Sioux, 1866–1890*, 132.

23. Sheridan to Townsend, May 7, 1876, Division of the Missouri, Letters Sent, RG 393, Records of United States Army.

24. Loyd J. Overfield II, comp., *The Little Big Horn 1876: The Official Communications, Documents and Reports, with Rosters of the Officers and Troops of the Campaign*, 17.

25. Sheridan to Terry, May 16, 1876, Box 91, Sheridan Papers; Sheridan to Crook, May 16, 1876, Division of the Missouri, Letters Sent, RG 393, Records of United States Army; Gray *Centennial Campaign*, 89–90.

26. Sheridan to Townsend, May 8, 1876; Sheridan to Crook, May 29, 1876; Sheridan to Sherman, May 30, 1876, Division of the Missouri, Letters Sent, Records of United States Army; Bourke, *With Crook*, 286–306; James Olson, *Red Cloud and the Sioux Problem*, 218–19.

27. Sheridan to Pope, May 29, 1876, Division of the Missouri, Letters Sent, RG 393, Records of United States Army; James Forsyth to James Gilless, June 9, 1876, Box 45, Sheridan Papers; James T. King, *War Eagle: A Life of General Eugene A. Carr*, 153–54.

28. Sheridan to Crook, June 18, 20, 1876; James Forsyth to Townsend, June 18, 1876, Division of the Missouri, Letters Sent, RG 393, Records of United States Army; William F. Cody, *The Life of Hon. William F. Cody, Known as Buffalo Bill, the Famous Indian Hunter, Scout, and Guide: An Autobiography*, 341.

29. Sheridan to Crook, June 18, 1876; Sheridan to Carr, June 20, 1876, Division of the Missouri, Letters Sent, RG 393, Records of United States Army; James Forsyth to Carr, June 18, 1876, Box 45, Sheridan Papers. Also see Paul L. Hedren, *First Scalp for Custer: The Skirmish at Warbonnet Creek, Nebraska, July*

17, 1876, with a Short History of the Warbonnet Battlefield, 33–38; Charles King, "The Story of a March," *Journal of the United States Cavalry Association* 3 (March 1890): 121–29.

30. Sheridan to Townsend, June 23, 1876, enclosing Crook to Sheridan, June 19, 1876, Division of the Missouri, Letters Sent, RG 393, Records of United States Army. The Battle of the Rosebud is described in J. W. Vaughn, *With Crook at the Rosebud*, 47–171.

31. *Report of the Secretary of War [1876]* 1:442.

32. Sheridan to Terry, June 23, 1876; Sheridan to Robert Williams, June 23, 1876; Sheridan to Carr, June 23, 1876, Division of the Missouri, Letters Sent, RG 393, Records of United States Army.

33. Michael Sheridan to John Hawkins, June 25, 1876; Sheridan to Crook, June 28, 1876, ibid.

34. King, *War Eagle*, 158; Hedren, *First Scalp for Custer*, 47–48.

35. Don E. Alberts, *Brandy Station to Manila Bay: A Biography of General Wesley Merritt*, 225–27; Barry C. Johnson, comp., *Merritt and the Indian Wars: "Three Indian Campaigns" by Gen. Wesley Merritt, U.S.A.*, 4–11; Eben Swift, "General Wesley Merritt," *Journal of the United States Cavalry Association* 21 (March 1911): 29–37.

36. Michael Sheridan to Sheridan, June 20, 1876; Sheridan to Merritt, June 28, 1876, Division of the Missouri, Letters Sent, RG 393, Records of United States Army.

37. Drum to Sheridan, July 4, 1876, enclosing Terry to Sheridan, June 21, 1876, ibid.

38. Oliver Knight, *Following the Indian Wars: The Story of the Newspaper Correspondents among the Indian Campaigners*, 194–95; W. A. Graham, *The Custer Myth: A Source Book of Custeriana*, 349–51.

39. Drum to Sheridan, July 6, 1876, enclosing Terry to Sheridan, July 2, 1876, Division of the Missouri, Letters Sent, RG 393, Records of United States Army. Terry's official report on the battle, written June 27 and far more detailed and objective than his July 2 dispatch, had been sent by messenger to Fort Ellis and would not reach Sheridan until July 8. Drum to Sheridan, July 6, 1876, enclosing Smith to Drum, July 6, 1876; Drum to Adjutant General, July 8, 1876, enclosing Terry to Sheridan, June 27, 1876, ibid.

40. Stewart, *Custer's Luck*, 138.

41. Indian strength on the Little Big Horn has long been hotly debated. The most exhaustive investigation of the subject has been conducted by John S. Gray, who concluded that between seventeen hundred and two thousand warriors fought Custer (*Centennial Campaign*, 308–57).

42. The historical literature on the Battle of the Little Big Horn is massive. Two useful guides to the historiography are Tal Luther, *Custer High Spots* (Fort Collins, Colo., Old Army Press, 1972); and Robert M. Utley, *Custer and the Great Controversy: The Origin and Development of a Legend* (Los Angeles, Westernlore, 1962).

43. Knight, *Following the Indian Wars*, 218–19; Sherman to Sheridan, August 17, 1876, Box 39, Sheridan Papers.

44. Sheridan to Sherman, July 7, 1876, Division of the Missouri, Letters Sent, RG 393, Records of United States Army; H. C. Greiner, *General Phil Sheridan as I knew Him, Playmate-Comrade-Friend*, 357.

45. Sheridan to Sherman, July 7, 1876 (three letters); Sheridan to Sherman, July 6, 1876; Drum to Pope, July 7, 1876; Drum to George Ruggles, July 7, 1876; Drum to Sheridan, July 7, 1876; Sheridan to Terry, July 7, 1876, Division of the Missouri, Letters Sent, RG 393, Records of United States Army.

46. Sheridan to Sherman, July 18, 1876; Sheridan to Terry, July 24, 1876; Sheridan to Pope, July 24, 1876, ibid.

47. Sheridan to Sherman, July 19, 1876, ibid.; James T. King, "General Crook at Camp Cloud Peak: 'I Am at a Loss What to Do,' " in *Hostiles and Horse Soldiers: Indian Battles and Campaigns in the West*, comp. Lonnie J. White, 175–90; Hedren, *First Scalp for Custer*, 62–81; Charles King, *Campaigning with Crook*, 22–48.

48. Virginia Weisel Johnson, *The Unregimented General: A Biography of Nelson A. Miles*, 93–96; James Forsyth to Drum, August 11, 1876, Box 45, Sheridan Papers.

49. Bailey, *Pacifying the Plains*, 162–64; *Personal Recollections and Observations of General Nelson A. Miles*, 212–16.

50. Sheridan to Terry, July 7, 1876; Sheridan to Crook, July 10, 1876; Sheridan to Sherman, July 20, 1876, Division of the Missouri, Letters Sent, RG 393, Records of United States Army.

51. Sheridan to Sherman, July 18, 1876, Box 16, Sheridan Papers; Sheridan to Sherman, July 20, 1876, Division of the Missouri, Letters Sent, RG 393, Records of United States Army.

52. James T. King, *War Eagle*, 172; Charles King, *Campaigning with Crook*, 74–89; John F. Finerty, *War-Path and Bivouac; or, the Conquest of the Sioux*, 162–70; Bourke, *With Crook*, 351–62; Merrill J. Mattes, *Indians, Infants and Infantry: Andrew and Elizabeth Burt on the Frontier*, 223; Jerome A. Greene, *Slim Buttes, 1876; An Episode of the Great Sioux War*, 27–31.

53. John Gibbon, *Gibbon on the Sioux Campaign of 1876*, 59–60; Bailey, *Pacifying the Plains*, 166–67.

54. Sheridan to Terry, August 18, 1876, Division of the Missouri, Letters Sent, RG 393, Records of United States Army.

55. Sheridan to Sherman, August 10, 1876, ibid.

56. Ibid.; Sheridan to Sherman, August 30, 1876, ibid.

57. Sheridan to Crook, August 23, 1876; Sheridan to Sherman, August 30, 1876, ibid. A new Black Hills commission visited the Sioux agencies in the fall of 1877 with the ultimatum that unless they relinquished the Black Hills and the unceded hunting grounds to the west, their government rations would be cut off. The Sioux relented, or at least enough chiefs did to satisfy the commission, and the paperwork on the fruits of the military conquest of the

Sioux was wrapped up. Olson, *Red Cloud*, 224–30; George E. Hyde, *Red Cloud's Folk: A History of the Oglala Sioux Indians*, 380–83.

58. Pope to Sheridan, July 25, 1876, Special File, Box 16; Sheridan to Pope, July 24, 25, 1876, Letters Sent; Sheridan to Sherman, July 25, 1876, Division of the Missouri, Letters Sent, RG 393, Records of United States Army.

59. Drum to R. Williams, July 24, 1876; Drum to Frank North, August 18, 1876; Sheridan to Townsend, August 22, 1876, Letters Sent, ibid.; Ernest Wallace, *Ranald S. Mackenzie on the Texas Frontier*, 172; Olson, *Red Cloud*, 220–24; Donald F. Danker, ed., *Man of the Plains: Recollections of Luther North, 1856–1882*, 195–202.

60. Mattes, *Indians, Infants, and Infantry*, 233; Sherman to Sheridan, August 22, 1876, Box 39, Sheridan Papers; Sheridan to Crook, August 23, 1876; Sheridan to Mackenzie, September 16, 1876, Division of the Missouri, Letters Sent, RG 393, Records of United States Army.

61. Sheridan to Sherman, September 16, 1876, Division of the Missouri, Letters Sent, RG 393, Records of United States Army. The best account of Crook's campaign is in Greene, *Slim Buttes, 1876*. Also see Bourke, *With Crook*, 362–80; King, *Campaigning with Crook*, 89–113; Finerty, *War-Path and Bivouac*, 178–205; Anson Mills, *My Story*, 165–68, 428–31; Alberts, *Brandy Station to Manila Bay*, 234–40.

62. Sheridan to Crook, August 23, 1876; Sheridan to Mackenzie, September 16, 1876, Division of the Missouri, Letters Sent, RG 393, Records of United States Army; Bourke, *With Crook*, 387; Mattes, *Indians, Infants and Infantry*, 233.

63. Sheridan to Sherman, October 24, 1876, enclosing Crook to Sheridan, October 23, 1876; Sheridan to Terry, October 24, 1876; Sheridan to Crook, October 24, 1876, Division of the Missouri, Letters Sent, RG 393, Records of United States Army.

64. Sheridan to Secretary of War, November 6, 1876, Box 16, Sheridan Papers.

65. Sheridan to Sherman, December 1, 1876, Division of the Missouri, Letters Sent, RG 393, Records of United States Army; John G. Bourke, *Mackenzie's Last Fight with the Cheyennes: A Winter Campaign in Wyoming and Montana*.

66. Miles, *Personal Recollections*, 221–56; Johnson, *Unregimented General*, 109–70; Robert M. Utley, *Frontier Regulars: The United States Army and the Indian, 1866–1891*, 272–81; Don Rickey, Jr., "The Battle of Wolf Mountain," *Montana: The Magazine of Western History* 13 (Spring 1963): 44–54.

67. Sherman to Sheridan, February 17, 1877, Box 39, Sheridan Papers.

68. Sheridan to Sherman, February 9, 1877, Box 16, ibid.

69. Sheridan to Crook, January 30, 1877, Box 41, ibid.

70. Sheridan to M. V. Sheridan, May 16, 1877, Box 17; Sheridan to Sherman, April 8, 1878, Box 19, ibid.; Richard O'Connor, *Sheridan the Inevitable*, 344.

71. Sheridan to Sherman, April 8, 1878, Box 19, Sheridan Papers; *Report of the Secretary of War [1876]* 1:442–45; Sheridan to Sherman, August 23, 1876, Box 15, Sheridan Papers.

72. Philip H. Sheridan and W. T. Sherman, *Reports of Inspection Made in the Summer of 1877 by Generals P. H. Sheridan and W. T. Sherman of Country North of the Union Pacific Railroad,* 5.

73. *Report of the Secretary of War [1878]* 1:38, This trip is covered in detail in Bourke Diaries, vol. 21.

74. Sheridan and Sherman, *Reports of Inspection,* 5.

CHAPTER 15

1. *Report of the Secretary of War [1879]* 1:45.

2. Ibid.

3. *Report of the Secretary of War [1878]* 1:33.

4. For the debate over who deserved credit for capturing the Nez Perce, see Mark H. Brown, *The Flight of the Nez Perce,* 418–23; John A. Carpenter, *Sword and Olive Branch: Oliver Otis Howard,* 262–63; Virginia Weisel Johnson, *The Unregimented General: A Biography of Nelson A. Miles,* 210; Robert M. Utley, *Frontier Regulars: The United States Army and the Indian, 1866–1891,* 316–19.

5. Sheridan to Townsend, June 6, 1878, Box 19, Sheridan Papers. Also see Brown, *Flight of Nez Perce,* 424–31.

6. George Bird Grinnell, *The Fighting Cheyennes,* 398–413; Peter J. Powell, *Sweet Medicine: The Continuing Role of the Sacred Arrows, the Sun Dance, and the Sacred Buffalo Hat in Northern Cheyenne History* 1:192–98.

7. Sheridan to Townsend, February 26, 1879, Division of the Missouri, Letters Sent, RG 393, Records of United States Army; Ben Clark, Field Notes, Box 2, folder 4, Camp Mss.

8. Sheridan to Sherman, October 9, 1878, Box 20, Sheridan Papers; Donald J. Berthrong, *The Cheyenne and Arapaho Ordeal: Reservation and Agency Life in the Indian Territory, 1875–1907,* 34, 28–35.

9. Powell, *Sweet Medicine* 1:198–225; Grinnell, *Fighting Cheyennes,* 404–18. See also Mari Sandoz, *Cheyenne Autumn* (New York, Hastings House, 1953).

10. Sheridan to Sherman, October 14, 1878, Box 20, Sheridan Papers; Ben Clark, Field Notes, Box 2, folder 4, Camp Mss.; Ben Clark interview, October 22, 1910, Field Notes, folder 11, Camp Mss.; Hugh Lenox Scott, *Some Memories of a Soldier,* 88–90; Powell, *Sweet Medicine* 1:278–80.

11. Sheridan endorsement, November 5, 1878, Box 20, Sheridan Papers; Powell, *Sweet Medicine* 1:226–27.

12. Grinnell, *Fighting Cheyennes,* 418–27; Powell, *Sweet Medicine* 1:232–77; Philip H. Sheridan, *Record of Engagements with Hostile Indians within the*

Military Division of the Missouri, from 1868 to 1882, Lieutenant-General P. H. Sheridan, Commanding, 83–84.

13. Sheridan to Sherman, January 22, 1879, Division of the Missouri, Letters Sent, RG 393, Records of United States Army.

14. *Report of the Secretary of War [1879]* 1:43; Sheridan to Townsend, February 26, 1879, Division of the Missouri, Letters Sent, RG 393, Records of United States Army.

15. Powell, *Sweet Medicine* 1:210–14, 289–93.

16. *Report of the Secretary of War [1881]* 1:84.

17. Sheridan to Sherman, January 22, 1879, Box 21, Sheridan Papers.

18. Sheridan to Sherman, October 9, 1878; Sheridan to Sherman, November 12, 1878, Box 20, Sheridan Papers.

19. *Report of the Secretary of War [1878]* 1:34.

20. Carl Schurz, *The Reminiscences of Carl Schurz: With a Sketch of His Life and Public Services from 1869 to 1906 by Frederick Bancroft and William A. Dunning* 3:385–86; Philip H. Sheridan and Michael V. Sheridan, *Personal Memoirs of Philip Henry Sheridan, General, United States Army: New and Enlarged Edition with an Account of His Life from 1871 to his Death, in 1888* 2:531–32.

21. Sheridan to Sherman, November 12, 1878, Box 20, Sheridan Papers.

22. Sheridan to Department Commanders, November 20, 1878; Sheridan to Sherman, November 12, 26, 1878, ibid.

23. "Synopsis of General Sheridan's Supplemental Report," n.d., Box 89, ibid.

24. Francis Paul Prucha, *American Indian Policy in Crisis: Christian Reformers and the Indian, 1865–1900,* 97–98.

25. Sheridan to Sherman, January 11, 1879, Box 21, Sheridan Papers.

26. Claude Moore Fuess, *Carl Schurz, Reformer,* 255–57; Loring Benson Priest, *Uncle Sam's Stepchildren: The Reformation of United States Indian Policy, 1865–1887,* 20–22.

27. *Report of the Secretary of War [1881]* 1:84; Sheridan to the Adjutant General, January 31, 1879, Box 21, Sheridan Papers.

28. Sheridan to Sherman, May 11, 1879, Box 23; Sheridan to the Adjutant General July 28, 1879, Box 24, Sheridan Papers.

29. For John Bourke's career, see Joseph C. Porter, "John Gregory Bourke, Victorian Soldier Scientist: The Western Apprenticeship, 1869–1886."

30. John G. Bourke Diaries 39:197, 44:1916–20, 47:20–22.

31. *Chicago Times,* September 14, 1881.

32. *Army and Navy Register,* October 18, 1884.

33. W. P. Clark, *The Indian Sign Language,* 5–7; Thomas W. Dunlay, *Wolves for the Blue Soldiers: Indian Scouts and Auxiliaries with the United States Army, 1860–90,* 97–98.

34. *Army and Navy Register,* September 27, 1884.

35. *Report of the Secretary of War [1886]* 1:76–78; *Army and Navy Register*, November 14, 1885.

36. *Army and Navy Register*, January 23, 1886.

37. Ibid., January 23, 1886, and November 14, 1885.

38. Prucha, *American Indian Policy in Crisis*, 248–57. Also see Robert Winston Mardock, *The Reformers and the American Indian*, 216–23; Priest, *Uncle Sam's Stepchildren*, 217–32.

39. Data compiled from Adjutant General's Office, *Chronological List of Actions, &c., with Indians from January 15, 1837 to January, 1891*, 29–77. This reprints an AGO memorandum published in 1891. The ratio of killed to wounded is unusual, the result of the large number killed at Little Big Horn in 1876.

CHAPTER 16

1. Sherman to Ellen Sherman, October 30, 1883, Sherman Family Papers; Rachel Sherman Thorndike, ed., *The Sherman Letters: Correspondence between General and Senator Sherman from 1837 to 1891*, 356–57.

2. Sherman to Ellen Sherman, January 11, 1879, Sherman Family Papers. See also Sherman to Ellen Sherman, May 26, 1881, June 19, 1882, ibid.

3. Sherman to Sheridan, November 13, 1880, Box 39, Sheridan Papers.

4. Sherman to Ellen Sherman, October 30, 1883, Sherman Family Papers.

5. Thorndike, ed., *Sherman Letters*, 356.

6. *Army and Navy Register*, December 1, 1883.

7. Ibid., July 21, 1883. These same admirers also endowed the general's son, Philip, Jr., born in 1880, with a rich trust fund of telephone stock. Frank A. Burr and Richard J. Hinton, *The Life of Gen. Philip H. Sheridan: Its Romance and Reality*, 357.

8. *Army and Navy Register*, November 3, 1883.

9. Ibid.

10. John M. Schofield, *Forty-six Years in the Army*, 462; Philip H. Sheridan and Michael V. Sheridan, *Personal Memoirs of Philip Henry Sheridan, General, United States Army: New and Enlarged Edition, with an Account of His Life from 1871 to His Death, in 1888* 2:555–56. Secretary of War Lincoln's letter is reprinted in *Army and Navy Register*, September 5, 1885.

11. Thorndike, ed., *Sherman Letters*, 377; Sheridan and Sheridan, *Memoirs* 2:556–57; Schofield, *Forty-six Years in the Army*, 471–73; William Harding Carter, *The American Army*, 192; Russell F. Weigley, *History of the United States Army*, 287–88; Allan Nevins, *Grover Cleveland: A Study in Courage*, 332–36.

12. For discussions of the relationship of the commanding general of the army and the secretary of war, see Russell F. Weigley, *History of the Army*,

285–89; and *Towards an American Army: Military Thought from Washington to Marshall*, 162–76; Schofield, *Forty-six Years in the Army*, 406–23; Carter, *American Army*, 184–204. Also see *Army and Navy Register*, September 5, October 10, November 14, 1885.

13. Sheridan and Sheridan, *Memoirs* 2:553; Schofield, *Forty-six Years in the Army*, 454–55; *Report of the Secretary of War [1884]* 1:48, *[1886]* 1:70–71, *[1887]* 1:74–75.

14. *Army and Navy Register*, December 22, 1888.

15. Schofield, *Forty-six Years in the Army*, 426–27; Weigley, *History of the Army*, 290; William Addleman Ganoe, *The History of the United States Army*, 363–64; Sheridan and Sheridan, *Memoirs* 2:553–54, 565; *Report of the Secretary of War [1884]* 1:50–51, *[1887]* 1:74, 77.

16. *Report of the Secretary of War [1887]* 1:79.

17. Ganoe, *History of the Army*, 334, 361, 367–68; *Report of the Secretary of War [1884]* 1:48.

18. Sheridan and Sheridan, *Memoirs* 2:554–55; *Report of the Secretary of War [1884]* 1:49, *[1887]* 1:79–80; Schofield, *Forty-six Years in the Army*, 484–85; Ganoe, *History of the Army*, 361; Weigley, *History of the Army*, 284.

19. Sheridan's recommendations for division and department commanders upon his promotion to commanding general are in Sheridan to Robert Lincoln, September 25, October 7, 1883, Box 34, Sheridan Papers.

20. Sheridan to Robert Lincoln, December 8, 1881, Box 30, ibid.

21. Ernest Wallace, *Ranald S. Mackenzie on the Texas Frontier*, 190–91.

22. Ibid., 192–95.

23. Sheridan to Robert Lincoln, June 27, 1882, Box 32; Sheridan to John McCullough, June 22, 1882, Sheridan Papers; Philip Sheridan, *Report of an Exploration of Parts of Wyoming, Idaho, and Montana in August and September, 1882, Made by Lieut. Gen. P. H. Sheridan*, 21–22; Aubrey L. Haines, *The Yellowstone Story: A History of Our First National Park* 1:263.

24. Sheridan, *Report of an Exploration*, 17, 28.

25. Ibid., 17–18; Haines, *Yellowstone Story* 1:263–67, 2:31–34.

26. Sheridan, *Report of an Exploration*, 17–18.

27. Ibid.; Haines, *Yellowstone Story* 2:94, 319–20.

28. Sheridan, *Report of an Exploration*, 18; *Forest and Stream* 19 (December 14, 1882): 382–83; 20 (February 8, 1883): 22.

29. H. Duane Hampton, *How the U.S. Cavalry Saved Our National Parks*, 61.

30. Sheridan to George G. Vest, December 10, 1882, Box 33, Sheridan Papers.

31. Haines, *Yellowstone Story* 1:268–70; Hampton, *How the U.S. Cavalry Saved Our National Parks*, 55–60.

32. Sheridan to Vest, January 31, April 9, 1883, Box 42, Sheridan Papers.

33. A day-by-day account of the presidential excursion is given in *Journey through the Yellowstone National Park and Northwestern Wyoming, 1883: Photographs of Party and Scenery along the Route Traveled, and Copies of the Associated Press Dispatches Sent whilst en Route.* Twelve copies of this book were prepared and given to the excursion's participants. The Associated Press dispatches, written by Mike Sheridan and James Gregory since no reporters were allowed on the trip, and 105 of Frank Jay Haynes' photographs comprise the book. The copy employed for this study belonged to Mike Sheridan and was used by courtesy of the DeGolyer Library, Southern Methodist University. Since no reporters were along, contemporary newspaper accounts of the expedition were all fabricated. Historians who have relied on these western newspaper stories as source material for the trip have thus been misled. Also see Jack Ellis Haynes, "The Expedition of President Chester A. Arthur to Yellowstone National Park in 1883," *Annals of Wyoming* 14 (January 1942): 31–38; Thomas C. Reeves, "President Arthur in Yellowstone National Park," *Montana: The Magazine of Western History* 19 (July 1969): 18–29; Sheridan and Sheridan, *Memoirs* 2:538–51; Haines, *Yellowstone Story*, 2:279–82.

34. For Washakie's career, see Peter M. Wright, "Washakie," in *American Indian Leaders: Studies in Diversity*, ed. R. David Edmunds, 131–51.

35. *Journey through the Yellowstone National Park*, 24.

36. Sheridan and Sheridan, *Memoirs* 2:550–51.

37. Hampton, *How the U.S. Cavalry Saved Our National Parks*, 70–79; Haines, *Yellowstone Story* 1:323–26.

38. Hampton, *How the U.S. Cavalry Saved Our National Parks*, 80. Also see George S. Anderson, "Work of the Cavalry in Protecting the Yellowstone National Park," *Journal of the United States Cavalry Association* 10 (March 1897): 3–10; Haines, *Yellowstone Story* 2:3–6. Camp Sheridan became Fort Yellowstone in 1891. Military administration of the park had first been proposed by Secretary of War Belknap after an 1875 visit. William E. Strong, *A Trip to the Yellowstone National Park in July, August, and September, 1875*, xv–xvi.

39. Haines, *Yellowstone Story* 2:319–36.

40. Donald J. Berthrong, *The Cheyenne and Arapaho Ordeal: Reservation and Agency Life in the Indian Territory, 1875–1907*, 92–96. See also Edward E. Dale, "Ranching on the Cheyenne-Arapaho Reservation, 1880–1885," *Chronicles of Oklahoma* 6 (March 1928): 35–59; Donald J. Berthrong, "Cattlemen on the Cheyenne-Arapaho Reservation, 1883–1885," *Arizona and the West* 13 (Spring, 1971): 5–32.

41. Berthrong, *Cheyenne and Arapaho Ordeal*, 99–102.

42. Sheridan and Sheridan, *Memoirs* 2:558–59; *Army and Navy Register*, July 11, 18, 1885; *Personal Recollections and Observations of General Nelson A. Miles*, 432–34; Nelson A. Miles, *Serving the Republic: Memoirs of the Civil and Military Life of Nelson A. Miles*, 215–17; Berthrong, *Cheyenne and Arapaho Ordeal*, 109–11; Nevins, *Cleveland*, 229–30.

43. Berthrong, *Cheyenne and Arapaho Ordeal*, 114–15.
44. Berthrong, "Cattlemen on the Cheyenne-Arapaho Reservation," 26–28.
45. Sheridan and Sheridan, *Memoirs* 2:559; *Army and Navy Register*, July 25, 1885; Berthrong, *Cheyenne and Arapaho Ordeal*, 114–15; *Report of the Secretary of War [1885]* 1:65–71.
46. Sheridan to Grover Cleveland, July 26, 1885, Box 25, Sheridan Papers.
47. Berthrong, *Cheyenne and Arapaho Ordeal*, 113; Ernest Staples Osgood, *The Day of the Cattleman* (Chicago, University of Chicago Press, 1968), 217–18; Nevins, *Cleveland*, 230.
48. Robert M. Utley, *Frontier Regulars: The United States Army and the Indian, 1866–1891*, 375–81; Martin F. Schmitt, ed., *General George Crook: His Autobiography*, 241–50. Also see Dan L. Thrapp, *General Crook and the Sierra Madre Adventure* (Norman: University of Oklahoma Press, 1972).
49. *Report of the Secretary of War [1885]* 1:62. For Ulzana's raid, see Dan L. Thrapp, *The Conquest of Apacheria*, 334–37; Angie Debo, *Geronimo: The Man, His Time, His Place*, 247–48. Ulzana is also called Josanie.
50. *Report of the Secretary of War [1886]* 1:7, 71; *Army and Navy Register*, December 12, 1885; Schmitt, ed., *Crook Autobiography*, 251–59; Sheridan and Sheridan, *Memoirs* 2:562–63; Thomas W. Dunlay, *Wolves for the Blue Soldiers: Indian Scouts and Auxiliaries with the United States Army, 1860–90*, 178.
51. Dunlay, *Wolves for the Blue Soldiers*, 66; W. Bruce White, "The American Indian as Soldier, 1890–1919," *Canadian Review of American Studies* 7 (Spring 1976): 16. Also see Eve Ball, "The Apache Scouts: A Chiricahua Appraisal," *Arizona and the West* 7 (Winter 1965): 315–28.
52. Bernard C. Nalty and Truman R. Strobridge, "Captain Emmet Crawford: Commander of Apache Scouts, 1882–1886," *Arizona and the West* 6 (Spring 1964): 30–40; *Army and Navy Register*, February 13, 1886; Thrapp, *Conquest of Apacheria*, 339–43; Debo, *Geronimo*, 248–52.
53. John G. Bourke, *On the Border with Crook*, 465–79; Schmitt, ed., *Crook Autobiography*, 260–63; Britton Davis, *The Truth about Geronimo*, ed. M. M. Quaife, 196–212.
54. Sheridan to Crook, March 31, 1886, Box 36, Sheridan Papers.
55. Bourke, *With Crook*, 483; *Report of the Secretary of War [1886]* 1:147–55.
56. *Report of the Secretary of War [1886]* 1:73; Miles, *Personal Recollections*, 476–532; Davis, *Geronimo*, 213–30; Thrapp, *Conquest of Apacheria*, 328–67; Debo, *Geronimo*, 281–98. Gatewood's account of the surrender is in John M. Carroll, ed., *The Papers of the Order of Indian Wars*, 106–13.
57. *Army and Navy Register*, September 18, 1886.
58. *Report of the Secretary of War [1886]* 1:72–74; Schmitt, ed., *Crook Autobiography*, 265–76, 289–301; Debo, *Geronimo*, 299–335. Some of the corres-

pondence concerning this affair is reprinted in *Senate Exec. Docs.*, 49th Cong., 2d sess., no. 117.

59. *Army and Navy Register*, February 20, 1886.

60. *Army and Navy Register*, October 13, 1883; Sheridan and Sheridan, *Memoirs* 2:572–73; Burr and Hinton, *Sheridan*, 373.

61. Richard O'Connor, *Sheridan The Inevitable*, 349; Sheridan and Sheridan, *Memoirs* 2:573–74.

62. George F. Hoar, *Autobiography of Seventy Years* 1:397–98; Sheridan and Sheridan, *Memoirs* 2:581.

63. *Army and Navy Register*, March 17, 1888. Also see Mary R. Dearing, *Veterans in Politics: The Story of the G.A.R.*, 121–22, 262–63, 321.

64. Joseph Faulkner, *The Life of Philip Henry Sheridan, the Dashing, Brave, and Successful Soldier*, 91.

65. *Philadelphia Press*, August 11, 1888; Burr and Hinton, *Life of Sheridan*, 362–64; Sheridan and Sheridan, *Memoirs* 2:459.

66. Sheridan and Sheridan, *Memoirs* 2:566; *Army and Navy Register*, May 19, 1888.

67. *Army and Navy Register*, August 18, 1888.

68. Sheridan and Sheridan, *Memoirs* 2:567; *Army and Navy Register*, May 26, 1888.

69. *Army and Navy Register*, June 2, 9, 1888.

70. *Army and Navy Register*, August 11, 1888. For Sheridan's illness and final heart attack, see Sheridan and Sheridan, *Memoirs* 2: 566–68; Burr and Hinton, *Life of Sheridan*, 376–84.

71. Burr and Hinton, *Life of Sheridan*, 410; For Sheridan's funeral see ibid., 400–21; Lloyd Lewis, *Sherman: Fighting Prophet*, 643; Sheridan and Sheridan, *Memoirs* 2:569–70; [Charles King], "Sheridan," *Journal of the United States Cavalry Association* 1 (November 1888): 13–14.

BIBLIOGRAPHY

MANUSCRIPTS

Aldrich, James F., Collection. Chicago Historical Society.

Barnitz, Albert and Jennie, Diaries and Letters. Beinecke Library, Yale University, New Haven, Conn.

Bourke, John G., Diaries. United States Military Academy Archives, West Point, N.Y.

Camp, Walter, Manuscripts. Lilly Library, Indiana University, Bloomington.

Chicago Fire Guards Collection. Chicago Historical Society.

Custer, Elizabeth B., Collection. Custer Battlefield National Monument, Montana.

Drennan, Daniel O., Papers. Manuscript Division, Library of Congress, Washington, D.C.

Garfield, James A., Papers. Manuscript Division, Library of Congress, Washington, D.C.

Grierson, Benjamin H., Papers. Ayer Manuscripts, Newberry Library, Chicago.

Grierson, Benjamin H., Papers. Illinois State Historical Society, Springfield.

Neihardt, John G., Papers. Western Historical Manuscripts Collection, University of Missouri Library, Columbia.

Official Register of the Officers and Cadets of the U.S. Military Academy, West Point, New York, June 1849, June 1850, June 1851, June 1852, June 1853. United States Military Academy Archives, West Point, N.Y.

Records of United States Army Continental Commands, RG 393, Military Division of the Missouri, 1866–91. National Archives, Washington, D.C.

    Annual Inspection Reports of the Inspector General, 1875, 1879.

    Letters Received, 1866–67, 1871–1891.

    Letters Sent, 1868–1891.

    Special File of Letters Received, 1863–1885.

Rosser, Thomas L., Collection, Chicago Historical Society.

Sheridan, Michael V., File. Chicago Historical Society.

Sheridan, Philip H., ACP File. S93 CB 1869, Letters Received by the Commission Branch, Records of the Adjutant General's Office, RG 94, National Archives, Washington D.C.

Sheridan, Philip H., Collection. Chicago Historical Society.

Sheridan, Philip H., File. No. 1612, United States Military Academy Archives, West Point, N.Y.

Sheridan, Philip H., Papers. Manuscript Division, Library of Congress, Washington, D.C.

Sherman, Francis T., Diaries. Chicago Historical Society.

Sherman, William Tecumseh, Family Papers. University of Notre Dame Archives, Memorial Library, Notre Dame, Indiana.

Sherman, William Tecumseh, Papers. Manuscript Division, Library of Congress, Washington, D.C.

Strong, William E., Collection. Chicago Historical Society.

GOVERNMENT DOCUMENTS

Annual Reports of the Secretary of War, 1866–1888.

Annual Reports of the Commissioner of Indian Affairs, 1866–1888.

Senate Documents.

    Senate Executive Documents, 39th Congress, 2d session, 1867, no. 45.

    Senate Executive Documents, 40th Congress, 1st session, 1867, nos. 7, 13.

    Senate Executive Documents, 40th Congress, 3d session, 1868, no. 7.

    Senate Executive Documents, 40th Congress, 3d session, 1868–69, nos. 11, 13, 18, pts. 1–3, 27, 36, 40.

    Senate Executive Documents, 41st Congress, 2d session, 1870, no. 49.

    Senate Executive Documents, 43d Congress, 2d session, 1874, nos. 13, 17.

    Senate Executive Documents, 43d Congress, special session, 1874, no. 2.

    Senate Executive Documents, 45th Congress, 2d session, 1878, no. 33, pts. 1–2.

    Senate Executive Documents, 49th Congress, 2d session, 1887, no. 117.

    Senate Report, 39th Congress, 2d session, 1867, no. 156.

    Senate Report, 45th Congress, 3d session, 1879, no. 555.

    Senate Report, 46th Congress, 3d session, 1881, no. 740.

House Documents.

    House Executive Documents, 39th Congress, 2d session, 1866–67, no. 45.

    House Executive Documents, 40th Congress, 2d session, 1867–68, no. 97.

    House Miscellaneous Documents, 41st Congress, 2d session, 1869, nos. 139, 142.

    House Executive Documents, 41st Congress, 2d session, 1869, no. 240.

    House Executive Documents, 44th Congress, 1st session, 1876, no. 184.

    House Report, 39th Congress, 1st session, 1866, no. 30, pt 4.

    House Report, 44th Congress, 1st session, 1876, nos. 240, 354.

DISSERTATIONS

Andrews, Richard Allen. "Years of Frustration: William T. Sherman, the Army, and Reform, 1869–1883." Ph.D. diss., Northwestern University, 1968.

Dinges, Bruce J. "The Making of a Cavalryman: Benjamin H. Grierson and the Civil War along the Mississippi, 1861–1865." Ph.D. diss., Rice University, 1978.

Hutton, Paul Andrew. "General Philip H. Sheridan and the Army in the West, 1867–1888." Ph.D diss., Indiana University, 1980.

Porter, Joseph C. "John Gregory Bourke, Victorian Soldier Scientist: The Western Apprenticeship, 1869–1886." Ph.D. diss., University of Texas, 1980.

Schubert, Frank N. "Fort Robinson, Nebraska: The History of a Military Community, 1874–1916." Ph.D. diss., University of Toledo, 1977.

Wallace, Andrew. "Soldier in the Southwest: The Career of General A. V. Kautz, 1869–1886." Ph.D. diss., University of Arizona, 1968.

Zeimet, Roger Thomas. "Philip H. Sheridan and the Civil War in the West." Ph.D. diss., Marquette University, 1981.

PERIODICAL ARTICLES

Anderson, George S. "Work of the Cavalry in Protecting the Yellowstone National Park." *Journal of the United States Cavalry Association* 10 (March 1897): 3–10.

Anderson, Harry H. "A Challenge to Brown's Sioux Indian Wars Thesis." *Montana: The Magazine of Western History* 12 (January 1962): 40–49.

———. "Stand at the Arickaree." *Colorado Magazine* 41 (Fall 1964): 336–42.

Badeau, Adam. "Lieut.-General Sheridan." *Century Magazine* 27 (February 1884): 496–511.

Berthrong, Donald. "Cattlemen on the Cheyenne-Arapaho Reservation, 1883–1885." *Arizona and the West* 13 (Spring 1971): 5–32.

Bischoff, William N. "The Yakima Campaign of 1856." *Mid-America* 31 (April 1949): 163–208.

———. "The Yakima War, 1855–1856: A Problem in Research." *Pacific Northwest Quarterly* 41 (April 1950): 162–69.

Brown, Mark H. "Muddled Men Have Muddied the Yellowstone's True Colors." *Montana: The Magazine of Western History* 11 (January 1961): 28–37.

Canan, H. V. "Phil Sheridan, a Superb Combat Intelligence Officer." *Armor* 71 (September-October 1962): 58–61.

Clark, Robert Carlton. "Military History of Oregon, 1849–59." *Oregon Historical Quarterly* 36 (March 1935): 14–59.

Clow, Richmond L. "General Philip Sheridan's Legacy: The Sioux Pony Campaign of 1876." *Nebraska History* 57 (Winter 1976): 461–77.

Connelley, William E., ed. "John McBee's Account of the Expedition of the Nineteenth Kansas." *Collections of the Kansas State Historical Society* 17 (1926–28): 361–74.

Cooper, Grace E. "Benton County Pioneer-Historical Society." *Oregon Historical Quarterly* 57 (March 1956): 83–84.

Cooper, Jerry M. "The Army as Strikebreakers—The Railroad Strikes of 1877 and 1884." *Labor History* 18 (Spring 1977): 179–96.

Cutler, Lee. "Lawrie Tatum and the Kiowa Agency, 1869–1873." *Arizona and the West* 13 (Autumn 1971): 221–44.

Dale, Edward E. "Ranching on the Cheyenne-Arapaho Reservation, 1880–1885." *Chronicles of Oklahoma* 6 (March 1928): 35–59.

[Davis, Theodore R.]. "Gen. Custer's Command." *Harper's Weekly* 11 (August 3, 1867): 481, 484.

———. "General Sheridan's Personality." *Cosmopolitan* 13 (June 1892): 209–16.

———. "The Indian War." *Harper's Weekly* 11 (May 11, 1867), 301–2.

———. "Indian War Scenes." *Harper's Weekly* 11 (August 17, 1867): 513–14.

———. "Our Indian War Sketches." *Harper's Weekly* 11 (June 29, 1867): 406–7.

———. "A Summer on the Plains." *Harper's New Monthly Magazine* 36 (February 1868): 292–307.

———. "Winter on the Plains." *Harper's New Monthly Magazine* 39 (June 1869): 22–34.

Dawson, Joseph G., III. "The Alpha-Omega Man: General Phil Sheridan." *Red River Valley Historical Review* 3 (Spring 1978): 147–63.

———. "General Phil Sheridan and Military Reconstruction in Louisiana." *Civil War History* 24 (June 1978): 133–51.

D'Elia, Donald J. "The Argument over Civilian or Military Indian Control, 1865–1880," *Historian* 24 (February 1962): 207–25.

Dippie, Brian W. "Southern Response to Custer's Last Stand." *Montana: The Magazine of Western History* 21 (April 1971): 18–31.

———. " 'What Will Congress Do about It?' The Congressional Reaction to the Little Big Horn Disaster." *North Dakota History* 37 (Summer 1970): 161–89.

Dorst, Joseph H. "Ranald Slidell Mackenzie," *Journal of the United States Cavalry Association* 10 (December 1897): 367–82.

Doubleday, Abner. "An Anecdote of Sheridan." *Century Magazine* 40 (October 1890): 958–59.

Ediger, Theodore A., and Vinnie Hoffman. "Some Reminiscences of the Battle of the Washita." *Chronicles of Oklahoma* 33 (Summer 1955): 137–41.

Ellis, Richard N. "The Humanitarian Generals." *Western Historical Quarterly* 3 (April 1972): 169–78.

Filipiak, Jack D. "The Battle of Summit Spring." *Colorado Magazine* 41 (Fall 1964): 343–54.

Fite, Gilbert C. "The United States Army and Relief to Pioneer Settlers, 1874–1875." *Journal of the West* 6 (January 1967): 99–107.

Forbes, Archibald. "The United States Army." *North American Review* 309 (August 1882): 127–45.

Foreman, Carolyn Thomas. "General Benjamin Henry Grierson." *Chronicles of Oklahoma* 24 (Summer 1946): 195–218.

Forsyth, G. A. "A Frontier Fight." *Harper's New Monthly Magazine* 91 (June 1895): 42–62.

Freidel, Frank. "General Orders 100 and Military Government." *Mississippi Valley Historical Review* 32 (March 1946): 541–56.

Gabrilson, C. L. "General Sheridan and His Troops." *Century Magazine* 38 (July 1889): 479.

Garfield, Marvin H. "The Military Post as a Factor in the Frontier Defense of Kansas, 1865–1869." *Kansas Historical Quarterly* 1 (November 1931): 50–62.

Gates, John Morgan. "General George Crook's First Apache Campaign: The Use of Mobile, Self-contained Units against the Apache in the Military Department of Arizona, 1871–1873." *Journal of the West* 6 (April 1967): 310–20.

"General Sheridan." *Harper's Weekly* 32 (August 11, 1888): 594.

Gibson, Arrell Morgan, "The St. Augustine Prisoners." *Red River Valley Historical Review* 3 (Spring 1978): 259–70.

Godfrey, E. S. "Custer's Last Battle: By One of His Troop Commanders." *Century Magazine* 43 (January 1892): 358–87.

———. "Reminiscences of the Medicine Lodge Peace Treaties." *Cavalry Journal* 37 (January 1928): 112–15.

———. "Some Reminiscences, Including an Account of General Sully's Expedition against the Southern Plains Indians, 1868." *Cavalry Journal* 36 (July 1927): 417–25.

———. "Some Reminiscences, Including the Washita Battle, November 29, 1868." *Cavalry Journal* 37 (October 1928): 481–50.

Gray, John S. "Will Comstock, Scout: The Natty Bumppo of Kansas." *Montana: The Magazine of Western History* 20 (July 1970): 2–15.

Griswold, Gillett. "Old Fort Sill: The First Seven Years." *Chronicles of Oklahoma* 36 (Spring 1958): 2–14.

Guentzel, Richard. "The Department of the Platte and Western Settlement, 1866–1877." *Nebraska History* 56 (Fall 1975): 389–417.

Guy, Duane F., ed. "The Canadian River Expedition of 1868." *Panhandle-Plains Historical Review* 48 (1975): 1–26.

Hacker, Barton C. "The United States Army as a National Police Force: The Federal Policing of Labor Disputes, 1877–1898." *Military Affairs* 33 (April 1969): 255–64.

Hadley, James Albert. "The Nineteenth Kansas Cavalry and the Conquest of the Plains Indians." *Transactions of the Kansas State Historical Society* 10 (1907–1908): 428–56.

———. "A Royal Buffalo Hunt." *Transactions of the Kansas State Historical Society* 10 (1907–1908): 564–80.

Hagan, William T. "Kiowas, Comanches, and Cattlemen, 1867–1906: A Case Study of the Failure of U.S. Reservation Policy." *Pacific Historical Review* 40 (August 1971): 333–55.

Haynes, Jack Ellis. "The Expedition of President Chester A. Arthur to Yellowstone National Park in 1883." *Annals of Wyoming* 14 (January 1942): 31–38.

Howe, George Frederick. "Expedition to the Yellowstone River in 1873: Letters of a Young Cavalry Officer." *Mississippi Valley Historical Review* 39 (December 1952): 519–34.

Hurst, John. "The Beecher Island Fight." *Collections of the Kansas State Historical Society* 15 (1919–22): 530–38.

Hutton, Paul A. "Phil Sheridan's Pyrrhic Victory: The Piegan Massacre, Army Politics, and the Transfer Debate." *Montana: The Magazine of Western History* 32 (Spring 1982): 32–43.

"The Indian War." *Harper's Weekly* 12 (December 19, 1868): 801–2, 804.

Isern, Thomas D. "The Controversial Career of Edward W. Wynkoop." *Colorado Magazine* 56 (Winter-Spring 1979): 1–18.

Jensen, Oliver. "War Correspondent 1864: The Sketchbooks of James E. Taylor." *American Heritage* 31 (September 1980): 48–64.

Kautz, August V. "Our National Military System: What the United States Army Should Be." *Century Magazine* 36 (October 1888): 934–39.

Keenan, Jerry. "Exploring the Black Hills: An Account of the Custer Expedition." *Journal of the West* 6 (April 1967): 248–61.

King, James T. "A Better Way: General George Crook and the Ponca Indians." *Nebraska History* 50 (Fall 1969): 239–56.

———. "George Crook: Indian Fighter and Humanitarian." *Arizona and the West* 9 (Winter 1967): 333–48.

———. "Needed: A Re-evaluation of General George Crook." *Nebraska History* 45 (September 1964): 223–35.

———. "The Republican River Expedition, June–July, 1869: I, On the March." *Nebraska History* 41 (September 1960): 165–99.

———. "The Republican River Expedition, June–July 1869: II, The Battle of Summit Springs." *Nebraska History* 41 (December 1960): 281–97.

Leckie, William H. "Buell's Campaign." *Red River Valley Historical Review* 3 (Spring 1978): 186–93.

———. "The Red River War, 1874–1875." *Panhandle-Plains Historical Review* 29 (1956): 79–100.

Leonard, Thomas C. "Red, White, and the Army Blue: Empathy and Anger in the American West." *American Quarterly* 26 (May 1974): 176–90.

Levens, Turner F. "When Sheridan Was in Oregon." *Washington Historical Quarterly* 16 (July 1925): 163–85.

Lockley, Fred. "Reminiscences of Mrs. Frank Collins, Nee Martha Elizabeth Gilliam." *Quarterly of the Oregon Historical Society* 17 (December 1916): 358–72.

McLaird, James D. and Lesta V. Turchen. "Exploring the Black Hills, 1855–1875: Reports of the Government Expeditions." *South Dakota History*, 4 (Summer 1974): 281–319.

Manley, Robert N. "In the Wake of the Grasshoppers: Public Relief in Nebraska, 1874–1875." *Nebraska History* 44 (December 1963): 255–75.

Mardock, Robert. "The Plains Frontier and the Indian Peace Policy, 1865–1880." *Nebraska History* 49 (Summer 1968): 187–201.

Mattes, Merrill J. "The Beecher Island Battlefield Diary of Sigmund Shlesinger." *Colorado Magazine* 29 (July 1952): 161–69.

Mattison, Ray H. "The Army Post on the Northern Plains. 1865–1885." *Nebraska History* 35 (March 1954): 17–43.

Millbrook, Minnie Dubbs. "Custer's First Scout in the West." *Kansas Historical Quarterly* 39 (Spring 1973): 75–95.

———. "The Jordan Massacre." *Kansas History* 2 (Winter 1979): 218–30.

———. "The West Breaks in General Custer." *Kansas Historical Quarterly* 36 (Summer 1970): 113–48.

Montgomery, Mrs. Frank C. "Fort Wallace and Its Relation to the Frontier." *Collections of the Kansas State Historical Society* 17 (1926–28): 189–283.

Moore, Horace L. "The Nineteenth Kansas Cavalry." *Transactions of the Kansas State Historical Society* 6 (1897–1900): 35–52.

Myers, Rex C. "Montana Editors and the Custer Battle." *Montana: The Magazine of Western History* 26 (April 1976): 18–31.

Myres, Sandra L. "Romance and Reality on the American Frontier: Views of Army Wives." *Western Historical Quarterly* 13 (October 1982), 409–27.

Nesbitt, Paul. "Battle of the Washita." *Chronicles of Oklahoma* 3 (April 1925): 3–32.

Olson, Gary D., ed. "Relief for Nebraska Grasshopper Victims: The Official Journal of Lieutenant Theodore E. True." *Nebraska History* 48 (Summer 1967): 119–40.

Parker, Watson, "The Majors and the Miners: The Role of the U.S. Army in the Black Hills Gold Rush." *Journal of the West* 11 (January 1972): 99–113.

Pate, J'Nell, "The Battles of Adobe Walls." *Great Plains Journal* 16 (Fall 1976): 2–44.

———. "Indians on Trial in a White Man's Court." *Great Plains Journal* 14 (Fall 1974): 56–71.

"Philip H. Sheridan." *Century Magazine* 36 (October 1888): 950.

Reeves, Thomas C. "President Arthur in Yellowstone National Park." *Montana: The Magazine of Western History* 19 (Summer 1969): 18–29.

Richter, William L. "Texas Politics and the United States Army, 1866–1877." *Military History of Texas and the Southwest* 10, no. 3 (1972): 159–86.

———. "Tyrant and Reformer: General Griffin Reconstructs Texas, 1865–66." *Prologue* 10 (Winter 1978): 225–41.

Rogers, Jerry L. "The Indian Territory Expedition: Winter Campaigns, 1874–1875." *Texas Military History* 8, no. 4 (1970): 233–50.

Rolston, Alan. "The Yellowstone Expedition of 1873." *Montana: The Magazine of Western History* 20 (April 1970): 20–29.

Russell, Don. "How Many Indians Were Killed?" *American West* 9 (July 1973): 42–47.

Schneirov, Richard. "Chicago's Great Upheaval of 1877." *Chicago History* 9 (Spring 1980): 3–17.

Scott, Leslie M. "Military Beginnings of the Salmon River Highway." *Oregon Historical Quarterly* 25 (September 1934): 228–34.

Scott, Thomas A. "The Recent Strikes." *North American Review* 258 (September-October 1877): 351–62.

"Sheridan." *Harper's Weekly* 32 (August 18, 1888): 607.

"Sheridan." *Journal of the United States Cavalry Association* 1 (November 1888): 1–14.

"Sheridan on the Move." *Harper's Weekly* 12 (December 5, 1868): 774, 776.

Sheridan, Philip H., "The Last Days of the Rebellion." *North American Review* 320 (July 1883): 8–18.

———. "From Gravelotte to Sedan." *Scribner's Magazine* 4 (November 1888): 515–35.

Sherman, William T. "Our Army and Militia." *North American Review* 305 (August 1890): 121–45.

Shirk, George H. "Campaigning with Sheridan: A Farrier's Diary." *Chronicles of Oklahoma* 37 (Spring 1959): 69–105.

Shlesinger, Sigmund. "The Beecher Island Fight." *Collections of the Kansas State Historical Society* 15 (1919–22): 538–47.

Slotkin, Richard. " '. . . & Then the Mare Will Go!': An 1875 Black Hills Scheme by Custer, Holladay, and Buford." *Journal of the West* 15 (July 1976): 60–77.

[Stanley, Henry M.]. "A British Journalist Reports the Medicine Lodge Peace Councils of 1867." *Kansas Historical Quarterly* 33 (Autumn 1967): 249–320.

Stout, Joseph A. "Davidson's Campaign." *Red River Valley Historical Review* 3 (Spring 1978): 194–201.

Taylor, Morris F. "The Carr-Penrose Expedition: General Sheridan's Winter Campaign, 1868–1869." *Chronicles of Oklahoma* 51 (Summer 1973): 159–76.

Temple, Frank M. "Colonel Grierson in the Southwest." *Panhandle-Plains Historical Review* 30 (1957): 27–54.

Utley, Robert M. "A Chained Dog: The Indian-Fighting Army." *American West* 9 (July 1973): 18–24.

Walker, Francis A. "The Indian Question." *North American Review* 116 (April 1873): 343–44.

Wallace, Edward S. "General Ranald Slidell Mackenzie, Indian Fighting Cavalryman." *Southwestern Historical Quarterly* 56 (January 1953): 378–96.

Wallace, Ernest. "Prompt in the Saddle: The Military Career of Ranald S. Mackenzie." *Military History of Texas and the Southwest* 9, no. 3 (1971): 161–89.

Wallace, Ernest, and Adrian S. Anderson. "R. S. Mackenzie and the Kickapoos: The Raid into Mexico in 1873." *Arizona and the West* 7 (Summer 1965): 105–26.

Waltmann, Henry. "Circumstantial Reformer: President Grant and the Indian Problem." *Arizona and the West* 13 (Winter 1971): 323–42.

Weigley, Russell, F. "Philip H. Sheridan: A Personality Profile." *Civil War Times Illustrated* 7 (July 1968): 4–11.

White, John I. "Red Carpet for a Romanoff." *American West* 9 (January 1972): 5–9.

White, Lonnie J. "The Battle of Beecher Island: The Scouts Hold Fast on the Arickaree." *Journal of the West* 5 (January 1966): 1–24.

———. "The Cheyenne Barrier on the Kansas Frontier, 1868–1869." *Arizona and the West* 4 (Spring 1962): 51–64.

———. "General Sully's Expedition to the North Canadian, 1868." *Journal of the West* 11 (January 1972): 75–98.

———. "The Hancock and Custer Expeditions of 1867." *Journal of the West* 5 (July 1966): 355–78.

———. "Winter Campaigning With Sheridan and Custer: The Expedition of the Nineteenth Kansas Volunteer Cavalry." *Journal of the West* 6 (January 1967): 68–98.

———, ed. "The Nineteenth Kansas Cavalry in the Indian Territory, 1868–1869: Eyewitness Accounts of Sheridan's Winter Campaign." *Red River Valley Historical Review* 3 (Spring 1978): 164–85.

White, Richard. "The Winning of the West: The Expansion of the Western Sioux in the Eighteenth and Nineteenth Centuries." *Journal of American History* 65 (September 1978): 319–43.

Wilson, Wesley, C. "The U.S. Army and the Piegans: The Baker Massacre on the Marias, 1870." *North Dakota History* 32 (January 1965): 40–58.

Yenchar, John G. "General Philip H. Sheridan." *Cavalry Journal* 46 (November–December 1937): 499–502.

BOOKS AND PAMPHLETS

Adjutant General's Office. *Chronological List of Actions, &c., with Indians from January 15, 1837, to January, 1891*. Fort Collins, Colo.: Old Army Press, 1979.

Alger, Russell A. *Eulogy on the Late General Philip H. Sheridan*. Detroit, Mich., 1888.

Alberts, Don E. *Brandy Station to Manila Bay: A Biography of General Wesley Merritt*. Austin, Tex.: Presidial Press, 1981.

Alvord, Benjamin. *Remarks of Brig. Gen. Benjamin Alvord, Paymaster-General U.S.A. upon the Reorganization of the Army*. Washington, D.C.: Government Printing Office, 1876.

Ambrose, Stephen E. *Upton and the Army*. Baton Rouge: Louisiana State University Press. 1964.

Armes, George A. *Ups and Downs of an Army Officer*. Washington D.C., 1900.

Athearn, Robert G. *Forts of the Upper Missouri*. Englewood Cliffs, N.J.: Prentice-Hall, 1967.

———. *Union Pacific Country*. Lincoln: University of Nebraska Press, 1976.

———. *William Tecumseh Sherman and the Settlement of the West*. Norman: University of Oklahoma Press, 1956.

Badeau, Adam. *Grant in Peace: From Appomattox to Mount McGregor: A Personal Memoir*. Hartford, Conn.: S. S. Scranton and Co., 1887.

Bailey, John W. *Pacifying the Plains: General Alfred Terry and the Decline of the Sioux, 1866–1890*. Westport, Conn.: Greenwood Press, 1979.

Beal, Merrill D. *The Story of Man in Yellowstone*. Caldwell, Idaho: Caxton Printers, 1949.

Berthrong, Donald J. *The Cheyenne and Arapaho Ordeal: Reservation and Agency Life in the Indian Territory, 1875–1907*. Norman: University of Oklahoma Press, 1976.

———. *The Southern Cheyennes*. Norman: University of Oklahoma Press, 1963.

Bigelow, Donald Nevius. *William Conant Church and the Army and Navy Journal*. New York: Columbia University Press, 1952.

Bonney, Orrin H., and Lorraine Bonney. *Battle Drums and Geysers: The Life and Journals of Lt. Gustavus Cheyney Doane, Soldier and Explorer of the Yellowstone and Snake River Regions*. Chicago: Swallow Press, 1970.

Bourke, John G. *Mackenzie's Last Fight with the Cheyennes: A Winter Campaign in Wyoming and Montana*. Bellevue, Nebr.: Old Army Press, 1970.

———. *On the Border with Crook*. New York: Charles Scribner's Sons, 1891.

Boyd, James P. *The Gallant Trooper, General Philip H. Sheridan*. Philadelphia: Franklin News Co., 1888.

Bradley, James H. *The March of the Montana Column: A Prelude to the Custer Disaster*. Edited by Edgar I. Stewart. Norman: University of Oklahoma Press, 1961.

Brill, Charles J. *Conquest of the Southern Plains: Uncensored Narrative of the Battle of the Washita and Custer's Southern Campaign.* Oklahoma City, Okla.: Golden Saga Publishers, 1938.

Brown, Dee. *The Year of the Century: 1876.* New York: Charles Scribner's Sons, 1966.

Brown, Harry James, and Frederick D. Williams, eds. *The Diary of James A. Garfield.* 3 vols. Lansing: Michigan State University Press, 1967–73.

Brown, Mark H. *The Flight of the Nez Perce.* New York: G. P. Putnam's Sons, 1967.

———. *The Plainsmen of the Yellowstone: A History of the Yellowstone Basin.* Lincoln: University of Nebraska Press, 1969.

Bruce, Robert V. *1877: Year of Violence.* Indianapolis, Ind.: Bobbs-Merrill Co., 1959.

Buffum, F. H. *Sheridan's Veterans, No. II: A Souvenir of Their Third Campaign in the Shenandoah Valley, 1864–1883–1885.* Boston: W. F. Brown, 1886.

Burkey, Blaine. *Custer, Come at Once! The Fort Hays Years of George and Elizabeth Custer, 1867–1870.* Hays, Kansas: Thomas More Prep, 1976.

Burlingame, Merrill G. *The Montana Frontier.* Helena, Mont.: State Publishing Co., 1942.

Burr, Frank A., and Richard J. Hinton. *The Life of Gen. Philip H. Sheridan: Its Romance and Reality.* Providence, R.I.: J. A. and R. A. Reid, Publishers, 1888.

Busch, Moritz. *Bismarck: Some Secret Pages of His History.* 2 vols. London: Macmillan Co., 1898.

Carpenter, John A. *Sword and Olive Branch: Oliver Otis Howard.* Pittsburgh, Penn.: University of Pittsburgh Press, 1964.

Carriker, Robert C. *Fort Supply Indian Territory: Frontier Outpost on the Plains.* Norman: University of Oklahoma Press, 1970.

Carroll, John M., ed. *The Benteen-Goldin Letters on Custer and His Last Battle.* New York: Liveright, 1974.

———, ed. *The Black Military Experience in the American West.* New York: Liveright, 1971.

———, ed. *General Custer and the Battle of the Little Big Horn: The Federal View.* New Brunswick, N.J.: Garry Owen Press, 1976.

———, ed. *General Custer and the Battle of the Washita: The Federal View.* Bryan, Tex.: Guidon Press, 1978.

———, ed. *I, Varnum: The Autobiographical Reminiscences of Custer's Chief of Scouts.* Glendale, Calif.: Arthur H. Clark Co., 1982.

———, ed. *The Papers of the Order of Indian Wars.* Fort Collins, Colo.: Old Army Press, 1975.

Carter, R. G. *On the Border with Mackenzie; or, Winning West Texas from the Comanches.* New York: Antiquarian Press, 1961.

Carter, William Harding. *The American Army.* Indianapolis, Ind.: Bobbs-Merrill Co., 1915.

449

Chandler, Melbourne C. *Of Garry Owen in Glory: The History of the Seventh United States Cavalry Regiment*. Annandale, Va.: Turnpike Press, 1960.

Clark, W. P. *The Indian Sign Language*. Lincoln: University of Nebraska Press, 1982.

Clendenen, Clarence C. *Blood on the Border: The United States Army and the Mexican Irregulars*. New York: Macmillan, 1969.

Cody, William F. *The Life of Hon. William F. Cody, Known as Buffalo Bill, the Famous Hunter, Scout, and Guide: An Autobiography*. Lincoln: University of Nebraska Press, 1978.

Cook, John R. *The Border and the Buffalo: An Untold Story of the Southwest Plains*. New York: Citadel Press, 1967.

Cooper, Jerry M. *The Army and Civil Disorder: Federal Military Intervention in Labor Disputes, 1877–1900*. Westport, Conn.: Greenwood Press, 1980.

Cramton, Louis C. *Early History of Yellowstone National Park and Its Relation to National Park Policies*. Washington D.C.: Government Printing Office, 1932.

Cresap, Bernarr. *Appromattox Commander: The Story of General E. O. C. Ord*. San Diego, Calif.: A. S. Barnes, 1981.

Custer, Elizabeth B. *"Boots and Saddles"; or, Life in Dakota with General Custer*. New York: Harper and Brothers, 1885.

———. *Following The Guidon*. Norman: University of Oklahoma Press, 1966.

———. *Tenting on the Plains; or, General Custer in Kansas and Texas*. New York: Charles L. Webster & Co., 1887.

Custer, George Armstrong. *My Life on the Plains; or, Personal Experiences with Indians*. Edited by Edgar I. Stewart. Norman: University of Oklahoma Press, 1962.

Danker, Donald F., ed. *Man of the Plains: Recollections of Luther North, 1856–1882*. Lincoln: University of Nebraska Press, 1961.

Davidson, Homer K. *Black Jack Davidson: A Cavalry Commander on the Western Frontier*. Glendale, Calif.: Arthur H. Clark Co., 1974.

Davies, Henry E. *General Sheridan*. New York: D. Appleton and Co., 1909.

———. *Ten Days on the Plains*. New York: Crocker & Co. [1871].

Davis, Britton, *The Truth about Geronimo*. Edited by M. M. Quaife. Lincoln: University of Nebraska Press, 1976.

Dawes, Henry L. *Past and Present Indian Policy*. Bible House, N.Y.: Rooms of the American Missionary Association, 1892.

Dawson, Joseph G., III. *Army Generals and Reconstruction: Louisiana, 1862–1877*. Baton Rouge: Louisiana State University Press, 1982.

Dearing, Mary R. *Veterans in Politics: The Story of the G.A.R.* Baton Rouge: Louisiana State University Press, 1952.

Debo, Angie. *Geronimo: The Man, His Time, His Place*. Norman: University of Oklahoma Press, 1976.

Denison, C. W. *Illustrated Life, Campaigns, and Public Services of Philip Henry Sheridan*. Philadelphia: T. B. Peterson, 1865.

Dippie, Brian W., ed. *Nomad: George A. Custer in Turf, Field, and Farm.* Austin: University of Texas Press, 1980.

Dodge, Grenville M. *The Battle of Atlanta and Other Campaigns, Addresses, Etc.* Council Bluffs, Iowa: Monarch Printing Co., 1910.

———. *How We Built the Union Pacific Railway and Other Railway Papers and Addresses.* Council Bluffs, Iowa, 1910.

———. *Paper Read before the Society of the Army of the Tennessee at Its Twenty-first Annual Reunion at Toledo, O., Sept. 15, 1888.* New York: Unz & Co., 1899.

———. *Personal Recollections of President Abraham Lincoln, General Ulysses S. Grant, and General William T. Sherman.* Council Bluffs, Iowa: Monarch Printing Co., 1914.

Dodge, Richard Irving. *Our Wild Indians: Thirty-three Years' Personal Experience among the Red Men of the Great West.* New York: Archer House, 1959.

Downey, Fairfax. *Indian-fighting Army.* New York: Charles Scribner's Sons, 1941.

Driver, Harold. *Indians of North America.* Chicago: University of Chicago Press, 1969.

Dunlay, Thomas W. *Wolves for the Blue Soldiers: Indian Scouts and Auxiliaries with the United States Army, 1860–90.* Lincoln: University of Nebraska Press, 1982.

Dunn, J. P., Jr. *Massacres of the Mountains: A History of the Indian Wars of the Far West, 1815–1875.* New York: Archer House, n.d.

Du Pont, Henry A. *The Campaign of 1864 in the Valley of Virginia and the Expedition to Lynchburg.* New York: Baber and Taylor, 1925.

Dupuy, R. Ernest, and Trevor N. Dupuy. *Military Heritage of America.* New York: McGraw-Hill Book Co., 1956.

Edmunds, R. David, ed. *American Indian Leaders: Studies in Diversity.* Lincoln: University of Nebraska Press, 1980.

Ege, Robert J. *"Tell Baker to Strike Them Hard!": Incident on the Marias, 23 Jan. 1870.* Bellevue, Nebr.: Old Army Press, 1970.

Eisenschiml, Otto. *The Celebrated Case of Fitz John Porter: An American Dreyfus Affair.* Indianapolis, Ind.: Bobbs-Merrill Co., 1950.

Ellis, Richard N. *General Pope and U.S. Indian Policy.* Albuquerque: University of New Mexico Press, 1970.

Emmons, David M. *Garden in the Grasslands: Boomer Literature of the Central Great Plains.* Lincoln: University of Nebraska Press, 1971.

Ewers, John C. *The Blackfeet: Raiders of the Northwestern Plains.* Norman: University of Oklahoma Press, 1958.

Faulkner, Joseph. *The Life of Philip Henry Sheridan, the Dashing, Brave, and Successful Soldier.* New York: John W. Lovell Co., 1888.

Finerty, John F. *War-Path and Bivouac; or, The Conquest of the Sioux.* Norman: University of Oklahoma Press, 1961.

Fite, Gilbert C. *The Farmer's Frontier, 1865–1900*. New York: Holt, Rinehart and Winston, 1966.

Foner, Jack D. *The United States Soldier between Two Wars: Army Life and Reforms, 1865–1898*. New York: Humanities Press, 1970.

Foner, Philip S. *The Great Labor Uprising of 1877*. New York: Monad Press, 1977.

Forsyth, George A. *The Story of the Soldier*. New York: D. Appleton and Co., 1900.

———. *Thrilling Days in Army Life*. New York: Harper & Brothers, 1900.

Forsyth, James W., and F. D. Grant. *Report of an Expedition up the Yellowstone River, Made in 1875, by James W. Forsyth, Lieutenant-Colonel and Military Secretary, and F. D. Grant, Lieutenant-Colonel and Aide-de-Camp, under the Orders of Lieutenant-General P. H. Sheridan, Commanding Military Division of the Missouri*. Washington, D.C.: Government Printing Office, 1875.

Fowler, Arlen L. *The Black Infantry in the West, 1869–1891*. Westport, Conn.: Greenwood Press, 1971.

Fritz, Henry, *The Movement for Indian Assimilation, 1860–1890*. Philadelphia: University of Pennsylvania Press, 1963.

Frost, Lawrence A. *The Court-Martial of General George Armstrong Custer*. Norman: University of Oklahoma Press, 1968.

———. *General Custer's Libbie*. Seattle, Wash.: Superior Publishing Co., 1976.

———. *The Phil Sheridan Album: A Pictorial Biography of Philip Henry Sheridan*. Seattle, Wash.: Superior Publishing Co., 1968.

———, ed. *With Custer in '74: James Calhoun's Diary of the Black Hills Expedition*. Provo, Utah: Brigham Young University Press, 1979.

Fry, James B. *Army Sacrifices; or, Briefs from Official Pigeon-Holes*. New York: D. Van Nostrand, 1879.

Fuess, Claude Moore. *Carl Schurz, Reformer*. New York: Dodd, Mead & Company, 1932.

Ganoe, William Addleman. *The History of the United States Army*. Ashton, Md.: Eric Lundberg, 1964.

Gard, Wayne. *The Great Buffalo Hunt*. Lincoln: University of Nebraska Press, 1968.

Gardner, Asa Bird. *Argument on Behalf of Lieut. Gen. Philip H. Sheridan, U.S.A., Respondent, by Asa Bird Gardner, LL.D., Judge-Advocate, U.S.A., of Counsel, before the Court of Inquiry Convened by the President of the United States in the Case of Lieut. Col. and Bvt. Major-General Gouverneur K. Warren, Corps of Engineers, Formerly Major-General Commanding the Fifth Army Corps, Applicant*. Washington, D.C.: Government Printing Office, 1881.

Gibbon, John. *Gibbon on the Sioux Campaign of 1876*. Bellevue, Nebr.: Old Army Press. 1970.

Gibson, A. M. *The Kickapoos: Lords of the Middle Border*. Norman: University of Oklahoma Press, 1963.

Goetzmann, William H. *Exploration and Empire: The Explorer and the Scientist in the Winning of the American West.* New York: Alfred A. Knopf, 1966.

Graham, W. A. *The Custer Myth: A Source Book of Custeriana.* Harrisburg, Penn.: Stackpole, 1953.

———. *The Story of the Little Big Horn: Custer's Last Fight.* Harrisburg, Penn.: Stackpole, 1959.

Grant, U. S. *Personal Memoirs of U. S. Grant.* 2 vols. New York: Charles L. Webster & Co., 1885–86.

Gray, John S. *Centennial Campaign: The Sioux War of 1876.* Fort Collins, Colo.: Old Army Press, 1976.

Greene, Jerome A. *Slim Buttes, 1876: An Episode of the Great Sioux War.* Norman: University of Oklahoma Press, 1982.

Greiner, H. C. *General Phil Sheridan as I Knew Him, Playmate-Comrade-Friend.* Chicago: J. S. Hayland & Co., 1908.

Grierson, Benjamin H. *Brief Record of General Grierson's Services during and since the War, with Special Testimonials and Recommendations from General Officers, Senators, Representatives, and Other Officials. 1861 to 1882.* N.p., n.d.

Grinnell, George Bird. *The Cheyenne Indians: Their History and Ways of Life.* 2 vols. Lincoln: University of Nebraska Press, 1972.

———. *The Fighting Cheyennes.* Norman: University of Oklahoma Press, 1956.

———. *Two Great Scouts and Their Pawnee Battalion.* Lincoln: University of Nebraska Press, 1973.

Guie, H. Dean. *Bugles in the Valley: Garnett's Fort Simcoe.* Portland: Oregon Historical Society, 1977.

Hagan, William T. *United States–Comanche Relations: The Reservation Years.* New Haven, Conn.: Yale University Press, 1976.

Hagemann, E. R., ed. *Fighting Rebels and Redskins: Experiences in Army Life of Colonel George B. Sanford, 1861–1892.* Norman: University of Oklahoma Press, 1969.

Haines, Aubrey L. *The Yellowstone Story: A History of Our First National Park.* 2 vols. Yellowstone National Park, Wyo.: Yellowstone Library and Museum Association, 1977.

Haley, James L. *The Buffalo War: The History of the Red River Indian Uprising of 1874.* Garden City, N.Y.: Doubleday & Co., 1976.

Hampton, H. Duane. *How the U.S. Cavalry Saved Our National Parks.* Bloomington: Indiana University Press, 1971.

Hancock, A. R. *Reminiscences of Winfield Scott Hancock, by His Wife.* New York: Charles L. Webster & Co., 1887.

Haworth, Paul L. *The Hayes-Tilden Election.* Indianapolis, Ind.: Bobbs-Merrill Co., 1927.

Hazen, W. B. *A Narrative of Military Service.* Boston: Ticknow and Co., 1885.

Hedren, Paul L. *First Scalp for Custer: The Skirmish at Warbonnet Creek, Nebraska, July 17, 1876, with a Short History of the Warbonnet Battlefield.* Glendale, Calif.: Arthur H. Clark, 1980.

453

Heitman, Francis B. *Historical Register and Dictionary of the United States Army, from Its Organization, September 29, 1789, to March 2, 1902.* 2 vols. Washington, D.C.: Government Printing Office, 1903.

Hergesheimer, Joseph *Sheridan: A Military Narrative.* Boston: Houghton Mifflin Co., 1931.

Hesseltine, William B. *Ulysses S. Grant, Politician.* New York: Frederick Ungar, 1957.

Heyman, Max L., Jr. *Prudent Soldier: A Biography of Major General E. R. S. Canby, 1817–1873.* Glendale, Calif.: Arthur H. Clark, 1959.

Higham, Robin, ed. *A Guide to the Sources of United States Military History.* Hamden, Conn.: Archon Books, 1975.

Higham, Robin, and Carol Brandt, eds. *The United States Army in Peacetime: Essays in Honor of the Bicentennial, 1775–1975.* Manhattan, Kans.: Military Affairs / Aerospace Historian Publishing, 1975.

Hirshon, Stanley P. *Grenville M. Dodge: Soldier, Politician, Railroad Pioneer.* Bloomington: Indiana University Press, 1967.

Hoar, George F. *Autobiography of Seventy Years.* 2 vols. New York: Charles Scribner's Sons, 1906.

Hoig, Stan. *The Battle of the Washita: The Sheridan-Custer Indian Campaign of 1867–69.* Garden City, N.Y.: Doubleday & Co., 1976.

———. *The Peace Chiefs of the Cheyennes.* Norman: University of Oklahoma Press, 1980.

Howard, O. O. *Autobiography of Oliver Otis Howard, Major General, United States Army.* 2 vols. New York: Baker & Taylor Co., 1908.

———. *Nez Perce Joseph: His Ancestors, His Lands, His Confederates, His Enemies, His Murders, His War, His Pursuit and Capture.* Boston: Lee and Shepard Publishers, 1881.

———. *My Life and Experiences among Hostile Indians.* New York: Da Capo Press, 1972.

Howe, George Frederick. *Chester A. Arthur; A Quarter-Century of Machine Politics.* New York: Frederick Ungar, 1957.

Howe, M. A. DeWolfe, ed. *Home Letters of General Sherman.* New York: Charles Scribner's Sons, 1909.

Hudnut, James Monroe. *Commanders of the Army of the Cumberland.* New York: J. M. Hudnut, 1884.

Hunt, Frazier, and Robert Hunt. *I Fought with Custer: The Story of Sergeant Windolph.* New York: Charles Scribner's Sons, 1953.

Hyde, George E. *Life of George Bent: Written from His Letters.* Edited by Savoie Lottinville. Norman: University of Oklahoma Press, 1968.

———. *The Pawnee Indians.* Norman: University of Oklahoma Press, 1974.

———. *Red Cloud's Folk: A History of the Oglala Sioux Indians.* Norman: University of Oklahoma Press, 1937.

Indian Rights Association. *Annual Reports, 1883–1885.* Philadelphia: Office of the Indian Rights Association, 1885.

Jackson, Donald. *Custer's Gold: The United States Cavalry Expedition of 1874*. New Haven, Conn.: Yale University Press, 1966.

Johnson, Barry C., comp. *Merritt and the Indian Wars: "Three Indian Campaigns" by Gen. Wesley Merritt, U.S.A.* London: Johnson-Taunton Military Press, 1972.

Johnson, Robert Underwood, and Clarence Clough Buel, eds. *Retreat from Gettysburg*. Vol. 3 of *Battles and Leaders of the Civil War*. New York: Thomas Yoseloff, 1956.

————, eds. *The Way to Appomattox*. Vol. 4 of *Battles and Leaders of the Civil War*. New York: Thomas Yoseloff, 1956.

Johnson, Virginia Weisel. *The Unregimented General: A Biography of Nelson A. Miles*. Boston: Houghton Mifflin, 1962.

Jones, Douglas C. *The Treaty of Medicine Lodge: The Story of the Great Council as Told by Eyewitnesses*. Norman: University of Oklahoma Press, 1966.

Jones, Virgil Carrington. *Ranger Mosby*. Chapel Hill: University of North Carolina Press, 1944.

Journey through the Yellowstone National Park and Northwestern Wyoming, 1883: Photographs of Party and Scenery along the Route Traveled, and Copies of the Associated Press Dispatches Sent whilst en Route. N.p.: [1883].

Kane, Lucile M., ed. and trans. *Military Life in Dakota: The Journal of Philippe Régis de Trobriand*. Saint Paul, Minn.: Alvord Memorial Commission, 1951.

Keim, De B. Randolph. *Sheridan's Troopers on the Border: Winter Campaign on the Plains*. Philadelphia: Clayton, Remsen & Habbelfinger, 1870.

————. *Sherman: A Memorial in Art, Oratory, and Literature by the Society of the Army of the Tennessee with the Aid of the Congress of the United States of America*. Washington, D.C.: Government Printing Office, 1904.

Kellogg, Sanford C. *The Shenandoah Valley and Virginia, 1861 to 1865: A War Study*. New York: Neale, 1903.

King, Charles. *Campaigning with Crook*. Norman: University of Oklahoma Press, 1964.

King, James T. *War Eagle: A Life of General Eugene A. Carr*. Lincoln: University of Nebraska Press, 1963.

Knight, Oliver. *Following the Indian Wars: The Story of the Newspaper Correspondents among the Indian Campaigners*. Norman: University of Oklahoma Press, 1960.

————. *Life and Manners in the Frontier Army*. Norman: University of Oklahoma Press, 1978.

Krause, Herbert, and Gary D. Olson. *Prelude to Glory: A Newspaper Accounting of Custer's 1874 Expedition to the Black Hills*. Sioux Falls, S.D.: Brevet Press, 1974.

Kroeker, Marvin E. *Great Plains Command: William B. Hazen in the Frontier West*. Norman: University of Oklahoma Press, 1976.

Leckie, William H. *The Buffalo Soldiers: A Narrative of the Negro Cavalry in the West*. Norman: University of Oklahoma Press, 1967.

――――. *The Military Conquest of the Southern Plains*. Norman: University of Oklahoma Press, 1963.

Lewis, Lloyd. *Sherman: Fighting Prophet*. New York: Harcourt, Brace and Co., 1932.

Liberty, Margot, and John Stands in Timber. *Cheyenne Memories*. New Haven, Conn.: Yale University Press, 1967.

Longacre, Edward G. *From Union Stars to Top Hat: A Biography of the Extraordinary General James Harrison Wilson*. Harrisburg, Penn.: Stackpole, 1972.

Lonn, Ella. *Reconstruction in Louisiana after 1868*. New York: G. P. Putnam's Sons, 1918.

Lynam, Robert, ed. *The Beecher Island Annual: Sixty-second Anniversary of the Battle of Beecher Island, Sept. 17, 18, 1868*. Wray, Colo.: Beecher Island Memorial Association, 1930.

McChristian, Douglas C. *An Army of Marksmen: The Development of United States Army Marksmanship in the Nineteenth Century*. Fort Collins, Colo.: Old Army Press, 1981.

McClellan, Carswell. *Notes on the Personal Memoirs of P. H. Sheridan*. Saint Paul, Minn.: Banning Press, 1889.

McDonough, James L. *Schofield: Union General in the Civil War and Reconstruction*. Tallahassee: Florida State University Press, 1972.

McElroy, John. *Gen. Philip Henry Sheridan*. Washington, D.C.: National Tribune, 1896.

McFeely, William S. *Grant: A Biography*. New York: W. W. Norton & Co., 1981.

McHenry, Robert, ed. *Webster's American Military Biographies*. Springfield, Mass.: G. & C. Merriam Co., 1978.

McIlvaine, Mabel, comp. *Reminiscences of Chicago during the Great Fire*. Chicago: R. R. Donnelley & Sons, 1915.

Mackey, T. J. *The Hazen Court-Martial: The Responsibility for the Disaster to the Lady Franklin Bay Polar Expedition Definitely Established, with Proposed Reforms in the Law and Practice of Courts-Martial*. New York: D. Van Nostrand, 1885.

McKitrick, Eric L. *Andrew Johnson and Reconstruction*. Chicago: University of Chicago Press, 1960.

Mantell, Martin E. *Johnson, Grant, and the Politics of Reconstruction*. New York: Columbia University Press, 1973.

Manypenny, George W. *Our Indian Wards*. Cincinnati, Ohio: Robert Clarke & Co., 1880.

Mardock, Robert Winston. *The Reformers and the American Indian*. Columbia: University of Missouri Press, 1971.

Marquis, Thomas B. *Custer, Cavalry, and Crows: The Story of William White*. Edited by John A. Popovich. Fort Collins, Colo.: Old Army Press, 1975.

Marshall, S. L. A. *Crimsoned Prairie: The Wars between the United States and the*

Plains Indians during the Winning of the West. New York: Charles Scribner's Sons, 1972.

Mattes, Merrill J. *Indians, Infants, and Infantry: Andrew and Elizabeth Burt on the Frontier.* Denver, Colo.: Old West Publishing Co., 1960.

Mayhall, Mildred P. *The Kiowas.* Norman: University of Oklahoma Press, 1962.

Meade, George. *The Life and Letters of George Gordon Meade: Major-General, United States Army.* 2 vols. New York: Charles Scribner's Sons, 1913.

A Memorial of Philip Henry Sheridan from the City of Boston. Boston: City of Boston, 1889.

Merington, Marguerite, ed. *The Custer Story: The Life and Intimate Letters of General George A. Custer and His Wife Elizabeth.* New York: Devin-Adair Co., 1950.

Merrill, James M. *Spurs to Glory: The Story of the United States Cavalry.* Chicago: Rand McNally, 1966.

———. *William Tecumseh Sherman.* Chicago: Rand McNally, 1971.

Miles, Nelson A. *Personal Recollections and Observations of General Nelson A. Miles.* Chicago: Werner Company, 1896.

———. *Serving the Republic: Memoirs of the Civil and Military Life of Nelson A. Miles.* New York: Harper & Brothers, 1911.

Military Order of the Loyal Legion of the United States: The Commander-in-Chief: In Memoriam, General Philip Henry Sheridan, United States Army. N.p., n.d.

Millis, Walter, ed. *American Military Thought.* Indianapolis, Ind.: Bobbs-Merrill, 1966.

Mills, Anson. *My Story.* 2d ed. Edited by C. H. Clandy. Washington D.C.: Press of Byron S. Adams, 1921.

Milner, Clyde A., II. *With Good Intentions: Quaker Work among the Pawnees, Otos, and Omahas in the 1870s.* Lincoln: University of Nebraska Press, 1982.

Monaghan, Jay. *Custer: The Life of General George Armstrong Custer.* Boston: Little Brown and Co., 1959.

Nenninger, Timothy K. *The Leavenworth Schools and the Old Army: Education, Professionalism, and the Officer Corps of the United States Army, 1881–1918.* Westport, Conn.: Greenwood Press, 1978.

Nevins, Allan. *Grover Cleveland: A Study in Courage.* New York: Dodd, Mead & Co., 1932.

———. *Hamilton Fish: The Inner History of the Grant Administration.* New York: Dodd, Mead & Co., 1936.

[Newhall, Frederic Cushman]. *With General Sheridan in Lee's Last Campaign, by a Staff Officer.* Philadelphia: Lippincott & Co., 1866.

Nye, W. S. *Carbine and Lance: The Story of Old Fort Sill.* 3d ed. Norman: University of Oklahoma Press, 1969.

———. *Plains Indian Raiders: The Final Phases of Warfare from the Arkansas to the Red River, with Original Photographs by William S. Soule.* Norman: University of Oklahoma Press, 1968.

O'Connor, Richard. *Sheridan the Inevitable*. Indianapolis, Ind.: Bobbs-Merrill, 1953.

Olson, James C. *Red Cloud and the Sioux Problem*. Lincoln: University of Nebraska Press, 1965.

Our Great Captains: Grant, Sherman, Thomas, Sheridan, and Farragut. New York: Charles B. Richardson, 1865.

Overfield, Loyd J., II, comp. *The Little Big Horn 1876: The Official Communications, Documents, and Reports, with Rosters of the Officers and Troops of the Campaign*. Glendale, Calif.: Arthur H. Clark, 1971.

Paine, Albert Bigelow. *Th. Nast: His Period and His Pictures*. New York: Macmillan, 1904.

Parker, Watson. *Gold in the Black Hills*. Lincoln: University of Nebraska Press, 1982.

Plummer, Mark A. *Frontier Governor: Samuel J. Crawford of Kansas*. Lawrence: University Press of Kansas, 1971.

Pogue, Anna Holm. *An Oregon Interlude: A Narrative Poem*. Boston: Bruce Humphries, 1946.

Pond, George E. *The Shenandoah Valley in 1864*. New York: Charles Scribner's Sons, 1898.

Potomac Corral of the Westerners. *Great Western Indian Fights*. Garden City, N.Y.: Doubleday & Co. 1960.

Powell, Peter J. *Sweet Medicine: The Continuing Role of the Sacred Arrows, the Sun Dance, and the Sacred Buffalo Hat in Northern Cheyenne History*. 2 vols. Norman: University of Oklahoma Press, 1969.

Pratt, Fletcher. *Eleven Generals: Studies in American Command*. New York: William Sloane Associates, 1949.

Pratt, Richard Henry. *Battlefield and Classroom: Four Decades with the American Indian, 1867–1904*. Edited by Robert M. Utley. New Haven, Conn.: Yale University Press, 1964.

Price, George F. *Across the Continent with the Fifth Cavalry*. New York: Antiquarian Press, 1959.

————. *The Necessity for Closer Relations between the Army and the People, and the Best Method to Accomplish the Result*. New York: G. P. Putnam's Sons / Military Service Institution, 1885.

Priest, Loring Benson. *Uncle Sam's Stepchildren: The Reformation of United States Indian Policy, 1865–1887*. New York: Octagon Books, 1969.

Proceedings of the State and Assembly of the State of New York, on the Life and Services of Gen. Philip H. Sheridan, Held at the Capitol, April 9, 1889. Albany, N.Y.: James B. Lyon, State Printer, 1890.

Prucha, Francis Paul. *American Indian Policy in Crisis: Christian Reformers and the Indian, 1865–1900*. Norman: University of Oklahoma Press, 1976.

————. *A Bibliographical Guide to the History of Indian-White Relations in the United States*. Chicago: University of Chicago Press, 1977.

————. *A Guide to the Military Posts of the United States, 1789–1895*. Madison: State Historical Society of Wisconsin, 1964.

————. *Indian-White Relations in the United States: A Bibliography of Works Published, 1975–1980*. Lincoln: University of Nebraska Press, 1982.

————. *The Sword of the Republic: The United States Army on the Frontier, 1783–1846*. New York: Macmillan, 1969.

Quaife, Milo Milton, ed. *Army Life in Dakota: Selections from the Journal of Phillippe Régis Denis de Keredern de Trobriand*. Translated by George Francis Will. Chicago: R. R. Donnelley & Sons, 1941.

————. *"Yellowstone Kelly": The Memoirs of Luther S. Kelly*. New Haven, Conn.: Yale University Press, 1926.

Reid, Whitelaw. *Ohio in the War: Her Statesmen, Her Generals, and Soldiers*. 2 vols. New York: Moore, Wilstach and Baldwin, 1868.

Reiger, John F., ed. *The Passing of the Great West: Selected Papers of George Bird Grinnell*. New York: Charles Scribner's Sons, 1972.

Rickey, Don, Jr. *Forty Miles a Day on Beans and Hay: The Enlisted Soldier Fighting the Indian Wars*. Norman: University of Oklahoma Press, 1963.

Rister, Carl Coke. *Border Command: General Phil Sheridan in the West*. Norman: University of Oklahoma Press, 1944.

Robins, Richard, comp. *Toasts and Responses at Banquets Given Lieut.-Gen. P. H. Sheridan, United States Army, "Commander," by the Military Order of the Loyal Legion of the United States, Commandery of the State of Illinois, March 6, 1882–3*. Chicago: Knight & Leonard Printers, n.d.

Rodenbough, Theodore F., and William L. Haskin, eds. *The Army of the United States: Historical Sketches of Staff and Line with Portraits of Generals-in-Chief*. New York: Argonaught Press, 1966.

Roosevelt, Theodore. *Address of the President at the Unveiling of the Monument to General Sheridan, Wednesday, November 25, 1908*. Washington, D.C.: Government Printing Office, 1908.

Rosa, Joseph G. *They Called Him Wild Bill: The Life and Adventures of James Butler Hickok*. Norman: University of Oklahoma Press, 1974.

Russell, Don. *The Lives and Legends of Buffalo Bill*. Norman: University of Oklahoma Press, 1960.

Schmitt, Martin F., ed. *General George Crook: His Autobiography*. Norman: University of Oklahoma Press, 1946.

Schneider, George, ed. *The Freeman Journal: The Infantry in the Sioux Campaign of 1876*. San Rafael, Calif.: Presidio Press, 1977.

Schofield, John M. *Forty-six Years in the Army*. New York: Century Co., 1897.

Schurz, Carl. *The Reminiscences of Carl Schurz: With a Sketch of His Life and Public Services from 1869 to 1906 by Frederick Bancroft and William A. Dunning*. 3 vols. New York: Doubleday, Page & Co., 1909.

Scott, Hugh Lenox. *Some Memories of a Soldier*. New York: Century Co., 1928.

Sefton, James E. *The United States Army and Reconstruction, 1865–1877*. Baton Rouge: Louisiana State University Press, 1967.

459

Sheridan, Philip H. *Outline Descriptions of the Posts in the Military Divison of the Missouri.* Facsimile edition. Fort Collins, Colo.: Old Army Press, 1972.

———. *Personal Memoirs of P. H. Sheridan, General, United States Army.* 2 vols. New York: Charles L. Webster & Co., 1888.

———. *Record of Engagements with Hostile Indians within the Military Division of the Missouri, from 1868 to 1882, Lieutenant-General P. H. Sheridan, Commanding.* Facsimile edition. Fort Collins, Colo.: Old Army Press, 1972.

———. *Report of an Exploration of Parts of Wyoming, Idaho, and Montana in August and September, 1882, made by Lieut. Gen. P. H. Sheridan.* Washington, D.C.: Government Printing Office, 1882.

———. *Report of Lieut. General P.'H. Sheridan, Dated September 20, 1881, of His Expedition through the Big Horn Mountains, Yellowstone National Park, etc.* Washington, D.C.: Government Printing Office, 1882.

Sheridan, Philip H., and Michael V. Sheridan. *Personal Memoirs of Philip Henry Sheridan, General, United States Army: New and Enlarged Edition, with an Account of His life from 1871 to His Death, in 1888.* 2 vols. New York: D. Appleton and Co., 1904.

Sheridan, Philip H., and W. T. Sherman. *Reports of Inspection Made in the Summer of 1877 by Generals P. H. Sheridan and W. T. Sherman of Country North of the Union Pacific Railroad.* Washington, D.C.: Government Printing Office, 1878.

Sheridan's Veterans: A Souvenir of Their Two Campaigns in the Shenandoah Valley: The One, of War, in 1864; the Other, of Peace, in 1883. Boston: W. F. Brown & Co., 1883.

Sherman, William T. *Memoirs of Gen. W. T. Sherman, Written by Himself.* 2 vols. New York: Charles L. Webster & Co., 1892.

Smalley, Eugene V. *History of the Northern Pacific Railroad.* New York: G. P. Putnam's Sons, 1883.

Spotts, David L. *Campaigning with Custer and the Nineteenth Kansas Volunteer Cavalry on the Washita Campaign, 1868–'69.* Edited by E. A. Brininstool. New York: Argonaut Press, 1965.

Sprague, Marshall. *A Gallery of Dudes.* Lincoln: University of Nebraska Press, 1979.

Stackpole, Edward J. *Sheridan in the Shenandoah: Jubal Early's Nemesis.* Harrisburg, Penn.: Stackpole, 1961.

Stallard, Patricia Y. *Glittering Misery: Dependents of the Indian Fighting Army.* Fort Collins, Colo.: Old Army Press / Presidio Press, 1978.

Stanley, D. S. *Personal Memoirs of Major-General D. S. Stanley, U.S.A.* Cambridge: Harvard University Press, 1917.

———. *Report on the Yellowstone Expedition of 1873.* Washington, D.C.: Government Printing Office, 1874.

Stanley, Henry M. *My Early Travels and Adventures in America and Asia.* 2 vols. New York: Charles Scribner's Sons, 1895.

Starr, Stephen Z. *The Union Cavalry in the Civil War*. 2 vols. Baton Rouge: Louisiana State University Press, 1979–81.

Steffen, Randy. *The Horse Soldier, 1776–1942: The United States Cavalryman: His Uniforms, Arms, Accoutrements, and Equipments*. Vol. 2, *The Frontier, the Mexican War, the Civil War, the Indian Wars, 1851–1880*. Norman: University of Oklahoma Press, 1978.

Stewart, Edgar I. *Custer's Luck*. Norman: University of Oklahoma Press, 1955.

———, ed. *Penny-an Acre Empire in the West*. Norman: University of Oklahoma Press, 1968.

Strong, William E. *Canadian River Hunt*. Norman: University of Oklahoma Press, 1960.

———. *A Trip to the Yellowstone National Park in July, August, and September, 1875*. Norman: University of Oklahoma Press, 1968.

Sully, Langdon. *No Tears for the General: The Life of Alfred Sully, 1821–1879*. Palo Alto, Calif.: American West Publishing Co., 1974.

Tatum, Lawrie. *Our Red Brothers and the Peace Policy of President Ulysses S. Grant*. Lincoln: University of Nebraska Press, 1970.

Taylor, Joe Gray. *Louisiana Reconstructed, 1863–1877*. Baton Rouge: Louisiana State University Press, 1974.

Terry, Alfred H. *The Field Diary of General Alfred H. Terry: The Yellowstone Expedition—1876*. Bellevue, Nebr.: Old Army Press, 1970.

Thian, Raphael P. *Notes Illustrating the Military Geography of the United States, 1813–1880*. Austin: University of Texas Press, 1979.

Thorndike, Rachel Sherman, ed. *The Sherman Letters: Correspondence between General and Senator Sherman from 1837 to 1891*. New York: Charles Scribner's Sons, 1894.

Thrapp, Dan L. *The Conquest of Apacheria*. Norman: University of Oklahoma Press, 1967.

Tobie, Edward P. *Personal Narratives of Events in the War of the Rebellion, Being Papers Read before the Rhode Island Soldiers and Sailors Historical Society: Personal Recollections of General Sheridan*. 4th ser., no. 5. Providence, R.I., 1889.

Tolman, Newton F. *The Search for General Miles*. New York: G. P. Putnam's Sons, 1968.

Tremain, Henry Edwin. *Last Hours of Sheridan's Cavalry: A Reprint of War Memoranda*. New York: Bonnell, Silver & Bowers, 1904.

[Tucker, William.] *The Grand Duke Alexis in the United States of America*. New York: Interland Publishing Co., 1972.

Unveiling of the Equestrian Statue of General Philip H. Sheridan, Capitol Park, Albany, New York October 7, 1916. Albany, N.Y.: J. B. Lyon Co., 1916.

Upton, Emory. *The Military Policy of the United States*. Washington, D.C.: Government Printing Office, 1911.

Utley, Robert M. *The Contribution of the Frontier to the American Military Tradition*. Colorado Springs, Colo.: United States Air Force Academy, 1977.

———. *Frontier Regulars: The United States Army and the Indian, 1866–1891*. New York: Macmillan, 1973.

———. *Frontiersmen in Blue: The United States Army and the Indian, 1848–1865*. New York: Macmillan, 1967.

———. *The Indian Frontier of the American West, 1846–1890*. Albuquerque: University of New Mexico Press, 1984.

———, ed. *Life in Custer's Cavalry: Diaries and Letters of Albert and Jennie Barnitz 1867–1868*. New Haven, Conn.: Yale University Press, 1977.

Van DeWater, Frederic F. *Glory-Hunter: A Life of General Custer*. New York: Argosy-Antiquarian, 1963.

Vaughn, J. W. *The Reynolds Campaign on Powder River*. Norman: University of Oklahoma Press, 1961.

———. *With Crook at the Rosebud*. Harrisburg, Penn.: Stackpole, 1956.

Vaughn, Robert. *Then and Now; or, Thirty-six Years in the Rockies*. Minneapolis, Minn.: Tribune Printing Co., 1900.

Victor, Frances Fuller. *The Early Indian Wars of Oregon, Compiled from the Oregon Archives and Other Original Sources, with Muster Rolls*. Salem, Ore.: Baker, 1894.

Wallace, Ernest. *Ranald S. Mackenzie on the Texas Frontier*. Lubbock: West Texas Museum Association, 1964.

———, ed. *Ranald S. Mackenzie's Official Correspondence relating to Texas*. 2 vols. Lubbock: West Texas Museum Association, 1967–68.

War Papers Read before the Commandery of the State of Wisconsin, Military Order of the Loyal Legion of the United States. Vol. 1. Milwaukee, Wisc.: Burdick, Armitage & Allen, 1891.

War Papers Read before the Indiana Commandery, Military Order of the Loyal Legion of the United States. Indianapolis: Indiana Commandery, 1898.

Warner, Ezra J. *Generals in Blue: Lives of the Union Commanders*. Baton Rouge; Louisiana State University Press, 1964.

Weigley, Russell F. *The American Way of War: A History of United States Military Strategy and Policy*. New York: Macmillan, 1973.

———. *History of the United States Army*. New York: Macmillan, 1967.

———. *Quartermaster General of the Union Army: A Biography of M. C. Meigs*. New York: Columbia University Press, 1959.

———. *Towards an American Army: Military Thought from Washington to Marshall*. New York: Columbia University Press, 1962.

White, Leonard D. *The Republican Era: A Study in Administrative History, 1869–1901*. New York: Free Press, 1965.

White, Lonnie J. *Hostiles and Horse Soldiers: Indian Battles and Campaigns in the West*. Boulder, Colo.: Pruett Publishing Co., 1972.

Whitman, S. E. *The Troopers: An Informal History of the Plains Cavalry, 1865–1890*. New York: Hastings House, 1962.

Willert, James. *Little Big Horn Diary: Chronicle of the 1876 Indian War*. La Mirada, Calif.: James Willert, 1977.

Williams, C. R. *The Life of Rutherford Birchard Hayes.* 2 vols. Columbus: Ohio State Archaeological and Historical Society, 1928.

————, ed. *Diary and Letters of Rutherford Birchard Hayes.* 5 vols. Columbus: Ohio State Archaeological and Historical Society, 1922–26.

Wilson, Frederick T. *Federal Aid in Domestic Disturbances, 1787–1903.* Washington, D.C.: Government Printing Office, 1903.

Wilson, James Harrison. *Under the Old Flag: Recollections of Military Operations in the War for the Union, the Spanish War, the Boxer Rebellion, Etc.* 2 vols. New York: D. Appleton and Company, 1912.

Wormser, Richard. *The Yellowlegs: The Story of the United States Cavalry.* Garden City, N.Y.: Doubleday & Co., 1966.

Zogbaum, Rufus Fairchild. *Horse, Foot, and Dragoons: Sketches of Army Life at Home and Abroad.* New York: Harper & Brothers, 1888.

INDEX

Wells, James M., 22–24, 277
Welsh, Herbert, 128
Wessells, Henry, 335–36
West Point: and military cliques, 135–38; Sheridan at, 4–6
Wheeler, William A., 271–72
Whipple, Henry B., 95
White Horse, 110, 111, 241, 242, 362
White League, 263, 266–67, 269–71, 273
White Shield, 361–62
William I, king of Prussia, 202–5
Wilson, Charles L., 207
Wilson, James H., 15
Wiltz, Louis, 265–66
Winchell, Newton H., 167
Winchester, Battle of, 14, 189
Wingate, George C., 159–60
Wolf Mountain, Battle of, 326
Wolf-Sleeve, 101
Woman's Heart, 77, 84, 89, 93, 101, 258

Women: army wives, 221–22; Indian captives, 74, 387 n. 29, 389 n. 42, n. 45; white captives, 52, 59, 81–83, 98–99, 112, 194, 399 n. 66; Sheridan's opinions of, 143–44
Wool, John, 7–8
Wright, George, 8, 9
Wright, W. W., 39
Wyllyams, Frederick, 81
Wynkoop, Edward W., 37–38, 41, 56, 95, 96

Y

Yakima Indians, 7–11, 122
Yates, George, 139
Yellow Bear, 89, 93–94, 102
Yellowstone National Park, 163–65, 354–60, 435 n. 33
Yellowstone Park Improvement Company, 354–56